THE PAGEANT OF AMERICA

R.K.

Independence Edition

VOLUME VIII

THE PAGEANT OF AMERICA

A PICTORIAL HISTORY OF THE UNITED STATES

RALPH HENRY GABRIEL
EDITOR

HENRY JONES FORD HARRY MORGAN AYRES
ASSOCIATE EDITORS

OLIVER McKEE
ASSISTANT EDITOR

CHARLES M. ANDREWS
HERBERT E. BOLTON
IRVING N. COUNTRYMAN
WILLIAM E. DODD
DIXON RYAN FOX
ALLEN JOHNSON
WILLIAM BENNETT MUNRO
VICTOR H. PALTSITS
ARTHUR M. SCHLESINGER
NATHANIEL WRIGHT STEPHENSON
ADVISORY EDITORS

DAVID M. MATTESON
INDEXER

From the painting by H. A. Ogden (1856–) in his possession

SIGNING THE DECLARATION OF INDEPENDENCE

THE PAGEANT OF AMERICA

BUILDERS OF THE REPUBLIC

BY

FREDERIC AUSTIN OGG

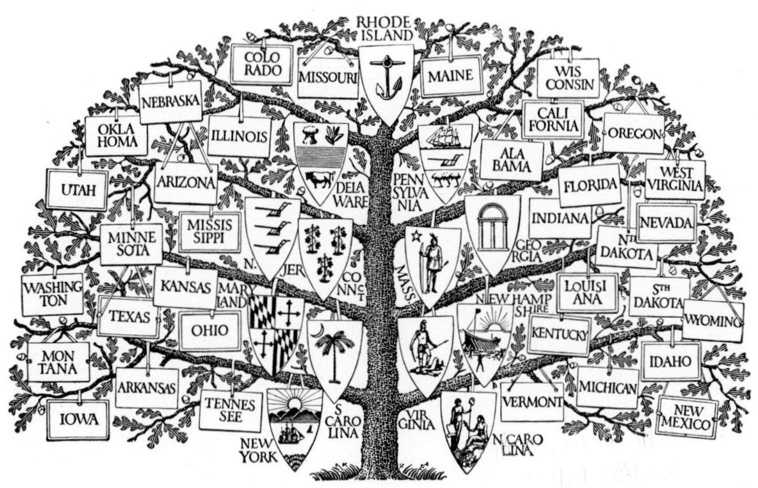

NEW HAVEN · YALE UNIVERSITY PRESS
TORONTO · GLASGOW, BROOK & CO.
LONDON · HUMPHREY MILFORD
OXFORD UNIVERSITY PRESS

PRINTED IN THE UNITED STATES OF AMERICA

3-28-52
Yale University Press
99.00 set

TABLE OF CONTENTS

CHAPTER PAGE

BUILDERS OF THE REPUBLIC

AS the seventeenth century opened, a new royal house occupied the throne of England. The Stuart monarchs, though sometimes quite unwillingly, were destined to play no unimportant part in the constitutional development of their kingdom. Between the advent of James I in 1603 and the hasty departure of James II in 1688 England saw the struggle for power between the Crown and the representatives of the people more than once become bitterly intense as the Crown yielded one after another of the prerogatives inherited from the vigorous Tudors. During these years all but one of England's colonies on the continent of North America were planted.

"In reality," as Charles M. Andrews has remarked, "these settlements were not colonies; they were private estates, the proprietors of which, both corporate and feudal, were endowed with wide powers and privileges, conferred upon them by royal charters. There were the feudal seignories of New York, and the Carolinas, and the Bahamas, whose owners had an eye to profits from trade and the rent of their lands; the similar seignories of Maryland and Pennsylvania, where a religious refuge and a holy experiment were brought into being under the legal protection of feudal lordships; and the Separatist communities of New England, whose founders established religious Puritan commonwealths in the wilderness, and wanted to be let alone by the authorities in England that they might worship God and fight the Devil in their own way. Even had the English government been able to conceive of a colonial organization at this period of its history, it would have been unable to develop a workable policy as long as it allowed these settlements in America to remain under private control and to manage their own governments and own their own soil under the terms of the charters granted them by the King. Certainly the early Stuarts never tried to fashion a colonial policy, and their successors after the Restoration were hardly more aware than they had been that a colonial world was in the making."

But these distant and isolated settlements in America, though so far removed from central authority were not to become laboratories for experiments with novel forms of government. In its earlier phases the settlement of America meant little more than the extension to the New World of the social and political code of the Old. The newcomers remained Englishmen, subjects of the King. The ancient institution of feudalism took vigorous root in American soil, bringing with it the stratification that was the foundation of European social intercourse. The civil and criminal law of Britain was adapted by the overseas governments to the peculiar needs of their communities. Though the English Government may have had no very clear objectives for its American provinces, they were, nevertheless, definitely extensions of English culture into an undeveloped continent.

The first three quarters of the eighteenth century saw developed on the Atlantic seaboard between Maine and Georgia a degree of civilization that Americans of to-day sometimes fail to realize. In 1720 the Plymouth people noted the centenary of the landing of the Pilgrims; Virginia had traditions that ran even farther back. Life had become settled and comfortable. America boasted a landed aristocracy several members of which held English titles. The wealthy merchants of the coast towns, like Boston, New York, Philadelphia, and Charleston, had interests reaching far beyond their immediate neighborhoods and into lands as far away as Europe or the African coast. In New England a learned clergy raised the intellectual level of their flocks. The rawness of the provincial largely disappeared as life in the coast region of America became urbane and sophisticated. The beautiful and stately Georgian buildings of the eighteenth century not only indicate a refined taste but symbolize the culture of the society that lived and worked within them (see Vol. XIII). J. Franklin Jameson has commented that "American society in the colonial period had a more definite and stable organization than it ever has had since the Revolution."

A convenient instrument through which the ruling class of this eighteenth-century civilization could express itself was the colonial assembly. A visitor to the Virginia House of Burgesses in the middle decades of the eighteenth century would have observed the operation of a political life entirely in keeping with the spirit of the age. He would have noted that a majority of the delegates were well-dressed planters, who had for the most part ridden into Williamsburg in considerable state. Listening to their debates, he would have heard constantly the sentiments of conservative men satisfied with the social order as they found it. Occasionally there would be a difference with the Governor when the interest of the ruling group ran counter to that of the British Government. In these disputes, the counterpart of those in other colonies, the honors did not all go to either side. But, as the years passed, the assemblies gained rather than lost in power and prestige. In the Virginia House the visitor would have heard other disputes between the great planters of the coast region and a minority of less fashionably clad gentlemen who represented the interior counties, some of which were on the frontier itself. The burden of the complaint of the western men was that the interests of their section were made secondary to those of the richer East and that the West was not permitted its fair share of delegates in the legislative body. Had the stranger attended an election to this House, he would have discovered that only persons of some property and consequence were allowed to vote. Democracy was not a part of the political code of the dominant elements of eighteenth-century America. Independence of Britain was even further from their minds. The typical American of the time was a loyal subject of the King and proud of his British heritage. If, as the years passed, he more or less unconsciously sought a greater measure of local autonomy, this aspiration was part of the inevitable evolution of a frontier community far from the center of empire. Perhaps, had it not been for the Seven Years' War (1756–63), the Americans and the English would have gone on living together in the same empire, "muddling through" the difficulties bound to arise from time to time until the British colonies in North America had achieved a measure of autonomy comparable to that of the self-governing units in the present British Commonwealth of Nations. But that war, which left England burdened with debt and responsible for the management and defense of a vastly enlarged domain, was followed by a quarrel that was to destroy the old relationship and to call into being the new United States of America.

Why the compromising genius of the British failed them in the crisis between 1765 and 1775 still remains the subject for a multitude of explanations. This is not the place for a discussion of the various phases of the dispute between the mother country and thirteen of her American colonies. Suffice it to say that from first to last Britain held fast to the mercantilist conception of the colony as existing primarily for the benefit of the parent state. Moreover, though taxes which proved obnoxious to the Americans were repealed, the British assertion of the competency of Parliament to legislate in all matters for the colonies was not abated. Across the Atlantic the controversies over the Stamp Act (No. 89), the Townshend duties (No. 119), and the Billeting Act (No. 146), loosed violent and disruptive forces in the stabilized society of eighteenth-century America.

The aristocracy in general resented any reduction in the large measure of autonomy enjoyed by the local governments which they controlled. Aspiring persons of ability who were not of the upper class shared the sentiments of their leaders and also saw an opportunity to gain fame and prestige for themselves by opposing England. More than once a mob of the lower classes broke into noisy riots. Calling themselves "Liberty Boys," they burned in effigy persons whom they disliked, compelled public officials to resign their posts, and even pillaged houses and destroyed property. The merchants of the North and the planters of the South who formed the aristocracy were not slow to perceive in the "Liberty Boys" a menace to their interests. Leaders in American communities set about holding the unruly elements in check. For three years after 1770, when all the Townshend taxes save one had been repealed, it seemed as though the British empire had safely weathered a threatening storm. The active quarrel had subsided though neither side had given up the assertion of its interpretation of the English Constitution. Then, in 1773, Lord North's ministry undertook to assist the struggling British East India Company by giving it practically a monopoly of the American tea trade.

This move, made apparently with little thought as to its effects in America, roused the American merchants as not even the Stamp Act had done and forced them to make common cause with the radicals whom of late years they had been trying to quiet. The result was violent and deliberate destruction of property at Boston. The British Government replied with punitive and coercive measures. The establishment of what amounted to military control in Massachusetts led directly to the armed clash at Lexington and Concord. Yet at this time the conflict was not waged for independence but rather by Americans fighting for their rights as British subjects under the common law. "Let these truths be indelibly impressed upon our minds," wrote the conservative John Dickinson, "that we cannot be happy without being free; that we cannot be free without being secure in our property; that we cannot be secure in our property, if, without our consent, others may, as by right, take it away." England's statesmen grievously failed her when they allowed a dispute over such an issue to develop into armed conflict. The climax was reached when Lord North's government declared the continental colonies in rebellion and hired German mercenaries to fight the King's subjects in America. After such a move, even had Britain won the war, the heritage of bitterness would have remained a constant menace to the integrity of the empire. Then it was that the Americans declared their independence.

Rebellion was quite a different thing from the old-time opposition to the acts of Parliament, while a war for independence raised the question not only of loyalty but of the wisdom of breaking away from the most powerful empire in the world to set up what was bound to be a weak and divided state. The Declaration of Independence was a line drawn by a sword on either side of which Americans must now take their stand; a line dividing, it might be, neighbor from neighbor, friend from friend, and often father from son. "Men in a state of civil war," wrote St. John de Crèvecoeur in the midst of the conflict, "are no longer the same. They cease to view the former objects through the same medium as before. The most unjust thoughts, the most tyrannical actions, the most perverse measures, which would have covered them before with infamy or would have made them dread the omnipotence of heaven, are no longer called by these ancient names; the sophistry of each party calls them policy, justice, self-defense." For more than seven years, until the Patriots had finally won, this unnatural strife of American with American went on side by side with the war against England. The inevitable result was one of the saddest consequences of the War of Independence, a decline in the moral strength of individuals and communities. Of scarcely less importance was the driving into exile of tens of thousands of men and women who represented the best blood and brains of the American people.

For American social and political life the War of Independence was a profoundly disruptive force. Particularly was the old aristocracy shaken. Large numbers of estates owned by Tory aristocrats were confiscated. Laws like those relating to primogeniture which were part of the heritage of feudalism were abrogated. The electorate was increased as the restrictions on voting were modified. Men of humble origin, like Nathanael

Greene, rose not only to take their places beside the traditional leaders of the generation but sometimes achieved international fame.

While still in the maelstrom of war the Patriot leaders began the task of creating governments with a constitutional foundation. They showed their essential conservatism by their refusal to experiment with novel devices. In general, the old written charter from the King was replaced by a new written constitution, though Connecticut and Rhode Island found the ancient documents quite adequate for their needs under the new régime. The colonial assembly became the legislature and the royal governor was replaced by the new chief executive elected in several different ways. As the end of the war approached, a confederation of semi-independent states was set up. The difficulties of the post-war period and the necessity for new adjustments brought this confederation to the verge of collapse. To their dismay the conservative leaders of the Revolution found that the society which they had fought to defend against the power of Parliament was threatened by the very weakness of the government they had established and by the sudden rise of radicalism in a new quarter. Small farmers suffering acutely as a result of the depression which followed the war used the franchise which many of them had gained during the conflict to force the enactment of laws which, while they might temporarily relieve the husbandman, contained a general threat to property interests. Then it was that a group of able and determined men, distinctly a minority, who carried on the traditions of the old ruling class of the days before the war, initiated and carried through a peaceful revolution. The result of their handiwork was America's greatest single contribution to political thought and practice, the Constitution of the United States (No. 345). In these later years, when the ideas of Marxian socialism have become familiar to the people of the western republic, the "Fathers of the Constitution" have sometimes been referred to as capitalists seeking to create a strong government in order that property rights might be protected. That most of them were large property owners is true. That the protection of property was one of their chief motives is also true. But this was incidental to their larger aim, which was to preserve from dissolution the nation which they had fought to create, to protect from anarchy the civilization which they had inherited, and to provide an instrument of government which would make possible the orderly development of the life of the American people. But the small farmers, whose revolt had been partly responsible for the calling of the Constitutional Convention and most of whom voted against the Constitution, made also their contribution to the political development of the people of the United States.

The yeoman farmer became the characteristic figure of the frontier which even during the Revolution began a swift and steady advance across the central lowland of North America. More than a decade before this frontier ceased to exist William G. Sumner wrote: "In a new country . . . with unlimited land, the substantial equality of the people in property, culture, and social position is inevitable. Political equality follows naturally. Democracy is given in the circumstances of the case." The practice of democracy came out of the "West." In the eighteen twenties and thirties democracy became almost a fetish in America. With the widespread abolition of property qualifications for voters, some enthusiasts began to feel that Jefferson's famous words were coming true, "that all men are created equal . . . that . . . Governments are instituted among Men, deriving their just powers from the consent of the governed. . . ." Jefferson himself, though a Virginia aristocrat, had been the first leader of the western democrats. But before his death he saw the passing of the political party which he had done so much to found.

The origin and development of American political parties is one of the most significant aspects of American political history. In Washington's administration two national parties came clearly into view, each with roots running well back into the era of the Confederation. Each was led by a group of men who inherited the traditions of the old governing class. Of the two parties, that of Jefferson was more in harmony with the developing ideals of nineteenth-century America. The Federalists, under the leadership of Hamilton, clung with a fatal tenacity to the eighteenth-century tradition of aristocracy and before the nineteenth century was two decades old the Federalist party had ceased to be of national importance. John Quincy Adams, the son of Hamilton's great rival for the leadership of the Federalists, rose to the Presidency as a member of the party of Jefferson. For eight years before his inauguration there had virtually been but one national party. But the campaign of 1824 as a result of which he had been chosen chief executive had seen that party rent into no less than five contending factions.

One familiar with the system of many parties that have developed in the parliaments of continental Europe is prone to ask why but two parties should appear at the outset of the national career of the United States, and why at the end of the first quarter of the nineteenth century should five political groups within the Democratic-Republican party coalesce into two new national parties. At this particular time in American development, Frederick J. Turner has distinguished no less than five distinct sections within the area of the United States, each having interests differing from the others and each looking toward the central government for the furtherance of its well-being. Obviously some force stronger than economic sectionalism prevented the appearance of a multiplicity of parties. That such a force can be found in the two-party tradition inherited from England is hardly probable though the influence of that tradition was doubtless of importance. The war between England and France, at the close of the eighteenth century, played its part in dividing American sentiment into two phases, as Americans sympathized with one or the other of the belligerents. Perhaps the chief reason for the appearance of two parties in the eighteen twenties was the peculiar character of the central government set up by the Constitution. The framers of that instrument, under the apprehension of tyranny and under the influence of the theories of Montesquieu, the French philosophical historian (1689–1755), had created a federal government divided into three separate branches and had given each certain checks over the activities of the others. So prone were the executive and legislative departments to disagree over important issues that some outside extra-legal agency was needed to facilitate harmony between them. A national political party with its organization and discipline formed an effective instrument for holding the President and his party supporters in Congress to the same general policy. A coalition of small parties would not have sufficient permanence or strength of organization and discipline. Until some radical change is made in the form of government of the United States, the two-party system seems likely to remain fixed in American political *mores*. Its definite adoption, however, in the administration of Andrew Jackson, did not mean that sectionalism or sectional antagonisms were dead.

Side by side with the expansion to the Pacific coast during the first half of the nineteenth century went the growth of sectional dissention within the nation. The trouble arose from contrasts between the North and the South that were, in the last analysis, the outgrowth of climatic differences. North of the Ohio were the varied conditions of the temperate zone; to the south of it conditions approached the sub-tropical. In the heart of the cotton and sugar country where white men could not work efficiently at manual tasks negro slaves supplied the necessary labor. The greater efficiency of the slave when handled in gangs led to the growth of the plantation system, a mode of agriculture that was further stimulated by the cheapness of land in the new country and by the need for the constant substitution of virgin soil in place of fields worn out by cropping. When in 1793 the invention of the cotton gin established cotton as the staple crop of the South (see Vol. III), the plantation system with its slave labor was firmly fixed and practically universalized. The only areas into which it did not advance were the upland valleys of the Appalachians and the lowland regions where the soil was sandy and infertile.

The plantation brought about a definite and permanent social stratification. At the top was the planter and at the bottom the slave. Between the two were grades of lesser whites and free blacks. The southern civilization carried into the nineteenth century many of the traditions of the eighteenth; it was aristocratic to the core. Its outstanding characteristics were differences in wealth, social position, and political power.

In sharp contrast was the democracy of the Northwest, built also upon agriculture. The small farmer of the northern half of the Ohio valley was the economic and political equal of his neighbor. In the communities where he lived, democracy was as inevitable as cultivating the land. Here slave labor was economically so inefficient that the prohibition of the Ordinance of 1787 (No. 336) was hardly needed. In the northern states, east of the Alleghenies, commercial and industrial enterprises were rapidly developing. But, although they were causing an unequal distribution of wealth, they were not as yet seriously modifying the general ideal of democracy.

In the young United States, therefore, two civilizations had appeared: one agricultural, commercial, and industrial, with its political institutions founded on democracy; the other almost solely agricultural, with its social and political life colored by aristocracy. Both civilizations, in the beginning, supported the central government and favored national expansion. Three factors made for discord. The first was the inevitable dislike of the people of each section for the different institutions and ideals of the other. This was particularly true in the North, where the dislike of slavery grew to the proportions of a moral crusade. The second was disparity in growth of population, a condition which threatened the equality of the South with the North in the councils of the nation. This led to the development of an interpretation of the Constitution which would make that instrument more effective in the protection of the rights of a minority — Calhoun's theory of nullification (Nos. 546, 548). The third and probably the most important factor was the competition of the two civilizations for the unsettled public domain. Northerners, naturally, wished to exclude the obnoxious institution of slavery from the new country and Southerners, quite as naturally, desired to increase the area of their section as much as possible. The sectional struggle became most acute on the climatic borderline where the states of Missouri and Kansas were established. This competition for the national domain ultimately brought on the Civil War (see Vol. VII).

It is perhaps easier to understand why the South wished to abandon the Union than why the North desired to compel it to stay. The Southerner who squarely faced the facts saw clearly that his very civilization was menaced; that the North wished to and was able to put slavery on the way to ultimate extinction. He believed that the result in his own section would be a social revolution, the consequences of which no man could foresee. His home, his wife and daughters, the whole structure of his society would be confronted by a black menace if the slaves should gain their freedom and feel the power that lay in their numbers. If this were to be the price that he must pay for loyalty to the Union, he would fight, if need be, for southern freedom. Why, he asked, if the Northerner so deeply disliked southern institutions, should the North not be willing to let the South go in peace? Why undertake a fratricidal war to compel an unwilling section to remain within a Union that threatened to tear in shreds its whole social fabric?

The answer is not easy. In the North, as the country had expanded, the spirit of nationalism had grown. Webster had preached it in his great orations; Clay had woven it into the compromises with which he was associated; economic interchange had knit the nation into an ever closer union. If the South left the Union, this nation would be deeply, irreparably wounded. Was such to be the end of the dreams of the men who had fought and labored to make America free and to establish its independence? Northerners, already angered at the South for wrongs they believed the "slaveocracy" had committed, could not stand calmly by and permit this colossal injury to their country. National patriotism was, therefore, enlisted against the Southerner. Many men in the North joined the Union armies to free the black man. The battle was joined with idealism burning bright on both sides. The time of America's greatest testing was at hand.

Ralph H. Gabriel

CHAPTER I

POLITICS OF THE COLONIES

THE English colonists who crossed the Atlantic in the seventeenth and eighteenth centuries to found homes in the New World brought with them as a part of their cultural heritage the political ideas and traditions of England. In fact they considered themselves as much Englishmen when living in Virginia as though they were in Kent. With this thought they adjusted themselves as best they could to the new environment. The task was arduous; forests had to be cleared, lands made fit for the cultivation of staple crops, the Indians appeased or conquered, pestilence overcome. There was no leisure for political speculation, no occasion for the construction of novel political institutions. Of necessity life in the wilderness was simple and the governmental needs of the primitive communities were slight.

By the eighteenth century the country had become more settled, communities were larger and more complex, and the whole atmosphere of the colonies was one of stability rather than of a desperate struggle for existence. Division of labor gradually appeared as the artisan and even the professional man began to specialize each on his own calling. In such circumstances the problem of regulating the affairs of American communities became more difficult. Order must be maintained within, and a militia system must be built up as a protection against Indian raids. As property increased in amount and in value, property rights were in need of ever sharper definition. The regulation of social relations and the punishment of crime became steadily more difficult as hamlets grew into villages and villages into towns. In the solution of these problems English law and precedent governed. Inevitably the colonists brought the common law of England to bear upon the legal questions which confronted them.

Quite naturally in the growth of the American communities elements appeared in the population each having its own special interest. In Virginia, for instance, there grew up a sharp contrast between the tobacco planters of the coast and the small farmers of the frontier. Such economic and social differences were the foundation for most of the political disputes within the colonies. In some settlements, like Maryland or Massachusetts, religious questions caused contention. Side by side with these internal controversies were questions regarding the relation of the colony to the mother country.

As one generation followed another, the children and grandchildren of the pioneers had come more and more to look upon their governments as indigenous and as agencies created for service, not by imperial command but by colonial desire. Royal instructions that proved unworkable were likely to be disregarded, or modified to fit colonial needs; and, under pressure from local conditions, the old institutions were molded into something new. So there developed around these native growths loyalties which were sensitive to and ready to resist encroachment and dictation from beyond the seas. Meanwhile this colonial tendency was little regarded in the mother country. As a result, when a crisis came, the imperial government was ill informed as to the probable American reaction to some of the laws which it had passed.

1 John Winthrop, 1588–1649, from a portrait by a pupil of Anthony van Dyck (1599–1641) in the American Antiquarian Society, Worcester

2 John Cotton, 1585–1652, engraving by H. W. Smith, after the portrait, painted about 1735, by John Smibert (1684–1751), owned by John E. Thayer, Lancaster, Mass.

THE PURITANS

UNABLE to wrest control of the Established Church in England from the moderates and desirous of cleansing religious worship of the trappings of popery, the Puritans sought a country where they might, as Winthrop expressed it, "live under a due form of government, both civil and ecclesiastical." Able and astute men of affairs, such as John Winthrop, and men of stanch Puritan precepts, such as John Cotton, came to the New World, not to found an asylum for the persecuted, but to establish a Bible Commonwealth in which they should hold the commanding positions. To these men, Massachusetts Bay was to be a "bulwark against the kingdom of anti-Christ" then threatening to engulf Europe — a community shaped in accordance with Puritan theory. By the mere transfer to the New World, the charter of a trading company known as the Massachusetts Bay Company was turned into the constitution of a commonwealth. The members of the Company became the voters of the colony. (See also Vol. I, Chapter X, Pilgrims and Puritans in New England.) The suffrage was confined to the orthodox Puritans; administration of the laws was vested in a group of ministers and such lay leaders as were sympathetic with theocratic principles.

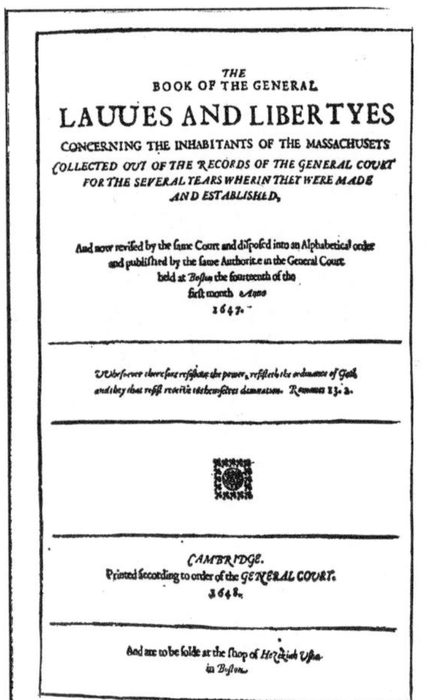

THE
BOOK OF THE GENERAL
LAUUES AND LIBERTYES
CONCERNING THE INHABITANTS OF THE MASSACHUSETS
COLLECTED OUT OF THE RECORDS OF THE GENERAL COURT
FOR THE SEVERAL YEARS WHERIN THEY WERE MADE
AND ESTABLISHED,

And now revised by the same Court and disposed into an Alphabetical order
and published by the same Authoritie in the General Court
held at Boston the fourteenth of the
first month Anno
1647.

Whosoever therefore resisteth the power, resisteth the ordinance of God,
and they that resist receive to themselves damnation. Romanes 13. 2.

CAMBRIDGE.
Printed according to order of the GENERAL COURT.
1648.

And are to be solde at the shop of Hezekiah Usher
in Boston.

3 Title-page of the unique copy printed in 1648, owned by Henry E. Huntington, in the New York Public Library

COMMON LAW

THOUGH the charter of 1629 provided that colonial laws should conform to the laws of England, in practice the magistrates were fond of relying upon the precedents of the Old Testament. This caused dissatisfaction and uncertainty as to the law. After much hesitation, the theocracy permitted the drafting and promulgation of a code of laws — the Body of Liberties of 1641 — wherein a man might find his rights and duties set forth in definite form. This code and subsequent laws, compiled by Nathaniel Ward, embodied much of English common law, but also many principles gleaned from the Bible. Narrow as it was, the code thus early established the cardinal rule of civil society in America, that government is the reign of law and not of autocratic caprice.

4 From the mural painting *A New England Town Meeting*, by Max Bohm (1868–1923) in the Cuyahoga County Courthouse, Cleveland, Ohio

TOWN MEETINGS REGULATE LOCAL AFFAIRS

THE theocratic exclusiveness of early New England is in no manner better illustrated than in the town government. As the ungracious soil near the coast was taken up, the colonists began to search for more fertile areas. The discovery of the Connecticut led some pastors to emigrate westward with their flocks. In the valley, towns sprang up around the village church. Town meetings, composed of all qualified voters, that is, of all church members, were held in the vestry to regulate local matters. And regulations were numerous. The early Puritan examined minutely into the concerns of his neighbors. Strangers, frivolous actions, oddities of dress and many matters of similar character, were the object of disapproving by-laws.

5 From the painting *Sir William Berkeley Signing the Capitulation of Virginia*, by Howard Pyle (1853–1911), for Woodrow Wilson, *A History of the American People*, 1901. © Harper & Bros.

VIRGINIA'S ROYALIST GOVERNOR WITHDRAWS, 1652

THE sturdy colonial spirit is well shown by happenings in early Virginia. In 1649, Charles I was beheaded; Cromwell and the Puritans became the rulers of England. Virginia and her Governor, Sir William Berkeley, were royalist in sympathy and proclaimed their allegiance to Charles II. Parliament, in retaliation, prohibited trade with the recalcitrant colony, and in 1651 dispatched commissioners — including Berkeley's foes, Claiborne and Bennett — to compel its submission. Berkeley blustered and talked of resistance; but the planters wanted peace and freedom of trade. The Governor was pushed into signing articles of surrender, and withdrew to private life. For eight years Virginia, under Claiborne and Richard Bennett, was almost an independent republic.

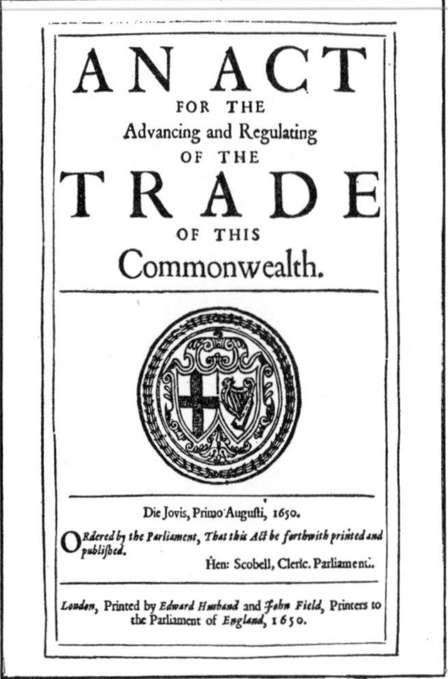

AN ACT FOR THE Advancing and Regulating OF THE TRADE OF THIS Commonwealth.

Die Jovis, Primo Auguſti, 1650.

ORdered by the Parliament, That this Act be forthwith printed and publiſhed.

Hen: Scobell, Cleric. Parliament.

London, Printed by Edward Husband and John Field, Printers to the Parliament of England, 1650.

6 Title-page of the Navigation Act, 1650, in the New York Public Library

(970)

lar Ordinances, Orders, Grants, Patents and Conſtitutions of the ſeveral Companies of Merchants, and Handicrafts men, to the end that if any of them tend to the hurt of the Publique, they may be laid down, in ſuch maner as the Parliament ſhall think fit.

Eleventhly, They are to conſider the great Trade of Fiſhing, and that not onely upon the Coaſts of *England* and *Ireland*, but likewiſe of *Iſeland*, *Greenland*, *Newfound-Land* and *New-England*, or elſwhere, and to take care that the Fiſhermen may be encouraged to go on in their Labors, to the encreaſe of Shipping and Mariners.

Twelfthly They are to take into their conſideration the Engliſh Plantations in *America* or elſwhere, and to adviſe how thoſe Plantations may be beſt managed, and made moſt uſeful for this Commonwealth; and how the Commodities thereof may be ſo multiplied and improved, as (if it be poſsible) thoſe Plantations alone may ſupply the *Commonwealth* of *England* with whatſoever it neceſſarily wants.

And they are hereby required, That as ſoon as they have maturely conſidered and reſolved upon any material part or point of theſe Inſtructions, or that they have thought or adviſed of any thing beſides, which they in their judgements may ſuppoſe to be advantageous to the Advancement of Trade, that they certifie the Parliament or Councel of State thereof from time to time; to the end that the Parliament or Councel of State may give ſuch Order thereupon, as they in their wiſdoms ſhall think to be moſt fit and reaſonable.

And they are hereby required, not onely to take theſe preſent Inſtructions into their ſpeedy conſideration; but what other Inſtructions or Conſiderations concerning Trade ſhall be hereafter tranſmitted to them by the Parliament or Councel of State, they are ſeriouſly to adviſe thereof, and to return their Opinions and Advices thereupon to the Parliament or Councel of State with

7 Specimen page of the Navigation Act, 1650

DEVELOPMENT OF THE BRITISH COLONIAL POLICY

BUT now new influences were at work in England. Cromwell and the merchants were taking steps to secure the self-sufficiency of the English trading empire, and its dominance over such rivals as the Dutch. In the Navigation Acts of 1650 and 1651 England aimed to cripple Holland by shutting off her carrying trade with the colonies, a policy which led to the first war with the Dutch. The colonies were to be parts of "one embodied commonwealth whose head and center" was England. Had Cromwell been in a position to enforce this policy, the colonies might have objected. But domestic troubles kept him occupied; and the spirit of independence throve unchecked and almost unnoticed, beyond the Atlantic.

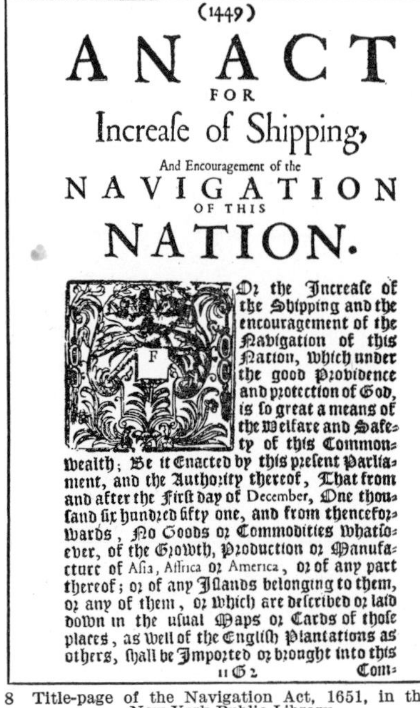

(1449)

AN ACT FOR Increaſe of Shipping, And Encouragement of the NAVIGATION OF THIS NATION.

For the Increaſe of the Shipping and the encouragement of the Navigation of this Nation, which under the good Providence and protection of God, is ſo great a means of the Welfare and Safety of this Commonwealth; Be it Enacted by this preſent Parliament, and the Authority thereof, That from and after the Firſt day of December, One thouſand ſix hundred fifty one, and from thenceforwards, No Goods or Commodities whatſoever, of the Growth, Production or Manufacture of Aſia, Affrica or America, or of any part thereof; or of any Iſlands belonging to them, or any of them, or which are deſcribed or laid down in the uſual Maps or Cards of thoſe places, as well of the Engliſh Plantations as others, ſhall be Imported or brought into this

11 G 2 Com-

8 Title-page of the Navigation Act, 1651, in the New York Public Library

(1450)

Commonwealth of England, or into Ireland, or any other Lands, Iſlands, Plantations or Territories to this Commonwealth belonging, or in their poſſeſsion, in any other Ship or Ships, Veſſel or Veſſels whatſoever, but onely in ſuch as do truly and without fraud belong onely to the people of this Commonwealth, or the Plantations thereof, as the Proprietors or right Owners thereof: And whereof the Maſter and Mariners are alſo for the moſt part of them of the People of this Commonwealth, under the penalty of the forfeiture and loſs of all the Goods that ſhall be Imported contrary to this Act; as alſo of the Ship (with all her Tackle, Guns and Apparel) in which the ſaid Goods or Commodities ſhall be ſo brought in and Imported, The one moyety to the uſe of the Commonwealth, and the other moyety to the uſe and behoof of any perſon or perſons who ſhall ſeize the ſaid Goods or Commodities, and ſhall proſecute the ſame in any Court of Record within this Commonwealth.

And it is further Enacted by the Authority aforeſaid, That no Goods or Commodities of the Growth, Production or Manufacture of Europe, or of any part thereof, ſhall after the Firſt day of December, One thouſand ſix hundred fifty and one, be Imported or brought into this Commonwealth of England, or into Ireland, or any other Lands, Iſlands, Plantations or Territories to this Commonwealth belonging, or in their poſſeſsion, in any Ship or Ships Veſſel or Veſſels whatſoever, but in ſuch as do truly ond without fraud belong onely to the people of this Commonwealth, as the true Owners and proprietors thereof, and in no other, except onely ſuch Foreign Ships and Veſſels

9 Specimen page of the Navigation Act, 1651

MASSACHUSETTS PROTESTS LOYALTY TO THE KING

WITH the return of the King, in 1660, persons unfriendly to Puritan New England came back to power. Massachusetts, suspicious of the developing colonial policy and fearful for her cherished privileges, tried to divert royal hostility by protestations of loyalty to Charles II. The *Humble Petition and Address* was followed by the dispatch of agents to appease the King for the action of Massachusetts in harboring the regicides who had condemned Charles I. In 1662 these agents returned with a gracious answer, and for the nonce all was well.

The Humble
PETITION
AND
ADDRESS
Of the General Court ſitting at
Boſton in *New-England*,
UNTO
The High and Mighty
PRINCE
CHARLES
THE SECOND.

And preſented unto His Moſt-Gracious
Majeſty *Feb.* 11. 1660.

Printed in the Year 1660.

10 Title-page of *The Humble Petition and Address . . . unto Prince Charles the Second,* in the New York Public Library

11 James, Duke of York, 1633–1701, from the portrait by Sir Peter Lely (1618–80) at St. James' Palace, London

COMMERCIAL POLICY AFTER THE RESTORATION

THE compliance of England, however, was not the result of weakness but of tact. The Restoration freed the energies of Englishmen from domestic trials; the notion of a self-sufficient nation-state received renewed support. Mercantilism was the dominant theory of the day. The slave trade was developed. The Navigation Acts were confirmed, committees on foreign trade and the plantations were established. Rivalry with the Dutch brought war; New Netherland was wrested from them (see Vol. I, p. 235) and granted to the Duke of York; Carolina was founded under Clarendon, Ashley, and others. (See Vol. I, pp. 263–69.) The business men were in the saddle. Men like Edward Hyde and the King's brother, James, guided England along the lines of Cromwell's policy.

12 Edward Hyde, first Earl of Clarendon, 1609–74, from the engraved portrait in the Emmet Collection, New York Public Library, after the portrait, 1674, by Sir Peter Lely

13 The Connecticut Charter, 1662, from the original in the State Library, Hartford, Conn.

CHARLES II GRANTS CHARTERS TO CONNECTICUT AND RHODE ISLAND

THE large design of a self-sufficient nation-state required that the far-flung colonies should be more continuously and uniformly administered. They were to be managed as a whole, as a unit for contributing to the welfare of the realm. Furthermore, the colonies must be contented and prosperous. Hence, the court did not turn a deaf ear to the demands of Connecticut and Rhode Island for charters. These colonies, unprotected by such a document, had suffered from the domineering tactics of Massachusetts. As a rebuke to the latter, and as a means of consolidating the colonies, Charles II was easily persuaded to grant Connecticut a charter which merged with the older colony the colony of New Haven. Two years later, a similar constitution was granted to Rhode Island. Under these charters substantial freedom in local matters was attained.

14 Seal of Virginia after the Restoration, from a photograph of the seal used on a proclamation, 1698, in the Public Record Office, London, courtesy of the Virginia State Library

THE RESTORATION IN VIRGINIA

OF all the continental colonies, Virginia most readily fell in with the colonial plan of England. More than most of them, she regarded the interregnum as a break with the past. The Restoration was for the "Dominion" a return to the former agreeable intimacy with England. Berkeley was welcomed as Governor; the Anglican and the Cavalier again controlled the public power and held the public offices. The decade following 1660 was for Virginia one of peace and prosperity. Such good times benefited particularly the ruling social class, the large planters of the tidewater counties, who took pride in imitating the splendor and the arrogance of the Restoration court.

15 From the painting *A Virginia Vestry Meeting After the Restoration*, by F. Louis Mora (1874–), for Woodrow Wilson, *A History of the American People*, 1901. © Harper & Bros.

VIRGINIA ARISTOCRATS

ASSISTING the popular Berkeley and his council were the burgesses, representing the freemen of the colony. The three joined to form a lawmaking assembly wherein all coöperated to further the interests of Virginia. This harmony was promoted by the dominant power possessed by the royal Governor. Ties of loyalty, of social caste, of the advantages coming from public office, bound to him the large planters sitting as burgesses. The local vestries, whose membership came to be filled by coöptation (selection), were manned by friends of the Governor. Controlled by an autocratic and aging Governor, a well-oiled machine operated smoothly and, apparently, with hearty popular endorsement. But the folk on the western frontier began to find this government not always to their interest.

THE BACON REBELLION

WITH the passage of time, flaws began to appear. Berkeley and his clique became arrogant and avaricious. His large powers of appointment secured the compliance of central and local officials in his personal rule. Accounts were rarely audited. Colonial defenses were suffered to deteriorate. Meanwhile, the back-country had been filling with persons who became imbued with the hardy self-reliance of the frontiersman. When Berkeley, in 1675–76, hesitated for ten months to render them aid against Indian depredations, the men of the upper counties took matters into their own hands. Led by Nathaniel Bacon, a sensitive young enthusiast of good social standing, volunteer levies repelled the Indians. When Berkeley attempted to denounce such patriotic but unauthorized conduct, the Assembly elected Bacon commander-in-chief. The Governor refused to sign the commission; whereupon Bacon, with five hundred men, marched upon Jamestown and by intimidation secured from the haughty Berkeley the desired document. What began as a necessary move for self-defense was drifting toward rebellion.

16 Governor Berkeley and the Insurgents, from W. A. Crafts, *Pioneers in the Settlement of America*, Boston, 1876, drawing by W. L. Sheppard (1833–1912)

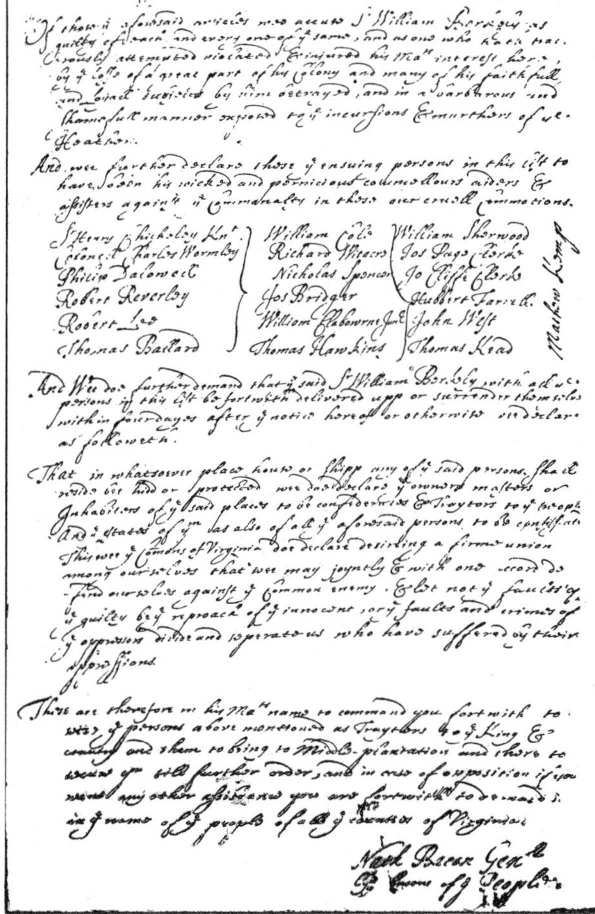

Of this & the aforesaid articles wee accuse Sr William Berkeley as guilty of each and every one of ye same, and as one who hath traiterously attempted violated & injured his Maties interest here, by ye losse of a great part of his Colony and many of his faithfull and loyall subjects by him betrayed, and in a barbarous and shamefull manner exposed to ye incursions & murthers of ye Heathen.

And wee further declare these ye ensuing persons in this list to have been his wicked and pernicious councellours aiders & assisters against ye Commonalty in these our cruell Commotions.

Sr Henry Chicheley Knt.	William Cole	William Sherwood
Coloneil Charles Wormeley	Richard Whitacre	Jos Page Clerke
Philip Ludwell	Nicholas Spencer	Jo Cliffe Clerke
Robert Beverley	Jos Bridger	Hubbert Farrell
Robert Lee	William Claiborne Junr	John West
Thomas Ballard	Thomas Hawkins	Thomas Reade

Mathew Kemp

And Wee doe further demand that ye said Sr William Berkeley with all ye persons in this list be forthwith delivered upp or surrender themselves within four dayes after ye notice hereof or otherwise wee declare as followeth.

That in whatsoever place house or shipp any of ye said persons shall reside bee hidd or protected wee doe declare ye owners masters or Inhabitants of ye said places to be confederates & Traytors to ye people And ye estates of them is also of all ye aforesaid persons to be confiscated This wee ye Commons of Virginia doe declare desiring a firme union amongst our selves that wee may joyntly & with one accord defend our selves against ye Common enemy. & let not ye faults of ye guilty bee ye reproach of ye innocent, or ye faults and crimes of ye oppressors divide and separate us who have suffered by their oppressions.

These are therefore in his Maties name to command you forthwith to seize ye persons above mentioned as Traytors to ye King & country and them to bring to Midle-plantation and there to secure them till further order, and in case of opposition if you want any other assistance you are forthwith to demand it in ye name of ye people of all ye counties of Virginia.

Nath Bacon Genll
by Consent of ye People.

17 "Declaration of the People of Virginia", signed by Nathaniel Bacon, 1676; from *Add. Mss.* 4159, folio 177, in the British Museum

GOVERNOR BERKELEY IS DEFIED BY BACON'S MEN

As soon as the popular leader had withdrawn to fight the Indians, Berkeley took steps to raise troops against him. Hearing of this, Bacon returned to Middle Plantation (now Williamsburg) and issued a call for a convention of his supporters. With this call was issued a "Declaration of the People" wherein Bacon vigorously arraigned the Berkeley administration. The Governor and his official family were called traitors, and all good men and true were summoned to aid in seizing "what Spounges have suckt up the publique treasure" and in such manifold way abused entrusted powers. Bacon prevailed upon those attending the Williamsburg Convention to subscribe to an oath which came dangerously near being a breach of allegiance to the Crown. The planters and freemen assented because of the high-handed conduct of the enraged Berkeley.

Bacon's signature to this document, "Genl by consent of ye People," is probably the first instance of the public enunciation of a principle which was to live and ultimately to reach its full fruition in the shaping of the government of a free people.

18 From the painting *The Burning of Jamestown*, by Howard Pyle for Woodrow Wilson, *A History of the American People*, 1901. © Harper & Bros.

THE REBELLION COLLAPSES AT BACON'S DEATH

AGAINST Berkeley, now in Jamestown, a small force moved under Bacon. Rather than fight, the Governor withdrew; and Bacon entered the town. Fearing attack, he burned it to the ground. While proceeding to gather more support from the tidewater counties, he suddenly died, and the rebellion collapsed. Berkeley returned to power, using it to wreak vindictive vengeance upon those who had thwarted his tyranny.

A BRITISH COMMISSION INVESTIGATES THE VIRGINIA REBELLION

NEWS of the disturbance reached England just in time to prevent the granting to Virginia of a charter which might have secured her even greater autonomy. At once the home authorities took measures to handle the crisis. Berkeley was ordered home; a commission of inquiry was sent out. This body, on reaching Virginia early in 1677, found Bacon dead, and the inhabitants both loyal to the Crown and bitter against Berkeley's autocratic system. Yet, though a variety of reforms in the direction of liberalism were mooted, little was done. The old privileged officialdom, somewhat chastened by their late experience, resumed control. The rebellion gave evidence, however, of the ease with which resistance to bad government might turn into resistance to the Crown.

STRANGE NEWS
FROM
VIRGINIA;
Being a full and true
ACCOUNT
OF THE
LIFE and DEATH
OF
Nathanael Bacon Efquire,
Who was the only Caufe and Original of all the late Troubles in that COUNTRY.
With a full Relation of all the Accidents which have happened in the late War there between the Chriftians and Indians.

LONDON,
Printed for *William Harris*, next door to the Turn-Stile without *Moor-gate*. 1677.

19 Title-page from a facsimile of the original issue, 1677, in the New York Public Library

20 Obverse side of Oak Tree and Willow Tree Shillings, and Obverse and Reverse sides of Pine Tree Shilling, all of date 1652, from original Massachusetts coins in the collection of the American Numismatic Society, New York

MASSACHUSETTS SHOWS SIGNS OF INDEPENDENCE

To bring Massachusetts within the scope of the colonial policy now developing was less easy. The exclusive theocracy of Boston was composed of vigorous and able men, jealous of their rights under the charter. There was little liking for Stuart principles; full fifteen months passed before Charles II was proclaimed King in Boston. But grievances against their government were being forcefully presented at Court. Massachusetts in 1652 was coining its own currency, issuing proclamations in its own name, and in other ways violating the charter and "accroaching royal power." Diplomacy dictated caution. In 1662 Simon Bradstreet and the Reverend John Norton were dispatched to England to counter the complaints and to represent the loyalty of the people.

SIMON BRADSTREET, 1603–97, SENT TO ENGLAND AS COLONIAL AGENT

Bradstreet's selection for this mission was prompted by the hope that an appearance of submissiveness might preserve the cherished privileges of the colony. Yet Bradstreet was one of the official class; he held public office without interruption from 1632 until the charter was annulled in 1684. Furthermore, the General Court reminded their agents that "you shall not engage us by any act of yours to anything which may be prejudicial to our present standing according to patent." Such embassies surely could not solve the problem. Nor did the Commission sent to the colony in 1664 succeed in breaking the obstinacy of Endicott, Bellingham, and their colleagues. Foreign entanglements forced England for a time to acquiesce.

21 From the portrait, artist unknown, in the Senate Chamber, Massachusetts State House, Boston

THE KING REVOKES THE MASSACHUSETTS CHARTER

Massachusetts continued on her disobedient course. Making concessions where necessary, more in form than substance, she nevertheless resisted the continued efforts of the English merchant and lawyer to bring her within the commercial union established by the Acts of Trade. That system stirred the opposition of powerful interests in the colony, an opposition that sentiments of loyalty alone could not overcome. Strict measures of enforcement were needed. Hence Edward Randolph was sent out as royal collector of customs; but, as he was forced to rely upon local aid in his work, his efforts were fruitless. Behind the bulwark of their charter the Governor and Company continued their obstructive tactics till the situation became intolerable to the home authorities. By 1678 stern measures were determined upon. In 1683 Randolph was dispatched to Boston with a *quo warranto* demanding the authority under which Massachusetts had exercised such large powers in derogation of the rights of the Crown. With this writ he carried a proclamation from Charles promising liberal treatment in case of submission. But the colony, though greatly troubled, did not consider submitting. Instead they interposed technical objections to the writ. In this move they succeeded. But the victory was temporary; for more effective and more drastic steps were immediately taken. By decree of October 13, 1684, the Massachusetts charter was "vacated, cancelled and annihilated."

At the Court at WHITEHALL,
The 20th of *July*, 1683.

Present
The Kings most Excellent Majesty,

Lord Archbishop of Canterbury	*Earl of* Bathe
Lord Keeper	*Earl of* Craven
Lord President	*Earl of* Aylesbury
Lord Privy Seal	*Earl of* Conway
Duke of Ormond	*Viscount* Falconberg
Duke of Albemarle	*Lord Bishop of* London
Earl of Peterborrow	*Lord* Dartmouth
Earl of Sunderland	*Mr. Chancellor of the* Exchequer
Earl of Clarendon	*Mr. Chancellor of the* Dutchy:

He Right Honourable the Lords of the Committee for Trade and Foreign Plantations, having this day Presented to the Board, a Report concerning *New England*, together with the Draught of a Declaration from His Majesty, to the Governour and Company of the *Massachusetts Bay*, up-
A on

22 Proclamation of Charles II in *Re Quo Warranto*, 1683, title-page of the copy in the New York Public Library

(3)

Charles R.

HARLES the Second by the Grace of God, King of *England, Scotland, France* and *Ireland*, Defender of the Faith, &c. To all to whom these Presents shall come, or may in any wise concern, Greeting. Although We have thought fit to Issue Our Writ of *Quo Warranto* against the Charter and Priviledges Claimed by the Governour and Company of the *Massachusetts Bay* in *New England*, by reason of some Crimes and Misdemenours by them Committed; Yet Our Will and Pleasure is, and We do hereby Declare, That the Private Interests and Proprieties of all Persons within that Our Colony, shall be Continued and Preserved to them, so that no man shall receive any Prejudice in his Freehold or Estate; and that in case the said Corporation of the *Massachusetts Bay* shall before further Prosecution had upon the said *Quo Warranto*, make a full Submission, and entire Resignation to Our Pleasure, We will then Regulate their Charter in such manner as shall be for Our Service, and the good of that Our Colony, without any other Alterations then such as We shall find necessary for the better Support of Our Government there.

And

23 Order-in-Council, 1683, to proceed with the *Quo Warranto*, in the New York Public Library

(4)

And We do hereby further Declare and Direct, That all those Persons who are questioned in or by the said *Quo Warranto*, and shall go about to maintain the Suit against Us, shall make their Defence at their own particular Charge, without any help by, or spending any part of the Publick Stock of Our said Colony; And that as well those that are not Freemen, as such as are willing to submit to Our Pleasure, shall be Discharged from all Rates, Levies and Contributions towards the Expence of the said Suit, both in their Persons and Estates. And Our further Pleasure is, That this Our Royal Declaration be Published within Our said Colony, that none may pretend ignorance hereof.

Given under Our Signet and Royal Sign Manual at Our Court at Whitehall, *the 26th day of* July 1683. *In the Five and thirtieth Year of Our Reign.*

By His Majesties Command.

L. Jenkins.

LONDON,
Printed by the Assigns of *John Bill* deceas'd: And by *Henry Hills*, and *Thomas Newcomb*, Printers to the Kings most Excellent Majesty, 1683.

24 Second page of Order-in-Council, 1683, in the New York Public Library

25 Joseph Dudley, 1647–1720, from the portrait, artist unknown, in the Massachusetts Historical Society, Boston

MASSACHUSETTS AND NEIGHBORING COLONIES UNITED UNDER CENTRAL CONTROL

THE revocation of the charter was only the first and easiest step in fulfilling the grand plan of consolidating the English colonies under vigorous central control. It remained to erect in New England a governmental structure strengthened by local support. At once Plymouth colony was joined to Massachusetts Bay; and before long New Hampshire, the Narragansett settlements, and Maine were added to what came to be called the Dominion of New England. On Randolph's advice, recognition under the new arrangements was given to those colonists, now growing in number, who were inclined to sympathize with the English commercial and colonial policy. In particular, Randolph recommended that Joseph Dudley, the son of the second Governor of Massachusetts, be given important office. British merchants were interested in more effective colonial control because of the profits that accrued from a favored trading position.

DUDLEY AS PRESIDENT OF THE COUNCIL OF NEW ENGLAND

DUDLEY'S business ties, his temperament, and occasional visits to England in an effort to conciliate the Crown had led him to take a favorable view of the new policies. The antipathy which his attitude aroused against him in Massachusetts is indicated in the title of a later pamphlet, *The Deplorable State of New England by reason of a Covetous and Treacherous Governor and Pusillanimous Counsellors.* Perhaps a later Governor, Thomas Hutchinson, passed the surest judgment when he wrote: "He had as many virtues as can consist with so great a thirst for honour and power." Randolph's efforts bore fruit. In the fall of 1685 a temporary government over New England was established. This consisted of Dudley as President, Randolph as Secretary, and sixteen other councillors named by the Crown. They were empowered to administer the laws of England and of the colonies, to establish courts, and in other ways to maintain royal authority until a more nearly permanent scheme could be devised. In the following May, with no outward opposition, this government was proclaimed in Boston and immediately proceeded to exert its authority. The disputes between the Crown and the people, which were to last for seventy years, began with Dudley.

A

PROCLAMATION

BY The *PRESIDENT* and *COUNCIL* of His Majeſtiy's Territory & Dominion of *NEW-ENGLAND* in AMERICA.

WHEREAS His Moſt Excellent Majeſty our Soveraign LORD *JAMES* the Second, King of *England*, *Scotland*, *France* and *Ireland*, Defender of the Faith &c. by COMMISSION or *Letters Patents* under His Great Seal of *England*, bearing Date the Eight day of *October* in the firſt ,– of His Reign hath been graciouſly pleaſed to erect and conſtitute a PRESIDENT and COUNCIL to take Care of all *that* His Territory and Dominion of *New-England* called the *Maſſachuſets Bay*, the Provinces of *New-Hampſhire* & *Main*, and the *Narraganſet Countrey*, otherwiſe called the *Kings-Province*, with all the Iſlands, Rights and Members thereunto appertaining; and to Order Rule and GOVERN the ſame according to the Rules, Methods and Regulations ſpecified in the ſaid *Commiſſion*: Together with His Majeſties Gracious *Indulgence* in matters of *Religion*.

And for the Execution of His Royal pleaſure in that behalf, His Majeſty hath been pleaſed to appoint *Joſeph Dudley* Eſq to be the firſt *PRESIDENT* of His Majeſties ſaid *Council*, & *VICE-ADMIRAL* of theſe *Seas*. And to Continue in the ſaid Offices until his Majeſty ſhall otherwiſe direct, & alſo to nominate & appoint *William Stoughton*, Eſq; now *Deputy-Preſident*, *Simon Bradſtreet*, *Robert Maſon*, *John Fitz-Winthrope*, *John Pynchon*, *Peter Bulkley*, *Edward Randolph*, *Wait Winthrope*, *Richard Wharton*, *John Uſher*, *Nathaniel Saltonſtal*, *Bartholomew Gidney*, *Jonathan Tyng*, *Dudley Bradſtreet*, *John Hinks*, and *Edward Tyng*, Eſq's: &c, be His Majeſties *Council* in the ſaid *Colony* and *Territories*.

The *Preſident* & *Council* therefore being convened and having according to the Direction & Form of the ſaid Commiſſion, taken their Oathes and Entered the GOVERNMENT aforeſaid; and finding it needful, that ſpeedy & effectual Care be taken for the Obſervation of His Majeſties Commands, and particularly for the Regulation and good Government of the *Narraganſet* Countrey or *Kings-Province*, which hath hitherto been *unſettled*. They the ſaid *Preſident* & *Council* have reſolved ſpeedily to *erect* and *ſettle* a conſtant *Court* of *Record* upon the place; and that the *Preſident*, *Deputy-Preſident*, or ſome others of the Members of His Majeſties Council ſhall be preſent to give all neceſſary Power and Directions for *Eſtabliſhing* His Majeſties *Government* there, and Adminiſtration of Juſtice to *All* His Majeſties Subjects within the ſaid *Narraganſet Countrey* or *Kings-Province*, and all the *Iſlands*, *Rights*, and *Members* thereof. And the ſaid *Preſident* & *Council* have in the interim aſſigned *Richard Smith* Eſq: *James Pendleton*, and *John Fones* Gentlemen, *Juſtices* to keep the *Peace* of our Soveraign Lord the KING and all His Subjects: And alſo given Commiſſion to the ſaid *Richard Smith* to be *Sergeant Major*, and Chief Commander of His Majeſties *Militia*, both of *Horſe* & *Foot* within the *Narraganſet Countrey* or *Province*, and all the Iſlands Rights and Members thereof. THEREFORE the ſaid *Preſident* & *Council* doe hereby in His Majeſties Name and by virtue of His ſaid Commiſſion ſtrictly Require & Command all other perſons *being* or *coming* upon the place, to forbear the Excerciſe of all manner of Juriſdiction, Authority, and Power, and to ceaſe all further Proceedings for the Allotments or Diviſions of Land, or making any *Strip* or *Waſte* upon any part of the ſaid Province, ſave only on each man's *ſtated* Propriety, except by Licence obtained from the ſaid Court, or the *Preſident* & *Council*, until there ſhall be ſuch effectual Regulation and Government eſtabliſhed as is directed by His Majeſty. And the ſaid *Preſident* & *Council* doe hereby henceforth *diſcharge* all His Majeſties Subjects within the ſaid *Narraganſet Countrey* or *Kings Province* and all the Iſlands, Rights & Members thereof *from* the Government of the *Governour* & *Company* of *Connecticut* & *Rhode-Iſland* and *Providence* Plantation, & all others pretending any Power or Juriſdiction. Hereby Charging & Commanding all His Majeſties Subjects to yeild ready & due *Obedience* to the ſaid *Juſtices* of the Peace, the *Sergeant Major* or Cheif Commander of His Majeſties *Militia*. And *George Weightman*, *Thomas Eldridge*, *Thomas Monford* and *William Chaplin* are hereby appointed & authorized preſent Conſtables: and Liberty given to the aforeſaid Juſtices to appoint ſo many more as they ſhall ſee needful to them, and to adminiſter Oathes unto the aforeſaid Conſtables & ſuch as are to be Ordeined. And all other perſons are to be *aiding* & *aſſiſting* unto them the ſaid Juſtices and Conſtables in the Execution and Diſcharge of their reſpective Offices, Charges and Truſts, as they will anſwer the contrary at their utmoſt Peril.

Given from the Council-houſe *in* Boſton *this 28th Day of May Anno Domini* 1686. *Annoq: Regni Regis* Jacobi Secundi *ſecundo*.

By the Preſident and Council, *Edward Randolph* Secr':

GOD SAVE THE KING

BOSTON, in N. E. *Printed by* Richard Pierce, *Printer to the Honourable His Majeſties* Preſident *and* Council *of this Government*.

26 Proclamation by the President and Council of New England, May 28, 1686, from a printed copy in the Massachusetts Historical Society, Boston

THE KING SENDS NEW ENGLAND A MARTINET GOVERNOR

On December 20, 1686, Sir Edmund Andros reached Boston with a commission as Governor of New England, and instructions as to the government to be instituted. These placed substantially all power, legislative as well as executive, in the hands of the Governor and his council, all of whom were appointed by the Crown. The plan was to consolidate the whole of New England into a singly-ruled vice-royalty. Andros, a soldier by trade, was imperious and inflexible, faithful to the interests of his superiors and an ardent churchman. He had just served several years as Governor of the conquered province of New York, where he had distinctly furthered the imperial schemes of the Stuart court. He was sent to New England to pursue similar tactics and similar results were expected from him.

27 Sir Edmund Andros, *d.* 1714, from the engraving in The Prince Society, *The Andros Tracts*, Boston, 1867–74, after the original portrait in the possession of the descendants of Andros in London

THE PURITANS OPPOSE THE ANGLICAN SERVICE

The interim government under Dudley had assumed a conciliatory attitude toward the customs and prejudices of the colony. Now the people anxiously waited to observe the actions of the new Governor. Andros was not long in showing his determined will. He had been instructed to provide for worship in accordance with the Anglican church. Zealously he endeavored to fulfill orders. When the Puritans refused to permit Robert Ratcliffe, minister of the English Church, to utilize any of their meeting-houses, the Governor forcibly seized the South Meeting-House. The Bostonians were aghast. The use of the prayer book within one of their churches was in their eyes scandalous in high degree, and such conduct boded ill for pleasant relations with the new administration.

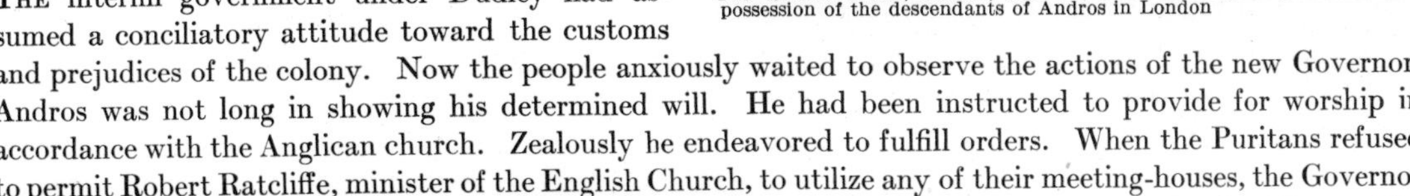

28 From the painting *Governor Andros Taking Possession of Old South Meeting-House*, by Frank O. Small. © Halliday Historic Photograph Co.

ANTAGONISM TO THE GOVERNOR APPEARS

New England traditions of self-government ran counter to the spirit of the Governor. Lawmaking and tax-levying by an appointed body were novel and distasteful. Supervision of town government and harsh scrutiny of land titles caused further dissatisfaction. Andros revised the tax system and the courts to enhance his power. Randolph was made censor of the press. It was not long before the overbearing conduct of the haughty Governor and his redcoats was met by the citizens with sullen looks and threatening gestures.

29 Governor Andros and the Boston People, from *Harper's Magazine*, June 1883, after a drawing by Howard Pyle

30 From a drawing *Andros Demanding the Charter of Connecticut,* made expressly for *The Pageant of America,* by C. W. Jefferys (1869–)

CONNECTICUT INSISTS ON KEEPING ITS CHARTER

Even before the coming of Andros, measures had been taken to incorporate Rhode Island and Connecticut into the new Dominion. Writs against their charters were issued in 1685–86. Rhode Island at once made formal submission; but Connecticut was less complaisant. In the fall of 1687 Andros was forced to proceed in person to Hartford to demand the charter. Appearing before the Assembly, he precipitated a discussion that ran on into the night. Tradition has it that suddenly the lights were put out, and William Wadsworth escaped in the darkness with the precious document, to hide it in the hollow of a tree. Until it was blown down in 1856, the Charter Oak symbolized for many the long resistance to oppression that culminated in the Revolution.

31 From the painting *The Charter Oak,* 1857, by C. D. Brownell in the Wadsworth Atheneum, Hartford, Conn.

ANDROS FINDS FEW SUPPORTERS

Five months later (April, 1688) King James issued a second commission to Andros as Governor of "The Territory and Dominion of New England," a jurisdiction now covering, in addition to New England proper, New York and the Jerseys. Over this vast country of dissimilar institutions and peoples, thus thrown together involuntarily, Andros exercised vice-regal power. In brief time, his Council discovered that it was useless to oppose his will. Meetings were sparsely attended, "so that it might be too truly affirmed, that in effect four or five persons, and those not so favorably inclined and disposed as were to be wished for, bear the Rule over and gave law to a Territory the largest and most considerable of any belonging to the Dominion of the Crown." (Quoted from *A Narrative of the Proceedings of Sir Edmund Androsse and his Complices,* written by William Stoughton, Thomas Hinckley and Wait Winthrop, three of his Councillors.)

32 Obverse of the Great Seal of New England, 1686–89, from the Massachusetts Historical Society *Proceedings,* Vol. VI, first series

33 Reverse of the Great Seal of New England, 1686–89, from the Massachusetts Historical Society *Proceedings,* Vol. VI, first series

REVOLUTION IN ENGLAND RELEASES THE BOSTON SPIRIT

Lasting submission to the odious rule of Andros was unthinkable. The very spirit of the New Englander revolted against such autocratic conduct. Moreover, Andros was to them the symbol not only of autocracy, but also of Anglicanism. Armed opposition had long been contemplated when news of the Revolution of 1688 in England released the pent-up hostility. On April 18, 1689, concerted action resulted in the seizure of several of the Governor's advisers. Andros himself took refuge in the fort. Simon Bradstreet, Thomas Danforth, William Stoughton and others of the old leaders, after consultation together, sent him a letter advising him to surrender.

35 Andros a Prisoner in Boston, from an unsigned illustration in W. A. Crafts, *Pioneers in the Settlement of America*, Boston, 1877

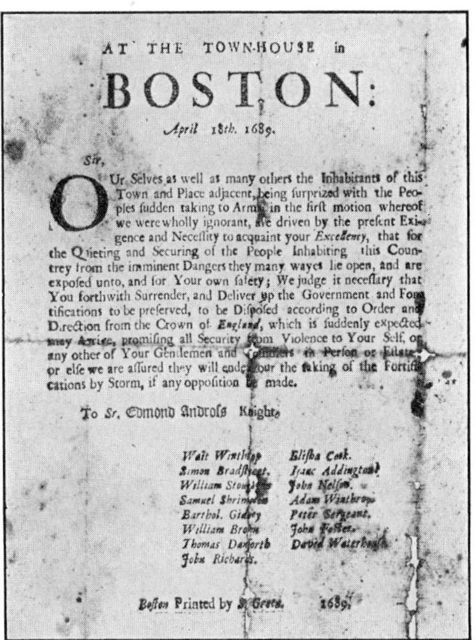

AT THE TOWN-HOUSE in

BOSTON:

April 18th. 1689.

Sir,

OUr Selves as well as many others the Inhabitants of this Town and Place adjacent, being surprized with the Peoples sudden taking to Arms; in the first motion whereof we were wholly ignorant, are driven by the present Exigence and Necessity to acquaint your *Excellency*, that for the Quieting and Securing of the People Inhabiting this Countrey from the imminent Dangers they many wayes lie open, and are exposed unto, and for Your own safety; We judge it necessary that You forthwith Surrender, and Deliver up the Government and Fortifications to be preserved, to be Disposed according to Order and Direction from the Crown of *England*, which is suddenly expected may Arrive, promising all Security from Violence to Your Self, or any other of Your Gentlemen and Souldiers in Person or Estate: or else we are assured they will endeavour the taking of the Fortifications by Storm, if any opposition be made.

To *Sr.* Edmond Andross Knight.

Wait Winthrop	*Elisha Cook.*
Simon Bradstreet.	*Isaac Addington.*
William Stoughton	*John Nelson.*
Samuel Shrimpton	*Adam Winthrop.*
Barthol. Gidney	*Peter Sergeant.*
William Brown	*John Foster.*
Thomas Danforth	*David Waterhouse.*
John Richards.	

Boston Printed by *S. Green.* 1689.

34 Warning to Andros to Surrender, from a broadside, Boston, 1689, in the Massachusetts Historical Society

THE REVOLT AGAINST THE GOVERNOR

Andros at first hoped for rescue from the frigate *Rose* lying at anchor in the harbor. But the people seized a boat sent to succor him, and surrounded the fort. Resistance was mad; Andros with his companions marched out to the Town-House, where they surrendered. Randolph and some of the more hated of the former rulers were committed to the common jail. Andros was placed in the custody of a trusted citizen. Within a few brief hours the constituted government had been overthrown.

NEW ENGLAND COLONIES REINSTATE THEIR OLD LEADERS

A temporary government was organized. There was then summoned a convention of delegates from the towns to consider further action. After some deliberation this body determined to restore the government as it had been under the charter. The people regarded the period from 1686 to 1689 as one of illegal usurpation of power, unauthorized by their fundamental law. Simon Bradstreet, who had been the last Governor under the charter, was recalled to office. William and Mary were proclaimed, and petitioned to recognize the new order of things. The other New England colonies, severed from Massachusetts by the revolt, followed her example. Before June, in Plymouth, Rhode Island and Connecticut, the old assemblies had been summoned and the old leaders restored to office. Not long after, William issued a proclamation approving the actions of Massachusetts.

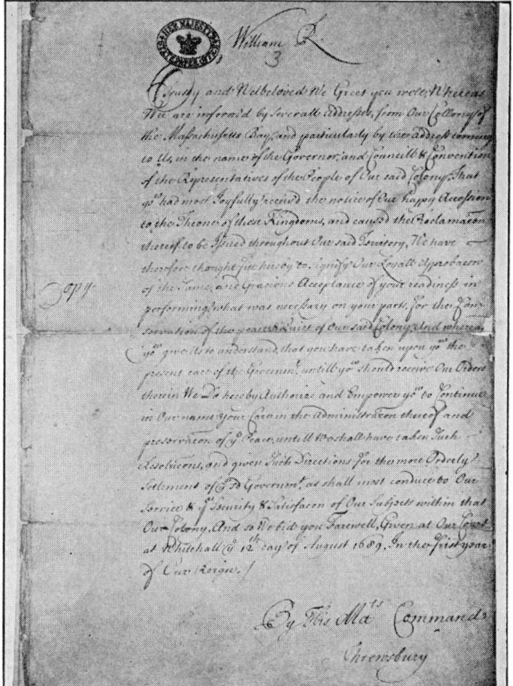

William R
3

Copy

Trusty and Welbeloved We Greet you well, Whereas
Wee are inform'd by Severall Addresses, from Our Collony of
the Massachusetts Bay, and particularly by two Addresses comming
to Us, in the name of the Governor, and Councill & Convention
of the Representatives of the People of Our said Colony, That
you had most Joyfully receiv'd the notice of Our happy Accession
to the Throne of these Kingdoms, and caused the Proclamacon
thereof to be Issued throughout Our said Territory, We have
therefore thought fitt hereby to signify Our Royall Approbacon
of the same, and Gracious Acceptance of your readiness in
performing what was necessary on your part, for the Preservation of the peace & Quiet of Our said Colony, And whereas
you give Us to understand that you have taken upon you the
present care of the Governmt untill you should receive Our Orders
therein We Do hereby Authorize and Empower you to Continue
in Our name your Care in the Administracon thereof and
preservacon of ye Peace, untill We shall have taken such
Resolucons, and given such Directions for the more Orderly
Settlement of ye sd Governmt as shall most conduce to Our
Service & ye Security & Satisfacon of Our Subjects within that
Our Colony, And so We bid you Farewell, Given at Our Court
at Whitehall ye 12th day of August 1689, In the first year
of Our Reign.

By His Mats Command
Shrewsbury

36 Proclamation of William of Orange Approving the Action of Massachusetts, from the copy, dated Aug. 12, 1689, in the Colonial Office, London

37 From the statue of Jacob Leisler by Solon H. Borglum (1868–1922), at New Rochelle, N. Y.

REVOLT IN NEW YORK BRINGS A GERMAN INTO POWER

From New England the revolt spread to New York. There also the events in England furnished the occasion for an uprising against constituted authority. Smarting under the narrow, class government in which they had no share, and alleging the existence of danger from French attacks, the train-bands of the city skirmished with the regular troops under Lieutenant-Governor Nicholson. Acting on the advice of his council, the latter let the rebellion develop. A provisional government was set up under Jacob Leisler. Leisler was a German immigrant who by dint of intelligence, honesty, and effort had risen to a position of influence among the merchants. He was, however, uneducated, and possessed of an ungoverned temper. Asserting that he was defending the people against arbitrary government until the King should make known his will, he attempted to legalize his position by proclaiming the new sovereigns, and by receiving, as if directed to him, instructions which had been sent out to the acting Governor.

THE KING'S NEW GOVERNOR IS INSTALLED IN NEW YORK

For more than a year Leisler remained in power. He called a convention of the people, and in other ways tried to establish at least the forms of representative government. But his rule was founded upon military force, and would of necessity fall as soon as an authorized agent of the Crown should appear. In 1689 Colonel Henry Sloughter had been appointed Governor under William and Mary but did not arrive in the colony until 1691. Preceding him came troops under Major Ingoldsby, who assumed a hostile attitude toward Leisler. The latter refused to resign his power to any one but the direct civil representative of the Crown. Two days before Governor Sloughter's arrival shots were exchanged between the troops of Leisler and Ingoldsby. This action was twisted, by the patriotic leader's enemies, into an act of treason against His Majesty. The charges were prosecuted with vigor, and Leisler was executed. The rebellion was over; but it had given a hint of the desire for a government in which the residents should have a larger voice.

38 Sloughter Signing Leisler's Death Warrant, from Bryant and Gay, *History of the United States*, New York, 1881–84, after a drawing by C. S. Reinhart (1844–96)

39 Increase Mather, 1639–1723, from an engraving by John Sturt (1655–1730), in Cotton Mather, *Parentator, Memoirs of Remarkables in the Life and Death of the Ever-Memorable Dr. Increase Mather*, Boston, 1724

THE PRESIDENT OF HARVARD PROTESTS TO THE KING

Increase Mather was at this time the leading Puritan divine of New England, and president of Harvard College. Like other preachers, he entered fully into the political combats of the day. Of great learning, a forceful and eloquent orator, and a ready publicist, he was sent by his friends, in 1688, to England. It was hoped that through his agency James might be persuaded to relax the rigor of the hated Andros régime. He was twice given audience by the King, but his protestations brought no more than empty promises from a falling monarch.

The Preſent State of the

New-Engliſh Affairs.

This is Publiſhed to prevent Falſe Reports

40 Section of the only known copy of the broadside, printed by Samuel Green, Boston, 1689, in the Massachusetts Archives, Boston

A Paſſage extracted from the publick News Letter, Dated July 6. 1689.

The people of *New-England* having made a thorow Revolution, and ſecured the publick Criminals. On *Thurſday* laſt, the Reverend and Learned Mr. *Mather*, Preſident of the *Colledge*, and Miniſter of *Boſton*, waited on the King; and in a moſt Excellent Speech laid before His Majeſty, the State of that People; ſaying, *That they were ſober, and Induſtrious, and fit for Martial Service; and all with their Lives and Intereſts were at His Majeſties Command, to tender the ſame unto His Majeſty: That they deſired nothing but His Majeſties Acceptance of what they had done, and His Protection; and that if His Majeſty pleaſed to encourage and Commiſſion them, He might eaſily be Emperour of* America. His Majeſty aſſured him, that He was pleaſed with what was done for Him, and for themſelves in the Revolution, and that their Priviledges and Religion ſhould be ſecured unto them.

Extracted from a Letter of Mr. Mather, to his *Son, Dated* Sept. 2. 1689.

On *July* 9. The King ſaid unto me, *That He did kindly Accept of what was done in* Boſton. *And that His Subjects in* New-England *ſhould have their Ancient Rights and Priviledges Reſtored and Confirmed unto them.* Yea, He told me, *That if it were in his power to cauſe it to be done it ſhould be done,* and bade me reſt aſſured of it.

The *Charter-Bill* is not finiſhed, becauſe ſome Additional Clauſes reſpecting Corporations here in *England* cauſed a Debate; and the Parliament is for ſome weeks Adjourned.

Beſides the Letter from the Kings Majeſty, whereof we have notice as above; there is now arrived, an Order from His Majeſty to the Government, bearing Date, *July* 30. 1689. Requiring, *That Sir* Edmund Andros, Edward Randolph, *and others, that have been Seized by the people of* Boſton, *and ſhall be at the Receipt of theſe Commands, Detained there under Confinement, be ſent on Board the firſt Ship, bound to* England, *to anſwer what may be objected againſt them.*

THE KING ORDERS THE TRIAL OF ANDROS AND RANDOLPH

BUT Mather's cause was favored by the Revolution. At once all his efforts were bent to win back the old charter. An attempt to include Massachusetts in a bill restoring various corporation charters was defeated through the dissolution of Parliament. The agent's pleas before William received a favorable, though cautious, response. The King was careful of his prerogative, and, counseled to hear both sides before taking action, he issued an order requiring the Massachusetts authorities to return Andros and Randolph for trial.

A BRIEF

ACCOUNT

CONCERNING

Several of the AGENTS

OF

New-England,

THEIR

NEGOTIATION at the COURT

OF

ENGLAND:

WITH

Some REMARKS on the NEW CHARTER Granted to the Colony of *MASSACHUSETS*.

SHEWING

That all things duely Conſidered, Greater Priviledges than what are therein contained, could not at this Time rationally be expected by the People there.

LONDON, Printed in the Year 1691.

41 Title-page in The Prince Society, *The Andros Tracts*, Vol. II, Boston

OPPOSITION TO MATHER INFLUENCES THE KING

EVEN before reaching England, Randolph began a vigorous and skillful opposition to Mather and his fellow-agents. While the latter were forced to rely chiefly upon such effect as pamphlets might produce, Randolph gained the ear of the merchants and officials who had guided the policy of James and now surrounded William of Orange. The King, busied with Continental affairs, had retained the abler colonial administrators of the Stuarts. The merchants desired as much as ever their trade monopoly. The French war (see Vol. VI) gave cause for alarm for the safety of New England. All these factors convinced the Government that New England could not be given its old separate and autonomous position.

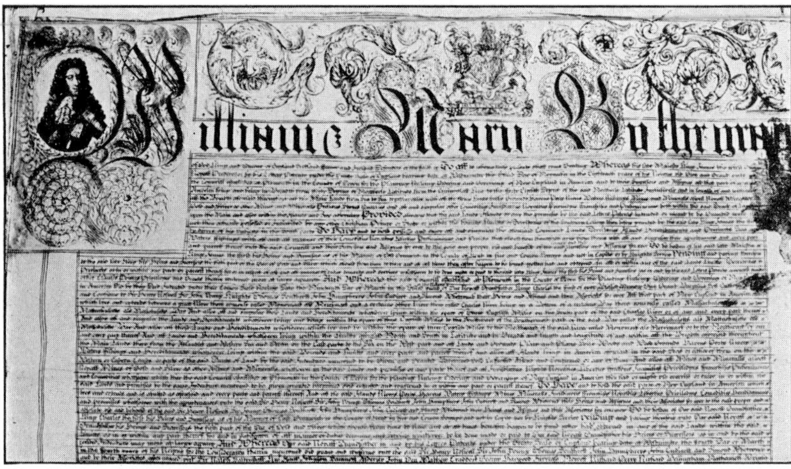

42 Massachusetts Charter of 1691 (first sheet), from the original parchment in the Massachusetts State House, Boston

THE NEW CHARTER IS A COMPROMISE

The result took the form of a new charter (1691). This was in the nature of a compromise between the desires of the Crown and those of the colonists. Imperial interests were recognized in the royal Governor, possessed of a veto over all actions of the legislature. Laws were also, within three years after passage, subject to royal disallowance. The Privy Council, moreover, could receive appeals from the provincial courts. Judges, sheriffs and justices of the peace were made appointive by Governor and council. Substitution of a property qualification for the religious test sounded the death-knell of the old theocracy. The former Assistants became the Council, or upper house, annually elected by the General Court, subject to approval by the Governor. All of these were innovations displeasing to New England. But there were compensations. The charter of 1691 for the first time gave an express legal sanction to the colonial institutions of government. The system of local government was for the most part untouched. Qualified inhabitants were annually to choose a House of Representatives. And the General Court was given powers not granted similar bodies in other royal provinces. Its right to legislate and to tax was expressly stated; it had power to establish courts and to choose many important public officials. Above all, the charter was to be a permanent constitution, to which not only statutes but also the Governor's commissions and instructions were to conform. Massachusetts became a royal province, but a colony possessed of unusually large privileges of self-government.

THE BRITISH BOARD OF TRADE

Steps were now taken to conform colonial administration in London to the new conditions. The Committee of the Privy Council for Trade and Plantations was replaced by a body — eight Commissioners of Trade and Plantations — which carried on its policies and traditions. Among the Commissioners were John Locke and William Blathwayt, both experienced in such matters. Their chief was the able Earl of Bridgewater. The powers of the Lords of Trade were extensive, falling into three major classes. First of all, they were to study British commerce and to ascertain and recommend means of furthering it. Secondly, they were to give especial thought to the condition of the colonies and methods of utilizing them for England's gain. Finally, they were overseers of the government in the colonies, empowered to hear petitions and grievances, to require accounting of public moneys, to advise the disallowance of colonial laws. In its multifarious work the Board of Trade could call upon the Attorney General for advice, and did so frequently, until, in 1718, its wide legal business was turned over to special counsel. A quorum for meetings was five; and for thirty years the Board met several times a week, being rarely forced to adjourn because of insufficient attendance. After 1740 the significance of the Board declined; in 1766 it became solely a consultative body; and in 1768 it was replaced by a Secretary for State, thus reducing the whole business to the control of a single official.

43 John Locke, 1632–1704, from the portrait attributed to J. Closterman, after Sir Godfrey Kneller (1648–1723), in the National Portrait Gallery, London

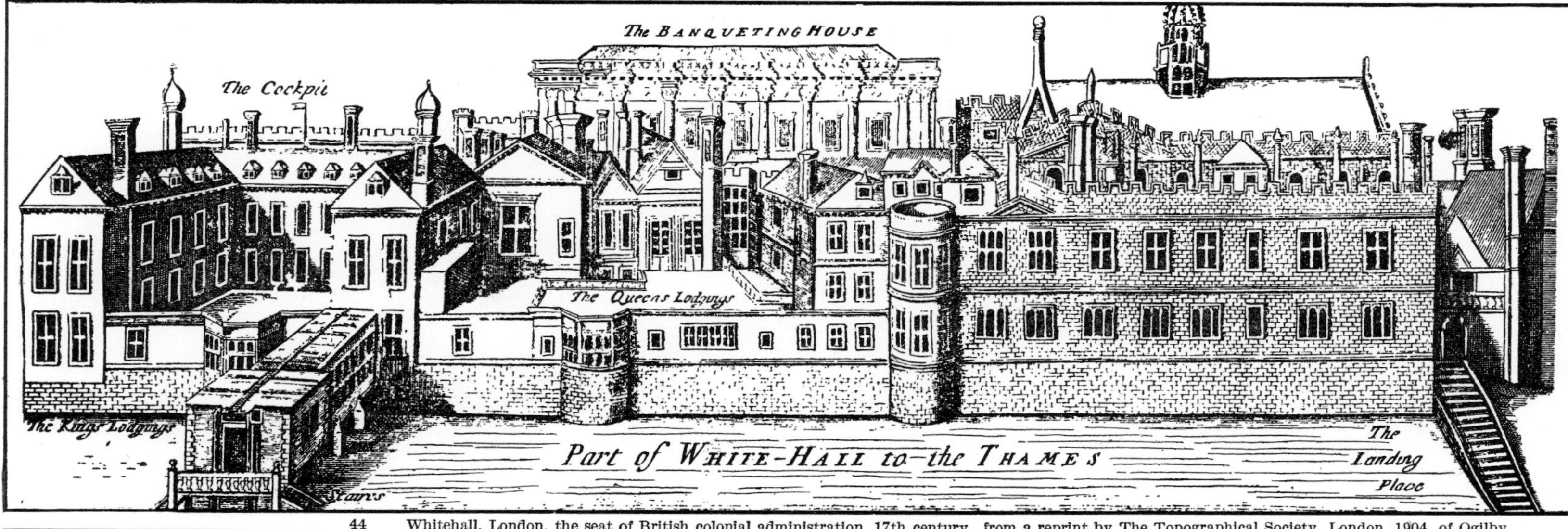

44 Whitehall, London, the seat of British colonial administration, 17th century, from a reprint by The Topographical Society, London, 1904, of Ogilby. *A Prospect of London & Westminster*, 1682

Anno Septimo & Octavo

Gulielmi III. Regis.

An Act for Preventing Frauds, and Regulating Abuses in the Plantation Trade.

Whereas notwithstanding divers Acts made for the Encouragement of the Navigation of this Kingdom, and for the better Securing and Regulating the Plantation Trade, more especially one Act of Parliament made in the Twelfth year of the Reign of the late King Charles the Second, Intituled, An Act for Increasing of Shipping and Navigation, another Act made in the Fifteenth year of the Reign of his said late Majesty, Intituled, An Act for the Incouragement of Trade, another Act made in the Two and twentieth and Three and twentieth years of his said late Majesties Reign, Intituled, An Act to prevent the Planting of Tobacco in *England*, and for Regulating the Plantation Trade, another Act made in the Twenty fifth year of the Reign of his said late Majesty, Intituled, An Act for the Incouragement of the *Greenland* and *Eastland* Trades, and for the better Securing the Plantation Trades, great Abuses are daily committed to the prejudice of the English Navigation, and the loss of a great part of the Plantation Trade

45 An Act for Preventing Frauds, etc., from a copy, 1696, in the British Museum

DIVIDED AUTHORITY

From the beginning, the work of the Board as agent for colonial administration was hampered. While it could recommend, it was not always able to secure the adoption of its policies. Even where its suggestions were accepted, its control over execution was slight. The Board did not appoint the colonial Governor, nor was he subject to removal by it. Indeed, the Government often used colonial offices to satisfy mere place-hunters. More important, colonial business was distributed among a number of independent agencies: the Admiralty looked after naval defense, the Commissioners of Customs and the Treasury shared power in matters fiscal. In brief, the colonies were not yet regarded as deserving control by an administrative body wholly devoted to their concerns. Even the Lords of Trade possessed a variety of functions and interests primarily commercial; and it was chiefly as commercial depots that the colonies came under their supervision. The American colonies did not constitute an isolated problem for the British Government. They had become inseparable from a world-wide attempt to further commercial development. The confusion which came about in their relations with the home government was the confusion between administrative and commercial policy that was inescapable in a system profoundly colored by commercialism but not wholly dominated by it. The types of supervision attempted by England illustrate this commercial bias. One of the earliest and most persistent problems was that of stopping wholesale violations of the existing Navigation Acts. Pressure from the merchants composing such influential bodies as the East India Company and the Royal African Company resulted in the passage of the "Act for preventing Frauds and Regulating Abuses in the Plantation Trade." This received royal assent in April, 1696. It endeavored to strengthen the earlier regulations concerning the colonial trade, and to enhance the position of England in transatlantic commerce.

Articles of Agreement,

Made the 10th Day of *October*, in the Year of our Lord 1695. Between the Right Honourable *RICHARD* Earl of *BELLOMONT* of the one part, and *Robert Levingſton* Eſq;

AND

Captain William Kid,

Of the other part.

WHEREAS the ſaid Capt. *William Kid* is deſirous of obtaining a Commiſſion as Captain of a Private Man of War in order to take Prizes from the King's Enemies, and otherways to annoy them; and whereas certain Perſons did ſome time ſince depart from *New-England*, *Rode-Iſland*, *New-York*, and other parts in *America* and elſewhere, with an intention to become Pirates, and to commit Spoils and Depredations, againſt the Laws of Nations, in the *Red-Sea* or elſewhere, and to return with ſuch Goods and Riches as they ſhould get, to certain places by them agreed upon; of which ſaid Perſons and Places, the ſaid Capt. *Kid* hath notice, and is deſirous to fight with and ſubdue the ſaid Pirates, as alſo other Pirates with whom the ſaid Capt. *Kid* ſhall meet at Sea, in caſe he be impowered ſo to do; and whereas it is agreed between the ſaid Parties, That for the purpoſe aforeſaid a good and ſufficient Ship, to the liking of the ſaid Capt. *Kid*, ſhall be forthwith bought, whereof the ſaid Capt. *Kid* is to have the Command. Now theſe Preſents do witneſs, and it is agreed between the ſaid Parties,

I. That the Earl of *Bellomont* doth covenant and agree, at his proper Charge, to procure from the King's Majeſty, or from the Lords Commiſſioners of the Admiralty (as the Caſe ſhall require) one or more Commiſſions, impowering him the ſaid Capt. *Kid* to act againſt the King's Enemies, and to take *Prizes* from them, as a private Man of War in the uſual manner; and alſo to fight with, conquer and ſubdue *Pirates*, and to take them and their Goods; with other large and beneficial Powers and Clauſes in ſuch Commiſſions as may be moſt proper and effectual in ſuch Caſes.

II. The ſaid Earl of *Bellomont* doth covenant and agree, That within three Months after the ſaid Capt. *Kid*'s departure from *England*, for the purpoſes in theſe Preſents mentioned, he will procure, at his proper charge, a Grant from the King, to be made to ſome indifferent and truſty Perſon, of all ſuch Mechandizes, Goods, Treaſure and other things as ſhall be taken from the ſaid Pirates, or any other Pirate whatſoever, by the ſaid Capt. *Kid*, or by the ſaid Ship, or any other Ship or Ships under his Command.

III. The ſaid Earl doth agree to pay four Fifth parts, the whole in Five parts to be divided, of all Moneys which ſhall be laid out for the buying ſuch good and ſufficient Ship for the purpoſes aforeſaid, together with Rigging and other Apparel and Furniture thereof, and providing the ſame with competent victualling the ſaid Ship, to be approved of by the ſaid Parties; and the ſaid other one Fifth part of the ſaid Charges of the ſaid Ship to be paid for by the ſaid *Robert Levingſton* and *William Kid*.

IV. The ſaid Earl doth agree, That in order to the ſpeedy buying the ſaid Ship, in part of the ſaid four parts of Five of the ſaid Charges, he will pay down the ſum of ſixteen hundred Pounds, by way of Advance, on or before the ſixth day of *November* next enſuing.

V. The ſaid *Robert Levingſton* and *William Kid* do jointly and ſeverally covenant and agree, That on and before the ſixth day of *November*, when the ſaid Earl of *Bellomont* is to pay the ſaid Sum of ſixteen hundred pounds as aforeſaid, they will advance and pay down four hundred pounds in part of the Share and Proportion which they are to have in the ſaid Ship.

VI. The ſaid Earl doth agree, to pay ſuch further Sums of Money as ſhall compleat and make up the ſaid four parts of Five of the Charges of the ſaid Ship's Arrival, Furniture and Victualling, unto the ſaid *Robert Levingſton* and *William Kid* within ſeven Weeks after the date of theſe Preſents; and in like manner the ſaid *Robert Levingſton* and *William Kid* do agree to pay ſuch further Sums as ſhall amount to a fifth part of the whole Charge of the ſaid Ship within ſeven Weeks after the date of theſe Preſents.

A VII The

46 First page of the printed copy, 1701, in the American Antiquarian Society, Worcester, Mass.

GOVERNOR BELLOMONT SENDS CAPTAIN KIDD AFTER PIRATES

DESPITE the efforts of Randolph, of colonial ill fame, and of his English colleagues, illicit trading increased. Trade flourished between the colonies and the Canary Islands, Scotland, Surinam and the West Indies. In addition, there was much smuggling through the agency of pirates from Madagascar and the Red Sea. Profits were enormous; nor did the pirate receive harsh treatment from the colonials. Merchants of Boston, New York, and Philadelphia, prospered. Official connivance was more than rumored. Finally, Governor Fletcher of New York was supplanted by the Earl of Bellomont, specifically instructed to suppress the trade. Before leaving England, the new Governor heard, through Robert Livingston of New York, that the man for the job was Captain William Kidd. So, not averse to profiteering, Bellomont and Livingston entered into an agreement with Kidd, whereby the latter was commissioned as a privateer against the pirates, while the former were to receive the larger share of any prize money resulting from Kidd's exploits. But the spoils of piracy won over Kidd's enterprise. On his return the gallant captain was arrested, tried and executed as a pirate.

THE GOVERNOR PROHIBITS SABBATH-BREAKING

THE failure of such methods led Parliament in 1700 to establish special Justiciary Courts of Admiralty for the trial, with a jury, of captured freebooters. Whether or not it was due to the use of a jury, unsatisfying results came of this venture. It would be interesting to know whether Governor Bellomont achieved more success in his attempts to regulate the personal behavior of the people in the province. In a proclamation that he issued April 2, 1698, he strictly prohibited "Cursing, Swearing, Immoderate Drinking, Sabbath Breaking and all sorts of Lewdness and Profane Behaviour in Word or Action," under penalty of the law. The grant of such wide powers to the Governor of a colony was part of the scheme emanating from London to place the American colonials more and more under royal control.

By His Excellency

Richard Earl of Bellomont, Captain General and Governour In Chief of His Majeſties Province of *New-York*, &c.

A PROCLAMATION

WHEREAS it is of abſolute Neceſſity for the Good and Proſperity of this Province, that our Principal and firſt Care be in Obedience to the Laws of God, and the wholſom Laws of England, to ſhake off all ſorts of Looſeneſs and Prophaneneſs, and to unite in the fear and Love of God, and of one another, by a Religious and Virtuous Deportment and Behaviour, every one in his reſpective Station and Calling, to the end that all Heats, Annimoſities and Diſſentions may vaniſh, and the Bleſſing of Almighty God accompany our Our Honeſt and Lawful Endeavours, and that we joyn Our Affections in the true Support of His Majeſties Government over us, who has ſo often and ſo generouſly expoſed His Sacred Perſon to eminent Dangers, to Redeem us from the growing Power of Popery and Arbitrary Government, and has by the Bleſſing of God procured Our Deliverance, and an Honourable Peace, and is a great Example and Encourager of Religion and Virtuous Living. I have therefore thought fit, by and with the Advice of His Majeſties Council for this Province, and I do hereby Strictly Prohibit all Inhabitants and Sojourners within this Province from *Curſing, Swearing, Immoderate Drinking, Sabbath Breaking* and *all ſorts of Lewdneſs* and *Profane Behaviour in Word or Action*. And for the true and effectual Performance hereof, I do by and with the Advice aforeſaid, Strictly Charge and Command all Mayors, Aldermen, Juſtices of the Peace, Sheriffs, Conſtables, and other Officers within this Province, that they take care that all the Laws made and provided for the Suppreſſion of Vice and encouragement of Religion and Virtue, particularly the Obſervation of the *Lords Day* be duely put in Execution, as they will anſwer the Contrary at their Peril.

Given at New-York the Second Day of April, 1698. *and in the Tenth Year of the Reign of Our Soveraign Lord*, WILLIAM *the Third, by the Grace of God, of* England, Scotland, France *and* Ireland, *King, Defender of the Faith, &c.*

Bellomont.

God Save the KING.

Printed by William Bradford, *Printer to the Kings Moſt Excellent Majeſty in the City of* New-York, 1698.

47 Proclamation of the Earl of Bellomont, 1698, printed by William Bradford, in the New York Public Library

A ROYAL SCAPEGOAT MADE GOVERNOR OF NEW YORK

48 First sheet of Queen Anne's Commission to Lord Cornbury, 1702, confirming his commission by William and Mary, 1701, from the original in the New York Historical Society

THE extent to which the home government relied upon this gubernatorial power is indicated by the minuteness with which instructions were given new appointees. The death, in 1701, of Lord Bellomont reopened the New York problem. This colony was in a pivotal position. She it was whose frontiers came in contact with the French; within her boundaries was the powerful Iroquois confederation whose friendship was invaluable and whose enmity might be disastrous. New York, moreover, was geographically the crux of any scheme of colonial consolidation. These were the phases of the question that appealed to London; local sentiment and institutions were ignored. To fill the vacancy in the office of Governor, choice fell upon the Queen's scapegoat cousin, Lord Cornbury. That this notorious spendthrift might not be welcome in New York was not apparently considered. When Cornbury proceeded to pocket public funds, there began that long struggle for control of the public purse that here, as elsewhere, ended in placing colonial legislatures in a dominating position. The Assembly insisted that revenues be paid to a treasurer appointed by it. Cornbury's royal instructions and dictatorial claims were of little avail. From a system of lump sum and permanent appropriation, there came, in course of combat, appropriations good for one year only, and for specific purposes. When the Council demurred, the Assembly cited English precedent for denying all power in the upper house to amend appropriation bills. Long before, however, Lord Cornbury had been recalled, to face his creditors in English courts.

49 Second sheet of Queen Anne's Commission to Lord Cornbury, 1702, confirming his commission by William and Mary, 1701, from the original in the New York Historical Society

50 Alexander Spotswood, 1676–1740, Lieut. Governor of Virginia, from the portrait about 1736 attributed to Charles Bridges, in the Virginia State Library

THE COLONIAL GOVERNOR

Colonial administration was the function of the British Crown rather than of Parliament. The royal Governor was the Crown's representative in the provinces. His task was to hold the colony in line with the policies of the home government. He had a veto on the acts of the legislature. He received instructions to work for certain kinds of legislation, such as laws for the furtherance of the French and Indian Wars. He was also required to veto bills adversely affecting British trade or British creditors. From time to time he received new instructions either of a general or specific nature. Strictly speaking, colonial laws were not in force even after receiving the Governor's signature. Approval by the Crown was essential and many were disallowed. Governors appointed from the nobility did not always come in intimate contact with the people. In 1704, for instance, the Earl of Orkney was appointed Governor of Virginia; but he took his office easily. Pocketing two thirds of the salary, he gave the remaining twelve hundred pounds to a Lieutenant Governor and he himself never visited the colony. Most remarkable of his deputies was Spotswood. A fiery Scottish soldier, he, like Andros and Cornbury, traveled a thorny path. Stubbornly desirous of improving administration, a high Tory and an intimate of Blathwayt, he early aroused opposition from both local camps. The Burgesses did not take to his efforts to spend money for improving colonial defenses; the Council found fault with his imperious manners and methods. In 1715 he administered to the former a stern rebuke, concluding with the assertion that "Heaven has not generally endowed [the Burgesses] with the ordinary qualifications requisite to legislators," and he summarily dissolved the assembly. The latter at last secured his removal. But the Governor had become a true Virginian; upon recall from office he settled in the colony and became a respected member of the gentry. Spotswood's policy of westward expansion came to fruition under a successor, Robert Dinwiddie. Rugged honesty won for this Scot promotion in the colonial customs service, until in 1752 he came to Virginia as Lieutenant Governor. Dinwiddie possessed many of the characteristics of Spotswood. He also was a stanch supporter of prerogative; he also became angered at colonial reluctance to vest control of expenditures, even for warfare, in the executive. This led Dinwiddie, in 1754, to suggest to the Board of Trade the levying of a colonial poll tax to secure funds for waging the fight against the French and Indians in the Ohio country. It was impossible, he said, to obtain united action on the part of the colonies in raising money. This, combined with perhaps undue zeal in collecting fees under moribund laws, rendered his recall in 1758 not unwelcome to Virginia.

51 Robert Dinwiddie, 1690–1770, Lieut. Governor of Virginia, after the portrait in the possession of the descendants of Dinwiddie in England

PENNSYLVANIA'S GOVERNOR FURTHERS HIS PERSONAL AMBITIONS

NOT solely in royal provinces did Governors have difficulty. Even in proprietary Pennsylvania there was turmoil. Beginning with Sir William Keith (Governor, 1717–26), the issue was drawn between the country people and the proprietor and his conservative supporters. Keith, friend of Spotswood of Virginia, was of an ingratiating character. At first he espoused the cause of the proprietor; but the death of Penn (1718) and the resultant confusion gave him his opportunity. Thenceforth he contrived, chiefly through countenancing large paper-money issues, to win the support of the Assembly against the proprietor's local adherents. This he did, however, not from friendship for the common people, but to create for himself as Governor an independent position.

52 Sir William Keith, 1680–1749, from an India-ink drawing about 1720 by John Watson (1685–1768) in the Historical Society of Pennsylvania, Philadelphia

REMOVAL OF GOVERNOR KEITH

KEITH, for defying proprietors' instructions, was suddenly removed from office in 1726. His crafty policy was soon laid bare to the popular party; and before long he lost the support of David Lloyd and others of their leaders.

The CASE *of the Heir at Law and Executrix of the late Proprietor of* Pennſilvania, *&c. in Relation to the Removal of Sir* William Keith, *and the Appointing Major* Patrick Gordon *to ſucceed him as Deputy-Governor there.*

KING *Charles* the Second was pleaſed by Patent, dated the 4th of *March*, 1680, for the Conſiderations therein mentioned, to grant to the late *William Penn* Eſq; his Heirs and Aſſigns, all that Tract of Land in *America* then inhabited only by Savages, ſince call'd the Province of *Pennſilvania*, with all Powers of Government, and full Authority to appoint Deputy-Governors for that Province, *&c.*

In the Year 1682, his then Royal Highneſs *James* Duke of *York*, afterwards King *James* the Second, granted to the ſaid *William Penn*, his Heirs and Aſſigns, all that Tract of Land lying on the Weſt Side of the Bay and River of *Delaware* adjoining to *Pennſilvania*, together with all Royalties, Franchiſes, Powers, *&c.*

IN virtue of which Letters Patents and Grants, aforeſaid, the ſaid Mr. *Penn* enjoyed all the ſaid Lands and Powers of Government for above forty Years, and from time to time appointed his

A Depu-

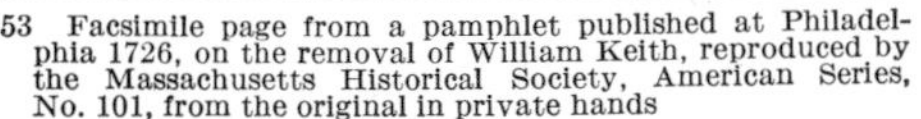

53 Facsimile page from a pamphlet published at Philadelphia 1726, on the removal of William Keith, reproduced by the Massachusetts Historical Society, American Series, No. 101, from the original in private hands

54 Patrick Gordon, 1644–1736, Governor of Pennsylvania, from a portrait in the Historical Society of Pennsylvania, Philadelphia

THE QUAKER COLONY UNDER GORDON

PATRICK GORDON, Keith's successor, was a blunt soldier who told his first Assembly that he was artless in politics and would govern without intrigue and in accord with simple justice. This pledge he faithfully kept until his death in office in 1736. Such conduct won the good will of the Indians, though it was during his administration that the well-known "walking purchase" occurred. He was also very popular in the colony, earning the deep respect of the conservative and proprietary interests.

55 From the painting *Building the Cradle of Liberty*, by J. L. G. Ferris (1863–), in Independence Hall, Philadelphia

GOVERNOR AND ASSEMBLY IN PENNSYLVANIA

In Pennsylvania, the business shrewdness of the Friends and their aversion to carnal weapons gave a peculiar turn to the inevitable clashes between Governor and Assembly. With the westward expansion and the consequent French and Indian wars, these characteristics came into collision with the interests of the proprietors and of England. The struggle began in the time of Governor Fletcher of New York, who wished money to defend the northern frontier. But the Friends were loath to authorize expenditures for military purposes. When the Assembly refused to appropriate, the Governor would veto; in like fashion the Governor on occasion agreed to sign and to enforce the Assembly's measures in return for a vote of supply. By 1754 the right of veto had fallen into disuse; the Governor and other officials relied upon the Assembly for their salaries, passed by annual vote. Though the province had in 1739 refused to authorize a militia, compromises had served to protect the people during the wars. In 1745, for instance, the Assembly denied money to purchase arms and ammunition for the capture of Louisburg; but they did appropriate four thousand pounds for buying "bread, beef, pork, flour, wheat or other grain." When the Governor proceeded to purchase gunpowder as "other grain," no protest was made. Yet such an arrangement was displeasing to the home authorities. Removal of the Quaker element from the Assembly was deemed necessary. A threat to accomplish this by Act of Parliament induced the obdurate Friends in Pennsylvania, at the solicitation of their fellows in England, to withdraw voluntarily. Meanwhile the home government had been developing new methods of continental supervision. The Board of Trade and Plantations pushed its powers vigorously, in an effort to establish effective control of colonial activities. At first it confined its endeavors largely to smoothing out difficulties facing the colonial governments. So, when boundary disputes between New York and Connecticut became chronic, the Board recommended a settlement. The result was an Order-in-Council issued in 1700, placing official approval upon an agreement previously reached by the colonies themselves. The Privy Council was in reality a court of last appeal where colonial cases of importance were finally adjudicated. Eighteenth-century American subjects of the British King thus became accustomed to one great tribunal above the courts of the separate provinces. When independent America framed its constitution in 1787, one of the striking features of the new government lay in the similarities between the new supreme court and the old Privy Council.

At the Court at Kensington
the 17th day of March 1699
Present,

The Kings most Excellent Ma^ty
in Councill

Upon reading this day at the Board a Representation from the Lords Comm^rs of Trade and Plantations dated the 13th of this Month Relating to the Boundaries between the Province of New Yorke and the Colony of Connecticut In America, and the Right of Government over the Towns of Rye and Bedford which lye on the Frontiers of the said Province and Colony, As also an agreement made between the said Province and Colony in 1683, relating to the said Boundaries, His Ma^ty in Councill Approving the said Representation, Is pleased to Order as it is hereby Ordered, That the Lords Comm^rs of Trade and Plantations do prepare the Draughts of letters to be sent to the Earl of Bellomont, and to the Governor and Company of Connecticut, from His Ma^ty Signifying to them His Ma^ts Approbation and Confirmation of the said Agreement in 1683, with such other Directions as are Proposed by the said Representation, And that the said Draughts be presented at this Board, for His Ma^ts further Directions thereupon /

[illegible]

56 Order-in-Council, 1700, relating to a boundary dispute between New York and Connecticut, from the copy in the Public Record Office London

ROYAL GOVERNMENT IN MASSACHUSETTS

Allusion has been made to the "Boston spirit." That spirit was the survival of the earlier stubborn opposition of New England to the centralizing ambitions of the London colonial administrators. To them Massachusetts had long been a source of worry. They had hoped that under the compromise charter of 1691 the old antipathies would die, and to this end they had selected as the first royal governor William Phips, a native of the colony, and suggested by the colonists themselves. This conciliatory policy was continued throughout most of the eighteenth century. But the Massachusetts leaders were not content. Glad to utilize the Royal Government to suppress the radical element in the colony, they remained quite willing to seek their own best interests, even though violation of navigation acts and evasion of the charter proved necessary. The royal Governor occupied, indeed, an unenviable position. Chosen to placate the citizens of Boston, he was yet forced to act as the representative of the Crown; so that if he wished to continue in favor with Whitehall, he was obliged to oppose policies locally popular. The man who resided in Province House must often have passed sleepless nights in trying to puzzle out a path of conduct that would satisfy both parties.

57 Province House, home of the Colonial Governors, from Samuel A. Drake, *Old Landmarks and Historical Personages of Boston*, 1873

THE GOVERNOR'S COUNCIL

For the Governor of Massachusetts had to govern with the consent of the General Court, the name given to the legislature. This body retained, moreover, under the charter of 1691 several of its most prized privileges. Members of the Lower House were elected annually. The legislature chose the provincial treasurer and certain other officers. Most illustrative, however, of the dubious position of the Governor were the structure and functions of the Council. It served as a body advisory to the Governor; it was also the upper, and smaller, branch of the General Court. Its members were chosen by joint ballot of the Houses, but subject to the Governor's veto. Thus, if the Governor sought a sympathetic Council, he jeopardized any program of legislation he might have in mind; on the other hand, to obtain such legislation he was obliged to accept Councillors selected by the representatives of the towns. The effect of all this was greatly to curb the Governor's power.

58 The Old State House, Boston, from the *Massachusetts Magazine*, 1793, courtesy of the New York Historical Society

59 Speaker's desk from the Old State House, Boston, now in the Massachusetts Historical Society

THE STRUGGLE FOR CONTROL OF THE HOUSE OF REPRESENTATIVES

In this predicament, certain of the governors of Massachusetts tried to secure control of the House of Representatives. This was notably the case with Joseph Dudley, selected as Governor in 1702. As the ally of Andros, Dudley had been unpopular in the days preceding the charter of 1691, but he now received the backing of several of the leading clergymen and merchants. Encouraged by this support, he claimed the right to approve or disapprove the speaker selected by the House, basing the right on certain ancient English parliamentary practices and on the power which the charter granted him to veto all acts of the General Court. In this effort he met defeat. But his successor in office, Samuel Shute, carried on the fight for what he considered the royal prerogative. His whole administration (1716–23) was a protracted struggle with the Representatives. He condemned the banking scheme favored by the legislature to relieve the financial depression that resulted from the Indian wars; he refused to recognize the election of Elisha Cooke as speaker; he had a dispute with the General Court over the impost bill. His tenacity was met with equal stubbornness by the colonial leaders. The latter, moreover, maintained in London an agent whose primary function was to persuade the Government to recall the Governor. In 1723 Shute returned to London to make a direct appeal for his rights. In this he was successful; for in 1725 an "explanatory charter" was issued, securing to the Governor his right to veto the selection of speaker of the House of Representatives. To this settlement the colonists submitted, lest worse follow.

THE QUESTION OF THE GOVERNOR'S SALARY

Of all the disputes between Governor and General Court, that of most bitterness and of most significance concerned the salary of the Governor. Though Massachusetts had lost the right to select her Governor, she took pains to prevent irresponsible action on his part. The fight began during Dudley's administration. Instructed to secure the grant of a permanent salary, he early tried to procure it. The General Court, however, adopted the policy of voting sums to recompense the governor for service rendered. These sums rarely met the ideas of the governor. For a time, indeed, Dudley refused such grants; but never throughout his tenure of office (1702–15) was he free from fiscal dependence upon the representatives. His successors suffered the same restraint. The controversy came to a head under Governor Burnet (1728–29). For him, like his predecessors, the General Court would fix no settled compensation; nor would he accept temporary grants, though he was offered three thousand pounds. Burnet died resisting; but general opinion gave the victory to the colonists. In 1735 Newcastle instructed Governor Belcher to accept the grant of the year and in the future to get as much as he could. The popular cause had triumphed. Governors were to be responsible to the taxpayers over whom they held sway, an important step in the development of popular government.

QUESTION:

ARE we obliged in this Government of the Massachusetts, by CHARTER, *to Settle a Salary upon the Governor?*

I Answer upon the Affirmative, *That we are obliged*, from the following Reasons: *Viz.*

I. Reason. *We, that is, (the General Assembly) have Power by Charter to do it.*
II. *The Support of Government, and of the Governor is our Duty plainly enjoyned upon us both by Charter, and universal Consent.*
III. *We have not Power to Provide for the Support of Government, and the Governor in any other Way, then that the Charter directs us unto.*
IV. *Then the Consequence will follow, That we are obliged in this Government to Settle a Salary upon the Governor by our Royal Charter.*

I shall Endeavour to handle and prove the aforesaid Particulars distinctly.

I. Reason. *We, that is, (the General Assembly) have Power by Charter to do it*, viz. To Settle a Salary upon the Governour. I will Recite the Words in the Charter, that gives us that Power, in the [illegible]th Page, viz. Full Power is given to the General Assembly, "*From time to time to Make, Ordain and Establish all manner of Wholesome and Reasonable Orders, Laws, Statutes, and Ordinances, Directions, and Instructions, either with Penalty or without, &c. As they shall judge to be for the Good and Welfare of Our said Province, and Territory, and for the Government and ordering thereof, and of the People Inhabiting, or who shall Inhabit the same; and for the necessary Support and Defence of the Government thereof*".

Here is plain Power to Support Government, as well as to defend it, given to the General Assembly, which is to be done by making Laws, Statutes and Ordinances there-about: As will very plainly appear, if you Consider the Charter a little further, when it comes to speak of Laying Taxes upon the People, Which saith those Taxes so Levyed, *Shall be Issued and Disposed of by Warrant under the Hand of the Governour of Our said Province, for the Time being, with the Advice and Consent of the Council, for Our Service, in the necessary Defence and Support of Our Government of Our said Province*". And it is to be agreeable to such Acts as are in force in the said Province. Now 'tis most evident from hence, That the General Assembly hath Power by Charter to make Laws that do Settle a Salary upon the Governing Power, as well as to make Laws and Raise Money for their Defence, 'tis most evident if you Consider that Support and Defence are the same Expressions in one Clause of the Charter, as they be in the other, and in the latter they speak of not any thing else but with respect of the disposition of Money, and for that very End to Support Government: And so I think the First Proposition is clear, That we have Power by Charter to make such Laws.

II. *The Support of Government and of the Governor is our Duty plainly enjoyned upon us, both by Charter and universal Consent.* This is most evident from Charter, because the Money is to be Issued out of the Treasury for that End, *viz.* The Support as well as the Defence of the Government. 'Tis the universal Consent (that Government ought to be Supported) both Ancient and Modern, both Christians and Civilized Heathens; and no Man amongst our selves that oppose the Settling a Salary upon the Governor to the last, but will confess that Government ought and must be Supported: Not only by helping to Maintain the Authority of the Governing Power, but by Money to Maintain them and enable them to maintain the Dignity of their Respective Offices.

III. *We, that is, (the General Assembly,) have not got Power to Provide for the Support of the Government, and of the Governor by any other way then that which the Charter directs unto.* For Consider, We are a dependent Government, and are Incorporated into one Political body by Charter, and all our Power is derivative from thence; We may as well of our selves Extend our bounds beyond the Limits circumscribed to us in our Charter, as our Power beyond the Charter Limitations. Some indeed understand so little about Politicks, that they say, Our General Assembly have got a Parliamentary Power, and can do as they will; or as the Parliament of *Great Britain* can do; but that is a great Mistake: The Parliament of *Great Britain* is a Superiour Court, accountable to none but GOD alone: But our General Assembly is a body Incorporate by Charter, as before hath been said, and we have not an Inch of Power but what is contained in the Charter: In the Charter there is no Power given the General Assembly to provide neither for the Defence of the Governor, nor the Support of the Governing Power, but by some *Act* or Law made by the Legislature; and when we provide for the Support of the Governor, or any other that have part in the Governing Power, by any way differs from the Charter: It may be Rightly and Justly said we cannot do it: for if it be unjust and unlawful for any that have a circumscribed Power Lawfully committed to them, to exceed it; Then they may be well said, Not to be able to do any thing but what they may Lawfully do agreable to the Charter, or Power they act upon.

But by this time most will say, 'Tis true we have got Power to make Orders or Laws for the Support of the Governour, and the governing Power, and that it is our Duty to Support them, both from Charter and Reason; But they say, We should do it in the *Old Way* (as they call it) in passing Resolves every half Year, or near there-about to the Governor, and other Salary Men: And that they say, They are free to go on in. And we have Power to make Orders about Support, and that is an Order; And so, and especially the Governour hath heretofore been well Supported, and he hath no reason to Distrust the General Assembly, but still he will have an honourable Support; according to that Degree of Dignity and Honour his Majesty hath been pleased to confer upon him: And therefore why should we be put out of that way which has so well answered the end, and hath so well pleased both the Governor and the Governed?

60 From a broadside, 1729, regarding the salary of the Massachusetts Governor, in the New York Public Library

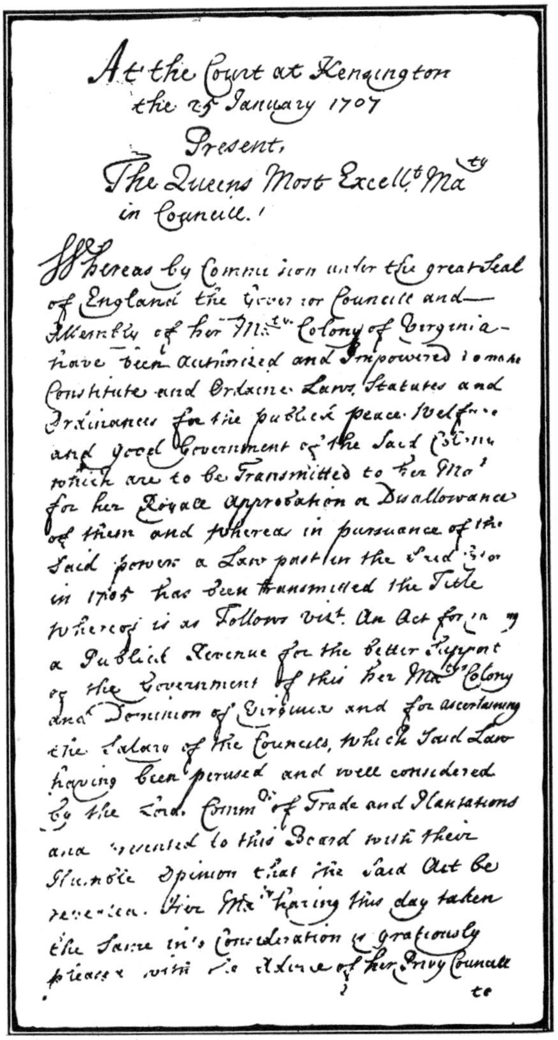

At the Court at Kensington
the 25 January 1707
Present,
The Queens Most Excellt Maty
in Councill.

Whereas by Commission under the great Seal of England the Govern[r] Councill and Assembly of her Matys Colony of Virginia have been authorized and Impowered to make Constitute and Ordaine Laws Statutes and Ordinances for the publick peace Welfare and good Government of the said Colony which are to be Transmitted to her Maty for her Royall approbation or Disallowance of them and whereas in pursuance of the said power a Law past in the said Colony in 1705 has been transmitted the Title whereof is as Follows vizt An Act for raising a Publick Revenue for the better Support of the Government of this her Matys Colony and Dominion of Virginia and for ascertaining the Salary of the Councill, which said Law having been perused and well considered by the Lords Commrs of Trade and Plantations and reported to this Board with their Humble Opinion that the said Act be repealed. Her Maty having this day taken the same into Consideration is graciously pleased with the Advice of her Privy Councill to

61 Order-in-Council, 1707, from the copy in the Public Record Office, London

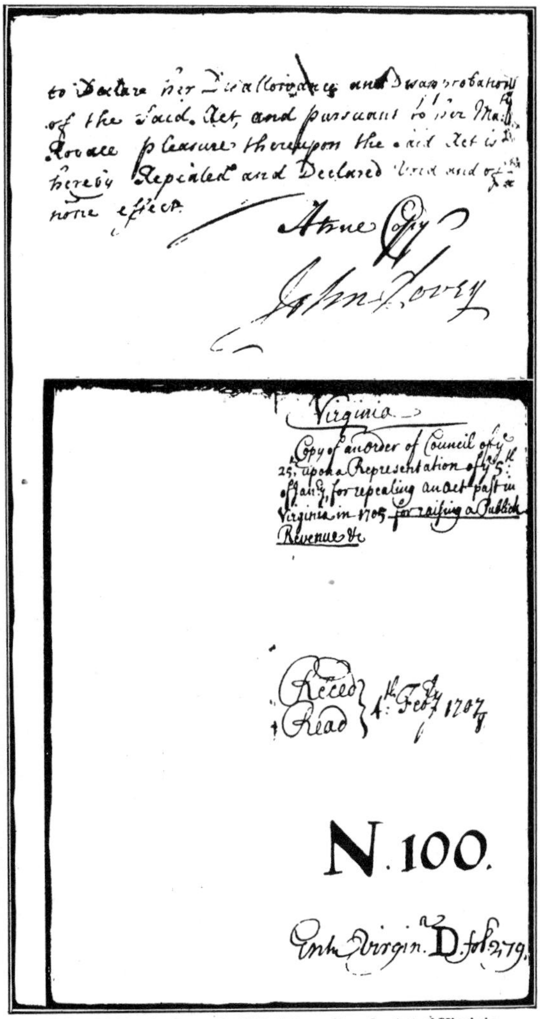

to Declare her Disallowance and Disapprobation of the said Act, and pursuant to her Matys Royall pleasure thereupon the said Act is hereby Repealed and Declared void and of none effect.

A true Copy
John Povey

Virginia.
Copy of an Order of Council of ye 25. upon a Representation of ye 5. of Jany for repealing an Act past in Virginia in 1705 for raising a Publick Revenue &c.

Recd } 4th Feby 1707/8
Read }

N. 100.

Entd Virgin. D. fol. 279.

62 Title of Order-in-Council, 1707, "Repealing the Act of Virginia, 1705, for Raising a Public Revenue, etc."

EVADING THE CROWN VETO

In time somewhat more imperious use was made of this policy. By 1692 Governors of all royal provinces and of the proprietary province of Pennsylvania were instructed to send all laws passed by their respective legislatures to England for approval. At the start there was much irregularity and delay. Sometimes laws were not sent; more often no action on them was taken when they were received by the Board of Trade. This delay was in the nature of a probationary period, during which the character of the act might be tested by its operation. After 1730 the reins were tightened; disallowance was a regularized method of imperial control. Under the Massachusetts charter of 1691, for instance, fifty-nine acts were disallowed before 1776. Disallowance was employed for several types of colonial legislation; the exercise of the power was chiefly intended to protect the royal prerogatives, and to maintain the colonial governor and his staff independent of local encroachments. In Massachusetts, in New York, in Virginia and elsewhere, the conflict between Assembly and Governor took the form of attacks upon the financial independence of the latter. And, on occasion, disallowance by Order-in-Council was called in to preserve the asserted rights of the Crown. As home control grew, the colonists found ways of evading the royal veto. Massachusetts, for example, proceeded to pass acts good for a limited time only. Thus the objects in view might be achieved before there was time to nullify the statute. When this practice was checked, she passed as resolutions what as acts would have been subject to disallowance. Thus was added to the many previous difficulties a fresh source of trouble between England and her colonies.

(283)

Anno ſexto

Georgii II. Regis.

An Act for the better ſecuring and encouraging the Trade of His Majeſty's Sugar Colonies in *America.*

WHEREAS the Welfare and Prosperity of Your Majesty's Sugar Colonies in America are of the greatest Consequence and Importance to the Trade, Navigation, and Strength of this Kingdom: And whereas the Planters of the said Sugar Colonies have of late Years fallen under such great Discouragements, that they are unable to improve or carry on the Sugar Trade upon an equal Footing with the foreign Sugar Colonies, without some Advantage and Relief be given to them from Great Britain: For Remedy whereof, and for the Good and Welfare of Your Majesty's Subjects, we Your Majesty's most dutiful and loyal Subjects, the Commons of Great Britain assembled in Parliament, have given and granted unto Your Majesty the several and respective Rates and Duties herein after mentioned, and in such Manner and Form, as is herein after expressed; and do most humbly beseech Your Majesty that it may be enacted, Preamble.

Bbbb 2 acted,

63 The Molasses Act of 1733, from the copy in the New York Public Library

THE MERCANTILE THEORY IN PRACTICE

MEANWHILE the center of political gravity in England was shifting. The long Whig rule assured to Parliament a position of prime importance. To effectuate their plan of colonial control, the Privy Council and the Board of Trade needed parliamentary sanction. This was given only with the dilatoriness characteristic of a deliberative body. So it was that for some time Parliament really served to protect the colonies from the extreme imperialism of the administrators and their commercial allies. Bills for the recall of colonial charters, sponsored by the Board of Trade, were killed. In 1717 permission to import Irish linen duty-free was renewed, despite opposition from the linen-drapers of England. Before long, however, the trading element had won a place of power in Parliament; and we find the mercantilist philosophy translated into law. The list of enumerated articles which could be shipped to Europe only by way of England was extended. In 1733 a further and heartily disliked step was taken in the Molasses Act, imposing prohibitive duties on sugar and molasses when imported into the colonies from the foreign West Indies. Running counter to a natural and lucrative course of trade, the measure could be but imperfectly enforced.

Along with commerce, manufacturing was growing. It was therefore not surprising to find Parliament, urged by strong lobbies, attempting to regulate colonial handicraft. In 1699 the export of woolens from one colony to another had been forbidden. In 1732 similar restrictions had been laid on hat-making. Iron manufacture came in for repressive legislation in 1750. The business interests of England were, in brief, alive to possible dangers of competition from the American continent. Gradually the royal policy of promoting the export of naval stores from the provinces was overshadowed by this new and restrictive legislation. From such matters, it was an easy step to parliamentary control of colonial currency, of coinage, of banking. Bit by bit, the English Parliament assumed the aspect of an imperial legislature. Such an evolution was probably justifiable in law. This eighteenth-century development of Parliament was, in a sense, an accidental growth, the result of adjustments to specific conditions rather than the working out of a deliberate imperial plan.

(219)

Anno quinto

Georgii II. Regis.

An Act for the more eaſy Recovery of Debts in His Majeſty's Plantations and Colonies in *America.*

WHEREAS His Majesty's Subjects, trading to the British Plantations in America, lie under great Difficulties, for want of more easy Methods of proving, recovering, and levying Debts due to them, than are now used in some of the said Plantations; and whereas it will tend very much to the retrieving of the Credit formerly given by the trading Subjects of Great Britain to the Natives and Inhabitants of the said Plantations, and to the advancing of the Trade of this Kingdom thither, if such Inconveniencies were remedied; May it therefore please Your Majesty that it may be enacted, and be it enacted by the King's most Excellent Majesty, by and with the Advice and Consent of the Lords Spiritual and Temporal, and Commons, in this present Parliament assembled, and by Preamble.

9 Iii 2 the

64 Act of 1732, for the "Easy Recovery of Debts . . . in America," from the copy in the New York Public Library

(1119)

Anno viceſimo quarto

Georgii II. Regis.

An Act to regulate and reſtrain Paper Bills of Credit in His Majeſty's Colonies or Plantations of *Rhode Iſland,* and *Providence* Plantations, *Connecticut,* the *Maſſachuſets Bay,* and *New Hampſhire* in *America;* and to prevent the ſame being legal Tenders in Payments of Money.

Whereas the Act of Parliament made in the Sixth Year of Her late Majesty Queen Anne, intituled, An Act for aſcertaining the Rate of Foreign Coins in Her Majeſty's Plantations in *America,* hath been intirely frustrated in His Majesty's said Colonies of Rhode Iſland and Providence Plantations, Connecticut, the Maſſachuſets Bay, and New Hampſhire in America, by their creating and issuing, from time to time, great Quantities of Paper Bills of Credit, by virtue of Acts of Assembly, Orders, Resolutions, or Votes, made or passed by their respective Assemblies, and making legal the Tender of such Bills of Credit in Payment for Debts, Dues, and Demands; which Bills of Credit have, for many Years past, been depreciating in their Value, by means whereof all Debts of late Years have been paid and satisfied with a much less Value than was contracted for, which hath been a great Discouragement and Prejudice to the Trade and Commerce of His Majesty's Subjects, by occasioning Confusion in Dealings, and lessening of Credit in those Parts: Therefore, for the more effectual preventing and remedying of the said Inconveniencies, may it please Your Preamble.

6 13 D 2 most

65 Act of 1751, to restrain the issue of paper money, from the copy in the New York Public Library

THE CASE OF PETER ZENGER

In 1735 occurred in the Province of New York a legal battle destined to have important results for the liberties of the people of the province. The Duke of Newcastle had secured the appointment of William Cosby as Governor of New York, an Irishman of long service in the army. Before leaving England he had lobbied against the Sugar and Molasses Bill of 1733. On arrival he was voted, as a token of local gratitude, £750; this gift he treated with scorn. And before long he became involved in a financial squabble with Van Dam, Acting-Governor, over the division of the gubernatorial emoluments during the latter's temporary incumbency. Court action followed. The popular party sided with Van Dam. Fearful of a jury, the Governor brought his case in equity before the Justices of the Supreme Court. At once a dispute arose as to his right to do this; and Chief Justice Morris ruled against him. Cosby thereupon summarily removed Morris, who for eighteen years had served acceptably. Motives for this action may be detected in the first letter Cosby had written as Governor, to Newcastle, in which he speaks of the "Boston spirit" growing in New York, and of the disregard of certain public officers for the prerogatives of the Governor. Nor were the results of his spite insignificant. Notable lawyers rallied around Van Dam and Morris. Previously, in 1733, Morris, James Alexander, William Smith, and other leading citizens had formed a political club. Morris was elected to the Assembly. Under these auspices was started in November, 1733, the *New York Weekly Journal*, edited by a young printer named John Peter Zenger. The *Journal* immediately became a powerful vehicle for spreading the views of the popular party. Many of the leading articles were written by Morris, Alexander and their friends. Freedom of the press, the liberties of Englishmen, and like subjects were prominent in its pages. Precedents were found in the works of the English jurist, Coke, in the philosophy of Locke, and in English history. From this the step to forceful, even virulent, criticism of royal administration in New York was short and was quickly taken.

Numb. II.

THE

New-York Weekly JOURNAL

Containing the freſheſt Advices, Foreign, and Domeſtick.

MUNDAY November 12, 1733.

Mr. *Zenger.*

INcert the following in your next, and you'll oblige your Friend,

CATO.

Mira temporum felicitas ubi ſentiri quæ velis, & quæ ſentias dicere licit.

Tacit.

THE Liberty of the Preſs is a Subject of the greateſt Importance, and in which every Individual is as much concern'd as he is in any other Part of Liberty: therefore it will not be improper to communicate to the Publick the Sentiments of a late excellent Writer upon this Point. ſuch is the Elegance and Perſpicuity of his Writings, ſuch the inimitable Force of his Reaſoning, that it will be difficult to ſay any Thing new that he has not ſaid, or not to ſay that much worſe which he has ſaid.

There are two Sorts of Monarchies, an abſolute and a limited one. In the firſt, the Liberty of the Preſs can never be maintained, it is inconſiſtent with it; for what abſolute Monarch would ſuffer any Subject to animadvert on his Actions, when it is in his Power to declare the Crime, and to nominate the Puniſhment? This would make it very dangerous to exerciſe ſuch a Liberty. Beſides the Object againſt which thoſe Pens muſt be directed, is their Sovereign, the ſole ſupream Magiſtrate; for there being no Law in thoſe Monarchies, but the Will of the Prince, it makes it neceſſary for his Miniſters to conſult his Pleaſure, before any Thing can be undertaken: He is therefore properly chargeable with the Grievances of his Subjects, and what the Miniſter there acts being in Obedience to the Prince, he ought not to incur the Hatred of the People; for it would be hard to impute that to him for a Crime, which is the Fruit of his Allegiance, and for refuſing which he might incur the Penalties of Treaſon. Beſides, in an abſolute Monarchy, the Will of the Prince being the Law, a Liberty of the Preſs to complain of Grievances would be complaining againſt the Law, and the Conſtitution, to which they have ſubmitted, or have been obliged to ſubmit; and therefore, in one Senſe, may be ſaid to deſerve Puniſhment, So that under an abſolute Monarchy, I ſay, ſuch a Liberty is inconſiſtent with the Conſtitution, having no proper Subject in Politics, on which it might be exercis'd, and if exercis'd would incur a certain Penalty.

But in a limited Monarchy, as *England* is, our Laws are known, fixed, and eſtabliſhed. They are the ſtreight Rule and ſure Guide to direct the King, the Miniſters, and other his Subjects: And therefore an Offence againſt the Laws is ſuch an Offence againſt the Conſtitution as ought to receive a proper adequate Puniſhment; the ſevera

Conſtil

66 Peter Zenger's *New-York Weekly Journal*, from the copy, November 12, 1733, in the New York Public Library

67 From the tapestry picture *The Trial of Peter Zenger*, woven by the Herter Looms, in the Hotel McAlpin, New York

THE BATTLE FOR THE FREEDOM OF THE PRESS

In the fall of 1734 proceedings against Zenger, legally responsible for the contents of his paper, began. The Governor's Council tried in vain to persuade the Assembly to join in an address to the Governor urging Zenger's prosecution. Acting then in an executive capacity, the Council ordered certain issues of the *Journal* burned by the hangman. Thereafter the editor was arrested. Bail fixed by Chief Justice DeLancey was more than Zenger could furnish, and he was put in prison. In April, 1735, the trial opened before the Supreme Court. Smith and Alexander, appearing for Zenger, at once attacked the competency of the judges to sit, asserting that they had been appointed without the consent of the Council. The court thereupon disbarred the two eminent lawyers, and the trial was laid over till fall. In the autumn of 1735 the trial finally took place. The sole issue was that of libel. Under existing law, the jury was empowered to render a verdict solely upon the fact of publication by the accused. The character of the publication was to be decided by the judges. Under such conditions, Zenger's conviction seemed foreordained. But, thanks to the delay, his supporters had obtained the services of Andrew Hamilton of Philadelphia. Hamilton had emigrated from Scotland some fifty years before. Starting as a plantation-hand in Virginia, he had steadily risen in power and public esteem. In 1717 he had become attorney-general of Pennsylvania; afterward he was elected to the Assembly, was chosen speaker in 1729, and was reëlected annually until his retirement. He was the designer and builder of Independence Hall, though he died before its completion. At this time, therefore, he was one of the leading lawyers in the colonies. His introduction into the case came as a surprise to the court. Before he could be halted, he had begun an impassioned plea for freedom of the press. Admitting the fact of publication, he asked permission to prove the truth of the statements in the *Journal*. This right the court rejected, saying "a libel is not to be justified; for it is nevertheless a Libel that is true." Apparently defeated, the aged lawyer then turned to the jury, asking it to be a witness to the truth of the publication and to realize the deep issues involved. In this plea he succeeded, for immediately upon the conclusion of his address the jury brought in a verdict of not guilty, amid the cheers of the court-room. Untrammeled discussion in the press of the conduct of officials was vindicated. In reality the outcome of the Zenger case had added a new principle to the common law at a time when the Colonials were coming to depend more and more on it as the bulwark of their rights as Englishmen. The common law was assuming this new importance because of the passing of several of the old colonial charters.

68 Andrew Hamilton, 1676–1741, from a copy by William Cogswell, after a copy of an original portrait by an unknown artist, in the Historical Society of Pennsylvania, Philadelphia

NEW YORK CALLS ITS ELECTION A "COCK MATCH"

THE incidents in Pennsylvania, New York, and Massachusetts indicate the growth of interest in things political. By the middle of the eighteenth century the colonists were no longer simply trading representatives of English companies. They had become a people, a community with many common interests requiring political action for solution. Thus it is not surprising to find the beginnings of political sophistication. This, in many of the colonies, and perhaps particularly in New York, often took the form of clever cynicism. For there, as elsewhere, political phenomena almost invariably appeared as items in the struggle between the Governor's clique and the popular party. Elections were "Cock Matches" between "plain Liberty and Property Cocks" and "Cocks . . . with gaudy Feathers." The broadside (No. 69) refers to an election in New York for the Assembly. John Roberts, Sheriff, had issued a notice that "Pursuant to His Majesty's Writ to me directed and delivered, for the Electing four Representatives to serve in a General Assembly of this Province, Notice is hereby given to the Freemen and Freeholders of the City and County of *New York*, in my Bailiwick, to assemble and meet together on Tuesday the Seventeenth Day of *February* next at Ten o'Clock in the Forenoon of the same day, on the Green near the Work-House, . . . and then and there to nominate and chuse . . . four able and sufficient Freeholders . . . to be Representatives. . . ." In the *New York Mercury* of February 16, 1761, a writer, styling himself "C. Freeman," urges the voters to support those candidates who favored the liberty of the people, not those who would be subservient to men in high office.

Advertiſement.

ON *Tueſday* the 17th of *February* 1761, there will be a grand Cock Match, on the Green near the Work-Houſe (greateſt Part of which will be converted into a Pit) between ſeveral Hundreds of plain *Liberty and Property* Cocks with their own Spurs, Combs and Gills, and ſome Cocks of a *French* Extraction, with gaudy Feathers, Gaffs, and Gantlets finely trimmed, that have been for ſome Time kept up and are highly feed, with artificial Balls compounded of Garlic, Old *Madeira* Wine, &c. The Bets will be very high; as the Battles will not be decided there, they are to adjourn to the City Hall, where the Sport will be continued for two or three Days; a Young Gentleman, but an Old Cock Fighter (who lately diſtinguiſhed himſelf at *Stout's*) that has fought himſelf, as long as he thought fighting Safe, though by fighting a little longer he might have gained great Applauſe, and is well ſkilled in all the Laws, Rules and Orders of the Cock Pit, is to be mounted on the Bench, and determine all Diſputes that may ariſe: When the Sport is over, if the Majority of the Spectators ſhould give their Conſent, he will joyn with ſome others, and make a complete Syſtem of Laws, relating to Cock Fighting, Horſe Races, Drinking Bumpers with proper Toaſts and Epithets, Concerts, Balls and Aſſemblies, and even Maſquerades if it be thought neceſſary to introduce them into this Country.

69 From a New York broadside, 1761, in the New York Historical Society

THE FIRST CALL FOR A COLONIAL CONGRESS

THIS interest in political action, this sense of community of problems, is shown in the several efforts through the century to establish some form of intercolonial coöperation. The old New England Confederation (see Vol. I, page 223) had been founded on certain provincial needs, but had foundered upon the rock of local jealousies. Joint action for purposes of defense against the Indians and the French had been a favorite notion of the English administrators under James II. So with the outbreak of King William's War, Massachusetts issued a call for a colonial conference, to be held in New York, in April, 1690, to devise means of common action for self-defense. These endeavors achieved no enduring result.

70 From the original minutes, Mar. 19, 1689, in the Massachusetts Archives, Boston

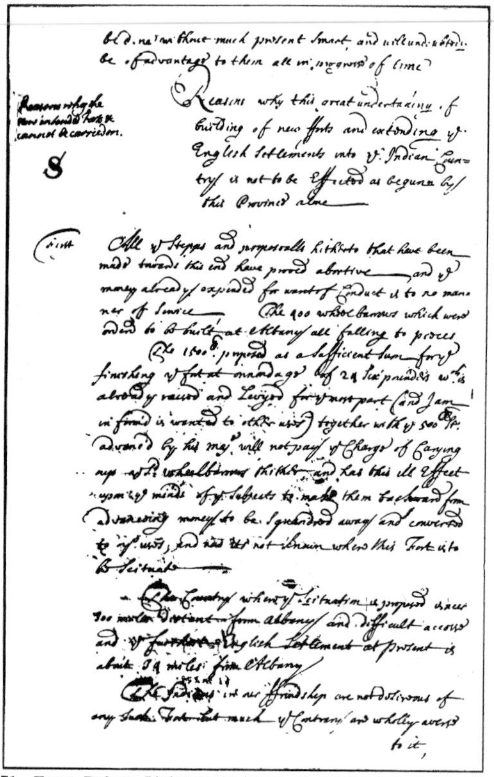

71 From Robert Livingston's letter of twenty-two pages advocating the union of the colonies, addressed to the Council of Trade and Plantations, May 13, 1701, in the Public Record Office, London

A NEW YORK MERCHANT PROPOSES COLONIAL UNION

SCHEMES of this character, fostered by the home government, invariably fell to the ground. Calls from the Crown addressed to the several colonies to contribute to the conduct of the wars were often evaded or disregarded. To attain the required group effort and frontier security, voluntary action seemed necessary. The plan proposed in 1701 by Robert Livingston is for this reason of particular interest. Robert Livingston was a leading merchant of New York and much interested in opening up the back country, rich in furs and timber. Realizing that settlement could not come from the actions of New York alone, he proposed to the Board of Trade and Plantations a plan of colonial coöperation. The continental provinces were to be united into "one form of government," divided into three groups, a southern, a central and a northern. From this government was to be raised annually a sum of money to be administered from Albany under the supervision of commissioners selected from each of the groups. The Crown was to send troops and equipment; the groups were, under a quota scheme, to furnish labor. Forts were to be built in the wilderness to protect the settlers, who were to be encouraged to establish homesteads. Every two years England was to send out "two hundred youths," and two hundred of the soldiers were to be disbanded, to whom, on condition of remaining, free land was to be given. In this way Livingston hoped to assure the "extending of Christian Settlements and English forts into the Indian Country for the Security of all his maj. plantations on this north Continent of America."

THE ALBANY PLAN OF COLONIAL UNION, 1754

BY far the most pretentious attempt at colonial union came in 1754. The motive was still primarily military, protection from the French and Indians. This is well stated by *The New York Gazette* of May 13, 1754, in commenting upon French schemes of aggression. "The Confidence of the French in this Undertaking seems well-grounded on the present disunited State of the British Colonies, and the extreme Difficulty of bringing so many different Governments and Assemblies to agree in any speedy and effectual Measures for our common Defence and Security: while our Enemies have the very great Advantage of being under one Direction, with one Council, and one Purse. Hence their efforts to take an easy Possession of such Parts of the British Territory as they find most convenient will, if unchecked, end in the Destruction of the British Interest, Trade and Plantations in America." It was in this issue of the *Gazette* that the famous device of the dismembered snake, later to be utilized for other purposes, made its New York appearance. In 1754, partly to establish a treaty with the Iroquois, the home government called the Albany Congress. Seven colonies sent commissioners, Franklin being a leading spirit. The result was a plan to establish a council, composed of members chosen by the several colonial legislatures, with power to provide for the common defense, to control relations with the Indians, and to levy taxes to meet expenses connected therewith. All actions of the council were subject to the veto of a president-general, appointed by the King. But such a plan met with favor neither with the colonies, jealous of their rights, nor with the English administration, suspicious of the popular origins of the scheme.

72 "Dismembered snake" device, from *The New York Gazette*, May 13, 1754, in the New York Public Library

JOIN or DIE.

SATURDAY, September 21, 1765. [NUMB. 1.]

The Conſtitutional COURANT:

Containing Matters intereſting to LIBERTY, and no wiſe repugnant to LOYALTY.

To the PUBLIC.

WHEN a new public Paper makes its appearance, the reader will naturally be curious to know from whence it came, the publiſher, and the deſign of it. To gratify that curioſity, know reader, that the publiſher having formerly acquired a competent knowledge of the Printing-buſineſs, for his amuſement furniſhed himſelf with a ſet of proper materials;---and the authors of the following pieces having acquainted him that they applied to the printers in YORK, *who refuſed to publiſh them in their news-papers---not because they diſapproved them, or were apprehenſive of danger, but purely becauſe ſeveral of their friends had been anxious on their account, and particularly deſired them to be careful not to publiſh any thing that might give the enemies of liberty an advantage, which they would be glad to take, over them; and as theſe pieces are thought to be wrote with greater freedom than any thing that has yet appeared in the pub-* [illegible]

[illegible] eſpecially when a method of anſwering the ſame ends, (as far as they ought to be anſwered) perfectly agreeable to the conſtitution, ſo readily offers itſelf.---- Let us then beſiege the throne with petitions and humble remonſtrances, and not doubt of a favorable iſſue in the reſult.

It muſt certainly give the moſt ſenſible pleaſure to every American that loves this his native country, to find a propoſal ſet on foot for all the colonies to lay before his majeſty a united repreſentation of their grievances, and pray a redreſs. Such a repreſentation as this, in the name of ſo large and reſpectable a body of his ſubjects, muſt have great weight and influence in the royal councils. That ſo excellent a ſcheme is likely to be ſo generally complied with, raiſes our hopes, and demonſtrates that the ſons of America are not afraid nor aſhamed to be her advocates againſt tyranny and oppreſſion, tho' obtruding [illegible]

[illegible] may be miſled; ſome perſons they muſt truſt for the information they receive; thoſe perſons are generally ſuch, whoſe intereſt it is to repreſent all things to them in falſe lights; ſo that it is rather to be admired that they are not oftner miſled than they are. Parliaments alſo are liable to miſtakes, yea, ſometimes fall into capital errors, and frame laws the moſt oppreſſive to the ſubject, yea, ſometimes take ſuch ſteps, which, if perſiſted in, would ſoon unhinge the whole conſtitution. Our hiſtories bear innumerable atteſtations to the truth of this. It cannot be treaſon to point out ſuch miſtakes and the conſequences of them, yea to ſet them in the moſt glaring light, to alarm the ſubject. By acting on this principle, our anceſtors have tranſmitted to us our privileges inviolated; let us therefore proſecute the ſame glorious plan. Let the *Britiſh* parliament be treated with all poſſible reſpect, while they treat us as fellow-ſubjects; [illegible]

73 From *The Constitutional Courant*, Sept. 21, 1765, in the New York Public Library

ANTI-BRITISH SPIRIT RESURRECTS THE SYMBOL

ELEVEN years later the "dismembered snake" design appeared at the head of a new paper. It now bore a different signification. The Stamp Act had passed. Protest in the colonies was virulent. The Stamp Act Congress was about to assemble in New York. The *Constitutional Courant* resurrected the "Dismembered Snake" to symbolize the manifest need for "a united representation of grievances" to be laid before the King. Union was desired now, not to ward off the French and Indians, but the alleged aggressions of the English Parliament. And again, it is worthy of note, New England is represented as the head of the rattlesnake, possessed of a menacing fang. This emblem reappeared in 1775 as the headpiece of the *Pennsylvania Journal.*

AMERICA MOURNS WITH ENGLAND IN DEFEAT

THOUGH it may be easy, looking back from to-day, to discover in the developments of the early eighteenth century trends toward an "inevitable" break with the mother country, such was not, in the middle of the eighteenth century, the intent or feeling of the colonists. Loyalty was still professed and felt. Though New England might chafe under the obstinacy of the English administrators, she regarded herself not as a separate people but as truly part of England, an England planted on new soil.

By the HONOURABLE

SPENCER PHIPS, Eſq;

Lieutenant-Governour and Commander in Chief in and over His Majeſty's Province of the *Maſſachuſetts-Bay* in *New-England*.

A PROCLAMATION for a general FAST.

IN Conſideration of the awful Rebuke of the Divine Providence in the late Defeat of His Majeſty's Forces near the River *Ohio*, whereby it has pleaſed GOD to manifeſt His high Diſpleaſure againſt the People of the ſeveral *Britiſh* Colonies in *America*, and loudly to call upon them to humble themſelves under his mighty Hand; and to repent of all their heinous Offences againſt the divine Majeſty, and to return to Him that ſmites them: In Conſideration alſo of the important Enterprizes now depending, and near the Point of Execution, for the Recovering of our Rights wreſted from us in the moſt perfidious Manner by our ambitious Neighbours, and for preſerving our Intereſts from further Invaſion; for the Succeſs whereof we depend on the Bleſſing of Almighty GOD, without which the beſt Preparations we are able to make will be ineffectual;

For theſe Reaſons,

I Have thought fit, with the Advice of his Majeſty's Council, and at the Deſire of the Aſſembly, to appoint Thurſday the Twenty-eighth Day of this Inſtant Auguſt to be kept as a Day of ſolemn Humiliation and Prayer, hereby exhorting both Miniſters and People, religiouſly to obſerve the ſame, by humbly imploring the Forgiveneſs both of publick and private Sins, and the divine Commiſſeration under all our Afflictions; that the Tokens of his Diſpleaſure may be followed with Reformation and Amendment of Life, in all Orders and Ages of Men; That there may be impreſſed on our Minds a Senſe of our abſolute Dependance on the great Governour of the World; That our Forces, gone and going forth, may be directed and proſpered of Heaven; and that we may be prepared to meet our GOD both in the Way of Mercy and Judgment; That it would pleaſe GOD to direct and ſucceed the Counſels and Adminiſtration of this Government; to bleſs our Sovereign Lord the KING, their Royal Highneſſes the Prince of *Wales*, the Princeſs Dowager of *Wales*, the Duke, and the reſt of the Royal Family; and to protect and proſper the Kingdoms and Dominions under his Majeſty's wiſe and gracious Government, and give Succeſs to all the Meaſures uſed to prevent the Calamities of a general War; and that the Goſpel of Peace may prevail and be victorious for the Eſtabliſhment of the Spiritual Kingdom of our Lord JESUS CHRIST: And all ſervile Labour and Recreations are forbidden on the ſaid Day.

Given at the Council-Chamber in Boſton, *the* 13*th Day of* Auguſt 1755, *in the* Twenty-ninth *Year of the Reign of our Sovereign Lord* GEORGE *the Second, by the Grace of GOD, of* Great-Britain, France *and* Ireland, KING, *Defender of the Faith*, &c.

By Order of the Lieutenant-Governor, with the Advice of the Council,

J. Willard, Secr'y.

S. Phips.

GOD Save the KING.

BOSTON: Printed by *John Draper*, Printer to His Honour the Lieutenant-Governour and Council. 1755.

74 Proclamation for a Fast following British reverses, 1755, from a broadside in the New York Public Library

CHAPTER II

THE EVE OF THE REVOLUTION

THE middle decades of the eighteenth century were a period of mental fruition for America. The Great Awakening, that revival movement which profoundly stirred both the northern and southern colonies, was still fresh in men's minds. It was followed by the appearance in many places of a new religious attitude which was the result of the scientific discoveries of the day and of the philosophy of the French encyclopædists. Many men in New England were beginning to challenge the supremacy of the Puritan church. It was not a long step from religious liberalism to political liberalism. Social movements made the changed intellectual attitude significant. These middle decades of the eighteenth century found the colonies rapidly making money. New fortunes were rising; commerce was taking fresh starts; there was a new vision of western lands. Old established communities felt the stirring of a new ardor on the part of the people to attain wealth and social importance. The thirteen continental colonies were forging ahead, sharply conscious of their own interests and peculiar needs. Across the Atlantic they had to deal with an England which was also given over to new outbursts of energy. Commercial development was the order of the day. The English Government had just brought to an end the Seven Years' War, which had been long and costly. The troubles with America began early in the "reconstruction period" which followed the Treaty of Paris (1763). People on both sides of the Atlantic had fought in the conflict and both evidenced the somewhat testy particularism which seems to be the inevitable aftermath of armed conflict. The Americans resented the attempts of the British Government to levy new taxes and that Government was thoroughly displeased at what seemed to be factious and unwarranted opposition.

Indignation, however, was not the mood in which to approach the problem. Parliament, unaware of the real state of matters across the Atlantic, was hurried into unfortunate action. British commercial interests, British foreign policy, royal pique, ministerial indecision — all contributed to the final ineptitude. The Intolerable Acts were so designated by the colonists because these measures seemed to indicate a lack of desire on the part of the mother country to consider colonial grievances. The Acts were, to the Americans — for such, under pressure of circumstances, the provincials were becoming — indicative of Parliament's unwillingness to recognize the British colonies as the equals of Britain. Parliament, in short, was acting as an imperial, not a British, legislature.

To counter such aggressions upon colonial rights, two courses of action were available. In the first place, the colonies must show by conduct manifest to the least observant that they were united and were capable of governing themselves. Thus sprang up those virile Committees of Correspondence, culminating in the Continental Congress. In the second place, reliance for redress of grievances must be placed in the Crown, since Parliament had proved unworthy. Thus colonial invective was poured out upon the latter, while King George and the monarchy continued to receive cordial expressions of loyalty and urgent prayers for intercession on behalf of the oppressed subjects in America. There was as yet little talk of political separation from Great Britain. Though Liberty Poles were raised, the liberty sought was freedom from improper and hurtful interference with American rights, not freedom from the duty of allegiance.

Province ... George the third, by the Grace of God of Great Britain France and Ireland King Defender of the Faith &c.

To all and singular our Justices of the Peace Sheriffs Constables and to all other our Officers and Subjects within our said Province and to each of You. Greeting.

Know ye that whereas in and by an Act of Parliament made in the fourteenth year of the reign of the late King Charles the second the Officers of our Customs and their Deputies are authorized and impowered to go and enter aboard any Ship or Vessell outward or inward bound for the purposes in the said Act mentioned and it is in and by the said Act further enacted and declared that it shall be lawfull to or for any person or persons authorized by Writ of Assistants under the seal of our Court of Exchequer to take a Constable Headborough or other publick Officer inhabiting near unto the place and in the day time to enter and go into any House, Shop, Cellar, Warehouse, or Room or other place and in case of resistance to break open doors chests trunks and other package there to seize and from thence to bring any kind of goods or merchandize whatsoever prohibited and uncustomed and to put and secure the same in our Storehouse in the port next to the place where such seizure shall be made.

And whereas in and by an Act of Parliament made in the seventh and eighth year of the reign of the late King William the third there is granted to the Officers for collecting and managing our revenue & inspecting the plantation trade in any of our plantations the same powers and authorities for visiting and searching of Ships, and also to enter houses or warehouses to search for and seize any prohibited or uncustomed goods, as are provided for the officers of our Customs in England by the said last mentioned Act made in the fourteenth year of the reign of King Charles the second, and the like assistance is required to be given to the said Officers in the execution of their Office as by the said last mentioned Act is provided for the Officers in England. And whereas in and by an Act of our said

75 From an original Writ of Assistance made out to Nathaniel Hatch, dated June 2, 1762, in the archives of the Supreme Judicial Court of Massachusetts, Boston

said Province of Massachusetts Bay made in the eleventh year of the reign of the late King William the third it is enacted and declared that our Superiour Court of Judicature Court of Assize and General Goal Delivery for our said Province shall have cognizance of all matters and things within our said Province as fully and amply to all intents and purposes as our Courts of King's Bench Common Pleas and Exchequer within our Kingdom of England have or ought to have —

And whereas John Temple Esq. Surveyor General of our Customs for the Northern District of America by his Commission or Deputation under his hand & seal dated at Boston the fourth day of January in the second year of our reign hath Deputed and Impowered . . . . . . Nathaniel Hatch Esq. to be Comptroller of all the rates and duties arising and growing due to us at Boston in our Province aforesaid, and in and by said Commission or deputation has given him power to enter into any Ship Bottom Boat or other Vessell and also into any Shop House Warehouse Hostery or other place whatsoever to make diligent search into any trunk chest pack case truss or any other parcel or package whatsoever for any Goods wares or Merchandize prohibited to be imported or exported, or whereof the Customs or other Duties have not been duly paid and the same to seize to our use in all things proceeding as the Law directs

Therefore we strictly Injoin and Command you and every one of you that all excuses apart you and every one of you permit the said Nath Hatch according to the true intent and form of the said Commission or Deputation and the Laws and statutes in that behalf made and provided as well by night as by day from time to time to enter and go on board any Ship Boat or other Vessell riding lying or being within or coming to the said port of Boston or any places or Creeks thereunto appertaining such Ship Boat or Vessell then and there found to search and oversee and the persons therein being strictly to examine touching the premisses aforesaid and also in the day time to enter and go into the Vaults Cellars warehouses Shops and other places where any prohibited goods wares or merchandizes or any goods wares or merchandizes for which the customs or other duties shall not have been duly and truly satisfied and paid lye concealed or are suspected to be concealed according to the true

76 Second page of the Writ of Assistance in the archives of the Supreme Judicial Court of Massachusetts

BOSTON OPPOSES THE "WRITS OF ASSISTANCE"

BRITISH colonial policy after the war did not define itself at once. The first hint of it came in the form of instructions to colonial officers to enforce the old acts of trade. This the Massachusetts rum-merchants did not fancy. They objected, in particular, to the use of writs of assistance or general search warrants issued by local courts. Armed with these, the royal officers could with impunity pry into storehouses with possible embarrassment to the owner. Such writs were authorized by act of Parliament and had been used before; but never had they been so zealously employed to execute the laws of trade. A stand against them was determined upon by the sturdy merchants.

true intent of the Law to inspect and oversee and search for the said Goods wares and Merchandize, and further to do and execute all things which of right and according to the Laws and statutes in this behalf shall be to be done. And we further strictly Injoin and Command you and every one of you that to the said Nathaniel Hatch Esq. you and every one of you from time to time be aiding assisting and helping in the Execution of the premisses as is meet. And this you or any of you in no wise omit at your perils. Witness Thomas Hutchinson Esq. at Boston the third day of June, in the second year of our Reign. Annoq Domini 1762. By Order of Court.

Sam Winthrop Cler

77 Third page of the Writ of Assistance in the archives of the Supreme Judicial Court of Massachusetts

78 James Otis, 1725–83, from a copy in the Bostonian Society of the portrait by Joseph Blackburn (1700–65) in the Museum of Fine Arts, Boston

OTIS PLEADS THE MERCHANTS' CAUSE

THE Boston merchants found a man to their liking in James Otis. Graduated from Harvard at eighteen, he was at this time serving as advocate-general of Massachusetts. Though perhaps the busiest lawyer in New England, Otis had not lost an early love for literature and philosophy. The year before he had published, anonymously, *Rudiments of Latin Prosody with a Dissertation on Letters and the Principles of Harmony in Poetic and Prosaic Composition.* The discipline of such studies found curious fruit in the following years. Engaged as counsel for the merchants, Otis resigned his office to plead the case. His success at once made him a marked man. No one played a more important and prominent part in the years immediately preceding the war. His eloquence, spoken and written, his passion, his magnetism kept him to the front. But in 1769 a blow on the head rendered him intermittently insane; thereafter he recedes from view and the drama moves on without his impetuous leadership.

79 From the mural painting *Otis Protesting the Writs of Assistance* by Robert Reid (1862–), in the State House, Boston

THE SPIRIT OF INDEPENDENCE

In 1761 Otis was at the height of his power. Disdaining to rely on technicalities, he based his plea at the trial before the five judges of the Supreme Court in Boston on broader grounds. To him a writ of assistance was "the worst instrument of arbitrary power, the most destructive of English liberty and the fundamental principles of law that ever was found in an English law-book." He continued: "I was solicited to argue this cause as advocate-general; and because I would not, I have been charged with desertion from my office. To this charge I can give a very sufficient answer. I renounced that office, and I argue this cause, from the same principle; and I argue it with the greater pleasure, as it is in favor of British liberty, at a time when we hear the greatest monarch upon earth declaring from his throne that he glories in the name of Briton, and that the privileges of his people are dearer to him than the most valuable prerogatives of his crown; and as it is in opposition to a kind of power, the exercise of which, in former periods of English history, cost one king of England his head, and another his throne. . . . Reason and constitution are both against this writ. Let us see what authority there is for it. Not more than one instance can be found in all our law-books; and that was in the zenith of arbitrary power, in the reign of Charles II. . . . But had this writ been in any book whatsoever, it would have been illegal. All precedents are under the control of the principles of law. . . . No acts of parliament can establish such a writ. . . . An act against the constitution is void." These fiery words laid the foundation for the arguments soon to be used throughout the colonies in a struggle for freedom. John Adams, present at the hearing, reports that "a great crowd of spectators and auditors went away absolutely electrified."

80 Sir Francis Bernard, 1711–79, from the portrait by John Singleton Copley (1737–1815) in Christ Church, Oxford University

OTIS ACCUSES THE GOVERNOR

The following year events gave Otis occasion for writing the first of a series of impassioned political pamphlets. At a critical juncture, and without waiting for the approval of the legislature not then in session, Governor Bernard had taken it upon himself to fit out an armed vessel. At its next meeting, the House, led by Otis, whose pleading of 1761 had won him a seat, protested that such an act was "in effect taking from the House their most darling privileges, the right of originating all taxes. . . . When once the representatives of a people give up this privilege, the government will soon become arbitrary. No necessity, therefore, can be sufficient to justify a House of Representatives in giving up such a privilege, for it would be of little consequence to the people whether they were subject to George, or Louis, . . . if both could levy taxes without parliament."

THE RIGHTS OF THE ASSEMBLY

Bernard at once returned the bold message, asking the House not to enter upon its minutes words disrespectful to the King. The House voted to erase this part of the address, while still maintaining that the Governor had exceeded his authority. Bernard persisted in declaring his right to incur expense without legislative approval. So the assembly now appointed a committee to present its position to the people. Otis was a member, and took over the entire work. The result was published in the autumn — *A Vindication of the Conduct of the House of Representatives.* Of this John Adams wrote later: "How many volumes are concentrated in this little fugitive pamphlet, the production of a few hurried hours, amidst the continual solicitations of a crowd of clients! . . . Look over the declaration of rights and wrongs issued by Congress in 1774. Look into the Declaration of Independence in 1776. . . . Look into all the French constitutions of government; and, to cap the climax, look into Mister Thomas Paine's *Common Sense*. . . . What can you find that is not to be found, in solid substance, in this . . .?"

A
VINDICATION
OF THE
CONDUCT
OF THE
House of Representatives
OF THE
PROVINCE
OF THE
MASSACHUSETTS-BAY:
MORE PARTICULARLY,
IN THE
LAST SESSION
OF THE
GENERAL ASSEMBLY

By James Otis, Efq;
A Member of faid Houfe.

"Let fuch, fuch only, tread this facred Floor,
Who dare to love their Country and *be Poor:"*
"Or good tho' rich, humane and wife tho' great,
Jove give but thefe, we've nought to Fear from Fate!"
* Pope. Anon.

BOSTON: Printed by Edes & Gill, in *Queen-Street.* 1762.

81 Title-page of the original issue, in the New York Public Library

PATRICK HENRY ARGUES THE "PARSON'S" CAUSE IN VIRGINIA

In Virginia occurred another incident, significant as the wind before the storm. In the Old Dominion, clergy of the Established Church were still supported through public taxes. Their compensation had since 1696 taken the form of fixed amounts of tobacco. With the hard times of the French wars, tobacco became scarce and dear. Under popular pressure, the Burgesses, therefore, in 1755 and again in 1758, enacted that tobacco debts should be paid in money at the ratio of two pence per pound. This was much under the market price for tobacco. The clergy protested and sent the Reverend Camm to England, whereupon the act of 1758 fell under the royal veto. Suits were then brought in the county courts to recover the difference between the compensation paid under the Twopenny Act and the old tobacco-payment measures. Chief among these suits was one brought by the Reverend James Maury, one-time teacher of Jefferson, in Hanover County. In November, 1763, the court declared the Act of 1758 to be void: the parson had won. But Hanover was a center of religious dissent; and one more step was needed to make the victory complete. It was necessary to determine the amount of damages due the parson. For this purpose a jury was summoned. The popular cause seemed hopeless. So the defendants retained as counsel young Patrick Henry, an awkward ne'er-do-well who, after six weeks of study, had been admitted to the bar. Henry, like Otis in Boston, went far afield from the point at issue. Building from the theory that government was instituted by contract between King and people, he established the doctrine that violation of such contract by the King was an illegal act. For the King of England to veto an act lawfully passed by the Virginia Burgesses was forbidden by the contract. The jury was carried off its feet and awarded James Maury one penny damages. The orator of the Revolution had been found.

82 Hanover Courthouse, from Henry Howe, *Historical Collections of Virginia*, Charleston, S. C., 1845

83 George Grenville, 1732–92, from the portrait by Sir Joshua Reynolds in the possession of Lord Leconfield at Petworth, England

GRENVILLE DEMANDS MORE REVENUE FROM AMERICA

Writs of assistance and parsons' salaries were, after all, isolated instances of colonial unrest. They are indicative of tension, but not of disloyalty. Nor did they furnish any basis for united action. Meanwhile, however, affairs in England were shaping to the King's wishes. In 1763 George Grenville became chief minister. Honest, industrious, courageous, matter-of-fact, Grenville in ordinary times might have served his country creditably and even with distinction. Colonial administration now, however, required delicate handling; and Grenville lacked imagination. As Secretary of State under Bute, he had learned something of the way in which colonial affairs were being handled. Such vacillation as he had seen displeased him. Furthermore, the wars had doubled England's debt; the cost of the American establishment had risen since 1748 from seventy thousand pounds to three hundred fifty thousand pounds. As Grenville saw it, what was more natural than that the colonies should stand a share of this expenditure? The course to pursue seemed obvious; and in the fall of 1763 and spring of 1764 he proceeded to outline a new governmental policy. His scheme was threefold: first, to establish in America a permanent military force for purposes of defense; second, to enlarge and enforce the laws of trade; third, to raise colonial revenue by means of a parliamentary tax. The scheme, in short, was a comprehensive one, of concern to all the colonies. In 1764 the first step was taken in the passage of the Sugar Act. This revived and amplified the Molasses Act of 1733 (No. 63). Grenville also asked the colonial agents in London and the colonial assemblies to suggest to him adequate means of raising the revenue needed to support the troops in America. His preference was, he stated, for a stamp tax; but he was willing to accept any practicable measure.

OTIS ASSERTS THE RIGHTS OF ALL THE COLONIES

Grenville's actions aroused widespread alarm, especially among the New England merchants and traders, for enforcement of the Sugar Act meant diminution of profits in their trade with the West Indies. In New England, therefore, appeared the first organized protest against the new policy of Parliament. And no one better sensed its significance than James Otis. In July, 1764, he issued an elaborate pamphlet, *The Rights of the British Colonies Asserted and Proved*, in which he applied his theory that the power of Parliament was limited by the free principles of the British Constitution. No legislature has "a right to make itself arbitrary," nor can any such body "take from any man part of his property without his consent." The Americans were as much British as the inhabitants of the British Isles. "No parts of His Majesty's dominions can be taxed without their consent; every part has a right to be represented in the supreme or some subordinate legislation; . . . this would firmly unite all parts of the British Empire in the greatest peace and prosperity, and render it invulnerable and perpetual."

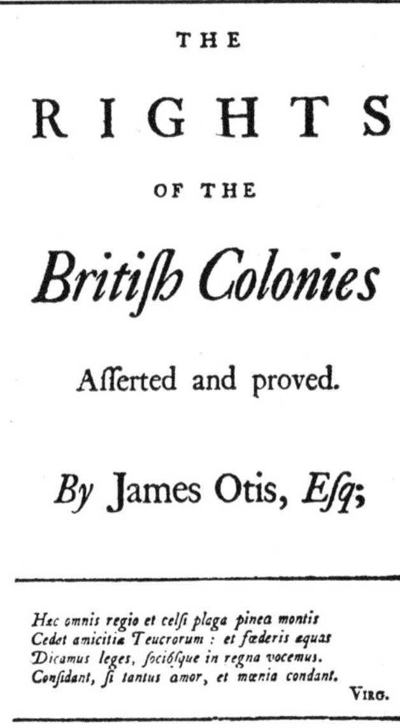

THE

RIGHTS

OF THE

Britiſh Colonies

Aſſerted and proved.

By James Otis, *Eſq*;

Hæc omnis regio et celſi plaga pinea montis
Cedet amicitiæ Teucrorum : et fœderis æquas
Dicamus leges, ſociòſque in regna vocemus.
Conſidant, ſi tantus amor, et mœnia condant.
Virg.

BOSTON

Printed and Sold by Edes and Gill, in Queen-Street.

M,DCC,LXIV.

84 Title-page of the original issue in the New York Public Library

[66]

APPENDIX.

The City of *Boſton*, at their Annual Meet-in *May*, 1764, made Choice of *Richard Dana*, *Joſeph Green*, *Nathaniel Bethune*, *John Ruddock*, Eſq'rs; and Mr. *Samuel Adams*, to prepare INSTRUCTIONS for their REPRESENTATIVES.

The following Inſtructions were reported by ſaid Committee, and unanimouſly Voted.

To *Royal Tyler**, *James Otis*, *Thomas Cuſhing*, and *Oxenbridge Thacher*, Eſq'rs.

GENTLEMEN,

YOUR being choſen by the freeholders and inhabitants of the town of *Boſton*, to repreſent them in the General Aſſembly the enſuing year, affords you the ſtrongeſt teſtimony of that confidence which they place in your integrity and capacity. By this choice they have delegated to you the power of acting in their public concerns in general, as your own Prudence ſhall direct you; always reſerving to themſelves the conſtitutional right of expreſſing their mind, and giving you ſuch inſtruction upon particular matters, as they at any time ſhall judge proper.

We

* Now of the honorable Board; in whoſe room was returned Mr. *Thomas Gray*, Merchant.

85

[67]

We therefore your conſtituents take this opportunity to declare our juſt Expectations from you,

That you will conſtantly uſe your power and influence in maintaining the invaluable rights and privileges of the province, of which this town is ſo great a part: As well thoſe rights which are derived to us by the royal charter, as thoſe which being prior to and independent on it, we hold eſſentially as free-born ſubjects of Great-Britain;

That you will endeavour, as far as you ſhall be able, to preſerve that independence in the houſe of repreſentatives, which characterizes a free people; and the want of which may in a great meaſure prevent the happy effects of a free government: Cultivating as you ſhall have opportunity, that harmony and union there, which is ever deſirable to good men, when founded in principles of virtue and public ſpirit; and guarding againſt any undue weight which may tend to diſadjuſt that critical balance upon which our happy conſtitution, and the bleſſings of it do depend. And for this purpoſe, we particularly recommend it to you to uſe your endeavours to have a law paſſed, whereby the ſeats of ſuch gentlemen as ſhall accept of poſts of profit from the Crown, or the Governor, while they are members of the houſe, ſhall be vacated, agreeable to an act of the Britiſh parliament, 'till their conſtituents ſhall have the opportunity of re-electing them, if they pleaſe, or of returning others in their room.

Being members of the legiſlative body, you will have a ſpecial regard to the morals of this people, which are the baſis of public happineſs; and endeavour to have ſuch laws made, if any are ſtill wanting, as ſhall be beſt adapted to ſecure them: And we particularly deſire you carefully to look into the laws of exciſe, that if the virtue of the people is endangered by the multiplicity of oaths therein enjoined, or their trade and buſineſs is unreaſonably impeded or embarraſſed thereby, the grievance may be redreſſed.

As the preſervation of morals, as well as property and right, ſo much depends upon the impartial diſtribution of juſtice, agreeable to good and wholeſome law: And as the judges of the land do depend upon the free grants of the general aſſembly for ſupport; it is incumbent upon you at all times to give your voice for their honourable maintenance,

I 2 ſo

86

[68]

ſo long as they, having in their minds an indifference to all other affairs, ſhall devote themſelves wholly to the duties of their own department, and the further ſtudy of the law, by which their cuſtoms, precedents, proceedings and determinations are adjuſted and limited.

You will remember that this province hath been at a very great expence in carrying on the war; and that it ſtill lies under a very grievous burden of debt: You will therefore uſe your utmoſt endeavor to promote public frugality as one means to leſſen the publick debt.

You will join in any propoſals which may be made for the better cultivating the lands, and improving the husbandry of the province: and as you repreſent a town which lives by its trade, we expect in a very particular manner, that you make it the object of your attention, to ſupport our commerce in all its juſt rights, to vindicate it from all unreaſonable impoſitions, and promote its proſperity——Our trade has for a long time laboured under great diſcouragements; and it is with the deepeſt concern that we ſee ſuch further difficulties coming upon it, as will reduce it to the loweſt ebb, if not totally obſtruct and ruin it. We cannot help expreſſing our ſurprize that when ſo early notice was given by the agent, of the intentions of the miniſtry, to burthen us with new taxes, ſo little regard was had to this moſt intereſting matter, that the court was not even call'd together to conſult about it 'till the latter end of the year; the conſequence of which was, that inſtructions could not be ſent to the agent, tho' ſollicited by him, 'till the evil had got beyond an eaſy remedy.

There is now no room for further delay: We therefore expect that you will uſe your earlieſt endeavours in the General Aſſembly, that ſuch methods may be taken as will effectually prevent theſe proceedings againſt us. By a proper repreſentation, we apprehend it may eaſily be made to appear that ſuch ſeverities will prove detrimental to Great Britain itſelf; upon which account we have reaſon to hope that an application, even for a repeal of the act, ſhould it be already paſs'd, will be ſucceſsful. It is the trade of the colonies, that renders them beneficial to the mother country: Our trade, as it is now, and always has been conducted, centers in Great Britain, and in return for her manufactures,

affords

87

Three pages of Instructions to Representatives, May 1764, prepared by Samuel Adams, from the copy in the New York Public Library

THE MASSACHUSETTS LEGISLATURE STARTS INTER-COLONIAL CORRESPONDENCE

OTIS' object, therefore, was to avert a revolution by appealing to England to recognize the rights of the Britons resident in America. His plea, consequently, was phrased in language and based on ideas that could, and did, appeal as strongly to the Virginian as to the Bostonian. *The Rights of the British Colonies* assumed that the problems of Massachusetts were likewise those of all of the colonies. New England's agitation at this time is instanced by the conduct of the Boston Town Meeting of May, 1764. Here Samuel Adams carried through a set of instructions to the newly elected delegates in the House of Representatives. "There is now no room for further delay. . . . These unexpected proceedings may be preparatory to new taxations. . . . This . . . annihilates our charter right to govern and tax ourselves — It strikes at our British privileges which . . . we hold in common with our fellow subjects who are natives of Britain. If taxes are laid upon us in any shape, without our having a legal representation where they are laid, are we not reduc'd from the character of free subjects to the miserable state of tributary slaves? . . . Use your endeavors that their weight [that of the other North American colonies] may be added to that of this province, that by the united application . . . all may happily obtain redress." Upon these instructions the Massachusetts legislature acted. Otis, Thacher and others were constituted a committee for corresponding with the other colonies; a circular letter was issued calling for "united assistance" in preserving their "most essential rights."

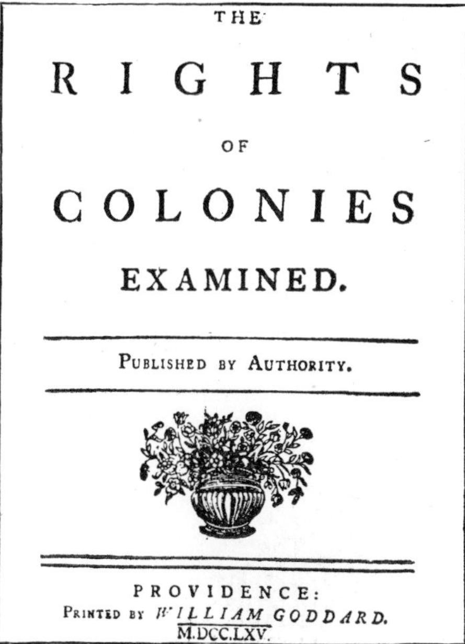
THE RIGHTS OF COLONIES EXAMINED.

PUBLISHED BY AUTHORITY.

PROVIDENCE:
PRINTED BY WILLIAM GODDARD.
M.DCC.LXV.

88 Title-page of the pamphlet by Stephen Hopkins, Governor of Rhode Island, in the New York Public Library

RHODE ISLAND'S GOVERNOR FURTHERS THE COLONIAL CAUSE

THE appeal of the Massachusetts committee of correspondence met with an enthusiastic response. Rhode Island likewise elected a committee of correspondence and stood prepared "to exert its utmost efforts to preserve its privileges inviolate."

Anno quinto

Georgii III. Regis.

C A P XII.

An Act for granting and applying certain Stamp Duties, and other Duties, in the *British* Colonies and Plantations in *America*, towards further defraying the Expences of defending, protecting, and fecuring the fame; and for amending fuch Parts of the feveral Acts of Parliament relating to the Trade and Revenues of the faid Colonies and Plantations, as direct the Manner of determining and recovering the Penalties and Forfeitures therein mentioned.

WHEREAS by an Act made in the laft Seffion of Parliament, feveral Duties were granted, continued, and appropriated, towards defraying the Expences of defending, protecting, and fecuring, the Britifh Colonies and Plantations in America: And whereas it is juft and neceffary, that Provifion be made for raifing a further Revenue within Your Majefty's Dominions in America, towards defraying the faid Expences; We, Your Majefty's moft dutiful and loyal Subjects, the Commons of Great Britain in Parliament affembled,

A 2 have

89 First page of a printed copy of *The Stamp Act*, 1765, in the Library of Congress

THE STAMP ACT IS PASSED AGAINST COLONIAL PROTEST

THE assemblies of six colonies sent remonstrances against the proposed Stamp Act. "An exemption from the burden of ungranted and involuntary taxes must be the grand principle of every free state" reads the New York petition, boldest of all. To Grenville this seemed a simple refusal to submit to any and all British taxation. To the colonial agents, on the 2nd of February, he said, "I take no pleasure in bringing upon myself their resentments; it is a duty of my office to manage the revenue." In February, 1765, the Stamp Act passed the Commons, by a vote of two hundred and five to forty-nine; on the 8th of March, without amendment, debate or division, it passed the Lords; and on the 22nd it received the royal assent. On November 5 following, it was to go into operation. Benjamin Franklin, Colonial Agent in England, set out to secure for certain of his American friends some of the collectorships which the new law created in the various colonies.

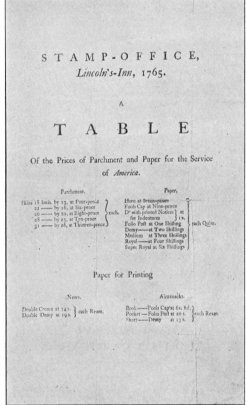

STAMP-OFFICE,

Lincoln's-Inn, 1765.

A

TABLE

Of the Prices of Parchment and Paper for the Service of *America*.

Parchment.		Paper,	
Skins 18 Inch. by 13, at Four-pence	each.	Horn at Seven-pence	each Quire.
22 —— by 16, at Six-pence	each.	Fools Cap at Nine-pence	each Quire.
26 —— by 20, at Eight-pence	each.	D° with printed Notices for Indentures at 1 s.	each Quire.
28 —— by 23, at Ten-pence	each.	Folio Poft at One Shilling	each Quire.
31 —— by 26, at Thirteen-pence	each.	Demy——at Two Shillings	each Quire.
		Medium at Three Shillings	each Quire.
		Royal——at Four Shillings	each Quire.
		Super Royal at Six Shillings	each Quire.

Paper for Printing

News.		Almanacks.	
Double Crown at 14 s.	each Ream.	Book——Fools Cap at 6 s. 6 d.	each Ream.
Double Demy at 19 s.	each Ream.	Pocket—Folio Poft at 20 s.	each Ream.
		Sheet——Demy at 13 s.	each Ream.

90 Table of Stamp Act Charges, from a printed copy in the Emmet Collection, New York Public Library

VIOLATIONS OF THE STAMP ACT TO BE TRIED WITHOUT JURY

THE Act consisted of fifty-five sections and required that for every skin or piece of vellum or parchment, or sheet or piece of paper, on which should be engrossed, written or printed any declaration, plea, rejoinder, demurrer or other pleading, or any copy thereof, in any court of law within the British colonies and plantations in America, a stamp duty should be imposed. A stamp duty of from one half-penny to twenty shillings was also imposed on every pamphlet, newspaper, marriage certificate or commerical paper. The proceeds were to be expended solely for the colonies. Violations of the Act were to be tried in Admiralty Courts, without a jury, in England or in America.

91 An embossed stamp for two shillings, six pence, on an "original sheet of stamped paper returned from America," in the Emmet Collection, New York Public Library

STAMPS ARE REQUIRED TO LEGALIZE PAPERS

EVIDENCE that the required tax had been paid was to be shown by a stamp or seal embossed upon the paper in question. The stamps represented taxes of different amounts. Unless such stamps were used on business documents and legal papers, marriages would be null, notes of hand valueless, suits at law impossible.

[1]

To the Honourable the

COMMONS

OF

GREAT BRITAIN,

In PARLIAMENT Aſſembled:

The PETITION of the Merchants, Traders, and others, of the City of *London*, intereſted in the *American* Commerce,

SHEWETH,

THAT your Petitioners are deeply concerned to obſerve, by the Votes of this Honourable Houſe, that a Bill is brought in, "To reſtrain the Trade and Commerce of the Province of *Maſſachuſet's Bay* and "*New Hampſhire*, and Colonies of *Connecticut* and *Rhode* "*Iſland*, and *Providence Plantation* in *North America*, to "*Great Britain*, *Ireland*, and the *Britiſh Iſlands* in the "*Weſt Indies*; and to prohibit ſuch Provinces and Colonies "from carrying on any Fiſhery on the Banks of *Newfound-* "*land*, or other Places therein to be mentioned, under "certain Reſtrictions, and for a Time to be limited."

YOUR

92 Protest of British Merchants to Parliament, from the first page of the copy, with proposed revisions, in the Massachusetts Historical Society

[2]

YOUR Petitioners beg Leave to repreſent, that the ſaid Bill, ſhould it paſs into a Law, will, in its Operation, deprive Thouſands of His Majeſty's loyal Subjects of their actual Subſiſtance, and reduce them to extreme Diſtreſs, even that of Famine; the ſaid Provinces not generally raiſing Corn ſufficient for their own Support; and by this Bill they will be prevented from receiving any Supplies from their Siſter Colonies, and precluded from their Natural Reſource, *The SEA*.

THAT your Petitioners have reaſon to believe, that very great Numbers of Men are bred and employed in the Fiſheries, who in Hardineſs and Intrepidity are not exceeded by any in this extenſive Empire, and will be impelled by the preſſing Calls of Hunger and Want, to ſuch a Conduct as may be productive of Devaſtation and Bloodſhed, which may endanger the Peace and Welfare of that Part of His Majeſty's *American* Dominions; or be induced to emigrate to the Iſlands of *Miquelon* and *St. Pierre*, there to fiſh for the *French*, and give our Rivals *the Means* of ſupplying the Markets in *Europe*, and thereby render it difficult for us to regain that valuable Branch of Commerce.

YOUR Petitioners beg Leave further to repreſent, that there is now due from the ſaid Provinces and Colonies to the City of *London*, very large Sums of Money: That their Remittances are principally made by Means of the Fiſheries, and conſequently the Ruin brought on thoſe Colonies will ultimately fall on Great Britain.

THAT among the other Grievances, of which our Fellow Subjects in *America* ſo generally complain, is, their being deprived of Trial by Jury in particular Caſes, and the Extention of the Juriſdiction of the Admiralty Courts; which Grievances, your Petitioners, with much Concern, find, are not only continued, but extended, by the preſent Bill.

And

93 Second page of the Protest of British Merchants to Parliament petitioning the removal of Trade Restrictions

LONDON MERCHANTS ASK REMOVAL OF AMERICAN TRADE RESTRICTIONS

OPINION in England seemed favorable to the Stamp Act and to the Government's policy in general. The merchant class, however, was ever watchful of its interests, and ready to oppose measures that threatened to reduce colonial trade with England. The colonies owed to London alone a full million pounds, and this could be paid only in goods. So, to placate America and the London merchants, certain commercial bounties and tariff exemptions were granted on colonial trade, along with the imposition of the stamp tax.

A BRITISH OFFICER DEFENDS THE COLONISTS

IN Parliament itself little opposition appeared. Pitt was absent. But one voice was raised in eloquence. Colonel Isaac Barré, who had fought with Wolfe at Louisburg and Quebec, vigorously defended the colonials and their loyalty. "Sons of Liberty," he called them, men who had prospered despite English neglect and English maladministration.

94 Bostonians Reading the Stamp Act, wood engraving after a drawing by F. O. C. Darley (1822–88)

95 Isaac Barré, 1726–1802, from an engraving by W. T. Fry, published 1817 after an original portrait by A. G. Stuart in the possession of the Earl of St. Vincent

Extract of a Letter from London.

"MR *Charles Townſend* ſpoke in favour of the Bill, (Stamp Duty) and concluded his Speech by ſaying to the following Effect :

" Theſe Children of our own Planting, (ſpeaking of *Americans*) nouriſhed by our Indulgence, until they are grown to a good Degree of Strength and Opulence, and protected by our Arms, will they grudge to contribute their Mite to relieve us from the heavy load of national Expence which we lie under ?

" Which having ſaid and ſat down, Mr. *Barre* aroſe, and with Eyes darting Fire and an outſtretched Arm, ſpoke as follows, with a Voice ſomewhat elevated, and with a Sternneſs in his Countenance, which expreſs'd in a moſt lively Manner, the feelings of his Heart.

" Children planted by your Care ? No ! Your Oppreſſion planted them in *America* ; they fled from your Tyranny, into a then uncultivated Land, where they were expoſed to almoſt all the Hardſhips, to which humane Nature is liable ; and among others, to the Savage Cruelty of the Enemy of the Country ; a People the moſt ſubtile, and I take upon me to ſay, the moſt truly terrible, of any People that ever inhabited any Part of GOD'S EARTH, and yet actuated by Principles of true *Engliſh* Liberty ; they met all theſe Hardſhips with Pleaſure, compared with thoſe they ſuffered in their own Country, from the Hands of thoſe that ſhould have been their Friends.

" They nouriſhed up by your Indulgence ? They grew by your Neglect of them : As ſoon as you began to care about them, that Care was exerciſed in ſending Perſons to Rule over them, in one Department and another ; who were, perhaps, the Deputies of ſome Deputy, of Members of this Houſe, ſent to ſpy out their Liberty, to miſrepreſent their Actions, and to prey upon them ; Men, whoſe Behaviour, on many Occaſions, has cauſed the Blood of thoſe Sons of LIBERTY, to recoil within them ; Men promoted to the higheſt Seats of Juſtice, ſome to my Knowledge, were glad by going to foreign Countries, to Eſcape being bro't to a Bar of Juſtice, in their own.

" They protected by your Arms ? They have nobly taken up Arms in your Defence, have exerted their Valour, amidſt their conſtant and laborious Induſtry, for the Defence of a Country whoſe Frontier, while drench'd in Blood, its interior Parts have yielded all its little Savings to your Enlargement : And BELIEVE ME, REMEMBER I THIS DAY TOLD YOU SO, That the ſame Spirit which actuated that People at firſt, will continue with them ſtill : But Prudence forbids me to explain my ſelf any further. GOD KNOWS, I do not at this Time ſpeak from Motives of Party Heat ; What I deliver, are the genuine Sentiments of my Heart : However ſuperior to me in general Knowledge and Experience, the reſpectable Body of this Houſe may be, yet I claim to know more of *America* than moſt of you, having ſeen and been converſant in that Country. The People there are as truly Loyal, I believe, as any Subjects the King has : But a People jealous of their Liberties, and who will vindicate them, if they ſhould be violated ; but the Subject is too delicate, I will ſay no more.

97 Isaac Barré's Speech on the Sons of Liberty, from *The Boston Post Boy*, May 27, 1765, in the Massachusetts Historical Society, Boston

"SONS OF LIBERTY" ORGANIZE IN AMERICA

As Barré spoke, there sat in the gallery one Jared Ingersoll of Connecticut. Though later to be a stamp collector and a Loyalist, he was greatly moved by the oration. Back to the colonies he sent a report of the speech. His letter was widely printed in the American press. Soon organizations known as Sons of Liberty appeared in the colonies to protest against the Stamp Act.

96 Patrick Henry, 1736–99, from a miniature on ivory, 1795, by Lawrence Sully (1769–1803), courtesy of Herbert L. Pratt, New York

OPPOSITION TO THE STAMP TAX

SINCE 1673 England had levied duties in America, with slight protest. A stamp tax, moreover, had been discussed for a full half-century. Yet the Stamp Act at once aroused a storm of objection. The new tax differed from the ones previously laid. For the first time, a direct internal tax had been imposed. Applicable alike in New England and Virginia, on farm and in town, the tax furnished a basis for unified action. The stamps, passing from hand to hand, would serve as a symbol and constant reminder of the tax imposed by a legislature three thousand miles away, in whose deliberations America had no voice. So, from Massachusetts to the South, ran the protest. The people gathered in excited groups and loudly expressed their anger. The tax was denounced from the pulpit; the press spoke out fearlessly. The stamp distributors were insulted and prevented from acting. The stamps were everywhere seized, hidden and burned. In May, 1765, Patrick Henry had been elected to the House of Burgesses. His entrance into that august assembly focused in intense form the general indignation. His first days as a member he spent in gathering about him a group of the younger men, and men from the discontented western counties. Near the end of the session, he found the time ripe for action.

PATRICK HENRY DEBATES

On the blank page of a law book Patrick Henry wrote out a series of resolutions condemning the Stamp Act. The aristocratic members from tidewater Virginia, fearful of unloosing radical elements among the people, deprecated such outspoken language. After hot debate, in which he was opposed by Bland, Pendleton, Randolph and Wythe, Henry won. "Tarquin and Caesar each had his Brutus; Charles the First his Cromwell; and George the Third" — he paused, while the speaker and others cried "Treason"— "may profit by their example. If this be treason, make the most of it."

Extract of a Letter from a Gentleman in Philadelphia, to his Friend in this Town, dated last Tuesday.

"I HAVE inclosed the Resolves of the Virginia Assembly, on debating the Stamp Act. The Governor, as soon as he heard what they were about, sent for them, and without Preamble, told them, he would dissolve them; and that Minute they were dissolved. As they are of an extraordinary Nature, thought they might not be disagreeable. They are as follows."

"*WHEREAS the Hon. House of Commons, in England, have of late drawn into Question, how far the General Assembly of this Colony hath Power to enact Laws for laying of Taxes and imposing Duties, payable by the People of this his Majesty's most antient Colony: For settling and ascertaining the same to all future Times, the House of Burgesses of this present General Assembly have come to the following Resolves:*——

"Resolved, *That the first Adventurers, Settlers of this his Majesty's Colony and Dominion of Virginia, brought with them and transmitted to their Posterity, and all other his Majesty's Subjects since inhabiting in this his Majesty's Colony, all the Privileges and Immunities that have at any Time been held, enjoyed and possessed by the People of Great-Britain.*

"Resolved, *That by two Royal Charters, granted by King* JAMES *the First, the Colony aforesaid are declared and entitled to all Privileges and Immunities of natural born Subjects, to all Intents and Purposes, as if they had been abiding and born within the Realm of England.*

"Resolved, *That his Majesty's liege People of this his antient Colony have enjoy'd the Right of being thus govern'd, by their own Assembly, in the Article of Taxes and internal Police; and that the same have never been forfeited, or any other Way yielded up, but have been constantly recogniz'd by the King and People of Britain.*

"Resolved, *therefore, That the General Assembly of this Colony, together with his Majesty or his Substitutes, have, in their Representative Capacity, the only exclusive Right and Power to lay Taxes and Imposts upon the Inhabitants of this Colony: And that every Attempt to vest such Power in any other Person or Persons whatever, than the General Assembly aforesaid, is illegal, unconstitutional and unjust, and have a manifest Tendency to destroy British as well as American Liberty.*

"Resolved, *That his Majesty's liege People, the Inhabitants of this Colony, are not bound to yield Obedience to any Law or Ordinance whatever, designed to impose any Taxation whatsoever upon them, other than the Laws or Ordinances of the General Assembly aforesaid.*

"Resolved, *That any Person, who shall, by speaking or writing, assert or maintain, that any Person or Persons, other than the General Assembly of this Colony, have any Right or Power to impose or lay any Taxation on the People here, shall be deemed an Enemy to this his Majesty's Colony.*"

99 First publication of the Virginia Resolutions, from the *Newport* (R.I.) *Mercury* of June 24, 1765, in the John Carter Brown Library, Providence

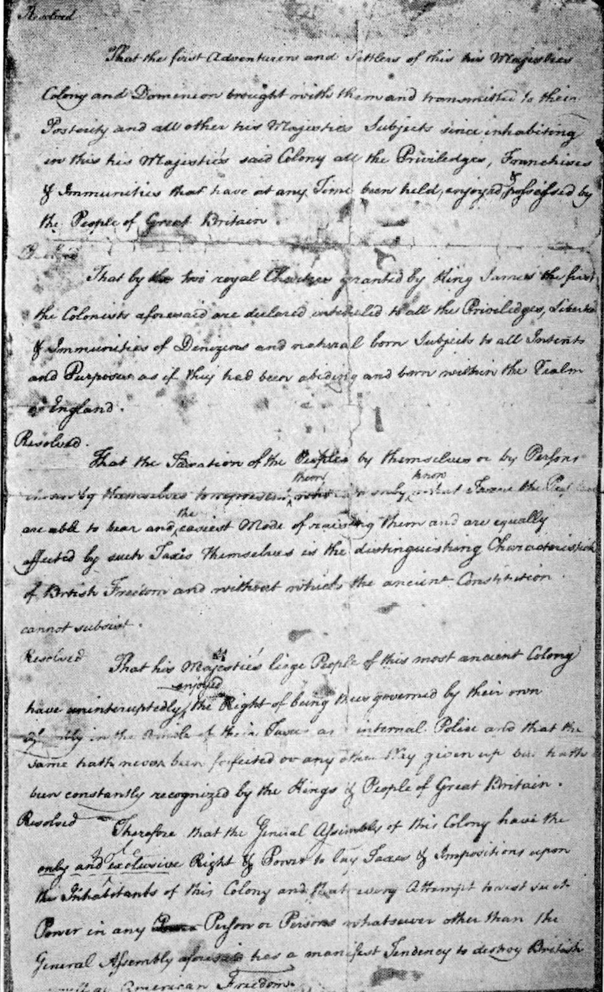

Resolved

That the first Adventurers and Settlers of this his Majesties Colony and Dominion brought with them and transmitted to their Posterity and all other his Majesties Subjects since inhabiting in this his Majesties said Colony all the Priviledges, Franchises & Immunities that have at any Time been held, enjoyed & possessed by the People of Great Britain.

[illegible]

That by the two royal Charters granted by King James the first the Colonists aforesaid are declared entitled to all the Priviledges, Liberties & Immunities of Denizens and natural born Subjects to all Intents and Purposes as if they had been abiding and born within the Realm of England.

Resolved.

That the Taxation of the People by themselves or by Persons chosen by themselves to represent them who [illegible] only know what Taxes the People are able to bear and the easiest Mode of raising them and are equally affected by such Taxes themselves is the distinguishing Characteristick of British Freedom and without which the ancient Constitution cannot subsist.

Resolved

That his Majesties liege People of this most ancient Colony have uninterruptedly enjoyed the Right of being thus governed by their own Assembly in the Article of their Taxes and internal Police and that the same hath never been forfeited or any other Way given up but hath been constantly recognized by the Kings & People of Great Britain.

Resolved

Therefore that the General Assembly of this Colony have the only and sole exclusive Right & Power to lay Taxes & Impositions upon the Inhabitants of this Colony and that every Attempt to vest such Power in any Person or Persons whatsoever other than the General Assembly aforesaid has a manifest Tendency to destroy British as well as American Freedom.

98 Draft of Virginia Resolutions, May 1765, from the original in Patrick Henry's handwriting, owned by Charles L. Hamilton, Germantown, Penn.

THE VIRGINIA RESOLUTIONS

Four only of Henry's resolves remained in the journal when the Governor dissolved the assembly. But dissolving the House was of no avail. Henry had roused Virginia. A version of the resolutions, correct in spirit and substance, appeared in the *Newport Mercury* and was widely reprinted throughout the colonies. Similar steps were taken elsewhere. Through common indignation, a sentiment of union was developing. The associations calling themselves Sons of Liberty now determined to prevent enforcement of the law. Legislatures took measures leading in the same direction. Out of all this turbulence, provincial sentiment was crystallized in the Stamp Act Congress, called to meet in New York on the 7th of October. It was organized by Timothy Ruggles of Massachusetts, chairman, and John Cotton, clerk. Nine colonies were represented. Prominent in the membership were Otis, Livingston of New York, John Dickinson and George Bryan of Pennsylvania, and Christopher Gadsden of South Carolina.

To the Right Honorable the Lords Spiritual and Temporal of Great Britain in Parliament Assembled.

The Memorial of the Freeholders and other Inhabitants of the Massachusetts Bay, Rhode Island, and Providence Plantations, New Jersey Pennsylvania, the Government of the Counties of New Castle, Kent and Sussex, upon Delaware, Province of Maryland.

Most Humbly Sheweth, .

That his Majesty's Liege Subjects in his American Colonies, though they acknowledge a due Subordination to that August Body, the British Parliament, are entitled in the Opinion of your Memorialists, to all the inherent Rights and Liberties of the Natives of Great Britain, and have ever since the Settlement of said Colonies Exercised those Rights and Liberties, as far as their Local Circumstances would permit.

That your Memorialists humbly conceive one of the most essential Rights of these Colonists, which they have ever till lately uninterruptedly enjoyed, to be Trial by Jury.

That your Memorialists also humbly conceive another of these essential Rights to be the Exemption from all Taxes but such as are imposed on the People by the Several Legislatures in these Colonies, which Right also they have till of late freely enjoyed.

But your Memorialists humbly beg leave to represent to your Lordships, that the Act for granting certain Stamp Duties in the British Colonies in America, fills his Majesty's American Subjects with the deepest Concern, as it tends to Deprive them [illegible] Liberties above mentioned, and thus Several.

100 Memorial to Parliament of the Stamp Act Congress, 1765, from a facsimile by Bierstadt, New York, 1897, in the Emmet Collection, New York Public Library

ACTION OF THE STAMP ACT CONGRESS

The Congress framed a declaration of rights and grievances, stating the common position of the colonies. Admitting the right of Parliament to make general and trade laws for the colonies, this document denied power to levy taxes. Before adjourning, the Congress adopted an address to Parliament, restating the colonial grievances. The Congress is particularly important as it established a precedent for future concerted action in still more troublous times.

THE COLONIES MAKE GOODS TO REPLACE IMPORTS

Economic retaliation was the aim of the committees of correspondence set up at this time. Adopting a device tried the previous year, agreements not to import and not to consume English-made goods were entered into with enthusiasm. "Frugality and Industry" was the watchword. Even songs were used to stir the people. The *Massachusetts Gazette* of October 31, 1765, contains a long poem, of which the following stanza is a sample.

With us of the woods
Lay aside your fine goods,
Contentment depends not on clothes;
We hear, smell and see,
Taste and feel, with high glee,
And in winter have huts for repose.

That the boycott was effective is shown by the number of memorials, praying for the repeal of the Stamp Act, presented to Parliament by British merchants.

BOSTON, October 1.

IT is now out of fashion to put on mourning at the funeral of the nearest relation, which will make a saving to this town of twenty thousand sterling per annum.—It is surprizing how suddenly, as well as how generally an old custom is abolished, it shows however, the good sense of the town, for it is certainly prudent to retrench our extravagant expences, while we have something left to subsist ourselves, rather than be driven to it by fatal necessity.

We hear that the laudable practice of frugality is now introducing itself in all the neighbouring towns, (and it were to be wished it might thro'out the government) an instance of which we have from Charlestown, at a funeral there the beginning of last week, which the relatives and others attended, without any other mourning than which is prescribed in a recent agreement.

October 8. There seems to be a disposition in many of the inhabitants of this and the neighbouring governments to cloath themselves with their own manufacture.—At Hampstead, on Long Island, in the Province of N. York, a company of gentlemen have set up a new woolen manufactory, and having given notice to gentlemen shopkeepers and others, of any of the provinces, that by sending proper patterns of any colour, they may be supplied with broad-cloths, equal in fineness, colour, and goodness, and cheaper than any imported: the proprietors give good encouragement to any person who are any way versed in the woolen manufactory, such as wool combers, weavers, clothiers, shearers, dyers, spinners, carders, or understand any branch of the broad-cloth, blanket, or stroud manufactory.——At Jamaica on the said island, one Tookis Polpham is erecting a fulling-mill, which will be compleat in about a month, and carry on all the branches of a fuller and dyer of cloth.

The northern colonists have sense enough, at least the sense of *feeling*; and can tell where the *shoe pinches*—The delicate ladies begin to find by experience, that the Shoes made at Lyn are *much easier* than those of the make of Mr. Hose of London—What is become of the noted shoemaker of *Essex?*

It is fear'd by many who wish well to *Great Britain*, that the new A—t of P——t will greatly distress, if not totally ruin some of HER own manufactures—It is thought that by means of this A—t, less of her woolen cloths, to the amount of some thousands sterling, will be purchas'd in this cold climate the insuing winter.

We are told that all the Funerals of last Week were conducted upon the new Plan of Frugal y.

Nothing but Frugality can now save the *distress'd* northern colonies from impending ruin—It ought to be a consolation to the good people of a certain province, that the greatest man in it exhibits the most *rigid* example of this political as well as moral virtue.

101 From the front page of *The Connecticut Courant*, Hartford, Oct. 29, 1764, in the New York Public Library

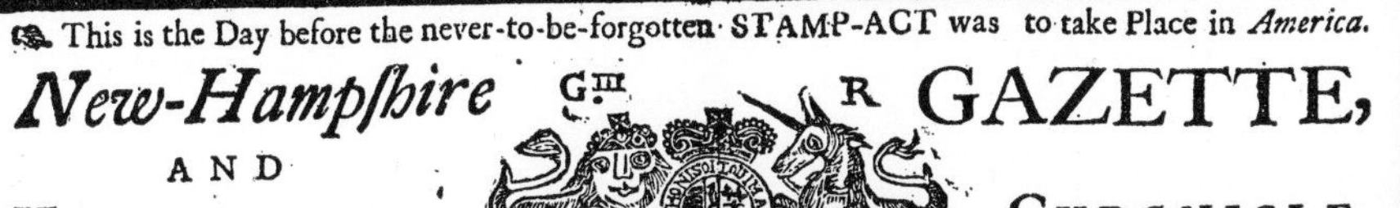

This is the Day before the never-to-be-forgotten STAMP-ACT was to take Place in *America.*

New-Hampshire GAZETTE, AND HISTORICAL CHRONICLE,

Thursday October 31, 1765.

No. 474 { Weeks since this Paper was first Publish'd.

—But what avail her unexhausted Stores,
Her blooming Mountains and her sunny Shores,
With all the Gifts that Heav'n and Earth impart,
The Smiles of Nature and the Charms of Art,
While proud Oppressions in her Vallies Reigns,
And Tyranny usurps her happy Plains?

WE are now arrived at the Eve of that remarkable Day, which is appointed to be as fatal to almost all that is dear to us, as the *Ides of March* were, to the Life of *Cæsar*, or as the memorable *Fifth of November* had like to have prov'd to the Lives, Liberty and Property of the honest People of *England.* —A Day on which our Slavery is to commence, by a Decree more severe, considering all Circumstances, than was ever pronounced in the famous *Star-Chamber*; an Ordinance by which we are not only to be reduced to Beggary by a TAX we can never pay, but are made Slaves for our Disability, and are to be plunged into a deeper Bondage, by discharging of it, if it were in our Power.

And all this is determined by those from whom by our Connection and Relation, we had the greatest Reason to expect Defence, Protection and all the Favours and Blessings, that a dutiful Child cou'd expect, from a kind, tender Parent. For among other just Grounds for such Hopes, *their* Predecessors for Ages past, esteem'd it their Glory, as it was their Delight, to diffuse Happiness among all to whom their Influence extended. And more especially to transmit to their Successors Posterity and Dependants, that *Liberty* which they themselves enjoy'd, and thought worth defending and preserving at any Rate. A very slighty Acquaintance with English History, will inform any one, Ignorant of it, with what mighty Struggles and earnest Contention, they have maintained this natural Right, against the united Force of Tyrants in various Forms, and all their Sycophants and adulating Adherents. And that they cou'd never be prevail'd upon, by all the Hopes and Allurements despotic Power and arbitrary Misrule cou'd furnish, or the World give in Exchange, to part with their own Freedom or intail Vassalage on their Posterity: As without Liberty they justly thought all the Enjoyments of Life to a generous Mind, a Person freeborn, wou'd be insipid, vapid and tastless.

Oh *Liberty*, thou Goddess heav'nly bright,
Profuse of Bliss, and pregnant with Delight!
Eternal Pleasures in thy Presence reign,
And smiling Plenty leads thy wanton Train;
Eas'd of her Load Subjection grows more light,
And Poverty looks chearful in thy Sight;
Thou mak'st the gloomy Face of Nature gay,
Giv'st Beauty to the Sun & Pleasure to the Day.

Thee Goddess, thee Britannia's Isle adores:
How has she oft exhausted all her Stores,
How oft in Fields of Death thy Presence sought,
Nor thinks the mighty Prize too dearly bought.

These, and such as these, were the Sentiments of those in Power, in former Times. They knew that Liberty, was the natural Right of Mankind: And that it was the greatest Injury even to curtail or deprive them of it, in any Degree, any further than by their own Consent they exchange Part of it, for other Blessings, and the Preservation of what remains. They were so far from a Disposition to rob Men of this natural Right, that on the contrary they were for enlarging, and extending of it to all the World that wou'd receive it. *Sed Tempora Mutantur &c.*—who that has read, that strong metaphorical Exclamation, How is the Gold become dim, and the most fine Gold Changed! can avoid thinking of it—it seems to obtrude itself on this Occasion.—

What an amazing Change of Principles, Policy and Tempers! —One wou'd think a prodigious Vertigo had seiz'd every Head, that in the impetuous Whirl all Objects appeared alike— that there cou'd be no distinguishing Mercy from Cruelty, Right from Wrong,.—Formerly every honest industrious Man was encourgaged, his Diligence gained him Reputation as well as Subsistence. Can it be pretended the Case is the same, when no Man may buy or sell but he that receives a Mark?— a Badge of his Slavery, an Evidence of the Limitation of Property and the Loss of Liberty.—Is honest Industry encouraged, when the most Industrious pay the more for excelling, and are subjected more than others to the imperious Mandates, probably of insulting strutting overbearing Officers?——

Was there any Thing more grievous and enslaving in the Scheme to introduce a general Excise, propos'd about thirty Years ago to the People in G—— B——, than *This* is to us? — and the Prime M——r of that Time who bro't in such a Bill, it was said cou'd have carried it through, (such is the magic Power attending a certain high Office) yet what was the Event? the general Disgust it gave, the Opposition to it, the People discover'd without Doors put an End to the Project. —And had it past into an Act, as was design'd, it wou'd never have been executed, but at the Head of a standing Army.—As odious and detestable as this Scheme was, there were notwithstanding a great many Advocates for it, prompted by the *Primum Mobile.*—And should an Edict like that once past by the King of *Egypt*, relative to Male Children be promoted in the same Manner, there would no doubt be found a Majority for it within certain Walls, if it related only to the Colonies.—And indeed with respect to the present Generation, such an Edict wou'd not be so severe as the Edict now against us.—And shall we calmly and quietly yield our Necks to the Yoke?— We have been told by some mercenary Scriblers, that the Right of passing such a Law cannot be disputed, that our Remedy is by humble Supplication, &c. and by this Way of Reasoning one may prove that whatever is done by superior Force is right, and so Robbery of any kind may be prov'ed to be right, because there was Power to perform the Action—and as to Petitioning and Remonstrating,—What became of the humble Petitions presented, while this Matter was under Consideration, were they not spurn'd and frown'd as it were into Vaults.—They that represent us ought to hear us by their own Principles—but the same first Mover remaining, we have Reason to think no Remonstrances will ever be heard, no Reasons prevail for our Relief in that Way.— Our own Resolutions not to hold our Foreheads still to receive the *Mark*, that is, not to be active to purchase our own Bondage from private selfish Views for fear of loosing a particular Interest, is the most probable Means of having the Difficulty removed,— and can any Thing follow from that worse than will follow from Compliance?—Will not this subject us to the same Condition of the Subjects of the *Grand Monarch.*— Will not he who seeks to save a petty Interest by such Measures, become a Slave by his own Consent?—Does he not in effect agree to give up his Birth-Right, for a *Mess of Pottage?*—As those who were to have been the Distributors of our Chains have generally disdained such an invideous Office, he will well deserve Chains and every other *Mark of Slavery* who shall hunt after the *Mark of the Beast*, or fish as it were after *Sharks?* —Let any one consider what Character *he* is like to acquire who should sneak in private after what he will be ashamed openly to avow. Who to save a paltry insignificant Property, voluntarily laid down his Neck and took on the Yoke of a perpetual Bondage, at a Time when his Townsmen, his Countrymen, and a whole Continent resisted and sav'd themselves from Ruin, the *Loss of Liberty and Property.* Can there be any Doubt whether it is lawful? Let him that doubts, consider, whether it is lawful for any Numbers of Men to sell another Number as free as themselves for Slaves? Let them prove that the Sale of *Joseph* into *Egypt*, was lawful, and then they may doubt on—Let them determine whether, if a Magistrate, whose Authority they acknowledge within his Jurisdiction, shou'd, because he has assistance, order them where they were liable to a Moderate Fine, to be pilloried, whipt, and finally imprisoned for Life, they shou'd think themselves obliged passively to submit: If they do, let such Friends to *Passive Obedience*, suffer the just Consequence of their own Principles, till they receive Conviction.

The LAMENTATION Of the NEW-HAMPSHIRE-GAZETTE, in particular, and the PRESS in general, On a *Suspicion* of losing their LIBERTY.

—Cari sunt nobis propinqui, familiares et amici, sed omnes omnium caritates, patria una est complexa, pro qua quis bonus dubitet Mortem oppetere? si ei sit profuturus, et res ita requiret. Cicero.

BEHOLD THE GREAT, THE IMPORTANT DAY,
BIG with the FATE OF CATO, and of ROME.
Addison.

WHAT a hard Case is it, that after this Day's Appearance upon the Stage of Action, *I must Die*, or submit to that which *is worse* than Death, *be Stamp'd*, and lose my Freedom—Will all the good Deeds I have done signify nothing?--If the whole Kingdom of England would save my Life, I am unable to live *under* this Burden; therefore I must *Die!*—O unhappy that I am—It is true, Life, like the Harmony in Music, is composed of the Contrarieties of several Notes, sweet and harsh, sharp and flat, sprightly and solemn; 'tis chequer'd with variety of Circumstances; sometimes it swells with a prosperous Fortune; at others it ebbs into the lowest Degree of Adversity; and seldom admits of Constancy and Durability— It is true, my Life in these Parts have been *but short*, having this Day compleated *nine Years and five Weeks* — FREEDOM is so natural, and SLAVERY so contrary to my Nature, that I chuse a *voluntary* Death, in Hopes of escaping this Servitude—Should I once submit to have my Liberty infring'd, I could never make that Appearance in the World I have, therefore an honorable Death is to be prefer'd before an *ignominious* Life —I was resolv'd to live well; and be as useful as I could, without being concern'd as to the *Length* or *Shortness* of my Duration— But before I make my *Exit*, I will recount over some of the many good Deeds I have done, and how useful I have been, and still may be, provided my Life should be spar'd; or I might hereafter revive again, altho' it may not seem so proper to sound my own Praise. Without this Art of communicating to the Public, how dull and melancholy must all the intelligent Part of Mankind appear?—It may with great Veracity be affirm'd, that there is no Art, Science or Profession in the World, but what owes its Origin, or at least its Progress and preseu

102 Facsimile of front page of the *New Hampshire Gazette*, Oct. 31, 1765, in the Massachusetts Historical Society

PLANS ARE MADE TO EVADE THE STAMP TAX

As the day approached on which the Act was to go into effect, efforts were redoubled to maintain popular opposition. Some newspapers appeared in mourning, lamenting the death of American liberty. Other agencies of publicity begged the people to pardon a temporary cessation of printing, until means could be devised for evading the Act. There was apparently no thought of compliance with the command of the British Parliament.

103 Burns' Coffee House, New York Meeting-place of the Sons of Liberty, from an engraving in the Emmet Collection, New York Public Library

NEW YORK MERCHANTS SIGN NON-IMPORTATION AGREEMENT

Opposition seemed keenest in New York. There the Congress assembled; there the first non-importation agreement was signed; and there the popular outcry was loudest. By May the principal gentlemen of the town clad themselves in homespun or "turned clothes." The Society for promoting Arts and Manufactures encouraged domestic industry. On the 23rd of October a market for all kinds of home products was opened in Broad Street. *The New York Gazette* carried in large type the legend, "It is better to wear a homespun coat than lose our liberty." On the last of October, upwards of two hundred of the leading merchants assembled in the long room of the City Arms. Resolutions were adopted: "First, that in all Orders they send out to Great Britain, for Goods or Merchandise of any Nature, Kind, or Quality whatsoever, they will direct their Correspondents not to ship them, unless the Stamp Act be repealed. Secondly, it is further unanimously agreed that all orders already sent Home, shall be countermanded by the very first Conveyance; and the Goods and Merchandise thereby ordered, not to be sent, unless upon the condition mentioned in the foregoing Resolution. Thirdly, that no Merchant will vend any Goods or Merchandise sent upon Commission from Great Britain that shall be shipped from thence after the first Day of January next, unless upon the condition mentioned in the first Resolution." Philadelphia, on November 7, and Boston, on December 9, followed suit.

NEW YORK'S UNPOPULAR ROYALIST GOVERNOR

The stamps reached New York on October 23. As soon as this became known — for they had been shipped in secret — "all vessels in the Harbour lowered their colours to signify Mourning, Lamentation and Woe." The following day, writes Robert Livingston, "a vast number of people beheld the sight and were greatly enraged." Officially in charge at the time was Lieutenant Governor Colden, a man of strange career. Born in Dunse, Scotland, he had at the age of twenty migrated to America. Here for some years he practiced medicine. In 1718 he settled in New York, and soon entered public life. Colden withal was a scholar and scientist of note. He was a founder of the American Philosophical Society; he corresponded with Franklin and leading scholars of the continent. He had sent Linnaeus some four hundred American plants, and the eminent botanist had responded by naming one "Coldenia." His most famous work was a history of the Indians in the colony of New York. On top of all this, Colden was a strong Royalist and supporter of prerogative. He had already given evidence of his intention to enforce the Stamp Act, though such a stand had lost him the support of his council and won him popular enmity.

104 Cadwallader Colden, 1688–1776, from a portrait by Matthew Pratt (1734–1805) in the Chamber of Commerce, New York

A MOB GREETS THE ARRIVAL OF STAMPS AT NEW YORK

In July, Governor Colden had asked General Gage "for a guard sufficient to secure the fort against the Negroes or a Mob." That his request was not needless, subsequent events indicated. On the night after the arrival of the *Edward*, bearing the stamps, a handbill containing ominous warnings was distributed over the city. Colden thought it best to unload in midstream; with the aid of the men-of-war in the harbor, he managed to get the packages of stamps to the fort. Evil was brewing along the water-front. On the first of November the storm broke. A mob of the Sons of Liberty, "the most formidable imaginable," writes Livingston, gathered. In its midst were effigies of Colden and Bute, hated adviser of George III. Street parading followed. The crowd stopped to cheer before the residence of McEvers, who had resigned as Stamp-Master, and then proceeded to the fort, which served also as the Governor's residence. Here they found Colden's best coach; into it they tumbled the effigy; and both were burned on the Bowling Green.

Pro Patria

The first Man that either distributes or makes use of Stampt Paper, let him take Care of his House, Person, & Effects.

Vox Populi;

We dare

105 From the *Magazine of American History*, Vol. I, 1877, copy of a handbill preserved in the State Paper Office, London

-[No *Stamped Paper* to be had.]

From the PUBLIC LEDGER, Auguſt 16.

A Dialogue between a North-American *and a* Courtier.

North-American.

YOU remember that at our laſt meeting, we agreed upon this day candidly to enquire into the juſtice as well as policy of Great-Britain, in taxing the North-Americans: and as this is a matter of the greateſt importance to both countries, I ſhall with pleaſure hear you endeavour to defend the meaſures that have been taken to the utmoſt of my power, I mean as far as is conſiſtent with truth or right reaſon: but if I ſhould differ with you in opinion, I hope you will hear me with the ſame candor that I ſhall you.

Courtier.

Upon theſe principles, Sir, I join iſſue; and firſt, as to the juſtice or right of Taxing. This I think we are veſted with, from your being the ſubjects of the Crown of England, as well as in conſideration of the protection and repeated ſuccours you have received from this nation, to which you owe your origin and which ſo often has de-

LONDON, Auguſt 29.

His Excel'ency the Earl of Hertford, Lord Lieutenant of Ireland, has appointed the Hon. Col. Cunningham, and Capt. Fleming, to be his Aids de Camp.

Very large Orders from Spain are come over for the purchaſe of corn, ſo great a ſcarcity of which has not been known there for many years.

A Letter from on board the Hardwicke Indiaman, in St. Jago road, capital of the Cape de Verd Iſlands, dated May 16, mentions, that ſhe touched there the 8th of that Month for Water, (having had a very good paſſage) where ſhe found the Hector and True Briton. The Royal Charlotte came in there for water a few days after.

A ſhip, John Hop, Maſter, from Bordeaux bound to Hamburgh, was boarded in the Britiſh Channel by pirates, under Engliſh Colours, and robbed of two Caſks indigo, and a cheſt of wine, with ſome

and not chiming in with the *oppreſſive* Meaſures of thoſe in Power, having had many broad Hints and Overtures, to bring them over for that Purpoſe. Which they rejected with Diſdain. I ſhou'd be very ſorry to find your Paper under ſo much *undue* Influence, as to omit inſerting Things of ſo great Conſequence to the Peace, Happineſs, and Tranquility of the Public in general. I cannot in Juſtice to theſe Gentlemen's Characters, read your Papers, without making ſome Reply to ſo great a Falaſy.

I am, Sir, Your obedient Servant,

A Citizen of Montreal.

N. B. For Conveniency, we have new Comiſſion of the Peace every Quarter Seſſions; ſuppoſe it is ſo in the other Colonies.

St. Jago, (Jamaica) Auguſt 24.

Extract of the Aſſembly of the 16th Auguſt.

A Meſſage from his Excellency by the Provoſt Marſhal, commanding in his Majeſty's Name, the immediate Attendance of the Houſe in the Council Chamber; Mr. Speaker and the whole Houſe attending his Excellency, his Excellency addreſſed the Speaker in the Words to

106 Heading of Hugh Gaine's *New York Mercury*, Nov. 18, 1765, from a copy in the New York Public Library

GOVERNOR COLDEN SURRENDERS THE STAMPS TO THE CITY FATHERS

So far the mob had been fairly orderly, under control. But matters rapidly got out of hand. Cooler heads feared an outbreak. Livingston, John Cruger, mayor of the city, and others waited upon the governor. As a result of this interview, they announced that Colden had said "that he would not issue, nor suffer to be issued any of the stamps now in Fort George." It must have been a humiliating moment for the proud old man. In 1736 he had published a treatise entitled "Account of Diseases prevalent in America"; but this malady of 1765 could not be disposed of with any scientific label. Even yet the people were not satisfied: on the 5th, Colden was obliged to turn over to the city fathers all of the hated stamps, which were then deposited in the City Hall, safe from royal officers. Eight days later the new Governor, Moore, arrived. Colden was glad to surrender his responsibilities. Moore was inclined to compromise. He wrote home, concerning the Stamp Act, that he was "obliged to suspend the power he was unable to exert." Hence it came about that the papers could announce: "No stamped paper to be had." In New York the wealthy merchants, determined to oppose Grenville's new tax, had called to their assistance the easily excited rabble. Irresponsible mobs prevented the execution of the law. The conservative merchants and the aristocrats were well aware that the mob of "Liberty Boys" had dangerous possibilities. Its spleen might be vented against the aristocracy in America as readily as against the British Government.

107 Andrew Oliver, 1706–74, from a photograph in the Massachusetts Historical Society of the original portrait in possession of the Oliver family

THE BOSTON STAMP-DISTRIBUTOR IS FORCED TO RESIGN

EVEN before the arrival of the stamps, Boston had seen disorder. Grenville, in announcing the Stamp Act, had declared his intention of appointing Americans as collectors. In Boston the choice fell upon Andrew Oliver, brother-in-law of Governor Thomas Hutchinson, a native of Boston who had already held several minor posts. His acceptance of the office of stamp-distributor was unfortunate. The patriot party saw in this naught but devotion to an unsympathetic British ministry. It was proposed that he should be hanged in effigy on the Liberty Tree, under which the Sons of Liberty held their meetings. The mob bearing the effigy went to Kilby Street, where Oliver had recently erected a building which the people supposed was designed for a stamp office. This they instantly demolished. Then they made demonstrations before Oliver's residence, breaking windows and threatening his life. Oliver fled, resigned his office, and signed a pledge that he would not act as stamp agent. But he never regained popular favor. In the outbreak of mob violence in Boston, Governor Hutchinson's house was entered and pillaged, his library and priceless manuscripts being almost completely destroyed. (See Vol. XI, No. 124.)

CERTAIN BRITISH OPINION FAVORS AMERICA

ALL this was not without its effect in England. At the time of the passage of the Stamp Act there had been observers who favored the colonies. Now their number was greatly increased. Those who were accustomed to trade with the colonies, those who disliked the influence of royal favorites, those who in any way suffered from Grenville's attempt at retrenchment — in short, all discontented elements — vociferously attacked the ministry, in press, in pamphlet, in cartoon. In the illustration, Grenville is attempting to balance the budget; Bute is assisting by weighing down the credit side with petty savings eked from royal favor. The military, crippled by the Government, is protesting against the abandonment of policies which, though expensive, will expand British influence in "Havanna," the "Philipines," and Newfoundland. America urges that commerce will outweigh these expenses. In the offing, French and Dutch scoff at the commercial stupidity of the British.

108 From a British caricature in the New York Historical Society

A MARYLAND LAWYER

A MAN of importance at this juncture was Daniel Dulany of Annapolis. His father, a poor Irishman, had risen to be Attorney-General, a member of the landed gentry, and a leader of the popular party. His son he had sent to England for schooling at Eton, Cambridge, and the Middle Temple. Opening a law practice in Annapolis in 1747, Daniel soon became the outstanding lawyer and barrister of Maryland. Indeed, his legal learning was so great and of such repute that judges were known to refer difficult questions to him. His opinion was sought even from England, while often cases would be withdrawn from the courts to be settled by this provincial lawyer. Dulany ultimately became a firm Tory, and in later times refused to join the Revolutionary forces; as a consequence, most of his large landed properties were confiscated. His last years were spent in seclusion.

109 Daniel Dulany, 1721–97, from the portrait, artist not known, in the Supreme Court, Baltimore, courtesy of the Frick Art Reference Library, New York

CONSIDERATIONS
ON THE
PROPRIETY
OF IMPOSING
TAXES
IN THE
BRITISH COLONIES,

For the Purpose of raising a REVENUE, by ACT OF PARLIAMENT.

——*Haud-Totum Verba resignent*
Quod latet arcanâ, non enarrabile, fibrâ.

THE SECOND EDITION.

Annapolis: Printed and Sold by Jonas Green, 1765

[Price Two Shillings and Six-pence.]

110 Title-page of Daniel Dulany's pamphlet on taxation, original in the New York Public Library

A LEGAL ARGUMENT AGAINST "TAXATION WITHOUT REPRESENTATION"

WHILE the Stamp Act Congress was in session, an imposing pamphlet upon the matter in hand made its appearance. Its close and powerful reasoning soon identified it as the work of Dulany. Lawyerlike, he pointed out in a clear, simple, and forcible manner that the colonists, as British subjects, were not represented in Parliament and that taxation without representation was a violation of the common law of England. The remedy he, as a good King's man, found to reside in the use of all proper and constitutional means for convincing Parliament of its error. The pamphlet made a deep impression in America, where reprints came thick and fast. In England also it was printed and read. His arguments were not only freely used, but served as the basis of Pitt's speech in the Commons just three months after the publication of the pamphlet.

PITT, THE COLONIES' STALWART SUPPORTER IN ENGLAND

PRESSURE upon the English government was thus severe. George III, moreover, disliked the independent attitude of Grenville, who therefore resigned late in 1765. The King was willing to receive Pitt the elder as Prime Minister. The great Commoner, as Secretary of State, had guided England to victory in the recent struggle with France for supremacy in America. (See Vol. VI.) He was an object of devotion among the Americans. But agreements failed; a weak ministry under the Whig Marquis of Rockingham was formed. Pitt believed the Stamp Act was not right; Rockingham felt it to be right but not wise; Grenville was sure it was both right and wise.

111 William Pitt, First Earl of Chatham, 1708–78, from the portrait, "The Great Commoner," by William Hoare (1706–92) in the National Portrait Gallery, London

Mr. PITT began with prefacing, that he did not mean to have gone any further upon the Subject on that Day; that he had only deſigned to throw out a few Hints, which Gentlemen, who were ſo confident of the Right of this Kingdom to ſend Taxes to *America*, might conſider, perhaps might reflect, in a cooler Moment, that the Right was at leaſt equivocal. But ſince the Gentleman who ſpoke laſt had not ſtopt on that Ground, but had gone into the whole; into the Juſtice, the Equity, the Policy, the Expediency of the STAMP-ACT, as well as into the Right, he would follow him through the whole Field, and combat his Arguments on every Point.

He was going on, when Lord *St-nge* got up, and called both the Gentlemen (Mr. *Pitt*, and Mr. *Greenville*) to order; he ſaid they had both departed from the Matter before the Houſe, which was the King's Speech, and that Mr. PITT was going to ſpeak twice in the ſame Debate, although the Houſe was not in a Committee. Mr. *G---ge Onſlow* anſwered, that they were both in order, as nothing had been ſaid but what was fairly deducible from his Majeſty's Speech, and appealed to the Speaker.---The Speaker decided in Mr. *Onſlow*'s Favour. Mr. PITT ſaid,

"I do not apprehend I am ſpeaking twice. I did expreſly reſerve a Part of my Subject, in order to ſave the Time of the Houſe, but I am compelled to proceed in it. I do not ſpeak twice, I only finiſh what I had deſignedly left imperfect; but if the Houſe is of a different Opinion, far be it from me to indulge a Wiſh of tranſgreſſing againſt Order. I am content, if it be your Pleaſure, to be ſilent."

Here he pauſed, the Houſe reſounded with GO ON, GO ON. He proceeded.

GENTLEMEN,

SIR,

"I have been charged with giving Birth to Sedition in *America*. They have ſpoken their Sentiments with Freedom againſt this unhappy Act. That Freedom has become their Crime. Sorry I am to hear the Liberty of Speech in this Houſe imputed as a Crime, but the Imputation ſhall not diſcourage me; it is a Liberty I mean to exerciſe; no Gentleman ought to be afraid of exerciſing it. It is Liberty, by which the Gentleman who calumniates it, might himſelf have profited. He ought to have deſiſted from his Project. The Gentleman tells us, *America* is obſtinate; *America* is almoſt in open Rebellion. I rejoice that *America* has reſiſted. Three Millions of People, ſo dead to all the Feelings of Liberty, as voluntarily to conſent to be Slaves, would have been fit Inſtruments to make Slaves of the reſt. I came not here armed at all Points with Law Caſes, and Acts of Parliament, with the Statute Book, doubled down in Dogs Ears, to defend the Cauſe of Liberty. If I had, I would myſelf have cited the two Caſes of *Cheſter* and *Durham*; I would have cited them, to have ſhewn, that even, under arbitrary Reigns, Parliaments were aſhamed of taxing a People without their Conſent, and allowed them Repreſentatives. Why did the Gentleman confine himſelf to *Cheſter* and *Durham*? He might have taken a higher Example in *Wales*. *Wales* that never was taxed by Parliament, until it was incorporated. I would not debate a particular Point of Law with the Gentleman; I know his Abilities. I have been obliged to his diligent Reſearches; but for the Defence of Liberty, on a general Principle, upon a conſtitutional Principle, it

112 Report of Pitt's Speech, Jan. 14, 1766, from the *Pennsylvania Gazette*, Philadelphia, Apr. 24, 1766

PITT URGES REPEAL OF THE STAMP ACT

THE British ministry was in a quandary. America seemed to be on the verge of open revolt. Yet to repeal the Stamp Act would be acknowledgment of defeat, not only in the enforcement of a tax measure, but also in the exercise of the sovereign power. The moment was crucial. Pitt, advanced in years and crippled with gout, roused himself for a great and stirring speech. His position was that, while Parliament had a right to levy taxes for purposes of trade regulation, it had no right to levy internal taxes for revenue upon those not represented in the taxing body. He concluded: "Upon the whole, I will beg leave to tell the house what is really my opinion. It is, that the Stamp Act be repealed, absolutely, totally and immediately; that the reason for the repeal be assigned, because it was founded on an erroneous principle."

PRESSURE FROM MERCHANTS AND LIBERALS LEADS TO REPEAL

GRENVILLE, proud of his measure, counseled otherwise. "The total repeal will persuade the colonies that Great Britain confesses itself without the right to impose taxes on them, and is reduced to make this confession by their menaces. Do the merchants insist that debts to the amount of three millions will be lost, and all fresh orders be countermanded? Do not injure yourselves from fear of injury; the merchants may sustain a temporary loss, but they and all England would suffer much more from the weakness of Parliament, and the impunity of the Americans. With a little firmness, it will be easy to compel the colonists to obedience." But on March 4 repeal was carried in the Commons, by a vote of two hundred fifty to one hundred twenty-two; one week later it passed the Lords, one hundred five to seventy-one. On the 18th it received the royal signature, amid the rejoicings of tradesmen and people of liberal politics. The cartoon pictures the funeral of the Stamp Act, sparsely attended by some pamphleteers, lawyers, ministers, royal favorites and bishops. Behind them the merchants are busied with the reviving trade, to be borne before favoring winds on the ships of state, Rockingham, Conway and Grafton. Useless is the bale of stamps from America; a reminder of the trade embargo is found in the "black cloth from America" returned unused because non-consumption agreements had led the colonists to forego black garb even at funerals. The Government, opposed by the merchants, by those who sympathized with the colonies, and by the colonies themselves, had been forced to retreat from a position which its ignorance of American conditions had led it to adopt so light-heartedly.

113 From a British caricature *The Repeal* (a satirical presentation of the funeral procession of the Stamp Act), in the Emmet Collection, New York Public Library

AMERICA IS OVERJOYED AT THE NEWS OF REPEAL

In America bells were rung, bonfires lit, toasts drunk to the King, liberty poles erected. Virginia and New York ordered statues of George III. New York and South Carolina in similar fashion honored Pitt. In Boston a day of celebration was set apart. All persons in prison for rent were released by public subscription. The Common was bedecked with illuminated figures of the King, Pitt, Barré and Lord Camden.

IONATHAN MAYHEW, D.D. PASTOR OF THE WEST CHVRCH IN BOSTON, IN NEW ENGLAND, AN ASSERTOR OF THE CIVIL AND RELIGIOVS LIBERTIES OF HIS COVNTRY AND MANKIND, WHO, OVERPLIED BY PVBLIC ENERGIES, DIED OF A NERVOVS FEVER, IVLY VIII, MDCCLXVI, AGED XXXXV

114 Jonathan Mayhew, 1720–66, from Thomas Hollis, *Memoirs*, London, 1770, after an engraving by J. B. Cipriani, 1767, of the portrait by John Smibert

Glorious News.

BOSTON, Friday 11 o'Clock, 16th *May* 1766.

THIS Inſtant arrived here the Brig Harriſon, belonging to *John Hancock*, Eſq; Captain *Shubael Coffin*, in 6 Weeks and 2 Days from LONDON, with important News, as follows.

From the LONDON GAZETTE.

Weſtminſter, *March* 18th, 1766.

THIS day his Majeſty came to the Houſe of Peers, and being in his royal robes ſeated on the throne with the uſual ſolemnity, Sir Francis Molineux, Gentleman Uſher of the Black Rod, was ſent with a Meſſage from his Majeſty to the Houſe of Commons, commanding their attendance in the Houſe of Peers. The Commons being come thither accordingly, his Majeſty was pleaſed to give his royal aſſent to

An ACT to REPEAL an Act made in the laſt Seſſion of Parliament, intituled, an Act for granting and applying certain Stamp-Duties and other Duties in the Britiſh Colonies and Plantations in America, towards further defraying the expences of defending, protecting and ſecuring the ſame, and for amending ſuch parts of the ſeveral Acts of Parliament relating to the trade and revenues of the ſaid Colonies and Plantations, as direct the manner of determining and recovering the penalties and forfeitures therein mentioned.

Alſo ten public bills, and ſeventeen private ones.

Yeſterday there was a meeting of the principal Merchants concerned in the American trade, at the King's Arms tavern in Cornhill, to conſider of an Addreſs to his Majeſty on the beneficial Repeal of the late Stamp-Act.

Yeſterday morning about eleven o'clock a great number of North American Merchants went in their coaches from the King's Arms tavern in Cornhill to the Houſe of Peers, to pay their duty to his Majeſty, and to expreſs their ſatisfaction at his ſigning the Bill for Repealing the American Stamp-Act, there was upwards of fifty coaches in the proceſſion.

Laſt night the ſaid gentleman diſpatched an expreſs for Falmouth, with fifteen copies of the Act for repealing the Stamp-Act, to be forwarded immediately for New York.

Orders are given for ſeveral merchantmen in the river to proceed to ſea immediately on their reſpective voyages to North America, ſome of whom have been cleared out ſince the firſt of November laſt.

Yeſterday meſſengers were diſpatched to Birmingham, Sheffield, Mancheſter, and all the great manufacturing towns in England, with an account of the final deciſion of an auguſt aſſembly relating to the Stamp-Act.

When the KING went to the Houſe of Peers to give the Royal Aſſent, there was ſuch a vaſt Concourſe of People, huzzaing, clapping Hands, &c. that it was ſeveral Hours before His Majeſty reached the Houſe.

Immediately on His Majeſty's Signing the Royal Aſſent to the Repeal of the Stamp-Act the Merchants trading to America, diſpatched a Veſſel which had been in waiting, to put into the firſt Port on the Continent with the Account.

There were the greateſt Rejoicings poſſible in the City of London, by all Ranks of People, on the TOTAL Repeal of the Stamp-Act,—the Ships in the River diſplayed all their Colours, Illuminations and Bonfires in many Parts. — In ſhort, the Rejoicings were as great as was ever known on any Occaſion.

It is ſaid the Acts of Trade relating to America would be taken under Conſideration, and all Grievances removed. The Friends to America are very powerful, and diſpoſed to aſſiſt us to the utmoſt of their Ability.

Capt. Blake ſailed the ſame Day with Capt. Coffin, and Capt. Shand a Fortnight before him, both bound to this Port.

It is impoſſible to expreſs the Joy the Town is now in, on receiving the above, great, glorious and important NEWS—The Bells in all the Churches were immediately ſet a Ringing, and we hear the Day for a general Rejoicing will be the beginning of next Week.

PRINTED for the Benefit of the PUBLIC, by *Drapers*, *Edes* & *Gill*, *Green* & *Ruſſell*, and *Fleets*.

The Cuſtomers to the Boſton Papers may have the above gratis at the reſpective Offices.

115 From a broadside dated May 16, 1766, in the Emmet Collection, New York Public Library

A MILITANT MINISTER URGES COLONIAL UNION

Dr. Mayhew was born on Martha's Vineyard, where for three generations his family had "tilled the soil and preached the gospel." He was graduated from Harvard, and became pastor of a prominent Boston church, the first to call itself Unitarian. Like most New England preachers of the day, he introduced political questions into his sermons. On the Sunday preceding the sacking of Governor Hutchinson's house in 1765, he took as his text: "I would they were even cut off which trouble you. For, brethren, ye have been called unto liberty; only use not liberty for an occasion to the flesh, but by love serve one another." That was the text of his life. His eloquence proved a sturdy buttress for the educational campaign of Otis. One of his last acts was the preaching of a Thanksgiving sermon on the repeal of the Stamp Act in which he pleaded fervently in behalf of civil and religious liberty. Shortly thereafter he wrote to Otis urging the union of the colonies as the only means of perpetuating American liberty.

Anno ſexto

Georgii III. Regis.

CAP XII.

An Act for the better ſecuring the Dependency of His Majeſty's Dominions in *America* upon the Crown and Parliament of *Great Britain*.

HEREAS ſeveral of the Houſes of Repreſentatives in His Majeſty's Colonies and Plantations in America, have of late, againſt Law, claimed to themſelves, or to the General Aſſemblies of the ſame, the ſole and excluſive Right of impoſing Duties and Taxes upon His Majeſty's Subjects in the ſaid Colonies and Plantations; and have, in purſuance of ſuch Claim, paſſed certain Votes, Reſolutions, and Orders, derogatory to the Legiſlative Authority of Parliament, and inconſiſtent with the Dependency of the ſaid Colonies and Plantations upon the Crown of Great Britain: May it therefore pleaſe Your moſt Excellent Majeſty, that it may be declared; and be it declared by the King's moſt Excellent Majeſty, by and with the Advice and Conſent of the Lords Spiritual and Temporal, and Commons, in this preſent Parliament aſſembled, and Preamble.

Qqq 2 by

248 Anno Regni ſexto Georgii III. Regis.

by the Authority of the ſame, That the ſaid Colonies and Plantations in America have been, are, and of Right ought to be, ſubordinate unto, and dependent upon, the Imperial Crown and Parliament of Great Britain, and that the King's Majeſty, by and with the Advice and Conſent of the Lords Spiritual and Temporal, and Commons of Great Britain, in Parliament aſſembled, had, hath, and of Right ought to have, full Power and Authority to make Laws and Statutes of ſufficient Force and Validity to bind the Colonies and People of America, Subjects of the Crown of Great Britain, in all Caſes whatſoever.

The Colonies and Plantations in *America* declared to be ſubordinate unto, and dependent upon the Imperial Crown and Parliament of *Great Britain*; and the Legiſlative Authority of *Great Britain* declared to extend to, and bind the Colonies and People of *America*, as Subjects, in all Caſes whatſoever.

And be it further declared and enacted by the Authority aforeſaid, That all Reſolutions, Votes, Orders, and Proceedings, in any of the ſaid Colonies or Plantations, whereby the Power and Authority of the Parliament of Great Britain, to make Laws and Statutes as aforeſaid, is denied, or drawn into Queſtion, are, and are hereby declared to be, utterly null and void to all Intents and Purpoſes whatſoever.

All Reſolutions and Proceedings of the ſaid Colonies denying, or calling in Queſtion the ſaid Power, declared null and void.

FINIS.

116 The Declaratory Act (affirming the supremacy of Parliament), 1766, from the first printed edition in the New York Public Library

LORD MANSFIELD PROPHESIES FURTHER TROUBLE WITH AMERICA

IN the excitement, few noticed the Declaratory Act, passed with the repeal. In the debates over this, Lord Mansfield, than whom no one had a more attentive audience in Parliament, spoke prophetically. "The colonies must remain dependent upon the jurisdiction of the mother country, or they must be totally dismembered from it, and form a league of union among themselves against it, which could not be effected without great violences. . . . I am extremely sorry that the question has ever become necessary to be agitated, and that there should be a decision upon it. No one in this house will live long enough to see an end put to the mischief which will be the result of the doctrine that has been inculcated; but the arrow is shot, and the wound already given." Yet Mansfield insisted that Parliament was supreme, and that its legislative power extended in all cases over the American colonies. His views received the endorsement of the legislature and the approval of the King.

PITT'S ILL HEALTH LEAVES POWER TO TOWNSHEND

FOUR months after the repeal of the Stamp Act, the Rockingham ministry fell from power. This time Pitt was prevailed upon to form a Government, although it was a composite of varying points of view. Pitt's age and ill health soon forced his retirement into the country. This left a cabinet with no forceful leader. At this mischance, Charles Townshend, Chancellor of the Exchequer, found his opportunity to push a scheme long cherished by him. As president of the Board of Trade under Bute, in 1763, Townshend had formulated a sweeping plan for the reorganization of colonial administration on lines of uniformity and of strict imperial control. Later, while a member of the Rockingham ministry, he had continued openly to favor minute imperial supervision of America, including taxation by Parliament. Now, with the Great Commoner out of the way, Townshend could execute his long-deferred design. Needless to say, his impetuosity took no account of colonial opinion.

117 Charles Townshend, 1725–67, from an engraving after a portrait by Sir Joshua Reynolds, in the Emmet Collection, New York Public Library

THE BILLETING ACT IS ENFORCED IN NEW YORK

THIS colonial opinion, despite the repeal, was still suspicious of English intentions. New York was the center of the British regular troops in America. An Act of 1765 had required the colony to furnish the troops with quarters. To this the Assembly objected. Here Townshend found an opportunity to show America that the Declaratory Act was not to be a dead letter. In May, 1767, he persuaded Parliament to enact a measure suspending the New York Assembly until it should comply with the billeting law. The colonies at once murmured; for if Parliament had the power to suspend for a limited time a colonial legislature, self-government might easily be destroyed. The blow was heavy. New York in 1769 succumbed, though with bad grace.

Anno ſeptimo

Georgii III. Regis.

C A P. LIX.

An Act for reſtraining and prohibiting the Governor, Council, and Houſe of Repreſentatives, of the Province of *New York*, until Proviſion ſhall have been made for furniſhing the King's Troops with all the Neceſſaries required by Law, from paſſing or aſſenting to any Act of Aſſembly, Vote, or Reſolution, for any other Purpoſe.

WHEREAS an Act of Parliament was made in the Fifth Year of His preſent Majeſty's Reign, intituled, An Act to amend and render more effectual, in His Majeſty's Dominions in *America*, an Act paſſed in this preſent Seſſion of Parliament, intituled, *An Act for puniſhing Mutiny and Deſertion, and for the better Payment of the Army and their Quarters*; wherein ſeveral Directions were given, (Preamble, reciting Acts 5 Geo. III,)

10 Q

b

118 Townshend Act suspending the New York Assembly, 1767, from the first printed edition of British laws, in the New York Public Library

666 Anno Regni ſeptimo Georgii III. Regis.

(at the Rate of 5s. 6d. per Oz. in Silver; and to be paid and levied as any other Duties payable to His Majeſty;) ing to the Proportion and Value of Five Shillings and Six Pence the Ounce in Silver; and ſhall be raiſed, levied, collected, paid, and recovered, in the ſame Manner and Form, and by ſuch Rules, Ways, and Means, and under ſuch Penalties and Forfeitures, as any other Duties, now payable to His Majeſty upon Goods imported into the ſaid Colonies or Plantations, may be raiſed, levied, collected, paid, and recovered, by any Act or Acts of Parliament now in Force, as fully and effectually, to all Intents and Purpoſes, as if the ſeveral Clauſes, Powers, Directions, Penalties, and Forfeitures, relating thereto, were particularly repeated, and again enacted, in the Body of this preſent Act: And (and to be applied, in the firſt Place, in making Proviſions for the Adminiſtration of Juſtice, and Support of the Civil Government;) that all the Monies that ſhall ariſe by the ſaid Duties (except the neceſſary Charges of raiſing, collecting, levying, recovering, anſwering, paying, and accounting for the ſame) ſhall be applied, in the firſt Place, in ſuch Manner as is herein after mentioned, in making a more certain and adequate Proviſion for the Charge of the Adminiſtration of Juſtice, and the Support of Civil Government, in ſuch of the ſaid Colonies and Plantations where it ſhall be found neceſſary; and that the Reſidue (and the Reſidue to be paid into the Exchequer, and reſerved for the Diſpoſition of Parliament.) of ſuch Duties ſhall be paid into the Receipt of His Majeſty's Exchequer, and ſhall be entered ſeparate and apart from all other Monies paid or payable to His Majeſty, His Heirs, or Succeſſors; and ſhall be there reſerved, to be from time to time diſpoſed of by Parliament towards defraying the neceſſary Expences of defending, protecting, and ſecuring, the Britiſh Colonies and Plantations in America.

(His Majeſty impowered to cauſe ſuch Monies to be applied out of the Produce of the ſaid Duties as He ſhall judge neceſſary for defraying the Charges of the Adminiſtration of Juſtice and Civil Government there.) And be it further enacted by the Authority aforeſaid, That His Majeſty and His Succeſſors ſhall be, and are hereby, impowered, from time to time, by any Warrant or Warrants under His or Their Royal Sign Manual or Sign Manuals, counterſigned by the High Treaſurer, or any Three or more of the Commiſſioners of the Treaſury for the time being, to cauſe ſuch Monies to be applied, out of the Produce of the Duties granted by this Act, as His Majeſty, or His Succeſſors, ſhall think proper or neceſſary, for defraying the Charges of the Adminiſtration of Juſtice, and the Support of the Civil Government, within all or any of the ſaid Colonies or Plantations.

And whereas the allowing a Drawback of all the Duties of Cuſtoms upon the Exportation, from this Kingdom, of Coffee and Cocoa Nuts, the Growth of the Britiſh Dominions in America, may be a Means of encouraging the Growth of Coffee and Cocoa in the ſaid Domi-

119 Townshend Duty Act, 1767 (relating to the uses of the revenue), from the first printed edition, in the New York Public Library

NEW REVENUE ACTS ASSERT BRITISH CONTROL

OTHER Acts Townshend, without consulting his colleagues, obtained from an indifferent Parliament. To enforce the Navigation laws, the customs service was tightened; writs of assistance were declared legal; above all, duties were laid on colonial imports of tea, glass, lead, paper and similar articles. This was "external" taxation, which the colonists had admitted to be within parliamentary competence. Such an appearance of compliance with American theory, Townshend took pains to dispel. The Duty Act asserted that the duties were laid, not to regulate commerce, but to raise revenue and, furthermore, this revenue was to be used where necessary "to support royal governors and courts within the provinces, and to pay the necessary Expenses of defending, protecting and securing the British Colonies and Plantations in America." The Townshend Acts, in short, established a precedent for more vigorous control of the colonies in America.

JOHN DICKINSON COUNSELS PRUDENCE

EXPRESSIONS of colonial opinion soon appeared. The ablest protest came from John Dickinson of Pennsylvania, in the form of a series of *Letters from a Farmer*. Dickinson, like Dulany, was an American trained in the law at the Inns of Court, London. Shrewdly weaving the now familiar arguments into the current situation, he denied the validity of any distinction between internal and external taxes, when levied for purposes of revenue. His counsel was one of prudence. "Let us behave like dutiful children, who have received unmerited blows from a beloved parent."

120 John Dickinson, 1732–1808, from the portrait by Charles Willson Peale (1741–1827) in Independence Hall, Philadelphia

121 Samuel Adams, 1722–1803, from the portrait by John Singleton Copley in the Museum of Fine Arts, Boston

SAMUEL ADAMS Esq.
One of the DELEGATES from the Province of MASSACHUSETTS-BAY
to the General Continental CONGRESS of NORTH AMERICA.

122 From the engraving in *An Impartial History of the War in America*, London, 1780

SAM ADAMS, THE RADICAL

OTHER less cautious leaders appeared, and among them Samuel Adams, the born politician. "Perhaps no long public career was ever more perfectly self-consistent than his. From boyhood to old age, his master principle was individualism. As an undergraduate in college, having occasion to choose a subject for a public discussion, he revealed the bent of his mind by taking that of 'Liberty.' In 1743, for his Master's degree at Harvard, he wrote a Latin thesis on the affirmative side of the question, 'Whether it be lawful to resist the Supreme Magistrate, if the Commonwealth cannot be otherwise preserved.' . . . From the day of his graduation till his work as a political writer was done, he did but play variations on this robust doctrine and its corollaries." — TYLER, *Literary History of the American Revolution*, II, p. 13. Adams, a failure in the ordinary pursuits of life which would provide a competence for his family, had a genius for organizing and directing a radical movement. He also had the ability to put into clear and cogent English the ideas of his times regarding liberty and government. In season and out of season, he kept before the eyes of his fellow provincials what he conceived to be the tyranny of the British Government.

No. 676.

THE
Boston-Gazette,
AND
COUNTRY JOURNAL.

Containing the freshest Advices, Foreign and Domestic.

MONDAY, MARCH 14, 1768.

SIR,

THE House of Representatives of this Province, have taken into their serious consideration, the great difficulties that must accrue to themselves and their constituents, by the operation of the several acts of parliament imposing duties and taxes on the American colonies.

As it is a subject in which every colony is deeply interested, they have no reason to doubt but your assembly is duly impress'd with its importance; and that such constitutional measures will be come into as are proper. It seems to be necessary, that all possible care should be taken that the representations of the several assemblies, upon so delicate a point, should harmonize with each other: The House therefore hope that this letter will be candidly considered in no other light than as expressing a disposition freely to communicate their mind to a Sister Colony, upon a common concern, in the same manner as they would be glad to receive the sentiments of your or any other House of assembly on the continent.

This House have humbly represented to the Ministry, their own sentiments: That his Majesty's high court of Parliament is the supreme legislative power over the whole empire: That in all free states the constitution is fixed; and as the supreme legislative derives its power and authority from the constitution, it cannot over-leap the bounds of it, without destroying its own foundation: That the constitution ascertains and limits both sovereignty and allegiance; and therefore his Majesty's American subjects who acknowledge themselves bound by the ties of allegiance, have an equitable claim to the full enjoyment of the fundamental rules of the British constitution: That it is an essential unalterable right in nature, ingrafted into the British constitution, as a fundamental law, and ever held sacred and irrevocable by the subjects within the realm, that what a man hath honestly acquired, is absolutely his own, which he may freely give, but cannot be taken from him without his consent: That the American subjects may therefore, exclusive of any consideration of charter rights, with a decent firmness adapted to the character of free men and subjects, assert this natural constitutional right.

It is moreover their humble opinion, which they express with the greatest deference to the wisdom of the parliament; That the acts made there, imposing duties on the people of this province, with the sole and express purpose of raising a revenue, are infringements of their natural and constitutional rights; because, as they are not represented in the British parliament, his Majesty's commons in Britain, by those acts, grant their property without their consent.

This House further are of opinion, that their constituents, considering their local circumstances, cannot by any possibility, be represented in the Parliament; and that it will for ever be impracticable that they should equally be represented there, and consequently not at all; being seperated by an ocean of a thousand leagues: That his Majesty's royal predecessors, for this reason, were graciously pleased to form a subordinate legislative here, that their subjects might enjoy the unalienable right of a representation. And that considering the utter impracticability of their being fully and equally represented in parliament, and the great expence that must unavoidably attend even a partial representation there, this House think that a taxation of their constituents, even without their consent, grievous as it is, would be preferable to any representation that could be admitted for them there.

Upon these principles, and also considering that were the right in the Parliament ever so clear, yet for obvious reasons, it would be beyond the rules of equity, that their constituents should be taxed on the manufactures of Great Britain here, in addition to the duties they pay for them in England, and other advantages arising to Great Britain from the acts of trade; this House have preferred a humble, dutiful and loyal petition to our most gracious Sovereign, and made such representations to his Majesty's Ministers, as they apprehended would tend to obtain redress.

They have also submitted it to consideration, whether any people can be said to enjoy any degree of freedom, if the crown, in addition to its undoubted authority of constituting a governor, should also appoint him such a Stipend as it shall judge proper, without the consent of the people, and at their expence: And whether, while the judges of the land, and other civil officers, hold not their commissions during good behaviour, their having salaries appointed for them by the crown, independent of the people, hath not a tendency to subvert the principles of equity and endanger the happiness and security of the subject.

In addition to these measures, the house have wrote a letter to their agent Mr. DeBerdt, the sentiments of which he is directed to lay before the Ministry; wherein they take notice of the hardship of the act for preventing mutiny and desertion, which requires the governor and council to provide enumerated articles for the King's marching troops, and the people to pay the expence: And also of the commission of the gentlemen appointed commissioners of the customs to reside in America, which authorises them to make as many appointments as they think fit, and to pay the appointees what sums they please, for whose mal-conduct they are not accountable—From whence it may happen that officers of the crown may be multiplied to such a degree as to become dangerous to the liberty of the people, by virtue of a commission which doth not appear to this House to derive any such advantages to trade, as many have been led to expect.

These are the sentiments and proceedings of this house; and as they have too much reason to believe that the enemies of the colonies have represented them to his Majesty's ministers and the parliament, as factious, disloyal, and having a disposition to make themselves independent of the mother country, they have taken occasion, in the most humble terms, to assure his Majesty and his ministers, that with regard to the people of this province, and as they doubt not of all the colonies, the charge is unjust.

The house is fully satisfied that your assembly is too generous and enlarg'd in sentiment, to believe, that this letter proceeds from an ambition of taking the lead, or dictating to the other assemblies.

123 Circular Letter of Feb. 11, 1768, written by Samuel Adams to the Massachusetts Legislature, from the *Boston Gazette*, Mar. 14, 1768, copy in the New York Public Library

SAMUEL ADAMS' CIRCULAR LETTER

ADAMS was now clerk of the Massachusetts Assembly. From this point of vantage he issued a series of addresses, endorsed as the official voice of the body. Most famous was the *Circular Letter* of February 11, 1768, sent "to the respective Assemblies on the Continent." Here we have Adams at his best. Massachusetts hopes "that this letter will be candidly considered in no other light than as expressing a disposition freely to communicate their mind to a Sister Colony, upon a common concern, in the same manner as they would be glad to receive the sentiments of your or any other House of assembly on the continent." Thus he dispelled any lingering jealousy of the leading place Boston was assuming, while he deftly pointed to the desirability of unified action in the emergency. The *Letter* was a brilliant exposition of colonial grievances against the Townshend Acts. When it came to the attention of Lord Hillsborough, colonial secretary, he at once took action against the letter as a seditious libel. Writing to the Rhode Island Assembly, under date of April 21, 1768, he warned it against the Massachusetts epistle. "As his Majesty considers this Measure to be of a most dangerous and factious Tendency, calculated to enflame the Minds of his good Subjects in the Colonies; to promote an unwarrantable Combination, and to excite and encourage an open Opposition to and Denial of the Authority of Parliament, and to subvert the true Principles of the Constitution, It is his Majesty's Pleasure that you should . . . exert your utmost Influence to defeat this flagitious Attempt to disturb the publick Peace, by prevailing upon the Assembly of your Province to take no Notice of it, which will be treating it with the Contempt it deserves." The King had been particularly enraged by this circular letter. And Hillsborough was clever. To the cause he brought the vast influence of the King's name and prestige. Thus George III became a participant in the conflict. It need scarcely be said that such evidence of ministerial alarm merely encouraged the colonies to hope that the Government would yield.

124 George III in Military Uniform, from the portrait study by Benjamin West (1738–1820) in the Historical Society of Pennsylvania, Philadelphia

125 George III, from an engraving by E. Scriven, after the portrait, 1779, by Sir Joshua Reynolds (1723–92)

126 George III in His Coronation Robe, from the portrait by Allan Ramsay (1713–84) in the National Portrait Gallery, London

KING GEORGE III, 1738–1820

In 1760 there had ascended the throne of England, as George III, a youth of twenty-two years. Everywhere he had been hailed with applause. For forty-five years England's King had been a foreigner, scarce able to speak the language of his people. George III was born in England; in his first speech he expressed pride "in the name of Britain." In the colonies also the new reign had been welcome. Quebec had just fallen; America need no longer fear the French. Enthusiasm and loyalty abounded. The Massachusetts Assembly, in August, 1760, speaking of the "inexpressible joy of the present times," had extolled the British Constitution: "Now this glorious constitution exceeds itself; it raises new ideas for which no language has provided words, because never known before. Contradictions are become almost consistent, clamorous faction is silent, morose envy good-natured, by the divine blessing on the councils and arms of our dread sovereign in every quarter of the world. He is become the scourge of tyrants, the hope of the oppressed; yet in the midst of victory prophesying peace."

THE NEW KING

Secure on his throne, possessed of boundless energy and industry, the new King at once began to assert himself. An English historian has written that "he had a smaller mind than any English King before him save James II." This mind had been molded, as had that of James I before him, by the philosophy of his tutor. And in each case this had been a philosophy flattering royal power. Lord Bute, George's Scottish preceptor, was a disciple of Lord Bolingbroke and a believer in his doctrine of the patriot King, the doctrine that the King should rule as well as reign — no lay figure in the hands of party leaders, but a leader of the nation. This doctrine was firmly implanted in George; pertinacity, tending at times to vindictiveness, enabled him to a considerable degree to put it into practice. The constitution praised by the colonists in 1760 was shortly to change character.

127 A View of Westminster Abbey from the High Altar, showing His Majesty's Coronation, Sept. 22, 1761, from the *Universal Magazine*, Oct. 1761, in the New York Public Library

128 The British House of Lords, from an aquatint after the drawing by Pugin & Rowlandson in Rudolph Ackermann, *The Microcosm of London*, 1808

PARLIAMENT OR KING?

Pursuing the ideal of Bolingbroke, Bute and George ran counter to the developments of the preceding half century. Under the first two Hanoverian kings, actual government had rested in the King's advisers. The Tories, exiled through adherence to the Stuart cause, had given way to the Whigs. The chief of these were members of old and noble families, traditionally politicians. Their interests, historic and economic, favored the principles of the Glorious Revolution of 1688. In the forefront of these principles was the doctrine of parliamentary sovereignty as opposed to royal will.

BUTE, THE KING'S FAVORITE MINISTER

The first move was to break up Whig control. Pitt and Newcastle, the latter the leader of the Whigs, were especially obnoxious to the Crown. So Bute had become the King's favorite minister; and within two years the ministry was wholly subservient to royal wishes. Bute, haughty and a Scot, was unpopular. His personal influence with the Queen Mother and the King added to the public dislike. He was therefore glad of a chance in 1763 to retire from the limelight. But he had served as an entering wedge in the struggle between the King and the political cliques, and he continued to be an influential person, as may be seen in the cartoons with which the opposition, a few years later, attacked the American policies of the Crown (Nos. 108, 113, 170, 177).

129 John Stuart, Third Earl of Bute, 1713–92, from the portrait by Allan Ramsay in the National Portrait Gallery of Scotland, Edinburgh

130 The British House of Commons in 1741–42, from an engraving by W. J. White after a drawing by Gravelot

GEORGE III USES PATRONAGE TO CONTROL PARLIAMENT

THE second step in the royal progress had been to secure control of Parliament. This was not difficult. No such thing as an organized party existed throughout the period of the Revolutionary War. The Whigs were split into bitter factions; the Tory element was little better. Amid such confusion George III, the able politician, played faction against faction to gain his ends. Moreover, he fell in with the prevailing practice of using patronage and public funds to obtain necessary votes in the Commons. His "gold pills" won him meek followers; the "King's Friends" often held in the legislature a balance of power invariably utilized to further royal influence. The fall of New France, 1759, had revived the old colonial policy of the Lords of Trade. Canada, Florida and the valley of the Mississippi had been added to the established English colonies. The new problems which had arisen as a consequence had led to the first of the new King's acts to arouse widespread opposition in America.

THE KING APPORTIONS AMERICAN LANDS

THE existing scheme of colonial administration was seen to be clumsy and inadequate. A tentative and temporizing step was taken by a royal proclamation of 1763. This organized from the new lands three royal provinces, Quebec, West Florida and East Florida. The territory west of the Alleghanies became an Indian reservation, whence settlers were to withdraw. In short, the policy so long favored by the Board of Trade was adopted. It included alterations in colonial boundaries, revision of colonial charters and constitutions, restrictions of representative government, revival of economic regulation, enhancement of royal and mercantile control — all emanating from England and to be administered under English guidance.

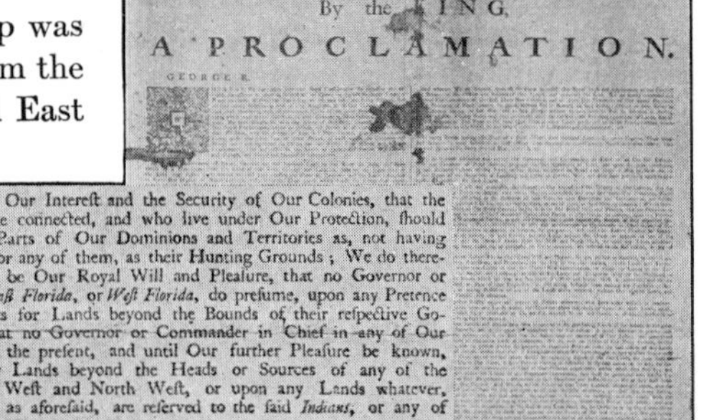

By the KING.

A PROCLAMATION.

GEORGE R.

And whereas it is juſt and reaſonable, and eſſential to Our Intereſt and the Security of Our Colonies, that the ſeveral Nations or Tribes of *Indians*, with whom We are connected, and who live under Our Protection, ſhould not be moleſted or diſturbed in the Poſſeſſion of ſuch Parts of Our Dominions and Territories as, not having been ceded to, or purchaſed by Us, are reſerved to them, or any of them, as their Hunting Grounds; We do therefore, with the Advice of Our Privy Council, declare it to be Our Royal Will and Pleaſure, that no Governor or Commander in Chief in any of Our Colonies of *Quebec*, *Eaſt Florida*, or *Weſt Florida*, do preſume, upon any Pretence whatever, to grant Warrants of Survey, or paſs any Patents for Lands beyond the Bounds of their reſpective Governments, as deſcribed in their Commiſſions; as alſo, that no Governor or Commander in Chief in any of Our other Colonies or Plantations in *America*, do preſume, for the preſent, and until Our further Pleaſure be known, to grant Warrants of Survey, or paſs Patents for any Lands beyond the Heads or Sources of any of the Rivers which fall into the *Atlantick* Ocean from the Weſt and North Weſt, or upon any Lands whatever, which, not having been ceded to, or purchaſed by Us as aforeſaid, are reſerved to the ſaid *Indians*, or any of them.

And We do further declare it to be Our Royal Will and Pleaſure, for the preſent as aforeſaid, to reſerve under Our Sovereignty, Protection, and Dominion, for the Uſe of the ſaid *Indians*, all the Lands and Territories not included within the Limits of Our ſaid Three New Governments, or within the Limits of the Territory granted to the *Hudſon's Bay* Company, as alſo all the Lands and Territories lying to the Weſtward of the Sources of the Rivers which fall into the Sea from the Weſt and North Weſt, as aforeſaid; and We do hereby ſtrictly forbid, on Pain of Our Diſpleaſure, all Our loving Subjects from making any Purchaſes or Settlements whatever, or taking Poſſeſſion of any of the Lands above reſerved, without Our eſpecial Leave and Licence for that Purpoſe firſt obtained.

And We do further ſtrictly enjoin and require all Perſons whatever, who have either wilfully or inadvertently ſeated themſelves upon any Lands within the Countries above deſcribed, or upon any other Lands, which, not having been ceded to, or purchaſed by Us, are ſtill reſerved to the ſaid *Indians* as aforeſaid, forthwith to remove themſelves from ſuch Settlements.

And whereas great Frauds and Abuſes have been committed in the purchaſing Lands of the *Indians*, to the great Prejudice of Our Intereſts, and to the great Diſſatisfaction of the ſaid *Indians*; in order therefore to prevent ſuch Irregularities for the future, and to the End that the *Indians* may be convinced of Our Juſtice, and determined Reſolution to remove all reaſonable Cauſe of Diſcontent, We do, with the Advice of Our Privy Council, ſtrictly enjoin and require, that no private Perſon do preſume to make any Purchaſe from the ſaid *Indians* of any Lands reſerved to the ſaid *Indians*, within thoſe Parts of Our Colonies where We have thought proper to allow Settlement; but that if, at any Time, any of the ſaid *Indians* ſhould be inclined to diſpoſe of the ſaid Lands, the ſame ſhall be purchaſed only for Us, in Our Name, at ſome Publick Meeting or Aſſembly of the ſaid *Indians* to be held for that Purpoſe by the Governor or Commander in Chief of Our Colonies reſpectively, within which they ſhall lie; and in caſe they ſhall lie within the Limits of any Proprietary Government, they ſhall be purchaſed only for the Uſe and in the Name of ſuch Proprietaries, conformable to ſuch Directions and Inſtructions as We or they ſhall think proper to give for that Purpoſe: And We do, by the Advice of Our Privy Council, declare and enjoin, that the Trade with the ſaid *Indians* ſhall be free and open to all Our Subjects whatever; provided that every Perſon, who may incline to trade with the ſaid *Indians*, do take out a Licence for carrying on ſuch Trade from the

131 Royal Proclamation of a New Colonial Policy, from the printed copy dated London, 1763, in the Library of Congress

Extract from George III's Proclamation restricting western lands to the Indians, prohibiting surveys, warning settlers to depart, and forbidding land purchase from Indians, except in the King's name.

THE MASSACHUSETTS' GOVERNOR

WHEN opposition to the Townshend Acts appeared, the prestige and power of the King were brought to the aid of the British Government in its contest with America. Sir Francis Bernard was Governor of Massachusetts. In 1764 he wrote, "To settle American governments to the greatest possible advantage, it will be necessary to reduce the number of them. . . . If there should be but one form of government established for the North American provinces, it would greatly facilitate the reformation of them. . . . A nobility, appointed by the King for life and made independent, would probably give strength and stability to the American governments as effectually as hereditary nobility does to that of Great Britain." He had already needlessly quarreled with the legislature. (Nos. 80, 81.) He had, for instance, insisted that no one should be appointed colonial agent in England without his approval; he had supported Lieutenant Governor Hutchinson in his pretensions to a seat in the Council; he had openly declared his intentions to control that body. Now further trouble was brewing for him.

At a Meeting of the Freeholders and other Inhabitants of the Town of *Boston*, legally assembled at *Faneuil*-Hall, on Wednesday the 28th of *October*, 1767.

THE Town then took into Consideration the Petition of a Number of Inhabitants, "That some effectual Measures might be "agreed upon to promote Industry, Oeconomy, and Manufactures; thereby "to prevent the unnecessary Importation of European Commodities, which threaten the Country "with Poverty and Ruin:" Whereupon in a very large and full Meeting, the following Votes and Resolutions were passed Unanimously.

Whereas the excessive Use of foreign Superfluities is the chief Cause of the present distressed State of this Town, as it is thereby drained of its Money; which Misfortune is likely to be increased by Means of the late additional Burthens and Impositions on the Trade of the Province, which threaten the Country with Poverty and Ruin:

Therefore, *VOTED*, That this Town will take all prudent and legal Measures to encourage the Produce and Manufactures of this Province, and to lessen the Use of Superfluities, & particularly the following enumerated Articles imported from Abroad, viz. *Loaf Sugar, Cordage, Anchors, Coaches, Chaises and Carriages of all Sorts, Horse Furniture, Men and Womens Hatts, Mens and Womens Apparel ready made, Houshold Furniture, Gloves, Mens and Womens Shoes, Sole-Leather, Sheathing and Deck Nails, Gold and Silver and Thread Lace of all Sorts, Gold and Silver Buttons, Wrought Plate of all Sorts, Diamond, Stone and Paste Ware, Snuff, Mustard, Clocks and Watches, Silversmiths and Jewellers Ware, Broad Cloths that cost above 10s. per Yard, Muffs Furrs and Tippets, and all Sorts of Millenary Ware, Starch, Womens and Childrens Stays, Fire Engines, China Ware, Silk and Cotton Velvets, Gauze, Pewterers hollow Ware, Linseed Oyl, Glue, Lawns, Cambricks, Silks of all Kinds for Garments, Malt Liquors and Cheese* —— And that a Subscription for this End be and hereby is recommended to the several Inhabitants and Housholders of the Town; and that *John Rowe*, Esq; Mr *William Greenleafe*, *Melatiah Bourne*, Esq; Mr. *Samuel Austin*, Mr. *Edward Payne*, Mr. *Edmund Quincy*, Tertius, *John Ruddock*, Esq; *Jonathan Williams*, Esq; *Joshua Henshaw*, Esq; Mr. *Henderson Inches*, Mr. *Solomon Davis*, *Joshua Winslow*, Esq; and *Thomas Cushing*, Esq. be a Committee to prepare a Form for Subscription, to report the same as soon as possible; and also to procure Subscriptions to the same.

And whereas it is the Opinion of this Town, that divers new Manufactures may be set up in America, to its great Advantage, and some others carried to a greater Extent, particularly those of Glass & Paper

Therefore, *Voted*, That this Town will by all prudent Ways and Means, encourage the Use and Consumption of Glass and Paper, made in any of the British American Colonies; and more especially in this Province.

[*Then the Meeting adjourn'd till 3 o'Clock Afternoon.*]

III o'Clock, *P. M.*

THE Committee appointed in the Forenoon, to prepare a Form for Subscription, reported as follows.

WHEREAS this Province labours under a heavy Debt, incurred in the Course of the late War; and the Inhabitants by this Means must be for some Time subject to very burthensome Taxes —— *And as our Trade has for some Years been on the decline, and is now particularly under great Embarrasments, and burthened with heavy Impositions, our Medium very scarce, and the Balance of Trade greatly against this Country.*

WE therefore the Subscribers, being sensible that it is absolutely necessary, in Order to extricate us out of these embarrassed and distressed Circumstances, to promote Industry, Oeconomy and Manufactures among ourselves, and by this Means prevent the unnecessary Importation of European Commodities, the excessive Use of which threatens the Country with Poverty and Ruin — DO promise and engage, to and with each other, that we will encourage the Use and Consumption of all Articles manufactured in any of the British American Colonies, and more especially in this Province; and that we will not, from and after the 31st of *December* next ensuing, purchase any of the following Articles, imported from Abroad, viz. *Loaf Sugar*, and all the other Articles enumerated above.—

And we further agree strictly to adhere to the late Regulation respecting Funerals, and will not use any Gloves but what are Manufactured here, nor procure any new Garments upon such an Occasion, but what shall be absolutely necessary.

The above Report having been considered, the Question was put, Whether the same shall be accepted? *Voted unanimously in the Affirmative.* —And that said Committee be desired to use their best Endeavours to get the Subscription Papers filled up as soon as may be. Also, *Voted unanimously*, That the foregoing Vote and Form of a Subscription relative to the enumerated Articles, be immediately Published, and that the Selectmen be directed to distribute a proper Number of them among the Freeholders of this Town; and to forward a Copy of the same to the Select-Men of every Town in the Province; as also to the principal City or Town Officers of the chief Towns in the several Colonies on the Continent, as they may think proper.

Attest,

William Cooper, *Town-Clerk.*

Then the Meeting was Adjourn'd to the 20th Day of November next.

133 From the broadside containing the report of the Boston town meeting of Oct. 28, 1767, in the Massachusetts Historical Society

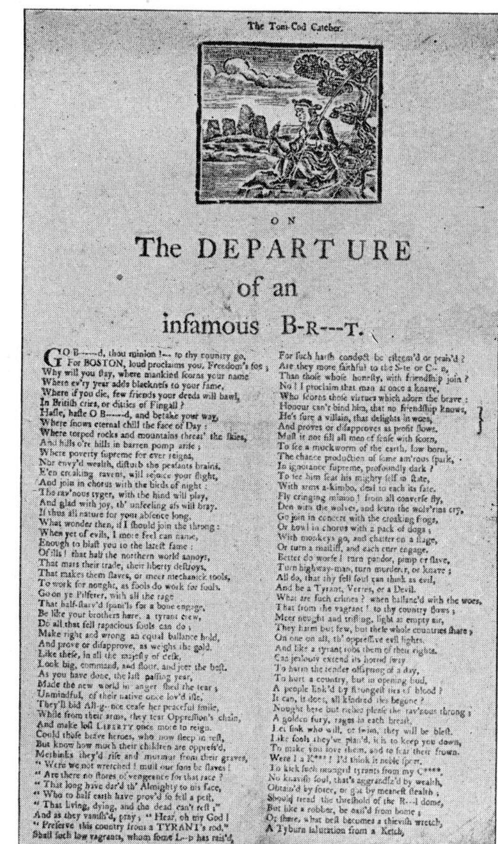

The Tom-Cod Catcher.

ON

The DEPARTURE of an infamous B-R---T.

GO B-----d, thou minion!— to thy country go,
For BOSTON, loud proclaims you, Freedom's foe;
Why will you stay, where mankind scorns your name
Where ev'ry year adds blackness to your fame,
Where if you die, few friends your deeds will bawl,
In British cries, or ditties of Fingall?
Haste, haste O B-----d, and betake your way,
Where snows eternal chill the face of Day:
Where torped rocks and mountains threat' the skies,
And hills o're hills in barren pomp arise;
Where poverty supreme for ever reigns,
Nor envy'd wealth, disturb the peasants brains.
E'en croaking ravens, will rejoice your flight,
And join in chorus with the birds of night:
The rav'nous tyger, with the hind will play,
And glad with joy, th' unfeeling ass will bray.
If thus all nature for your absence long,
What wonder then, if I should join the throng:
When yet of evils, I more feel can name,
Enough to blast you to the latest fame:
Of ills! that half the northern world annoys,
That mars their trade, their liberty destroys,
That makes them slaves, or meer mechanick tools,
To work for nought, as fools do work for fools.
Go on ye Pilferer, with all the rage
That half-starv'd spaniels for a bone engage,
Be like your brothers here, a tyrant crew,
Do all that fell rapacious fools can do;
Make right and wrong an equal ballance hold,
And prove or disapprove, as weighs the gold.
Like these, in all the majesty of desk,
Look big, command, and flour, and jeer the best.
As you have done, the last passing year,
Made the new world in anger shed the tear;
Unmindful, of their native once lov'd isle,
They'll bid All-g-nce cease her peaceful smile,
While from their arms, they tear Oppression's chain,
And make lost LIBERTY once more to reign.
Could those brave heroes, who now sleep in rest,
But know how much their children are oppress'd,
Methinks they'd rise and murmur from their graves,
"Were we not wretched! must our sons be slaves!
"Are there no stores of vengeance for that race?
"That long have dar'd th' Almighty to his face,
"Who to half earth have prov'd so fell a pest,
"That living, dying, and the dead can't rest;"
And as they vanish'd, pray; "Hear, oh my God!
"Preserve this country from a TYRANT's rod."
Shall such low vagrants, whom some L--p has rais'd,
For such harsh condesct be esteem'd or prais'd?
Are they more faithful to the S-te or C-- n,
Than those whose honesty, with friendship join?
No! I proclaim that man at once a knave,
Who scorns those virtues which adorn the brave:
Honour can't bind him, that no friendship knows,
He's sure a villain, that delights in woes,
And proves or disapproves as profit flows.
Must it not fill all men of sense with scorn,
To see a muckworm of the earth, low born,
The chance production of some am'rous spark,
In ignorance supreme, profoundly dark?
To see him seat his mighty self in state,
With arms a-kimbo, deal to each its fate.
Fly cringing minion! from all converse fly,
Den with the wolves, and learn the wolv'rins cry,
Go join in concert with the croaking frogs,
Or howl in chorus with a pack of dogs;
With monkeys go, and chatter on a stage,
Or turn a mastiff, and each curr engage.
Better do worse! turn pandor, pimp or slave,
Turn highway-man, turn murderer, or knave;
All do, that thy fell soul can think as evil,
And be a Tyrant, Verres, or a Devil.
What are such crimes? when ballanc'd with the woes,
That from the vagrant! to thy country flows;
Meer nought and trifling, light as empty air,
They harm but few, but these whole countries share;
On one on all, th' oppressive evil lights,
And like a tyrant robs them of their rights.
Can jealousy extend its horrid sway
To harm the tender offspring of a day,
To hurt a country, but in opening bud,
A people link'd by strongest ties of blood?
It can, it does, all kindred ties begone?
Nought here but riches please the rav'nous throng;
A golden fury, rages in each breast,
Let sink who will, or swim, they will be blest.
Like fools they've plan'd, it is to keep you down,
To make you love them, and to fear their frown.
Were I a K***! I'd think it noble sport,
To kick such mongrel tyrants from my C****,
No knavish soul, that's aggrandiz'd by wealth,
Obtain'd by force, or got by meanest stealth;
Should tread the threshold of the R--l dome,
But like a robber, be oust'd from home;
Or there, what best becomes a thievish wretch,
A Tyburn salutation from a Ketch,

132 From a broadside *The Tom-Cod Catcher*, in the American Antiquarian Society, Worcester, Mass., published at the time of Governor Bernard's departure

MASSACHUSETTS' NON-IMPORTATION AGREEMENT, 1767

THE new taxes (No. 119) were to be collected on the twentieth of November. Numerous arrangements were prerequisite. Chief of these was the establishment in Boston, chosen as the center of imperial control, of the new American Board of Commissioners of the Customs. To Boston, therefore, America looked for leadership. And Boston was perturbed. For Bernard had refused to call the legislature in special session. So, on the twenty-eighth of October, the inhabitants assembled in town meeting, under the leadership of James Otis and Samuel Adams, and unanimously voted to enter into an agreement not to import British-made goods. Steps were taken to inform "the chief Towns in the several Colonies" of this action, and to solicit support.

The legislature finally convened, in January, 1768, in the Town House (already known as the State House). Many members "appeared completely clothed in the manufacture of the country." Samuel Adams was clerk. Thomas Cushing, a Boston merchant, was speaker. The House voted the Circular Letter of February 11 (No. 123) which Bernard sent to London characterizing it as intended to prepare for colonial union against England.

134 From the caricature *A Warm Place — Hell*, by Paul Revere, 1768, engraved for the Colonial Society of Massachusetts from an original owned by Mary Lincoln Eliot

MASSACHUSETTS REFUSES TO RESCIND THE CIRCULAR LETTER

BERNARD'S misrepresentation met with a sympathetic response from the King and Hillsborough. Royal orders were issued to the Governor to require the House to withdraw the resolution authorizing the Circular Letter of February 11. On June 21 this order was transmitted. Otis opened the debate with a ringing arraignment of the ministry's conduct. "When Lord Hillsborough knows that we will not rescind our acts, he should apply to Parliament to rescind theirs. Let Britain rescind her measures, or the colonies are lost to her forever." For nine days the debate continued. Then, behind locked doors, the question was put, "Whether this House will rescind the resolution." Ninety-two answered nay; only seventeen sided with the Government. Dissolution followed. The whole proceeding evoked intense excitement. The "Illustrious Ninety-two" became the popular toast. The caricature pictures the public attitude toward the dissident seventeen. Timothy Ruggles of Worcester is in the van. Means are about to be employed to overcome his obvious reluctance to proceed. In the background is the cupola of the Governor's mansion, Province House.

OTHER COLONIES WELCOME THE CIRCULAR LETTER

EVENTS in Massachusetts found an echo in the South. Maryland, through its Assembly, reprimanded its Governor when he asked, as he was required to do by Hillsborough, that the Circular Letter should be ignored. Then Maryland professed entire agreement with the opinions expressed by Adams. In Delaware, Pennsylvania, New York, Georgia, South Carolina, Rhode Island, an equally favorable reception was given to the epistle. Even cautious John Dickinson was moved to unusual depths of emotion. In May, 1768, the new customs commissioners reached Boston. Shortly thereafter John Hancock's sloop *Liberty* was seized on a charge of importing goods without duty payments. Scuffles between officers of the law and the populace ensued. Dickinson broke into verse. Using Garrick's popular *Hearts of Oak* as a catchy tune, the staid lawyer wrote *A Song for American Freedom*. Shy of publishing his new venture into unfamiliar realms, Dickinson sent it to his friend Otis, who at once had it published. For years the *Liberty Song* was the most popular of all political snatches.

135 The Liberty Song, 1768 from Bickerstaff's *Boston Almanack*, 1769, words written by John Dickinson, music, tune of *Hearts of Oak*, by David Garrick, in the Boston Public Library

May 29—June 5. THE PENNSYLVANIA CHRONICLE, &c. for 1769.. 161

RESOLVES *of the* House *of* Burgesses, *passed the* 16*th of* May, 1769.

Resolved, Nemine Contradicente, THAT the sole right of imposing taxes on the inhabitants of this his Majesty's Colony and Dominion of *Virginia*, is now, and ever hath been, legally and constitutionally vested in the House of Burgesses, lawfully convened, according to the antient and established practice, with the consent of the Council, and of his Majesty, the King of *Great-Britain*, or his Governor for the time being.

Resolved, Nemine Contradicente, That it is the undoubted privilege of the inhabitants of this colony, to petition their Sovereign for redress of grievances; and that it is lawful and expedient to procure the concurrence of his Majesty's other colonies, in dutiful addresses, praying the Royal interposition in favour of the violated rights of *America*.

Resolved, Nemine Contradicente, That all trials for treason, misprision of treason, or for any felony or crime whatsoever, committed and done in this his Majesty's said colony and dominion, by any person or persons residing therein, ought of right to be had, and conducted in and before his Majesty's courts, held within his said colony, according to the fixed and known course of proceeding; and that the seizing any person or persons residing in this colony, suspected of any crime whatsoever, committed therein, and sending such person or persons to places beyond the sea to be tried, is highly derogatory of the rights of *British* subjects, as thereby the inestimable privilege of being tried by a jury from the vicinage, as well as the liberty of summoning and producing witnesses on such trial, will be taken away from the party accused.

Resolved, Nemine Contradicente, That an humble, dutiful, and loyal address, be presented to his Majesty, to assure him of our inviolable attachment to his sacred person and government; and to beseech his royal interposition, as the father of all his people, however remote from the seat of his empire, to quiet the minds of his loyal subjects of this colony, and to avert from them those dangers and miseries which will ensue, from the seizing and carrying beyond sea any person residing in America, suspected of any crime whatsoever, to be tried in any other manner than by the antient and long established course of proceeding.

136 The Virginia Resolves, May 16, 1769, from the *Pennsylvania Chronicle*, May 29–June 5, 1769, in the New York Public Library

THE VIRGINIA ASSEMBLY DEFIES THE GOVERNOR

THE ministry, alarmed, determined upon stern measures. To divide the colonies, Massachusetts, as the chief offender, was singled out for treatment. In February, 1769, Parliament asked the Crown to inquire into treasonable acts in Boston, and to bring to England for trial all persons accused. "Your measures," said a member, "are more calculated to raise than to quell rebellion." So it proved. Nothing more fully illustrates the growing community of spirit in America than the events that ensued. In Virginia the new issue was first and most boldly met. The Assembly had been opened, with mutual courtesies, by the new Governor, Lord Botetourt. The first resident Governor for many years, he had been selected because of his urbanity, as a fit means of winning to the Crown the good graces of the Old Dominion. But the Burgesses insisted upon consideration of the pending political questions. The result was the adoption of a series of resolutions, asserting the rights of petition, of self-taxation and of trial by persons of the neighborhood, and beseeching the King "to quiet the minds of his loyal subjects of this colony, and to avert from them those dangers and miseries which will ensue from the seizing and carrying beyond sea any person residing in America . . . to be tried in any other manner than by the ancient and long established course of proceeding." Peyton Randolph, as speaker, sent copies to the other Assemblies. Dissolved by the indignant Governor, the members met in the Raleigh Tavern, elected Randolph moderator, and proceeded to draft a non-importation agreement submitted by Washington. The document was then circulated throughout the province.

THE CHAIN OF UNION IS COMPLETED

UP to this time, such non-importation agreements had not been widely adopted. Many felt that they would serve merely to widen the breach; others that farming and the fisheries would unduly suffer from the stimulated manufactures. The Virginia Resolves aroused the continent. Resolutions, memorials and addresses were prepared; the printing-press became active; arguments patriotic and ingenious were advanced in favor of the agreements. Late in 1769 action on the part of North Carolina "completed the chain of union throughout the continent." An economic reprisal had been set on foot.

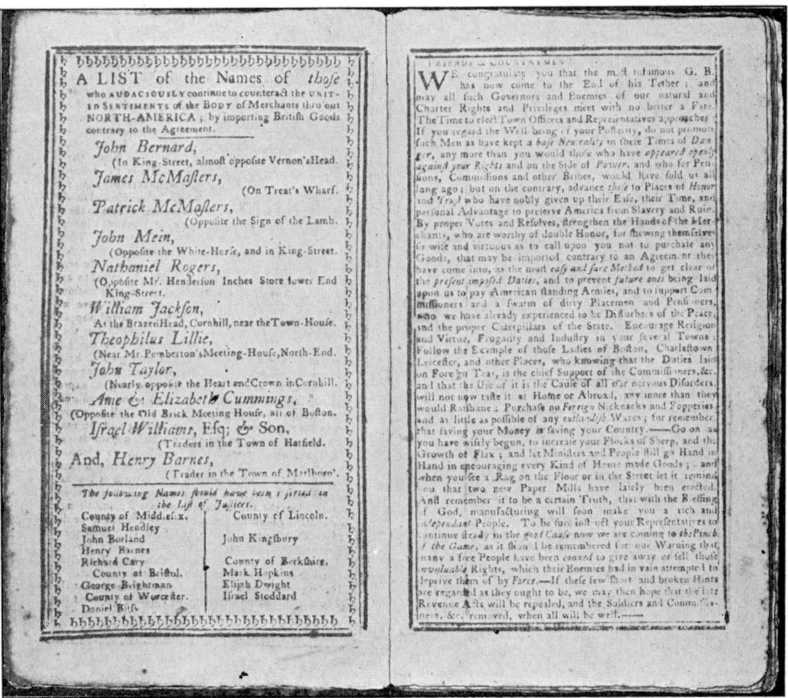

A LIST of the Names of *those* who AUDACIOUSLY continue to counteract the UNITED SENTIMENTS of the BODY of Merchants thro'out NORTH-AMERICA; by importing British Goods contrary to the Agreement.

John Bernard,
(In King-Street, almost opposite Vernon's Head.
James McMasters,
(On Treat's Wharf.
Patrick McMasters,
(Opposite the Sign of the Lamb.
John Mein,
(Opposite the White-Horse, and in King-Street.
Nathaniel Rogers,
(Opposite Mr. Henderson Inches Store lower End King-Street.
William Jackson,
At the Brazen Head, Cornhill, near the Town-House.
Theophilus Lillie,
(Near Mr. Pemberton's Meeting-House, North-End.
John Taylor,
(Nearly opposite the Heart and Crown in Cornhill.
Ame & Elizabeth Cummings,
(Opposite the Old Brick Meeting House, all of Boston.
Israel Williams, Esq; & Son,
(Traders in the Town of Hatfield.
And, *Henry Barnes*,
(Trader in the Town of Marlboro'.

The following Names should have been inserted in the List of Justices.

County of Middlesex.	County of Lincoln.
Samuel Hendley	
John Borland	John Kingsbury
Henry Barnes	
Richard Cary	County of Berkshire.
County of Bristol.	Mark Hopkins
George Brightman	Elijah Dwight
County of Worcester.	Israel Stoddard
Daniel Bliss	

FRIENDS & COUNTRYMEN!

WE congratulate you that the most infamous G. B. has now come to the End of his Tether; and may all such Governors and Enemies of our natural and Charter Rights and Privileges meet with no better a Fate. The Time to elect Town Officers and Representatives approaches: If you regard the Well-being of your Posterity, do not promote such Men as have kept *a base Neutrality* in these Times of *Danger*, any more than you would those who have *appeared openly against your Rights* and on the Side of *Power*, and who for Pensions, Commissions and other Bribes, would have sold us all long ago; but on the contrary, advance *those* to Places of *Honor* and *Trust* who have nobly given up their Ease, their Time, and personal Advantage to preserve America from Slavery and Ruin. By proper Votes and Resolves, strengthen the Hands of the Merchants, who are worthy of double Honor, for shewing themselves so wise and virtuous as to call upon you not to purchase any Goods, that may be imported contrary to an Agreement they have come into, as the most *easy and sure Method* to get clear of the *present imposed Duties*, and to prevent *future ones* being laid upon us to pay American standing Armies, and to support Commissioners and a swarm of dirty Placemen and Pensioners, who we have already experienced to be Disturbers of the Peace, and the proper Caterpillars of the State. Encourage Religion and Virtue, Frugality and Industry in your several Towns: Follow the Example of those Ladies of Boston, Charlestown, Leicester, and other Places, who knowing that the Duties laid on Foreign Teas, is the chief Support of the Commissioners, &c. and that the Use of it is the Cause of all our nervous Disorders, will not now taste it at Home or Abroad, any more than they would Ratsbane. Purchase no *Foreign* Nicknacks and Fopperies, and as little as possible of any *outlandish* Wares; for remember, that saving your Money is saving your Country.——Go on as you have wisely begun, to increase your Flocks of Sheep, and the Growth of Flax; and let Ministers and People still go Hand in Hand in encouraging every Kind of Home made Goods; and when you see a *Rag* on the Floor or in the Street let it remind you that two new Paper Mills have lately been erected. And remember it to be a certain Truth, that with the Blessing of God, manufacturing will soon make you a rich and *independant* People. To be sure instruct your Representatives to continue steady in the *good Cause* now we are coming to *the Pinch of the Game*, as it should be remembered for our Warning that many a free People have been *coaxed* to give away or sell those *invaluable* Rights, which their Enemies had in vain attempted to deprive them of by *Force*.—If these few short and broken Hints are regarded as they ought to be, we may then hope that the late Revenue Acts will be repealed, and the Soldiers and Commissioners, &c. removed, when all will be well.——

137 A List of Unpatriotic Importers, from Edes and Gill's *North American Almanack*, Boston, 1770, in the New York Public Library

WILLIAM JACKSON,

an *IMPORTER*; at the

BRAZEN HEAD,

North Side of the TOWN-HOUSE,

and *Oppoſite the Town-Pump, in*

Corn-hill, BOSTON.

It is deſired that the SONS and DAUGHTERS of *LIBERTY*, would not buy any one thing of him, for in ſo doing they will bring Diſgrace upon *themſelves*, and their *Poſterity*, for *ever* and *ever*, AMEN.

138 Boycott of a Boston Importer, 1770, from a handbill in the Massachusetts Historical Society

ASSEMBLIES ENDORSE NON-IMPORTATION AGREEMENTS

MEASURES were framed to make the agreements effective. Colonial assemblies passed resolutions endorsing the private arrangements entered into by the citizenry. Town meetings voted to prohibit the consumption of tea. Handbills were used to persuade the "Sons and Daughters of Liberty" to boycott traders who continued to import the prohibited articles.

The true Sons of Liberty

And Supporters of the Non-Importation Agreement,

ARE determined to reſent any the leaſt Inſult or Menace offer'd to any one or more of the ſeveral Committees appointed by the Body at Faneuil-Hall, and chaſtiſe any one or more of them as they deſerve; and will alſo ſupport the Printers in any Thing the Committees ſhall deſire them to print.

☞ AS a Warning to any one that ſhall affront as aforeſaid, upon ſure Information given, one of theſe Advertiſements will be poſted up at the Door or Dwelling-Houſe of the Offender.

139 A Warning by the Boston Sons of Liberty, from a handbill in the Massachusetts Historical Society

140 Lord North, 1732–92, from the drawing by Nathaniel Dance-Holland (1735–1811) in the National Portrait Gallery, London

THE PATRIOTS' COMMITTEES COMMAND SUPPORT

WHEN public authorities — especially the redcoats — threatened to interfere with the work of "non-importation and economy" the patriots did not shrink from hints of direct action.

KING GEORGE'S WISHES ARE FURTHERED BY NORTH

ENGLISH politics had changed since the repeal of the Stamp Act. In 1767 Townshend's death had brought Lord North into office as Chancellor of the Exchequer. Here was a minister pleasing to George III. Able, courageous, good-humored, North was a dexterous politician. As a supporter of Tory principles, too indolent to oppose even extreme measures sponsored by the willful monarch, he employed his skill for thirteen years to further the King's desires. The ministry was soon to become the pliable instrument of an irresponsible ruler.

BY OPPRESSION ENGLAND INCURS LOSS OF PRESTIGE

141 From a caricature *The Colonies Reduced* in the *Political Register*, London, Dec. 1768

On November 8, 1768, the King opened Parliament with a speech in which he said: "The capital town of [that] colony appears . . . to be in a state of disobedience to all law and government, and has proceeded to measures subversive of the constitution, and attended with circumstances that might manifest a disposition to throw off their dependence on Great Britain. On my part, I have pursued every measure that appears to be necessary for supporting the constitution, and inducing a due obedience to the authority of the legislature." There were many in England who did not agree with this. Opposition to the King's policy was becoming outspoken. The *Political Register* for December, 1768, carried the above cartoon. The following explanation of it was given: "Great Britain is supposed to have been placed upon the globe; but the colonies being severed from her, she is seen lifting her eyes and mangled stumps to heaven: her shield, which she is unable to wield, lies useless at her side; her lance has pierced New England: the laurel branch has fallen from the hand of Pennsylvania: the English oak has lost its head, and stands a bare trunk." This was the moral: "The ordaining of laws in favor of *one* part of the nation, to the prejudice and oppression of *another*, is certainly the most erroneous and mistaken policy. . . . The whole state is weakened, and perhaps ruined forever!"

142 Thomas Pownall, 1720–1805, from a mezzotint engraving by Richard Earlom (1743–1822), after a painting by Francis Cotes (1725–70), in the Emmet Collection, New York Public Library

POWNALL URGES REPEAL OF THE TOWNSHEND DUTIES

In January, 1770, North became Prime Minister. He was faced with a dilemma. The net revenue from America was less than three hundred pounds; while the expenses of the military establishment there were over one hundred fifty thousand pounds. The colonial boycott had in 1769 reduced imports from Great Britain seven hundred fifty thousand pounds. Something must be done, and that without surrendering to the malcontents. In the spring of 1769 Thomas Pownall had in the Commons proposed repeal of the Townshend duties: "So favorable an opportunity will never recur. Colonies are combining against our trade and manufactures; new provocations will be given; British honor will be more deeply engaged. Let Parliament then, at once, in advance of the new difficulties, repeal the Act, end the controversy, and give peace to the two countries." Pownall had long been a firm and consistent friend of America. He had been one of the best of the royal governors of Massachusetts. In 1767 he had opposed the idea of parliamentary taxation.

(331)

Anno decimo

Georgii III. Regis.

CAP XVII

An Act to repeal ſo much of an Act made in the Seventh Year of His preſent Majeſty's Reign, intituled, *An Act for granting certain Duties in the* Britiſh *Colonies and Plantations in* America, *for allowing a Drawback of the Duties of Cuſtoms upon the Exportation, from this Kingdom, of Coffee and Cocoa Nuts of the Produce of the ſaid Colonies or Plantations, for diſcontinuing the Drawbacks payable on China Earthen-ware exported to* America, *and for more effectually preventing the clandeſtine Running of Goods in the ſaid Colonies and Plantations,* as relates to the Duties upon Glaſs, Red lead, White-lead, Painters Colours,

4 O Paper

143

332 Anno Regni decimo Georgii III. Regis.

Paper, Paſte-boards, Mill-boards, and Scale-boards, of the Produce or Manufacture of *Great Britain*, imported into any of His Majeſty's Colonies in *America*; and alſo to the diſcontinuing the Drawbacks payable on China Earthen-ware exported to *America*, and for regulating the Exportation thereof

Preamble reciting Act 7 Geo. III.

WHEREAS in and by an Act paſſed in the Seventh Year of His Majeſty's Reign, intituled, An Act for granting certain Duties in the Britiſh Colonies and Plantations in *America*, for allowing a Drawback of the Duties of Cuſtoms upon the Exportation, from this Kingdom, of Coffee and Cocoa Nuts of the Produce of the ſaid Colonies or Plantations; for diſcontinuing the Drawbacks payable on China Earthen-ware exported to *America*; and for more effectually preventing the clandeſtine Running of Goods in the ſaid Colonies and Plantations, it was, amongſt other Things enacted, That there ſhould be raiſed, levied, collected, and paid unto His Majeſty, His Heirs, and Succeſſors, certain Duties upon Glaſs, Red-lead, White-lead, Painters Colours, and upon the ſeveral Sorts of Paper therein mentioned; as alſo upon all Paſte-board, Mill-board, and Scale-board, which ſhould be imported into any Colony or Plantation in America, under the Dominion of His Majeſty, His Heirs and Succeſſors And whereas the ſaid Duties, in ſo far as they affect the Produce and Manufacture of Great Britain, do in their Nature tend to the Prejudice and Diſcouragement thereof, and are therefore contrary to the true Principles of Commerce: May it therefore pleaſe Your moſt Excellent Majeſty, that it may be enacted; and be it enacted, by the King's moſt Excellent Majeſty, by and with the Advice and Conſent of the Lords Spiritual and Temporal, and Commons, in this preſent Parliament aſſembled, and by the Authority of the ſame, That, from and after the

Firſt

144

From an original printed copy (second and third pages), in possession of the publishers, of the Act of 1770 repealing all duties except the one on tea

THE KING RETAINS THE TEA TAX ON PRINCIPLE

BUT repeal was not to the liking of North and his master. Said North: "If we are to run after America in search of reconciliation, I do not know a single Act of Parliament that will remain. Are we to make concessions to these people, because they have the hardihood to set us at defiance? No authority was ever confirmed by the concession of any part of honor or of right. Shall I give up my right?" The answer was the King's: "There must always be one tax to keep up the right." "The contest in America," North said in 1770, "is now for no less than sovereignty on one side, and independence on the other." So in April all the duties were repealed except that on tea. This was retained to assert British sovereignty. "The Grenville plan to tax America for revenue was given up, and in lieu of it was the King's plan to tax it on principle." — J. S. BASSETT, *Short History of the United States*, p. 173.

145 From an engraving, about 1870, by John C. McRae after the painting *Raising the Liberty Pole*, by F. A. Chapman

BOSTON PASSIVELY RESISTS THE QUARTERING OF BRITISH TROOPS

THE troubles of 1768 in Boston had led to the sending of troops to that place. They arrived in September. Governor Bernard tried to have at least one regiment quartered in town. The townspeople insisted that all be lodged in the barracks at Fort William in the harbor. General Gage was at last forced to hire quarters at high rentals. Throughout the stay of the troops, till the eve of the Revolution, this policy of passive resistance proved effective.

WHOEVER has candidly traced the rapid Growth of theſe Colonies from their little Beginnings to their preſent flouriſhing State in Wealth and Population, muſt eye the diſtinguiſhed Hand of Heaven, and impreſs every Mind with a humble Confidence, that "no Deſign formed againſt us ſhall proſper:" The poor devoted Town of Boſton has ſuffered, and is ſtill ſuffering, all that the unmeritted Malice of Men and Devils could invent for her Deſtruction; but although impoveriſhed and diſtreſſed, ſhe is not yet ſubjugated and enſlaved; though immured within the Fortreſſes of their Enemies, the free and generous Bosoms of the Inhabitants beat ſtrongly in the Cauſe of Liberty: But it appears that the Meaſure of miniſterial Wrath is not yet full: That deteſted Parricide HUTCHINSON, has vaunted to his few Friends, that ſhould the People ſubmit to the villainous Exactions of the preſent governmental Knot of Tyrants, * "yet ſtill the Town of Boſton would forever remain a garriſoned Town," as a Check upon the Country, leſt they ſhould hereafter be induced to clamour againſt the Edicts of their ſovereign Lords and Maſters, the Britiſh Parliament. The following Plan was providentially detected, and is now offered to the Public, with this ſolemn Queſtion---Will the People ſit tame and inactive Spectators of the hoſtile Deſigns of our inveterate Enemies, and exerciſe ſuch Degrees of Moderation and Forbearance as to ſuffer thoſe Enemies to compleat their Works, and ſo far effect their dangerous Purpoſe, that Reſiſtance would finally be in vain?

THE WATCHMAN.

Memorandums, for a Report.

WE have agreable to your Commands viewed and enquired what Cover can be hired with the Conſent of the Proprietors for the Troops next Winter.

We find that Out-Houſes, Diſtilleries and Store-Houſes can be hired to contain the Serjeants, &c. and private Men of four Regiments. That as theſe want Fire-Places, Windows, and even Floors, the Expence of ſetting up theſe, and for Rent, and returning them in the Condition they now ſtand, will be nearly to One Thouſand Pounds a Regiment. This Expence would be greatly leſſened, and the Troops more comfortably quartered, if the public Buildings, ſuch as the Manufacturing Houſe, &c. can be appropriated for the Accommodation of the Troops.

It appears that Barracks can be built on a more thirfty Footing than they can be hired, and fitted up. But as no Body in this Place will aid ſuch Works, Capt. Montreſor with the Aſſiſtance he can at preſent depend upon, thinks he cannot undertake to furniſh Barracks before the End of November, for more than three Regiments; the Officers of one of theſe Regiments to be quartered.

It appears on Enquiry, difficult to find Houſes for quartering Officers of the Regiments, whoſe private Men are to be lodged in Out-Houſes; Lodging Money ſhould be given to Officers who we cannot provide for.

In chuſing Situations for the Barracks to be built, it might be wiſhed to place them ſo as to make the preſent Erection part of ſome general Plan that may be found, with a View of commanding the Obedience of the Town on future Occaſions; but if they are confined to Situations where the Ground is reputed to belong to the Public, we would propoſe to build Barracks for two Regiments, including Officers, on the Common, or on a Field near it, which could be hired or purchaſed from Mr. Brattle.

To put two Companies into a ſolid Barrack, or Block-Houſe, on the Top of Bacon-Hill, which ſhould be encloſed with a Trench and Paliſade.

A Barrack ſhould be built on Fort-Hill, which might lodge eight Companies and the Artillery.

As ſoon as it is proper to let each Regiment have its Quarters, their Efforts to get themſelves lodged would contribute greatly to have the Work finiſhed early.

* This is a Fact, founded on the Authority of a reſpectable Gentleman of this Town, lately arrived from London, who there had it from Mr. Hutchinſon's own Mouth.

146 From a broadside urging resistance to the quartering of troops, Boston (1768?), in the Emmet Collection, New York Public Library

THE PRESENCE OF TROOPS IRRITATES THE BOSTON PEOPLE

THE presence of the King's scarlet was a continual source of irritation to the inhabitants. Their services were not wanted; their pompous parades were offensive; their bearing often insulting. "The troops greatly corrupt our morals," said Dr. Cooper, brother of the Town Clerk, and Mayhew's successor as the political preacher of the town. "They are in every sense an oppression. May Heaven soon deliver us from this great evil." Quarrels often arose between individual soldiers and the citizens. In all fairness to the former, the taunts of the latter were more than occasionally provocative.

147 From the painting *King's Scarlet and Homespun*, by Harry A. Ogden (1856–). © Goupil & Co., Paris

THE BOSTON "MASSACRE," 1770

ON March 5, 1770, the pent-up feelings overflowed in the episode dubbed the Boston Massacre. Though differing but in degree from earlier affrays, it aroused the populace and was for years celebrated annually in Old South Church. On the day following the affair, a town meeting authorized Samuel Adams to request the Governor to remove the troops to Castle William. This Hutchinson and his staff finally agreed to do; and for four years troops remained in Boston harbor.

148 From the engraving by Paul Revere in the New York Historical Society

149 From the portrait of Hutchinson by John Singleton Copley, in the Massachusetts Historical Society

THOMAS HUTCHINSON, 1711–80, TORY GOVERNOR OF MASSACHUSETTS

HUTCHINSON in 1770 succeeded Bernard as Governor. A descendant of Ann Hutchinson, he did not inherit any bent toward rebellion against constituted authority. He was a scholar, a man of ability, a good administrator. His long public career gives evidence of this. In 1738 he was a Boston selectman; for ten years he represented the town in the Assembly, for three years being Speaker; from 1749 to 1766 he was a member of the Council; he had been Lieutenant Governor since 1758; and since 1760 Chief Justice as well. "No man was so experienced in the public affairs of the colony; and no one was so familiar with its history, usages and laws." — BANCROFT, VI, p. 303. This knowledge should have served him in these portentous years; but unfortunately that long official service had brought his natural conservatism more and more into line with the views of the imperial government. In 1765 he had disapproved of the Stamp Act. In 1770 he not only supported Lord North, but urged him on.

ISRAEL MAUDUIT, 1708–87, HUTCHINSON'S AGENT IN ENGLAND

IN such actions, Hutchinson was not unwilling to misrepresent American conditions. His agent in this work was Mauduit. Though educated for the ministry, Mauduit had become a successful London merchant. In 1763 he was entrusted with the presentation of the interests of Massachusetts to the Government. Shortly thereafter he began issuing pamphlets favoring the contentions of the colonies; in this work, which continued until 1781, he proved very adroit. When events in America seemed to threaten a rupture of British relations, Mauduit opposed the colonies. In March, 1778, however, he declared for American independence and bent his efforts to secure it. The use of such London agents became a common practice of many of the colonies. With direct and continuous intercommunication out of the question, some such institution was needed to impress the imperial authorities with the real views of the colonists. Official dispatches often required interpretation at the hands of some one familiar with local conditions. Of such agents Mauduit was one of the ablest.

150 From the *European Magazine*, 1787, engraving after a portrait, 1751, by Mason Chamberlin (d. 1787)

FEMININE TEA-DRINKERS WEAKEN THE BOYCOTT, 1770

Lord North had originally favored the total repeal of the Townshend duties. Royal persistence, combined with a belief that the non-importation agreements would fall of themselves, had won him round. In this belief he was correct. Only in New York had the agreement been well kept. After the partial repeal, Carolina, Georgia, New Hampshire, Pennsylvania, Maryland, Virginia, Massachusetts, one by one increased importations from England. Merchants of New York felt the strain of their self-imposed abnegation. A poll of the people was taken in the summer of 1770 — one of the earliest in American history. Only three hundred out of fifteen hundred favored the retention of restrictions on goods other than tea. So in July the merchants placed London orders for merchandise, except tea. Philadelphia, Boston and South Carolina denounced the action. "Send us your Liberty Pole," said Philadelphia. But the agreement was broken, to the joy of the Tory. That there was pressure upon the New York merchant to procure tea as well is shown by the accompanying squib. And there is little doubt that plenty of the "Indian weed" found its way into the homes of the well-to-do.

New-York May 10th 1770.

The Female Patriot, No. I.

ADDRESSED TO THE

TEA-DRINKING LADIES of NEW-YORK.

When Adam firſt fell into Satan's Snare,
And forfeited his Bliſs to pleaſe the Fair;
God from his Garden drove the ſinful Man,
And thus the Source of human Woes began.
'Twas weak in Adam, for to pleaſe his Wife,
To loſe his acceſs to the Tree of Life:
His dear bought Knowledge all his Sons deplore,
Death thir Inheritance, and Sin their Store.
But why blame Adam, ſince his Brainleſs Race
Will loſe their All to obtain a beautious Face;
And will their Honour, Pride, and Wealth lay down,
Rather then ſee a lovely Woman frown.
The Ladies are not quite, ſo complifant,
If they want Tea, they'll ſtorm and rave and rant,
And call their Lordly Huſbands Ass and Clown,
The jeſt of Fools and Sport of all the Town.
A pleaſent Story lately I heard told
Of Madam Hornbloom, a noted Scold,
Laſt Day her Huſband ſaid, "My deareſt Life,
My Kind, my Fair, my Angel of a Wiſe;
Juſt now, from London, there's a Ship come in
Brings noble News will raiſe us Merchants Fame,
The Fruits of our non-importation Scheme.
The Parliament, dear Saint, may they be bleſt
Have great part of our Grievances redreſt:"
"Have they indeed," replies the frowning Dame,
"Say, is there not ſome Tea and China come."
"Why, no! We can't import that Indian Weed,
That Duty's ſtill a Rod above our Head."
"Curſe on your Heads, you naſty fumbling Crew,
Then round his Shoulders the hard Broom-Stick flew,
Go, dirty Clod-pole! get me ſome Shuſhong,
This Evening I've invited Madam Strong.
— Silence — you Blockhead — hear, the Lady knocks!
Get to your Cock-Loſt or expect ſome Strokes."
— "Your Servant Madam, Tea is on the Board
I really tho't you once had broke your Word."
"I aſk your Pardon, dear Miss Hornbloom,
My ſpraling Brats kept me ſo long at Home;
My ſtupid Huſband too has gone aſtray
To wait upon the Sons of Liberty."

151 From a broadside dated New York, May 10, 1770, in the New York Public Library

A BRITISH PATROL SHIP IS BURNED OFF PROVIDENCE

"The people," wrote Johnson, Connecticut's agent, on October 25, 1771, "appear to be weary of their altercations with the Mother Country; a little discreet conduct on both sides would perfectly reëstablish . . . warm affection and respect towards Great Britain." But such conduct was not forthcoming. Comparative calm was broken from time to time, and in very significant fashion. A most dramatic instance occurred off Providence in 1772. Patrolling that shore against smugglers was the *Gaspé*, Lieutenant Dudingston commanding. Smugglers were then patriots; Dudingston was exasperatingly efficient, perhaps overbearing, in the execution of his duty. One day, chasing Captain Benjamin Lindsay's sloop *Hannah*, the *Gaspé* ran aground. The news spread rapidly. Under the lead of John Brown, merchant, and Abraham Whipple, shipmaster, an expedition was organized. During the night the *Gaspé* was boarded by a party of sixty-four armed men from Providence, after a scuffle in which the Lieutenant was wounded. Sending the crew ashore, the daring townsfolk set fire to the vessel, which burned to the water's edge. It was another episode showing the degree of irritation aroused in the average American of those days by the inept conduct of the British Government.

152 From the painting *Attack on the Gaspé* by Charles DeWolf Brownell, in the Rhode Island Historical Society, Providence

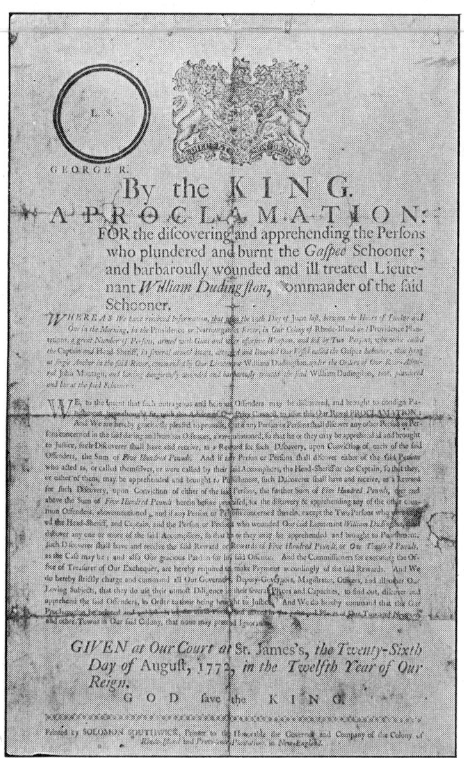
L. S.

GEORGE R.

By the KING.

A PROCLAMATION:

FOR the discovering and apprehending the Persons who plundered and burnt the *Gaspee* Schooner; and barbarously wounded and ill treated Lieutenant *William Dudingston*, Commander of the said Schooner.

GIVEN at Our Court at St. James's, *the Twenty-Sixth Day of* August, 1772, *in the Twelfth Year of Our Reign.*

GOD save the KING.

153 From the original in the Rhode Island Historical Society

ROYAL PROCLAMATION CONCERNING THE *GASPÉ*

IN England this lawless act was magnified into high treason. Royal orders were issued to the colonial authorities, commanding them to arrest the culprits and hand them over to be taken to England for trial. But Rhode Island had no royal governor; nor would any one move to retain the raiders. Stephen Hopkins, now Chief Justice, let it be known that he would give no cognizance to any such arrest. Even the offer of rewards by the Crown failed to bring forward the offenders. Yet they were well known. They were, indeed, with Abraham Whipple as their leader, among the most prominent persons in Providence. They had assembled for their adventure by beat of drum and laid their plans at a public tavern. And on the day following the raid one of them had openly paraded the Lieutenant's gold-laced hat.

BOSTON, JUNE 22d, 1773.

SIR,

THE Committee of Correspondence of the Town of *Boston*, conformable to that Duty which they have hitherto endeavoured to discharge with Fidelity, again address you with a very fortunate Important Discovery; and cannot but express their grateful Sentiments in having obtained the Approbation of so large a Majority of the Towns in this Colony, for their past Attention to the general Interest

A more extraordinary Occurrence possibly never yet took Place in *America*; the Providential Care of that gracious Being who conducted the early Settlers of this Country to establish a safe Retreat from Tyranny for themselves and their Posterity in *America*, has again wonderfully interposed to bring to Light the Plot that had been laid for us by our malicious and insidious Enemies.

Our present Governor has been exerting himself (as the honorable House of Assembly have expressed themselves in their late Resolves). "by his secret confidential Correspondence, to introduce Measures "destructive of our constitutional Liberty, while he has practiced every "method among the People of this Province, to fix in their Minds "an exalted Opinion of his warmest Affection for them, and his "unremitted Endeavours to promote their best Interest at the Court "of Great-Britain." This will abundantly appear by the Letters and Resolves which we herewith transmit to you; the serious Perusal of which will shew you your present most dangerous Situation. This Period calls for the strictest Concurrence in Sentiment and Action of every individual of this Province, and we may add, of THIS CONTINENT; all private Views should be annihilated, and the Good of the Whole should be the single Object of our Pursuit— "By uniting we stand," and shall be able to defeat the Invaders and Violaters of our Rights.

We are,

Your Friends and humble Servants,

Signed by Direction of the Committee for Correspondence in *Boston*,

William Cooper, *Town-Clerk.*

To the Town-Clerk of ; *to be immediately delivered to the Committee of Correspondence for your Town, if such a Committee is chosen, otherwise to the Gentlemen the Selectmen, to be communicated to the Town.*

154 From the Circular Letter, June 22, 1773, addressed to the town committees, in the Massachusetts Historical Society

BOSTON'S COMMITTEE OF CORRESPONDENCE CALLS FOR UNIFIED ACTION

HAPPENINGS such as this encouraged the radical element. Sam Adams, smelling tyranny on every tainted breeze, was convinced by now (October 29, 1772) that "this country must shake off its intolerable burdens at all events." Unceasingly he worked. More and more he insisted that the cause of one colony was the cause of all, and that through union alone could rights be maintained. At last, in Boston town meeting, he found occasion to set up machinery to achieve his end. On his motion there was appointed a Committee of Correspondence of twenty-one members, to exchange opinions and information with other towns. "God grant," he cried, "that the love of liberty, and a zeal to support it, may enkindle in every town." The response was pleasing. Soon Adams was leading an unofficial but authoritative colonial organization. Though Hutchinson might refuse to call the Assembly, unified counsel was now again possible and even present.

AT a Meeting at the Exchange, 16th May, 1774, ISAAC LOW, chosen CHAIRMAN.

1st Question put, Whether it is necessary for the present, to appoint a Committee to correspond with the neighbouring Colonies, on the present important Crisis? Carried in the Affirmative by a great Majority.

2d. Whether a Committee be nominated this Evening for the Approbation of the Public?---Carried in the Affirmative by a great Majority.

3d. Whether the Committee of 50 be appointed, or 25?---Carried for 50, by a great Majority.

The following Persons were nominated:

John Alsop,	Benjamin Booth,
William Bayard,	Joseph Hallett,
Theophylact Bache,	Charles Shaw,
Peter V. B. Livingston,	Alexander Wallace,
Philip Livingston,	James Jauncey,
Isaac Sears,	Gabriel H. Ludlow,
David Johnston,	Nicholas Hoffman,
Charles Mc. Evers,	Abraham Walton,
Charles Nicholl,	Gerardus Duyckinck,
Alexander M'Dougall,	Peter Van Schauck,
Capt. Thomas Randall,	Henry Remsen,
John Moore,	Hamilton Young,
Isaac Low,	George Bowne,
Leonard Lispenard,	Peter T Curtenius,
Jacobus Van Zandt,	Peter Goelet,
James Duane,	Abraham Brasher,
Edward Laight,	Abraham P Lott,
Thomas Pearsall,	David Van Horne,
Elias Desbrosses,	Gerardus W. Beekman,
William Walton,	Abraham Duryee,
Richard Yates,	Joseph Bull,
John De Lancey,	William M'Adam,
Miles Sherbrook,	Richard Sharpe,
John Thurman,	Thomas Marston,
John Jay,	Francis Lewis, added *nem. con.* May 19th.
John Broome,	

155 From a facsimile of the original handbill of the New York Committee, May 16, 1774, in the Bancker Collection Catalogue, 1898, courtesy of Stan. V. Henkels

OTHER COLONIES FOLLOW BOSTON'S LEAD

WHEN Virginia, spurred by the *Gaspé* affair, and under the leadership of Patrick Henry, Thomas Jefferson, Dabney Carr and Richard Henry Lee, created in March, 1773, a standing Committee of Correspondence to communicate with the other colonies, Adams' hopes were realized. By July Committees were operating in six colonies; and gradually others came into existence. Through them public opinion was focused, and by them political union was foreshadowed.

ROYAL CONCESSION TO EAST INDIA COMPANY THREATENS AMERICAN COMMERCE

THE fires of discontent soon received fresh fuel from England. In 1773 the East India Company, financially embarrassed, appealed to the Government for aid. This the King granted. The company was allowed to carry tea to America free of the usual duties charged for transshipment in England. Further, it might establish in the colonies stores for selling its goods. The Americans therefore could buy their tea more cheaply than the English; while the obstinate boycotting American merchant would face the cutthroat competition of a monopolistic trading corporation. The resentment of colonial merchants was that of men whose whole economic position was threatened. Their thoughts were, a few years later, mirrored by Tom Paine, the ever-ready pamphleteer, who was always prepared to write on any burning aspect of the political or economic life of the hour. "When rights are secure, property is secure in consequence. But when property is made a pretence for unequal or exclusive rights, it weakens the right to hold the property, and provokes indignation and tumult; for it is unnatural to believe that property can be secure under the guarantee of a society injured in its rights by the influence of that property."

ASSOCIATION
OF
THE SONS OF LIBERTY,
OF
NEW-YORK.

IT is eſſential to the Freedom and Security of a Free People, that no Taxes be impoſed upon them but by their own Conſent, or their Repreſentatives. For "what Property have they, in that, which another may, by Right, take when he pleaſes, to himſelf?" The Former is the undoubted Birthright of *Engliſhmen*, to ſecure which, they expended Millions, and ſacrificed the Lives of Thouſands. And yet, to the Aſtoniſhment of all the World, and the Grief of *America*, the Commons of *Great-Britain*, after the Repeal of the memorable and deteſtable *Stamp Act*, reaſſumed the Power of impoſing Taxes on the *American* Colonies, and inſiſting on it, as a neceſſary Badge of Parliamentary Supremacy, paſſed a Bill, in the ſeventh Year of his preſent Majeſty's Reign, impoſing Duties on all Glaſs, Painters Colours, Paper, and Teas, that ſhould after the 20th of *November*, 1767, be "imported from *Great-Britain*, into any Colony or Plantation in *America*." This Bill, after the Concurrence of the Lords, obtained the Royal Aſſent. And thus, they, who from Time immemorial, have exerciſed the Right of giving to, or withholding from the Crown, their Aids and Subſidies, according to their *own free Will and Pleaſure*, ſignified by their Repreſentatives in Parliament, do, by the Act in Queſtion, deny us, their Brethren in *America*, the Enjoyment of the ſame Right. As this Denial, and the Execution of that Act, involves our Slavery, and would ſap the Foundation of our Freedom, whereby we ſhould become Slaves to our Brethren and Fellow Subjects, born to no greater Stock of Freedom than the *Americans*, the Merchants and Inhabitants of this City, in Conjunction with the Merchants and Inhabitants of the ancient *American* Colonies, entered into an Agreement to decline a Part of their Commerce with *Great-Britain*, until the abovementioned Act ſhould be totally repealed. This Agreement operated ſo powerfully to the Diſadvantage of the Manufacturers of *England*, that many of them were unemployed. To appeaſe their Clamours, and to provide the Subſiſtence for them, which the Non-Importation Agreement had deprived them of, the Parliament in 1770, repealed ſo much of the Revenue Act as impoſed a Duty on Glaſs, Painters Colours, and Paper, and left the Duty on Tea, as *a Teſt of the Parliamentary Right to Tax us*. The Merchants of the Cities of *New-York* and *Philadelphia*, having ſtrictly adhered to the Agreement, ſo far as it related to the Importation of Articles ſubject to an *American* Duty; have convinced the Miniſtry, that ſome other Meaſure muſt be adopted, to execute Parliamentary Supremacy, over this Country; and to remove the Diſtreſs brought on the *Eaſt India* Company, by the ill Policy of that Act. Accordingly, to increaſe the Temptation, to the Shippers of Tea from *England*, an Act of Parliament paſſed the laſt Seſſion, which gives the whole Duty on Tea, the Company were ſubject to pay, upon the Importation of it into *England*, to the Purchaſers, and Exporters; and when the Company have Ten Millions of Pounds of Tea, in their Warehouſes, excluſive of the Quantity they may want to ſhip, they are allowed to export Tea, diſcharged from the Payment of that Duty, with which they were, before chargeable. In Hopes of Aid in the Execution of this Project, by the Influence of the Owners of the *American* Ships, Application was made, by the Company, to the Captains of thoſe Ships, to take the Tea on Freight; but they virtuouſly rejected it. Still determined on the Scheme, they have chartered Ships to bring over the Tea to this Country, which may be hourly expected, to make an important Trial of our Virtue. If they ſucceed in the Sale of that Tea, we ſhall have no Property that we can call our own, and then we may bid adieu to *American* Liberty.——Therefore, to prevent a Calamity, which, of all others, is the moſt to be dreaded,—Slavery, and its terrible Concomitants,—We the Subſcribers, being influenced from a Regard to Liberty, and diſpoſed to uſe all lawful Endeavours, in our Power, to defeat the pernicious Project, and to tranſmit to our Poſterity, thoſe Bleſſings of Freedom, which our Anceſtors have handed down to us; and to contribute to the Support of the Common Liberties of *America*, which are in danger to be ſubverted, DO, for thoſe important Purpoſes, agree to aſſociate together, under the Name and Stile of the SONS OF LIBERTY, OF NEW YORK, and engage our Honour, to and with each other, faithfully to obſerve and perform the following RESOLUTIONS, *Viz.*

1ſt. RESOLVED, That whoever ſhall aid, or abet, or in any Manner aſſiſt, in the Introduction of Tea, from any Place whatſoever, into this Colony, while it is ſubject by a *Britiſh* Act of Parliament, to the Payment of a Duty, for the Purpoſe of raiſing a Revenue in *America*, he ſhall be deemed, an Enemy to the Liberties of *America*.

2d. RESOLVED, That whoever ſhall be aiding, or aſſiſting, in the Landing, or carting of ſuch Tea, from any Ship, or Veſſel, or ſhall hire any Houſe, Storehouſe, or Cellar, or any Place whatſoever, to depoſit the Tea, ſubject to a Duty as aforeſaid, he ſhall be deemed, an Enemy to the Liberties of *America*.

3d. RESOLVED, That whoever ſhall ſell, or buy, or in any Manner contribute to the Sale, or Purchaſe of Tea, ſubject to a Duty as aforeſaid, or ſhall aid, or abet, in tranſporting ſuch Tea, by Land, or Water, from this City, until the 7th. Geo. III. Chap. 46, commonly called the Revenue Act, ſhall be totally, and clearly repealed, he ſhall be deemed, an Enemy to the Liberties of *America*.

4th. RESOLVED, That whether the Duties on Tea, impoſed by this Act, be paid in *Great Britain*, or in *America*, our Liberties are equally affected.

5th. RESOLVED, That whoever ſhall tranſgreſs any of theſe Reſolutions, we will not deal with, or employ, or have any Connection with him.

NEW-YORK, November 29, 1773.

156 From a broadside of the Sons of Liberty, New York, Nov. 29, 1773, protesting against the tea duty, in the New York Historical Society

157 John Hancock, 1737–93, from the portrait by John Singleton Copley in the Museum of Fine Arts, Boston

A RICH BOSTON MERCHANT LEADS THE RADICALS

THE East India Company, however, proceeded to send out ships laden with tea, destined for various ports. Their coming was known; everywhere preparations were made. Most spectacular were the events in Boston. Here as elsewhere the new measure brought into alliance the radical leaders, such as Samuel Adams, with the more substantial citizens, as William Phillips, John Rowe and John Hancock. The latter is one of the most striking figures of the Revolution. He was a prominent merchant of Boston, of liberal, indeed, of exceedingly charitable, bent. He had amassed a great fortune, being the owner of more property in Boston than any other individual. His determined objection to the impositions of the English Government, his courage in defying the excise officers by smuggling through wines from the Indies, his wholehearted generosity toward those who suffered from the cessation of business, endeared him to the people of Massachusetts. Hancock was the first signer of the Declaration of Independence, and the first Governor of the Commonwealth of Massachusetts.

Whereas a Number of Merchants in this Province have inadvertently imported Tea from Great Britain, while it is subject to the Payment of a Duty imposed upon it by an Act of the British Parliament for the Purpose of raising a Revenue in America, and appropriating the same without the Consent of those who are required to pay it :

RESOLVED, That in thus importing said Tea, they have justly incurr'd the Displeasure of our Brethren in the other Colonies.

And Resolved further, That if any Person or Persons shall hereafter import Tea from Great-Britain, or if any Master or Masters of any Vessel or Vessels in Great-Britain shall take the same on Board to be imported to this Place, until the said unrighteous Act shall be repeal'd, he or they shall be deem'd by this Body, an Enemy to his Country ; and we will prevent the Landing and Sale of the same, and the Payment of any Duty thereon. And we will effect the Return thereof to the Place from whence it shall come.

RESOLVED, That the foregoing Vote be printed and sent to England, and all the Sea-Ports in this Province.

Upon a Motion made, Voted, That fair Copies be taken of the whole Proceedings of this Meeting, and transmitted to New-York & Philadelphia, And that Mr. SAMUEL ADAMS, Hon. JOHN HANCOCK, Esq; WILLIAM PHILLIPS, Esq; JOHN ROWE, Esq; JONATHAN WILLIAMS, Esq Be a Committee to transmit the same.

Voted, That it is the Determination of this Body, to carry their Votes and Resolutions into Execution, at the Risque of their Lives and Property.

Voted, That the Committee of Correspondence for this Town, be desired to take Care that every other Vessel with Tea that arrives in this Harbour, have a proper Watch appointed for her — Also Voted, That those Persons who are desirous of making a Part of these Nightly Watches, be desired to give in their Names at Messieurs Edes and Gill's Printing-Office.

Voted, That our Brethren in the Country be desired to afford their Assistance upon the first Notice given ; especially if such Notice be given upon the Arrival of Captain Loring, in Messieurs Clarkes' Brigantine.

Voted, That those of this Body who belong to the Town of Boston do return their Thanks to their Brethren who have come from the neighbouring Towns, for their Countenance and Union with this Body in this Exigence of our Affairs.

VOTED, That the Thanks of this Meeting be given to JONATHAN WILLIAMS, Esq; for his good services as Moderator.

VOTED, That this Meeting be Dissolved — And it was accordingly Dissolved.

158 Resolutions of a Boston Town Meeting to prevent the "Landing and Sale of Tea," from a broadside, Dec. 1, 1773, in the Massachusetts Historical Society

BOSTON PLANS TO PREVENT THE LANDING OF TEA

The first effort in Boston was to secure the resignation of the Company's agents, two of whom were sons of the Governor. Success in this, however, was not attained. On November 28, the first of the tea-ships, the *Dartmouth*, appeared in the harbor. Two others followed shortly. Every exertion was now made to have the tea sent back in the ships that had brought it.

BOSTON, December 2, 1773.

WHEREAS it has been reported that a Permit will be given by the Custom-House for Landing the Tea now on Board a Vessel laying in this Harbour, commanded by Capt. HALL : THIS is to Remind the Publick, That it was solemnly voted by the Body of the People of this and the neighbouring Towns assembled at the Old-South Meeting-House on Tuesday the 30th Day of *November*, that the said Tea never should be landed in this Province, or pay one Farthing of Duty : And as the aiding or assisting in procuring or granting any such Permit for landing the said Tea or any other Tea so circumstanced, or in offering any Permit when obtained to the Master or Commander of the said Ship, or any other Ship in the same Situation, must betray an inhuman Thirst for Blood, and will also in a great Measure accelerate Confusion and Civil War : This is to assure such public Enemies of this Country, that they will be considered and treated as Wretches unworthy to live, and will be made the first Victims of our just Resentment.

The PEOPLE.

N. B. Captain *Bruce* is arrived laden with the same detestable Commodity ; and 'tis peremptorily demanded of him, and all concerned, that they comply with the same Requisitions.

159 From a Boston handbill, Dec. 2, 1773, in the Massachusetts Historical Society

WARNINGS AGAINST GIVING AID TO THE TEA-SHIP

Simultaneously precautions were taken against the landing of the cargo. This made the situation virtually impossible for the ships. The collector of the port declined to issue clearance papers till all dutiable goods had been discharged; the townspeople stood ready to oppose unloading of the tea. Governor Hutchinson meanwhile had taken measures to prevent the departure of the vessels past Castle William. The law provided that should duties not be paid after twenty days, the vessel and its cargo were liable to seizure for non-payment. The date of expiration was the 16th of December. As the day approached, Hutchinson glimpsed victory over his townsmen.

160 The Old South Meetinghouse, from a photograph by The Halliday Historic Photograph Co.

A MEETING OF PROTEST ENDS WITH A WAR WHOOP

On the 16th, a vast concourse flocked to that accustomed rendezvous of the patriot, Old South Church. Here, with noteworthy patience and order, final efforts were made to solve the problem. By evening failure was apparent. Then rose Sam Adams, saying: "This meeting can do nothing more to save the country." As though this were a prearranged signal, an Indian war whoop at once sounded without. This was caught up by the crowd. The moderator adjourned the meeting, amid tremendous shouting and cheering.

"INDIANS" STAGE THE BOSTON TEA PARTY

THE throng then proceeded to the foot of Purchase Street. There, off Griffin's Wharf, were moored the three tea-ships. Aboard these went the "Indian" party which, in point of fact, had been making careful preparations through the day. Quietly and systematically, before a silent but eager gathering, every bit of tea was destroyed. No other property was damaged, no person harmed. "The whole," Hutchinson confessed, "was done with very little tumult." Nevertheless it was an overt and premeditated act of violence, weakening the colonial cause among liberal Englishmen who were friends of America and diminishing the chances for a peaceful settlement of the difficulties.

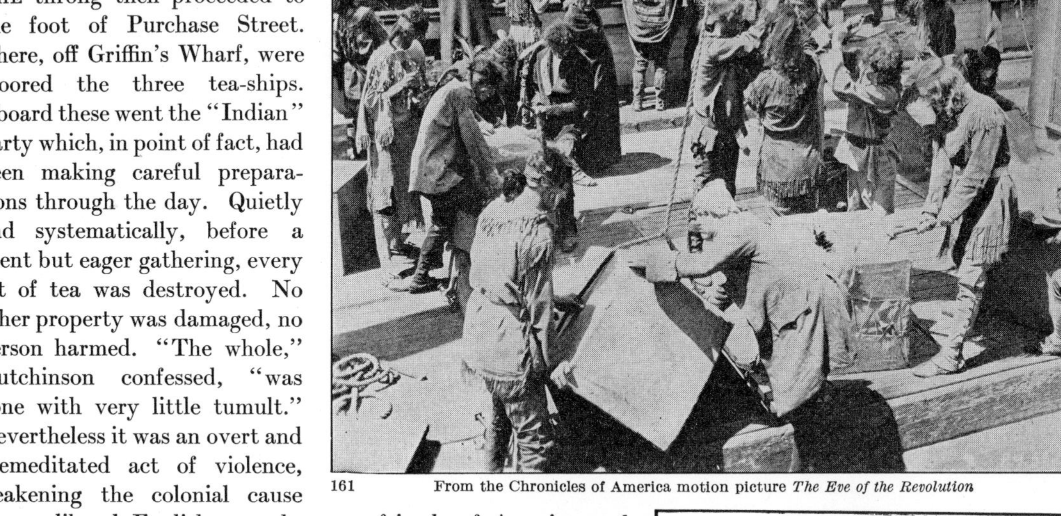

161 From the Chronicles of America motion picture *The Eve of the Revolution*

BOSTONIANS EXULT OVER THEIR DEFIANCE

GREAT was the rejoicing. "You cannot imagine," wrote Samuel Adams, "the height of joy that sparkles in the eyes and animates the countenances as well as the hearts of all we meet." From outside Massachusetts came echoes. In New York crowds "highly extolled the Bostonians"; in Philadelphia bells announced "the most perfect approbation." "The TEA is sunk in spite of all our foes," said a contemporary broadside. "A NOBLE SIGHT—to see the accursed TEA mingled with MUD—and ever for to be." Withal, there was an undercurrent of concern and of courage. One participant epitomized this as follows: "We do console ourselves that we have acted constitutionally."

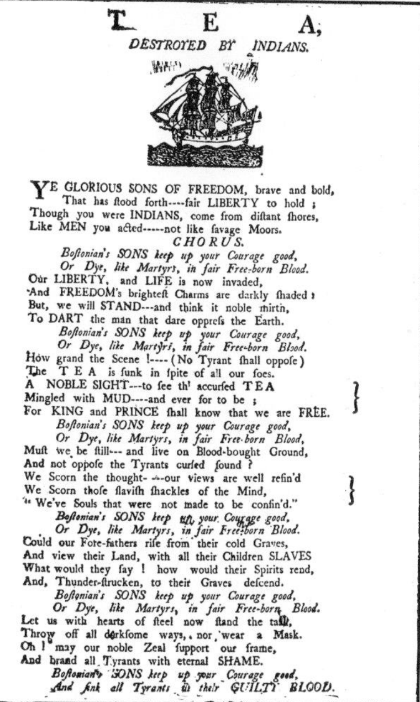

T E A,

DESTROYED BY INDIANS.

YE GLORIOUS SONS OF FREEDOM, brave and bold,
That has ftood forth----fair LIBERTY to hold ;
Though you were INDIANS, come from diftant fhores,
Like MEN you acted-----not like favage Moors.

CHORUS.

Boftonian's SONS keep up your Courage good,
Or Dye, like Martyrs, in fair Free-born Blood.

Our LIBERTY, and LIFE is now invaded,
And FREEDOM's brighteft Charms are darkly fhaded !
But, we will STAND---and think it noble mirth,
To DART the man that dare opprefs the Earth.

Boftonian's SONS keep up your Courage good,
Or Dye, like Martyrs, in fair Free-born Blood.

How grand the Scene !----(No Tyrant fhall oppofe)
The T E A is funk in fpite of all our foes.
A NOBLE SIGHT---to fee th' accurfed TEA
Mingled with MUD----and ever for to be ;
For KING and PRINCE fhall know that we are FREE.

Boftonian's SONS keep up your Courage good,
Or Dye, like Martyrs, in fair Free-born Blood,

Muft we be ftill--- and live on Blood-bought Ground,
And not oppofe the Tyrants curfed found ?
We Scorn the thought----our views are well refin'd
We Scorn thofe flavifh fhackles of the Mind,
"We've Souls that were not made to be confin'd."

Boftonian's SONS keep up your Courage good,
Or Dye, like Martyrs, in fair Free-born Blood.

Could our Fore-fathers rife from their cold Graves,
And view their Land, with all their Children SLAVES
What would they fay ! how would their Spirits rend,
And, Thunder-ftrucken, to their Graves defcend.

Boftonian's SONS keep up your Courage good,
Or Dye, like Martyrs, in fair Free-born Blood.

Let us with hearts of fteel now ftand the tafk,
Throw off all darkfome ways, nor wear a Mask.
Oh ! may our noble Zeal fupport our frame,
And brand all Tyrants with eternal SHAME.

Boftonian's SONS keep up your Courage good,
And fink all Tyrants in their GUILTY BLOOD.

162 From a broadside, 1773, in the Massachusetts Historical Society

DELAWARE PILOTS.

THE Regard we have for your Characters, and our Defire to promote your future Peace and Safety, are the Occafion of this Third Addrefs to you.

IN our fecond Letter we acquainted you, that the Tea Ship was a Three Decker ; We are now informed by good Authority, fhe is not a Three Decker, but an *old black Ship, without a Head,* or *any Ornaments.*

THE *Captain* is a *fhort fat* Fellow, and a little *obftinate* withal.---So much the worfe for him.----For, fo fure as he *rides rufty,* We fhall heave him Keel out, and fee that his Bottom be well fired, fcrubb'd and paid.---His Upper-Works too, will have an Overhawling-----and as it is faid, he has a good deal of *Quick Work* about him, We will take particular Care that fuch Part of him undergoes a thorough Rummaging.

WE have a ftill *worfe Account* of *his Owner* ;---for it is faid, the Ship POLLY was bought by him on Purpofe, to make a Penny of us ; and that *he* and Captain *Ayres* were well advifed, of the Rifque they would run, in thus daring to infult and abufe us.

Captain Ayres was here in the Time of the Stamp-Act, and ought to have known our People better, than to have expected we would be fo mean as to fuffer his *rotten* TEA to be funnel'd down our Throats, with the *Parliament's Duty* mixed with it.

WE know him well, and have calculated to a Gill and a Feather, how much it will require to fit him for an *American Exhibition.* And we hope, not one of your Body will behave fo ill, as to oblige us to clap him in the Cart along Side of the *Captain.*

WE muft repeat, that the SHIP POLLY is an *old black Ship,* of about Two Hundred and Fifty Tons burthen, *without a Head,* and *without Ornaments,*---and, that CAPTAIN AYRES is a *thick chunky Fellow.*----------As fuch, TAKE CARE to AVOID THEM.

YOUR OLD FRIENDS,

THE COMMITTEE FOR TARRING AND FEATHERING.

Philadelphia, December 7, 1773.

Monday Morning, December 27, 1773.

THE TEA-SHIP being arrived, every Inhabitant, who wifhes to preferve the Liberty of America, is defired to meet at the STATE-HOUSE, This Morning, precifely at TEN o'Clock, to advife what is beft to be done on this alarming Crifis.

163 From a broadside in the Historical Society of Pennsylvania, Philadelphia

PHILADELPHIA REBUFFS ITS TEA-SHIP

THE tea-ship met short shrift wherever it appeared. At Philadelphia precautions had early been taken to forestall any attempt to land the cargo. On Christmas Day came news that the ship *Polly*, was off Chester, down the river. Five thousand in town meeting then counseled together. At their persuasion the Company agent resigned his office, and the captain agreed to sail back to London the very next day. No whiff of tea reached land; and again the colonists exulted in their strength to oppose the pretentions of a willful Government.

164 From a mural painting *Burning of the Peggy Stewart*, by C. Y. Turner (1850–1918) in the Courthouse, Baltimore

A LOCAL TEA MERCHANT IS FORCED TO BURN HIS SHIP

ANNAPOLIS also had its tea party. On October 14, 1774, the *Peggy Stewart* arrived with a cargo of tea and indentured servants. Anthony Stewart, local merchant and owner, paid the duty on the tea in order that he might get the servants ashore. The town's ire was raised thereby; and though Stewart made public announcement that he would burn the tea upon its unloading, a minority of the inhabitants, led by Charles Warfield, found this unsatisfactory. The merchant finally, with his own hands, fired the ship with its tea.

THE TEA-SHIPS HASTEN AWAY FROM NEW YORK

THE Company's tea-ships destined for New York were delayed by winds. The Sons of Liberty became impatient to show their spirit. When a vessel, not belonging to the East India Company, happened along with eighteen cases of tea aboard, the Massachusetts precedent, costume and all, was followed. By the time the vessels of the company appeared, the course of procedure was so well understood that little confusion arose. Asking humble permission to provision his ship, the captain tarried no longer than that process required before turning back to London. In Charleston the tea was actually landed, and was kept in storage until, years later, it was sold for the benefit of the troops. Thus, up and down the coast, the colonists were learning that forcible resistance to the commands of Parliament was possible, and that such methods were at least as likely to gain the contended point for America as the use of humble petition and memorial.

To the Public.

THE long expected TEA SHIP arrived laſt night at Sandy-Hook, but the pilot would not bring up the Captain till the ſenſe of the city was known. The committee were immediately informed of her arrival, and that the Captain ſolicits for liberty to come up to provide neceſſaries for his return. The ſhip to remain at Sandy-Hook. The committee conceiving it to be the ſenſe of the city that he ſhould have ſuch liberty, ſignified it to the Gentleman who is to ſupply him with proviſions, and other neceſſaries. Advice of this was immediately diſpatched to the Captain; and whenever he comes up, care will be taken that he does not enter at the cuſtom-houſe, and that no time be loſt in diſpatching him.

New-York, April 19, 1774.

165 From a facsimile of an original New York handbill, Apr. 19, 1774, in the Bancker Collection catalogue, 1898

THE COLONIES BEGIN COÖPERATIVE RESISTANCE

THE tea parties illustrated the effectiveness of the control exercised by a *de facto* government. That machinery, fostered by Samuel Adams, was now strengthened under the impetus of these happenings. For instance, we find the people of Newport affirming the principles upon which colonial resistance rested and stressing the desirability of united colonial action "for the preservation of the general and particular rights and privileges of North America." It is no longer "Rhode Island" or "Massachusetts Bay," but "North America." In March, Adams wrote to Franklin, now the agent of Massachusetts in London: "It will be in vain for any to expect that the people of this country will now be contented with a partial and temporary relief; or that they will be amused by Court promises, while they see not the least relaxation of grievances. By means of a brisk correspondence among the several towns of this Province, they have wonderfully animated and enlightened each other. They are united in sentiment, and their opposition to unconstitutional measures of Government is become systematical. Colony begins to communicate freely with colony. There is a common affection among them; and shortly the whole Continent will be as united in sentiment and in measures of opposition to tyranny, as the inhabitants of this province." Such was the hope of the radicals. And no one was a better judge than Adams himself; for he was on intimate terms with all classes of the people, from the denizens of the taverns to the ministers of the gospel.

Colony of RHODE-ISLAND, &c.

At a Town-Meeting held at NEWPORT, the 12th Day of January, 1774, HENRY WARD, Eſq; MODERATOR.

WHEREAS the Eaſt-India Company, notwithſtanding the reſolutions of the Americans not to import TEA while it remains ſubject to the payment of a DUTY, in America, have attempted to force large quantities thereof into ſome of our ſiſter colonies, without their conſent, in order to be ſold, in this country, on their account, and riſque: And whereas they may attempt to introduce it into this colony: We, the inhabitants of this town, legally convened, in town-meeting, do *firmly reſolve*,

1ſt. That the diſpoſal of their own property is the inherent right of freemen; that there can be no property in that which another can, of right, take from us, without our conſent; that the claim of Parliament to tax America, is, in other words, a claim of right to levy contributions on us at pleaſure.

2. That the duty impoſed, by parliament, upon Tea, landed in America, is a tax on the Americans, or levying contributions on them without their conſent.

3. That the expreſs purpoſe for which the tax is levied on the Americans, namely, for the ſupport of government, adminiſtration of juſtice, and defence of his Majeſty's dominions, in America, has a direct tendency to render aſſemblies uſeleſs; and to introduce arbitrary government and SLAVERY.

4. That a virtuous and ſteady oppoſition to this miniſterial plan of governing America, is abſolutely neceſſary to preſerve even the ſhadow of Liberty; and is a duty which every freeman in America owes to his country, to himſelf, and to his poſterity.

5. That the reſolutions lately entered into by the Eaſt-India Company, to ſend out their tea to America, ſubject to the payment of DUTIES, on its being landed here, is an open attempt to inforce this miniſterial plan, and a violent attack upon the liberties of America.

6. That it is the duty of every American to oppoſe this attempt.

7. That whoever ſhall, directly or indirectly, countenance this attempt, or in any wiſe aid, or abet, in unloading, receiving, or vending the tea ſent, or to be ſent out by the Eaſt India Company, or by any other perſon, while it remains ſubject to the payment of a duty here, is an enemy to his country.

8. That Col. Joſeph Wanton, jun. Henry Ward, John Mawdſley, John Collins, and William Ellery, Eſquires, or the major part of them, be appointed a committee for this town, to correſpond with all other committees, appointed by any other towns in this colony, or the towns in any of the other colonies; which committee, or the major part of them, ſhall, upon information or ſuſpicion of any tea being imported into this town, ſubject to a duty, immediately wait on the maſter of the veſſel who ſhall bring the ſame, or the merchant to whom it ſhall belong, requeſting that it may not be landed, and immediately call a town-meeting, to conſider what ſteps to take; and that ſaid committee inquire into the late riſe of tea, and uſe their utmoſt influence to bring it down to the uſual price as it was at a ſhort time paſt.

9. RESOLVED, That this meeting will heartily join with, and, to the utmoſt of our power, ſtand by and ſupport our ſiſter colonies, in all laudable meaſures, for the preſervation of the general and particular rights and privileges of North America.

VOTED, That the foregoing RESOLVES be publiſhed in the NEWPORT MERCURY; and that the committee of correſpondence tranſmit copies of them to the ſeveral towns in this colony, with a requeſt to them to come into ſimilar reſolutions, if they ſhall think proper. A true copy:

Witneſs

WM. CODDINGTON, Town Clerk.

It was alſo voted, at ſaid meeting, that the printer of the Newport Mercury, ſhould be requeſted to acquaint the public, in his next paper, that the paragraph inſerted laſt Monday, containing an intimation, that a letter of importance to the liberties of America had been ſecreted, was founded upon miſtake, and that that matter hath been cleared up, entirely to the ſatisfaction of the town.

⁂ Every one of the above VOTES paſſed without a ſingle diſſentient, except that to inquire into the riſe of TEA, againſt which there were but about 3 or 4 hands up.——Notwithſtanding the weather was extremely cold, there never was ſo full a town-meeting here, as the above, except ſometimes in the higheſt ſtruggle of parties, for repreſentatives, &c.

Printed by SOLOMON SOUTHWICK.

166 Resolves of a Newport, R. I., town meeting, Jan. 12, 1774, urging action against the tea duty, from the copy in the New York Public Library

167 From a cartoon published in Paris, 1774, drawn and engraved by François Godefroy (1729–88)

A BOSTON MOB MALTREATS A CUSTOMS OFFICER

The events of December, 1773, had aroused a zeal that did not slowly cool. On New Year's Eve a half-chest of tea was burned on the Common. On the 20th, three barrels of Bohea suffered immolation to the cause. On the 25th, John Malcolm, a customs officer who had made indiscreet remarks concerning English retribution, was taken from his house, tarred and feathered, and paraded through the public streets.

168 From an English cartoon *Bostonians Paying the Exciseman*, London, 1774, original in the Library of Congress, Washington

LONDON MOCKS COLONIAL VIOLENCE

Poor John Malcolm became the subject of many cartoons, both in America and in England. This one, and the one that follows, pictures the state of public feeling in the home country. It portrays the treatment meted out to the unfortunate exciseman by the homespun ruffian-patriots of Massachusetts. In addition to the indignity of a coat of tar and feathers, he appears to have been forced by the mob to drink of the obnoxious tea. In the background are shown the customary Liberty Tree and the tea-ships, ice-bound in the harbor. Many such prints, ridiculing the matters at issue between the Government and the colonies, were published in London just prior to the Revolution, for this was preëminently the age of political satire, both in text and picture, and the English excelled in the arts of irony and sarcasm. So appreciated was the "American custom" at this time, that a "tarring and feathering" scene was introduced into a popular pantomime at the Theatre Royal, Covent Garden, and became one of the features of the performance.

REBELLION IN AMERICA IS CLASSED WITH RADICALISM IN ENGLAND

The title of a companion to the preceding cartoon was evidently suggested by the report that Malcolm was to become a King's pensioner. (In those days, "Macarony" was a term of contempt and derision.) The scaffold, under which the Sons of Liberty kept Malcolm for many hours on a winter's night, is here shown in place of the Liberty Tree. The number "45" had to do with John Wilkes, at that time Lord Mayor of London. Some years before, the forty-fifth issue of his political paper, *The North Briton* — the title was a travesty on Lord Bute — got him into trouble with the King. Jailed, Wilkes at once became a popular idol, and represented, in England, the opposition to royal prerogative practised in America by the Sons of Liberty. Thus were interwoven the strands of rebellion at home and in the colonies.

169 From a cartoon *A New Method of Macarony Making*, in *The Boston Port Bill as Pictured by a Contemporary London Cartoonist*, 1774, by R. T. H. Halsey, published by the Grolier Club, New York, 1904

BRITISH ACTS FORCE MERCHANTS TO TAKE A RADICAL STAND

THE people of Boston had defied the Government. And the fact was not lost upon the Government. Furthermore, not only the Ministry, but all elements in Great Britain, resented this colonial arrogance. Even such sturdy friends of America as Chatham and Barré felt that she had gone too far. To everyone her attitude seemed a menace to English welfare. The moment was opportune for the merchant-princes of England to renew their arguments for a strong stand by the Government. What the Government did not realize was that the King's policy toward the East India Company, just as in the case of the Stamp Act and that of the Townshend Act, had forced the powerful and conservative merchants of the colonies to make common cause with the radicals, a situation fraught with danger for the British.

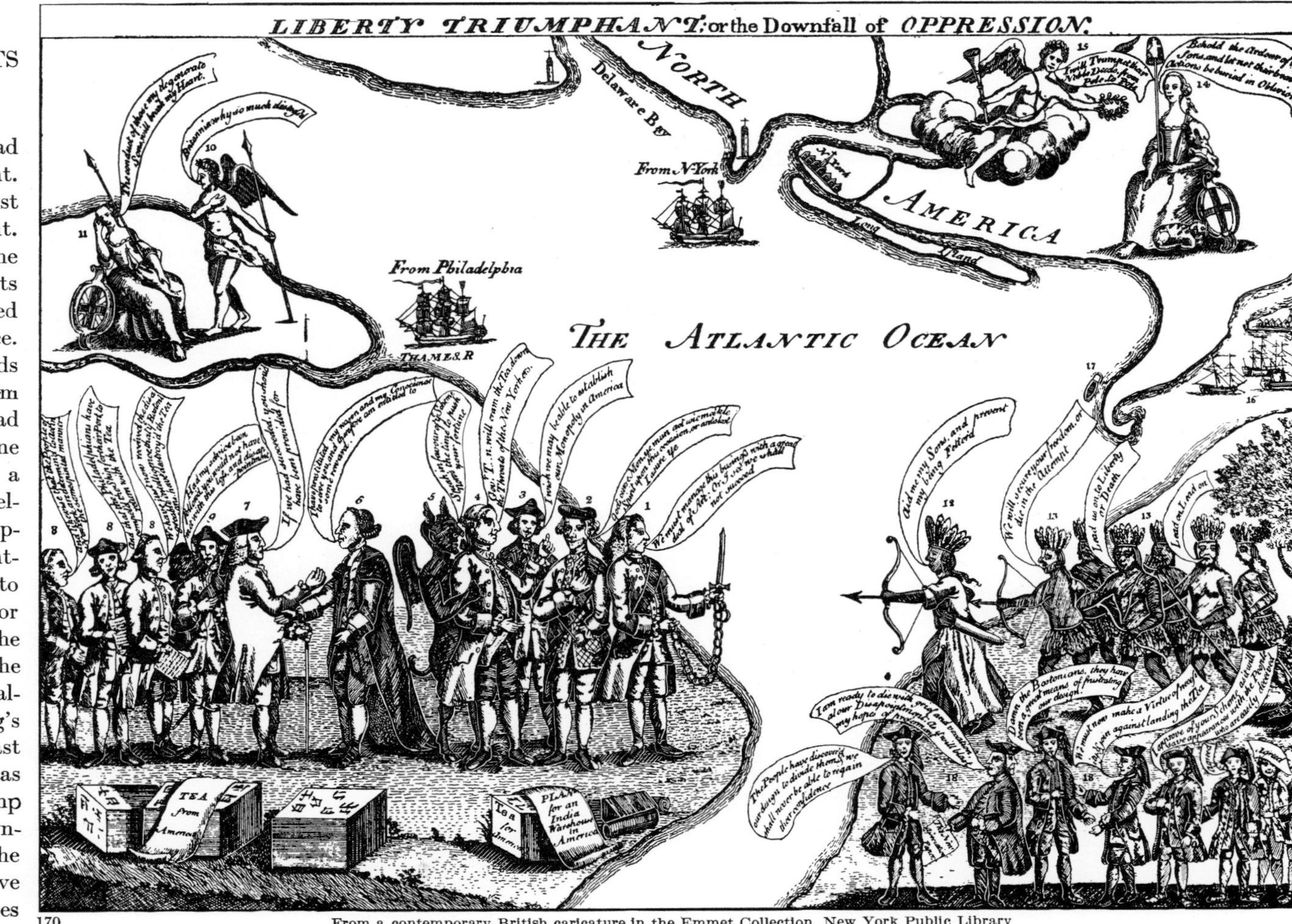

170

From a contemporary British caricature in the Emmet Collection, New York Public Library

1 Lord N—th
2 Lord B—te
3 An East India Director
4 The infamous K—g
5 Belzebub, the Prince of Devils whispering to K—g
6 The writer of the Papers (signed Poplicola) in favor of the Tea
7 The Chairman of the India Company
8 A Group of India Directors
9 The Patriotic Duke of Richmond
10 The Genius of Britain
11 Britannia
12 America represented by a woman
13 The Sons of Liberty represented by the Natives of America, in their savage garb
14 The Goddess of Liberty addressing herself to Fame and pointing to her Sons
15 Fame
16 A view of the Tea Ships in the Harbour of Boston
17 Capt. Loring's Vessel with Tea, shipwreck'd on Cape Cod
18 A group of Disappointed Americans, who were for landing the Tea: In hopes of sharing in the Plunder of their Country

171 From a British caricature *Lord N—h in a Fix*, in possession of the publishers

THE BRITISH MINISTRY CAN SUGGEST NO SOLUTION

Lord North was in a fix. Though he was intelligent enough to perceive the issue, the indecisiveness he often showed in times of crisis again displayed itself. For a situation such as this his natural amiability was no solvent. America was touchy; England was indignant. On the seventh of March, 1774, Parliament listened to a message from the Crown on the proceedings in Boston. "Nothing," said North, "can be done to reëstablish peace without additional powers from Parliament." Yet he submitted no plan of action.

LORD NORTH ADOPTS A POLICY OF PRESSURE

But strong pressure was at work upon him. The press was vehemently demanding punishment. The King was using every artifice to bolster North's courage. The apparent acquiescence of America's friends promised an easy road. So, on March 14, he moved (though, says Burke, with noticeable languor) the first of a series of penal measures, aimed at Boston. This was the Boston Port Bill. Meeting practically no opposition, it received the royal assent on the 31st. Boston harbor was, after June first, to be closed to all commerce. Marblehead was to become the port of entry, Salem the seat of government. This was to continue until the East India Company and all others should be indemnified for their losses, and until the King should be satisfied that in future Boston would be obedient. It became known that the army and the fleet would be used to enforce the Act.

172 From a cartoon in the *Oxford Magazine*, London, Apr. 1774

(1047)

ANNO DECIMO QUARTO

Georgii III. Regis.

C A P. XLV.

An Act for the better regulating the Government of the Province of the *Massachuset's Bay*, in *New England*.

WHEREAS by Letters Patent under the Great Seal of England, made in the Third Year of the Reign of Their late Majesties King William and Queen Mary, for uniting, erecting, and incorporating, the several Colonies, Territories, and Tracts of Land therein mentioned, into One real Province, by the Name of Their Majesties Province of the *Massachuset's Bay*, in *New England*; whereby it was, amongst other Things, ordained and established, That the Governor of the said Province should, from thenceforth, be appointed and commissionated by Their Majesties, Their Heirs and Successors: It was, however, granted and ordained, That, from the Expiration of the Term for and during which the Eight and twenty Persons named in the said Letters Patent were appointed to be the first Counsellors or Assistants to the Governor of the said Province for the Time being, the aforesaid

Preamble, reciting Letters Patent of 3 *Gul. & Mariæ.*

4 12 I 2

173 From a copy of the *Administration of Justice Act*, 1774, in the New York Public Library

MORE ROYAL ACTS AIM TO REDUCE THE COLONIES

Four more Acts of similar tenor followed in rapid succession. One provided that where a person in Massachusetts was accused of "murther or other capital crime," and officials thought a fair trial in the courts unlikely, the case could be transferred to a court in another colony or to one in England. A second revived the law of 1665 which permitted the quartering of troops; and General Gage succeeded Hutchinson as civil Governor of Massachusetts. Most important was the Massachusetts Government Act (No. 173). In violation of her royal charter, the Council of Massachusetts was to be appointed by the Crown; all minor executive and judicial offices were to be filled by appointment; and town meetings were severely restricted. The Quebec Act organized the territory acquired in 1763 from France into the Province of Quebec, with a Government centralized under the Crown. The Act also sanctioned the Catholic religion for this large domain, many portions of which had long been claimed by Virginia, New York, Connecticut, and Massachusetts. This Act, destined to become the corner stone of the relations between the French and English in Canada, gave grave offence, because of some of its provisions, to the English colonists in America.

The SPEECH of the Right Honourable the Earl of CHATHAM, in the Houſe of LORDS, upon reading the Amendments in the QUEBEC BILL, on Friday, the 17th June, 1774. Together with his Lordſhip's SPEECH, on the Third Reading, in the Houſe of Lords, of the Bill for PROVIDING WITH QUARTERS, the Officers and Troops in AMERICA.

MOST ILLUSTRIOUS LORDS,

THE unfavourable ſtate of health, under which I have long laboured, could not prevent me from laying before your Lordſhips my thoughts on the Bill now before you; and on the American affairs in general.

If we take a tranſient view of thoſe motives which induced the anceſtors of our fellow-ſubjects, in America, to leave their native country to encounter the innumerable difficulties of the unexplored regions of the weſtern world, our aſtoniſhment at the preſent conduct of their deſcendants will naturally ſubſide. There was no corner of the world into which men of their free and enterprizing turn would not fly, with alacrity, rather than ſubmit to the ſlaviſh and tyrannical principles which prevailed, at that period, in their native country. And ſhall we wonder, my Lords, if the deſcendants of ſuch illuſtrious characters ſpurn, with contempt, the hand of unconſtitutional power, that would ſnatch from them ſuch dear bought privileges as they now contend for? Had the Britiſh colonies been planted by any other kingdoms than our own, the inhabitants would have carried with them the chains of ſlavery, and the ſpirit of deſpotiſm; but as they are, they ought to be remembered as great inſtances to inſtruct the world, to what a ſtretch of liberty mankind will naturally attain, when they are left to the free exerciſe of themſelves. And, my Lords, notwithſtanding my intention to give my hearty negative to the queſtion now before you, I cannot help condemning, in the ſevereſt manner, the late turbulent and unwarrantable conduct of the Americans in general, and the riots in Boſton, in particular. But, my Lords, the mode which has been purſued to bring them back to a ſenſe of their duty to the parent ſtate, has been ſo diametrically oppoſite to the fundamental principles of ſound policy, that individuals, poſſeſs'd of common underſtanding, muſt be aſtoniſhed at ſuch proceedings. By blocking up the harbour of Boſton, you have involved the innocent Trader in the ſame puniſhment with the guilty Profligates who deſtroyed your merchandize; and inſtead of making a well-concerted effort to ſecure the Real offenders, you clap a naval and military extinguiſher over their harbour; and puniſh the ſin of a few lawleſs Raparees, and their abettors, upon the whole body of the inhabitants.

My Lords, this country is little obliged to the Framers and Promoters of this Tea-tax; the Americans had almoſt forgot, in their exceſs of gratitude for the repeal of the Stamp act, any intereſt but that of the Mother Country; there ſeemed an emulation among the different provinces, who ſhould be moſt dutiful and forward in their expreſſions of loyalty to their Royal Benefactor; as you will readily perceive by the following extract of a letter from governor Bernard to a noble Lord then in office.

"The Houſe of Repreſentatives, (ſays "he) from the time of opening the ſeſſion "to this day, has ſhewn a diſpoſition to "avoid all diſputes with me; every thing "having paſſed with as much good humour "as I could deſire. They have acted, in "all things, with temper and moderation; "they have avoided ſome ſubjects of diſ"pute, and have laid a foundation for re"moving ſome cauſes of former alterca"tion."

This, my Lords, was the temper of the Americans; and would have continued ſo, had it not been interrupted by your fruitleſs endeavours to tax them without their conſent; but the moment they perceived your intention was renewed to tax them, through the ſides of the Eaſt India Company, their reſentment got the aſcendant of their duty, and hurried them into actions contrary to all laws of policy, civilization, and humanity, which, in their cooler hours, they would have thought on with horror; for I ſeriouſly believe, the deſtroying of the Tea was much more the effect of deſpair, than that of deſign.

But, my Lords, from the complexion of the whole of the proceedings, I am apt to think, that Adminiſtration has purpoſely irritated them into thoſe late violent acts for which they now ſo ſeverely ſmart; purpoſely to be revenged on them for the victory they gained by the repeal of the Stamp-act, a meaſure to which they ſeemingly acquieſced, but at the bottom, they were its real enemies. For what other motive could induce them to dreſs Taxation, that father of American ſedition, in the robes of an Eaſt India director, but to break in upon that mutual peace and harmony which then ſo happily ſubſiſted between them and the Mother-country? My Lords, I am an old man, and will adviſe the noble Lords now in office, to adopt a more gentle mode of governing America; for the day is not far diſtant, when America may vie with theie kingdoms, not only in arms, but in arts alſo. It is an eſtabliſhed fact that the principal towns in America are learned and polite, and underſtand the conſtitution of the Britiſh empire as well as the noble Lords who guide the ſprings of government; and conſequently, they will have a watchful eye over their liberties, to prevent the leaſt encroachment of an Arbitrary Adminiſtration on their hereditary rights and privileges.

This obſervation is ſo recently exemplified in an excellent pamphlet which comes from the pen of an American gentleman*, that I ſhall take the liberty of reading to your Lordſhips his thoughts on the competency of the Britiſh Parliament to tax America, which in my opinion, ſets that intereſting matter in the cleareſt point of view.

"The high court of Parliament, (ſays "he) is the ſupreme legiſlative power over "the whole empire; in all free ſtates the "conſtitution is fixed; and as the ſupreme "legiſlative derives its power and authority "from the conſtitution, it cannot overleap "the bounds of it, without deſtroying its "own foundation; for the conſtitution "aſcertains and limits both ſovereignty and "allegiance: And therefore his Majeſty's "American ſubjects, who acknowledge "themſelves bound by the ties of allegiance, "have an equitable claim to the full enjoy"ment of the fundamental rules of the "Engliſh conſtitution; that it is an eſſen"tial unalterable right in nature, ingrafted "into the Britiſh conſtitution as a funda"mental law, and ever held ſacred and ir"revocable by the ſubjects within the "realm; and that what a man has honeſtly "acquired, is abſolutely his own; which "he may freely give, but which cannot be "taken from him without his conſent."

* See Dr. Franklin's ſtate of the conteſt between Great Britain and America. Publiſhed by W. Bingley.

This, my Lords, though no new doctrine, has been always my received and unalterable opinion; and I will carry it to my grave, *that this country had no right, under Heaven, to tax America.* It is contrary to all the principles of juſtice and civil policy, which neither the exigencies of the ſtate, or even the acquieſcence in the taxes, could juſtify upon any occaſion whatſoever. Such proceedings will never meet with their wiſhed for ſucceſs; and inſtead of adding to their miſeries, as the Bill now before you moſt undoubtedly does, adopt ſome lenient meaſures, which may lure them to their duty; proceed like a kind and affectionate parent over a child whom he tenderly loves; and, inſtead of thoſe harſh and ſevere proceedings, paſs an amneſty on all their youthful errors; claſp them once more in your fond and affectionate arms; and I will venture to affirm, you will find them children worthy of their ſire. But, ſhould their turbulence exiſt after your proffered terms of forgiveneſs which I hope, and expect this Houſe will immediately adopt, I will be among the foremoſt of this illuſtrious aſſembly to move for ſuch meaſures as will effectually prevent a future relapſe, and make them feel what it is to provoke a fond and forgiving parent! A parent, my Lords, whoſe welfare has ever been my greateſt and moſt pleaſing conſolation. This declaration may ſeem unneceſſary, but I will venture to declare, the period is not far diſtant, when ſhe will want the aſſiſtance of her moſt diſtant friends; but ſhould the all diſpoſing hand of Providence prevent me from affording her my poor aſſiſtance, my prayers ſhall be ever for her welfare.

Length of days be in her right hand, and in her left riches and honour; may her ways be ways of pleaſantneſs, and all her paths be peace.

ON Friday the 17th of June, the order of the day was read in the Houſe of Peers for the amendments made in the Quebec bill to be taken into conſideration: The ſame were accordingly read by the clerk; and the queſtion being put, for the Houſe to agree to the amendments, Lord Chatham roſe up, and entered fully into the ſubject of the bill. He ſaid, "It would involve a great country in a thouſand difficulties, and in the worſt of deſpotiſm, and put the whole people under arbitrary power: That it was a moſt cruel, odious, and oppreſſive meaſure, tearing up juſtice and every good principle by the roots: That by aboliſhing the *trial by jury*, he ſuppoſed the framers of the bill thought that mode of proceeding, together with the habeas corpus, mere moonſhine; whilſt every true Engliſhman was ready to lay down his life, ſooner than loſe thoſe two bulwarks of his perſonal ſecurity and property. The merely ſuppoſing, that the Canadians would not be able to feel the good effects of law and freedom, becauſe they had been uſed to arbitrary power, was an idea as ridiculous as falſe. The bill eſta-

174 Chatham's Speech in The House of Lords, June 17, 1774, from a London broadside in the New York Public Library

THE EARL OF CHATHAM

THESE coercive measures did not pass without some voiced opposition. Burke in one House, and Chatham in the other, counseled moderation. "I trust," wrote Chatham, on the Christmas Eve of 1774, "that it will be found impossible for freemen in England to wish to see three millions of Englishmen slaves in America." But the King's majority was not to be hindered by argument. Parliament was irritated by Massachusetts; and the royal advisers who since 1766 had been waiting their chance now found it.

GENTLEMEN,

THE evils which we have long foreſeen are now come upon this town and province, the long meditated ſtroke is now given to the civil liberty of this country? How long we may be allowed the enjoyment of our religious liberty is a queſtion of infinite moment. Religion can never be retained in it's purity where tyranny has uſurped the place of reaſon and juſtice. The bill for blocking up the harbour of Boſton is replete with injuſtice and cruelty, thouſands of innocent men, beſides women and infants, are by it reduced to indegence and diſtreſs; and though we in this town more immediately feel this diſtreſs, yet our brethren in the other towns of this province, and all the other colonies, muſt ſee that we ſuffer in the common cauſe, and that *they* themſelves muſt ſoon realize the ſufferings under which *we* now labour, if no means are diſcovered for our relief. But if any ſhould think that this town alone is to groan under the weight of arbitrary power, we are now furniſhed by our enemies with a ſtill more glaring evidence of a fixed plan of the Britiſh adminiſtration to bring the whole continent into the moſt humiliating bondage. A bill has been brought into parliament apparently for the purpoſe of taking away our charter rights, wherein it is to be enacted that the counſellors ſhall be appointed by mandamus from the king, that our juſtices of the ſuperior court, juſtices of our inferior courts, and juſtices of the peace, ſhall be all appointed by the governor alone, without the advice of the council, and all of them, excepting the juſtices of the ſuperior court be removeable by him at his pleaſure, that our juries ſhall not be choſen by the freeholders, as they heretofore have been, but by the ſheriff of the county, and that this ſheriff ſhall not be appointed by the governor and council as heretofore, but by the governor alone, ſo that our lives and properties are to be decided upon by judges appointed by the governor alone, and by juries choſen by a ſheriff who muſt be entirely under the influence of the governor as he is appointed by him, and is removeable by him alone, whenever he ſhall diſcover a reluctance to conform to the will of the governor. Surely if we ſuffer theſe things we are the moſt abject ſlaves. If a favorite of a perverſe governor ſhould pretend a title to our lands, or any other part of our property, we need not doubt but a very ſmall degree of evidence in ſupport of the claim, would be judged ſufficient, eſpecially as the bill makes proviſion, that upon the motion of either of the parties, it ſhall be lawful to try the cauſe in another county than that in which the action was brought, ſo that a man is to be carried into a diſtant part of the province, inſtead of having his cauſe tried in his own county, and to be tried by ſtrangers with whom the good or bad characters of the parties or of the witneſſes can have no weight, contrary to the very ſpirit of magna charta. Of what value are our lands or eſtates to us, if ſuch an odious government ſhould be eſtabliſhed among us? Can we look with pleaſure on the inheritance left by our anceſtors, or on the fields cultivated by *our* induſtry? When we reflect that all our labours have made them only a more inviting prey to our enemies, will not the vine-yard of Naboth be ever in *our* minds? But left any thing ſhould be wanting to compleat our miſery, another bill is alſo prepared, which enables the governor to ſave any perſon or perſons, who, under the pretext of ſupporting or carrying into execution the late or other acts of the Britiſh parliament, ſhall murder and deſtroy the people of this country, from being tried in this province (even if they ſhould be indicted by ſuch grand jurors as ſhall be choſen by the ſheriff of the county in the ſame manner that we have mentioned that petty jurors are to be returned) but the perſon indicted with ſuck witneſſes as he and the proſecutor (which will be the crown) ſhall judge proper; ſhall be ſent to either of the other colonies, or even to Great Britain, to be tried for murdering the inhabitants of the Maſſachuſetts-Bay. And proviſion is alſo made to prevent our meeting together in our corporate capacity as a town, unleſs it be once in the mouth of March for the election of the town officers, except the matter or buſineſs of the meeting is laid before the governor, and his leave in writing is obtained for a meeting of the town.

There is but one way that we can conceive of, to prevent what is to be deprecated by all good men, and ought by all poſſible means to be prevented, *viz*, The horrors that muſt follow an open rupture between Great Britain and her colonies; or on our part, a ſubjection to abſolute ſlavery: And that is by affecting the trade and intereſt of Great Britain, ſo deeply as ſhall induce her to withdraw her oppreſſive hand. There can be no doubt of our ſucceeding to the utmoſt of our wiſhes if we univerſally come into a ſolemn league, not to import goods from Great Britain, and not to buy any goods that ſhall hereafter be imported from thence, until our grievances ſhall be redreſſed. To theſe, or even to the leaſt of theſe ſhameful impoſitions, we truſt in God, our countrymen never will ſubmit.

We have received ſuch aſſurances from our brethren in every part of the province of their readineſs to adopt ſuch meaſures as may be likely to ſave our country, that we have not the leaſt doubt of an almoſt univerſal agreement for this purpoſe; in confidence of this, we have drawn up a form of a covenant to be ſubſcribed by all adult perſons of both ſexes; which we have ſent to every town in the province, and that we might not give our enemies time to counteract us, we have endeavoured that every town ſhould be furniſhed with ſuch a copy on or before the fourteenth day of this month, and we earneſtly deſire that you would uſe your utmoſt endeavours that the ſubſcription paper may be filled up as ſoon as poſſible, that ſo they who are in expectation of overthrowing our liberties may be diſcouraged from proſecuting their wicked deſigns; as we look upon this the laſt and only method of preſerving our land from ſlavery without drenching it in blood, may God proſper every undertaking which tends to the ſalvation of his people. We are, &c.

BOSTON, JUNE 8, 1774.

Signed by order and in behalf of the Committee of Correſpondence for Boſton.

William Cooper Clerk

175 From the Boston Circular Letter of June 8, 1774, urging complete suspension of trade with Great Britain; in the New York Public Library

BOSTON'S REACTION TO THE INTOLERABLE ACTS

A COPY of the Port Bill reached Boston on May 10. Action was electric. The Act was printed with deep bands of mourning and burnt by the common hangman. The committee of correspondence, led by Samuel Adams, with representatives of eight neighboring towns present, sent a circular to like committees in all the colonies, recommending suspension of trade with Great Britain till the Act should be repealed. On the 13th, a town meeting dispatched a similar appeal "to all the sister colonies, promising to suffer for America with fortitude, but confessing that singly they must find their trial too severe." Thus Boston, rejecting revolution, founded its faith on the tried policy of non-importation, backed by united colonial action.

ENGLISH LIBERALS DISAPPROVE THE INTOLERABLE ACTS

THIS cartoon well shows how American affairs were regarded in England, not as an isolated matter, but as part and parcel of a corrupt system. Parliament has been dissolved; the members are going home. The coachman is remarking, "I will not overset Ye, if Ye don't overset Yourselves." A roistering passenger observes, "May the Patriots ride uppermost," while a beggar in the street cries, "You have starved me and my children." The harsh treatment meted out to America by the "Intolerable Acts" was to the English liberal merely another example of incompetent, unrepresentative British Government. Placemen, inclosures, restrictions upon freedom of the press (Wilkes) were in England fully as devastating as the Boston Port Bill.

176 From a cartoon in the *London Magazine*, Vol. XLIII, Oct. 1774

177 From an engraving by Paul Revere in *The Royal American Magazine*, Boston, June 1774, after the caricature in the *London Magazine*, April 1774

THE PORT OF BOSTON IS CLOSED TO COMMERCE

ON the same day General Gage entered the harbor, bringing additional troops to enforce the Boston Port Bill. Promptly on June 1, the port was closed by a cordon of vessels. The official records were removed to Salem. Soldiery and artillery were landed, cannon mounted, fortifications erected between Boston and the mainland. The cartoon, by Paul Revere, shows Lord North, the Boston Port Bill protruding from his pocket, pouring scalding tea down the throat of prostrate America; Lord Mansfield, with his lawyer's precedents, pinions her arms; Britannia stands aside in tears; while France and Spain are avaricious spectators.

THOMAS JEFFERSON SUMS UP AMERICAN RIGHTS

FROM Maine to Georgia came responses to the appeal of Massachusetts. Pamphlets arguing the cause of Massachusetts and the colonies generally flooded the country. One of the ablest was penned by a man who was soon to achieve an international reputation. Early in the summer of 1774 appeared Thomas Jefferson's *A Summary View of the Rights of British America.* This carried to a new stage the arguments which were later to justify political separation from the home country. In all of the provinces, and in England as well, the name of Jefferson soon became familiar as that of a man ardent in opposing governmental tyranny.

A

SUMMARY VIEW

OF THE

RIGHTS

OF

BRITISH AMERICA,

Set forth in some

RESOLUTIONS

INTENDED FOR

The INSPECTION of the present DELEGATES of the People of VIRGINIA, now in CONVENTION.

It is the indispensable duty of the supreme magistrate to consider himself as acting for the whole community, and obliged to support its dignity, and assign to the people, with justice, their various rights, as he would be faithful to the great trust reposed in him.

CICERO'S OF. B. C.

By a NATIVE, and Member of the House of Burgesses.

WILLIAMSBURG, Printed by CLEMENTINA RIND.

LONDON,

Re-printed for G. KEARSLY, at No. 46, near Serjeants Inn, in Fleet Street, 1774.

178 Title-page of a copy of the first London issue in the New York Public Library

179 From a cartoon *The Bostonians in Distress*, published in London, 1774, reprinted by the Grolier Club, New York, 1904

BOSTON RECEIVES HELP FROM SISTER COLONIES

Expressions of sympathy with Boston took also more substantial form. As the blockade of the port drew near, supplies of foodstuffs poured into the town. And after the blockade became operative and starvation faced the population — for commerce had been the mainstay — such voluntary contributions continued. Windham, Connecticut, sent a flock of sheep; South Carolina two hundred barrels of rice; money came from Maryland, New York, Montreal, even London. George Washington's name heads a subscription list circulated in Fairfax County, Virginia. In the picture the cartoonist has depicted men of Boston being given the punishment in America meted out to slaves convicted of capital offenses, who, thus imprisoned, were left to starve as an example to their fellows in bondage. This parallel was a forcible one, as the petitions of the Americans had long said that, bereft of their rights, their condition would be that of slavery. The cannon, with muzzles pointed toward the "Liberty Tree," represent the "8 pieces of ordnance" which were parked upon the Common. The background shows royal troops landing as reinforcements. In the distance are the "four or five frigates" which Lord North had predicted would be sufficient to enforce the Boston Port Bill. Marblehead men are seen giving food to the prisoners. A shallop is laden with baskets of codfish, in answer to Boston's cry for assistance. Sermons preached by Boston clergy probably suggested the long-handled contribution boxes. This print was exceedingly popular in England.

BOSTON PRACTICES INDEPENDENT GOVERNMENT

Despite such aid, food and fuel became scarce; unemployment increased. Then was shown the vigor and flexibility of Sam Adams' machinery. Disregarding the official Government installed by the Acts of 1774, Boston proceeded to govern herself through the Committee of Correspondence and her town meeting. Through these agencies means were found to employ the poor and needy. Street improvements were undertaken; leather was found for the shoemakers, iron for the blacksmith. Voluntary levies were made upon the citizenry, and these were paid while taxes remained uncollected. In short, the new Acts were inoperative beyond the lines of the British soldiers.

VOTES and PROCEEDINGS of
the Town of
B O S T O N,
JUNE 17, 1774.

AT a legal and very full meeting of the freeholders and other inhabitants of the town of Boſton, *by adjournment at* Faneuil-hall, *June* 17, 1774.

The Hon. JOHN ADAMS, Esq; Moderator.

UPON a motion made, the town again entered into the conſideration of that article in the warrant, Viz, "To conſider and determine what meaſures are proper to be taken upon the preſent exigency of our public affairs, more eſpecially relative to the late edict of a Britiſh parliament for blocking up the harbour of Boſton, and annihilating the trade of this town," and after very ſerious debates thereon,

Voted, (With only one diſſentient) That the committee of correſpondence be enjoined forthwith to write to all the other colonies, acquainting them that we are not idle, that we are deliberating upon the ſteps to be taken on the preſent exigencies of our public affairs; that our brethren the landed intereſt of this province, with an unexampled ſpirit and unanimity, are entering into a non-conſumption agrement; and that we are waiting with anxious expectation for the reſult of a continental congreſs, whoſe meeting we impatiently deſire, in whoſe wiſdom and firmneſs we can confide, and in whoſe determinations we ſhall chearfully acquieſce.

Agreable to order, the committee of correſpondence laid before the town ſuch letters, as they had received in anſwer to the circular letters, wrote by them to the ſeveral colonies and alſo the ſea port towns in this province ſince the reception of the Boſton port bill; and the ſame being publicly read,

Voted, unanimouſly, That our warmeſt thanks be tranſmitted to our brethren on the continent, for that humanity, ſympathy and affection with which they have been inſpired, and which they have expreſſed towards this diſtreſſed town at this important ſeaſon.

Voted, unanimouſly, That the thanks of this town be, and hereby are, given to the committee of correſpondence, for their faithfulneſs, in the diſcharge of their truſt, and that they be deſired to continue their vigilance and activity in that ſervice.

Whereas the Overſeers of the poor in the town of Boſton are a body politic, by law conſtituted for the reception and diſtribution of all charitable donations for the uſe of the poor of ſaid town,

Voted, That all grants and donations to this town and the poor thereof at this diſtreſſing ſeaſon, be paid and delivered into the hands of ſaid Overſeers, and by them appropriated and diſtributed in concert with the committee lately appointed by this town for the conſideration of ways and means of employing the poor.

Voted, That the town clerk be directed to publiſh the proceedings of this meeting in the ſeveral news papers.

The meeting was then adjourned to Monday the 27th of June, inſtant.

Atteſt,

WILLIAM COOPER, Town Clerk.

180 Proceedings of the Boston Town Meeting, June 17, 1774, from a printed copy in the Massachusetts Historical Society, Boston

MASSACHUSETTS APPOINTS DELEGATES TO THE FIRST CONTINENTAL CONGRESS

WHILE Boston was thus governing itself, General Gage was endeavoring to operate the Intolerable Act. Thus we find the Massachusetts Assembly in June meeting in Salem, official capital of the province. By this time, as the *Boston Evening Post* of June 20 tells us, a colonial congress "was the general desire of the continent, in order to agree on effectual measures for defeating the despotic designs of those who were endeavoring to effect the ruin of the colonies." Hence on June 17 Samuel Adams secured the adoption of resolves appointing delegates to such a convention to assemble at Philadelphia on the first of September. As these resolves were being adopted, Gage's messenger stood outside the locked doors bearing a proclamation dissolving the legislature, the last to meet under royal sanction.

NEW YORK'S CALL FOR THE FIRST CONGRESS

THERE was, in a sense, nothing novel in this. There were the precedents of Leisler's call in 1690, the Albany Congress of 1754, and the Stamp Act Congress of 1765. Moreover, the project had often been mooted in these past years. Indeed, by May, 1774, the demand seemed to rise spontaneously from many places. The first somewhat authoritative call came from New York. Here the Sons of Liberty wrote to Boston regarding the step. It was in answer to this that the Massachusetts Assembly on June 17 designated the time and place of meeting.

SALEM, *June* 17, 1774.

PROVINCE OF MASSACHUSETT'S BAY.

The following Reſoves paſſed the Houſe of Repreſentatives this Day by a very great Majority, and are now tranſmitted to the Selectmen of the ſeveral Towns and Diſtricts in this Province.

Saml Adams Clerk.

In the Houſe of REPRESENTATIVES, *June* 17, 1774.

WHEREAS this Houſe, taking into Conſideration the many Diſtreſſes and Difficulties to which the American Colonies, and this Province in particular, are and muſt be reduced by the Operation of certain late Acts of Parliament, have determined that it is highly expedient that a Committee ſhould be appointed to meet as ſoon as may be the Committees that are or ſhall be appointed by the ſeveral Colonies on this Continent, to conſult together upon the preſent State of the Colonies, and to deliberate and determine upon wiſe and proper Meaſures to be by them recommended to all the Colonies for the Recovery and Eſtabliſhment of their juſt Rights and Liberties, Civil and Religious, and the Reſtoration of that Union and Harmony between Great-Britain and the Colonies, moſt ardently deſired by all good Men. And the Honorable JAMES BOWDOIN, Eſq; the Hon. THOMAS CUSHING, Eſq; Mr. SAMUEL ADAMS, JOHN ADAMS, and ROBERT-TREAT PAINE, Eſquires, are appointed a Committee on the Part of this Province, for the Purpoſes aforeſaid; any three of whom to be a Quorum, to meet ſuch Committees or Delegates from the other Colonies, as have been or may be appointed, either by their reſpective Houſes of Burgeſſes, or Repreſentatives, or by Convention, or by Committees of Correſpondence appointed by the reſpective Houſes of Aſſembly, in the City of *Philadelphia*, or any other Place that ſhall be judged moſt ſuitable by the joint Committees, on the 1ſt Day of *September* next. And whereas this Houſe did *Reſolve*, That there be paid to ſaid Committee out of the public Treaſury, the Sum of *FIVE HUNDRED POUNDS*, to enable them to diſcharge the important Truſt to which they are appointed; they upon their Return to be accountable for the ſame.—And ſaid Reſolve was ſent up to the honorable Board for their Concurrence, who accordingly concurred the Reſolve of the Houſe, but his Excellency the Governor declined his Conſent to the ſame.——Wherefore this Houſe would Recommend, and they do accordingly hereby recommend to the ſeveral Towns and Diſtricts within this Province, that each Town and Diſtrict, raiſe, collect and pay, to the Honorable *Thomas Cuſhing*, Eſq; of *Boſton*, the Sum of *FIVE HUNDRED POUNDS* by the Fifteenth Day of *Auguſt* next, agreeable to a Liſt herewith exhibitted, being each Town's and Diſtrict's Proportion of ſaid Sum, according to the laſt Province Tax, to enable them to diſcharge the important Truſt to which they are appointed; they upon their Return to be accountable for the ſame.

County of *Suffolk*.

Boſton,	£.47	2	11	*Wrentham*,	3	13	7
Roxbury,	14	15	11	*Brookline*,	1	8	9
Dorcheſter,	3	8	8	*Needham*,	1	9	3
Milton,	1	18	10	*Stoughton*,	2	17	9
Braintree,	4	4	[illegible]	*Stoughtonham*,	1	6	0
Weymouth,	2	6	0	*Medway*,	1	10	4
Hingham,	3	2	4	*Bellingham*,	0	19	6
Dobaſſet,	1	1	4	*Hull*,	0	6	8
Dedham,	3	13	0	*Walpole*,	1	4	0
Menſfield,	1	9	10	*Chelſea*,	0	19	4

County of *Eſſex*.

Salem,	£.13	14	8	*Haverhill*,	3	19	10
Danvers,	4	6	4	*Glouceſter*,	5	13	7
Ipſwich,	7	6	2	*Topsfield*,	1	9	0
Newbury,	6	18	0	*Amsberry*,	2	8	7
Newbury-Port,	7	0	0	*Bradford*,	2	3	9
Marblehead,	9	8	10	*Wenham*,	0	17	7
Lynn,	3	6	8	*Mancheſter*,	1	3	3
Andover,	5	10	10	*Methuen*,	1	16	7
Beverly,	5	18	0	*Boxford*,	1	16	9
Rowley,	3	3	11	*Midaleton*,	1	3	11
Saliſbury,	2	15	6				

County of *Lincoln*.

Pownalborough,	1	8	0	*Newcaſtle*,	0	11	2
Georgetown,	1	16	9	*Topſham*,	0	11	10
Woolwich,	0	12	0				

County of *Cumberland*.

Falmouth,	5	4	3	*Harpſwell*,	0	19	2
North-Yarmouth,	1	19	1	*Windham*,	0	8	10
Scarborough,	1	19	10	*Cape-Elizabeth*,	1	17	10
Brunſwick,	1	2	0	*Gorham*,	1	9	[illegible]

181 The Massachusetts Resolves, from a broadside, Salem, June 17, 1774, in the New York Public Library

182

183

184

Letter from the New York Committee of Fifty-one, May 23, 1774, to the Massachusetts Committee of Correspondence, in the Manuscript Room, New York Public Library

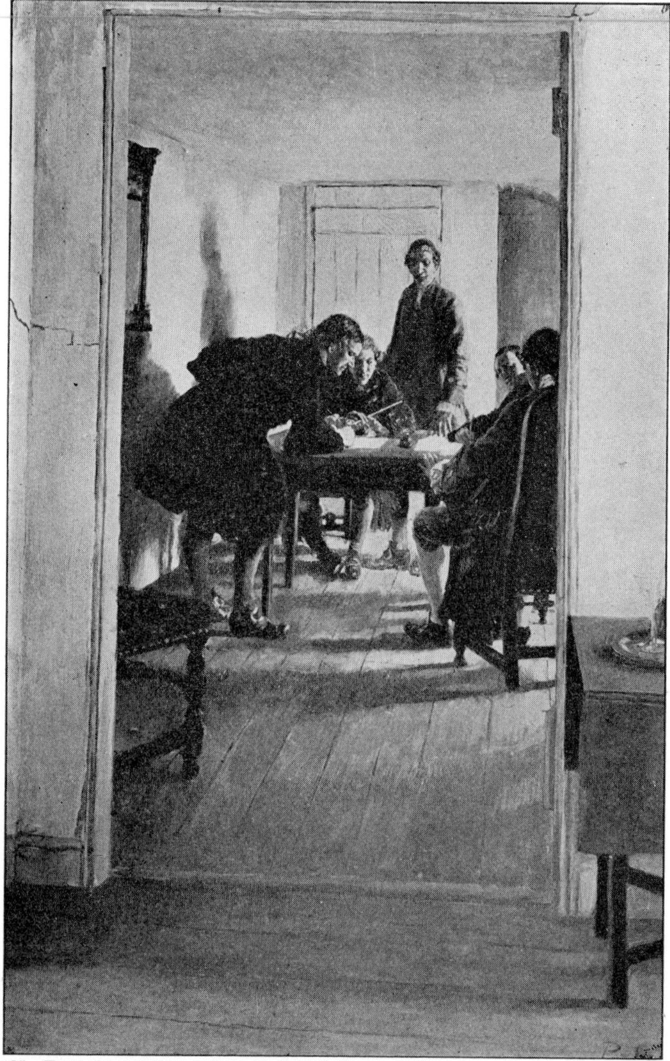

185 From the painting *A Room in Raleigh Tavern, Williamsburg, Va.*, by Howard Pyle, for Woodrow Wilson, *A History of the American People*, 1901. © Harper & Bros.

VIRGINIA UNOFFICIALLY PREPARES FOR THE CONGRESS

THE apparent spontaneity of the movement is shown by events in Virginia. The House of Burgesses, on May 24, adopted Jefferson's resolutions setting aside June 1 — when the Boston blockade began — as "a day of fasting, humiliation and prayer, . . . for the heavy calamity which threatens destruction to our civil rights." Two days later Governor Dunmore found this action a cause for dissolving the House. So, as they had done before, the members gathered in Raleigh Tavern as an unofficial body. There, on May 27, they adopted resolutions for an annual colonial congress "to deliberate on those general measures which the united interests of America may from time to time require." Simultaneous was the issuance of a call for a provincial congress to select delegates to the continental meeting. Thus, once more, Massachusetts and Virginia took the lead in opposing the Government in London. The work of the committees of correspondence was bearing fruit. A feeling of community of interest, of common danger, had been created through the persistent and extensive activity of a few of the more intrepid spirits in the colonies. United action was now a real possibility.

METHODS VARY IN THE SELECTION OF DELEGATES

OTHER colonies rapidly fell into line. Delegates were selected in a variety of ways. In Massachusetts, as we have noticed, appointment was by the Lower House of the legislature. In New Hampshire, New Jersey, Maryland, Delaware, North Carolina and Virginia, provincial congresses made the selection; in Connecticut, the committee of correspondence; in South Carolina, a public meeting held in Charleston; in Rhode Island and Pennsylvania, the legislature. New York employed a different system whereby the nominees of the Sons of Liberty were endorsed by groups in other parts of the state; while three counties sent separate representatives. Georgia alone failed to select.

ADVERTISEMENT.

THE Committee of Correſpondence in New-York, having on Monday Night laſt proceeded to the Nomination of five Perſons to go as Delegates for the ſaid City and County, on the propoſed General Congreſs, at Philadelphia, on the 1ſt of September next; the five following Perſons were nominated for that Purpoſe,

Philip Livingſton,
James Duane,
John Alſop,
John Jay,
Iſaac Low.

The Inhabitants, therefore, of this City and County, are requeſted to meet, at the City-Hall, on THURSDAY next, at 12 o'Clock, in order to approve of the ſaid five Perſons, as Delegates, *or to chooſe ſuch other in their Stead, as to their Wiſdom ſhall ſeem meet.*

By Order of the Committee,
ISAAC LOW, CHAIRMAN.

TUESDAY, 5th
July, 1774.

186 From a New York broadside, July 5, 1774, in the New York Historical Society

CONGRESS INCLUDES MANY OF THE ABLEST AMERICANS

On the fifth of September the delegates gathered at Philadelphia City Tavern. Here it was determined to hold the meetings of the Congress in Carpenter's Hall, a building recently erected, containing a spacious assembly room. Thither the members walked. In all, there were fifty-five, many of them the ablest Americans of the time — Samuel and John Adams from Massachusetts, Roger Sherman from Connecticut, John Dickinson of Pennsylvania, Christopher Gadsden from South Carolina, Peyton Randolph, Richard Henry Lee, Patrick Henry and George Washington from Virginia. One, Stephen Hopkins from Rhode Island, had participated in the Albany Congress; eight had attended the Stamp Act Congress; the others were, with few exceptions, experiencing for the first time the emotions evoked by inter-colonial deliberation.

187 Interior of Carpenter's Hall, Philadelphia. © Rau Brothers, Inc.

THE OPENING OF CONGRESS

On the first day, Peyton Randolph was chosen president, and Charles Thomson, a Pennsylvania patriot, secretary. An oath of secrecy bound the members; sessions were to be held behind closed doors. These were wise precautions; although our knowledge of their proceedings is scanty, we know that the deliberations were not always harmonious and dispassionate. On September 6 a rupture was avoided only by the political skill and whole-hearted earnestness of Samuel Adams. His colleague, Cushing, had moved that meetings should be opened with prayer. To this John Jay of New York and Rutledge of South Carolina objected, since diversity of creed made it impracticable. Then rose the sturdy and artful Puritan and, declaring that "he was no bigot," suggested that on the following morning prayer should be offered by Mr. Duché, the local Episcopal clergyman. Adams' motion prevailed, and one snag to coöperation was removed. And when, on the morning of the 7th, Duché appeared, there were new impulses to call for solidarity. For news — subsequently proved false — had just come that the British forces had bombarded Boston. Consternation prevailed in the city, doubt in the minds of delegates. Duché read a Psalm and several petitions from the Book of Common Prayer, concluding with an invocation, vividly described by John Adams, so patriotic and reverent that he received a vote of thanks. At its end the assemblage was filled with a new exaltation of purpose and a determination to carry through the difficult tasks that lay before them.

188 From an engraving *The First Prayer in Congress* by Sadd after a painting by T. H. Matteson (1813–84)

Reading from left to right: First row (kneeling) Patrick Henry, John Rutledge, George Washington, Peyton Randolph, Richard Henry Lee, John Jay, Isaac Low. Second row (kneeling) Nathaniel Folsom, Robert Treat Paine, Thomas Lynch, Philip Livingston, John Dehart, Thomas M'Kean, Roger Sherman, William Paca, Rev. Mr. Duché, Samuel Ward. Third row (standing) Caesar Rodney, Edward Rutledge, T. Cushing, Eliphalet Dyer, Samuel Adams, John Adams, George Read, Silas Deane, Richard Smith, Stephen Hopkins, William Livingston, Samuel Rhodes, Col. William Floyd, Stephen Crane, John Morton, Thomas Mifflin, Charles Thomson.

189 James Duane, 1733–97, from the portrait, 1805, by John Trumbull (1756–1843), in the City Hall, New York, courtesy of the Municipal Art Commission

SOME AMERICANS ARE SLOW TO JOIN THE RADICALS

YET all the political maneuvering of Sam Adams could not gloss the fact that the Congress contained two opposing groups, one radical and the other conservative. The conflict between them became most tense on September 28, when the conservative Joseph Galloway of Pennsylvania presented a "Plan for a Proposed Union between Great Britain and the Colonies." This was a last and sagacious stand of those who hoped to conciliate all parties. The plan involved the appointment by the Crown of a president-general of the colonies; with him was to be associated a council of delegates selected every three years by the several provinces. The laws of the council were to be subject to parliamentary veto, while acts of Parliament pertaining to the colonies could be nullified by the council. This plan received earnest support from some of the abler leaders of Congress, among them John Jay and James Duane of New York and Edward Rutledge of South Carolina. Their strength is shown by the fact that the plan was laid on the table by a majority of only one vote. Duane incurred odium at this time by his efforts in behalf of the Galloway Plan, and by his suggestion that the Congress recognize the validity of the Navigation Acts. Allied by marriage with the powerful Livingston family, Duane was one of a group of prominent lawyers who were willing to venture all to maintain the English connection. In 1776 he objected to the Declaration of Independence. Once war became inevitable, however, he threw in his lot with the colonies, and served them well. He was a member of the Congresses from start to finish, of the New York Convention which ratified the Federal Constitution, and mayor of New York City from 1784 to 1789, and later served as Federal District Judge.

CONGRESS, UNOFFICIAL AND WITHOUT LEGAL AUTHORITY

MASSACHUSETTS and Virginia led the more advanced group, with able backing from such men as Sherman of Connecticut — men who denied all parliamentary authority over the colonies. At the outset of the Congress, Patrick Henry had given the key to the views of this party. Debate had arisen as to the method of determining questions. Some suggested that each delegate should have one vote; others that the provinces should have equality of power. The latter won. It was in this debate that Henry declared, "The distinctions between Virginians, Pennsylvanians, New Yorkers, and New Englanders are no more. I am not a Virginian, but an American." To his mind a nation had been born, entitled to treatment proportionate to its dignified status.

190 From the painting *Patrick Henry in the First Continental Congress*, by Clyde Osmer DeLand (1872–) in Carpenter's Hall, Philadelphia, courtesy of The American Telephone and Telegraph Company

Proceedings of the General Congreſs of Delegates from the ſeveral Britiſh Colonies in North-America, held in Philadelphia, September 1774.

From the PENNSYLVANIA PACKET.

To the Printer of the Pennſylvania Packet,

SIR.

Pleaſe to inſert in your paper, the following extract from the Minutes of the Congreſs now ſitting at Philadelphia.

By Order of the Congreſs,

CHARLES THOMSON, Secretary.

In the Congreſs, Saturday Sept. 17, 1774.

THE reſolutions entered into by the delegates from the ſeveral towns and diſtricts in the county of Suffolk, in the province of Maſſachuſetts Bay, on Tueſday the 6th inſtant, and their addreſs to his Excellency Governor GAGE, dated the 9th inſtant, were laid before the Congreſs and are as follows.

At a meeting of the Delegates of every town and diſtrict in the county of Suffolk on Tueſday the 6th of September, at the houſe of Mr. Richard Woodward, of Dedham, and by adjournment at the houſe of Mr. —— Voſe, of Milton, on Friday the 9th inſtant. Joſeph Palmer, Eſq; being choſen Moderator, and William Thompſon, Eſq; clerk, a Committee was choſen to bring in a report to the Convention, and the following being ſeveral times read, and put paragraph by paragraph, was unanimouſly voted, viz.

WHEREAS the power but not the juſtice the vengeance, but not the wiſdom of Great Britain, which of old perſecuted, ſcourged and exiled our fugitive parents from their native ſhores, now purſues us their guiltleſs children with unrelenting ſeverity: And whereas, this then ſavage and uncultivated deſart was purchaſed by the toil and treaſure, or acquired by the blood and valour of thoſe our venerable progenitors, to us they bequeathed the dear bought inheritance, to our care and protection they conſigned it, and the moſt ſacred obligations are upon us to tranſmit the glorious purchaſe, unfettered by power, unclogged with ſhackles, to our innocent and beloved offspring. On the fortitude, on the wiſdom, and on the exertions of this important day is ſuſpended the fate of this new world, and of unborn millions. If, a boundleſs extent of continent ſwarming with millions will tamely ſubmit to live, move and have their being at the arbitrary will of a licentious miniſter, they baſely yield to voluntary ſlavery, and future generations ſhall load their memories with inceſſant execrations. On the other hand, if we arreſt the hand which would ranſack our pockets; if we diſarm the parricide which points the dagger to our boſoms, if we nobly defeat that fatal edict which proclaims a power to *frame laws for us in all caſes whatſoever,* thereby entailing the endleſs and numberleſs curſes of ſlavery upon us, our heirs, and their heirs forever; if we ſucceſsfully reſiſt that unparalleled uſurpation of unconſtitutional power, whereby our capital is robbed of the means of life; whereby the ſtreets of Boſton are thronged with military executioners; whereby our coaſts are lined and harbours crowded with ſhips of war; whereby the charter of the colony, that ſacred barrier againſt the encroachments of tyranny is mutilated and in effect annihilated; whereby a murderous law is framed to ſhelter villains from the hands of juſtice; whereby that unalienable and ineſtimable inheritance which we derived from nature, the conſtitution of Britain, and the privileges warranted to us in the charter of the province, is totally wrecked, annulled and vacated, poſterity will acknowledge that virtue which preſerved them free and happy; and while we enjoy the rewards and bleſſings of the faithful, the torrent of panegyric will roll our reputations to that lateſt period, when the ſtreams of time ſhall be abſorbed in the abyſs of eternity——Therefore we have reſolved and do reſolve,

1. That whereas his Majeſty George the third is the rightful ſucceſſor to the throne of Great Britain, and juſtly entitled to allegiance of the Britiſh realm, and agreeable to compact, of the Engliſh colonies in America,—therefore we the heirs and ſucceſſors of the firſt planters of this colony do cheerfully acknowledge the ſaid George the third to be our rightful Sovereign, and that ſaid covenant is the tenure and claim on which are founded our allegiance and ſubmiſſion.

2. That it is an indiſpenſible duty which we owe to God, our country, ourſelves, and poſterity, by all lawful ways and means in our power, to maintain, defend and preſerve thoſe civil and religious rights and liberties, for which many of our fathers fought, bled and died, and to hand them down entire to future generations.

3. That the late acts of the Britiſh Parliament for blocking up the harbour of Boſton, for altering the eſtabliſhed form of government in this colony, and for ſcreening the moſt flagitious violators of the laws of the province from a legal trial, are groſs infractions of thoſe rights to which we are juſtly entitled by the laws of nature, the Britiſh conſtitution, and the charter of the province.

4. That no obedience is due from this province to either or any part of the acts abovementioned, but that they be rejected as the attempts of a wicked adminiſtration to enſlave America.

5. That ſo long as the Juſtices of our Superior Court of Judicature, Court of Aſſize, &c. and Inferior Court of Common Pleas in this county are appointed, or hold their places, by any other tenure than that which the charter and the laws of the province direct, they muſt be conſidered as under undue influence, and are therefore unconſtitutional officers, and as ſuch no regard ought to be paid to them by the people of this county.

6. That if the Juſtices of the Superior Court of Judicature Aſſize, &c. Juſtices of the Court of Common Pleas, or of the General Seſſions of the Peace ſhall ſit and act during their preſent diſqualified ſtate, this county will ſupport and bear harmleſs all Sheriffs and other deputies, Conſtables, Jurors and other officers, who ſhall refuſe to carry into execution the orders of ſaid Court; and as far as poſſible to prevent the many inconveniencies which muſt be occaſioned by a ſuſpenſion of the Courts of Juſtice, we do moſt earneſtly recommend it to all creditors that they ſhew all reaſonable and every generous forbearance to their debtors and to all debtors, to pay their juſt debts with all poſſible ſpeed, and if any diſputes relative to debts or treſpaſſes ſhall ariſe which cannot be ſettled by the parties, we recommend it to them to ſubmit all ſuch cauſes to arbitration, and it is our opinion that the contending parties or either of them who ſhall refuſe ſo to do, ought to be conſidered as cooperating with the enemies of this country.

7. That it be recommended to the collectors of taxes, conſtables and all other officers who have public monies in their hands to retain the ſame, and not to make any payment thereof to the provincial county treaſurer until the civil government of the province is placed upon a conſtitutional foundation, or until it ſhall otherwiſe be ordered by the propoſed provincial congreſs.

8. That the perſons who have accepted ſeats at the Council board, by virtue of a mandamus from the King, in conformity to the late act of the Britiſh Parliament, entitled an act for the regulating the government of the Maſſachuſetts Bay, have acted in direct violation of the duty they owe to their country, and have thereby given great and juſt offence to this people, therefore reſolved that this county do recommend it to all perſons who have ſo highly offended, by accepting ſaid departments, and have not already publicly reſigned their ſeats at the Council board, to make public reſignations of their places at ſaid board, on or before the 20th day of this inſtant, September; and that all perſons refuſing ſo to do, ſhall from and after ſaid day, be conſidered by this county as obſtinate and incorrigible enemies to this country.

9. That the fortifications begun and now carrying on upon Boſton Neck, are juſtly alarming to this county, and give us reaſon to apprehend ſome hoſtile intention againſt that town, more eſpecially as the commander in chief has in a very extraordinary manner removed the powder from the magazine at Charleſtown, and has alſo forbidden the keeper of the magazine at Boſton, to deliver out to the owners the powder which they had lodged in ſaid magazine.

10. That the late act of Parliament for eſtabliſhing the Roman Catholic religion and the French laws in that extenſive country now called Canada, is dangerous in an extreme degree to the proteſtant religion and to the civil rights and liberties of all America; and therefore as men and proteſtant Chriſtians we are indiſpenſibly obliged to take all proper meaſures for our ſecurity.

11. That whereas our enemies have flattered themſelves that they ſhall make an eaſy prey of this numerous, brave and hardy people, from an apprehenſion that they are unacquainted with military diſcipline, we therefore for the honour, defence and ſecurity of this county and province adviſe, as it has been recommended to take away all commiſſions from the officers of the militia that thoſe who now hold commiſſions, or ſuch other perſons be elected in each town as officers in the militia, as ſhall be judged of ſufficient capacity for that purpoſe, and who have evidenced themſelves the inflexible friends to the rights of the people; and that the inhabitants of theſe towns and diſtricts who are qualified do uſe their utmoſt diligence to acquaint themſelves with the art of war as ſoon as poſſible, and do for that purpoſe appear under arms at leaſt once every week.

12. That during the preſent hoſtile appearances on the part of Great Britain, notwithſtanding the many inſults and oppreſſions which we moſt ſenſibly reſent, yet, nevertheleſs, from our affection to his Majeſty, which we have at all times evidenced, we are determined to act merely upon the defenſive, ſo long as ſuch conduct may be vindicated by reaſon and the principles of ſelf-preſervation, but no longer.

13. That as we underſtand it has been in contemplation to apprehend ſundry perſons of this county, who have rendered themſelves conſpicuous in contending for the violated rights and liberties of their countrymen, we do recommend, ſhould ſuch an audacious meaſure be put in practice, to ſeize and keep in ſafe cuſtody, every ſervant of the preſent tyrannical and unconſtitutional government throughout the county and province, until the perſons ſo apprehended be liberated from the hands of our adverſaries, and reſtored ſafe and uninjured to their reſpective friends and families.

14. That until our rights are fully reſtored to us, we will to the utmoſt of our power, and recommend the ſame to the other counties, withhold all commercial intercourſe with Great Britain, Ireland and the Weſt Indies, and abſtain from the conſumption of Britiſh merchandize and manufactures, and eſpecially of Eaſt India teas and piece goods, with ſuch additions, alterations, and exceptions only, as the *Grand Congreſs* of the colonies may agree to.

15. That under our preſent circumſtances it is incumbent on us to encourage arts and manufactures among us by all means in our power, and that
be and hereby are appointed a committee to conſider of the beſt ways and means to promote and eſtabliſh the ſame, and to report to this convention as ſoon as may be.

16. That the exigencies of our public affairs demand that a provincial congreſs be called to concert ſuch meaſures as may be adopted, and vigorouſly executed by the whole people; and we do recommend to the ſeveral towns in this county, to chuſe members for ſuch a provincial congreſs, to be holden at Concord on the ſecond Tueſday of October next enſuing.

17. That this county confiding in the wiſdom and integrity of the continental congreſs, now ſitting at Philadelphia, pay all due reſpect and ſubmiſſion to ſuch meaſures

191 The Suffolk Resolves before Congress, from a broadside in the New York Historical Society

CONGRESS APPROVES THE *SUFFOLK RESOLVES*, SEPT. 17, 1774

THE radicals made great headway when the Congress was persuaded to approve the Suffolk Resolves. These had been adopted under the leadership of Joseph Warren, at a public meeting in Dedham, Massachusetts, on September 6, 1774. Their language was more defiant than that which had been used publicly hitherto. To the Intolerable Acts, they said, "no obedience is due from this province." And "whereas our enemies have flattered themselves that they shall make an easy prey of this numerous, brave and hardy people," those "who are qualified" are urged "to acquaint themselves with the art of war as soon as possible, and do for that purpose appear under arms at least once a week."

[135]

To the KING's moſt excellent MAJESTY.

Moſt gracious SOVEREIGN,

WE your Majeſty's faithful ſubjects of the Colonies of *Newhampſhire, Maſſachuſetts Bay Rhode-Iſland* and *Providence* Plantations, *Connecticut, New York, New-Jerſey, Pennſylvania,* the counties of *Newcaſtle, Kent* and *Suſſex* on *Delaware, Maryland, Virginia, North-Carolina,* and *South-Carolina,* in behalf of ourſelves and the inhabitants of theſe Colonies, who have deputed us to repreſent them in General Congreſs, by this our humble Petition beg leave to lay our grievances before the Throne.

A STANDING army has been kept in theſe Colonies, ever ſince the concluſion of the late war, without the conſent of our Aſſemblies; and this army, with a conſiderable naval armament has been employed to enforce the collection of taxes.

THE authority of the Commander in Chief, and under him of the Brigadiers-General has, in time of peace, been rendered ſupreme in all the civil governments in America.

THE Commander in Chief of all your Majeſty's forces in North America has, in time of peace, been appointed Governor of a Colony.

THE charges of uſual offices have been greatly increaſed; and new, expenſive and oppreſſive offices have been multiplied.

R 2 THE

192 First Page of the Petition to the King, from the *Journal of the Proceedings of the Congress* at Philadelphia, Sept. 5, 1774, printed by William and Thomas Bradford

THE ACTS OF THE CONGRESS WIN PRAISE FROM LORD CHATHAM

GRADUALLY differences were overcome or compromised; and on the twenty-sixth of October adjournment was taken, after May 10, 1775, was fixed as the date for a second Congress. The actions of the Congress were now a public matter. Among them were a petition to the King, an address to the Canadians asking them to join in the next Congress, an address to the people of Great Britain, and one to the people of the colonies. Of these papers, on their receipt, Chatham said in the House of Lords, "For solidity of reason, force of sagacity, and wisdom of conclusion under a complication of difficult circumstances, no nation or body of men can stand in preference to the general congress at Philadelphia. I trust it is obvious . . . that all attempts to impose servitude upon such men, to establish despotism over such a mighty continental nation, must be vain, must be fatal."

AMERICA MAKES A DECLARATION OF RIGHTS AND GRIEVANCES

MORE important than these papers was the Declaration of Rights and Grievances, adopted October 14. This specified a dozen Acts of Parliament whose repeal would be prerequisite to harmony. They were "infringements and violations of the rights of the colonies." In lofty language that at times resembles that of England's earlier Bill of Rights, the Congress enumerated these rights, inalienable because inherent, because guaranteed by the British constitution, and because granted by the colonial charters.

[60]

trary proceedings of parliament and adminiſtration, have ſeverally elected, conſtituted, and appointed deputies to meet and ſit in general congreſs in the city of Philadelphia, in order to obtain ſuch eſtabliſhment, as that their religion, laws, and liberties may not be ſubverted: Whereupon the deputies ſo appointed being now aſſembled, in a full and free repreſentation of theſe colonies, taking into their moſt ſerious conſideration the beſt means of attaining the ends aforeſaid, do in the firſt place, as Engliſhmen their anceſtors in like caſes have uſually done, for aſſerting and vindicating their rights and liberties, DECLARE,

THAT the inhabitants of the Engliſh colonies in North-America, by the immutable laws of nature, the principles of the Engliſh conſtitution, and the ſeveral charters or compacts, have the following RIGHTS.——

Reſolved, N. C. D. 1. THAT they are entitled to life, liberty, and property: and they have never ceded to any ſovereign power whatever, a right to diſpoſe of either without their conſent.

Reſolved, N. C. D. 2. THAT our anceſtors, who firſt ſettled theſe colonies, were at the time of their emigration from the mother country, entitled to all the rights, liberties, and immunities of free and natural born ſubjects, within the realm of England.

Reſolved,

[61]

Reſolved, N. C. D. 3. THAT by ſuch emigration they by no means forfeited, ſurrendered, or loſt any of thoſe rights, but that they were, and their deſcendants now are, entitled to the exerciſe and enjoyment of all ſuch of them, as their local and other circumſtances enable them to exerciſe and enjoy.

Reſolved, 4. THAT the foundation of Engliſh liberty and of all free government, is a right in the people to participate in their legiſlative council: and as the Engliſh coloniſts are not repreſented, and from their local and other circumſtances cannot properly be repreſented in the Britiſh parliament, they are entitled to a free and excluſive power of legiſlation in their ſeveral provincial Legiſlatures, where their right of repreſentation can alone be preſerved, in all caſes of taxation and internal polity, ſubject only to the negative of their ſovereign, in ſuch manner as has been heretofore uſed and accuſtomed: But from the neceſſity of the caſe, and a regard to the mutual intereſts of both countries, we cheerfully conſent to the operation of ſuch acts of the Britiſh parliament, as are bona fide, reſtrained to the regulation of our external commerce, for the purpoſe of ſecuring the commercial advantages of the whole empire to the mother country, and the commercial benefits of its reſpective members, excluding every idea of taxation internal or external, for raiſing a revenue on the ſubjects in America without their conſent

H *Reſolved,*

193 The Declaration of Rights & Grievances (in part), from the *Journal of the Proceedings of the Congress* at Philadelphia, 1774, printed by William and Thomas Bradford

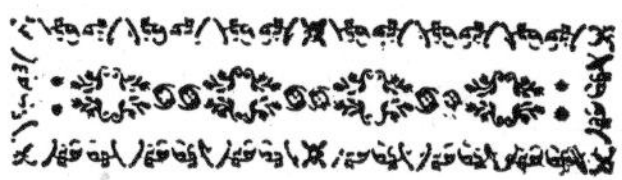

T H E

ASSOCIATION, &c.

WE, his Majesty's most loyal subjects, the Delegates of the several Colonies of New-Hampshire, Massachusett's Bay, Rhode-Island, Connecticut, New-York, New Jersey, Pennsylvania, the Three Lower Counties of Newcastle, Kent, and Sussex, on Delaware, Maryland, Virginia, North-Carolina, and South-Carolina, deputed to represent them in a continental Congress, held in the city of Philadelphia, on the fifth day of September, 1774, avowing our allegiance to his Majesty, our affection and regard for our fellow-subjects in Great-Britain and elsewhere, affected with the deepest anxiety, and most alarming apprehensions at those grievances and distresses, with which his Majesty's American subjects are oppressed, and having taken under our most serious deliberation, the state of the whole continent, find, that the present unhappy situation of our affairs, is occasioned by a ruinous system of colony administration adopted by the British Ministry about the year 1763, evidently calculated for inslaving these Colonies, and, with them, the British Empire. In prosecution of which system, various Acts of Parliament have been passed for raising a Revenue in America, for depriving the American subjects, in many instances, of the constitutional trial by jury, exposing their lives to danger, by directing a new and illegal trial beyond the seas, for crimes alledged to have been committed in America: And in prosecution of the same system, several late, cruel, and oppressive Acts have been passed respecting the town of Boston and the Massachusett's-Bay, and also an Act for extending the province of Quebec, so as to border on the western frontiers of these Colonies, establishing an arbitrary government therein, and discouraging the settlement of British subjects in that wide extended country; thus by the influence of civil principles and ancient prejudices to dispose the inhabitants to act with hostility against the free protestant Colonies, whenever a wicked Ministry shall chuse so to direct them.

To obtain redress of these grievances, which threaten destruction to the lives, liberty, and property of his Majesty's subjects in North-America, we are of opinion, that a non-importation, non-consumption, and non exportation agreement, faithfully adhered to, will prove the most speedy, effectual, and peaceable measure: And therefore we do, for ourselves and the inhabitants of the several Colonies, whom we represent, firmly agree and associate under the sacred ties of

[8]

Thirteenth. THAT all manufactures of this country be sold at reasonable prices, so that no undue advantage be taken of a future scarcity of goods.

Fourteenth. AND we do further agree and resolve, that we will have no trade, commerce, dealings or intercourse whatsoever, with any colony or province, in North America, which shall not accede to, or which shall hereafter violate this association, but will hold them as unworthy of the rights of freemen, and as inimical to the liberties of their country.

And we do solemnly bind ourselves and our constituents, under the ties aforesaid, to adhere to this association until such parts of the several Acts of Parliament passed since the close of the last war, as impose or continue duties on tea, wine, molasses, syrups, paneles, coffee, sugar, piemento, indigo, foreign paper, glass, and painters colours, imported into America, and extend the powers of the Admiralty courts beyond their ancient limits, deprive the American subject of trial by jury, authorise the Judge's certificate to indemnify the prosecutor from damages, that he might otherwise be liable to from a trial by his peers, require oppressive security from a claimant of ships or goods seized, before he shall be allowed to defend his property, are repealed---And until that part of the Act of the 12. G. 3 ch. 24. entitled, "An Act for the better securing his Majesty's dock yards, magazines, ships, ammunition, and stores," by which, any persons charged with committing any of the offences therein described, in America, may be tried in any shire or county within the realm, is repealed---And until the four Acts passed in the last session of Parliament, viz. that for stopping the port and blocking up the harbour of Boston ---That for altering the charter and government of the Massachusett's-Bay --- And that which is entitled, "An Act for the better administration of justice, &c."-------- And that "For extending the limits of Quebec, &c." are repealed. And we recommend it to the provincial conventions, and to the committees in the respective Colonies, to establish such farther regulations as they may think proper, for carrying into execution this Association.

THE foregoing Association being determined upon by the CONGRESS, was ordered to be subscribed by the several Members thereof; and thereupon we have hereunto set our respective names accordingly.

In Congress, Philadelphia, October 20, 1774.

Peyton Randolph President

Jno Sullivan, Nathl Folsom — New Hampshire

Thomas Cushing, Samuel Adams, John Adams, Robt Treat Paine — Massachusetts Bay

194 195

First and eighth pages of The Association, 1774, from a printed copy in the New York Public Library, with signatures of members from New Hampshire and Massachusetts Bay

THE COLONIES DECIDE NOT TO TRADE WITH ENGLAND

TO RENDER effective the American position, the Congress drew up The Association. This was an agreement not to import British goods after December 1, 1774, and to export no goods to Great Britain, Ireland and the West Indies after September 10, 1775. This aroused severe opposition from many quarters. Each section had economic interests involved: South Carolina in rice, Virginia in tobacco, Rhode Island in the slave trade, Massachusetts in the West India trade. Its adoption has been termed "virtually the beginning of the federal union." — HOWARD, *Preliminaries of the Revolution*, 1905, p. 295. Without doubt, the chief value of the Congress was to publish to the world that Massachusetts could not be isolated from her friends, that all had a united purpose. This unity, moreover, was promoted by the opportunity afforded provincial leaders to come to know one another and to acquire habits of coöperation.

196 From *The New York Journal* or *General Advertiser*, Dec. 15, 1774

A LIBERTY EMBLEM APPEARS IN THE PRESS

THE new spirit of unity was quickly symbolized. Here we have the emblem that appeared in the New York press of December 15, 1774, and on the title-page of the *Proceedings of the Congress.* Twelve hands support the liberty pole, adorned with the Phrygian cap, and resting on the Magna Charta. Encircling all is the living snake of earlier days. (See Nos. 72, 73.) Upon his body is inscribed a motto of promise and hope.

OPPOSITION TO THE TRADE BOYCOTT

OPPOSITION to The Association came not solely on the floor of Carpenter's Hall. The colonial secretary, Lord Dartmouth, denounced those who signed that compact as guilty of treason. And in the colonies were those who deprecated such action. Most influential of these was Samuel Seabury, rector of a church at Westchester, New York. Seabury was born (1729) in Connecticut, had entered the ministry of the Established Church in 1753, and was later (1784) to become the first Episcopal bishop in America. Humble and modest, he held pronounced political views. Now, in a series of pamphlets of which the foremost was his *Free Thoughts on The Proceedings of the Continental Congress,* he brought out, in a simple, homely fashion, the consequences of economic disruption in the country. Such an upheaval would cause great distress in England and Ireland, for which America would be held responsible. As a result, their trade would be diverted from America, to the latter's permanent loss. "For example," he writes, these measures would "ruin our market for flaxseed, for which our best customers have always been the Irish. You know, my friends, that the sale of your seed not only pays your taxes, but furnishes you with many of the little conveniences and comforts of life. The loss of it for one year would be of more damage to you, than paying the three-penny duty on tea for twenty. . . . And yet the Congress have been so inattentive to your interests, that they have laid you under almost an absolute necessity of losing it the next year."

FREE THOUGHTS,
ON
The PROCEEDINGS of
THE
CONTINENTAL CONGRESS,
Held at PHILADELPHIA Sept. 5, 1774:
WHEREIN
Their ERRORS are exhibited,
THEIR
REASONINGS CONFUTED,
AND
The fatal Tendency of their NON-IMPORTATION, NON-EXPORTATION, and NON-CONSUMPTION MEASURES, are laid open to the plainest UNDERSTANDINGS;
AND
The ONLY MEANS pointed out
For Preferving and Securing
Our prefent HAPPY CONSTITUTION:
IN
A LETTER
TO
THE FARMERS,
AND OTHER INHABITANTS OF
NORTH AMERICA
In General,
And to thofe of the Province of *New-York*
In Particular.

By a FARMER.

Hear me, for I WILL fpeak!

PPINTED IN THE YEAR M.DCC.LXXIV.

197 From Samuel Seabury, *Free Thoughts,* 1774, in the New York Public Library

A
FULL VINDICATION
OF THE
Meafures of the Congrefs,
FROM
The CALUMNIES of their ENEMIES;
In ANSWER to
A LETTER,
Under the Signature of
A. W. FARMER.
WHEREBY
His *Sophiftry* is expofed, his *Cavils* confuted, his *Artifices* detected, and his *Wit* ridiculed;
IN
A GENERAL ADDRESS
To the Inhabitants of America.
AND
A Particular Addrefs
To the FARMERS *of the Province of New-York.*
by Alexander Hamilton.
Veritas magna eft & prævalebit.
Truth is powerful, and will prevail.

NEW-YORK:
Printed by JAMES RIVINGTON. 1774.

198 Title-page of the copy in the New York Historical Society

HAMILTON DEFENDS THE MEASURES OF CONGRESS

SUCH an argument, couched in everyday language, made a profound impression. By many the pamphlet and its successors were received with applause, by others with execration. In answer appeared other pamphlets. One, entitled *A Full Vindication of the Measures of the Congress,* displayed great dialectic skill and knowledge of constitutional law; and was therefore credited to one or another of the eminent leaders. Soon it was learned that the writer was Alexander Hamilton, then in his 'teens and a student at King's College, New York. During the following winter Hamilton wrote more articles, the enthusiastic reception of which brought him favorably into the public view.

BOYCOTT MOTIVES GOVERN FIRST WOMAN'S CLUB

EVEN before publication of The Association, local action had been taken. In many cases resolutions were passed giving prior approval to all measures that might be adopted by the Congress. In other instances, non-importation and non-consumption agreements were framed. Perhaps the most interesting among the latter was made at a tea party at Edenton, North Carolina. Here in October, 1774, some fifty housewives gathered together and established America's first woman's club. Its purposes were two: to withhold all countenance from "that pernicious custom of drinking tea," and to insure that the members "would not promote ye weare of any manufacture of England." Within six months after the passage of The Association, it had been ratified by all colonies except Georgia and New York. And in these colonies, as elsewhere, local vigilance committees were created to enforce the agreement. There was thus in operation a rather complete set of political institutions, fitted to the emergency, extra-legal in origin and sanction, yet rapidly supplanting the official machinery of government established by law.

199 From a contemporary British cartoon, *A Society of Patriotic Ladies at Edenton in North Carolina*

THE ALTERNATIVE OF WILLIAMS-BURG.

200 From a cartoon *The Alternative of Williamsburg*, printed in London, 1775

THE ENGLISH SATIRIZE THE COERCION OF AMERICAN LOYALISTS

THE Continental Congress and its resolves served to draw ever more distinctly the cleavage between radicals and conservatives, between Patriots and Loyalists, between those who relied upon the old royal and established authority and those dissatisfied with the trend of events. High-handed conduct by Governor Lord Dunmore had made Williamsburg, Virginia, "the heart of rebellion." In the principal street was set up a gibbet, hung with tar and feathers ready for the Loyalist who was so bold as to refuse to sign conformity with the acts of the Congress. This London cartoon is of interest as illustrative of phases of contemporary English opinion. The gift for John Wilkes denotes both colonial recognition of his fight for liberty and the English intermingling of domestic violence with American contumacy. The presence of a cleric may refer to the Parson's Cause of 1763, or to colonial resistance to attempted English ecclesiastical control of American religious life. The English cartoonist makes the homespun of the Patriots distinctly uncouth beside the comely garb of the coerced Loyalists — this in accord with the English newspaper press of the day, which from sympathy with the London merchant constantly stressed the inferiority of American-made clothing.

CHAPTER III

INDEPENDENCE

AS petitions and addresses and memorials were received in England with contempt and evasion, the hopes of the colonials fell. Bit by bit, faith even in the good will of the King disappeared. Conservative Americans were at a loss how to act. But the more impetuous spirits were not unwilling to try forcible resistance. There was still little thought of war, or of political independence. Resort to arms was deemed a necessary action to protect the liberties of Englishmen. Lexington and Bunker Hill (see Vol. VI) were moral victories won by men who hoped that thus they might regain their rights while remaining subjects of the crown of Britain. For the time, the colonials saw nothing impossible in a loyal rebellion.

Yet the situation was impossible. Its clarification was due to a considerable extent to a fortunate bit of journalism. Thomas Paine, an English radical, after a few months in America gave a clear and vigorous statement to thoughts that had occupied men's minds increasingly since the battle of Bunker Hill. His *Common Sense* (No. 223) was a small link in the chain of events that led to the Declaration of Independence (No. 231–34). This ever famous pamphlet forced the issues of the conflict upon the attention of the provincials. They must now choose whether they would become Patriots or Loyalists. Under it the Patriots aligned themselves in a common cause; under it were erected new governments to replace the old; and through it the new body politic entered the world of independent states.

With the military history of the Revolutionary War it is not the purpose of this volume to treat. Yet it may be observed that on the field of battle the Americans were unexpectedly fortunate. For too long a time Britain regarded the rebellion as nothing but a feeble insurrection, easily to be suppressed, if, indeed, it did not collapse of its own weight. Her commanders exhibited, in a half-hearted manner on the whole, only mediocre ability. Her counsellors at home were often disdainful or seemingly indifferent.

This was in part due to Britain's position at the time in the world of states — which was such that she had to act with caution. In Europe the War of the American Revolution was considered little more than a new phase of the long struggle against England's rising commercial supremacy, as another opportunity to weaken a trade rival. Holland, ever with an eye open for the main chance, used every opportunity to humble Britain's trade and to win that of America. France and Spain were not displeased to see England in trouble. Yet these states were not at first ready to ally themselves openly with the rebellious colonies of their rival. It required all the diplomacy of Franklin, all the persuasiveness of such French liberals as LaFayette, and finally, the victory of Saratoga, to bring France, doubtful at first of the military strength of the Americans, into the war.

Even with such military good fortune and foreign sympathy, a successful outcome for the rebellion was not easily attained. Not until five long years had passed did victory seem certain; and with victory came new problems as momentous as those causing the war.

MASSACHUSETTS MAKES MILITANT PREPARATIONS

ARMED conflict seemed inevitable. Congress had counseled that "the schemes agitated against these colonies have been so conducted, as to render it prudent that you should extend your views to mournful events, and be, in all respects, prepared for every contingency." Throughout the colonies the answer came in militant form. In the early fall Washington had declared his willingness to march to the relief of Boston at the head of a thousand men. But Massachusetts was herself making ready. The Assembly had been summoned to meet at Salem on October 5, 1774. General Gage, fearing consequences, now revoked the call and removed the seat of government back to Boston. Disregarding this action, many of the representatives assembled at Cambridge and organized a Provincial Congress, with John Hancock as President and Benjamin Lincoln as Secretary. The last vestige of pretense that royal authority controlled outside of Boston vanished. The Provincial Congress took over the government of the country districts. It also passed resolutions to organize the town militia and the "minute-men."

202 From a caricature in the *London Magazine*, Feb. 1775

In Provincial Congress,

Cambridge, October 26, 1774.

Whereas in Consequence of the present unhappy Disputes between Great-Britain and the Colonies, a formidable Body of Troops with warlike Preparations of every Sort are already arrived at, and others destined for the Metropolis of this Province, and the expressed Design of their being sent is to execute Acts of the British Parliament, utterly subversive of the Constitution of the Province: And whereas his Excellency General Gage has attempted by his Troops to disperse the Inhabitants of Salem, whilst assembled to consult Measures for preserving their Freedom; and to subjugate the Province to arbitrary Government;—And proceeding to still more unjustifiable and alarming Lengths has Fortified against the Country the Capital of the Province, and thus greatly endangered the Lives, Liberties and Properties of its oppressed Citizens;—invaded private Property by unlawfully seizing and retaining large Quantities of Ammunition in the Arsenal at Boston and sundry Pieces of Ordnance in the same Town—committed to the Custody of his Troops the Arms, Ammunition, Ordnance and Warlike Stores of all Sorts, provided at the Public Expence for the Use of the Province, and by all possible Means endeavoured to place the Province entirely in a defenceless State—at the same Time having neglected and altogether disregarded Assurances from this Congress, of the pacific Dispositions of the Inhabitants of the Province, and Intreaties that he would cease from Measures which tended to prevent a Restoration of Harmony between Great-Britain and the Colonies:

Wherefore it is the Opinion of this Congress—That notwithstanding nothing but Slavery ought more to be deprecated than Hostilities with Great-Britain—notwithstanding the Province has not the most distant Design of attacking, annoying or molesting his Majesty's Troops aforesaid, but on the other Hand will consider and treat every Attempt of the Kind as well as all Measures tending to prevent a Reconciliation between Britain and the Colonies as the highest Degree of Enmity to the Province—Nevertheless there is great Reason from the Considerations aforesaid, to be apprehensive of the most fatal Consequences; and that the Province may be in some Degree provided against the same, and under full Persuasion that the Measures expressed in the following Resolves are perfectly consistent with such Resolves of the Continental Congress as have been communicated to us,

It is *Resolved*, and hereby Recommended to the several Companies of Militia in this Province, who have not already chosen and appointed Officers, that they meet forthwith, and elect Officers to Command their respective Companies; and that the Officers so chosen assemble as soon as may be; and where the said Officers shall judge the Limits of the present Regiments too extensive, that they divide them, and settle and determine their Limits, and proceed to elect Field Officers to Command the respective Regiments so formed; and that the Field Officers so elected, forthwith endeavour to enlist one Quarter at the least of the Number of the respective Companies, and form them into Companies of fifty Privates at the least, who shall equip and hold themselves in Readiness to march at the shortest Notice; and that each and every Company so formed, choose a Captain and two Lieutenants to command them on any necessary and emergent Service: And that the said Captain and Subalterns so elected, form the said Companies into Battalions, to consist of nine Companies each; and that the Captains and Subalterns of each Battalion so formed proceed to elect Field Officers to command the same. And this Congress doth most earnestly recommend that all the aforesaid Elections be proceeded in and made with due Deliberation and generous Regard to the public Service.

Also *Resolved*, That as the Security of the Lives, Liberties and Properties of the Inhabitants of this Province depends under Providence on their Knowledge and Skill in the Art Military, and in their being properly and effectually armed and equipt, if any of said Inhabitants are not provided with Arms and Ammunition according to Law, they immediately provide themselves therewith; and that they use their utmost Diligence to perfect themselves in Military Skill; and that if any Town or District within the Province is not provided with the full Town Stock of Arms and Ammunition according to Law, the Selectmen of such Town or District take effectual Care without Delay to provide the same.

A true Extract from the Minutes.

BENJAMIN LINCOLN, Sec'ry

201 From a broadside of the Resolves of the Massachusetts Provincial Congress, recommending the towns to prepare for defense, in the Massachusetts Historical Society

THE PRIVY COUNCIL FAVORS THE USE OF FORCE

IN the fall of 1774, new elections gave added parliamentary power to the ministerial party. With press and Parliament favoring, the Privy Council determined that force must be used to suppress the rebellion in America. "The New England governments," wrote the King to Lord North, "are now in a state of rebellion. Blows must decide whether they are to be subject to this country or independent." The accompanying caricature represents this phase of contemporary English public sentiment. King George and his chief Minister, Lord North, are dancing in carefree fashion around the thistle, symbol of Scottish predominance in the councils of state. They appear to be exulting in a supercilious manner at the impending confusion of those who have opposed the royal policies embodied in the Acts of 1774. Lord Mansfield weighty representative of the law, and supporter of those policies — particularly as embodied in the Quebec Act — is giving to the performance benign approval. Above, the thistle sheds its effulgent rays to all corners.

The motion made by Lord North on Monday laſt is as follows:

"That it is the opinion of this Committee; that when the Governor, Council, and Aſſembly, or General Court, of any of his Majeſty's provinces or colonies in America, ſhall propoſe to make proviſion according to the condition, circumſtances, and ſituation of ſuch province or colony, for contributing their proportion to the common defence (ſuch proportion to be raiſed under the authority of the General Court or Aſſembly of ſuch province or colony, and diſpoſable by Parliament) and ſhall engage to make proviſion alſo for the Civil Government and the Adminiſtration of Juſtice in ſuch province or colony; it will be proper, if ſuch propoſal ſhall be approved by his Majeſty and the two Houſes of Parliament, and for ſo long as ſuch proviſion ſhall be made accordingly, to forbear, in reſpect of ſuch province or colony, to levy any duty, tax, and aſſeſſment, except only ſuch duties as it may be expedient to continue to levy and impoſe for the regulation of commerce, the nett produce of the duties laſt mentioned to be carried to the account of ſuch province or colony reſpectively."

A motion was made, after a long debate, for the Chairman to leave the Chair,

Ayes — 88

Noes — 274

Then the main queſtion was put, and agreed to.

203 From the *London Packet*, Feb. 22, 1775, in the New York Public Library

LORD NORTH OFFERS CONCILIATORY RESOLVES

On January 19, 1775, the Congress petition (Nos. 192, 193) came before Parliament. The next day Chatham moved that the British troops be at once withdrawn from Boston: "An hour now lost may produce years of calamity." But Pitt's insight was not shared by the ministry. Yet the friends of America persisted. Chatham presented, on February 1, a scheme that, with mutual concessions, would have paved the way to harmony between America and England. But Parliament refused to give this bill even the usual courtesy of lying on the table. On first reading it was overwhelmingly rejected. Then, a few days later, Lord North surprised everyone by bringing in a conciliatory resolution (No. 203). The measure was regarded with distaste by the high Tories and with suspicion by American sympathizers. Disingenuous and trivial as it was, only strict party discipline secured its passage.

EDMUND BURKE SPEAKS ON CONCILIATION

The true policy of the ministry became clear on the tenth of February. On that day North, asserting that "as the Americans had refused to trade with this kingdom, it was but just that we should not suffer them to trade with any other nation," asked leave to bring in the New England Restraining Act. Permission was granted by a vote of two hundred and sixty-one to eighty-five. This was one of the important factors in driving colonial Americans from the fight for their rights under the English constitution to a battle for political independence. In the ensuing debate Edmund Burke made his famous speech on conciliation. Burke had already shown interest in American affairs. His first speech in Parliament had been in January, 1766, favoring the reception of the petition of the Stamp Act Congress. He had disapproved of the Townshend duties and of the Intolerable Acts; and now in March, 1775, he won the hearts of Americans by his plea for her cause.

The SPEECH of EDMUND BURKE, Eſq; on moving his Reſolutions for Conciliation with the Colonies, March 22, 1775.

[*Continued from our laſt.*]

THE propoſition is peace. Not peace through the medium of war. Not peace to be hunted through the labyrinth of intricate and endleſs negociations. Not peace to ariſe out of univerſal diſcord, fomented from principle in all parts of the empire. Not peace to depend on the juridical determination of perplexing queſtions; or the preciſe marking the ſhadowy boundaries of a complex government. It is ſimple peace ſought in its natural courſe, and its ordinary haunts. It is peace ſought in the ſpirit of peace, and laid in principles purely pacific. I propoſe by removing the ground of the difference and by reſtoring the *former unſuſpecting confidence of the colonies in the mother country*, to give permanent ſatisfaction to your people; and (far from a ſcheme of ruling by diſcord) to reconcile them to each other in the ſame act, and by the bond of the very ſame intereſt, which reconciles them to Britiſh government.

My idea is nothing more. Refined policy ever has been the parent of confuſion, and ever will be ſo long as the world endures. Plain good intention, which is as eaſily diſcovered at the firſt view, as fraud is ſurely detected at laſt, is, let me ſay, of no mean force in the government of mankind. Genuine ſimplicity of heart is an healing and cementing principle. My plan, therefore, being formed upon the moſt ſimple grounds imaginable, may diſappoint ſome people when they hear it. It has nothing to recommend it to the pruriency of curious ears. There is nothing at all new and captivating in it. It has nothing of the ſplendor of the project, which has been lately laid upon your table, by the noble Lord in the blue riband*. It does not propoſe to fill your lobby with ſquabbling colony agents, who will require the interpoſition of your mace, at every inſtant, to keep the peace amongſt them. It does not inſtitute a magnificent auction of finance, where captivated provinces come to general ranſom by bidding againſt each other, have inſtituted a mode that is altogether new; one that is, indeed, wholly alien from all the ancient methods and forms of parliament.

The principle of this proceeding is large enough for my purpoſe. The means propoſed by the noble Lord for carrying his ideas into execution, I think, indeed, are very indifferently ſuited to the end; and this I ſhall endeavour to ſhew you before I ſit down. But, for the preſent, I take my ground on the admitted principle. I mean to give peace. Peace implies reconciliation; and, where there has been a material diſpute, reconciliation does in a manner always imply conceſſion on the one part or on the other. In this ſtate of things I make no difficulty in affirming that the propoſal ought to originate from us. Great and acknowleged force is not impaired, either in effect or in opinion, by an unwillingneſs to exert itſelf. The ſuperiour power may offer peace with honour and with ſafety. Such an offer from ſuch a power will be attributed to magnanimity. But the conceſſions of the weak are the conceſſions of fear. When ſuch a one is diſarmed, he is wholly at the mercy of his ſuperior, and he loſes for ever that time and thoſe changes which, as they happen to all men, are the ſtrength and reſources of all inferiour power.

The capital leading queſtions, on which you muſt this day decide, are theſe two. Firſt, whether you ought to concede; and ſecondly, what your conceſſion ought to be. On the firſt of theſe queſtions we have gained (as I have juſt taken liberty of obſerving to you) ſome ground. But I am ſenſible that a good deal more is ſtill to be done. Indeed, Sir, to enable us to determine both on the one and the other of theſe great queſtions with a firm and preciſe judgment, I think it may be neceſſary to conſider diſtinctly the true nature and the peculiar circumſtances of the object which we have before us. Becauſe after all our ſtruggle whether we will or not, we muſt govern America according to that nature, and to thoſe circumſtances, and not according to our own imaginations; not according to abſtract ideas of right; by no means according to mere general theories of government and provoked with little danger. It will prove that ſome degree of care and caution is required in the handling ſuch an object; it will ſhew that you ought not, in reaſon, to trifle with ſo large a maſs of the intereſts and feelings of the human race. You could at no time do ſo without guilt, and be aſſured you will not be able to do it long with impunity.

But the population of this country, the great and growing population, though a very important conſideration, will loſe much of its weight if not combined with other circumſtances. The commerce of your colonies is out of all proportion beyond the numbers of the people. This ground of their commerce indeed has been trod ſome days ago, and with great ability, by a diſtinguiſhed perſon at your bar [Mr. Glover]. This gentleman after thirty-five years—it is ſo long ſince he appeared at the ſame place to plead for the commerce of Great-Britain, has come again before you to plead the ſame cauſe, without any other effect of time than that to the fire of imagination and extent of erudition, which even then marked him as one of the firſt literary characters of his age; he has added a conſummate knowledge in the commercial intereſt of his country, formed by a long courſe of enlightened, and diſcriminating experience.

Sir, I ſhould be inexcuſable in coming after ſuch a perſon with any detail, if a great part of the members, who now fill the houſe, had not the misfortune to be abſent when he appeared at your bar. Beſides, Sir, I propoſe to take the matter at periods of time ſomewhat different from his. There is, if I miſtake not, a point of view from whence, if you will look at this ſubject, it is impoſſible that it ſhould not make an impreſſion upon you.

I have in my hand two accounts, one a comparative ſtate of the export trade of England to its colonies, as it ſtood in the year 1704, and as it ſtood in the year 1772. The other a ſtate of the export trade of this country to its colonies alone, as it ſtood in 1772, compared with the whole trade of England to all parts of the world (the colonies included) in the year 1704. They are from good vouchers; the latter

204 From the *Massachusetts Spy*, Worcester, Sept. 29, 1775, in the New York Public Library

205 From the caricature *Virtual Representation*, dated Apr. 1, 1775, in the Massachusetts Historical Society, Boston

THE KING APPROVES THE NEW ENGLAND RESTRAINING ACT

In March the Act received the royal assent. Once again the British Government had shown its inability to comprehend that the colonial problem was no longer one of Massachusetts, or of New England, but of a continent. Even in Canada signs of dissatisfaction were not lacking and Governor Carleton was employing all his ingenuity to prevent an open expression of sympathy with the southern provinces. The contemporary cartoon here shown carries, in handwriting of the time, the following "explanation": "No. 1 intends the K—g of G.B., to whom the House of Commons (4) gives the Americans' money for the use of that very H. of C., and which he is endeavoring to take away with the power of cannon. No. 2, by a Frenchman, signifies the tyranny that is intended for America. No. 3, the figure of a Roman Catholic priest." [This alludes perhaps to the Quebec Act and its sanction of that religion, or to Carleton's attempt to enlist the Catholic priesthood in political propaganda.] "Nos. 5 and 6 are honest American yeomen, who oppose an oaken staff to G—'s cannon, and determine they will not be robbed. No. 7 is poor Britannia blindfolded, falling into the bottomless pit which her infamous rulers have prepared for the Americans. Nos. 8 and 9 represent Quebec triumphant and Boston in flames, to show the probable consequence of submission to the present wicked ministerial system, — that popery and tyranny will triumph over true religion, virtue, and liberty."

FRANKLIN WARNS LORD NORTH

When Lord North apprised Franklin of the ministerial policy, that great American replied: "The people of Massachusetts must suffer all the hazards and mischiefs of war, rather than admit the alteration of their charter and laws by Parliament. They that can give up essential liberty to obtain a little temporary safety deserve neither liberty nor safety." This attitude received warm assent in America on the receipt of news of the actions of Parliament. The second Massachusetts Provincial Congress was in session at Cambridge. In February this assemblage spurred on the military preparations authorized the preceding fall. In the other colonies like efforts were on foot.

New-York, May 8, 1775.

Extract of a Letter From Philadelphia,

To a Gentleman in this City, dated the 6th inst.

YESTERDAY evening Dr. FRANKLIN arrived here from London in six weeks, which he left the 20th of March, which has given great joy to this town, he says we have no favours to expect from the Ministry, nothing but submission will satisfy them, they expect little or no opposition will be made to their troops, those that are now coming are for *New-York*, where it is expected they will be received with cordiality. As near as we can learn there are about four thousand troops coming in this fleet, the men of war and transports are in a great measure loaded with dry goods, to supply *New-York*, and the country round it, agents are coming over with them. Dr. *Franklin* is highly pleased to find us arming and preparing for the worst events, he thinks nothing else can save us from the most abject slavery and destruction, at the same time encourages us to believe a spirited opposition, will be the means of our salvation. The Ministry are alarmed at every opposition, and lifted up again at every thing which appears the least in their favour, every letter and every paper from hence, are read by them.

NEW-YORK.
Printed by JOHN ANDERSON, at Beekman's-Slip.

206 From a facsimile of a New York Handbill, May 8, 1775, in the Bancker Collection catalogue, 1898

207 Joseph Warren, 1741–75, from the portrait by John Singleton Copley, in the Museum of Fine Arts, Boston. © Detroit Publishing Co.

WARREN WROTE, SPOKE AND DIED FOR AMERICA

A LEADER in this movement was Dr. Joseph Warren of Boston. After graduation at Harvard, Warren had in 1764 begun the practice of medicine. The following year witnessed the beginning of his political activity. In 1772 he gained further prominence by delivering the memorial address on the Boston Massacre. The same year found him a member of the Committee of Correspondence. In 1774 he was the draftsman of the stirring Suffolk Resolves. In October he became head of the Committee of Safety, charged with the preparation for defense. Winning manners, cultivated speech and manliness had won him wide affection. When the redcoats in Boston threatened the life of the "Massacre" orator for 1775, Joseph Warren pushed forward to the post of danger. So crowded was Old South Church that March day that the speaker, ever loath to create unnecessary trouble, climbed in at a window to the rear of the pulpit. There followed a noble exhortation to the people to resist the wrongs which America "had suffered from the hands of cruel and ungodly men." The British officers in the assemblage made no move to stop his oration. But Warren scarce outlived the echoes of the speech. For he fell at Bunker Hill, perhaps the greatest single loss to the American cause throughout the war.

THE BRITISH RETREAT FROM CONCORD

WARREN had said: "America must and will be free. The contest may be severe; and the end will be glorious. We would not boast, but we think, united and prepared as we are, we have no reason to doubt of success, if we should be compelled to make the last appeal; but we mean not to make that appeal, until we can be justified in doing it in the sight of God and man." That appeal was taken on the 19th of April, 1775. General Gage, determined to destroy munitions stored at Concord, sent out a detachment under cover of night and secrecy. Warren discovered the move; and Dawes and Revere carried the message, the consequences of which are familiar to all (See Vol. VI). The British forces were saved from utter rout solely by the appearance of reinforcements under Lord Percy, under whose protection the retreat to Boston was managed.

I'll Run for they are at our heels
Away with your Plunder
The Retreat
From Concord to Lexington of the Army of Wild Irish Asses Defeated by the Brave American Militia
Mr Deacon Mr Loeings Mr Mulikens Mr Bonds Houses and Barn all Plunder'd and Burnt on April 19th

208 From a British cartoon, 1775, in the collection of R. T. H. Halsey, New York

THE COLONIES PRESENT A UNITED FRONT

The country was roused. Everywhere Lord North's plan of conciliation was pushed aside. Ticonderoga and Crown Point were taken. Stimulated by the improvised revolutionary governments, a united front was presented to England. The familiar symbols of earlier protests were revived to quicken public spirit. Here we find Thomas Paine, disguised as a classicist, urging the common cause through the medium of verse on the Liberty Tree. The prophecy of Warren was met. The Provincial Congress of South Carolina adopted, on June 3, an Association; "The actual commencement of hostilities against this continent by the British troops, on the 19th of April last, and the dread of insurrections . . . are causes sufficient to drive an oppressed people to arms. We, inhabitants of South Carolina, . . . thoroughly convinced that under our present distressed circumstances we shall be justified before God and man in resisting force by force, do . . . associate as a band in her defense against every foe; hereby solemnly engaging that, whenever our continental or provincial councils shall deem it necessary, we will go forth, and be ready to sacrifice our lives and fortunes to secure her freedom and safety."

POETICAL ESSAYS.

For JULY.

For the Pennsylvania Magazine.

Liberty Tree. *A new Song.*

Tune, *The Gods of the Greeks.*

In a chariot of light from the regions of day,
The Goddeſs of Liberty came;
Ten thouſand celeſtials directed the way,
And hither conducted the dame.
A fair budding branch from the gardens above,
Where millions with millions agree,
She brought in her hand, as a pledge of her love,
And the plant ſhe named, *Liberty Tree.*

II.

The celeſtial exotic ſtruck deep in the ground,
Like a native it flouriſh'd and bore.
The fame of its fruit drew the nations around,
To ſeek out this peaceable ſhore.
Unmindful of names or diſtinctions they came,
For freemen like brothers agree,
With one ſpirit endued, they one friendſhip purſued,
And their temple was *Liberty tree.*

III.

Beneath this fair tree, like the patriarchs of old,
Their bread in contentment they eat,
Unvex'd with the troubles of ſilver and gold,
The cares of the grand and the great.
With timber and tar they Old England ſupply'd,
And ſupported her power on the ſea;
Her battles they fought, without getting a groat,
For the honour of *Liberty tree.*

IV.

But hear, O ye ſwains, ('tis a tale moſt profane,)
How all the tyrannical powers,
King, Commons, and Lords, are uniting amain,
To cut down this guardian of ours;
From the eaſt to the weſt, blow the trumpet to arms,
Thro' the land let the ſound of it flee,
Let the far and the near,—all unite with a cheer,
In defence of our *Liberty tree.*

ATLANTICUS.

209 Ode by Thomas Paine on the *Liberty Tree*, from the *Pennsylvania Magazine* July 1775

Bunkers hill, or the blessed effects of Family quarrels.

210 From a British caricature in possession of the publishers

FRANCE AND SPAIN EAGERLY WATCH AMERICA

In the quiet of Mount Vernon, Washington wrote: "Unhappy is it to reflect that a brother's sword has been sheathed in a brother's breast, and that the once happy and peaceful plains of America are to be either drenched with blood or inhabited by slaves. Sad alternative! But can a virtuous man hesitate in his choice?" The English sympathizer agreed, but saw in the conflict issues both narrower and wider than a struggle for continental liberty. On the one hand, Lexington seemed only the outcome of the light-hearted misrule of the King's friends, North, Bute and Mansfield. Yet the American war loomed also as a European war. France and Spain were thought eager to utilize the civil strife to humble Britannia and to regain Latin supremacy in the world. The cartoonist in his *Bunker's hill, or the blessed effects of Family quarrels*, represents Spain striking the shield from Britannia and holding America with a rope while France stabs Britannia in the back.

211 From a caricature published at London, Feb. 1776, courtesy of R. T. H. Halsey and the Grolier Club, New York

ENGLISH LIBERALS CRITICIZE BUTE'S POLICY

THIS cartoon, offered for sale in London shortly after Bunker Hill, depicts another phase of English opinion. The British lion naps in the sunshine, careless of his realm. King George, North, Mansfield and the bishops watch Bute as that conspirator seeks to secure, with one fell blow, all the coveted wealth of America. The last lines of the legend read:

About her Neck they put a Chain,
And more their Folly to compleat
They *Stampt* upon her Wings and Feet.
But this had no Effect at all,
Yet made her struggle, flutter, squall,
And do what every Goose would do
That had her Liberty in view;
When one of more distinguished Note
Cry'd D——n her let me Cut her Throat.
They did, but not an Egg was found
But Blood came flowing from ye wound.

CONGRESS DECLARES PRINCIPLE OF RETALIATION

FACTS could not be dodged. The Second Continental Congress, meeting on May 10, 1775, determined to lend its support to the Cambridge forces. Washington, a man with a distinguished military record, was chosen commander-in-chief of the army arrayed against what he called "the ministerial troops." For the "patriots" were not yet fighting for national independence, but for relief from the oppressive conduct of the King's ministers. So on July 8 the Congress adopted a petition to the King, "beseeching" him to use his office to interpose between the colonies and "those artful and cruel enemies, who abuse your royal confidence and authority, for the purpose of effecting our destruction." On the day on which Richard Penn was to present this to the Government, there was issued, as answer, the proclamation "for suppressing rebellion and sedition." The Crown and its ministry were prepared to call the bluff of the colonies, or to put down the insurrection.

By the KING,

A PROCLAMATION,

For ſuppreſſing Rebellion and Sedition.

GEORGE R.

WHEREAS many of Our Subjects in divers Parts of Our Colonies and Plantations in *North America*, miſled by dangerous and ill-deſigning Men, and forgetting the Allegiance which they owe to the Power that has protected and ſuſtained them, after various diſorderly Acts committed in Diſturbance of the Publick Peace, to the Obſtruction of lawful Commerce, and to the Oppreſſion of Our loyal Subjects carrying on the ſame, have at length proceeded to an open and avowed Rebellion, by arraying themſelves in hoſtile Manner to withſtand the Execution of the Law, and traitorouſly preparing, ordering, and levying War againſt Us; And whereas there is Reaſon to apprehend that ſuch Rebellion hath been much promoted and encouraged by the traitorous Correſpondence, Counſels, and Comfort of divers wicked and deſperate Perſons within this Realm: To the End therefore that none of Our Subjects may neglect or violate their Duty through Ignorance thereof, or through any Doubt of the Protection which the Law will afford to their Loyalty and Zeal; We have thought fit, by and with the Advice of Our Privy Council, to iſſue this Our Royal Proclamation, hereby declaring that not only all Our Officers Civil and Military are obliged to exert their utmoſt Endeavours to ſuppreſs ſuch Rebellion, and to bring the Traitors to Juſtice; but that all Our Subjects of this Realm and the Dominions thereunto belonging are bound by Law to be aiding and aſſiſting in the Suppreſſion of ſuch Rebellion, and to diſcloſe and make known all traitorous Conſpiracies and Attempts againſt Us, Our Crown and Dignity; And We do accordingly ſtrictly charge and command all Our Officers as well Civil as Military, and all other Our obedient and loyal Subjects, to uſe their utmoſt Endeavours to withſtand and ſuppreſs ſuch Rebellion, and to diſcloſe and make known all Treaſons and traitorous Conſpiracies which they ſhall know to be againſt Us, Our Crown and Dignity; and for that Purpoſe, that they tranſmit to One of Our Principal Secretaries of State, or other proper Officer, due and full Information of all Perſons who ſhall be found carrying on Correſpondence with, or in any Manner or Degree aiding or abetting the Perſons now in open Arms and Rebellion againſt Our Government within any of Our Colonies and Plantations in *North America*, in order to bring to condign Puniſhment the Authors, Perpetrators and Abettors of ſuch traitorous Deſigns.

Given at Our Court at St. *James's*, the Twenty-third Day of *Auguſt*, One thouſand ſeven hundred and ſeventy-five, in the Fifteenth Year of Our Reign.

God ſave the King.

212 Royal Proclamation, Aug. 23, 1775, from the copy in the Massachusetts Historical Society

PROMINENT LOYALISTS OPPOSE VIOLENCE

This last reference included the large body of colonists remaining faithful to England. John Adams estimated that one-third of the population were at first opposed to armed rebellion. Included in their number were most of the official class, the clergy, and those whose vested interests had bred a conservative political attitude. Some, of course, were simply playing the game of expediency; but many, like Galloway, admitted the grievances of America while honestly shrinking from violent methods of remedy. Many a thoughtful and patriotic conservative distrusted the radical elements in the colonies and feared the consequences for society that might result from war and from a successful revolution. Not a few of these men were driven to sacrifice property, position and friends by their loyalty to the ancient kingdom whence their forefathers had come.

213 Jonathan Boucher, 1738–1804, from *Letters of Jonathan Boucher to George Washington*, collected and edited by Worthington Chauncey Ford, Brooklyn, 1899

Two of these Loyalists deserve mention. One, Jonathan Boucher, Virginia rector and friend of Washington, drew down upon himself by his frankness the wrath of his parish. Boucher was a devout follower of the doctrines of Filmer and Hooker; passive obedience was to him the most effective and only honorable means of securing redress of wrongs. In his sermon, published in 1797, may be found the ablest statement of the Loyalist case. Boucher gave such offence to the members of his congregation that in 1785 he was obliged to return to England. The other was of a more militant turn. James Rivington had in 1773 established the *New York Gazetteer* as an organ for the Government party. Its virulence led to its being wrecked in 1775 at the hands of enraged Patriots. Rivington's utterances came to the notice of the Continental Congress, to which, while it was considering his case, he wrote that "however wrong and mistaken he may have been in his opinions, he has always meant honestly and openly to do his duty as a servant of the people." Soon after he was appointed King's printer for New York, and in 1777 he resumed publication of what soon became the *Royal Gazette*. This was the chief American vehicle for the Loyalists, and Rivington was singled out by the Patriots for vicious scorn. William Livingston wrote to Gouverneur Morris: "If Rivington is taken, I must have one of his ears; Governor Clinton is entitled to the other; and General Washington, if he pleases, may take his head." Rivington was cleverly satirized by Francis Hopkinson, Philip Freneau and John Witherspoon. Nevertheless, when the British cause became doubtful he played the spy and provided Washington with important information.

214 James Rivington, 1724–1802, from a portrait by an unknown artist in the New York Historical Society

THURSDAY, April 13, 1775. [Nº 104.]

RIVINGTON'S

NEW-YORK GAZETTEER;

OR, THE

Connecticut, Hudson's River, New-Jersey, and Quebec

WEEKLY ADVERTISER.

PRINTED at his OPEN and UNINFLUENCED PRESS, fronting Hanover-Square.

215 Heading of *Rivington's New York Gazetteer or Weekly Advertiser*, Apr. 13, 1775, from a copy in the New York Public Library

BY HIS EXCELLENCY

GEORGE WASHINGTON, Esquire,

Commander in Chief of the Army of the United Colonies of North-America.

To the INHABITANTS of CANADA.

FRIENDS and BRETHREN,

THE unnatural Contest between the English Colonies and Great-Britain, has now risen to such a Heighth, that Arms alone must decide it. The Colonies, confiding in the Justice of their Cause, and the Purity of their Intentions, have reluctantly appealed to that Being, in whose Hands are all human Events. He has hitherto smiled upon their virtuous Efforts—The Hand of Tyranny has been arrested in its Ravages, and the British Arms which have shone with so much Splendor in every Part of the Globe, are now tarnished with Disgrace and Disappointment.——Generals of approved Experience, who boasted of subduing this great Continent, find themselves circumscribed within the Limits of a single City and its Suburbs, suffering all the Shame and Distress of a Siege. While the freeborn Sons of America, animated by the genuine Principles of Liberty and Love of their Country, with increasing Union, Firmness and Discipline repel every Attack, and despise every Danger.

Above all, we rejoice, that our Enemies have been deceived with Regard to you—They have perswaded themselves, they have even dared to say, that the Canadians were not capable of distinguishing between the Blessings of Liberty, and the Wretchedness of Slavery; that gratifying the Vanity of a little Circle of Nobility—would blind the Eyes of the People of Canada.—By such Artifices they hoped to bend you to their Views, but they have been deceived, instead of finding in you that Poverty of Soul, and Baseness of Spirit, they see with a Chagrin equal to our Joy, that you are enlightened, generous, and virtuous—that you will not renounce your own Rights, or serve as Instruments to deprive your Fellow Subjects of theirs.—Come then, my Brethren, unite with us in an indissoluble Union, let us run together to the same Goal.—We have taken up Arms in Defence of our Liberty, our Property, our Wives, and our Children, we are determined to preserve them, or die. We look forward with Pleasure to that Day not far remote (we hope) when the Inhabitants of America shall have one Sentiment, and the full Enjoyment of the Blessings of a free Government.

Incited by these Motives, and encouraged by the Advice of many Friends of Liberty among you, the Grand American Congress have sent an Army into your Province, under the Command of General SCHUYLER; not to plunder, but to protect you; to animate, and bring forth into Action those Sentiments of Freedom you have disclosed, and which the Tools of Despotism would extinguish through the whole Creation.——To co-operate with this Design, and to frustrate those cruel and perfidious Schemes, which would deluge our Frontiers with the Blood of Women and Children; I have detached Colonel Arnold into your Country, with a Part of the Army under my Command—I have enjoined upon him, and I am certain that he will consider himself, and act as in the Country of his Patrons, and best Friends. Necessaries and Accommodations of every Kind which you may furnish, he will thankfully receive, and render the full Value.—I invite you therefore as Friends and Brethren, to provide him with such Supplies as your Country affords; and I pledge myself not only for your Safety and Security, but for ample Compensation. Let no Man desert his Habitation—Let no one flee as before an Enemy; The Cause of America, and of Liberty, is the Cause of every virtuous American Citizen; whatever may be his Religion or his Descent, the United Colonies know no Distinction but such as Slavery, Corruption and arbitrary Domination may create. Come then, ye generous Citizens, range yourselves under the Standard of general Liberty—against which all the Force and Artifice of Tyranny will never be able to prevail.

G. Washington.

216 Washington's Letter to the Canadians, 1775 (distributed also in French), from a broadside in the New York Public Library

CANADA HOLDS ALOOF FROM COLONIAL UNION

THE colonists were not, then, united. Much of the time of the new commander-in-chief was consumed in consolidating the American front against England. One fair prospect was Canada. The Congress hoped that loyalty to the British Crown sat but lightly on the recently conquered French. Franklin and the Catholic John Carroll of Maryland were sent to try their hand at winning Canadian support. They found George III's French-speaking subjects, however, not greatly interested and Sir Guy Carleton showed too great military ability. Canada was not won to the cause.

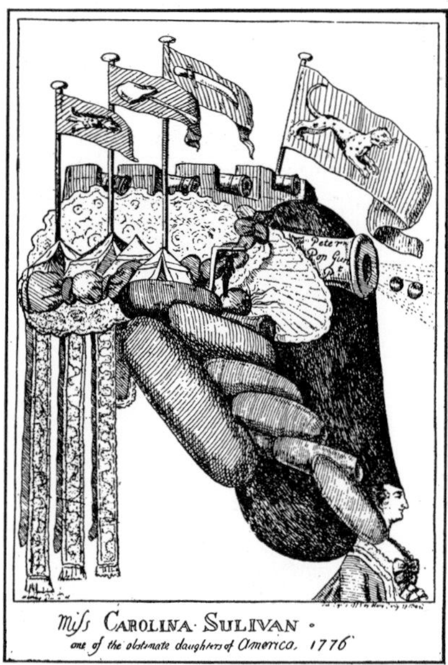

Miss CAROLINA SULIVAN ·
one of the obstinate daughters of America, 1776

217 From a British cartoon in the collection of R. T. H. Halsey, New York

THE BRITISH ARE REPULSED OFF CHARLESTON

COUNTING upon Loyalist strength in Carolina, the British offensive was opened there. A fleet under Admiral Sir Peter Parker appeared off Charleston on the 4th of June. The citizens had built a crude fort of green palmetto on Sullivan's Island, commanding the channel. This rough defense the Admiral thought to annihilate. But his shots were buried harmlessly in the soft logs, while a telling fire from the Island played havoc with the fleet. After ten hours of fighting the latter was glad to withdraw. It was another heartening victory for the Patriots, another blow to the Loyalists. (See Vol. VI.)

218 From the painting *Tory Refugees on Their Way to Canada*, by Howard Pyle for Woodrow Wilson, *A History of the American People*, 1901. © Harper & Bros.

LOYALISTS ARE DRIVEN FROM THEIR HOMES

INDEED the Loyalists proved of little aid to Great Britain. Though numerous in New York, Pennsylvania, Connecticut, New Jersey, Delaware, Maryland, South Carolina and Georgia, the superior zeal of the Patriots kept them disorganized and downcast. They received scant sympathy at the hands of the dominant group. Harried from pillar to post, many fled to Canada and England, leaving all their possessions behind. New York proved for a time the sanctuary of hundreds. Indignities of manifold character were heaped upon the Loyalists remaining in America. Some were thrown into the underground mines of Newgate prison. Others suffered still greater severities. This fratricidal war is the great tragedy of the Revolution.

THE FIRST VICTORIES BRING ELATION

HOPE ran high among the revolutionaries. It seemed as if their goal would be attained overnight. Broadsides of the period contain many songs and verses that illustrate the exultant spirit of the people.

219 Reception of the American Loyalists in England, from an engraving by H. Moses after the painting by Benjamin West

Two favorite SONGS,

made on the Evacuation of the Town of BOSTON.

by the *Britiſh Troops*, on the 17th of March, 1776.

IN ſeventeen hundred and ſeventy ſix,
On March the eleventh, the time was prefix'd
Our forces march'd on upon Dorcheſter-neck,
Made fortifications againſt an attack.
The morning next following, as Howe did eſpy,
The banks we caſt up, were ſo copious and high,
Said he in three months, all my men with their might,
Cou'd not make two ſuch Forts as they've made in a night.
Now we hear that their Admiral was very wroth,
And drawing his ſword, he bids Howe to go forth;
And drive off the YANKEES from Dorcheſter hill:
Or he'd leave the harbour and him to their will.
Howe rallies his forces upon the next day,
One party embark'd for the Caſtle they ſay,
But the wind and the weather againſt them did fight,
On Governor's Iſland it drove 'em that night.
Then being diſcourag'd they ſoon did agree,
From Bunker and Boſton, on board ſhip to flee,
Great Howe loſt his ſenſes, they ſay for a week,
For fear our next fort ſhould be rais'd in King-ſtreet.
But yet notwithſtanding the finger of God,
In the wind and the weather which often occurr'd;
Still Howe, Pharaoh like, did harden his heart,
Being thirſty for victory to maintain his part.
He gives out freſh orders on Thurſday it's ſaid,
Forms his men in three branches upon the parade;
Acknowledging it was a deſperate caſe,
In their ſituation the YANKEES to face:
Yet neverthelеſs being haughty of heart,
On Friday one branch of his men did embark:
A ſecond ſtood ready down by the ſea ſide:
His Dragoons were mounted all ready to ride.
Great Howe he now utters a deſperate oration,
Saying fight my brave boys for the crown of our nation:
Take me for your pattern, and fight ye as I,
Let it be 'till we conquer, or elſe 'till we die.
But all of a ſudden, with an Eagle ey'd glance,
They eſpied a fire being kindled by chance,
In a barrack at Cambridge, as many do know,
And then in confuſion they ran to and fro.
Moreover as Providence order'd the thing,
Our drums beat alarm, our bell it did ring,
Which made them cry out, O the YANKEES will come;
O horror! they'll have us, come let us begone.
Then hilter ſkilter they ran in the ſtreet,
Sometimes on their heads and ſometimes on their feet,
Leaving cannon and mortars, pack ſaddles and wheat,
Being glad to eſcape with the ſkin of their teeth.
Now off goes Pilgarlick with his men in a fright,
And altho' they ſhow cowards, yet ſtill they ſhow ſpite,
In burning the Caſtle, as they paſs along,
And now by Nantaſket they lie in a throng.
Let 'em go, let 'em go, for what they will fetch,
I think their great Howe is a miſerable wretch;
And as for his men, they are fools for their pains,
So let them return to Old-England again.

IT was'nt our will that Bunker Hill
From us ſhould e'er be taken;
We thought 'twould never be retook,
But we find we are Miſtaken.

The ſoldiers bid the hill farewell,
Two images left ſentreis,
This they had done all out of fun
To the American Yankees.

A flag of truce was ſent thereon,
To ſee if the hill was clear,
No living ſoul was found thereon,
But theſe images ſtood there.

Their hats they wave, come if you pleaſe,
There's none here to moleſt us,
These wooden men that here do ſtand,
Are only to defy us.

Theſe images they ſoon threw down,
Not one man's life was loſt then,
No ſooner they were on the hill
But they landed into Boſton.

The women come, and children run,
To brave PUTNAM rejoicing,
Saying now is your time to man your lines
For the ſoldiers have left Boſton.

The troops you fairly ſcar'd away,
On board the ſhips they're quarter'd,
The children laugh'd, ſaying over the wharf
They threw their beſt bomb mortar.

With the blazing of your guns that night,
And roaring of your mortars,
The ſoldiers cry'd the Yankees come
To tear us all in quarters.

The barracks being ſet on fire,
Which made the ſoldiers quiver,
They ſoon embark on board their ſhips,
May they ſtay there forever.

Soon after this the fleet fell down,
It's what we long deſir'd,
I think the Gen'rals were afraid
That they'd be ſet on fire.

The ſhipping now have all ſet ſail,
No cauſe have we to mourn,
But ſeem afraid becauſe 'tis ſaid
That they will ſoon return.

Some ſay they're ſail'd for Halefax,
And others for New York
Howe let none know whe[illegible]
When the ſoldiers did [illegible]

Where they are bound [illegible]
But the great GOD on high
May all our heads be cover'd [illegible]
When cannon balls do fly

220 From a broadside in the Massachusetts Historical Society

BY THE HONORABLE

JONATHAN TRUMBULL, Eſq;

Governor and Commander in Chief of the *Engliſh* Colony of *Connecticut* in *New-England*.

A PROCLAMATION.

THE Race of Mankind was made in a State of Innocence and Freedom, ſubjected only to the Laws of GOD the CREATOR, and through his rich Goodneſs, deſigned for virtuous Liberty and Happineſs here and forever; and when moral Evil was introduced into the World, and Man had corrupted his Ways before GOD, Vice and Iniquity came in like a Flood, and Mankind became expoſed, and a prey to the Violence, Injuſtice and Oppreſſion of one another. GOD, in great Mercy, inclined his People to form themſelves into Society, and to ſet up and eſtabliſh civil Government for the Protection and Security of their Lives and Properties from the Invaſion of wicked Men: But through Pride and Ambition, the King's and Princes of the World, appointed by the People the Guardians of their Lives and Liberties, early and almoſt univerſally, degenerated into Tyrants, and by Fraud or Force betrayed and wreſted out of their Hands the very Rights and Properties they were appointed to protect and defend. But a ſmall Part of the human Race maintained and enjoyed any tolerable Degree of Freedom. Among thoſe happy Few the Nation of *Great-Britain* was diſtinguiſhed, by a Conſtitution of Government wiſely framed and modelled, to ſupport the Dignity and Power of the Prince, for the Protection of the Rights of the People; and under which, that Country in long Succeſſion, enjoyed great Tranquility and Peace, though not unattended with repeated and powerful Efforts, by many of it's haughty Kings, to deſtroy the conſtitutional Rights of the People, and eſtabliſh arbitrary Power and Dominion. In one of thoſe convulſive Struggles, our Forefathers having ſuffered in that, their native Country, great and variety of Injuſtice and Oppreſſion, left their dear Connections and Enjoyments, and fled to this then inhoſpitable Land, to ſecure a laſting Retreat from civil and religious Tyranny.

The GOD of Heaven favored and proſpered their Undertaking--made Room for their Settlement--increaſed and multiplied them to a very numerous People, and inclined ſucceeding King's to indulge them and their Children for many Years, the unmoleſted Enjoyment of the Freedom and Liberty they fled to inherit: But, an unnatural King has riſen up--violated his ſacred Obligations, and by the Advice of evil Counſellors, attempted to wreſt from us, their Children, the ſacred Rights we juſtly claim, and which have been ratified and eſtabliſhed by ſolemn Compact with, and recognized by, his Predeceſſors and Fathers, King's of *Great-Britain*--laid upon us Burdens too heavy and grievous to be born, and iſſued many cruel and oppreſſive Edicts, depriving us of our natural, lawful, and moſt important Rights, and ſubjecting us to the abſolute Power and Controul of himſelf, and the *Britiſh* Legiſlature; againſt which we have ſought Relief by humble, earneſt and dutiful Complaints and Petitions: But, inſtead of obtaining Redreſs, our Petitions have been treated with Scorn and Contempt, and freſh Injuries heaped upon us, while hoſtile Armies and Ships are ſent to deſtroy and lay waſte our Country. In this diſtreſſing Dilemma, having no Alternative but abſolute Slavery, or ſucceſsful Reſiſtance; this, and the United American Colonies, have been conſtrained by the over-ruling Laws of Self-preſervation, to take up Arms for the Defence of all that is ſacred and dear to Freemen, and make their ſolemn Appeal to Heaven for the Juſtice of their Cauſe, and reſiſt Force by Force.

GOD ALMIGHTY has been pleaſed, of his infinite Mercy, to ſucceed our Attempts, and give us many Inſtances of ſignal Succeſs and Deliverance; but the Wrath of the King is ſtill increaſing, and not content with before employing all the Force which can be ſent from his own Kingdom to execute his cruel Purpoſes, has procured, and is ſending all the Mercenaries he can obtain from foreign Countries, to aſſiſt in extirpating the Rights of *America*, and with their's, almoſt all the Liberty remaining among Mankind.

In this moſt critical and alarming Situation, this, and all the Colonies, are called upon, and earneſtly preſſed, by the honorable CONGRESS of the *American* Colonies, united for mutual Defence, to raiſe a large additional Number of their Militia and able Men, to be furniſhed and equipped with all poſſible Expedition, for Defence againſt the ſoon expected Attack and Invaſion of thoſe who are our Enemies without a Cauſe. In chearful Compliance with which Requeſt, and urged by Motives the moſt cogent and important that can affect the human Mind, the General Aſſembly of this Colony have freely and unanimouſly agreed and reſolved, that upwards of Seven Thouſand able and effective Men be immediately raiſed, furniſhed and equipped, for the great and intereſting Purpoſes aforeſaid. And not Deſirous that any ſhould go to a Warfare at their own Charges, (though equally intereſted with others) for Defence of the great and all-important Cauſe in which we are engaged, have granted large and liberal Pay and Encouragements, to all who ſhall voluntarily undertake for the Defence of themſelves and their Country, as by their Acts may appear.

I DO THEREFORE, by and with the Advice of the Council, and at the Deſire of the Repreſentatives in General Court aſſembled, iſſue this PROCLAMATION, and make the ſolemn Appeal of ſaid Aſſembly to the Virtue and public Spirit of the good People of this Colony. Affairs are haſtening faſt to a Criſis, and the approaching Campaign will, in all Probability, determine forever the Fate of *America*. If this ſhould be ſucceſsful on our Side, there is little to fear on Account of any other. Be exhorted to riſe, therefore, to ſuperior Exertions on this great Occaſion; and let all that are able and neceſſary, ſhew themſelves ready in Behalf of their injured and oppreſſed Country, and come forth to the Help of the LORD againſt the Mighty, and convince the unrelenting Tyrant of *Britain*, that they are reſolved to be FREE. Let them ſtep forth to defend their Wives, their little Ones, their Liberty, and every thing they hold ſacred and dear, to defend the Cauſe of their Country, their Religion and their GOD. Let every one to the utmoſt of their Power, lend a helping Hand to promote and forward a Deſign on which the Salvation of *America* now evidently depends. Nor need any be diſmayed: the Cauſe is certainly a juſt and a glorious one: GOD is able to ſave us in ſuch Way and Manner as he pleaſes, and to humble our proud Oppreſſors. The Cauſe is that of Truth and Juſtice; he has already ſhewn his Power in our Behalf, and for the Deſtruction of many of our Enemies. *Our Fathers truſted in him and were delivered.* Let us all repent, and thoroughly amend our Ways, and turn to him, put all our Truſt and Confidence in him--in his Name go forth, and in his Name ſet up our Banners, and he will ſave us with temporal and eternal Salvation. And while our Armies are Abroad, jeoparding their Lives in the high Places of the Field, let all who remain at Home, cry mightily to GOD for the Protection of his Providence, to ſhield and defend their Lives from Death, and to crown them with Victory and Succeſs. And in the Name of the ſaid General Aſſembly, I do hereby earneſtly recommend it to all, both Miniſters and People, frequently to meet together for ſocial Prayer to ALMIGHTY GOD, for the out pouring of his bleſſed Spirit upon this guilty Land--That he would awaken his People to Righteouſneſs and Repentance--bleſs our Councils--proſper our Arms, and ſucceed the Meaſures uſing for our neceſſary Self-Defence--diſappoint the evil and cruel Devices of our Enemies--preſerve our precious Rights and Liberties--lengthen out our Tranquility, and make us a People of his Praiſe, and the bleſſed of the LORD, as long as the Sun and Moon ſhall endure.

AND all the Miniſters of the Goſpel in this Colony, are directed and deſired to publiſh this Proclamation in their ſeveral Churches and Congregations, and to enforce the Exhortations thereof by their own pious Example and public Inſtructions.

GIVEN under my Hand, at the Council Chamber in Hartford, *the 18th Day of* June, *Anno Domini* 1776.

JONATHAN TRUMBULL.

221 Proclamation of Jonathan Trumbull, June 18, 1776, from a broadside in the New York Public Library

NEW POWERS ARE GRADUALLY ESTABLISHED

MORE prosaic, but more perplexing, was the dilemma facing Congress. How could the fact of war be reconciled with continued allegiance and the theory of subjection to the British crown? Illegal bodies had assumed actual political control in the colonies, and the result was a general confusion. John Adams even feared that the system would "injure the morale of the people, and destroy their habits of order and attachment to regular government." Civil government must continue. So, as early as November, 1775, the Congress recommended the establishment of new governments where the old had fallen. This policy was fully accepted as orthodox by the Resolution of May 15, 1776. The fact of war was pushing the colonies to a declaration of independence.

CONNECTICUT'S GOVERNOR SUMMONS RECRUITS

WHAT was that goal? Time and time again it had been stated to be freedom from the oppression of England's Government. But freedom is a word of fire. Whereas it at first meant simply relief from the unconstitutional acts of the British Parliament, it came, bit by bit, to mean political independence from the mother country. Throughout the literature of the period runs this ambiguity. Here we find it in a proclamation of the devout Jonathan Trumbull, that stanch adviser of Washington, "Brother Jonathan" of the war. As Governor of the "English Colony of Connecticut" he summons recruits to fight England! This confusion of thought in the minds of the rebel leaders well indicates how loath they were to surrender irrevocably the benefits of political union with the motherland. Pulled by diverse desires in opposite directions, they were for the most part opportunists, taking steps as need for them arose.

IN CONGRESS,

MAY 15, 1776.

WHEREAS his Britannic Majeſty, in conjunction with the Lords and Commons of Great-Britain, has, by a late Act of Parliament, excluded the inhabitants of theſe United Colonies from the protection of his crown: And whereas no anſwer whatever to the humble petitions of the Colonies for redreſs of grievances, and reconciliation with Great-Britain has been or is likely to be given; but the whole force of that kingdom, aided by foreign mercenaries, is to be exerted for the deſtruction of the good people of theſe Colonies: And whereas it appears abſolutely irreconcileable to reaſon and good conſcience, for the people of theſe Colonies now to take the oaths and affirmations neceſſary for the ſupport of any government under the Crown of Great-Britain; and it is neceſſary that the exerciſe of every kind of authority under the ſaid Crown ſhould be totally ſuppreſſed, and all the powers of government exerted under the authority of the people of the Colonies for the preſervation of internal peace, virtue, and good order, as well as for the defence of their lives, liberties and properties, againſt the hoſtile invaſions and cruel depredations of their enemies: Therefore

RESOLVED, That it be recommended to the reſpective Aſſemblies and Conventions of the United Colonies, where no Government ſufficient to the exigencies of their affairs has been hitherto eſtabliſhed, to adopt ſuch Government as ſhall in the opinion of the Repreſentatives of the People beſt conduce to the happineſs and ſafety of their Conſtituents in particular, and America in general.

Extract from the Minutes,

CHARLES THOMSON, SECRETARY.

PHILADELPHIA: Printed by JOHN DUNLAP

222 Resolution of Congress, May 15, 1776, from a broadside in the New York Public Library

PAINE'S BRIEF FOR INDEPENDENCE

OTHER events had contributed to this end. Parliament, in December, 1775, had again played into the hands of the Patriots. The Prohibitory Act forbade all nations to trade with America, and made vessels so trading lawful prizes of war. This was the Act that called forth the Resolution just noticed (No. 222). Said John Adams: "It makes us independent in spite of our supplications and entreaties." In a soil fully prepared was now sown Tom Paine's *Common Sense*. Published January 10, 1776, within a few weeks one hundred thousand copies were sold. The pamphlet was a passionate and brilliant brief for independence. "It is repugnant to reason, to the inward order of things, to suppose that this continent can longer remain subject to any external power. The utmost stretch of human wisdom cannot at this time compass a plan short of separation." It became the bible of the Revolution, found wherever there was a Patriot.

COMMON SENSE;

ADDRESSED TO THE

INHABITANTS

OF

AMERICA,

On the following interesting

SUBJECTS.

I. Of the Origin and Design of Government in general, with concise Remarks on the English Constitution.

II. Of Monarchy and Hereditary Succession.

III. Thoughts on the present State of American Affairs.

IV. Of the present Ability of America, with some miscellaneous Reflections.

A NEW EDITION, with several Additions in the Body of the Work. To which is added an APPENDIX; together with an Address to the People called QUAKERS.

N B. The New Addition here given increases the Work upward of one Third.

Man knows no Master save creating HEAVEN,
Or those whom Choice and common Good ordain.
THOMSON.

PHILADELPHIA PRINTED.

And SOLD by W. and T. BRADFORD

223 Title-page of the issue, 1776 (new edition), in the Thomas Paine National Historical Society, New Rochelle, N. Y.

VIRGINIA ADOPTS THE FIRST FREE CONSTITUTION

THE South had not waited for Congressional sanction to form new governments. In Virginia the conduct of Governor Dunmore had strengthened the independents. On May 5, 1776, a provincial convention met to frame a new constitution. On the 15th, resolutions drafted by Edmund Pendleton were adopted asking Congress to declare separation from Great Britain. North Carolina had the preceding month taken similar action. On June 29 Virginia adopted the first written constitution of a free and independent state in America. The fundamental ideas which underlay this document were derived from the old régime. Aside from the abrogation of allegiance to the British crown, there was no radical departure from the government of the colonial days. In the Virginia convention sat two men whose names are indelibly written in American history. Both Edmund Pendleton and George Mason had been prominent in Virginia politics. The former had been of the committee of correspondence in 1773 and of the first Continental Congress; both were members of the Virginia Committee of Safety in 1775, the former being President. In 1776 Pendleton drafted the resolution calling for national independence, while Mason prepared the famous Declaration of Rights. In 1788 reappeared the nationalism of the one, the devotion to freedom of the other; for while Pendleton, as chairman of the Virginia ratifying convention, was a leading advocate of the adoption of the Constitution, Mason, with Patrick Henry, led the opposition to a document regarded by them as dangerous to human liberty.

224 Edmund Pendleton, 1721–1803, from the portrait by Thomas Sully (1783–1872), in the Virginia Historical Society, Richmond

225 George Mason, 1726–92, from a copy by Henry Inman (1801–46) of an original portrait, about 1756 (since lost), by John Hesselius, in the Virginia State Library, Richmond

(Copy of the first Draught by G M.)

A Declaration of Rights made by the Representatives of the good People of Virginia, assembled in full and free Convention; which Rights do pertain to them and their Posterity, as the Basis and Foundation of Government.

1. That all Men are created equally free & independent, & have certain inherent natural Rights, of which they can not, by any Compact, deprive or divest their Posterity; among which are the Enjoyment of Life & Liberty, with the Means of acquiring & possessing Property, & pursueing & obtaining Happiness & Safety.

2. That all Power is by God & Nature vested in, & consequently derived from the People; that Magistrates are their Trustees & Servants, and at all Times amenable to them.

3. That Government is or ought to be, instituted for the common Benefit, Protection & Security of the People Nation, or Community. Of all the various Modes & Forms of Government that is best, which is capable of producing the greatest Degree of Happiness & Safety, & is most effectually secured against the Danger of mal-administration; and that whenever any Government shall be found inadequate or contrary to these purposes, a Majority of the Community hath an indubitable, unalienable & indefeasible Right, to reform, alter, or abolish it, in such

226 First draft of the Virginia Declaration of Rights, adopted June 12, 1776, from the original in the Virginia State Library, Richmond

VIRGINIA'S DECLARATION SERVES AS A MODEL

SEVENTEEN days prior to the adoption of the Virginia Constitution this work of George Mason received the assent of the convention. Composed of sixteen articles, its resemblance to the document of July 4 is striking. The spirit of its author is seen in his statement of 1778: "We have laid our new government upon a broad foundation and we have endeavoured to provide the most effectual securities for the essential rights of human nature, both in civil and religious liberty. The people become every day more attached to it, and I trust that neither the power of Great Britain, nor the power of Hell will be able to prevail against it."

227 Independence Hall, Philadelphia, from a photograph by Frank Cousins

THE TIDE OF EVENTS BEARS CONGRESS TOWARD FREEDOM

EVENTS were thus pushing the Continental Congress toward an unequivocal declaration. Many an American, wavering between loyalty to a great nation and a fight for independence, suddenly made up his mind when the news came that the British Government had hired Hessian troops for service against the colonies. The Second Congress, which met in the State House, included, like the first, men of all shades of political faith. But now the conservatives were weaker than before; while the patriots had the times with them. Yet there were weighty reasons for delay and hesitancy. A final break with the home country, to which many of the leaders still felt a sentimental attachment, might alienate powerful English sympathizers such as Pitt and Burke. Open rebellion, moreover, would bring non-intercourse, never favored by the commercial class. Then, too, such a declaration must be that of a united people. The conservatives — for example, Wilson of Pennsylvania and Jay of New York — reported their constituents unready for such a step.

Resolved That these United Colonies are, and of right ought to be, free and independent States, that they are absolved from all allegiance to the British Crown, and that all political connection between them and the State of Great Britain is, and ought to be, totally dissolved.

That it is expedient forthwith to take the most effectual measures for forming foreign Alliances.

That a plan of confederation be prepared and transmitted to the respective Colonies for their consideration and approbation.

228 Resolution of Richard Henry Lee, as reported from Committee, June 7, 1776, from the original in the Library of Congress

LEE'S RESOLUTION FOR INDEPENDENCE

THUS, when Richard Henry Lee of Virginia, obeying the mandate of the Virginia Convention, introduced on June 7 a resolution for independence, debate ensued. On the 8th and the days following, his resolution was considered in Committee of the Whole. Adoption was urged by Lee, the Adamses, Jefferson and others. But the moderates, led by Dickinson of Pennsylvania, persuaded the Congress to postpone the first resolution, declaring independence, till action had been taken on the third, the plan of confederation.

THE RADICALS ENDEAVOR TO WIN THE MODERATES

To win over, in the interim, the reluctant colonies became the endeavor of the radicals. They had already secured the appointment of a committee to draft the Declaration "lest any time be lost in case the Congress agree to the resolution" of Lee. Of this committee, four — Jefferson, Franklin, John Adams and Roger Sherman — were radicals, while the moderates had but one representative in the person of Robert Livingston. Early in their deliberations this committee assigned to Jefferson the task of preparing the draft. The work submitted by him received few changes at the hands of Franklin and John Adams.

229 From the painting *Writing the Declaration of Independence*, by J. L. G. Ferris (1863–), in Independence Hall, Philadelphia

NEW YORK DELAYS UNANIMITY FOR INDEPENDENCE

On July 1 the Lee resolution again came before the Congress. Debate closed with a vote showing nine colonies in favor and two against the declaration. The delegates from New York refused to vote, while Delaware was evenly divided. The following day another vote was taken. The result showed the all-night efforts of the radical leaders. The South Carolina delegation now determined to side with the majority, running the risk of misrepresenting their distant constituents. Caesar Rodney, who was eighty miles from Philadelphia, rode all night and arrived in time to swing the Delaware vote to the affirmative. Enough Pennsylvania delegates were won over to secure a final vote of twelve to none, with New York still abstaining. A week later the New York convention gave its approval. Unanimity had been secured. On the same day the report of the drafting committee was taken under advisement. Debate was lively, and several changes were made. On the 4th, the edited Declaration of Independence was formally adopted by the Congress.

230 From the painting in Independence Hall, Philadelphia, *The Congress Voting Indepenuence*, by Robert Edge Pine (1730–88), left unfinished at the artist's death and completed by Edward Savage (1761–1817)

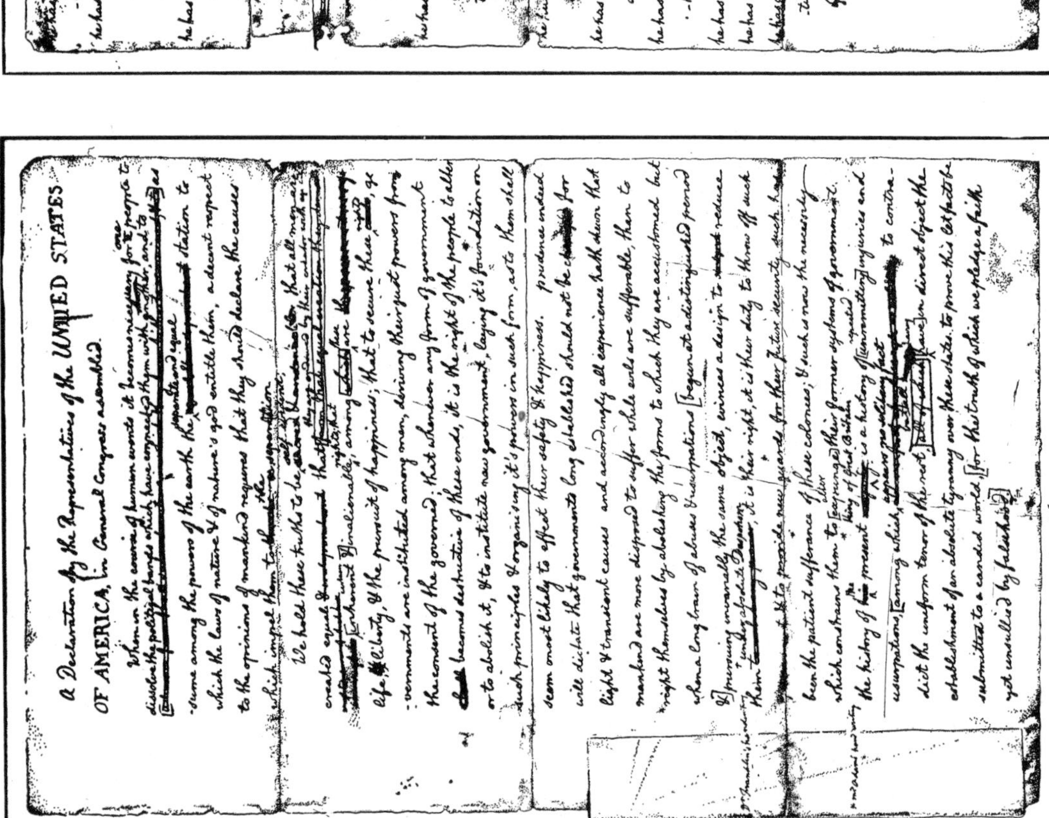

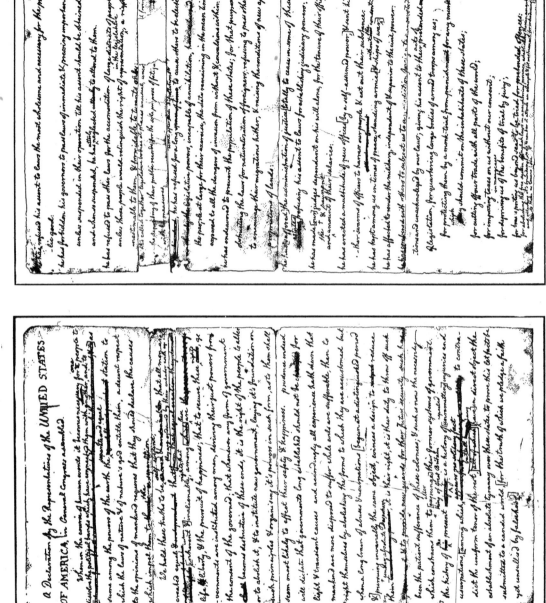

231 First and second sheets of Jefferson's hand-written draft of the Declaration of Independence, with revision by Benjamin Franklin and John Adams, and before its further revision by Congress, from the original in the Library of Congress 232

233 Third and fourth sheets of Jefferson's hand-written draft of the Declaration of Independence, with revision by Benjamin Franklin and John Adams, and before its further revision by Congress, from the original in the Library of Congress 234

235 From the painting, 1816, *The Declaration of Independence*, by John Trumbull, in the capitol, Washington

THE DECLARATION IS SIGNED ON AUGUST 2ND

THE form of the Declaration as it came from the committee was Jefferson's, and he was proud of it. He was noticeably restive as the Congress proceeded to alter the report; and in the succeeding days he prepared several copies of the document as the committee had reported it, with the portions changed or rejected by Congress underlined. One copy he sent to Lee, who had said that it was "copied from Locke's *Two Treatises on Government*," with the words, "You will judge whether it is better or worse for the critics." So many members were absent on the 4th that no effort was made to secure the signatures of the members. But on the 19th a committee to engross the resolution on parchment was authorized; and on August 2 the final copy was ready. The members present then affixed their names, and in the course of time, two other signatures, those of Thomas McKean and William Thornton, were added.

236 Algernon Sidney, 1622–83, from the portrait by Justus van Egmont (1601–74), in the National Portrait Gallery, London

237 James Harrington, 1611–77, from the portrait by A. Van der Venne (1589–1662) in the National Portrait Gallery, London

238 Thomas Paine, 1737–1809, from an engraving by William Sharp (1749–1824) after the portrait by George Romney (1734–1802)

IDEAS FROM MANY MINDS ARE MERGED IN THE DECLARATION

THE political ideas in the Declaration were not new. The philosophy — even the phraseology — is that of the colonial thought of the time. In Locke's *Two Treatises on Government* (1689), Sidney's *Discourses concerning Government* (1698), Harrington's *Oceana* (1656), Paine's *Common Sense* (1776), the patriots found the principles of government that justified revolution. Though no book or pamphlet was used in the preparation, Jefferson was "so thoroughly imbued with the republican spirit of the Parliamentarians of the times of the Commonwealth, that the paper reflects their dignity of thought and solidity of style." — FROTHINGHAM, *Rise of the Republic*, p. 548. Jefferson himself has ably stated the purpose and achievement of the Declaration: "Neither aiming at originality of principle or sentiment, nor yet copied from any particular or previous writings, it was intended to be an expression of the American mind, and to give to that expression the proper tone and spirit called for by the occasion."

THE PUBLIC HEARS THE DECLARATION

THE meetings of Congress were held behind closed doors. So, while the Philadelphians knew that Lee's resolution had been adopted, the Declaration of Independence first appeared in the *Pennsylvania Packet* of July 6. Two days later the Province bell, henceforth to be called the Liberty Bell, announced a public reading in the State House yard. From a stand built for astronomical observations, John Nixon's strong voice carried out over the great crowd assembled below. After the ceremony the royal coat-of-arms, suspended over the court-room door, was torn down and burned.

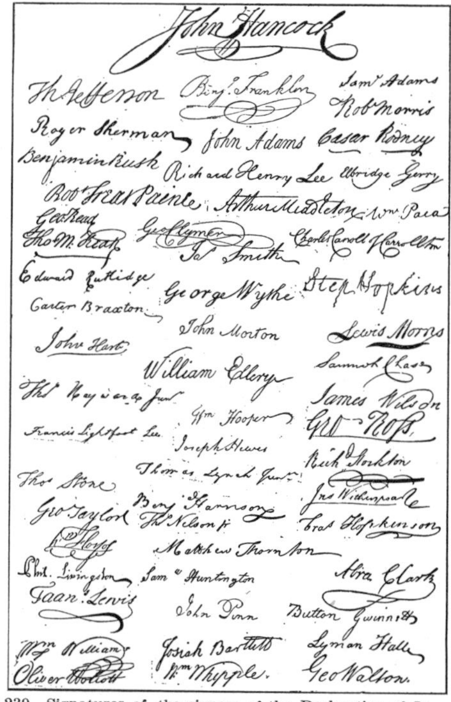

239 Signatures of the signers of the Declaration of Independence, reduced from the original document

240 From the engraving by John C. McRae, about 1870, after the painting *Pulling down the Statue of George III*, by Johannes A. Oertel (1823–1909)

THE DECLARATION ANIMATES THE COLONISTS

No state paper ever received such widespread and hearty endorsement. As couriers carried it over the country it was everywhere welcomed by popular assemblages. New York on the 10th celebrated by pulling down the statue of the King, erected but six years before, and ordering the monument to be run into bullets. *The New York Gazette* of July 15 further reports that "In Pursuance of the Declaration of Independence, a general Gaol Delivery, with respect to Debtors, took place." In Boston, on the 18th, the Council "proclaimed from the Balcony of the State-House the DECLARATION of the AMERICAN CONGRESS, absolving the United Colonies from their Allegiance to the British Crown. . . . After which, Thirteen Pieces of Cannon were fired from the Fort on Fort-Hill. . . . The Ceremony was closed with a proper collation to the Gentlemen in the Council Chamber. . . . On the same Evening the King's Arms, and every sign with any Resemblance of it, whether Lion and Crown, Pestle and Mortar and Crown, Heart and Crown, etc., together with every Sign that belonged to a Tory was taken down, and the latter made a general Conflagration of in King Street." William Whipple, one of the signers, expressed the effect of the Declaration upon the people, in a letter written July 16: "It has had a glorious effect — has made these colonies all alive."

241 Reading the Declaration from the Old State House, Boston, from a reconstruction based on contemporary accounts. © Halliday Historic Photograph Co.

I George Washington Commander in chief of the Armies of the United States of America do acknowledge the UNITED STATES of AMERICA, to be Free, Independent and Sovereign States, and declare that the people thereof owe no allegiance or obedience to George the Third, King of Great-Britain; and I renounce, refuse and abjure any allegiance or obedience to him; and I do swear — that I will to the utmoſt of my power, ſupport, maintain and defend the ſaid United States, againſt the ſaid King George the Third, his heirs and ſucceſſors and his or their abettors, aſſiſtants and adherents, and will ſerve the ſaid United States in the office of Com in chief as aforesaid which I now hold, with fidelity, according to the beſt of my ſkill and underſtanding.

G Washington

Sworn before me
Camp at Valley Forge
May 12th 1778
Stirling Major Genl

242 Facsimile of Washington's Oath of Allegiance, in the War Department, Washington

GREAT DIFFICULTIES FACE THE NEW NATION

A SEQUEL of the Declaration was that Americans were compelled to take sides for or against the new government. The oath of allegiance became the test. It remained to make good the Declaration of Independence on the field of battle. That was to be no easy task. The American army was small, poorly equipped and irregularly paid. State jealousies often jeopardized success.

HOWE'S OVERTURES

LITTLE wonder, then, that Lord Howe, commander of the royal forces in America, hoped to win without the necessity of bloodshed. While Congress was voting independence, the British army, aiming to threaten the rebels at a crucial point, was concentrating on New York. To oppose this formidable array, Washington, with unfriendly Tories at his rear, had a few thousand raw militiamen. Yet all overtures of conciliation from Howe were spurned, and the British reverted to the military weapon.

THE BATTLE OF LONG ISLAND

THERE followed, on August 27, the battle of Long Island. New York fell to the British. The Americans retreated to Jersey. The victory seemed to the British ministry to be decisive. The cartoon pictures Lord North, surrounded by the King, Bute and Mansfield, triumphantly displaying Howe's dispatch to the chagrined opposition, typified by Wilkes, Rockingham and a strumpet with Liberty Cap.

244 From a caricature in the *London Magazine*, Nov. 1776

NEW-YORK, July 18.

On Sunday afternoon a barge from the fleet, appeared in our bay, with a white flag, which was there met by the General's barge with ſeveral Gentlemen of the army on board. The flag was ſent from Lord Howe, with a letter to his Excellency General Waſhington. But as the letter was improperly directed, it was not received, though much ſolicited by the officer, who, we hear, ſaid it contained nothing of a hoſtile nature—that Lord Howe came over poſſeſſed of unlimited power, and was much concerned he had not arrived a few days ſooner, which would have effected a reconciliation, &c. However it ſeems his unlimited power did not extend even to the neceſſary preliminaries of a negociation—an acknowledgment of the right of the perſons to whom he came, to treat with him.

Indeed the idea of coming over to propoſe a plan of reconciliation, is in every view abſurd and ridiculous, for as the Colonies never invaded the rights of Britain, and only defended their own, there was no occaſion at all for negociation. The moment Great-Britain receded from her unjuſt claims, the war was at an end.

The very *propoſition*, therefore, of a negociation, was a proof that Great-Britain perſiſted in her incroachments on the rights of the Colonies, and was in itſelf an act of a hoſtile nature.

On Tueſday another flag from the fleet appeared, and was met as before, when a letter was again offered, but for the ſame reaſon as the former, rejected.

A gentleman from Virginia ſays, that General LEE had ſent there for ſome troops, who were on their march for Carolina, when another expreſs arrived, ordering them not to march, and by all accounts the fleet has met with much damage at Carolina, but the particulars we have not yet heard.

We hear from Poughkeepſie, that 23 perſons diſaffected to our common cauſe, endeavouring to diſarm the friends of liberty, have been taken up by order of the committe of that place, who have ordered them to Ridgfield gaol.

243 Contemporary account of Howe's offer of conciliation, from *The New England Chronicle*, July 25, 1776, in the New York Public Library

By RICHARD Viſcount HOWE of the Kingdom of IRELAND, and WILLIAM HOWE Eſq; General of His MAJESTY's Forces in AMERICA, the KING's Commiſſioners for reſtoring Peace to His MAJESTY's Colonies and Plantations in NORTH-AMERICA, &c. &c. &c.

PROCLAMATION.

WHEREAS by our Declarations of the 14th of July, and 19th of September laſt, in Purſuance of His MAJESTY's moſt gracious Intentions towards His Subjects in the Colonies or Provinces of NEW-HAMPSHIRE, MASSACHUSETT's-BAY, RHODE-ISLAND, CONNECTICUT, NEW-YORK, NEW-JERSEY, PENNSYLVANIA, the Three lower Counties on DELAWARE, MARYLAND, VIRGINIA, NORTH-CAROLINA, SOUTH-CAROLINA, and GEORGIA, all Perſons ſpeedily returning to their juſt Allegiance were promiſed a free and general Pardon, and were invited to accept, not only the Bleſſings of Peace, but a ſecure Enjoyment of their Liberty and Properties, upon the true Principles of the Conſtitution; AND WHEREAS, notwithſtanding the ſaid Declarations, and the Example of many who have availed themſelves of the Aſſurances therein made, ſeveral Bodies of armed Men, in open Contempt of His Majeſty's proffered Clemency, do ſtill continue their Oppoſition to the Eſtabliſhment of legal Government and Peace; and divers other ill diſpoſed Perſons, purſuing their own ambitious Purpoſes in the Exerciſe of a lawleſs Influence and Power, are uſing freſh Endeavors, by various Arts and Miſrepreſentations, to alienate the Confidence and Affection of His Majeſty's Subjects; To defeat every Plan of Reconciliation, and to prolong the unnatural War between GREAT-BRITAIN and her Colonies: NOW, in order to the more effectual Accompliſhment of His Majeſty's moſt gracious Intentions, and the ſpeedy Reſtoration of the public Tranquillity; And duly conſidering the Expediency of limiting the Time within which ſuch Pardon as aforeſaid ſhall be granted, and of ſpecifying the Terms upon which only the ſame ſhall and may be obtained, WE DO, IN HIS MAJESTY's Name, and by Virtue of the Powers committed to Us, hereby charge and command all Perſons whatſoever, who are aſſembled together in Arms againſt His Majeſty's Government, to diſband Themſelves and return to their Dwellings, there to remain in a peaceable and quiet Manner; AND WE ALSO charge and command all ſuch other Perſons as are aſſembled together under the Name of General, or Provincial Congreſſes, Committees, Conventions, or other Aſſociations, by whatever Name or Names known and diſtinguiſhed, or who under the Colour of any Authority from any ſuch Congreſs, Committee, Convention, and other Aſſociation, take upon them to iſſue or execute any Orders for levying Money, raiſing Troops, fitting out armed Ships and Veſſels, impriſoning, or otherwiſe moleſting His Majeſty's Subjects, to deſiſt and ceaſe from all ſuch treaſonable Actings and Doings, and to relinquiſh all ſuch uſurped Power and Authority, ſo that Peace may be reſtored, a ſpeedy Remiſſion of paſt Offences quiet the Apprehenſions of the Guilty, and all the Inhabitants of the ſaid Colonies be enabled to reap the Benefit of His Majeſty's paternal Goodneſs in the Preſervation of their Property, the Reſtoration of their Commerce, and the Security of their moſt valuable Rights, under the juſt and moderate Authority of the Crown and Parliament of GREAT-BRITAIN: AND WE DO hereby declare, and make known to all Men, that every Perſon who within SIXTY DAYS from the Day of the Date hereof ſhall appear before the Governor, or Lieutenant Governor, or Commander in Chief in any of His Majeſty's Colonies or Provinces aforeſaid, or before the General or commanding Officer of His Majeſty's Forces in AMERICA, or any other Officer in His Majeſty's Service having the Command of any Detachment or Parties of His Majeſty's Forces there, or before the Admiral or Commander in Chief of His Majeſty's Fleets, or any other Officer commanding any of His Majeſty's Ships of War, or any armed Veſſel in His Majeſty's Service, within any of the Ports, Havens, Creeks, or upon the Coaſts of AMERICA, and ſhall claim the Benefit of this Proclamation, and at the ſame Time teſtify his Obedience to the Laws, by ſubſcribing a Declaration in the Words following, "I, A. B. do promiſe and declare, that I will remain in a peaceable Obedience to His Majeſty, and will not take up Arms, nor encourage Others to take up Arms, in "Oppoſition to His Authority," ſhall and may obtain a full and free Pardon of all Treaſons and miſpriſions of Treaſons, by him heretofore committed or done, and of all Forfeitures, Attainders, and Penalties for the ſame; and upon producing to Us, or to either of Us, a Certificate of ſuch his Appearance and Declaration, ſhall and may have and receive ſuch Pardon made and paſſed to him in due Form.

GIVEN at NEW-YORK, this Thirtieth Day of November, 1776.

HOWE.
W. HOWE.

By Command of their Excellencies,
HEN. STRACHEY.

Printed by MACDONALD & CAMERON in WATER-STREET, between the COFFEE-HOUSE and the OLD SLIP.

245 Proclamation signed by Lord Howe and General William Howe, New York, Nov. 30, 1776, offering protection to all who should return to British allegiance, from a broadside in the New York Public Library

BRITISH OFFER OF PARDON

AGAIN the British resorted to peaceful penetration of the American position. Renewed offers of pardon brought to the side of the Crown some three thousand Jersey farmers. Desertions from the Continental army were constant. With the remainder — a bare three thousand — Washington crossed the Delaware, in early December, into Pennsylvania, while Howe threw outposts across New Jersey. The Congress fled to Baltimore. (See Vol. VI.)

TOM PAINE

THESE were dark days for the patriot cause. On the 17th of December Washington wrote: "Our only dependence now is the speedy enlistment of a new army. If this fails, I think the game will be pretty well up." The dismal circumstances of the Americans offered little inducement to volunteers. It was at this moment that there was published the first issue of Paine's *Crisis*, a series of pamphlets that appeared intermittently until the close of the war. This first number was a clarion call to the Patriots. "Up to help us; lay your shoulders to the wheel. . . . Let it be told to the future world, that in the depth of winter, when nothing but hope and virtue could survive, the city and country, alarmed at one common danger, came forth to meet and repulse it." A week later came Trenton and the beginning of the brilliant campaign that ended with the recovery of Jersey and the reinvigoration of the flagging spirit of the rebels.

The *American* CRISIS.

NUMBER I.

By the Author of COMMON SENSE.

THESE are the times that try men's ſouls: The ſummer ſoldier and the ſunſhine patriot will, in this criſis, ſhrink from the ſervice of his country; but he that ſtands it NOW, deſerves the love and thanks of man and woman. Tyranny, like hell, is not eaſily conquered; yet we have this conſolation with us, that the harder the conflict, the more glorious the triumph. What we obtain too cheap, we eſteem too lightly:—'Tis dearneſs only that gives every thing its value. Heaven knows how to ſet a proper price upon its goods; and it would be ſtrange indeed, if ſo celeſtial an article as FREEDOM ſhould not be highly rated. Britain, with an army to enforce her tyranny, has declared, that ſhe has a right *(not only to* TAX, but) "*to* "BIND *us in* ALL CASES WHATSOEVER," and if being *bound in that manner* is not ſlavery, then is there not ſuch a thing as ſlavery upon earth. Even the expreſſion is impious, for ſo unlimited a power can belong only to GOD.

WHETHER the Independence of the Continent was declared too ſoon, or delayed too long, I will not now enter into as an argument; my own ſimple opinion is, that had it been eight months earlier, it would have been much better. We did not make a proper uſe of laſt winter, neither could we, while we were in a dependent ſtate. However, the fault, if it were one, was all our own; we have none to blame but ourſelves*. But no great deal is loſt yet; all that Howe has been doing for this month paſt is rather a ravage than a conqueſt, which the ſpirit of the Jerſies a year ago would have quickly repulſed, and which time and a little reſolution will ſoon recover.

I have as little ſuperſtition in me as any man living, but my

* "The preſent winter" (meaning the laſt) "is worth an "age, if rightly employed, but if loſt, or neglected, the whole "Continent will partake of the evil; and there is no puniſhment that man does not deſerve, be he who, or what, or "where he will, that may be the means of ſacrificing a ſeaſon "ſo precious and uſeful." COMMON SENSE.

246 Title-page of *The American Crisis*, Philadelphia, Dec. 19, 1776, in the New York Public Library

247 From the caricature *The Flight of Congress*, published at London, Nov., 1777, by William Hitchcock, in the collection of R. T. H. Halsey, New York

PHILADELPHIA FALLS INTO THE HANDS OF THE BRITISH

Yet this success was but momentary. With the aid of the fleet and the Hessian mercenaries, the British, in the fall of 1777, captured the American capital. Once more Howe rested content. The Americans were being pushed back; their Congress was forced to fly to Lancaster and York; their credit was almost annihilated by the profuse issues of paper money. Even Burgoyne's surrender in October was soon overshadowed by the sufferings at Valley Forge. (See Vol. VI.)

248 Charles James Fox, 1749–1806, from the portrait by Karl Anton Hickel (1745–98), in the National Portrait Gallery, London

AMERICA'S FRIENDS IN PARLIAMENT

There were, however, a number of hopeful conditions. America was not without influential aids in England. Chief among the opposition to the King's Friends in Parliament were Rockingham, Pitt, Burke and Fox. The last named entered Parliament as a stripling in 1768. For a time he supported the ministry; but in 1774 he changed sides, and from then on he steadily grew to a position of leadership. Of picturesque character, he came to favor the American cause and to push its interests with vigor and adroitness.

AMERICA HONORS AN ENGLISH INTELLECTUAL

249 Richard Price, 1723–91, from the portrait by Benjamin West, in the Royal Society, London

Before the outbreak of the American Revolution Richard Price, a liberal clergyman and educator, had risen to prominence among the intellectuals of England. He had won for himself the reputation of being one of England's leading students of finance. He saw in the struggle of the colonials a fight for the liberties of Englishmen as well as Americans. He read Tom Paine's *Common Sense* and wrote *Observations on the Nature of Civil Liberty, the Principles of Government, and the Justice and Policy of the War with America.* His reasoned arguments for liberty fell on friendly times in England. The press could not supply the demand for his pamphlet. "It ran into five editions in as many weeks, and into over a dozen editions in the course of the year." — Roland Thomas, *Richard Price*, p. 74. To the end of the war Price maintained an unshaken stand for liberty and an unwavering support of the Americans. The writings of "Dr. Price," as he was known in America, made a profound impression west of the Atlantic. On October 6, 1778, the American Congress resolved: "That the Honorable Benjamin Franklin, Arthur Lee, and John Adams, Esquires, or any one of them, be directed forthwith to apply to Dr. Price and inform him that it is the desire of Congress to consider him as a Citizen of the United States, and to receive his assistance in regulating their finances." For personal reasons Price declined to come to America. But this was not the end of American recognition for his services. The following is a minute from the records of Yale University: "At a meeting of the Yale Corporation on April 24, 1781, it was voted to confer the degree of Doctor of Laws upon George Washington and upon Richard Price."

L'Arbitre d'Europe ou Atlas Politique

tiré selon les Observ.s de Mr Necker

CONFEDERATED COLONIES

LUXURY

RECONCILIATION

PUBLIC CREDIT

JOHN BULL.

Dédié aux Petits Mess.rs Anglois

250 From a contemporary French caricature *The Arbiter of Europe or Political Atlas*, published in Paris, in the collection of R. T. H. Halsey, New York

EUROPE SMILES AT BRITAIN'S EMBARRASSMENT

By the fall of 1777 pressure from many sources in England counseled resort to a conciliatory policy. Those suffering from the disturbed trade conditions began to cry out against higher taxes levied to carry on a fruitless war. Naval administration was notoriously corrupt and inefficient. In the cabinet itself appeared divisions of opinion. In January, Lord North had proposed the restoration of America to the condition of 1763, only to be overridden by the war party. Perhaps most influential was Britain's isolated position in international affairs. France, Spain, Holland, Prussia — none was sorry to see her embarrassed. From the beginning, the continental countries had regarded the American rebellion as an unexpected and fine opening to recover the prestige and the power that England had so recently won from them. And now the British merchants had learned that the American war was costly; and even the ministry was inclined to consider it more than an easily suppressed insurrection. The cartoon, representing England bearing the burden of the thirteen consolidated colonies on his back, well illustrated the current feeling.

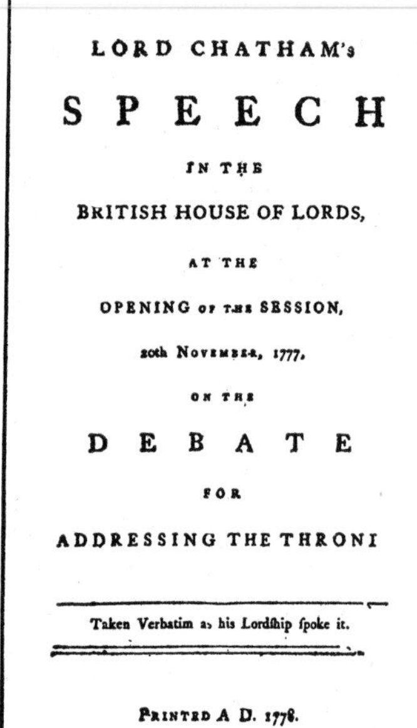

LORD CHATHAM's

SPEECH

IN THE

BRITISH HOUSE OF LORDS,

AT THE

OPENING OF THE SESSION,

20th NOVEMBER, 1777,

ON THE

DEBATE

FOR

ADDRESSING THE THRONE

Taken Verbatim as his Lordſhip ſpoke it.

PRINTED A D. 1778.

251 Title-page of *Lord Chatham's Speech* of Nov. 1777, printed in London, 1778, in the New York Public Library

(8)

ſpirited Remonſtrance of the Duke of Alva, Elizabeth found herſelf obliged to deny the Flemiſh Exiles all countenance, ſupport, or even entrance into her dominions; and the Count Le Marque, with his few deſperate followers, was expelled.—Happening to arrive at the Brille, and finding it weak in defence, they made themſelves maſters of the place:—And this was the foundation of the United Provinces.——

My Lords, this ruinous and ignominious ſituation, where we cannot act with ſucceſs, nor ſuffer with honour, calls upon me to remonſtrate in the ſtrongeſt and loudeſt language of Truth, to reſcue the Ear of Majeſty from the deluſions which ſurround it.—The deſperate ſtate of our Arms abroad is in part known.—No Man thinks more highly of them than I do;—I love and honour the Engliſh troops:—I know their Virtues and their Valour:—I know they can atchieve any thing except Impoſſibilities;—And I know that the Conqueſt of Engliſh America is an *Impoſſibility*. You cannot,—I venture to ſay it, You CANNOT conquer America.—Your Armies laſt War effected every thing that could be effected;—and what was it? It coſt your numerous army, under the

(9)

the command of a moſt able General *, now a noble Lord in this houſe, a long and laborious campaign to expel 5,000 Frenchmen from French America:——My Lords, *you cannot conquer America*:—What is your preſent ſituation there? We do not know the worſt; but we know, that in three campaigns we have done nothing, and ſuffered much. Beſides the ſufferings, perhaps the total loſs, of the Northern Force: The beſt appointed Army that ever took the field, commanded by Sir William Howe, has retired from the American lines:—He was obliged to relinquiſh his attempt, and with great delay and danger to adopt a new and diſtinct plan of operations. We ſhall ſoon know, and in any event have reaſon to lament, what may have happened ſince.—As to conqueſt, therefore, my Lords, I repeat, it is *impoſſible*:—You may ſwell every expence and every effort ſtill more extravagantly;—Pile and accumulate every aſſiſtance you can buy or borrow; traffic and barter with every little pitiful German Prince that ſells his ſubjects to the ſhambles of a foreign Prince;—your efforts are for ever vain and impotent:—doubly ſo from this mercenary aid on which you rely; for it irritates to an incurable reſentment the minds of your enemies:

B

* Sir Jeffry (now Lord) Amherſt

252 Pages 8 and 9 of *Lord Chatham's Speech*, printed in London, 1778 253

PITT WARNS OF FRENCH INTERVENTION

FEAR of French intervention in the American war led to further British efforts toward conciliation. Pitt, in a speech on the 30th of May, deftly joined this dread with the American issue as viewed by the liberals. "We are the aggressors. Instead of exacting unconditional submission from the colonies, we ought to grant them unconditional redress. Now is the crisis, before France is a party. Whenever France or Spain enter into a treaty of any sort with America, Great Britain must immediately declare war against them, even if we have but five ships of the line in our ports, and such a treaty must and will shortly take place, if pacification be delayed." With the opening of Parliament in November, Pitt again pressed for conciliation.

BURGOYNE'S SURRENDER

ON the second of December had come the news of Burgoyne's surrender. Lord North "was so agitated that he could neither eat nor sleep, and the next day at the levee his distress was visible to the foreign ministers. He desired to make peace by giving up all the points which had been in dispute with America, or to retire from the ministry. Concession after defeat was humiliating; but there must be prompt action or France would interfere." — BANCROFT, *History of the United States*, 1866, IX, p. 478. Fox said: "If no better terms can be had, I would treat them as allies, nor do I fear the consequences of their independence." The King and Lord George Germain, however, stood out for a continuation of the war. On January 20, 1778, the Parliament was adjourned.

254 From a British cartoon published Aug. 1, 1779, in the collection of R. T. H. Halsey, New York

255 Duc de Choiseul, 1719–85, from Charles Gavard, *Gallerie Historique de Versailles*, after an engraving by Fontaine

256 Comte de Vergennes, 1717–87, from an engraving after a portrait by Antoine Callet (1741–1823), in the Emmet Collection, New York Public Library

FRENCH DIPLOMATS SURVEY THE SITUATION

All this anxiety about the French was far from groundless. The Seven Years' War had disrupted the European balance of power by enhancing England at the expense of France. Traditional French foreign policy called for a rectification of such a maladjustment. It is, then, not surprising to find Choiseul, adept French diplomatist, watching with keen interest the early signs of unrest in British America. In 1774, Vergennes, equally versed in diplomacy, became minister of foreign affairs. At once he saw the possibilities latent in American revolt. France might regain the power lost in 1763; at the least, England might be driven from the North American continent whence she had so recently ousted France. (See Vol. VI.)

CONGRESS SENDS AGENTS TO ENGLAND AND FRANCE

In November, 1775, the Continental Congress had created "a Committee of Correspondence with our friends abroad," the function of which was to probe European sentiment toward the American struggle. Arthur Lee of the famous Virginia family, then in London, was made its agent. Lee had been educated in England and had lived abroad since 1766. This experience, combined with his reputation as propagandist for the American cause, now proved serviceable. In June, 1776, Silas Deane of Connecticut reached Paris as Congressional agent at the capital of Louis XVI.

257 Silas Deane, 1737–89, from an engraving by B. Reading after a drawing from life by Pierre du Simitiere (–1784) in Philadelphia, published at London, 1783

258 Arthur Lee, 1740–92, from a portrait by Charles Willson Peale in Independence Hall, Philadelphia

259 Pierre-Augustin Caron de Beaumarchais, 1732–99, from a lithograph by Jacques Matthieu Delpech (1775–1832), Paris, in the Emmet Collection, New York Public Library

FRANCE SENDS AMMUNITION TO AMERICA

VERGENNES had already been approached, indirectly of course, in behalf of the Americans. Through the agency of Beaumarchais, dramatist and wealthy gentleman-adventurer, active aid was now given. "Take every precaution," wrote Vergennes to a colleague, "that our motives, our intentions, and, as far as possible, our proceedings, may be hidden from the English." In 1775, Beaumarchais had held conversations with Lee in London. So the firm of "Rodrigue Hortalez et Cie" began to sell merchandise to "Timothy Jones" of Bermuda. In reality, Jones was Silas Deane, and Beaumarchais, aided by the French Government, was the vendor of ammunition.

CONGRESS SEEKS EUROPEAN RECOGNITION

THE second of the Lee resolutions of June 10, 1776, read: "That it is expedient forthwith to take the most effectual measures for forming foreign alliances." In the autumn of that year, therefore, the Congress took further action to secure French aid. In December, Benjamin Franklin, in European eyes the greatest of Americans, joined Deane and Lee in the diplomatic game to be played. Lee was soon sent on a vain mission to Spain to win her support. Vergennes had in August urged upon Louis XVI the expediency of war with England; but the King and his chief minister, Maurepas, were unwilling to burden a demoralized treasury in such a dubious cause. News of the battle of Long Island dampened any ardor for American liberty.

In Congress, Octr. 16. 1776

Additional Instructions to Benjamin Franklin, Silas Deane and commissioners from the united states of America to the King of France

Whilst you are negotiating the affairs you are charged with at the court of France, you will have opportunities of conversing frequently with the ministers and agents of other european princes and states residing there.

You shall endeavour, when you find occasion fit and convenient, to obtain from them a recognition of our independency and sovereignty and to conclude treaties of peace, amity and commerce between their princes or states and us; provided that the same be not inconsistent with the treaty you shall make with his most Christian majesty; that they do not oblige us to become a party in any war, which may happen in consequence thereof & that the immunities, exemptions, privileges, protection, defence & advantages or the contrary thereby stipulated be equal & reciprocal.

If that cannot be effected, you shall to the utmost of your power, prevent their taking part with great Britain in the war, which his britannic majesty prosecutes against us, or entering into offensive alliances with that king, and protest and present remonstrances against the same, desiring the interposition, mediation, and good offices, on our behalf, of his most Christian Majesty the King of France and of any other princes or states, whose dispositions are not hostile towards us.

In case overtures be made to you by the ministers or agents of any european princes or states for commercial treaties between them and us, you may conclude such treaties accordingly.

By order of Congress
John Hancock Presid.

260 Instructions of Congress to Franklin and Deane, Oct. 16, 1776, from the original in the Emmet Collection, New York Public Library 261

FRANKLIN MAKES A FAVORABLE IMPRESSION IN FRANCE

FRANKLIN then assumed, with much personal satisfaction, a Messianic rôle. Overwhelmed with plaudits from the Encyclopedists, fêted as the disciple of new truth, he deftly led French public opinion — at least that opinion which would be serviceable — to believe that the cause of American independence was the cause of human liberty. This was the easier because there were on the continent few Americans, because Paine's *Common Sense* and Richard Price's *Observations on Civil Liberty and the Justice of the War with America* were exceedingly popular, and the French were ever ready to believe evil of England. The quintessence of this incident is found in the allegory pictured here. Clasping the altar of Liberty kneels America near her benignant protector Franklin. Above is Minerva ready to shield them from harm; while below Hercules, wearing a Gallic cock for crest, hurls backward into the sea downcast Neptune and Britannia with the chains she would have used to hold America.

262 From an engraving *L'Amérique Indépendante,* 1778, by J. C. le Vasseur after a design by Borel, in the Emmet Collection, New York Public Library

THE DUTCH TRADE WITH AMERICA

MEANWHILE assistance came to the revolutionaries from another source. Holland was a commercial country and governed by the commercial spirit. Though she was tied by treaty to England, little love was lost between the two peoples. The Dutch "wished nothing more than to see the Republic's commercial rivals in the hands of a receiver." — VAN LOON, *Fall of the Dutch Republic,* 1913, p. 197. The American war was thus an opportunity not to be wasted. With no fleet, America was at the mercy of England on the sea. But the Dutch had ships, munitions of war, and the desire to make a profit. So a brisk smuggling trade between the Dutch West Indies and American ports sprang up, much to the annoyance of the English. Many of the more influential among the Dutch sympathized with the American cause; and private loans to the rebels were forthcoming. Here is pictured Dutch propaganda for the United States. The King, about to be disrobed of his royal prerogatives by two stalwart Americans, calls on the faltering North for aid. At one side are Englishmen petitioning Cromwell, who had given them such mighty support in their commercial rivalry with the Dutch, to come to their aid now, when the ministry of North was turning a deaf ear to their pleas. The Goddess of Justice, however, is about to strike the unsuspecting English.

263 From a contemporary Dutch cartoon in the collection of R. T. H. Halsey, New York

ENGLAND'S ENEMIES TAKE ADVANTAGE OF HER QUARREL

THE international situation was becoming distinctly menacing for Great Britain. The indiscretions of Deane had let her know of his secret negotiations at the French Court; the avarice of the Dutch had been detected; but England hesitated to declare war upon these unfriendly neutrals. The longer she hesitated, the bolder they became. The bolder they grew, the more they came to believe that Great Britain could not win in the struggle. The process of stealing from England her naval and commercial supremacy seemed as easy as milking a cow. With the Howes resting in captured Philadelphia, and with the British fleet incapacitated by a negligent administration, the British lion seemed harmless. This cartoon proved quite popular, and was reproduced in America, probably by the hand of Paul Revere. It represents the American Congress disarming the British cow of commerce by cutting off its horns. A Hollander is milking the cow, while a Frenchman and a Spaniard wait with bowls for milk. A British ship is stranded at Philadelphia, where English generals are forced into inaction. The British lion drowses, and its master is too dismayed to rouse the beast to defend his prerogatives.

264 From a French cartoon *Ill turns to him who wishes ill*, (trans.), in the collection of R. T. H. Halsey, New York

Treaty of Alliance

The most Christian King and the United States of North America, — towit, New hampshire, Massachusetts Bay, Rhodeisland, Connecticut, Newyork, — New Jersey, Pennsylvania, Delaware, Maryland, Virginia, North Carolina, — South Carolina, and Georgia, having this Day concluded a Treaty of amity and Commerce, for the reciprocal advantage of their Subjects and Citizens have thought it necessary to take into consideration the means of strengthening those engagements and of rendring them useful to the safety and tranquility of the two parties, particulary in case Great Britain in Resentment of that connection and of the good correspondence which is the object of the said Treaty, should break the Peace with France, either by direct hostilities, or by hindring her commerce and navigation, in a manner contrary to the Rights of Nations, and the Peace subsisting between the two Crowns; — and his Majesty and the said united States
to join
the En
the re
impow
conditi

265

FRANCE SIGNS A SECRET TREATY

THE diplomacy of Franklin needed, therefore, but the stimulus of the victory at Saratoga to throw France openly into alliance with the United States. Two months after the news of this success reached Paris, the secret treaty was signed. France sought the weakening of her ancient enemy and the trade of independent America.

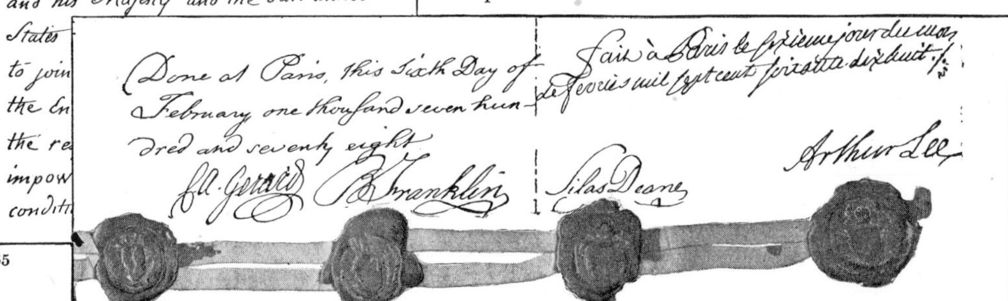
Done at Paris, this Sixth Day of February one thousand seven hundred and seventy eight

Fait à Paris le sixieme jour du mois de fevrier mil sept cent soixante dix huit.

C. A. Gerard B Franklin Silas Deane Arthur Lee

266 Facsimile of Treaty of Alliance with France, Feb. 6, 1778, from the original in the Department of State, Washington

267 From a French engraving attributed to "Corbut," Boston, 1778, *Dedicated to the Generals of the British Army by an Enthusiast for Liberty* (trans.), in the Emmet Collection, New York Public Library

FRENCH AND AMERICANS REJOICE OVER THEIR ALLIANCE

HAILED with delight by the French intellectuals who in their enthusiasm garbed themselves in hats and coats *à l'américaine*, the alliance brought new courage and hope to the American colonies. This French cartoon represents the angel of France bearing a shield embossed with a Medusa's head to inspire terror, and brandishing a flaming sword with which it chases the English from Philadelphia. A group of Americans dance around the Liberty Pole, "rejoicing over the rebirth of the Golden Age."

268 From a French engraving attributed to "Corbut," Boston, 1778, *Dedicated to the Lords of the British Admiralty by a Member of the American Congress* (trans.), in the Emmet Collection, New York Public Library

FRANCE HOPES TO WEAKEN ENGLAND

To the French ministry the objective of the alliance was less the desire to see a new nation born in America than to protect French interests, to humble England. Vergennes in a state paper of August, 1776, had urged French entry into the struggle. "The war will form a connection between France and North America which will not be merely a temporary expedient. Nothing can divide the two nations. Commerce will form a durable if not eternal chain between them; it will revive industry, bringing into our harbors the commodities which America formerly poured into English ports. Even could we be passive spectators of the revolution in North America, can we look on unmoved at what is taking place in Hindustan, and which will be as fatal to us as the American revolution to England? If the revolution in Hindustan is once begun, it will console England for her losses, by increasing her means and her riches tenfold. This we are still able to prevent." The cartoon represents England as an Admiral (1) with the wings and feet of a vulture. The creature is tied to a tree; the American Congress (2) cuts off its talons, while the Spaniard (3) holds one of the wings which the Frenchman (4) clips to prevent its flying.

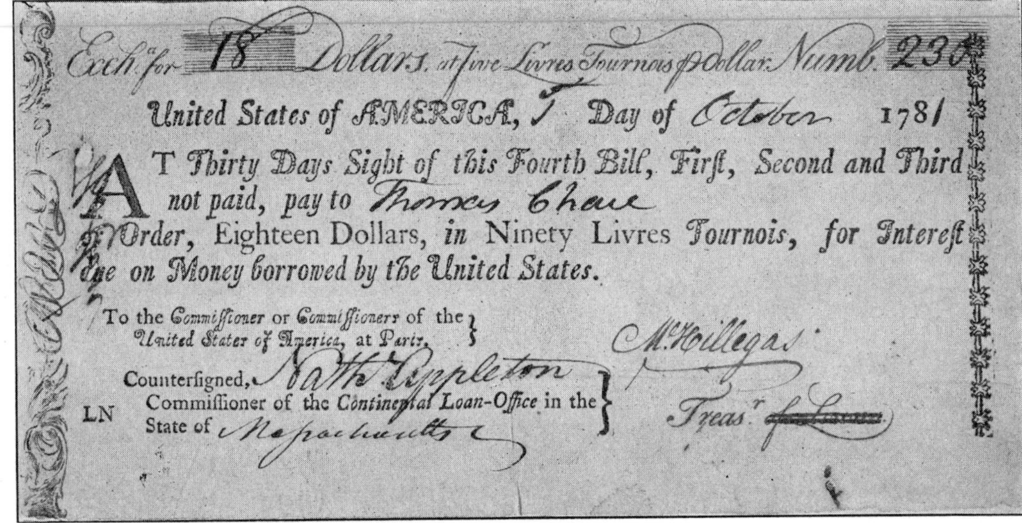

Exch.a for 18 Dollars, at five Livres Tournois p Dollar. Numb. 236

United States of AMERICA, 7 Day of October 1781

AT Thirty Days Sight of this Fourth Bill, First, Second and Third not paid, pay to Thomas Chase or Order, Eighteen Dollars, in Ninety Livres Tournois, for Interest due on Money borrowed by the United States.

To the Commissioner or Commissioners of the United States of America, at Paris.

Countersigned, Nath. Appleton
Commissioner of the Continental Loan-Office in the State of Massachusetts

LN

M. Hillegas
Treas.r

269 From an original scrip covering interest on money borrowed by the United States under the French loan to America, in possession of the publishers

270 Strong Box of Robert Morris, courtesy of the Historical Society of Pennsylvania

FRENCH GOLD PAYS AMERICAN SOLDIERS

In America news of the alliance caused outbursts of joy. The winter of 1777–78 had been depressing. Without funds, the Congress could not relieve the sufferings at Valley Forge. The farmers preferred the specie of the British in Philadelphia to the depreciated continental money. So French coöperation meant French gold to fill the coffers of the Revolutionary treasury, without which further prosecution of the cause seemed hopeless indeed.

LORD NORTH MAKES CONCESSIONS

Rumors of the French treaties had crossed the Channel. In a desperate effort to stave off a Continental war Lord North, on the 17th of February, announced to the Parliament a plan of conciliation with America, repealing the imposition of taxes on the Colonies. With nearly unanimous consent, the proposition was accepted, receiving the royal signature on March 11, 1778. But Congress, then in session at York, Pennsylvania, to forestall any wavering among the states and the people, issued an address "to the Inhabitants of the United States of America" urging continued resistance. For the Colonies, encouraged by the prospect of affairs, were now more than ever insistent upon independence as the essential condition of peace. And the North proposals, conciliatory as they were in certain respects, did not include or even consider any recognition of independence. Congress recommended to ministers of the gospel, of all denominations, to read or cause to be read, immediately after divine service, its address spurning Lord North's peace offer. The cartoon, which gives a very early representation of "Brother Jonathan," was intended to aid in bringing about a *rapprochement* between the warring parties.

THE ENGLISH & AMERICAN DISCOVERY.
BROTHER. BROTHER WE ARE BOTH IN THE WRONG.

271 From a British caricature published by M. Darley, London, 1778, courtesy of R. T. H. Halsey, New York

AMERICA REJECTS THE BRITISH OVERTURES

THE answer of America to the proposition is here depicted. Three members of Congress (intended to represent Rutledge, Adams, and Franklin), dressed as Tartars, receive with scorn and contumely the offers of General Clinton and his three associates sent from England. "Lord North," well said Governor Clinton of New York, "is two years too late with his political maneuver."

272 From a caricature *The Commissioners' Interview with Congress*, published by M. Darley, London, Apr. 1, 1778, in the Emmet Collection, New York Public Library

DANGER FROM EUROPE AROUSES GREAT BRITAIN

THE entry of France changed the whole character of the struggle. It now became, for England, a war to preserve her empire and her maritime and commercial supremacy. As Spain and Holland later joined France, America and her independence became of secondary importance. In this there were advantages to England. For members of the opposition who had obstructed the government in its conduct toward America, who had inclined to favor the American cause, now rallied to the defense of the realm. Chatham's dying speech (April, 1778) called the country to arms. "My lords! I rejoice that the grave has not closed upon me, that I am still alive to lift up my voice against the dismemberment of this ancient and most noble monarchy." France was more to be feared than America.

273 From a British caricature in the collection of R. T. H. Halsey, New York

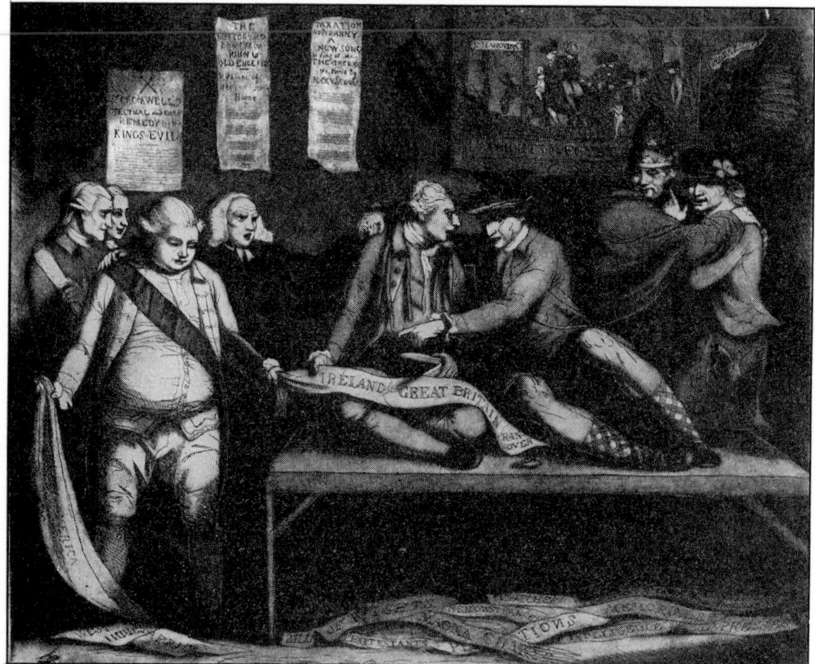

274 From the etching *The Botching Taylor, Cutting his Cloth to Cover a Button* by John Simpson (1782–1847), in the Emmet Collection, New York Public Library

INEFFICIENT MINISTERS CRIPPLE THE BRITISH

THE bungling of the North ministry, the obstinacy of the King, the discontent of the people — all played their part in retarding any vigorous campaign against the continental confederates. The etching here pictured tells the tale. George III, sitting cross-legged, is about to cut Great Britain to pieces; Bute beside him points to a piece held up by North, marked North America, with the suggestion that that would do; under the table in the "Taylor's Hell" lie discarded pieces, marked Magna Charta, Memorials. In the rear stand the Pope and the Pretender, joyfully watching England's perplexity, while on the wall are placarded prophecies.

275 From a British cartoon, 1781, by Robert Sayres, in the collection of R. T. H. Halsey, New York

GREAT BRITAIN FEELS CONFIDENT OF SUCCESS

FOR a time, however, Great Britain thought the scale would incline in her favor. In December, 1778, Savannah was captured; the seizure of Charleston followed in May, 1780. The preceding January, Admiral Rodney won a sweeping victory over the Spaniards off Cape St. Vincent. In February, 1781, the flourishing Dutch West Indian island of St. Eustatius, headquarters of a lively smuggling trade with America, was taken.

276 From a British caricature, 1782, in the collection of R. T. H. Halsey, New York

THE NORTH MINISTRY COMES TO AN END

BUT with the surrender of Cornwallis in October, 1781, affairs turned definitely against Great Britain. The people were tired of war and of the taxes it brought. Moreover, the corruption that marked the day in English politics had not abated. A contemporary cartoonist pictured North as a colossus standing, with ill-gotten prizes in one hand and flaming America in the other, above a stream polluted by political monsters. Commerce was unsettled. The French had captured St. Eustatius from the British; Minorca had fallen into enemy hands. So on the 22nd of February, 1782, a motion against continuing the American war, supported by Barré, Fox and Burke, failed of passage by but a single vote. For months the ministry had been losing ground as new instances of corruption and inefficiency came to light. On the 4th of March, Fox denounced them as "men void of honour and honesty." On the 20th North resigned.

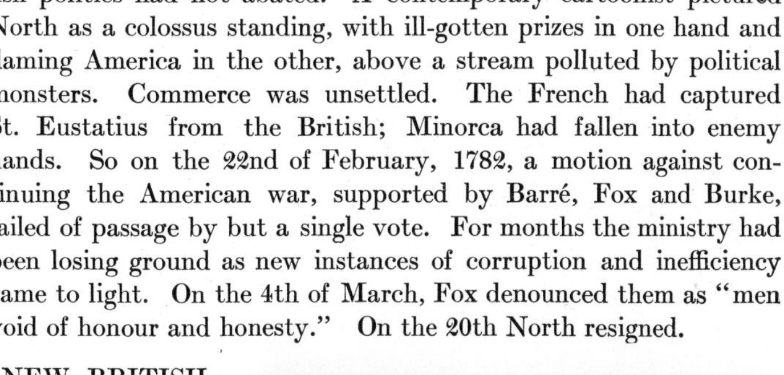

277 Lord Rockingham, 1730–82, from a portrait painted in the school of Sir Joshua Reynolds, in the National Portrait Gallery, London

NEW BRITISH POWERS ARE FRIENDLY

LORD ROCKINGHAM, the man who had proposed the repeal of the Stamp Act, became Prime Minister. With him were associated other American sympathizers, including the Duke of Richmond, Admiral Keppel and Fox. Lord Shelburne, ablest of Pitt's followers and old friend of Franklin, became Secretary of State in charge of American affairs, and, after Rockingham's death, chief minister. Before accepting office, Rockingham had secured from the King a promise that there should be "no veto to the independence of America."

278 Lord Shelburne, 1737–1805, from a portrait after Sir Joshua Reynolds, in the National Portrait Gallery, London

279 From a British caricature published by W. Humphrey, London, in the collection of R. T. H. Halsey, New York

ENGLAND AND AMERICA MAKE A TREATY OF PEACE

NEGOTIATIONS to this end were at once opened between Shelburne, through his agent Richard Oswald and the American peace commissioners. France interposed objections. The treaty of alliance had stipulated that neither France nor America would conclude a peace without the consent of the other party. France now insisted that the war was, after all, not solely an Anglo-American affair. The matter was further complicated by the fact that Spain had joined France in the war against Great Britain, after Vergennes had made the Spanish Government certain promises regarding the spoils. So pressure was now brought to bear by France and Spain to prevent a separate peace between England and America. The Dutch, little regarded by any of the parties, hoped for the best. Faced with such a situation, the American commissioners disregarded their instructions and entered into a separate treaty of peace, which secured the independence of the United States and marked the Mississippi River as the western boundary of the new nation.

280 From a British caricature on the Treaty published by W. Richardson, London, in the collection of R. T. H. Halsey, New York

ENGLAND WANTS FRIENDLY RELATIONS

281 From H. C. Lodge, *History of the Nations*, after the painting *Signing the Preliminary Treaty at Paris* by C. Seller, courtesy of John D. Morris and P. F. Collier & Son Company

England, having conceded American independence, was in haste to establish friendly relations with the new country. That America and France might thereby become estranged was no drawback to her. So on November 30, 1782, an agreement between Great Britain and America was reached, and the document signed by the American commissioners — Franklin, Jay, and John Adams — and Oswald. Strictly speaking, this was not a treaty, but simply a protocol, the articles of which were to be subsequently incorporated in a formal treaty after Great Britain had come to terms with France. So the alliance was lived up to according to the letter, though hardly according to the spirit.

AMERICA GAINS LAND WITH INDEPENDENCE

Of all the parties, America fared best by the negotiations. Her political independence was recognized, her boundaries were established liberally, with scant regard to the claims of Spain for the trans-Allegheny country. John Adams' stubbornness won for America privileges in the Newfoundland fisheries. In January, 1783, France, Spain and Great Britain came to an understanding, with some gains for each of the former. The preliminary agreement with the Dutch was not reached until the fall of the year. The crude cartoon presents the point of view of a certain body of English opinion upon the outcome.

282 From a British caricature published Apr. 14, 1783, by W. Humphrey, London, in the collection of R. T. H. Halsey, New York

283 From the unfinished painting *The Commissioners to Sign the Treaty of Peace*, 1783, by Benjamin West, in the possession of J. Pierpont Morgan, New York

THE DEFINITIVE TREATY IS SIGNED IN PARIS

THOUGH hostilities were suspended early in 1783, the definitive treaty of peace was not signed until September 3. The preliminary treaty had roused such opposition in Great Britain that the Shelburne ministry had fallen, to be succeeded by a peculiar coalition between the followers of Fox and North. The British agent was now David Hartley, a friend of Franklin who had throughout the American war sought means of conciliation between the two English-speaking nations. His attempts, countenanced by Fox, to bring about a commercial understanding at this time failed because of the opposition of British shipping and mercantile interests. So in the final treaty were incorporated simply the terms of the agreement of the preceding November. One morning in Paris, to the lodgings of Hartley, came Franklin, Adams, Jay and Laurens, together with the secretary of the commission and grandson of the philosopher-diplomat. Here the final act was taken. After some trouble in securing a quorum, the Congress accepted the treaty, and in May, 1784, ratifications were exchanged. Peace had come.

Duplicate.

In the Name of the most Holy and undivided Trinity.

It having pleased the Divine Providence to dispose the Hearts of the most Serene and most potent Prince George the third, by the Grace of God, King of Great Britain, France and Ireland, Defender of the Faith, Duke of Brunswick and Luneburg, Arch Treasurer and Prince Elector of the Holy Roman Empire &c. And of the United States of America, to forget all past Misunderstandings and Differences that have unhappily interrupted the good Correspondence and Friendship which they mutually wish to restore, and to establish such a beneficial and satisfactory Intercourse between the two Countries upon the Ground of reciprocal Advantages and mutual Convenience as may promote and secure to both perpetual Peace & Harmony, and having for this desirable End already laid the Foundation of Peace and Reconciliation, by the Provisional articles signed at Paris on the 30th of November 1782, by the Commissioners empowered on each Part, which Articles were agreed to be inserted in and to constitute the Treaty of Peace proposed to be concluded between the Crown of Great Britain ...

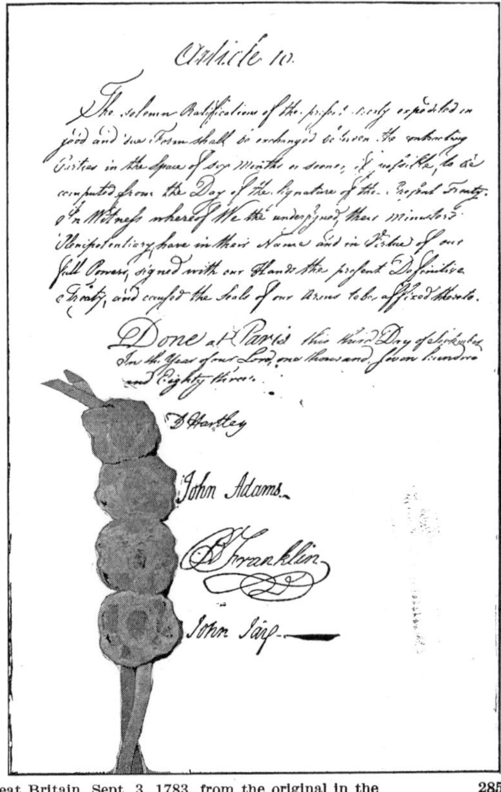

Article 10.

The solemn Ratifications of the present Treaty expedited in good and due Form shall be exchanged between the contracting Parties in the Space of Six Months or sooner if possible, to be computed from the Day of the Signature of the present Treaty. In Witness whereof We the undersigned their Ministers Plenipotentiary have in their Name and in Virtue of our Full Powers, signed with our Hands the present Definitive Treaty, and caused the Seals of our Arms to be affixed thereto.

Done at Paris this third Day of September In the Year of our Lord, one thousand seven hundred and Eighty three.

D Hartley

John Adams

B Franklin

John Jay

284 First and last pages of the Definitive Treaty of Peace with Great Britain, Sept. 3, 1783, from the original in the Department of State, Washington 285

THE REVOLUTION AS A SOCIAL FORCE

The Revolution shook American life to its foundations. The period of the "emergency" was from 1775 until the signing of the Treaty of Peace in 1783. For a community to be subjected for nearly eight years to the uncertainties of war and the hardships which resulted from war finance was to endure profound social changes. But when to this situation is added the fact that the Revolution involved the destruction of a deep and traditional loyalty to the British Crown and the elimination of an important part of the more educated and well-to-do part of the population, it can be seen how important the social consequences were bound to be. It was a time when the less fortunate classes, in an economic or social sense, were becoming more assertive and were securing more advantageous positions. It was a time when individuals from this group, like Sam Adams and Patrick Henry, were achieving national reputations and were rising to positions of power. The American Revolution brought about no such upheaval as the French Revolution which followed it so closely but, in both cases, when the period of the crisis had passed, the mass of the people emerged with a new point of view and a new attitude of mind.

286 From a petition to purchase confiscated Loyalist lands on Long Island, in the New York Historical Society

CHANGES IN LAND POLICY

The Americans of the Revolutionary epoch, both the humble and the great, were practically all farmers. Industry, fishing and even commerce occupied the full time of but a small fraction of the people. Some of these farmers like the tobacco planters in Virginia or the rice planters in South Carolina were dependent on foreign trade for an adequate market. But a large majority of husbandmen, even in the South, lived on practically self-sufficient farms, going outside of their acres for but the fewest commodities. Life in such rural communities was not subject to the dislocation which war inevitably brings to a highly urbanized people. The extremity of distress, the destroying of crops and buildings by a hostile army, such as at Bush-Hill which suffered almost total demolition, was followed by quick recuperation. When General Sullivan passed through Wyoming the year following its destruction by Indians and Tories, he found the cabins rebuilt and the women with what men were left tilling fields again. In spite of this, however, some of the most important consequences of the Revolution were changes in landownership. Many a great estate like that of the Penn family in Pennsylvania and of the Philipse family in New York (No. 289) were sold off in parcels to individual buyers by the new state governments which were created during the war. The sufferers were almost universally Loyalists. In this way the landed aristocracy, which was characteristic of the eighteenth-century colonies, received a heavy blow. The ultimate disappearance of this class was practically assured by the widespread abrogation of the old laws regarding entail and primogeniture. After the Revolution the small farmer became the characteristic figure in American agriculture. In the South for both economic and social reasons the planter persisted, but even in this section the small landowner was of great importance.

N York Mag
BUSH-HILL,
The Seat of William Hamilton Esq.r near Philadelphia

287 Estate of an aristocrat land-holder in Pennsylvania, from an engraving by Tiebout after J. Hoffman in the *New York Magazine*, 1793

33 Abstract of Sales of Forfeited Lands in the Southern District for Public Securities — 33

Date of Sales		To whom Sold	By whom Forfeited	Description	Amount of purchase £	s	d	Amount of each Days sale £	s	d	Interest allowed to		To whom Conveyed	Date of Conveyance
1786 April	14th	Cornelius P. Low	Fredk. Philipse Esqr.	The Mansion House & Mills with a Farm of 320 Acres late the Residence of Fredk. Philipse Esqr.	13.200	„	„							
		David Hunt...	Ditto.....	The House said David Hunt lives in and 41 Acres of Land adjoining	1.200	„	„							
		Robert Johnson	Ditto.....	Lot N:3 Contg: 190 Acres of Land	1.470	„	„							
		John Johnson..	Ditto.....	Lot N:4 Contg: 202 Acres	2.750	„	„							
		John Lawrance	Ditto.....	Lot N:5 Contg: 125 Acres	2.300	„	„							
		Ditto.....	Ditto.....	Lot N:6 Contg: 60 Acres	600	„	„							
		Andw. Bostwick	Ditto.....	Lot N:7 Contg: 24 Acres	375	„	„							
		Ditto.....	Ditto.....	Lot N:8 Contg: 24 Acres	340	„	„							
		Edwd. Couenhoven	Ditto.....	Lot N:9 Contg: 27 Acres	580	„	„							
		Abraham Lent	Ditto.....	Lot N:11 Contg: 40 Acres	.840	„	„							
		Cornelius P. Low	Ditto.....	Lot N:12 Contg: 83 Acres	700	„	„	24.355	„	„	1785 April	11th		

288 Record of sale of confiscated Loyalist lands, from *Abstract of Sales of Forfeited Lands, Southern District, New York and vicinity*, 1784

SOME CONSEQUENCES OF THE REVOLUTION

The new states that confiscated the Tory property also widened the franchise. "The status in which the electoral franchise was left at the end of the Revolutionary period fell far short of complete democracy. Yet during the years we are considering the right of suffrage was much extended. The freeholder, or owner of real estate, was given special privileges in four of the new state constitutions, two others widened the suffrage to include all owners of either land or personal property to a certain limit, and two others conferred it upon all taxpayers. . . . Multitudes of squires had been driven into exile or driven from their high position of dominance over the community. Multitudes of other Loyalists had been disfranchised, or impoverished by confiscations. . . . In fact the sense of social change pervaded the country." — J. F. Jameson, *The American Revolution Considered as a Social Movement*, pp. 26–28, Princeton, 1925. The years immediately following the close of the war were to see the newly enfranchised voters making a use of their power that was disconcerting to the more conservative elements of the population. The political consequences of the war were of such transcendent importance that historians have long failed to recognize the full significance of the social changes. Out of that conflict, however, a new America was born. Unquestionably the war hastened the changes in customs and social structure that the nineteenth century was inevitably to bring.

289 Philipse Manor in 1784, after a contemporary sepia drawing signed D. R. *fecit*, formerly owned by D. N. Stauffer, now in the Historical Society of Pennsylvania, Philadelphia

CHAPTER IV

BENJAMIN FRANKLIN

IT is not an easy matter to judge the part played in history by the individual man or woman. Yet one may, with perfect consistency, accept the view that "the times made the man," while still asserting that the man so made is great, and an influence upon his times. These statements apply with much force to Franklin. Amid the intellectual unrest of the eighteenth century his figure bulks large. This is so because of the integrity of his mind, and because of the manifold fields in which it sowed fruitful seed.

Franklin's worth was recognized by the people of his own day. Long before he had reached old age he was regarded as the wise man of America, to whom men looked for counsel. Upon no one in the country were more numerous and more varied public obligations imposed; nor did any other respond more fully and with greater ingenuity. Of all his qualities, sagacity was probably the most highly valued by his contemporaries. When matters of state demanded deliberation, he was sought out time and time again. His tact and his humor smoothed out the hindrances which personal irritations and asperities threw in the way of agreement. His fertility in suggestion and "uncommon common sense" made solution appear easy; his persuasiveness made its acceptance inescapable.

To this quality the common folk of his day, and of succeeding generations, added others which found their embodiment in "Poor Richard." Franklin's wisdom was of the homely kind that makes instant appeal to the untutored mind. His maxims of conduct were phrased in the language of the people, and they preached the virtues of the simple life led by the people of his day. The virtues in which he instructed the people were, moreover, virtues the practice of which would prove profitable in material ways. It was thus not too hard to come to believe that one's desires were morally justifiable. To be both virtuous and comfortable was delightful. And so the sales of the Almanac grew apace.

The chief merit of Franklin's teachings, however, is to be found in the fact that the virtues he inculcated were those peculiarly advantageous to such a society as he found around him. Thus he contributed to the stabilization and improvement of America; thus he buttressed the social practices that enabled Americans to gain political independence. This service is imponderable; but it is one which entitles him to a prominent place in the political chronicles of the country.

He deserves that place for one other reason. Franklin's work — and play — at the French Court were properly valued by the discriminating few during his lifetime. With the passage of years Franklin the diplomat has outweighed Franklin the moralist. He went to France with a reputation that brought him the favor of the enlightened classes; upon that he built, with rare dexterity and good humor, until he won for the struggling colonies the active support of the French Government. That support was the more valuable in that it was based upon widespread sympathy with America's aims and aspirations. And such sympathy was aroused in Europeans because they came to feel that the spirit of Franklin was the spirit of America. To the present day, the American holds much the same notion.

290 Franklin's Birthplace, Milk Street, Boston, from a lithograph, 1858, by J. H. Buffords, Boston, in the Huntington Collection in the Metropolitan Museum of Art, New York

BENJAMIN FRANKLIN COMES OF STURDY STOCK

In an unpretentious house on Milk Street, Boston, Franklin was born in January, 1706. His father was an Englishman whose ancestors for centuries had been sturdy and independent freeholders in Northamptonshire. A desire to practise his nonconformist creed in peace had led Josiah Franklin to migrate, in 1682, to the new country. Here, as his second wife, he had married Abiah Folger, daughter of Peter Folger, one of the first and most distinguished settlers of New England. They had ten children, of whom Benjamin was the eighth.

THE BOY FRANKLIN

"As the tithe of his sons," the father early determined to make of Benjamin a minister of the gospel. But the son had other notions, and it was not long before this project was abandoned. His eagerness for books led to his apprenticeship, in his thirteenth year, to his brother James, printer and publisher of the *New England Courant.*

291 From the statue *Franklin as a Young Man*, at the University of Pennsylvania, by R. Tait MacKenzie (1867–)

HIS ARRIVAL IN PHILADELPHIA

Before long, however, troubles fell upon the printing house. Benjamin, moreover, had made himself an object of suspicion to his worthy townsmen by certain "indiscreet disputations about religion." He thus determined to seek more congenial surroundings, and in the autumn of 1723 he embarked for New York. Finding no employment, he continued his journey to Philadelphia; the account of his entrance into the city is known to every American boy.

292 From the mural painting *Franklin the Printer's 'Prentice* by Charles E. Mills (1856–) in the Franklin Union, Boston. © Detroit Publishing Co.

FRANKLIN BECOMES A SUCCESSFUL PRINTER

In Philadelphia Franklin soon found his skill as a printer in demand. He attracted the attention of the Governor, who proposed to establish the young man as an independent tradesman. Franklin was dispatched to England to purchase a printing press and types, with money to be advanced by Sir William Keith. At the last moment the Governor conveniently forgot this promise, and Franklin was left stranded in London. On his return to Philadelphia, he again embarked upon the printing trade, and this time with notable success, for he soon became the leading printer of the Province.

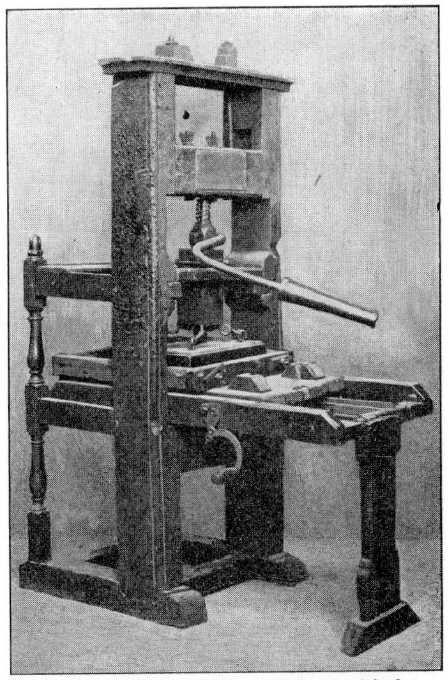

293 The Franklin Printing Press, from the original in the Smithsonian Institution, Washington

294 From the mural painting *Franklin the Editor* by Charles E. Mills in the Franklin Union, Boston. © Detroit Publishing Co.

THE *PENNSYLVANIA GAZETTE* SHOWS A NEW SPIRIT

He was soon able to buy one of the two newspaper establishments in Pennsylvania. Under his management, the *Pennsylvania Gazette* "prov'd in a few years extremely profitable." The causes for this happy outcome are best told in his own words: "Our first papers made a quite different appearance from any before in the Province; a better type, and better printed; but some spirited remarks of my writing, on the dispute then going on between Governor Burnet and the Massachusetts Assembly, struck the principal people, occasioned the paper and the manager of it to be much talked of, and in a few weeks brought them all to be our subscribers." Ever alert to capitalize virtue, Franklin became a model citizen. "In order to secure my credit and character as a tradesman, I took care to be not only in reality industrious and frugal, but to avoid all appearances to the contrary."

BOOKS FOR THE COMMON PEOPLE

Franklin's trade as printer and publisher convinced him there was a public whose desire for reading he could develop and meet. He therefore established, in 1731, a subscription library. "This," he wrote, "was the mother of all the North American subscription libraries, now so numerous. . . . These libraries have improved the general conversation of the Americans, made the common traders and farmers as intelligent as most gentlemen from other countries, and perhaps have contributed in some degree to the stand so generally made throughout the colonies in defense of their privileges."

295 From the mural painting *Franklin the Librarian* by Charles E. Mills in the Franklin Union, Boston. © Detroit Publishing Co.

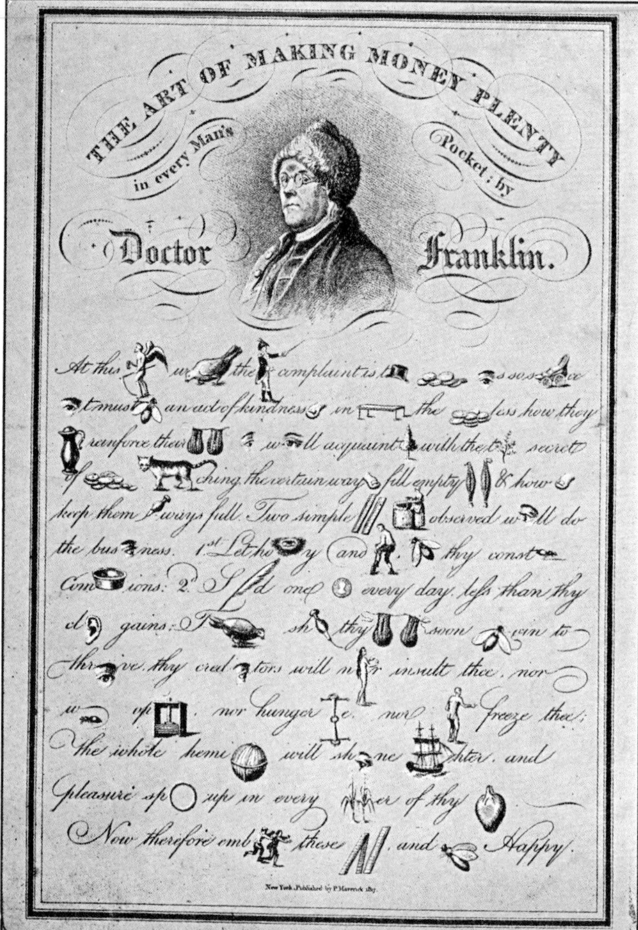

296 From *Poor Richard's Almanac*, published by P. Maverick, New York, 1817

FRANKLIN'S SHREWD MAXIMS ARE POPULAR

In December, 1732, he issued the first number of his *Almanac*. It proved an immediate success; and for a quarter of a century it was continued with an average sale of ten thousand copies a year. In it Franklin put, with homely humor and phrase, "the gleanings that I had made of the sense of all ages and nations." "*Poor Richard*," writes Morse, "was the revered and popular schoolmaster of a young nation during its period of tutelage. . . . Its wit and humor, its practical tone, its shrewd maxims, its worldly honesty, its morality of common sense, its useful information, all chimed well with the national character. . . . His teachings are among the powerful forces which have gone to shaping the habits of Americans."

SCIENCE AND PHILOSOPHY

Franklin was by this time a leading citizen of Philadelphia, and to him came many opportunities to inculcate and to practise his gospel of practical virtue. In 1732 he planned a treatise to be entitled *The Art of Virtue*, wherein would be presented not "mere exhortation to be good, that does not instruct or indicate the means," but "the means and manner of obtaining virtue." Though his pet project was never completed, Franklin in his life gave innumerable illustrations of its precepts. He founded the Junto as a "club of mutual improvement, in which were discussed queries on any point of morals, politics, or natural philosophy." This club he often used to further his schemes for public improvement, such as the Union Fire Company, the first organized volunteer fire brigade in the city. His energy was indeed prodigious, his interests of startling variety. His experiments in natural science and his founding, with others, of the American Philosophical Society (1727) to promote like studies, are among them. To him the people were indebted for what is now the University of Pennsylvania, for an efficient constabulary, for paved and well-lighted streets. Whenever and wherever there was need of improvement of the public or its circumstances, Franklin's ingenuity provided the means to achievement.

297 From the mural painting *Franklin Making his Famous Scientific Experiment* by Charles E. Mills in the Franklin Union, Boston. © Detroit Publishing Co.

298 From the mural painting *Franklin Building Fort Allen* by Charles E. Mills in the Franklin Union, Boston. © Detroit Publishing Co.

PUBLIC HONORS

SUCH activity inevitably brought Franklin before the public. In 1736 he was made clerk of the Pennsylvania General Assembly, a position he continued to hold until in 1750 he was elected a member of that body. In 1737 he was appointed postmaster at Philadelphia, a post that proved characteristically useful, "for, tho' the salary was small, it facilitated the correspondence that improv'd my newspaper, increased the number demanded, as well as the advertisements to be inserted, so that it came to afford me a considerable income." In 1753 he was made deputy postmaster-general of America; whereupon he set to work to remove from the service waste and spoils, so successfully that soon the office came "to yield three times as much clear revenue to the crown as the post-office of Ireland." In 1774 his politics caused his summary removal: "since that imprudent transaction," he comments, "they have received from it — not one farthing." Into military affairs, even, Franklin ventured. After Braddock's defeat the frightened Pennsylvanians turned to the many-sided citizen for aid. With no illusions concerning his military skill, Franklin went to the western frontier and there erected forts to protect the weaker settlements. As soon as possible, however, he withdrew to civilian pursuits as more suited to his abilities.

A PLAN FOR UNION

EVEN before his excursion into military matters, Franklin had gained a wide reputation for his practical wisdom. When, therefore, the Albany conference was called to meet in 1754, it was natural that he should be selected to represent Pennsylvania. On his journey he "projected and drew a plan for the union of all the colonies under one government, so far as might be necessary for defense and other important general purposes." With few changes, his scheme was adopted by the conference. "Its fate," said Franklin, "was singular." By the colonies assembled it was rejected because "there was too much prerogative in it"; from the Board of Trade in London it received no more favorable treatment, for to them it had "too much of the democratic." To Franklin himself its chief virtue was "that the colonies would, by this connection, learn to consider themselves, not as so many independent states, but as members of the same body; and thence be more ready to afford assistance and support to each other."

Short hints towards a scheme for uniting the Northern Colonies

A Governour General

To be appointed by the King
To be a Military man
To have a Salary from the Crown
To have a negation on all acts of the Grand Council, and carry into execution whatever is agreed on by him & that Council

Grand Council

One member to be chosen by the Assembly of each of the smaller Colonies & two or more by each of the larger, in proportion to the Sums they pay Yearly into the General Treasury

Members Pay

— Shillings sterling per Diem during their sitting & mileage for Travelling Expences.

Place & Time of meeting

To meet — times in every Year, at the Capital of each Colony in Course, unless particular circumstances & emergencies require more frequent meetings & Alteration in the Course of places The Governour General to Judge of those circumstances &c & call by his Writts —

General Treasury

Its Fund, an Excise on Strong Liquors pretty equally drank in the Colonies or Duty on Liquor imported — or — shillings on each Licence of Publick House or Excise on Superfluities as Tea &c &c all which would pay in some proportion to the present wealth of each Colony and increase as that wealth increases, & prevent disputes about the Inequality of Quotas —
To be Collected in each Colony, & Lodged in their Treasury to be ready for the payment of Orders issuing from the

299 From a facsimile of Franklin's plan for Colonial Union, in the New York Historical Society

300 From a mezzotint after the portrait by Mason Chamberlin painted in London between 1760 and 1762

FIVE YEARS IN ENGLAND

When, therefore, Franklin was in February, 1757, appointed the emissary of the Provincial Assembly to England, his fame had preceded him, his experiments with electricity were already recognized abroad as among the significant contemporary contributions to knowledge. The years during which his suit before the proprietaries and the Government, in behalf of the Province, dragged on were enlivened for him by that intellectual intercourse and social deference he loved. He became the friend of David Hume, of Lord Kames, and of other men of letters. Edinburgh extended to him the freedom of the city, while Oxford conferred upon him the degree of Doctor of Laws. It was with extreme reluctance that he finally, in the autumn of 1762, sailed for Philadelphia.

301 From the portrait, 1759, by Benjamin Wilson, taken by Major André from Franklin's house, restored to the United States by Earl Grey in 1906 and hung in the White House, Washington

"THE REPRESENTATIVE OF A DISAFFECTED PEOPLE"

While on board ship, Franklin had been reëlected to the Provincial Assembly. On his arrival he was at once plunged into the midst of political controversy. To a friend in England he wrote: "Business, public and private, consumes all my time; I must return to England for repose." It so fell out that to England he did return. The quarrels between the Assembly and the Proprietor came to a head with the passage by the former of a petition to the King-in-Council for a royal government for Pennsylvania. To present this petition Franklin in December, 1764, arrived in London. He expected to remain but a few months; in fact, he stayed ten years. For in England he found momentous events impending. In March, 1764, Grenville had given notice of his intent to introduce a bill imposing a stamp tax in America; the Pennsylvania Assembly had instructed Franklin to inform the minister of the colony's protest, and this duty, originally incidental, quickly overshadowed all others. "Instead of remaining simply an agent charged with urging a petition which brought him in conflict only with private persons, like himself subjects of the King, he saw his position rapidly change and develop until he became really the representative of a disaffected people maintaining a cause against the monarch and the government of the great British Empire." — J. T. Morse, *Franklin*, p. 101.

302 From the bust of Franklin by Jean Antoine Houdon (1740–1828), in the Metropolitan Museum of Art, New York

303 The Royal Society's Medal Given to Franklin, from an engraving in the Emmet Collection, New York Public Library

304 From the mural painting *Franklin at the Bar of the House of Commons*, 1766, by Charles E. Mills in the Franklin Union, Boston. © Detroit Publishing Co.

FRANKLIN PROTESTS AGAINST THE STAMP TAX

It was in this capacity, and as a familiar and respected companion of the men of affairs in England, that Franklin was in February, 1766, summoned before the House of Commons to give testimony in regard to the attitude of the colonies toward the stamp tax. His sturdy position in this examination he reasserted, in characteristic phrase, some weeks later. "I have some little property in America," he wrote. "I will freely spend nineteen shillings in the pound to defend my right of giving or refusing the other shilling. And, after all, if I cannot defend that right, I can retire cheerfully with my family into the boundless woods of America, which are sure to afford freedom and subsistence to any man who can bait a hook or pull a trigger." Franklin's strong common sense and wide knowledge contributed powerfully toward the repeal of the Stamp Act.

305 From the engraving by Robert Whitechurch, published 1859, after the painting *Franklin Before The Lords in Council* by Christian Schuessele (1824–79), courtesy of Kennedy & Co., New York

HIS MISSION TO ENGLAND COMES TO AN END

Franklin now came to be recognized in the colonies, as he was already in England, as the chief spokesman abroad of colonial opinion. New Jersey, Georgia, Maryland and Massachusetts made him their agent. It was in this last capacity that Franklin was, in January, 1774, summoned to appear before the Privy Council. The scene there enacted marked the end of Franklin's usefulness as counsellor to the colonies and to England. This in course of time Franklin understood. He remained in England a year longer. Many things were done to make his stay unpleasant, and in March, 1775, he sailed for home, no longer hopeful that the quarrel would end otherwise than in war.

Philada July 5. 1775

Mr Strahan,

You are a Member of Parliament, and one of that Majority which has doomed my Country to Destruction. — You have begun to burn our Towns, and murder our People. — Look upon your Hands! — They are stained with the Blood of your Relations! — You and I were long Friends: — You are now my Enemy, — and

I am,

Yours,

B Franklin

306 Franklin's Letter to Strahan, 1775, from the original in the Franklin Papers in the Library of Congress

POLITICS BREAKS PERSONAL FRIENDSHIPS

In 1773, Franklin had written from England: "The great defect here is, in all sorts of people, a want of attention to what passes in such remote countries as America; an unwillingness to read anything about them, if it appears a little lengthy; and a disposition to postpone a consideration even of the things which they know they must at last consider." Arriving in Philadelphia on May 5, 1775, he learned of the inevitable results of this indifference. To his great friend, Dr. Priestley, he wrote on the 16th, "You will have heard, before this reaches you, of a march stolen by the regulars into the country by night, and of their *expedition* back again. They retreated twenty miles in six hours. . . ." But Franklin found in that happening more than cause for joking. It meant the severance of many ties between America and the home country, between him and his English friends. Fortunately, some of these friendships, as that with Strahan, an English journalist who had been his intimate during Franklin's first stay in England, were later resumed. It was to Strahan that he wrote the famous letter concluding with the words: "You and I were long Friends:—You are now my Enemy,—and I am, Yours, B. Franklin."

FRANKLIN PARTICIPATES IN THE WORK OF CONGRESS

But sterner matters were in hand. On the day of his return, he had been unanimously elected delegate from Pennsylvania to the Continental Congress. In all of its manifold activities he participated, until in September, 1776, he was selected as one of three commissioners from the new America to England's enemy, France.

307 From the mural painting *Franklin Signing the Declaration of Independence* by Charles E. Mills in the Franklin Union, Boston. © Detroit Publishing Co.

THE ENGLISH FEAR FRANKLIN'S INFLUENCE IN FRANCE

THE prospect of the presence of the "chief of the American rebels" at the Court of Louis XVI was far from pleasing to those English statesmen who had had opportunity to gauge his skill. Lord Rockingham said that this more than offset the British victory on Long Island. All attempts, however, to capture *The Reprisal*, the sloop of war on which Franklin had sailed, were vain. Late in 1776 he reached Nantes. When the Marquis of Rockingham heard the news, the significance of it appalled him. "The horrid scene at a Privy Council," he wrote, referring to the occasion (No. 305) when Franklin met the withering invective of Wedderburn, "is in my memory, though, perhaps, not in his. It may not excite his conduct. It certainly deters him not. . . . He boldly ventures to cross the Atlantic. . . . The sight of Banquo's ghost could not more offend the eyes of Macbeth than the knowledge of this old man being at Versailles should affect the minds of those who were principals in that horrid scene." Even Stormont regarded Franklin's mission as a grave danger, because of "the partiality of the French people."

308 The "watch-case" portrait of Franklin, from a print after the orignal by John Lodge (died 1796)

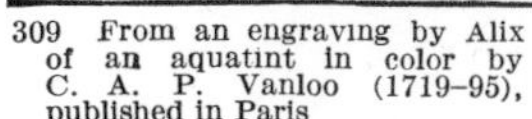

309 From an engraving by Alix of an aquatint in color by C. A. P. Vanloo (1719–95), published in Paris

310 From a mezzotint after the portrait, Paris, 1777, by Charles Nicholas Cochin (1715–90)

WELCOME TO FRANKLIN IN FRANCE

"BUT while the English were angry, the French indulged in a *furore* of welcome. They made feasts and hailed the American as the friend of humankind, as the 'ideal of a patriarchal republic and of idyllic simplicity,' as a sage of antiquity; the exuberant classicism of the nation exhausted itself glorifying him by comparison with those great names of Greece and Rome which have become symbols of all private and public virtues. They admired him because he did not wear a wig; they lauded his spectacles; they were overcome with enthusiasm as they contemplated his great cap of marten fur, his scrupulously white linen, and the quaint simplicity of his brown Quaker raiment of colonial make. They noted with amazement that his 'only defense' was a 'walking-stick in his hand.' The print-shops were soon full of countless representations of his noble face and venerable figure." — J. T. MORSE, *Benjamin Franklin*, 1889, pp. 231–32.

311 The "fur cap" portrait, from a mezzotint after the drawing, 1777, by Cochin

312 The House where Franklin lived at Passy, from an original sketch by Victor Hugo, 1836, in the New York Public Library

HE LIVES APART FROM THE DISTRACTIONS OF PARIS

FRANKLIN at once established himself at Passy, then a suburb of Paris. Here he was able at once to participate in the social festivities that furthered his mission among the people and to escape the dangers of too great proximity to the ministers who might at times be embarrassed by his presence. Thus, at the very outset of his mission, Franklin gave evidence of the discretion and tact for which he was already known, and through the use of which he was able to serve his country with conspicuous success.

313 From the mural painting *Franklin Signing The Treaty of Alliance*, by Charles E. Mills in the Franklin Union, Boston. © Detroit Publishing Co.

THE FRENCH ALLIANCE

FRANKLIN's position was a difficult one. It was his duty to get from France as much assistance, of all kinds, as possible. France was willing to aid so long as she did not become embroiled in war with England. Thus for a year or more, Franklin busied himself chiefly with gaining such covert and indirect assistance as he could win for the American cause. Then came, in December, 1777, the news of Burgoyne's surrender the preceding October. (Vol. VI.) France became convinced that she could venture upon open recognition of the new nation, and in February, 1778, the treaties of alliance and of commerce were signed.

314 From the painting *Franklin at the Court of France* by Baron Jolly in the collection of Cyrus Curtis, Philadelphia

THE COURT HONORS THE AMERICAN PHILOSOPHER

This achievement was in part due to the character of Franklin. Lacretelle, a French publicist, has well written: "His virtues and renown negotiated for him; and before the second year of his mission had expired, no one conceived it possible to refuse fleets and armies to the countrymen of Franklin." At the Court of Louis XVI, homage was paid him as a philosopher and as the representative of the new country whose watchword was liberty. He symbolized the liberty for which the French people were yearning. Tradesmen ran to the doors of their shops as he passed and the most distinguished ladies of Paris outdid one another in making their obeisance to him.

315 From a contemporary French engraving *The Tomb of Voltaire* in the Emmet Collection, New York Public Library

A TRIBUTE TO VOLTAIRE

He became, indeed, representative, not solely of America, but of liberating truth. Even his somewhat lukewarm admirer, John Adams, later conceded that "If a collection could be made of all the gazettes of Europe of the latter half of the eighteenth century, a greater number of panegyrical paragraphs upon *le grand* Franklin would appear, it is believed, than upon any other man that ever lived."

316 From an engraving by Edward Savage after the portrait by David Martin (1736–98), published in London, 1793

HOME AGAIN AFTER NINE YEARS IN FRANCE

By the spring of 1781, Franklin had tired of the worries of his post. He sent his resignation to Congress. That body, however, not only ignored it, but appointed him one of the commissioners to negotiate peace. So he took up the new task. After the signing of the preliminary treaty in 1782, and again after the definitive treaty of 1783, he renewed his plea for recall. But not until March, 1785, did Congress grant him permission to "return to America as soon as convenient." On September 13 he sighted "dear Philadelphia," where a cheering throng greeted his arrival. But Franklin's labors were not done. Immediately the people selected him as a member of the State Council, of which he soon became President. To this office he was reëlected in 1786 and in 1787. Of this distinction he characteristically wrote: "I had not firmness enough to resist the unanimous desire of my country-folks; and I find myself harnessed again in their service. They engrossed the prime of my life. They have eaten my flesh, and seem resolved now to pick my bones." To the Constitutional Convention of 1787 he was sent, one of four members who had signed the Declaration of Independence. While he took no active share in the proceedings, his presence and occasional homely advice were invaluable in smoothing out difficulties. "When the work was done, probably no signature except that of Washington did so much as Franklin's to win popular confidence" in the new instrument of government. — Greene, *Foundations of American Nationality*, p. 586.

A PROTEST AGAINST SLAVERY

Franklin's body now refused longer to support his still active mind. As he himself said: "I seem to have intruded myself into the company of posterity, when I ought to have been abed and asleep." Throughout a lingering and painful illness he kept his humor playing upon the foibles of mankind and kept alive his interest in the welfare of men. One of his last acts was to sign, as president of the Pennsylvania Society for the Abolition of Slavery, a memorial to Congress praying that it "devise means for removing this inconsistency from the character of the American people." On April 17, 1790 he died, full of years, of manifold experiences, of homely wisdom; honored throughout the western world for his many services to his fellow men.

317 From a stipple portrait engraved by Stöttrup

PHILADELPHIA, 22 April.

The following was the order of Proceſſion yeſterday at the funeral of our late learned and illuſtrious citizen, Dr FRANKLIN

All the Clergy of the city, before the corpſe.

THE CORPSE,

Carried by Citizens.

The Pall ſupported by The Preſident of the State, the Chief Juſtice—the Preſident of the Bank, Samuel Powell, William Bingham, and David Rittenhouſe, Eſquires,

Mourners,

Conſiſting of the Family of the deceaſed—with a number of particular friends,

The Secretary and Members of the Supreme Executive Council.

The Speaker and Members of the General Aſſembly.

Judges of the Supreme Court,

And other Officers of Government.

The Gentlemen of the Bar.

The Mayor and Corporation of the city of Philadelphia.

The Printers of the city, with their Journeymen and Apprentices.

The Philoſophical Society

The College of Phyſicians.

The Cincinnati.

The College of Philadelphia.

Sundry other Societies—together with a numerous and reſpectable body of Citizens.

The concourſe of ſpectators was greater than ever was known on a like occaſion. It is computed that not leſs than 20,000 perſons attended and witneſſed the funeral. The order and ſilence which prevailed, during the Proceſſion, deeply evinced the heartfelt ſenſe, entertained by all claſſes of citizens, of the unparralleled virtues, talents, and ſervices of the deceaſed.

318 The Procession at Franklin's Funeral, from *The Gazette of the United States*, Philadelphia, Apr. 22, 1790

FRANKLIN'S ACHIEVEMENTS

John T. Morse thus concludes his very readable biography of Benjamin Franklin: "It is hard indeed to give full expression to a man of such scope in morals, in mind and in affairs. He illustrates humanity in an astonishing multiplicity of ways at an infinite number of points. He, more than any other, seems to show us how many-sided our human nature is. No individual, of course, fills the entire circle; but if we can imagine a circumference which shall express humanity, we can place within it no one man who will reach out to approach it and to touch it at so many points as will Franklin. A man of active as well as universal good-will, of perfect truthfulness towards all dwellers on the earth, of supreme wisdom expanding over all the interests of the race, none has earned a more kindly loyalty. By the instruction which he gave, by his discoveries, by his inventions and by his achievements in public life he earns the distinction of having rendered to men varied and useful services excelled by no other one man; and thus he has established a claim upon the gratitude of mankind so broad that history holds few who can be his rivals."

319 From the portrait, 1787, by Charles Willson Peale in the Historical Society of Pennsylvania

320 Graves of Benjamin and Deborah Franklin, Christ Church burying ground, Philadelphia, from Scharf and Westcott, *History of Philadelphia*, Philadelphia, 1884

CHAPTER V

FRAMING THE CONSTITUTION

WHILE Franklin was laboring in France to promote the American cause, other patriots at home faced a different political problem. With the adoption of the Declaration of Independence, in July, 1776, the Continental Congress presented the American people with a twofold task. On the one hand, they were obliged to achieve independence on the field of battle. Simultaneously, they were obliged to establish a government more regular in origin and full-bodied in form than their hastily constructed machinery, in order that the military arm might be properly equipped and the union maintained. The event proved this latter task no easier than the former. Blunders by Britain, coupled with twists of European politics, might facilitate military victory; but to set up a government and to keep it operating, America had to rely upon herself alone.

At the outset there had to be fostered that spirit of community of interest without which political union — and only through union could independence be won — would prove impossible. Provincial exclusiveness and intercolonial jealousies made the task of education difficult. The leaders possessed of vision to see what must come were forced to proceed with care and circumspection. In 1776 it was recognized that the several states were willing to be united only to the extent needed to win a common victory against Great Britain. So the Articles of Confederation left to the member-states all of the form of sovereignty and most of the substance. The central Congress, with its committees, was simply an agent of the states in the execution of a set and specific piece of work, that of winning the war. Even such a slight union offended certain of the states; not until 1781 did the Confederation come into operation, and only because through no other agency could the war be won was it treated with indulgence by the touchy commonwealths. Indeed, within the sphere of its legitimate and recognized function, the Congress was often buffeted by the suspicious and ignored by the thoughtless.

The Congress of the Confederation did, however, manage to fulfill its duty. The Continentals were, in one way or another, kept in the field; foreign aid was solicited and obtained; the treaty of peace was signed. To some of the leaders of the states, this last act bespoke the end of the Confederation; now that independence had been gained, the several states should go their ways, friends but not members of the same family. To others, however, the Confederation was not the end of union, but the forerunner of a greater and better union. They felt that there were too many bonds of sympathy, of like interest, of tradition, between the states to admit of separation.

The position of these Federalists, as they came to be called, was destined to be adopted by America. The central Congress of the Confederation had, indeed, by its very existence and by its conduct, strengthened the national spirit, the feeling of community among the peoples of the several commonwealths. The economic distress of the postwar years soon gave additional impetus to the urgings of such men as Washington, Madison and Hamilton, until at last the need for a stronger central government, which could restrain the vagaries and the excesses of the states, forced upon the reluctant a new constitution with a new government standing for the new nation that was to be.

CIVIL GOVERNMENT FALLS TO THE CONTINENTAL CONGRESS

In 1776 it was necessary to provide a civil government to direct the conduct of the war. What more natural than that the existing Continental Congress should assume that office? It had come into being because of a recognized need for united action to oppose the unconstitutional aggressions of Great Britain; with independence declared, there was need for united action to attain the new goal. So the Congress, called in one capacity, proceeded to act in another. It recommended to the Provincial Assemblies military preparation; it adopted as its own the troops around Boston and sent them a commander; it provided for a navy; and it established agents to supervise all military and naval activities. Thus the Congress assumed under pressure of circumstance the exercise of numerous functions that could be handled most effectively from one central agency, acting for all the states.

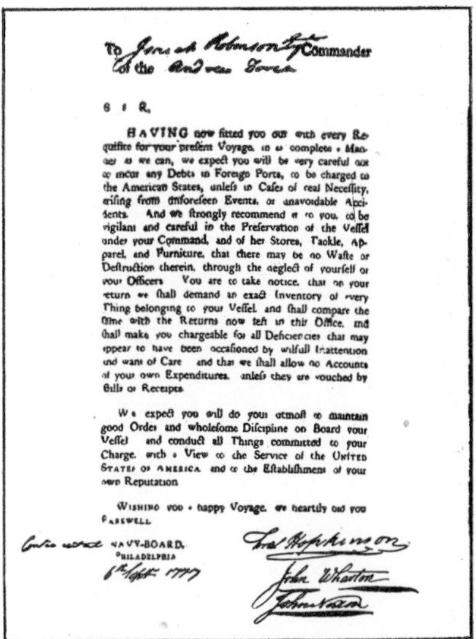

To ... Commander of the ...

SIR,

HAVING now fitted you out with every Requiſite for your preſent Voyage, in as complete a Manner as we can, we expect you will be very careful not to incur any Debts in Foreign Ports, to be charged to the American States, unleſs in Caſes of real Neceſſity, ariſing from unforeſeen Events, or unavoidable Accidents. And we ſtrongly recommend it to you, to be vigilant and careful in the Preſervation of the Veſſel under your Command, and of her Stores, Tackle, Apparel, and Furniture, that there may be no Waſte or Deſtruction therein, through the neglect of yourſelf or your Officers. You are to take notice, that on your return we ſhall demand an exact Inventory of every Thing belonging to your Veſſel, and ſhall compare the ſame with the Returns now left in this Office, and ſhall make you chargeable for all Deficiencies that may appear to have been occaſioned by wilfull Inattention and want of Care, and that we ſhall allow no Accounts of your own Expenditures, unleſs they are vouched by Bills or Receipts.

We expect you will do your utmoſt to maintain good Order and wholeſome Diſcipline on Board your Veſſel, and conduct all Things committed to your Charge, with a View to the Service of the UNITED STATES OF AMERICA, and to the Eſtabliſhment of your own Reputation.

WISHING you a happy Voyage, we heartily bid you FAREWELL.

NAVY-BOARD, PHILADELPHIA
6th Sept. 1777

Fra Hopkinson
John Wharton
John Nixon

321 Instructions to the man-of-war *Andria Doria*, Sept. 1777, from a facsimile in the catalogue of the Bancker Collection, 1898

CONGRESS CONTROLS WARSHIPS

From authorizing such activities to regulating them proved a short and necessary step. Having permitted the outfitting of privateers, the Congress soon found that, unguided, they would harm the cause. Hence, the Provisional Assembly assumed still another function of government, and one which was bound to bring it into contact with foreign nations.

A PROCLAMATION

WHEREAS Congreſs have received information and complaints, "That violences have been done by American armed veſſels to neutral nations, in ſeizing ſhips belonging to their ſubjects and under their colours, and in making captures of thoſe of the enemy whilſt under the protection of neutral coaſts, contrary to the uſage and cuſtom of Nations." To the end that ſuch unjuſtifiable and piratical acts, which reflect diſhonour upon the national character of theſe States, may be in future effectually prevented, the ſaid Congreſs hath thought proper to direct, enjoin and command, and they do hereby direct, enjoin and command, all Captains, Commanders and other Officers and Seamen belonging to any American armed veſſels, to govern themſelves ſtrictly in all things, agreeably to the tenor of their Commiſſions, and the Inſtructions and Reſolutions of Congreſs; particularly that they pay a ſacred regard to the rights of neutral powers, and the uſage and cuſtom of civilized nations, and on no pretence whatever preſume to take or ſeize any ſhips or veſſels belonging to the ſubjects of princes or powers in alliance with theſe United States, except they are employed in carrying contraband goods, or ſoldiers to our enemies; and in ſuch caſe that they conform to the Stipulations contained in Treaties ſubſiſting between ſuch princes or powers and theſe States; and that they do not capture, ſeize or plunder any ſhips or veſſels of our enemies being under the protection of neutral coaſts, nations or princes, under the penalty of being condignly puniſhed therefor, and alſo of being bound to make ſatisfaction for all matters of damage, and the intereſt thereof by reparation, under the pain and obligation of their perſons and goods. And further, The ſaid Congreſs doth hereby Reſolve and Declare, That perſons wilfully offending in any of the foregoing inſtances, if taken by any foreign powers in conſequence thereof, ſhall not be conſidered as having a right to claim protection from theſe States, but ſhall ſuffer ſuch puniſhment as by the uſage and cuſtom of nations may be inflicted upon ſuch offenders.

GIVEN in CONGRESS *at* YORK, *in the State of* PENNSYLVANIA, *this Ninth Day of May, Anno Domini One Thouſand Seven Hundred and Seventy-Eight.*

HENRY LAURENS, Preſident.

ATTEST. CHARLES THOMSON, Secretary.

YORK-TOWN: PRINTED BY JOHN DUNLAP.

322 Proclamation of Congress respecting Neutral Vessels, 1778, in the Emmet Collection, New York Public Library

FRANKLIN SENT TO FRANCE TO REPRESENT AMERICA

The results of such contact have been told. The French alliance, the negotiations with Spain and Holland, led to the dispatch to European courts of duly accredited representatives. Quite fittingly, Franklin was selected as America's first envoy to France. (See page 139.)

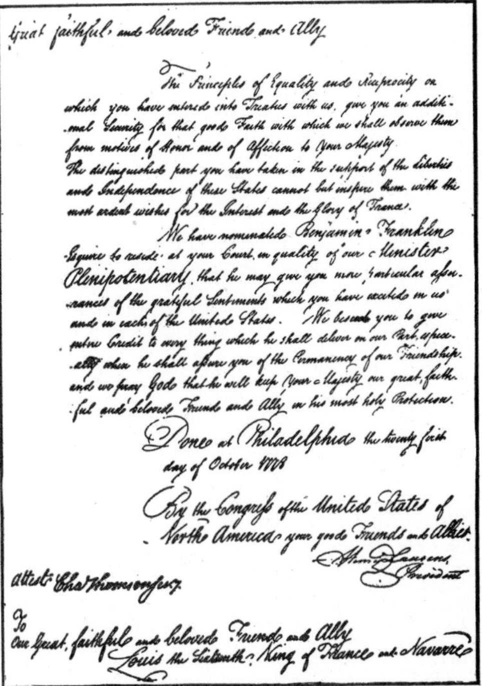

Great faithful and beloved Friend and Ally

The Principles of Equality and Reciprocity on which you have entered into Treaties with us, give you an additional Security for that good Faith with which we shall observe them from motives of Honor and of Affection to Your Majesty.

The distinguished part you have taken in the support of the Liberties and Independence of these States cannot but inspire them with the most ardent wishes for the Interest and the Glory of France.

We have nominated Benjamin Franklin Esquire to reside at your Court, in quality of our Minister Plenipotentiary, that he may give you more particular assurances of the grateful Sentiments which you have excited in us and in each of the United States. We beseech you to give entire Credit to every thing which he shall deliver on our Part, especially when he shall assure you of the Permanency of our Friendship. And we pray God that he will keep Your Majesty our great, faithful and beloved Friend and Ally in his most holy Protection.

Done at Philadelphia the twenty first day of October 1778

By the Congress of the United States of North America your good Friends and Allies

Henry Laurens President

Attest Cha Thomson secy

To Our Great, faithful and beloved Friend and Ally Louis the Sixteenth, King of France and Navarre

323 Letter of the Congress to Louis XVI, Oct. 21, 1778, appointing Franklin as envoy, in the Historical Society of Pennsylvania

324 Chevalier Gérard, from the portrait by C. W. Peale in Independence Hall, Philadelphia

FRANCE'S MINISTER APPEARS BEFORE CONGRESS

On the 6th of August, 1778, Conrad Alexandre, Chevalier Gérard, was received as Minister from France. The occasion is thus described in the *Continental Journal* of the 17th of that month: "Thus had a new and noble sight been exhibited in this New World, the representatives of the United States of America solemnly giving public audience to a minister plenipotentiary from the most powerful Prince in Europe. Four years ago, such an event, at so near a day, was not in view even of imagination. But it is the Almighty who raiseth up. He hath stationed America among the powers of the earth, and clothed her in robes of sovereignty." With the reception of a foreign envoy, the Continental Congress received additional prestige and strength. It seemed in a fair way to become the central government of the new nation.

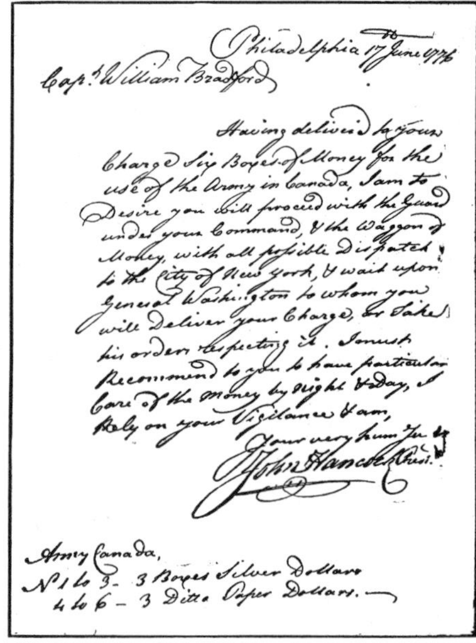

Philadelphia 17 June 1776

Capt. William Bradford

Having deliver'd to your Charge Six Boxes of Money for the use of the Army in Canada, I am to Desire you will proceed with the Guard under your Command, & the Waggon of Money, with all possible Dispatch to the City of New York, & wait upon General Washington to whom you will Deliver your Charge, or take his orders respecting it. I must Recommend to you to have particular Care of the Money by Night & day, I Rely on your Vigilance & am,

Your very hum Ser

John Hancock Presi.

Army Canada,
No 1 to 3 – 3 Boxes Silver Dollars
4 to 6 – 3 Ditto Paper Dollars.

325 Hancock to Captain William Bradford, June 17, 1776, from a facsimile in possession of the publishers

SOLDIERS MUST BE PAID

Not all the problems facing the Provisional Assembly had such a happy conclusion. Too soon the Congress discovered that the establishment of a fighting army involved the furnishing of munitions, equipment, food and fodder. All of this required money and management; so new functions were undertaken. Money was borrowed abroad and at home; paper currency was issued. All in all, more and more power was rapidly passing into the hands of Congress.

GOVERNMENTAL MACHINERY DEVELOPS SLOWLY

As the war continued, weaknesses in this arrangement became more and more evident. The Congress was composed of delegates, chosen and paid by the member states, whose instructions usually determined the action of their "ambassadors." Each state had one vote, each was watchful of its own interests, and the adherence of all was essential to the preservation of each; hence debatable matters suffered from either compromise or inaction. In short, the Congress was in the unenviable position of attempting to run a government when the operating machinery was not yet designed or installed. Not until near the close of the war did it learn and apply the principle of concentrated responsibility. At first it tried to handle everything in general session. After a time numerous committees, with overlapping personnel — such as a war office and a navy board — were set up to do the administrative work. Meanwhile the ineptitude of Congress, and more attractive public service elsewhere, resulted in a deteriorated membership of the body.

326 Office of Secretary of Foreign Affairs, South Sixth Street, Philadelphia, from J. F. Watson, *Annals of Philadelphia*, edition of 1850, after an engraving by Mumford

MORRIS IS FINANCIAL ADVISER

PERHAPS the outstanding exception to this wholesale withdrawal of the capable was Robert Morris of Pennsylvania. A wealthy banker who had from the beginning espoused the American cause, he had, though opposed to the step, signed the Declaration of Independence in 1776, and had ever since given his fiscal wisdom and wealth to achieving its objectives. His presence in Congress proved of extreme value. For the Congress, unable to levy taxes, found foreign loans and paper money uncertain support for the armies in the field. Then it was that Morris earned his title of "Financier of the Revolution."

327 Robert Morris, 1734–1806, from the portrait by C. W. Peale in the Pennsylvania Academy of the Fine Arts

CIRCULAR.

Gentlemen

UNDER cover, we tranſmit you the Plan of a BANK deviſed by Mr. MORRIS, ſuperintendant of finance elect, and approved of by Congreſs, on the twenty ſeventh inſtant.

It being a part aſſigned us therein to begin the execution, by the appointment of perſons within the States, to ſolicit and receive ſubſcriptions, we take the liberty of nominating You as our Agent for this purpoſe, for Newport your well known attachment to the cauſe of your country leaving us no room to doubt of your zeal, and readineſs, to fulfil the ends of your appointment.

We requeſt you will adviſe us, from time to time, of your progreſs in the buſineſs; it being neceſſary to know when the ſubſcriptions reach the preciſe point which is to entitle the ſtockholders to the right of electing their officers, that notice may be given accordingly

The printed receipts Twenty five in number alſo under cover, are for the convenience of aſſignment made out for ſingle ſhares; if any remain unuſed, you will be pleaſed to return them; if too few, written receipts may be given, and afterwards replaced by the printed forms, which we will ſend you on the firſt notice. The money when received, ſhould be ſent to us, as often as good opportunities offer.

The nature and general utility of national banks are well known, but in reference to our peculiar circumſtances, it has been obſerved that this eſtabliſhment appears well adapted to ſupply the place of the preſent circulation, which in ſome meaſure has loſt its uſe, both as a private convenience, and governmental ſupport. The latter is moſt to be regretted—but a bank raiſed on theſe ſolid principles, by a ſuitable enlargement of its foundation, may in time, by the anticipation of the public revenue, yield the prompteſt and moſt effectual aids to the United States: And we are not without a hope, but that even in its infant ſtate, if thoſe on whom its execution depends, apply vigorouſly to their truſt, it may have no immaterial influence upon the preſent campaign:

In this favourable light is the bank conſidered in this City, where we are happy to find a general diſpoſition to give it the earlieſt encouragement.

PHILADELPHIA, May 31. 1781.

We are, Your moſt obedient Humble Servants,

Caleb Gardner & George Champlin Esqrs Newport

Geo Clymer

John Nixon

328 Circular on Morris' Plan of a Bank, 1781, in the Emmet Collection, New York Public Library

CONGRESS PROVIDES FOR A BANK

WHEN in 1781 he persuaded Congress to establish the office of Superintendent of Finance and to provide for a central bank, Morris was chosen for the post. And in it he served with distinction for three years, when he withdrew in disgust at the pettiness of his colleagues and the states. Everyone was jealous of the others. They were unwilling to surrender to some one else, no matter how efficient and able he might be, powers of action which were needed to tide over the crisis facing the country.

ARTICLES OF CONFEDERATION, 1777

THE Congress itself realized its failings. In accord with Lee's resolution of June 7, 1776, it appointed a committee, headed by Dickinson of Pennsylvania, to "prepare a plan of confederation." Shortly after the adoption of the Declaration, the committee reported and desultory debate followed. No agreement was reached until November 15, 1777, when the plan was presented by Henry Laurens, President of Congress, to the several states for ratification.

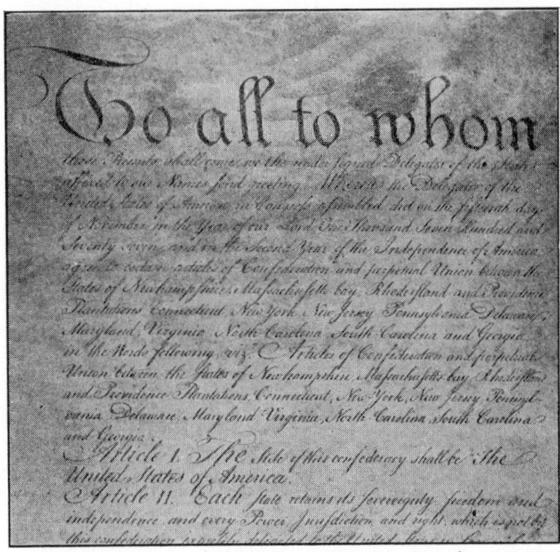

To all to whom these Presents shall come we the under signed Delegates of the States affixed to our Names send greeting. Whereas the Delegates of the United States of America in Congress assembled did on the fifteenth day of November in the Year of our Lord One Thousand Seven Hundred and Seventy seven, and in the Second Year of the Independence of America agree to certain articles of Confederation and perpetual Union between the States of Newhampshire, Massachusetts-bay, Rhodeisland and Providence Plantations, Connecticut, New York, New Jersey, Pennsylvania, Delaware, Maryland, Virginia, North Carolina, South Carolina and Georgia in the Words following, viz. "Articles of Confederation and perpetual Union between the States of Newhampshire, Massachusetts-bay, Rhodeisland and Providence Plantations, Connecticut, New York, New Jersey, Pennsylvania, Delaware, Maryland, Virginia, North Carolina, South Carolina and Georgia.

Article I. The Stile of this confederacy shall be "The United States of America."

Article II. Each state retains its sovereignty freedom and independence, and every Power, Jurisdiction, and right, which is not by

329 First page of the Articles of Confederation, from the engrossed copy in the Library of Congress, Washington

In Congress March 1 1781

According to the order of the Day, the Honourable John Hanson and Daniel Carrol, two of the Delegates for the State of Maryland, in Pursuance of the Act of the Legislature of that state, entitled "An Act to impower the Delegates of this State in Congress to subscribe and ratify the Articles of Confederation," which was read in Congress the Twelfth of February last, and a Copy thereof entered on the minutes, did in Behalf of the said State of Maryland Sign and ratify the said Articles of Confederation, by which Act the Confederation of the United States of America was compleated, each and every of the thirteen United States, from New Hampshire to Georgia, both included, having adopted and confirmed, and by their Delegates, in Congress ratified the same

Extract from the Minutes

Cha Thomson Secy

a true Copy, attest

John Adams Minister Plenipotentiary

330 Ratification of Articles of Confederation by Maryland, 1781, from the original in the Emmet Collection, New York Public Library

THE STATES WANT SELF-GOVERNMENT

GOVERNMENT in the United States, then, between 1775 and 1781, rested upon the several states. Though the powers of the Continental Congress were undefined, and on occasion vigorously exercised, its authority was constantly dependent upon the consent and coöperation of the states. And to the states the people rendered an allegiance much more willingly and more fully than to the body of inept and hampered diplomats composing the Congress. These "Sovereign, Free and Independent States" — so they were habitually called by Congress — had, indeed, initiated the Revolution and created the central committee. Even before the Declaration of Independence, several had established new governments. In the following busy years effort was turned to the drafting of new forms of government expressive of the current political ideals. State after state adopted its written constitution, often by a process irregular but always acceptable to the Patriots. But the time was soon coming when the states would anxiously turn to national authority for relief from conflicting theories.

JEALOUSY DELAYS RATIFICATION

PREOCCUPATION with the business of warring was one cause of the delay in ratifying the Articles. There were, however, differences of opinion among the delegates. John Adams, in a letter of July 29, 1776, stated the major problems: "One great question is how we shall vote — whether each colony shall have one, or whether each shall have weight in proportion to its number or wealth, or imports or exports, or a compound ratio of all? Another is whether Congress shall have authority to limit the dimensions of each colony, to prevent those which claim to the South Sea, so as to be dangerous to the rest." The first matter was settled in favor of the smaller states, the second in the favor of those states claiming western lands. Largely because of this latter decision, ratification of the Articles by all thirteen members was delayed until 1781. Maryland, in particular, held out until New York, Virginia and Massachusetts — the leading states with such claims — agreed to surrender them to the common government.

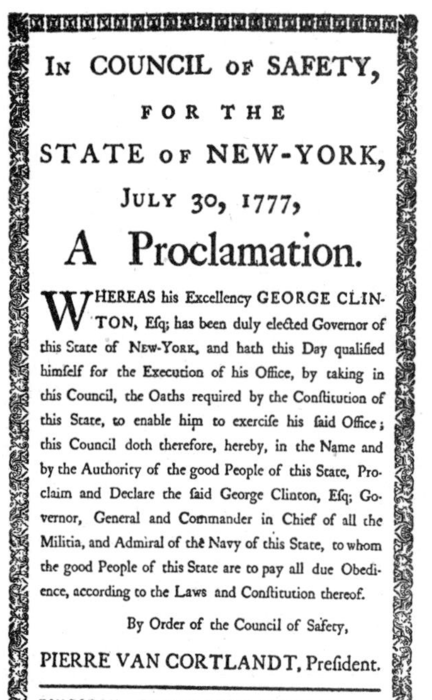

IN COUNCIL OF SAFETY,
FOR THE
STATE OF NEW-YORK,
JULY 30, 1777,

A Proclamation.

WHEREAS his Excellency GEORGE CLINTON, Esq; has been duly elected Governor of this State of NEW-YORK, and hath this Day qualified himself for the Execution of his Office, by taking in this Council, the Oaths required by the Constitution of this State, to enable him to exercise his said Office; this Council doth therefore, hereby, in the Name and by the Authority of the good People of this State, Proclaim and Declare the said George Clinton, Esq; Governor, General and Commander in Chief of all the Militia, and Admiral of the Navy of this State, to whom the good People of this State are to pay all due Obedience, according to the Laws and Constitution thereof.

By Order of the Council of Safety,

PIERRE VAN CORTLANDT, President.

KINGSTON. PRINTED BY JOHN HOLT, PRINTER TO THE STATE OF NEW-YORK.

331 Proclamation on the Election of the First Governor of New York, from the copy in the Emmet Collection, New York Public Library

State of *Maſſachuſetts-Bay.*

In the Houſe of REPRESENTATIVES, February 19, 1779.

WHEREAS the Conſtitution or Form of Civil Government, which was propoſed by the state Convention of this State to the People thereoj, hath been diſapproved by a Majority of the Inhabitants of ſaid State:

And whereas it is doubtful, from the Repreſentations made to this Court, what are the Sentiments of the major Part of the good People of this State as to the Expediency of now proceeding to form a new Conſtitution of Government:

Therefore, *Reſolved*, That the Selectmen of the ſeveral Towns within this State cauſe the Freeholders, and other Inhabitants in their reſpective Towns duly qualified to vote for Repreſentatives, to Be lawfully warned to meet together in ſome convenient Place therein, on or before the laſt Wedneſday of *May* next, to conſider of and determine upon the following Queſtions.

Firſt, Whether they chuſe at this Time to have a new Conſtitution or Form of Government made.

Secondly, Whether they will impower their Repreſentatives for the next Year to vote for the calling a State Convention, for the ſole Purpoſe of forming a new Conſtitution, provided it ſhall appear to them, on Examination, that a major Part of the People preſent and voting at the Meetings called in the Manner and for the Purpoſe aforeſaid, ſhall have anſwered the firſt Queſtion in the Affirmative.

And in Order that the Senſe of the People may be known thereon: Be it further *Reſolved*, That the Selectmen of each Town be and hereby are directed to return into the Secretary's Office, on or before the firſt Wedneſday in *June* next, the Doings of their reſpective Towns on the firſt Queſtion above-mentioned, certifying the Numbers voting in the Affirmative, and the Numbers voting in the Negative, on ſaid Queſtion.

Sent up for Concurrence,

JOHN PICKERING, *Speaker.*

In COUNCIL, February 20, 1779.

Read and concurred, JOHN AVERY, *Dep. Sec'ry.*

Conſented to by the Major Part of the Council.

A true Copy, Atteſt, JOHN AVERY, *Dep. Sec'ry.*

332 Resolution of Massachusetts Bay, Feb. 19, 1779, from the broadside in the New York Public Library

State of *Maſſachuſetts-Bay.*

In the Houſe of REPRESENTATIVES, *June* 15, 1779.

WHEREAS by the Returns made into the Secretary's Office from more than two thirds of the Towns belonging to this State, agreeably to a Reſolve of the General Court of the 20th of February *laſt, it appears that a large majority of the inhabitants of ſuch Towns, as have made return as aforeſaid, think it proper to have a new Conſtitution or Form of Government, and are of opinion that the ſame ought to be formed by a Convention of Delegates who ſhould be ſpecially authorized to meet for this Purpoſe:* Therefore,

RESOLVED, That it be and it hereby is recommended to the ſeveral Inhabitants of the ſeveral towns in this State to form a Convention for the ſole purpoſe of framing a new Conſtitution, conſiſting of ſuch Number of Delegates from each town throughout the State, as every different town is intitled to ſend Repreſentatives to the General Court, to meet at *Cambridge*, in the county of *Middleſex*, on the firſt day of *September* next.

And the Selectmen of the ſeveral towns and places in this State, impowered by the laws thereof to ſend Members to the General Aſſembly, are hereby authorized and directed to call a Meeting of their reſpective towns at leaſt fourteen days before the meeting of the ſaid Convention, to elect one or more Delegates to repreſent them in ſaid Convention, at which Meeting for the election of ſuch Delegate or Delegates, every Freeman, inhabitant of ſuch town, who is twenty one years of age, ſhall have a right to vote.

Be it alſo *Reſolved*, That it be and hereby is recommended to the inhabitants of the ſeveral towns in this State to inſtruct their reſpective Delegates to cauſe a printed copy of the Form of a Conſtitution they may agree upon in Convention to be tranſmitted to the Selectmen of each town, and the Committee of each plantation, and the ſaid Selectmen and Committees are hereby impowered and directed to lay the ſame before their reſpective towns and plantations at a regular Meeting of the Male inhabitants thereof, being free and twenty one years of age, to be called for that purpoſe, in order to its being duly conſidered and approved or diſapproved by ſaid towns and plantations; and it is alſo recommended to the ſeveral towns within this State to inſtruct their reſpective Repreſentatives to eſtabliſh the ſaid Form of a Conſtitution as the Conſtitution and Form of Government of the State of *Maſſachuſetts Bay*, if upon a fair Examination it ſhall appear that it is approved of by at leaſt two thirds of thoſe who are free and twenty one years of age, belonging to this State, and preſent in the ſeveral Meetings.

Sent up for Concurrence,

JOHN HANCOCK, Speaker.

In COUNCIL, *June* 21, 1779. Read and concurred.

JOHN AVERY, Dep. Secr'y.

333 Resolution of Massachusetts Bay, June 15, 1779, from the broadside in the New York Public Library

MASSACHUSETTS ADOPTS A CONSTITUTION

SINGULARLY enough, Massachusetts was the last to form its fundamental charter. A constitution framed by the legislature was rejected early in 1778. Then, thanks to pressure from the farmers of Berkshire County in the west, the legislature took the sense of the town meetings on the advisability of calling a special constitutional convention whose work would be submitted to popular determination. Though many of the towns failed to answer this request, the vote stood 6,612 to 2,639 in favor of the method. In September the convention began its deliberations. Under the lead of John Adams, a body containing such strong members as Hancock, James Bowdoin, Samuel Adams, Robert Treat Paine and Theophilus Parsons, submitted to the people a document which they adopted. Thus Massachusetts inaugurated the method now customary in the preparation and adoption of an American constitution.

BILLS OF RIGHTS BECOME LAWS

NEW HAMPSHIRE, perhaps influenced by developments in Maryland, convened a special convention (June, 1778) to draft a fundamental law. But the convention's work was too conservative to meet the desires of the people of the hill towns. As in six of the other states, the constitution finally adopted contained a bill of rights in which was stated the philosophy of the people. Perhaps it was the distinguishing mark of the early American constitution that the bill of rights summarized those provisions of English common law and those governmental processes which the struggle with England had led the colonists to believe fundamental to ordered and free political society.

A D E C L A R A T I O N

of RIGHTS, and PLAN of Government for the State of

New-Hampſhire.

WHEREAS *by the tyrannical Adminiſtration of the Government of the King and Parliament of Great-Britain, this State of New-Hampſhire, with the other United-States of* AMERICA, *have been neceſſitated to reject the Britiſh Government, and declare themſelves* INDEPENDENT STATES; *all which is more largely ſet forth by the* CONTINENTAL CONGRESS, *in their Reſolution or Declaration of the fourth of July A. D.* 1776.

AND WHEREAS, it is recommended by the ſaid CONTINENTAL CONGRESS *to each and every of the ſaid United-States to eſtabliſh a* FORM OF GOVERNMENT *moſt conducive to the Welfare thereof. We the* DELEGATES *of the ſaid State of* NEW-HAMPSHIRE *choſen for the Purpoſe of forming a permanent* PLAN *of* GOVERNMENT *ſubject to the Reviſal of our* CONSTITUENTS, *have compoſed the following* DECLARATION *of* RIGHTS, *and* PLAN *of* GOVERNMENT; *and recommend the ſame to our* CONSTITUENTS *for their Approbation.*

A DECLARATION of the R I G H T S of the PEOPLE of the STATE of NEW-HAMPSHIRE.

Firſt, WE declare, that we the People of the State of New-Hampſhire, are Free and Independant of the Crown of Great-Britain.

Secondly. We the People of this State, are intitled to Life, Liberty, and Property; and all other Immunities and Privileges which we heretofore enjoyed.

Thirdly. The Common and Statute Laws of England, adopted and uſed here, and the Laws of this State (not inconſiſtent with ſaid Declaration of INDEPENDENCE) now are, and ſhall be in force here, for the Welfare and good Government of the State, unleſs the ſame ſhall be repealed or altered by the future Legiſlature thereof.

Fourthly. The whole and intire Power of Government of this State, is veſted in, and muſt be derived from the People thereof, and from no other Source whatſoever.

Fifthly. The future Legiſlature of this State, ſhall make no Laws to infringe the Rights of Conſcience, or any other of the natural, unalienable Rights of Men, or contrary to the Laws of GOD, or againſt the Proteſtant Religion.

Sixthly. The Extent of Territory of this State, is, and ſhall be the ſame which was under the Government of the late Governor *John Wentworth*, Eſq; Governor of *New-Hampſhire*. Reſerving neverthelefs, our Claim to the *New-Hampſhire Grants*, ſo called, ſituate to the Weſt of Connecticut River.

Seventhly. The Right of Trial by Jury in all Caſes as heretofore uſed in this State, ſhall be preſerved inviolate forever.

A PLAN of Government for the State of New-Hampſhire.

Firſt, THE State of *New-Hampſhire* ſhall be governed by a COUNCIL, and Houſe of REPRESENTATIVES, to be choſen as herein after mentioned, and to be ſtiled the GENERAL-COURT of the State of *New-Hampſhire*.

Second. The COUNCIL ſhall conſiſt for the preſent of twelve Members to be elected out of the ſeveral Counties in the State, in Proportion to their reſpective Number of Inhabitants.

Third. The Numbers belonging to each County for the preſent, according to ſaid Proportion being as followeth, viz.—To the County of Rockingham, five—to the County of Strafford, two—to the County of Hillſborough, two—to the County of Cheſhire, two—to the County of Grafton, one.

Fourth. The number for the County of Rockingham, ſhall not be increaſed or diminiſhed hereafter, but remain the ſame; and the Numbers for the other Counties ſhall be increaſed or deminiſhed as their aforeſaid Proportion to the County of Rockingham may chance to vary.

Fifth. The Houſe of REPRESENTATIVES ſhall be choſen as follows. Every Town or Pariſh, chooſing Town Officers, amounting to one hundred Families, and upwards, ſhall ſend one Repreſentative for each hundred Families they conſiſt of, (or ſuch leſſer Number as they pleaſe) or claſs themſelves with ſome other Towns or Pariſhes that will join in ſending a Repreſentative.

Sixth. All other Towns and Pariſhes under the number of one hundred Families, ſhall have Liberty to claſs themſelves together to make the number of one hundred Families or upwards, and being ſo claſſed, each Claſs ſhall ſend one Repreſentative.

Seventh. The number of COUNCILLORS belonging to each County ſhall be aſcertained and done by the General-Court every Time there is a new Proportion made of the State Tax which ſhall be once in ſeven Years at the leaſt, and oftner if need be.

Eighth. All the Male Inhabitants of the State of lawful Age, paying Taxes, and profeſſing the Proteſtant Religion, ſhall be deemed legal Voters in chooſing COUNCILLORS and REPRESENTATIVES, and having an Eſtate of *Three Hundred Pounds* equal to Silver at ſix Shillings and eight Pence per Ounce, one half at leaſt whereof to be real Eſtate, and lying within this State, with the Qualifications aforeſaid, ſhall be capable of being elected.

Ninth. The Selectmen of each reſpective Town and Pariſh, chooſing Town Officers containing one hundred Families or upwards, and alſo of each reſpective Claſs of Towns claſſed together as aforeſaid, ſhall notify the legal Voters of their reſpective Towns, Pariſhes, or Claſſes, qualified as aforeſaid, in the uſual Way of notifying Town-Meetings, giving fifteen Days notice at leaſt, to meet at ſome convenient Place on the laſt Wedneſday of November annually, to chooſe COUNCILLORS and REPRESENTATIVES.

Tenth. And the Voters being met, and the Moderator choſen, ſhall proceed to chooſe their Repreſentative or Repepreſentatives, required by this Conſtitution by a Majority of the Voters preſent, who ſhall be notified accordingly, and a Return thereof made into the Secretary's Office, by the firſt Wedneſday of January then next.

Eleventh. And ſuch Repreſentatives ſhall be paid their Wages by their Conſtituents, and for their Travel by the State.

Twelvth. And in the Choice of COUNCILLORS each Voter ſhall deliver his Vote to the Moderator for the number of COUNCILLORS reſpectively required, with the Word COUNCILLORS writen thereon, & the Voters Name endorſed to prevent Duplicity.

Thirteenth. Theſe Votes ſhall be ſealed up by the Moderator, and tranſmitted by the Conſtable to one of the Juſtices of the Inferior Court of Common Pleas for the County, before the ſecond Wedneſday in December next following.

334 New Hampshire Declaration of Rights, 1779, from a broadside in the New York Public Library

335 Nathan Dane, 1752–1835, from the portrait, artist unknown, in the possession of Harvard University

THE CONGRESS PROVIDES FOR NEW STATES

UNDER the Articles of Confederation there was little improvement in the general government. Its powers were only such as the states, jealous of their prerogatives, deemed necessary to carry on national affairs. Though its membership included such able men as Jefferson, Madison, Sherman and Hamilton, state posts were still more attractive. Attendance was irregular, support by the states negligible. While the Congress in 1782–83 asked the states for $10,000,000, only some $1,500,000 was forthcoming by the end of 1783. The defects of the Confederation are too well-known to require restatement. Yet some achievements must be placed to its credit. Under it peace was obtained, commercial relations with several European states were established, and the union was preserved. Above all, it instituted our national territorial policy. The land cessions of Virginia, Massachusetts and Connecticut enabled the Confederation to organize and legislate for the national domain. The Continental Congress had in 1780 declared that such land was ultimately to be formed into member states of the union; the proposed state of Franklin in the old Southwest and the colonization of the western lands called attention to their importance. The discussion bore fruit in the Northwest Ordinance of 1787, largely framed by Nathan Dane of Massachusetts. This provided for temporary governments in the area, and for their ultimate admission to the Union. In the framing of the Ordinance of 1787 the influence of the versatile Thomas Jefferson was important. Three years before he had blocked out a policy for the Northwest Territory which, though it failed of enactment, was the foundation of the measure of 1787.

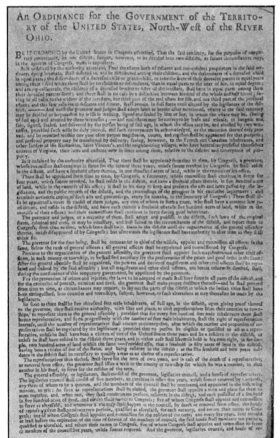

An ORDINANCE for the GOVERNMENT of the TERRITORY of the UNITED STATES, North-West of the RIVER OHIO.

BE IT ORDAINED by the United States in Congress assembled, That the said territory, for the purposes of temporary government, be one district; subject, however, to be divided into two districts, as future circumstances may, in the opinion of Congress, make it expedient.

[illegible]

DONE by the UNITED STATES in CONGRESS assembled, the 13th day of July, in the year of our Lord 1787, and of their sovereignty and independence the 12th.

Chas Thomson Sec^y

336 Ordinance of 1787, from the broadside in the New York Public Library 337

TRADE IN THE POST-WAR PERIOD

THE achievement of independence left the Americans free to trade in the world where they could. The merchants soon found, however, that the war had profoundly changed commercial conditions. The Navigation Acts against which the Americans had protested before 1775 now put them on the same footing with other foreign nations in so far as trade within the British empire was concerned. Particularly disastrous was the exclusion of vessels flying the Stars and Stripes from the commerce of British West Indies. The French and Spanish made only such concessions as accrued to their advantage. John Adams, sent to England as the first Minister, made no headway in securing a commercial treaty. Jefferson, in 1784, drafted a general plan for such treaties which has served as a model for subsequent commercial arrangements entered into by the United States. The attempts of the American merchants to find relief from this boycott caused a venturesome expansion along new channels. From the crippled harbors of the eastern coast American vessels sailed westward to China in search of the profitable cargo of the foreign factories, which, at Canton, were increasing each year in number. Yet the new Oriental activities could not provide immediate remedy for a depression as fundamental as that which resulted from the almost complete dislocation of former commerce. (See Volume IV, Chapter I.) The "hard times" of seventeen eighty-four and five served to bring home to the commercial classes the need for a strong government which could, if necessary, legislate to further American commerce, and institute a uniform commercial policy for all the states. When an effort was made to amend the Articles of Confederation so as to give the central government such power but two states supported it.

338 Canton factories in 1804, from a fireboard painted by Corné after an engraving, courtesy of the Peabody Museum, Salem, Mass.

339 From the original paper money issued by Rhode Island, 1786, in the Emmet Collection, New York Public Library

PAPER MONEY

COMMERCIAL depression was not the only cause for worry in the years immediately following the close of the Revolution. During the war the British and French armies had brought considerable specie into the country. When the troops departed, the business interests began to press for a stable currency to take the place of the vastly depreciated paper bills which Congress had issued during the war. Efforts tending to put the currency on a sound basis met with opposition from a large group of farmers who had mortgages on their property and also from other debtors. The debtor-farmers, already adversely affected by a slump in prices, sought to lighten their burden of debt by bringing about the issue of more irredeemable paper money which, in its turn, was certain to depreciate. The extension of suffrage during the Revolution now gave political power to the debtor group. They obtained control of Rhode Island and promptly issued paper money. In other states there were fierce battles at the polls between radicals and conservatives. When the latter won in Massachusetts, Shays' rebellion resulted.

THE

CASE,

TREVETT againſt *WEEDEN*:

On INFORMATION and COMPLAINT, for refuſing *Paper Bills* in Payment for *Butcher's Meat*, in Market, at Par with Specie.

Tried before the Honourable SUPERIOR COURT, in the County of *Newport*, *September* Term, 1786.

ALSO,

The Caſe of the Judges of ſaid Court,

Before the Honourable GENERAL ASSEMBLY, at *Providence*, *October* Seſſion, 1786, on Citation, for diſmiſſing ſaid Complaint.

Wherein the Rights of the People to *Trial by Jury*, &c. are ſtated and maintained, and the Legiſlative, Judiciary and Executive Powers of Government examined and defined.

By *JAMES M. VARNUM*, Eſq;

Major-General of the State of *Rhode-Iſland*, &c. Counſellor at Law, and Member of Congreſs for ſaid State.

PROVIDENCE: Printed by JOHN CARTER, 1787.

340 From the title-page of the copy in the New York Public Library

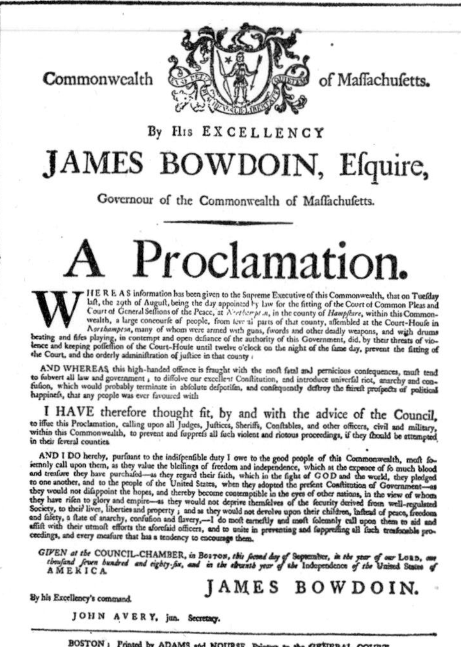

Commonwealth of Maſſachuſetts.

By His EXCELLENCY

JAMES BOWDOIN, Eſquire,

Governour of the Commonwealth of Maſſachuſetts.

A Proclamation.

WHEREAS information has been given to the Supreme Executive of this Commonwealth, that on Tueſday laſt, the 29th of Auguſt, being the day appointed by law for the ſitting of the Court of Common Pleas and Court of General Seſſions of the Peace, at *Northampton*, in the county of *Hampſhire*, within this Commonwealth, a large concourſe of people, from ſeveral parts of that county, aſſembled at the Court-Houſe in *Northampton*, many of whom were armed with guns, ſwords and other deadly weapons, and with drums beating and fifes playing, in contempt and open defiance of the authority of this Government, did, by their threats of violence and keeping poſſeſſion of the Court-Houſe until twelve o'clock on the night of the ſame day, prevent the ſitting of the Court, and the orderly adminiſtration of juſtice in that county:

AND WHEREAS, this high-handed offence is fraught with the moſt fatal and pernicious conſequences, muſt tend to ſubvert all law and government, to diſſolve our excellent Conſtitution, and introduce univerſal riot, anarchy and confuſion, which would probably terminate in abſolute deſpotiſm, and conſequently deſtroy the faireſt proſpects of political happineſs, that any people was ever favoured with

I HAVE therefore thought fit, by and with the advice of the Council, to iſſue this Proclamation, calling upon all Judges, Juſtices, Sheriffs, Conſtables, and other officers, civil and military, within this Commonwealth, to prevent and ſuppreſs all ſuch violent and riotous proceedings, if they ſhould be attempted in their ſeveral counties.

AND I DO hereby, purſuant to the indiſpenſible duty I owe to the good people of this Commonwealth, moſt ſolemnly call upon them, as they value the bleſſings of freedom and independence, which at the expence of ſo much blood and treaſure they have purchaſed—as they regard their faith, which in the ſight of GOD and the world, they pledged to one another, and to the people of the United States, when they adopted the preſent Conſtitution of Government—as they would not diſappoint the hopes, and thereby become contemptible in the eyes of other nations, in the view of whom they have riſen to glory and empire—as they would not deprive themſelves of the ſecurity derived from well-regulated Society, to their lives, liberties and property; and as they would not devolve upon their children, inſtead of peace, freedom and ſafety, a ſtate of anarchy, confuſion and ſlavery,—I do moſt earneſtly and moſt ſolemnly call upon them to aid and aſſiſt with their utmoſt efforts the aforeſaid officers, and to unite in preventing and ſuppreſſing all ſuch treaſonable proceedings, and every meaſure that has a tendency to encourage them.

GIVEN at the COUNCIL-CHAMBER, *in* BOSTON, *this ſecond day of* September, *in the year of our* LORD, *one thouſand ſeven hundred and eighty-ſix, and in the eleventh year of the* Independence *of the* United States *of* AMERICA.

JAMES BOWDOIN.

By his Excellency's command.

JOHN AVERY, jun. Secretary.

BOSTON: Printed by ADAMS and NOURSE, Printers to the GENERAL COURT.

341 Proclamation of Sept. 2, 1786, on the Shays Rebellion, from the copy in the New York Historical Society

SHAYS' REBELLION

"THE conservative elements in Massachusetts, and conservative commentators from other states described the rebellion as an attack upon property and government by reckless radicals, whose aim was to establish mob rule. But Shays and his band were not trying to overthrow government, as such, although they did want changes. . . . The movement was a protest against hard times, and it drifted into violence perhaps because of the survival of the state of mind of the Revolution. The common farmers had been taught that the proper way to end a grievance was to attack the government. Samuel Adams, the old specialist in revolutionary methods, denounced the 'Shaysites' with considerable more show of horror than had been used when British authorities had denounced him in earlier years. . . . Clearly then, in view of the obvious weakness of the Confederation and this threatened overthrow of state government, along with the hopeless failures to solve the problems of commerce and the frontier, something would have to be done to save the United States from chaos. So it happened that those who were most seriously affected by the dangers of the critical period — the merchants and the larger property owners, men with money to lose — began seriously to contemplate the revision of the Articles of Confederation, with a view to safeguarding, not only their own interests, but the public interests, which depended upon a continuance of peace and good order." — RALPH V. HARLOW, *Growth of the United States*, pp. 231–32.

A NATIONAL CONVENTION PLANNED BY THE CONSERVATIVES

THE movement to revise the Articles had, indeed, begun when Alexander Hamilton wrote in September, 1780, to Madison, suggesting that a convention be called "with full authority to conclude finally on a form of general Confederation . . . [and] to provide certain perpetual revenues . . . which . . . would give Congress a substantial existence and a stable foundation." As war receded, leaving in its wake the problems of reconstruction, such views came from many of the leaders. The failures to secure unanimous agreement to proposed strengthening amendments to the Articles pointed to the need for more drastic action. Opportunity was furnished in a meeting at Annapolis, called by Virginia "to take into consideration the trade of the United States . . . and to consider how far a uniform system in their commercial regulations may be necessary to their common interests and their permanent harmony." Only five states were represented, but Madison and Hamilton obtained the adoption of a report calling for a new convention to meet at Philadelphia in May following, "to consider the situation of the United States and devise such further provisions as should appear necessary to render the constitution of the federal government adequate to the exigencies of the Union." The Annapolis Convention instituted what proved to be a veritable bloodless revolution.

necessary to render the constitution of the Foederal Government adequate to the exigencies of the Union, and to report such an Act for that purpose to the United States in Congress assembled as when agreed to by them and afterwards confirmed by the Legislatures of every State will effectually provide for the same.

Though your Commissioners could not with propriety address these observations and sentiments to any but the States they have the honor to Represent they have nevertheless concluded from motives of respect to transmit Copies of this Report to the United States in Congress assembled, and to the executives of the other States.

By order of the Commissioners

Dated at Annapolis September 14th 1786

Resolved that the Chairman sign the aforegoing Report in behalf of the Commissioners

Then adjourned without day —

Egbt Benson — Alexander Hamilton } New York

Abra Clark, Wm Ch Houston, Js Schureman } New Jersey

Tench Coxe — Pennsylvania

Geo: Read, John Dickinson, Richard Bassett } Delaware

Edmund Randolph, Js Madison Jr, St George Tucker } Virginia —

342 Last page of the Report of the Annapolis Convention, 1786, from the original in the Library of Congress

343 Gouverneur Morris, 1752–1816, from the portrait by Ezra Ames (1768–1836) in the New York Historical Society

344 Rufus King, 1755–1827, from the portrait by C. W. Peale in Independence Hall, Philadelphia

345 Roger Sherman, 1721–93, from the portrait attributed to Ralph Earl (1751–1801) in possession of Yale University

346 Luther Martin, 1748–1826, from the portrait by an unknown artist in the Judge's Room of the Superior Court, Baltimore

347 James Madison, 1751–1812, from the portrait by Gilbert Stuart (1755–1828) in the Bowdoin Museum of Fine Arts, Bowdoin College, Brunswick, Me.

348 Charles Pinckney, 1758–1824 from the portrait by Gilbert Stuart in Philipse Manor Hall, Yonkers, N. Y.

THE CONVENTION DRAWS MEN OF PRESTIGE

To the gathering at Philadelphia came many able men. Most of them had had long and varied experience in public and private affairs. Robert and Gouverneur Morris — the latter the stylist of the Constitution — represented the financial interests; George Clymer and Roger Sherman the hard-headed business man; James Wilson, Luther Martin and Charles Pinckney were eminent lawyers; Hamilton and Madison were earnest students of politics and government. Revolutionary leaders such as Patrick Henry and Samuel Adams were conspicuous by their absence. In brief, the members came from the prosperous classes, from the groups wishing a stable central government sufficiently strong to protect property rights. There was thus general agreement on one important point: The central government must be strengthened, particularly in its fiscal and commercial controls. Differences arose chiefly with regard to the structure of the government that was to exercise this enhanced power. The delegates had come with a variety of instructions as to the character and extent of the change to be worked in the Articles of Confederation; but it was soon apparent that a new government and a new constitution would be necessary. The debates were carried on behind closed doors; the greatest strain came over the question of representation in the new national Congress.

We the People of the United States, in Order to form a more perfect Union, establish Justice, insure domestic Tranquility, provide for the common defence, promote the general Welfare, and secure the Blessings of Liberty to ourselves and our Posterity, do ordain and establish this Constitution for the United States of America.

Article I

Section 1. All legislative Powers herein granted shall be vested in a Congress of the United States, which shall consist of a Senate and House of Representatives.

Section 2. The House of Representatives shall be composed of Members chosen every second Year by the People of the several States, and the Electors in each State shall have the Qualifications requisite for Electors of the most numerous Branch of the State Legislature.

No Person shall be a Representative who shall not have attained to the Age of twenty five Years, and been seven Years a Citizen of the United States, and who shall not, when elected, be an Inhabitant of that State in which he shall be chosen.

Representatives and direct Taxes shall be apportioned among the several States which may be included within this Union, according to their respective Numbers, which shall be determined by adding to the whole Number of free Persons, including those bound to Service for a Term of Years, and excluding Indians not taxed, three fifths of all other Persons. The actual Enumeration shall be made within three Years after the first Meeting of the Congress of the United States, and within every subsequent Term of ten Years, in such Manner as they shall by Law direct. The Number of Representatives shall not exceed one for every thirty Thousand, but each State shall have at Least one Representative; and until such enumeration shall be made, the State of New Hampshire shall be entitled to chuse three, Massachusetts eight, Rhode Island and Providence Plantations one, Connecticut five, New York six, New Jersey four, Pennsylvania eight, Delaware one, Maryland six, Virginia ten, North Carolina five, South Carolina five, and Georgia three.

349 Preamble of the Constitution of the United States, from the original in the Department of State, Washington

A NEW NATIONAL GOVERNMENT IS FOUNDED

The delegates went far beyond their instructions to patch up the Confederation. In its place they created the structure of a truly national government, resting upon the people of America, and not solely upon the states. Even among the delegates, there had been dissension as to this point; and with the plan perfected, many felt dubious over the outcome. In November Washington wrote: "The warmest friends and the best supporters the Constitution has, do not contend that it is free from imperfections; but they found them unavoidable, and are sensible, if evil is likely to arise therefrom, the remedy must come hereafter; for in the present moment it is not to be obtained; and, as there is a constitutional door open for it, the people (for it is with them to judge), can, as they will have the advantage of experience on their side, decide with as much propriety on the alterations and amendments which are necessary as ourselves. I do not think we are more inspired, have more wisdom, or possess more virtue, than those who will come after us."

350 From the mural painting by Albert Herter (1871–) in the Supreme Court, Wisconsin State Capitol, Madison, Wis.

THE SIGNING OF THE CONSTITUTION

On September 8, a committee of five, dominated by men who in the preceding weeks of discussion had been pronouncedly nationalistic, was appointed "to revise the style of and arrange the articles agreed to by the House." On the 12th they reported. Three days of revision followed, and on the 15th the Constitution was accepted by delegates of all the states represented. Two days later the engrossed copy was signed. Thirteen members were absent, and three present refused to sign.

THE CONVENTION RECOMMENDS RATIFICATION

FURTHER to insure its adoption the convention, in submitting the document to the Congress, made two important recommendations. First, the Constitution was to be presented for ratification in each state to conventions specially chosen therefor by the people. Thus its acceptance would rest upon a broad and enduring basis. Secondly, it was to be put into operation when as many as nine states had ratified. Thus the *impasse* of unanimous consent, which the Confederation had found insuperable, was to be avoided. These recommendations the Congress readily adopted; and on September 28 the Constitution was sent to the states for action.

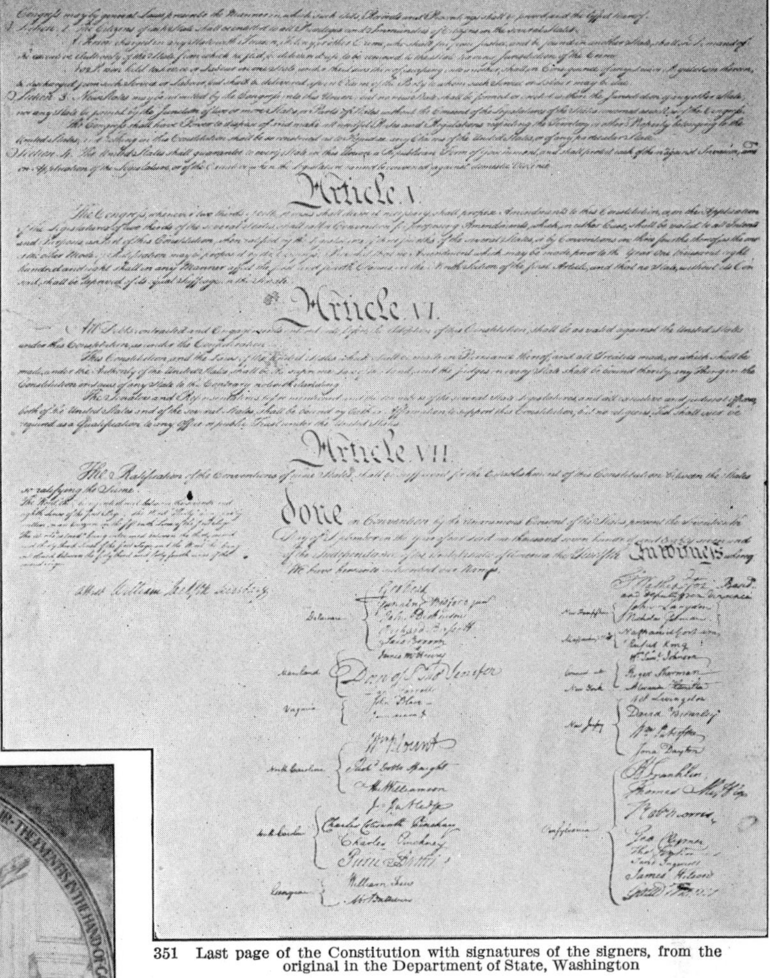

Article V

Article VI

Article VII

351 Last page of the Constitution with signatures of the signers, from the original in the Department of State, Washington

352 From the mural painting *Washington before the Constitutional Convention* by Violet Oakley (1874–) in the Pennsylvania State Capitol, Harrisburg. © Curtis & Cameron

DISSENTING VIEWS SHAKE THE CONVENTION

OVER the proceedings of the convention, a convention at times (wrote Luther Martin) "scarce held together by the strength of a hair," Washington had presided. Direct participation by him in its work had been slight; but his opinions on the matters discussed were well known. Nor had he refrained from expressing them to members. On the 10th of July he had written to Hamilton, then absent from Philadelphia: "I almost despair of seeing a favorable issue to the proceedings of our convention, and do therefore repent having had any agency in the business. The men, who oppose a strong and energetic government, are in my opinion narrow-minded politicians, or are under the influence of local views. The apprehension expressed by them, that the *people* will not accede to the form proposed, is the *ostensible* not the *real* cause of opposition. But, admitting that the present sentiment is as they prognosticate, the proper question ought nevertheless to be, Is it, or is it not, the best form that such a country as this can adopt? If it be the best, recommend it, and it will assuredly obtain, maugre opposition."

An addreſs of the ſubſcribers, members of the late houſe of repreſentatives of the commonwealth of Pennſylvania, to their conſtituents.

Gentlemen,

WHEN, in conſequence of your ſuffrages, at the laſt election, we were choſen to [illegible] you in the [illegible] will effectually [illegible] for the ſame."

You will therefore perceive, that they had no authority whatever from the legiſlature, to annihilate the preſent confederation, and form a conſtitution entirely new; and in doing which they have acted as mere individuals, not as the official deputies of this commonwealth. If, however, after mature deliberation, you are of opinion, that the plan of government, which they have offered for your conſideration, is beſt calculated to promote your political happineſs, and preſerve thoſe invaluable privileges you at preſent enjoy, you will, no doubt, chooſe men to repreſent you in convention who will adopt it; if you think otherwiſe, you will, with your uſual firmneſs, determine accordingly.

You have a right, and we have no doubt you will conſider whether or not you are in a ſituation to ſupport the expence of ſuch a government as is now offered to you, as well as the expence of your ſtate government? or whether a legiſlature, conſiſting of three branches, neither of them choſen annually, and that the ſenate, the moſt powerful, the members of which are for ſix years, are likely to leſſen your burdens, or increaſe your taxes? or whether, in caſe your ſtate government ſhould be annihilated, which will probably be the caſe, or dwindle into a mere corporation, the continental government will be competent to attend to your local concerns? You can alſo beſt determine whether the power of levying and impoſing internal taxes, at pleaſure, will be of real uſe to you or not? or whether a continental collector, aſſiſted by a few faithful ſoldiers, will be more eligible than your preſent collectors of taxes? You will alſo, in your deliberations on this important buſineſs, judge, whether the liberty of the preſs may be conſidered as a bleſſing or a curſe, in a free government, and whether a declaration for the preſervation of it is neceſſary? or whether, in a plan of government, any declaration of rights ſhould be prefixed or inſerted? You will be able, likewiſe, to determine, whether, in a free government, there ought or ought not to be any proviſion againſt a ſtanding army in time of peace? or whether the trial by jury, in civil cauſes, is become dangerous, and ought to be aboliſhed? and whether the judiciary of the united ſtates is not ſo conſtructed as to abſorb and deſtroy the judiciaries of the ſeveral ſtates? you will alſo be able to judge whether ſuch inconveniencies have been experienced by the preſent mode of trial between citizen and citizen, of different ſtates, as to render a continental court neceſſary for that purpoſe? or whether there can be any real uſe in the appellate juriſdiction with reſpect to fact as well as law? We ſhall not dwell longer on this ſubject; one thing, however, it is proper you ſhould be informed of; the convention were not unanimous with reſpect to men, though they were as ſtates: ſeveral of thoſe who have ſigned, did not fully approve of the plan of government: and three of the members, viz. governor Randolph, and colonel Geo. Maſon, of Virginia, and Elbridge Gerry, eſq. of Maſſachuſetts, whoſe characters are very reſpec- [illegible] to refuſe ſigning. The confederation, no doubt, is defective, and requires amendment and reviſion; and had the convention extended their plan to the enabling the united ſtates to regulate commerce—equalize the impoſt—collect it throughout the united ſtates—and have the entire juriſdiction over maritime affairs, leaving the exerciſe of internal taxation to the ſeparate ſtates, we apprehend there would have been no objection to the plan of government.

The matter will be before you, and you will be able to judge for yourſelves. "Shew that you ſeek not yourſelves, but the good of your country: and may HE, who alone has dominion over the paſſions and underſtandings of men, enlighten and direct you aright, that poſterity may bleſs God for the wiſdom of their anceſtors."

James M'Calmont,	*John Gilchriſt,*
Robert Clark,	*Abraham Smith,*
Jacob Miley,	*Robert Whitehill,*
Alexander Wright,	*David Mitchell.*
John M'Dowell,	*John Piper,*
John Flenniken,	*Samuel Dale,*
James Allyſon,	*William Findley,*
Theophilus Philips,	*James Barr.*

Saturday, September 29. 1787.

353 Report of the Minority Dissenters in the Pennsylvania Convention, from *The Independent Gazetteer; or, The Chronicle of Freedom,* Philadelphia, Oct. 3, 1787, in the New York Public Library

PENNSYLVANIA OPPOSES RATIFICATION

ON its first publication, the document seemed to meet with general favor. The desire for a stronger government was widespread; the proposal was the work of the leading men in the country. These men, moreover, had gone back to their communities ready to battle for the Constitution. They had heard the vigorous debates in the convention and therefore knew what issues were likely to be raised. Thus equipped, the Federalists for a time carried the day. Within four months the new Constitution was ratified by five states. In Delaware, New Jersey and Georgia, the action was unanimous; the vote in Connecticut was three to one. Opposition first raised its head in Pennsylvania. The farmers of the back-country had long opposed the "moneyed interests" of Philadelphia; they had carried Pennsylvania for independence in 1776; and now they resisted the effort of the city to foist upon them a government which would lessen their liberties. From Philadelphia, Gouverneur Morris wrote to Washington (October 30): "With respect to this State I am far from being decided in my opinion that they will consent. True it is that the city and its neighborhood are enthusiastic in the cause; but I dread the cold and sour temper of the back counties." The advantages of the Federalists now appeared. Working with vigor and haste, they pushed through an adjourning legislature a call for the state convention. With scant time for campaigning, the opposition found themselves outmaneuvered. On the 12th of December, by a vote of forty-six to twenty-three, ratification was obtained. Later, the Antis drew up an address to the public embodying their amendments. These amendments, ten, in time, introduced by Madison, became a part of the Constitution.

354 Elbridge Gerry, 1744–1814, from a crayon drawing, 1798, by John Vanderlyn (1776–1852) in C. W. Bowen, *The History of the Centennial Celebration of the Inauguration of George Washington,* New York, 1892

MASSACHUSETTS IS NOW FOR THE CONSTITUTION

THE sharp tactics in Pennsylvania served to rouse the anti-Federalists. In the press began to appear the views of men eminent for patriotism and ability, denouncing the Constitution. In Massachusetts came the next great struggle. For a time the cause of the Federalists seemed desperate. Elbridge Gerry had come back from Philadelphia without signing the Constitution; Samuel Adams and John Hancock hesitated; the farmers who had followed Shays were still opinionated and powerful. But shrewd political tactics won; and on February 6, by a close vote, Massachusetts took her place under the "New Roof," as the Constitution was popularly labeled.

NEW HAMPSHIRE IS THE NINTH PILLAR

In the spring of 1788 two more states, Maryland and South Carolina, joined; and on June 21 New Hampshire gained the honor of being the ninth state to ratify. The quota had been reached. But of the large states only two — Pennsylvania and Massachusetts — had come under the New Roof. Without Virginia and New York, the structure would indeed be weak.

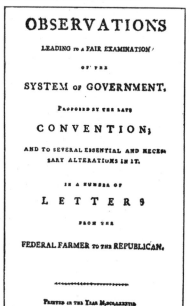

The Ninth PILLAR erected !

" The Ratification of the Conventions of nine States, ſhall be ſufficient for the eſtabliſhment of this Conſtitution, between the States ſo ratifying the ſame." *Art.* vii.

INCIPIENT MAGNI PROCEDERE MENSES.

The arrival of Mr. *Reed*, on Sunday laſt, from Concord, New Hampſhire, with the NEWS of the adoption of the New Federal Syſtem by the Convention of that State, at two o'clock, P. M. on Saturday laſt, diffuſed unuſual joy through all ranks in this metropolis,—as by this great event, the Federal Edifice is reared, and the future good government of the States in general ſecured to the people. On the queſtion for adoption, the deciſion appeared as follows:

For the Conſtitution,	57
Againſt it,	46
Majority,	11

Mr. *Reed* was honoured with diſpatches from His Excellency John Sullivan, Eſquire, Preſident of New-Hampſhire Convention, to His Excellency Governour Hancock—the contents of which follows.—

CONCORD, June 21, 1788.

S I R,

I HAVE the honor to inform your Excellency by favour of Mr. Reed, who is obliging enough to forward this Letter, that the Convention of this State have this Moment adopted the New Conſtitution. Yeas, 57; Nays, 46. The Amendments recommended, nearly the ſame as in your State.

With every Sentiment of reſpectful Attachment, I have the Honour to be,

Your Excellency's
moſt obedient Servant,
JOHN SULLIVAN.

" Gov. Hancock."

The bells in the ſeveral churches, on Monday morning, teſtified to the pleaſure which filled the breaſt of every citizen, on this pleaſing event.

The inhabitants of Roxbury alſo teſtified their extreme pleaſure on the arrival of this important intelligence, by the ſame demonſtrations of joy.

Extract of a letter from a gentleman of the firſt information, dated Peterſburgh, June 9, 1788, received per a veſſel in 5 days from Norfolk

" I have been attending the debates of

Meſſ'rs. Adams & Nourse,

THE natal day of our ſovereignty and independence approaches nigh;—A day, which will ever be held in grateful remembrance by every true born American:—A day, in which our illuſtrious heroes and patriots nobly ſhook off the galling ſhackles of vaſſalage, and fettered tyranny at the ſhrine of liberty. To the honour of Boſton, be it ſpoken, that its inhabitants, not content only with celebrating the anniverſary with feſtivity and mirth; but call upon one of their fellow citizens, publicly to recite the cauſes which led to the late revolution, and recapitulate the zeal and indefatigable perſeverance of our illuſtrious Chiefs in obtaining the acquiſition. The youth of this town, that they might not be remiſs in caſe of an emergency, have devoted much of their time to become diſciplinarians in the art of war; and their frequent military exhibitions have carried ſtrong convictions of their proficiency: And although the inſtitution of JULY ORATIONS was to keep alive the flame of patriotiſm, and no one is denied acceſs to the aſſembly, yet the young militairs, to their great diſappointment and mortification, were excluded the laſt year, by reaſon of the *Parade*. Can patriotiſm ever be nurtur'd in a more grateful ſoil, than in the breaſts of thoſe who ſtand ever ready to guard the precious legacy left to them by their fathers?—And muſt they be again deprived of theſe pleaſures, and excluded from hearing the addreſſes of a perſon, who has borne ſo conſpicuous a part in military matters for ſome time paſt?—Juſtice forbid! In deference to the opinions of thoſe who ſuperintend the affairs of that day, I would obſerve, that the Old-South Meeting-Houſe, would be more convenient than the Chapel-Church,—and there can be no impropriety in allotting a gallery for the *then* parading companies, as their being embodied together in that manner, in their uniforms, would not only add brilliancy to the aſſembly, but be productive of great ſatisfaction to

M A N Y.

355 From *The Independent Chronicle and Universal Advertiser*, June 26, 1778

OBSERVATIONS

LEADING TO A FAIR EXAMINATION

OF THE

SYSTEM OF GOVERNMENT,

PROPOSED BY THE LATE

CONVENTION;

AND TO SEVERAL ESSENTIAL AND NECESSARY ALTERATIONS IN IT.

IN A NUMBER OF

LETTERS

FROM THE

FEDERAL FARMER TO THE REPUBLICAN.

PRINTED IN THE YEAR M,DCC,LXXXVII.

356 Title-page of Richard Henry Lee's *Observations*, from the original issue, 1787, in the New York Public Library

VIRGINIA AFTER A STRUGGLE FALLS INTO LINE

In Virginia the struggle was spectacular. On either side were ranged men of national fame. Opposing the Constitution were Patrick Henry, the orator of the Revolution, George Mason, author of the Virginia Declaration of Rights, Richard Henry Lee, sponsor of the independence resolution of 1776, now author of one of the most popular pamphlets against ratification, and Edmund Randolph, popular Governor. Both Mason and Randolph had been members of the Philadelphia Convention; and both had refused to sign the Constitution. Jefferson, moreover, absent in France, at first urged rejection. Against this powerful group, supported by the people of the Piedmont region, were brought the influence of Washington and the skill of Madison. In the brilliant young lawyer, John Marshall, they found an invaluable ally. Randolph was won by Madison's tact; Jefferson wrote that, amended, the Constitution would suit him well enough. Mason had opposed it because it lacked a bill of rights. Virginia's ratification on June 25 was accompanied by a demand that this deficiency be rectified.

357 John Marshall, 1755–1835, from the portrait by St. Memin, about 1800, in the Corcoran Gallery of Art, Washington

358 Richard Henry Lee, 1732–94, from the portrait by C. W. Peale in Independence Hall, Philadelphia

JOHN JAY'S *ADDRESS TO THE PEOPLE OF THE STATE OF NEW-YORK,* 1787

NEW YORK remained outside. The fifth in population, from commercial and military standpoints she was a state vital to the success of the new Union. Nor was it a certainty that she would enter. Her critical position had early been recognized. John Jay, Secretary for Foreign Affairs, took a hand in the process of conversion by publishing an influential pamphlet in favor of the Constitution.

AN

ADDRESS

TO THE

PEOPLE

OF THE

STATE OF NEW-YORK,

On the SUBJECT of the

CONSTITUTION,

Agreed upon at PHILADELPHIA,

The 17th of September, 1787.

NEW YORK

PRINTED BY SAMUEL AND JOHN LOUDON,

PRINTERS TO THE STATE.

359 Title-page of the copy in the New York Public Library

360 George Clinton, 1739–1812, from the portrait, 1812, by Ezra Ames in the New York Historical Society

THE CONSTITUTION MEETS FOES

THE opposition was led by George Clinton, Governor of New York since 1777. Popular because of his successful war administration, he had not neglected to build up a powerful political machine. Gouverneur Morris in 1787 predicted that should the question of ratification be left to the "government" of New York, the vote would be decidedly in the negative. For Clinton was bitter in his attacks on a government that would lessen the importance of his state. With him sided the debtors, the politicians, and the landowners of up-state New York, traditionally at outs with the city, now the stronghold of the Federalists.

A BATTLE OF BROADSIDES IN NEW YORK

LATE in 1787 the campaign against the Constitution had begun. Pamphlets and broadsides pro and con were rushed from the presses. Verse, oratory, personal backbiting and abuse, all the arts of the demagogue, were employed, with much skill and an equal bitterness of feeling, on both sides.

To the Inhabitants of

KING'S COUNTY.

Friends and Fellow-Citizens!

I Muſt beg leave to treſpaſs once more on your patience, by a ſhort reply to the *King's County Farmer*'s Addreſs of the 26th inſtant. He has trod again in the ſame dirty path in which he firſt ſet out, as if he expected to carry his point by mere abuſe. I well know your ſentiments and feelings, with reſpect to a language of that kind, and I am convinced you will univerſally condemn the mean ſubterfuge of this man.—It matters not whether I am a madman or fool, whether I am in office, or in purſuit of an office: the point is, whether or not my arguments in favour of the New Conſtitution are founded on truth.—If they are not, this King's County Farmer ought to have endeavoured, by reaſoning, to convince you of it. Has he attempted this? Or has he not contented himſelf with dealing out low, mean invective, againſt my character. He may reſt aſſured, that ſuch kind of attacks are, and ever ſhall be, treated with due contempt by me—a mind conſcious of its own rectitude, deſpiſes every accuſer. What I have aſſerted, and reaſoned on, in favor of the New Conſtitution, he cannot confute. He is the mere tool of a party; and is determined, notwithſtanding he knows he is wrong, ſtill to perſiſt in the error. That it is your intereſt to adopt it I moſt righteouſly believe. He tells you that I have inſulted you; if I have, it has been done without an intention, or wiſh ſo to do. Had I, in any of my addreſſes to you, have made uſe of the ſame low mean declamation that he has done, I ſhould then ſtand convicted of having groſſly inſulted you. You will find in his beſt addreſs he has not even attempted to oppoſe the Conſtitution by any kind of argument whatever. He reſts his cauſe upon bare aſſertion, and wiſhes you to oppoſe the adoption of it, becauſe men in office have directed him to do ſo. I am ſure his objections to the Conſtitution will have no weight with you, for they merit none. He tells you that you will be taxed by the State, and by Congreſs; you are already taxed by the State for State purpoſes, and by the State for the ſupplies of Congreſs; what difference, therefore, will this make? It matters not, whether you pay your taxes immediately into the Continental Treaſury, or into the State Treaſury; for, if they are paid into the State Treaſury, they muſt go from thence into the Treaſury of the United States. But I continue, my friends, to be of the ſame opinion with which I ſet out, which is, that the revenue ariſing from the commerce of this country, under proper regulations, will be amply ſufficient to anſwer the demands of the New Government; your taxes therefore will be made much lighter than they now are. It now reſts with us to determine whether we ſhall adopt the New Conſtitution, and thereby ſecure to ourſelves, and our poſterity, peace, happineſs, and a good government; or reject it, and have diſcord, miſery, and wretchedneſs amongſt us. I moſt ſincerely pray that you will, with one heart, and one voice, join with me in proclaiming, adopt it! adopt it!—

A FLATBUSH FARMER.

Flatbuſh, 28th April, 1788.

NEW-YORK: PRINTED BY FRANCIS CHILDS.

361 Copy of a handbill from "a Flatbush Farmer," favoring the adoption of the Constitution, in the New York Historical Society

For the Independent Journal.

The FŒDERALIST. No. I.

To the People of the State of New-York.

AFTER an unequivocal experience of the ineſſicacy of the ſubſiſting Fœderal Government, you are called upon to deliberate on a new Conſtitution for the United States of America. The ſubject ſpeaks its own importance; comprehending in its conſequences, nothing leſs than the exiſtence of the UNION, the ſafety and welfare of the parts of which it is compoſed, the fate of an empire, in many reſpects, the moſt intereſting in the world. It has been frequently remarked, that it ſeems to have been reſerved to the people of this country, by their conduct and example, to decide the important queſtion, whether ſocieties of men are really capable or not, of eſtabliſhing good government from reflection and choice, or whether they are forever deſtined to depend, for their political conſtitutions, on accident and force. If there be any truth in the remark, the criſis, at which we are arrived, may with propriety be regarded as the æra in which that deciſion is to be made; and a wrong election of the part we ſhall act, may, in this view, deſerve to be conſidered as the general misfortune of mankind.

This idea will add the inducements of philanthropy to those of patriotiſm to heighten the ſollicitude, which all conſiderate and good men muſt feel for the event. Happy will it be if our choice ſhould be decided by a judicious eſtimate of our true intereſts, unperplexed and unbiaſſed by conſiderations not connected with the public good. But this is a thing more ardently to be wiſhed, than ſeriouſly to be expected. The plan offered to our deliberations, affects too many particular intereſts, innovates upon too many local

inſtitutions, not to involve in its diſcuſſion a variety of objects foreign to its merits, and of views, paſſions and prejudices little favourable to the diſcovery of truth.

Among the moſt formidable of the obſtacles which the new Conſtitution will have to encounter, may readily be diſtinguiſhed the obvious intereſt of a certain claſs of men in every State to reſiſt all changes which may hazard a diminution of the power, emolument and conſequence of the offices they hold under the State-eſtabliſhments—and the perverted ambition of another claſs of men, who will either hope to aggrandiſe themſelves by the confuſions of their country, or will flatter themſelves with fairer proſpects of elevation from the ſubdiviſion of the empire into ſeveral partial confederacies, than from its union under one government.

It is not, however, my deſign to dwell upon obſervations of this nature. I am well aware that it would be diſingenuous to reſolve indiſcriminately the oppoſition of any ſet of men (merely becauſe their ſituations might ſubject them to ſuſpicion) into intereſted or ambitious views: Candour will oblige us to admit, that even ſuch men may be actuated by upright intentions; and it cannot be doubted, that much of the oppoſition which has made its appearance, or may hereafter make its appearance, will ſpring from ſources, blameleſs at leaſt, if not reſpectable, the honeſt errors of minds led aſtray by preconceived jealouſies and fears. So numerous indeed and ſo powerful are the cauſes, which ſerve to give a falſe bias to the judgment, that we upon many occaſions, ſee wiſe and good men on the wrong as well as on the right ſide of queſtions, of the firſt magnitude to ſociety. This circumſtance, if duly attended to, would furniſh a leſſon of moderation to thoſe, who are ever ſo much perſuaded of their being in the right, in any controverſy.

And a further reaſon for caution, in this reſpect, might be drawn from the reflection, that we are not always ſure, that thoſe who advocate the truth are influenced by purer principles than their antagoniſts. Ambition, avarice, perſonal animoſity, party oppoſition, and many other motives, not more laudable than theſe, are apt to operate as well upon thoſe who ſupport as upon thoſe who oppoſe the right ſide of a queſtion. Were there not even theſe inducements to moderation, nothing could be more illjudged than that intolerant ſpirit, which has, at all times, characteriſed political parties. For, in politics as in religion, it is equally abſurd to aim at making proſelytes by fire and ſword. Hereſies in either can rarely be cured by perſecution.

And yet however juſt theſe ſentiments will be allowed to be, we have already ſufficient indications, that it will happen in this as in all former caſes of great national diſcuſſion. A torrent of angry and malignant paſſions will be let looſe. To judge from the conduct of the oppoſite parties, we ſhall be led to conclude, that they will mutually hope to evince the juſtneſs of their opinions, and to increaſe the number of their converts by the loudneſs of their declamations, and by the bitterneſs of their invectives. An enlightened zeal for the energy and efficiency of government will be ſtigmatiſed, as the off-ſpring of a temper fond of deſpotic power and hoſtile to the principles of liberty. An overſcrupulous jealouſy of danger to the rights of the people, which is more commonly the fault of the head than of the heart, will be repreſented as mere pretence and artifice; the bait for popularity at the expence of public good. It will be forgotten, on the one hand, that jealouſy is the uſual concomitant of violent love, and that the noble enthuſiaſm of liberty is too apt to be infected with a ſpirit of narrow and illiberal diſtruſt. On the other hand,

362 From the first number of *The Federalist,* Oct. 27, 1787, from the copy in the New York Historical Society

THE FEDERALIST

Out of all this but one piece of writing of permanent value has survived. The strength and number of the opposition had convinced Alexander Hamilton that what was needed was a thorough explanation of the new form of Government in a fashion to reach the general mass of the people. So began that famous series of incisive essays, the work of Hamilton, Madison and Jay, now called *The Federalist.* Appearing at frequent intervals through the winter of 1787–88, these articles must have done much to win over the uncertain. To-day they stand as the best contemporaneous analysis of the new Constitution and one of the most striking contributions to the history of political literature.

NEW YORK RATIFIES AMID REJOICING

Nevertheless, when the state convention met at Poughkeepsie in June, four fifths of the delegates were anti-Federalist. For five weeks Hamilton hammered at them. Skillful management, brilliant debating power and a growing fear of isolation from the states that were already members of the Union had their effect. Melancthon Smith, Clinton's right-hand supporter, deserted to Hamilton, and on July 26, 1788, by a vote of thirty to twenty-seven, New York ratified. Everywhere there was great rejoicing. Through the streets of the coming metropolis moved a huge parade, with the ship of state, "Hamilton," occupying the place of honor. The Union was assured. Though New York had voted for the Constitution, she accompanied her ratification with a proposal that a new constitutional convention should be called, to consider amendments to the document of 1787. In this move she received some support; but Massachusetts and Virginia, though they had asked for amendments to the Constitution, objected that this method of obtaining them would reopen the whole question and imperil all the good in the New Roof.

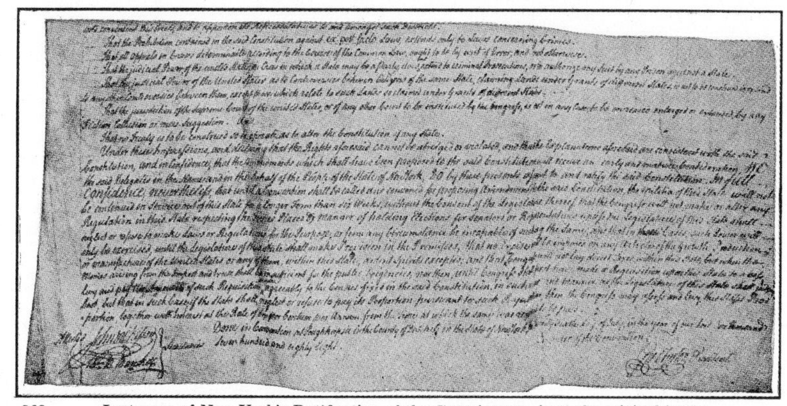

363 Last page of New York's Ratification of the Constitution, from the original in the State Education Department, Albany

Ratification of the Constitution of the United States by the Convention of the State of Rhode-Island and Providence-Plantations.

WE the DELEGATES of the PEOPLE of the STATE of RHODE-ISLAND AND PROVIDENCE-PLANTATIONS, duly elected and met in CONVENTION, having maturely considered the CONSTITUTION for the UNITED STATES of AMERICA, agreed to on the Seventeenth Day of September, A. D. 1787, by the Convention then assembled at Philadelphia, in the Commonwealth of Pennsylvania (a Copy whereof precedes these Presents) and having also seriously and deliberately considered the present Situation of this State, DO DECLARE and MAKE KNOWN,

1st. THAT there are certain natural rights, of which men, when they form a social compact, cannot deprive or divest their posterity, among which are the enjoyment of life and liberty, with the means of acquiring, possessing, and protecting property, and pursuing and obtaining happiness and safety.

2. That all power is naturally vested in and consequently derived from the people; that magistrates therefore, are their trustees and agents, and at all times amenable to them.

3. That the powers of government may be reassumed by the people whensoever it shall become necessary to their happiness. That the rights of the State respectively to nominate and appoint all State officers, and every other power, jurisdiction and right, which is not by the said Constitution clearly delegated to the Congress of the United States, or to the department of government thereof, remains to the people of the several States or their respective State governments to whom they may have granted the same; and that those clauses in the Constitution which declare that Congress shall not have or exercise certain powers, do not imply that Congress is entitled to any powers not given by the said Constitution; but such clauses are to be construed either as exceptions to certain specified powers, or as inserted merely for greater caution.

4. That religion, or the duty which we owe to our Creator, and the manner of discharging it, can be directed only by reason and conviction, not by force or violence, and therefore all men have an equal natural and unalienable right to the free exercise of religion according to the dictates of conscience; and that no particular religion, sect or society ought to be favoured or established by law in preference to others.

5. That the legislative, executive and judiciary powers of government should be separate and distinct; and the members of the two first may be restrained from oppression by feeling and participating the public burthen, they should at fixed periods be reduced to a private station, return into the mass of the people, and the vacancy be supplied by certain and regular elections, in which all or any part of the former members to be eligible or ineligible, as the rules of the Constitution of Government and the Laws shall direct.

6. That elections of representatives in the legislature ought to be free and frequent; and all men having sufficient evidence of permanent common interest with, and attachment to the community, ought to have the right of suffrage; and no aid, charge, tax or fee can be set, rated, or levied upon the people, without their own consent or that of their Representatives so elected; nor can they be bound by any law to which they have not, in like manner, assented for the public good.

7. That all power of suspending laws, or the execution of laws by any authority, without the consent of the Representatives of the people in the Legislature, is injurious to their rights, and ought not to be exercised.

8. That in all capital and criminal prosecutions a man hath a right to demand the cause and nature of his accusation, to be confronted with the accusers and witnesses, to call for evidence, and to be allowed council in his favor, and to a fair and speedy trial by an impartial jury of his vicinage, without whose unanimous consent he cannot be found guilty (except in the government of the land and naval forces) nor can he be compelled to give evidence against himself.

9. That no freeman ought to be taken, imprisoned or disseized of his freehold, liberties, privileges or franchises, or outlawed or exiled, or in any manner destroyed, or deprived of his life, liberty or property, but by the trial by jury or by the law of the land.

10. That every freeman restrained of his liberty is entitled to a remedy, to enquire into the lawfulness thereof, and to remove the same if unlawful, and that such remedy ought not to be denied or delayed.

11. That in controversies respecting property, and in suits between man and man, the antient trial by jury as hath been exercised by us and our ancestors from the time whereof the memory of man is not to the contrary, is one of the greatest securities to the rights of the people, and ought to remain sacred and inviolate.

12. That every freeman ought to obtain right and justice freely and without sale, completely and without denial, promptly and without delay; and that all establishments or regulations contravening these rights are oppressive and unjust.

13. That excessive bail ought not to be required, nor excessive fines imposed, nor cruel or unusual punishments inflicted.

14. That every person has a right to be secure from all unreasonable searches and seizures of his person, his papers, or his property, and therefore that all warrants to search suspected places, or to seize any person, his papers, or his property, without information upon oath or affirmation, of sufficient cause, are grievous and oppressive, and that all general warrants (or such in which the place or person suspected are not particularly designated) are dangerous and ought not to be granted.

15. That the people have a right to freedom of speech, and of writing and publishing their sentiments; that the freedom of the press is one of the greatest bulwarks of liberty, and ought not to be violated.

16. That the people have a right peaceably to assemble together to consult for their common good, or to instruct their representatives; and that every person has a right to petition or apply to the Legislature for redress of grievances.

17. That the people have a right to keep and bear arms; that a well regulated militia, including the body of the people capable of bearing arms, is the proper, natural and safe defence of a free State; that the militia shall not be subject to martial law, except in time of war, rebellion, or insurrection; that standing armies in time of peace are dangerous to liberty, and ought not to be kept up, except in cases of necessity; and that at all times the military should be under strict subordination to the civil power; that in time of peace no soldier ought to be quartered in any house without the consent of the owner; and in time of war only by the civil magistrate, in such manner as the law directs.

18. That any person religiously scrupulous of bearing arms ought to be exempted, upon payment of an equivalent to employ another to bear arms in his stead.

UNDER these impressions, and declaring that the rights aforesaid cannot be abridged or violated, and that the explanations aforesaid, are consistent with the said Constitution, and in confidence that the amendments hereafter mentioned, will receive an early and mature consideration, and conformably to the fifth article of said Constitution, speedily become a part thereof; WE, the said DELEGATES, in the Name and in the Behalf of the PEOPLE of the STATE OF RHODE-ISLAND AND PROVIDENCE PLANTATIONS, do by these Presents, assent to and ratify the said Constitution. IN FULL CONFIDENCE, nevertheless, that until the amendments hereafter proposed shall be agreed to and ratified, in pursuant to the aforesaid fifth article, the militia of this State will not be continued in service out of this State for a longer term than six weeks, without the consent of the Legislature thereof; that the Congress will not make or alter any regulation in this State respecting the times, places and manner of holding elections for Senators or Representatives, unless the Legislature of this State shall neglect or refuse to make laws or regulations for the purpose, or from any circumstance be incapable of making the same; and that in those cases [illegible] will only be exercised until the Legislature of this State shall make provision [illegible] premises; that the Congress will not lay direct taxes within this State but when the monies arising from the impost, tonnage, and excise shall be insufficient for the public exigencies, nor until the Congress shall have first made a requisition upon this State to assess, levy, and pay the amount of such requisition made agreeable to the census fixed in the said Constitution in such way and manner as the Legislature of this State shall judge best, and that the Congress will not lay or make any capitation or poll tax.

DONE IN CONVENTION, at Newport, in the County of Newport, in the State of Rhode-Island and Providence Plantations, the 29th Day of May, in the Year of our Lord One Thousand Seven Hundred and Ninety, and the Fourteenth Year of the Independence of the United States of America.

BY ORDER,

DANIEL OWEN, PRESIDENT.

ATTEST.

DANIEL UPDIKE, SECRETARY.

AND the CONVENTION DO, in the Name and Behalf of the PEOPLE of the STATE OF RHODE-ISLAND AND PROVIDENCE-PLANTATIONS, enjoin it upon the Senators and Representative or Representatives which may be elected to represent this State in Congress to exert all their influence and use all reasonable means to obtain a ratification of the following amendments to the said Constitution in the manner prescribed therein; and in all laws to be passed by the Congress in the mean time to conform to the spirit of the said amendments, as far as the Constitution will admit.

AMENDMENTS.

1. THE United States shall guarantee to each State its sovereignty, freedom, and independence, and every power, jurisdiction and right, which is not by the Constitution expressly delegated to the United States.

2. That Congress shall not alter, modify or interfere in the times, places and manner of holding elections for Senators and Representatives, or either of them, except when the Legislature of any State shall neglect, refuse, or be disabled by invasion or rebellion, to prescribe the same; or in case when the provision made by the State is so imperfect as that no consequent election is had; and then only until the Legislature of such State shall make provision in the premises.

3. It is declared by the Convention that the judicial power of the United States, in cases in which a State may be a party, does not extend to criminal prosecutions, or to authorize any suit by any person against a State; but to remove all doubts or controversies respecting the same, that it be especially expressed as a part of the Constitution of the United States, that Congress shall not directly or indirectly, either by themselves or through their judiciary, interfere with any one of the States in the redemption of paper money already emitted and now in circulation, or in liquidating or discharging the public securities of any one State; that each and every State shall have the exclusive right of such laws and regulations for the before-mentioned purposes, as they shall think proper.

4. That no amendments to the Constitution of the United States hereafter to be made, pursuant to the fifth article, shall take effect, or become a part of the Constitution of the United States after the year 1793, without the consent of eleven of the States heretofore united under one Confederation.

5. That the judicial power of the United States shall extend to no possible case where the cause of action shall have originated before the ratification of this Constitution, except in disputes between States about their territory, disputes between persons claiming lands under grants of different States, and debts due to the United States.

6. That no person shall be compelled to do military duty, otherwise than by voluntary enlistment, except in cases of general invasion; any thing in the second paragraph of the sixth article of the Constitution, or any law made under the Constitution to the contrary notwithstanding.

7. That no capitation or poll tax shall ever be laid by Congress.

8. In cases of direct taxes Congress shall first make requisitions on the several States to assess, levy, and pay their respective proportions of such requisitions in such way and manner as the Legislatures of the several States shall judge best; and in case any State shall neglect or refuse to pay its proportion pursuant to such requisition, then Congress may assess and levy such State's proportion, together with interest at the rate of six per cent. per annum, from the time prescribed in such requisition.

9. That Congress shall lay no direct taxes without the consent of the Legislatures of three fourths of the States in the union.

10. That the journals of the proceedings of the Senate and House of Representatives shall be published as soon as conveniently may be, at least once in every year, except such parts thereof relating to treaties, alliances, or military operations, as in their judgment require secrecy.

11. That regular statements of the receipts and expenditures of all public monies shall be published at least once a year.

12. As standing armies in time of peace are dangerous to liberty and ought not to be kept up except in cases of necessity, and as at all times the military should be under strict subordination to the civil power—that therefore no standing army or regular troops shall be raised or kept up in time of peace.

13. That no monies be borrowed on the credit of the United States without the assent of two thirds of the Senators and Representatives present in each House.

14. That the Congress shall not declare war without the concurrence of two thirds of the Senators and Representatives present in each house.

15. That the words "without the consent of Congress," in the seventh clause in the ninth section of the first article of the Constitution, be expunged.

16. That no judge of the Supreme Court of the United States shall hold any office under the United States, or any of them; nor shall any officer appointed by Congress, or by the President and Senate of the United States, be permitted to hold any office under the appointment of any of the States.

17. As a traffic tending to establish or continue the slavery of any part of the human species is disgraceful to the cause of liberty and humanity, that Congress shall, as soon as may be, promote and establish such laws and regulations as may effectually prevent the importation of slaves of every description into the United States.

18. That the State Legislatures have power to recall, when they think it expedient, their Federal Senators, and to send others in their stead.

19. That Congress have power to establish an uniform rule of inhabitancy or settlement of the poor of the different States throughout the United States.

20. That Congress erect no company with exclusive advantages of commerce.

21. That whenever two members shall move that the yeas and nays on any question shall be taken, the same shall be entered on the journals of the respective Houses.

IN CONVENTION, MAY 29, 1790.

RESOLVED, That three hundred copies of the Ratification of the Constitution of the United States by the Convention of this State, including the Bill of Rights and the proposed Amendments, be printed: That one copy be sent to each Member of this Convention, one to each Member of the Upper and Lower Houses of Assembly, and one to each Town-Clerk in this State, for the general information of the people; and that they be sent to the Sheriffs of the several Counties to be distributed.

The foregoing is a true Copy.

By Order of the Convention,

DANIEL UPDIKE, SECRETARY.

364 Rhode Island's Ratification of the Constitution, from a printed copy, dated May 29, 1790, in the Rhode Island Historical Society

RHODE ISLAND ADDS THE LAST RATIFICATION

IN several of the states acquiescence in the proposed Constitution had been secured only by a promise that certain changes would be made at once. This promise played its part in drawing into the Union the laggards, North Carolina and Rhode Island. In both the paper-money party was dominant. North Carolina had called a convention in July which soon adjourned without action. Rhode Island disdained even to call a convention. But after the new Government had got under way, after a Bill of Rights seemed assured, and when the revenue laws of the United States were about to be applied against them, the reluctant states changed their attitude. North Carolina came in late in 1789 and Rhode Island in the following May.

CHAPTER VI

GEORGE WASHINGTON

THE success of the new venture in government, hailed with such delight by its advocates, depended in large degree upon the men who were first to hold the reins of power. Those who had brought about the change from the Confederacy firmly believed the new union a vast improvement upon the weak and vacillating machinery it succeeded; and, fortunately, they differed little in the selection of a man to head the new government. On all hands Washington was proposed for the presidency; indeed, in many parts of the country the assumption that he would so serve had been a compelling argument in favor of ratifying the Constitution. Washington himself was loath to accept the post. Having given much to the country, he was desirous of seeking the pleasant quiet of his estate at Mt. Vernon. Once he acceded to the popular demand, however, the qualities which had made him a successful general were at the country's service. He was of the governing class, and accustomed to govern. It is true that he was inexperienced in civil administration; and of this no one was more conscious than himself. He was, however, an executive, and a good judge of men; he surrounded himself with advisers remarkable not only for their ability, but for their differences in point of view. Washington selected men who were supporters of the "new model" government. Moreover, they were men of experience in public affairs, men of integrity, who commanded the respect and loyalty of influential sections of the country. Upon them Washington was wise enough to rely for advice and for the immediate execution of national business. This had an important effect upon subsequent procedure. Instead of centering in the President the direct administration of government, Washington made his office that of an executive whose function it was to direct the administering of others. Thus he was free from the duties of routine, free to view the activities of the government as a whole, and was consequently able to correlate the work of each part with that of other parts. In his habit of consulting Hamilton and Jefferson, Washington established the basis for the American cabinet system as we know it to-day. So removing himself from concern with petty details, Washington drew about his office an independence and a dignity that have rarely been absent from it. In accord with the political philosophy of the day, he regarded the function of the executive and the legislature as distinct. He was willing to receive the advice of the Congress, but not to submit to its dictation. So he established firmly another convention of our Constitution, a precedent that has, in recent years, aided the growth of the presidency to its present exalted position.

Keenly aware of his responsibilities as the first president, Washington devoted much thought to matters that many considered trivial. To his contemporaries, however, this caution for the future meant less than his actions for the immediate day. Throughout the country he was respected by all sorts and conditions of people. Only two cartoons of him are known. This widespread reverence for the man enhanced allegiance to the government of which he was the head; abroad, sympathy for the new nation was the more fully forthcoming because of the character of its chief executive. His efforts to conciliate those who in ignorance were disaffected, combined with his firmness when he thought disaffection became treasonable, are well known. In like fashion, his efforts to give moral and political guidance to his fellow-citizens need no emphasis.

365 George Washington, 1731–1799, from an unfinished portrait, 1796, by Gilbert Stuart, known as the *Athenæum* portrait, in the Museum of Fine Arts, Boston

366 Mary Ball Washington, died 1788, mother of the General, from a portrait attributed to Robert Edge Pine, owned by W. Lanier Washington, New York

WASHINGTON'S PLANTER FORBEARS

THE man who is known as "The Father of His Country" was the son of Augustine Washington, a Virginia gentleman in no way distinguished from the class of substantial planters to which he belonged. In 1658 there had appeared in Virginia two brothers, John and Lawrence Washington, who purchased land in Westmoreland County. The former soon became a landed proprietor and prominent in local politics. His grandson was Augustine Washington, who thus inherited, and passed on to his sons, a considerable estate.

367 Martha Custis Washington, 1732–1802, from the portrait by Gilbert Stuart in the Museum of Fine Arts, Boston

THE MOUNT VERNON FARMER IS A LEADING CITIZEN

368 From the painting *Departure of Washington, Henry and Pendleton for the First Congress* by Howard Pyle for Woodrow Wilson, *History of the American People*, 1901. © Harper & Bros.

WASHINGTON first became known outside of Virginia as a result of his participation as a Colonel of militia in the French and Indian Wars. (See Vol. VI.) When he resigned his commission in December, 1758, he had already learned the arts of war and of command. Now for some years he withdrew to more peaceful pursuits. In 1759, he was happily married to Martha, widow of Daniel Custis, a charming and capable woman. He soon became a diligent and successful farmer of wide lands, and one of the wealthiest men in the country. His preoccupation with the pleasures of his estates did not, however, prevent him from participating in the affairs of the community. Early elected to the House of Burgesses, he soon became, by force of character and prestige, a leading figure in Virginia politics. As trouble with the home country loomed large, Washington took counsel with his friends. In April, 1769, he wrote to his neighbor, George Mason, that "at a time when our lordly masters in Great Britain will be satisfied with nothing less than the deprivation of American freedom, something should be done to avert the stroke and maintain the liberty which we have derived from our ancestors. But the manner of doing it, to answer the purpose effectually, is the point in question." Regarding force as "the last resource," he then urged the policy of non-importation as a possible solution. The following month he presented to his colleagues at the Raleigh Tavern a set of resolutions to effectuate this policy. Thus, when more drastic measures seemed necessary, it was but natural that he should be chosen, with Patrick Henry and Edmund Pendleton, to represent Virginia at the first Continental Congress.

369 From a portrait by C. W. Peale painted at Valley Forge on a piece of bedticking, in the State Normal School, West Chester, Pa. © C. S. Bradford

COMMANDER-IN-CHIEF OF THE CONTINENTAL ARMY

IN this first Congress Washington took no conspicuous part. His time was spent in discovering from the delegates the sentiments of the other colonies. His own position at this time was forcibly stated in a letter to a British officer stationed in Boston: "Permit me, with the freedom of a friend, to express my sorrow that fortune should place you in a service that must fix curses to the latest posterity upon the contrivers, and, if success (which, by the by, is impossible) accompanies it, execrations upon all those who have been instrumental in the execution. Give me leave to add, . . . that it is not the wish or intent of that government (Massachusetts), or any other upon this continent, separately or collectively, to set up for independence; but this you may at the same time rely on, that none of them will ever submit to the loss of those valuable rights and privileges which are essential to the happiness of every free state, and without which life, liberty, and property are rendered totally insecure." By the time of the assembling of the second Congress, matters were coming to a head; and Washington appeared at that meeting in the uniform of a Virginia colonel. He was thus ready when Congress gave him his general's commission and placed him at the head of the continental army.

370 From the portrait painted at Valley Forge by C. W. Peale, in the Pennsylvania Academy of the Fine Arts, Philadelphia

HOLDING ON AT VALLEY FORGE

Perhaps it is not too much to say that Washington became, after the cause of the colonies had been put to the hazard of war, the focal point of the rebellion. With liberty to be won by force of arms, the former Virginia colonel not only led his own independent command in the field but, as commander-in-chief of the American forces, supervised campaigns against Boston, Montreal and Quebec, around New York and New Jersey, against the Six Nations in the interior of New York, around Philadelphia, and against the invading British armies in Georgia and the Carolinas. And, when the cause of the Americans more than once seemed desperate almost beyond hope, he remained steadfast, holding about him a group of patriotic men, willing, like himself, to see the fight through to the bitter end. Had Washington been lost in battle, there was no one who could have taken his place.

371 From a mezzotint in the Emmet Collection, New York Public Library, after an original "Drawn from the Life by Alexander Campbell of Williamsburgh in Virginia," published in London in 1775, one of many spurious portraits

372 From the copyright painting *Washington and Members of Congress leaving Christ Church, Philadelphia*, 1781, by John Ward Dunsmore (1856–), in his possession

AFTER THE YORKTOWN VICTORY

At last more promising days came. Yorktown he rightly thought decisive of the issue. Heartily he participated with the members of Congress in the memorial service, on December 13, 1781, of "thanksgiving and prayer," decreed by Congress in memory of the victory.

373 From the painting *Washington Resigning His Commission* by Edwin White (1817–77) in the State House, Annapolis, Md.

WASHINGTON RESIGNS HIS COMMISSION

He, however, realized that much was yet to be done. "For my own part," he wrote, "I view our situation as such that, instead of relaxing, we ought to improve the present moment as the most favorable to our wishes. The British nation appears to me to be staggered, and almost ready to sink beneath the accumulating weight of debt and misfortune. If we follow the blow with vigor and energy, I think the game is our own." He therefore redoubled his efforts to increase the effectiveness of his army. While peace negotiations were in progress in Paris, he wrote: "There is nothing which will so soon produce a speedy and honorable peace as a state of preparation for war; and we must either do this, or lay our account to patch up an inglorious peace, after all the toil, blood and treasure we have spent." But, as he wrote in October, 1782: "It was high time for a peace"; and on December 23 he felt able to resign his commission and to beg to be allowed to retire from public life.

THE GENERAL BECOMES A FARMER AGAIN

With the war over, Washington returned to Mt. Vernon. To Governor Clinton he wrote: "The scene is at last closed. I feel myself eased of a load of public care. I hope to spend the remainder of my days in cultivating the affections of good men and in the practice of the domestic virtues." Into the old life of the proprietor of a large estate he threw himself with zest and thankfulness, more than happy to be free at last from all public cares.

374 Mount Vernon, from Charles William Janson, *The Stranger in America*, London, 1807, after an engraving by M. Marigot from a sketch made under the direction of the author

375 Statue of Washington, 1788, by Jean Antoine Houdon in the state capitol, Richmond, Va.

WASHINGTON IS BESIEGED BY ARTISTS AND FRIENDS

But a man of Washington's fame could not thus withdraw from an admiring public. He was besieged by visitors and correspondents, with calls upon his time and energy. One of the more exacting duties he was called upon to perform was that of sitting for his portrait. In 1785 he wrote: "I am so hackneyed to the touches of painters' pencils that I am now altogether at their beck, and sit 'like patience on a monument,' whilst they are delineating the lines of my face." Jean Antoine Houdon, the recognized master portrait-sculptor of the time, came from France expressly to model Washington, arriving, as the latter notes in his diary, "after we were in bed, at eleven o'clock in the evening." The resulting statue was pronounced by Lafayette to be "a facsimile of Washington's person."

376 Bust of Washington from the Houdon statue

WASHINGTON ADVOCATES A CONSTITUTION

As commander-in-chief Washington had become familiar with the many deficiencies of the Confederation as a form of union government. In his circular letter to the Governors of the states, issued at the close of the war, and again in his farewell address to the army, he had stressed the need for a stronger central government. He was now free to continue his campaign. To Hamilton, a strong sympathizer, he wrote, in 1783: "My wish to see the union of these states established upon liberal and permanent principles, and inclination to contribute my mite in pointing out the defects of the present constitution, are equally great. All my private letters have teemed with these sentiments, and whenever this topic has been the subject of conversation, I have endeavored to diffuse and enforce them." And again he wrote: "It is clearly my opinion, unless Congress have powers competent to all general purposes, that the distresses we have encountered, the expense we have incurred, and the blood we have spilt, will avail us nothing." Thus he was drawn back into the current of public affairs to preside over the Philadelphia Convention of 1787, whose work produced a frame of government more satisfying to him than was the Confederation.

Monday. 17th

Met in Convention when the Constitution received the unanimous assent of 11 States and Col. Hamilton's from New York (the only delegate from thence in Convention) and was subscribed to by every Member present except Govr. Randolph and Col. Mason from Virginia — & Mr. Gerry from Massachusetts. — The business being thus closed, the Members adjourned to the City Tavern, dined together and took a cordial leave of each other. — after which I returned to my lodgings — did some business with, and received the papers from the Secretary of the Convention, and retired to meditate on the momentous wk. which had been executed, after not less than five, for a large part of the time Six and sometimes 7 hours sitting every day, sundays & the ten days adjournment to give a Comee. opportunity & time to arrange the business for more than four Months. —

377 Washington's Entry in his Diary, Sept. 17, 1787, the day the Constitutional Convention adjourned, from the Washington Papers in the Library of Congress

378 From the copyright painting *Washington Receiving Notice of his Election as President* by John Ward Dunsmore, courtesy of the artist

WASHINGTON BECOMES PRESIDENT

With the adoption of the new Constitution, Washington's interest did not cease. He strove to secure as members of the new government those who were friendly to it, that it might get under way with a favorable breeze. Yet it was with diffidence that he accepted the presidency offered him by the unanimous vote of the Electoral College.

379 Washington's Welcome at Trenton, from the *Columbian Magazine*, Philadelphia, May, 1789

THE PRESIDENT-ELECT HAS A TRIUMPHAL JOURNEY

Leaving Mount Vernon on the sixteenth of April, 1789, Washington began his journey to New York, the seat of Congress. All along his route people turned out to do him honor. Troops of cavalry and citizens' committees everywhere met him; towns were decorated in his honor, and young girls strewed flowers in the road over which he passed.

380 From an engraving by J. Rogers after a painting, 1857, *Reception of President Washington at New York*, by J. McNevin

381 From *Harper's Bazaar*, May 11, 1889, after the drawing by Harry A. Ogden

NEW YORK HONORS THE FIRST CHIEF MAGISTRATE

At Elizabethtown Point, Washington embarked on a special barge, manned by thirteen masters of vessels, which took him to New York. Other barges, crowded with public officials and distinguished citizens, followed. Ringing bells, waving flags, and roaring cannon greeted him on all sides. At Murray's Wharf a throng awaited him. Here he was welcomed by Governor Clinton, who accompanied him to his house on Cherry Street.

WASHINGTON TAKES THE OATH OF OFFICE

On the thirtieth of April, 1789, the inauguration took place. After being received in the Senate Chamber, Washington was escorted to the balcony, where the oath of office was administered by the Chancellor of the State, Robert Livingston, in full view of thousands of eager spectators. Grouped around Washington were the Vice-President and many of the Revolutionary generals. At the conclusion of the ceremony, Livingston stepped forward and cried: "Long live George Washington, President of the United States." The crowd broke into cheers as the Stars and Stripes were raised on the staff above the balcony. From the harbor the cannon announced the new republic.

FIRST INAUGURAL ADDRESS

382 From the engraving by H. S. Sadd after the painting by Tompkins H. Matteson (1813-84)

Washington then withdrew to the Senate Chamber where he delivered his inaugural address. Senator Maclay, who was present, has written: "This great man was agitated and embarrassed more than ever he was by the leveled cannon or pointed musket. He trembled, and several times could scarce make out to read, though it must be supposed he had often read it before." He made no legislative recommendations to the Congress (though he reminded them that constitutional amendments were to be proposed to the states), for as yet he had formed no detailed policy. He also recognized the delicacy of his position. As he wrote some months later: "Few who are not philosophical spectators can realize the difficult and delicate part which a man in my situation had to act. . . . In our progress toward political happiness my station is new, and, if I may use the expression, I walk on untrodden ground. There is scarcely an action the motive of which may not be subject to a double interpretation. There is scarcely any part of my conduct which may not hereafter be drawn into precedent."

PRECEDENTS OF OFFICIAL DIGNITY

To this last matter Washington gave great importance. A new government had come into being, for which forms of procedure had to be established. What should be the method of intercourse between the President and the Senate, between the President and the representatives of foreign countries, between the President and the people? Such questions were handled by him with customary deliberateness. To Madison, Hamilton, Adams and Jay he set forth his views: "The true medium, I conceive, must lie in pursuing such a course as will allow him [the President] time for all the official duties of his station. This should be the primary object. The next, to avoid as much as may be the charge of superciliousness, and seclusion from information, by too much reserve and too great a withdrawal of himself from company on the one hand, and the inconveniences, as well as a diminution of respectability, from too free an intercourse and too much familiarity on the other." This policy he adopted. Thus, in keeping with his conception of his station, he ordered from England a coach-of-state. "It was globular, canary-coloured, gay with Cupids and nymphs of the seasons, and emblazoned with the Washington arms." Lest this smack too much of pomp and display, he determined to hold a weekly reception to which any person could come, and at which he invariably appeared clad in black velvet with a dress sword at his side. So he tried to create for the office traditions of dignity which would avoid both the ceremonial of monarchy and the unbridled freedom of republicanism.

383 The First Presidential Mansion, Pearl and Cherry Streets, New York, from Valentine's *Manual of the Common Council of New York*, 1853, in the New York Public Library

384 From the portrait, 1791, by John Trumbull in the City Hall, New York, courtesy of the Municipal Art Commission

THE PRESIDENT PRESENTS HIS POLICY TO CONGRESS

IN the more pressing affairs of the new government Washington felt less at ease. Hitherto he had, by force of position, viewed politics with the eyes of the military statesman. With the administration of an army he was familiar; about that of a government he was necessarily uninformed. But habits long formed came to his aid. He sent for all the papers of the Confederation dealing with public affairs since the treaty of peace. These he studied and annotated with painstaking care until he had at his command a working body of political knowledge. He then proceeded, relying much upon the advice of the men he had appointed to the major offices, to formulate a policy. When the Congress met for the second session, on January 4, 1790, Washington drove down to Federal Hall to "recommend to their consideration such measures" as he judged "necessary and expedient." Characteristically, his first consideration was to provide for the common defense by setting up a sufficient military force. His other suggestions sketched for the Congress "the outline of a vigorous system, which aimed at the establishment of a strong government with enlarged powers." — LODGE, *Washington*, II, p. 81. Upon many of his recommendations the Congress took action; so that the President was able in 1791 to tell them of "the happy effect of that revival of confidence, public as well as private, to which the constitution and laws of the United States have so eminently contributed."

National Gazette

BY *PHILIP FRENEAU*

VOL I. MONDAY, OCTOBER 31, 1791. NUMB. 1.

TUESDAY, *October* 25.

Mr Clark, Mr Dayton, and Mr Kitchell from New-Jerſey; and Mr. Jacobs from Pennſylvania, took their ſeats in the Houſe

The Rev Mr Blair was appointed chaplain.

A meſſage was received from the Senate, informing that they were ready to attend the Houſe in receiving the communication from the Preſident. Whereupon,

The Speaker with the members of the Houſe, preceded by the ſerjeant at arms, proceeded to the ſenate-chamber, where the Preſident addreſſed both Houſes as follows:

Fellow-citizens of the Senate, and of the Houſe of Repreſentatives.

I MEET you, upon the preſent occaſion, with the feelings, which are naturally inſpired by a ſtrong impreſſion of the proſperous ſituation of our common country, and by a perſuaſion equally ſtrong, that the labours of the ſeſſion, which has juſt commenced, will, under the guidance of a ſpirit, no leſs prudent than patriotic, iſſue in meaſures conducive to the ſtability and increaſe of national proſperity.

Numerous as are the providential bleſſings which demand our grateful acknowledgments; the abundance with which another year has again rewarded the induſtry of the huſbandman, is too important to eſcape recollection.

Your own obſervations, in your reſpective ſituations, will have ſatisfied you of the progreſſive ſtate of agriculture, manufactures, commerce and navigation: In tracing their cauſes, you will have remarked, with particular pleaſure, the happy effects of that revival of confidence, public as well as private to which the conſtitution and laws of the United States have ſo eminently contributed: And you will have obſerved, with no leſs intereſt, new and deciſive proofs of the encreaſing reputation and credit of the nation. But you, nevertheleſs, cannot fail to derive ſatisfaction from the confirmation of theſe circumſtances, which will be diſcloſed in the ſeveral official communications that will be made to you in the courſe of your deliberations.

The rapid ſubſcriptions to the Bank of the United States, which completed the ſum allowed to be ſubſcribed in a ſingle day, is among the ſtriking and pleaſing evidences which preſent themſelves, not only of confidence in the government, but of reſource in the community.

In the interval of your receſs, due attention has been paid to the execution of the different objects which were ſpecially provided for by the laws and reſolutions of the laſt ſeſſion.

Among the moſt important of theſe is the defence and ſecurity of the Weſtern Frontiers. To accompliſh it on the moſt humane principles, was a primary wiſh.

Accordingly at the ſame time, that treaties have been proviſionally concluded, and other proper means uſed to attach the wavering, and to confirm in their friendſhip, the well diſpoſed tribes of Indians—effectual meaſures have been adopted to make thoſe of a hoſtile deſcription ſenſible, that a pacification was deſired upon terms of moderation and juſtice.

Theſe meaſures having proved un-

385 Report of Washington's Address to Congress, Oct. 25, 1791, from the *National Gazette*, Philadelphia, Oct. 31, 1791

PHILADELPHIA BECOMES THE SEAT OF GOVERNMENT

In July, 1790, the Congress decided that for the next ten years the seat of Government should be located at Philadelphia. The executive officers moved to that city, and by December they were established in residence. President Washington lived at No. 190 High Street, near the southeast corner of Sixth Street, which house had been built by Richard Penn and had been occupied in turn by General Howe, Benedict Arnold and Robert Morris. Jefferson lived on the same street.

386 Residence of Washington in Philadelphia, from J. F. Watson, *Annals of Philadelphia*, 1830

WASHINGTON WORKS WITH OPPOSING FACTIONS

Washington had entered office with gloomy premonitions of stress and strain. He was profoundly aware that his conduct could not meet with unanimous approval. To counter, in some degree, the inevitable criticism, and to sound out the state of public opinion, he spent much of his time, between sittings of the Congress, in travel about the country. He found the people for the most part pleased and prosperous; but he also discovered the beginnings of division of sentiment, which were rapidly hardening into two distinct parties. This development he liked the less when he found the leaders of the opposing groups among his intimate advisers. He did his best to reconcile Hamilton and Jefferson. He appealed for a press less scurrilous than Freneau's *Gazette*, that the people might be given a fair opportunity to form unprejudiced judgments. As the time for the presidential election of 1792 approached, he yielded to the demand that he stand for reëlection. The unanimity of the vote heartened him; though in January, 1793, he wrote, "To say that I feel pleasure from the prospect of commencing another tour of duty would be a departure from the truth."

387 From the painting *Washington's Second Inauguration* by J. L. G. Ferris in Independence Hall, Philadelphia

388 From the portrait painted at Philadelphia in 1795 by Gilbert Stuart, in the Metropolitan Museum of Art, New York

THE FEDERALIST ARISTOCRACY IS ASSAILED

WASHINGTON soon learned that his reëlection did not mean a cessation of criticism of his administration. The success of Hamilton's measures made it difficult for the opposition to take issue with the Government on broad grounds of policy. Bent upon establishing a party, however, the Anti-Federalists became hypercritical. The dress, the speech, the private conduct of Washington and his advisers were held up to censure and ridicule in the Democratic press, much to the President's indignation and annoyance. He was accused of aping the aristocratic ways of monarchial England.

PARTY GOVERNMENT HAS ITS BEGINNING

389 From the portrait, 1795, by C. W. Peale in the New York Historical Society

"ALL statesmen entrusted in a representative system with the work of government," writes Henry Cabot Lodge, "are naturally prone to think that their opponents are also the enemies of the public welfare, and Washington was no exception to the rule." — *Washington*, II, p. 234. In this belief he was strengthened when the Jeffersonians seized upon the foreign issue of the French Revolution as the basis of their attacks upon the administration. At the doors of the Jacobin Clubs he too readily placed the blame for the Whisky Rebellion and the discontent of the transmontane settlements. When more virulent opposition rose over the ratification of the Jay treaty, Washington asserted his position even more fully. In September, 1795, he wrote to Pickering, an avowed Federalist and his Secretary of State: "I shall not, whilst I have the honor to administer the government, bring a man into any office of consequence knowingly, whose political tenets are adverse to the measures which the general government are pursuing; for this, in my opinion, would be a sort of political suicide. That it would embarrass its movements is most certain." Thus Washington was reluctantly and with perturbation forced to recognize the presence of partisan opinion within the country.

WASHINGTON GLAD TO RETIRE FROM PUBLIC OFFICE

ACTING on this insight, he wrote: "To misrepresent my motives, to reprobate my politics, and to weaken the confidence which has been reposed in my administration, are objects which cannot be relinquished by those who will be satisfied with nothing short of a change in our political system." Feeling thus, Washington regarded his service to the country as complete. When the country had needed firm guidance in the execution of an accepted policy, he had worked with unremitting zeal; with the new government established, he wished to give way to men more fit for the active conduct of the new political fight. He therefore resisted all suggestions for a third term. In September, 1796, he published his Farewell Address, calling upon the people to beware of the dangers in the extremes of factional spirit. Then he thankfully withdrew from public office.

26

with circumspection indeed, but with perfect good faith. — Here let us stop.

Europe has a set of primary interests, which to us have none, or a very remote relation. — Hence she must be engaged in frequent controversies, the causes of which are essentially foreign to our concerns. — Hence therefore it must be unwise in us to implicate ourselves, by artificial ties, in the ordinary vicissitudes of her politics, or the ordinary combinations & collisions of her friendships, or enmities. —

Our detached & distant situation invites and enables us to pursue a different course. — If we remain one people, under an efficient government, the period is not far off, when we may defy material injury from external annoyance; — when we may take such an attitude as will cause the neutrality we may at any time resolve upon to be scrupulously respected; — when belligerent nations, under the impossibility of making acquisitions upon us, will not lightly hazard the giving us provocation; — when we may choose peace or war, as our interest guided by justice shall counsel. —

Why forego the advantages of so peculiar a situation? — Why quit our own to stand upon foreign ground? — Why, by interweaving our destiny with that of any part of Europe, entangle our peace and prosperity

27

prosperity in the toils of European ambition, Rivalship, Interest, Humour or Caprice? —

'Tis our true policy to steer clear of permanent alliances with any portion of the foreign world — so far, I mean, as we are now at liberty to do it — for let me not be understood as capable of patronising infidelity to existing engagements. I hold the maxim no less applicable to public than to private affairs, that honesty is always the best policy. — those engagements be observed in their genuine sense. — But in my opinion, it is unnecessary and would be unwise to extend them. —

Taking care always to keep ourselves, by suitable establishments, on a respectably defensive posture, we may safely trust to temporary alliances for extraordinary emergencies. —

Harmony, liberal intercourse with all Nations, are recommended by policy, humanity and interest. — But even our Commercial policy should hold an equal and impartial hand: — neither seeking nor granting exclusive favours, or preferences; — consulting the natural course of things, — diffusing & diversifying by gentle means the streams of Commerce, but forcing nothing; — establishing with Powers so disposed — in order to give to trade a stable course, to define the rights of our Merchants, and to enable the Government to support them — conventional rules of intercourse

390 Washington on Foreign Alliances, extract from the manuscript of the Farewell Address, original in the custody of the State Education Department, Albany

391 The Last Portrait of Washington, 1798, from a mezzotint by Max Rosenthal after the original physionotrace by Charles de St.-Memin

POLITICAL AFFAIRS STILL INTEREST WASHINGTON

To Mount Vernon Washington retired to resume the life so pleasant to him, a life so long foregone. "To make and sell a little flour annually," he wrote, "to repair houses going fast to ruin, to build one for the security of my papers of a public nature, will constitute employment for the few years, I have to remain on this terrestrial globe." But no more than in the days between 1782 and 1789 could he entirely refrain from participation in the fortunes of his country. As the strife between Federalists and Republicans grew more bitter, he wrote letter after letter in support of the former against the seditious aims he imputed to the latter. When the X Y Z affair made war imminent, Washington offered his services, "in case of actual invasion by a formidable force." Again, when the Kentucky and Virginia Resolutions were spread abroad, Washington urged Patrick Henry to join him in resisting the Republicans. At a time "when everything dear and valuable to us is assailed," he said, "when this party hangs upon the wheels of government as a dead weight, opposing every measure that is calculated for defense and self-preservation; . . . when measures are systematically and pertinaciously pursued, which must eventually dissolve the Union or produce coercion; I say, when these things have become so obvious, ought characters who are best able to rescue their country from the pending evil to remain at home?"

New-York, December 21.

IT is with the deepeſt grief that we announce to the public the death of our *moſt diſtinguiſhed* fellow-citizen *Lieut. General George Waſhington.* He died at Mount Vernon on Saturday evening, the 13th inſt. of an inflammatory affection of the throat, which put a period to his exiſtence in 23 hours.

The grief which we ſuffer on this truly mournful occaſion, would be in ſome degree aleviated, if we poſſeſſed abilities to do juſtice to the merits of this *illuſtrious benefactor of mankind*; but, conſcious of our inferiority, we ſhrink from the ſublimity of the ſubject. To the impartial and eloquent hiſtorian, therefore, we conſign the high and grateful office of exhibiting the life of *George Waſhington* to the preſent age, and to generations yet unborn, as a perfect model of all that is *virtuous*, *noble*, *great*, and *dignified* in man. Our feelings, however, will not permit us to forbear obſerving, that the very diſintereſted and important ſervices rendered by *George Waſhington* to theſe United States, both in the Field and in the Cabinet, have erected in the hearts of his countrymen, monuments of ſincere and unbounded gratitude, which the mouldering hand of Time cannot deface; and that in every quarter of the Globe, where a free Government is ranked amongſt the choiceſt bleſſings of Providence, and *virtue*, *morality*, *religion*, and *patriotiſm* are reſpected, THE NAME of WASHINGTON WILL BE HELD IN *veneration.*

And as along the ſtream of TIME, his name
Expanded flies, and gathers all its fame,
Oh! may our little bark attendant ſail,
Purſue the triumph, and partake the gale!
While Stateſmen, Heroes, Kings, in duſt repoſe,
Whoſe *sons* ſhall bluſh their *fathers* were his foes.

CONGRESS, Dec. 18.

Immediately after reading the journal, General Marſhall came into the Houſe of Repreſentatives, apparently much agitated, and addreſſed the Speaker in the following words:

Information, ſir, has juſt been received, that our illuſtrious fellow-citizen, the Commander in Chief of the American army, and the late Preſident of the United States, is no more!

Though this diſtreſſing intelligence is not certain, there is too much reaſon to believe its truth.

After receiving information of a national calamity ſo heavy and ſo afflicting, the Houſe of Repreſentatives can be but ill fitted for public buſineſs. I move you therefore, that we adjourn.

The Houſe immediatejy adjourned.

The Senate alſo adjourned in conſequence of this diſtreſſing intelligence.

Extract of a letter from a gentleman of veracity, dated Alexandria, Dec. 10, 1799.

"General Waſhington died laſt night, under the adjunct attention of Doctors Crock and Dick, of Alexandria, and Doctor Brown, of Port Tobacco, Maryland."

A gentleman laſt evening politely favored us with the following extract of a letter from Alexandria, dated December 15.

"I mention to you the truly melancholy event of the death of our much beloved general GEORGE WASHINGTON—He made his exit laſt night brtween the hours of 11 and 12 after a ſhort but painful illneſs of 23 hours. The diſorder of which he died is by ſome called the Crupe, by others an Inflamatory Quinzy, a diſorder lately ſo mortal among children in this place, and I believe not until this year known to attack perſons at the age of maturity.

My information I have from doctor Dick, who was called in at a late hour. Alexandria is making arrangements to ſhow its high eſteem for him. We are all to cloſe our houſes, and act as we ſhould do if one of our family had departed. The bells are to toll daily until he is buried, which will not be until Wedneſday or Thurſday. He died perfectly in his ſenſes, and from doctor Dick's account perfectly reſigned. He informed them he had no fear of death, and that his affairs were in good order that he had made his will, and that his public buſineſs was but two days behind hand."

☞ *See the Reſolutions of the Common Council.*

392 From the *New York Gazette and General Advertiser*, Dec. 21, 1799, in the New York Historical Society

WASHINGTON PASSES AT THE CLOSE OF HIS CENTURY

WASHINGTON did not live to see the elevation to power of the faction whose tenets he so disapproved. Early in December, 1799, he contracted a sore throat which brought on fatal complications. So passed on December 14 a man who won the reverence of his contemporaries, and has received that of all succeeding generations.

CHAPTER VII

THE FEDERALIST RÉGIME

IN 1789, when the first President of the United States was to be chosen, the Electoral College turned naturally to Washington. The name of no other American carried so much prestige. Without his active participation the Constitutional Convention might well have ended in failure. The success of the campaign for ratification of the Constitution had added to his reputation and to his importance. He seemed the proper man to give dignity to the new office of President and to increase the confidence of the people in the new central government. The success of this Virginia planter in measuring up to the wide variety of responsibilities that his fellow countrymen placed upon him has been a source of unending wonder to succeeding generations. It was with real reluctance that Washington gave up the life of a private citizen to assume the cares of office. His achievements have sometimes blinded men of later days to the difficulties of the problems then confronting him.

When distances are considered, the United States even then was a country of truly vast size. The normal time spent in traveling from New York to Philadelphia was not much different from that which the twentieth-century traveler gives to crossing the continent. Measured in time, Boston was farther from Charleston than is San Francisco from Shanghai. Along the Atlantic seaboard were communities with interests as diverse as those of the small farmers of Massachusetts, the merchants of Philadelphia, and the rice planters of South Carolina. Across the mountains in then distant Kentucky and Tennessee lived frontiersmen who presented recurring problems both for domestic and foreign politics. In all these various sections local loyalties were strong and the sense of national unity largely absent. With the passing of the common danger which had been present during the Revolution, the particularism of the independent states sharply asserted itself. During the period of the Confederation state rivalries and local pride had more than once caused discord. While the first President found himself at the head of a government created, to be sure, by the combined action of these states, the new organism must establish an indisputable position for itself in the face of a not inconsequential jealousy on the part of the states.

When Washington assumed the Presidency some of the results of the Revolutionary War were already painfully evident. Seven years of fighting could not fail to have an unsettling influence upon the American people. Quite naturally the conflict had been followed by a moral and religious let-down. The economic depression of 1784 and 1785 had goaded the less fortunate classes to demand legislation that threatened property rights. Shays' Rebellion had demonstrated a readiness on the part of the discontented classes to resort to force as well as the inability of the central government to put down the uprising. The former Commander-in-chief of the Continental armies well knew that the time would come when a threat of force would put to the test the new government of which he had been chosen the chief executive. When he considered the difficulties which that government would have to face under its new Constitution, he must have dreaded the day of testing.

But Washington at New York taking the oath of office was more fortunate in the ability of his associates than Washington at Cambridge assuming command of the Continental army. Then, scarcely any of his officers had had adequate military training; now he could call upon men who had learned the art of government in the hard school of the politics of the Revolution and of the "Critical Period" (1781–89). Most of the revolutionary leaders had been in their thirties at the time of the voting of the Declaration of Independence. In 1789 the same men were rich in experience and at the height of their powers. John Adams, Jefferson, Madison, and Hamilton were not untried. With such men in high office the success of the new government was more than probable. The influence of all of them was powerful in the first formative years under the new Constitution. But the man to whom Cornwallis had surrendered did not become a figurehead. His work in civil office was not so spectacular as that in war, but from first to last Washington was President, guiding with his usual sound judgment the destinies of the nation he had done so much to create.

The ratification of the Constitution naturally brought new problems. The instrument did not attempt to make provision for all possible conditions that might arise. It was little more than a framework upon which there must now be woven the pattern that would express the political aspirations of a united people. The men who were chosen to inaugurate the new system held rather clear-cut ideas of the design that was to be worked out. Some, Washington among them, were chiefly anxious for peace and harmony; others, like Hamilton, sought material prosperity for America, thinking that in a prosperous people lay security for the government; while still others, like Jefferson, were concerned lest the new political order should result in a consolidated government that would overshadow the rights of the states and of men.

393 From the painting *Washington leaving Mt. Vernon for his inauguration*, by John Ward Dunsmore. © by the artist.

CONGRESS GIVES WAY TO THE REPUBLIC

On July 2, 1788, the president of Congress announced that nine states had ratified the new Constitution. The Congress had been called into being by Articles of Confederation which required unanimous consent of the states for amendment. Few incidents make so clear the political revolution for which the constitutional convention was responsible. The old Congress of thirteen states knuckled under and provided for the initiation of a new government set up by only nine. Though Virginia and New York soon ratified, two other states, Rhode Island and North Carolina, remained loyal to the old government. On the 13th of September a plan for initiating the Government was adopted. The states, on the first Wednesday in January, 1789, were to choose the presidential electors who were to cast their ballots a month later; the new Congress was to assemble the first Wednesday in March, which happened to be the 4th day of the month. (Three years later this day was fixed by Congress as the beginning of the presidential year.) In accord with these recommendations, the eleven states then in the Union made preparations for the first national election.

By the United States in Congreſs aſſembled,

SEPTEMBER 13, 1788.

WHEREAS the Convention aſſembled in Philadelphia, purſuant to the Reſolution of Congreſs of the 21ſt February, 1787, did, on the 17th of September in the ſame year, report to the United States in Congreſs aſſembled, a Conſtitution for the People of the United States; whereupon Congreſs, on the 28th of the ſame September, did reſolve unanimouſly, "That the ſaid report, with the Reſolutions and Letter accompanying the ſame, be tranſmitted to the ſeveral Legiſlatures, in order to be ſubmitted to a Convention of Delegates choſen in each State by the people thereof, in conformity to the Reſolves of the Convention made and provided in that caſe:" And whereas the Conſtitution ſo reported by the Convention, and by Congreſs tranſmitted to the ſeveral Legiſlatures, has been ratified in the manner therein declared to be ſufficient for the eſtabliſhment of the ſame, and ſuch Ratifications duly authenticated have been received by Congreſs, and are filed in the Office of the Secretary—therefore,

RESOLVED, That the firſt Wedneſday in January next, be the day for appointing Electors in the ſeveral States, which before the ſaid day ſhall have ratified the ſaid Conſtitution; that the firſt Wedneſday in February next, be the day for the Electors to aſſemble in their reſpective States, and vote for a Preſident; and that the firſt Wedneſday in March next, be the time, and the preſent Seat of Congreſs the place for commencing Proceedings under the ſaid Conſtitution.

Chas Thomson secy

394 Call for the Presidential Election, Sept. 13, 1788, from a copy in the Emmet Collection, New York Public Library

Commonwealth of Maſſachuſetts.

In SENATE, November 19, 1788.

RESOLVED, That the Commonwealth be divided into eight diſtricts for the purpoſe of chooſing eight perſons to repreſent the people thereof in the Congreſs of the United States, each diſtrict to chooſe one Repreſentative, who ſhall be an inhabitant of ſuch diſtrict, and that the diſtricts be as follows, viz.

The County of *Suffolk*, be one diſtrict.
The County of *Eſſex*, one diſtrict.
The County of *Middleſex*, one diſtrict.
The Counties of *Hampſhire* and *Berkſhire*, one diſtrict.
The Counties of *Plymouth* and *Barnſtable*, one diſtrict.
The Counties of *York*, *Cumberland* and *Lincoln*, one diſtrict.
The Counties of *Briſtol*, *Duke's-County* and *Nantucket*, one diſtrict.
The County of *Worceſter*, one diſtrict.

And be it further Reſolved, That the Selectmen of the reſpective towns and diſtricts in the ſeveral diſtricts before deſcribed, ſhall in manner as the law directs for calling town-meetings, cauſe the inhabitants thereof, duly qualified to vote for Repreſentatives to the General Court of this Commonwealth, to aſſemble on Thurſday the eighteenth day of *December* next, to give in their votes, for their reſpective Repreſentatives, to the Selectmen, who ſhall preſide at ſuch meeting: And the Selectmen or the major part of them, ſhall in open town-meeting, ſort and count the votes, and form a liſt of the perſons voted for, with the number of votes for each perſon, againſt his name, and ſhall make a public declaration thereof in the ſaid meeting, and ſhall in the preſence of the inhabitants, ſeal up copies of the ſaid liſt, and tranſmit the ſame to the office of the Secretary of the Commonwealth, on or before the firſt Monday of *January* next: And the Clerk of each town and diſtrict, ſhall make and fairly tranſcribe, in the records thereof, the liſt aforeſaid; and the Secretary ſhall lay the ſame before his Excellency the Governour and the Council. And in caſe of an election for any diſtrict by a majority of all the votes returned, his Excellency the Governour is hereby requeſted forthwith to tranſmit to the perſon ſo choſen, a certificate thereof. And in caſe no perſon ſhall have a majority of votes, the Governour is hereby requeſted, to cauſe precepts to iſſue, accompanied with a certificate of the names of the two perſons who had the greateſt number of votes in the firſt return, to the Selectmen of the ſeveral towns & diſtricts within the diſtrict for which no perſon ſhall have been choſen as aforeſaid, to aſſemble the inhabitants of their reſpective towns and diſtricts, qualified as aforeſaid, on a day in ſuch precept to be appointed, to give in their votes for a Repreſentative, and the like proceedings ſhall be had thereon, as are herein before directed; and the Selectmen ſhall make return thereof, in manner as aforeſaid, to the Secretary's office, on or before a day in ſuch precept to be preſcribed. And the Secretary ſhall lay the ſame before the Governour and Council; and in caſe any perſon ſhall have a majority as aforeſaid, the Governour is requeſted forthwith to tranſmit to the perſon ſo choſen, a certificate thereof: And in caſe no perſon ſhall have a majority of votes, the Governour is requeſted to iſſue like precepts as often as the caſe may require.

And be it further Reſolved, That when the inhabitants of the ſeveral towns and diſtricts qualified as aforeſaid, ſhall be aſſembled on the ſaid eighteenth day of *December* next, they ſhall alſo give in their votes for two perſons, who ſhall be inhabitants of the diſtrict in which ſuch town or diſtrict may be, as candidates for an Elector of the Preſident and Vice-Preſident of the United States; and a liſt of the votes ſo given in as aforeſaid, ſhall by the Selectmen of the ſeveral towns and diſtricts, or the major part of them, be tranſmitted to the Secretary's office, on or before the firſt Monday in *January* next. And on the Wedneſday next following, the General Court then in ſeſſion, ſhall examine the ſaid returns, and from the two who ſhall be found to have the greateſt number of votes in each diſtrict, the members of the two Houſes, aſſembled in one room, ſhall by joint ballot elect one who ſhall be the Elector for the diſtrict to which he belongs; and in caſe it ſhould ſo happen, that more than two perſons voted for as Electors, ſhould have an equality of votes among the higheſt voted for, then the members of the two Houſes as aforeſaid, ſhall out of ſuch number chooſe the Elector. And if in any caſe the aforeſaid returns from a diſtrict, ſhall not be received at the Secretary's office, on or before the firſt Monday in *January* next, the members of the two Houſes of the Legiſlature ſhall, on the firſt Wedneſday of *January* next, appoint ſome perſon, being an inhabitant of ſuch diſtrict, for an Elector of the Preſident and Vice-Preſident.

And be it further Reſolved, That the members of the two Houſes of the General Court, ſhall in manner as aforeſaid, appoint at large, two Electors for the Preſident and Vice-Preſident, not voted for by the diſtricts as aforeſaid.

And be it further Reſolved, That the ſaid Electors be, and they are hereby directed, to meet on the firſt Wedneſday of *February* next, at ten o'clock in the forenoon, at the State-Houſe in the town of *Boſton*, for the purpoſe of voting by ballot, for two perſons, for Preſident and Vice-Preſident of the United States, agreeably to the Conſtitution of ſaid United States: And that for their travel and attendance, they ſhall receive the ſame compenſation as members of the Senate are entitled to.

Sent down for concurrence,

SAMUEL PHILLIPS, jun. Preſident.

In the HOUSE of REPRESENTATIVES, November 20, 1788.

Read and concurred,

THEODORE SEDGWICK, Speaker.

Approved—

JOHN HANCOCK:

A true Copy.—Atteſt

JOHN AVERY, jun. Secretary.

BOSTON:—Printed by ADAMS & NOURSE, PRINTERS to the Honorable GENERAL COURT.

395 Massachusetts Resolution for Dividing the State into Electoral Districts, Nov. 19, 1788, from a copy in the New York Historical Society

WASHINGTON BECOMES PRESIDENT

For the first office in the land Washington was the inevitable choice. Though loath to assume new and arduous duties, the General found the pressure of public opinion too strong to resist. He, it was said, was the one man who could ensure the success of the new undertaking. "Your cool steady temper," wrote Gouverneur Morris to him in 1787, "is *indispensably necessary* to give firm and manly tone to the new Government. To constitute a well-poised political machine is the task of no common workman; but to set it in motion requires still greater qualities. When once agoing it will proceed a long time from the original impulse. . . . The exercise of authority depends on personal character. . . . Among these thirteen horses now about to be coupled together, there are some of every race and character. They will listen to your voice, and submit to your control; you therefore must, I say *must*, mount the seat." To fill the vice-presidency proved less simple. Yet it was generally felt that Massachusetts, with Virginia the leader of the country, should be represented. Thus the choice fell upon John Adams.

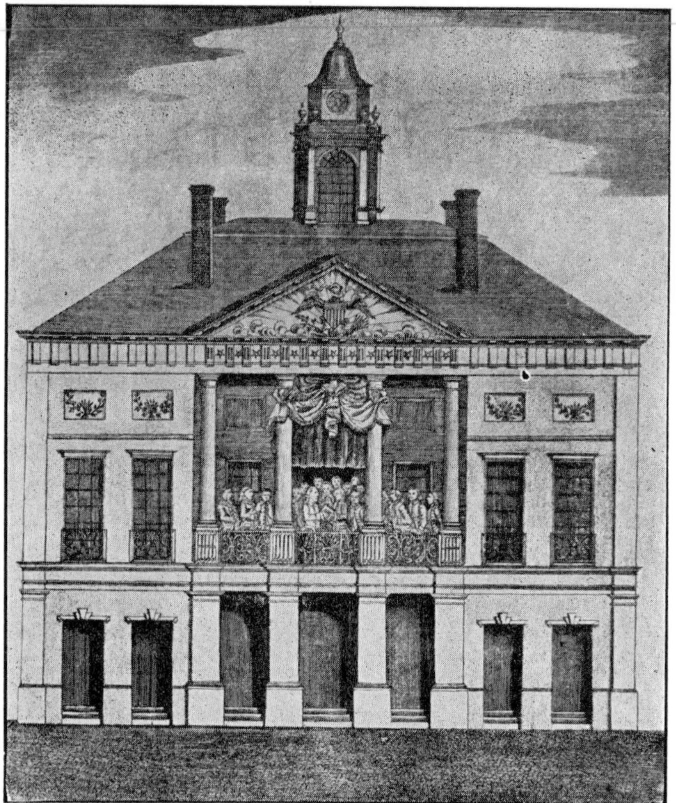

396 Federal Hall, New York City, from the engraving by Amos Doolittle after the drawing by Peter Lacour, published in New Haven, 1790, in the New York Historical Society

NEW YORK PREPARES A TEMPORARY CAPITOL

In preparation for the impending events the citizens of New York hastened to furbish up the old City Hall, now rechristened Federal Hall. Subscriptions of $32,000 enabled them to have the old building, erected in 1699, ready in time. It was, in truth, a fine structure. A grand vestibule, paved with marble, prepared one for the Senate Chamber with its azure ceiling from which shone the sun and thirteen stars. From this room three windows opened upon a balcony whereon the oath of office was taken in full view of the people. But with the 4th of March came few congressmen, nor for a month afterward was there a quorum to transact business. This delay, due to the short notice given the states and the bad conditions for traveling, was interpreted by the unfriendly as showing a lack of interest in the new Government. At last, however, the two Houses could organize; and on April 6 the electoral votes were counted and messengers dispatched to notify the chosen. Adams arrived on the 22nd and took his seat under the canopy of crimson cloth. On the following day Washington was greeted by a joyous multitude. A week later he assumed office.

EXPERIENCED MEN GUIDE THE NEW CONGRESS

The work before the new Congress was prodigious. Much depended upon the wisdom of the initial steps, and caution was necessary. Though its membership was not as illustrious as that of the Philadelphia Convention, there were many able and experienced men present. In the Senate were found Robert Morris, Richard Henry Lee, Rufus King and Oliver Ellsworth, later to become Chief Justice. The House leader was James Madison; his colleagues included Fisher Ames and Elbridge Gerry of Massachusetts, Elias Boudinot of New Jersey, and Jonathan Trumbull and Roger Sherman of Connecticut, all veterans of earlier political strife. Frederick Muhlenberg of Pennsylvania, a former Lutheran pastor of German descent, was chosen Speaker because of his reputation as a presiding officer of deliberative assemblies. Not until 1791 did the office become partisan. Committees were chosen by ballot of the House, and most of its work was done in Committee of the Whole, as had been the practice of the old Congress under the Articles of Confederation.

397 Frederick Augustus Conrad Muhlenberg, 1750–1801, from the portrait by C. W. Peale, courtesy of Edward Brooke, Birdsboro, Pa.

A FINANCIER BECOMES CHIEF JUSTICE

Ellsworth was one of the committee of four, called the "Pay-table," that managed the military finances of Connecticut during the Revolution. As judge of the Connecticut superior court, he advocated the rights of the individual states, and it was by his motion that the words "national government" were expunged from the constitution and the words "Government of the United States" substituted. In 1796 he was appointed Chief Justice of the Supreme Court. His watchfulness over the public expenditures earned for him the title of "the Cerberus of the Treasury"; and John Adams spoke of him as "the finest pillar of Washington's whole administration."

398 Oliver Ellsworth, 1745–1807, from the miniature, 1792, by John Trumbull, in the School of the Fine Arts, Yale University

IMPORT DUTIES PROVIDE GOVERNMENT REVENUE

First of all it was necessary to provide revenue for the new Government. The Constitution had been greeted as the New Roof under which "the farmer would meet immediately a ready market for his produce, manufactures would flourish, and peace and prosperity adorn the land." To this end, and without waiting for the inauguration of Washington, the House proceeded to discuss a tariff bill introduced by Madison. At once debate arose. The duties were quite moderate, for the main objective was revenue, not protection. With this in view, Madison wished the bill to become law in time to cover the spring importations. To this the traders of the cities objected; and the first American lobby won a victory. The bill did not receive approval till July 4, nor was it to go into effect for a month thereafter. Despite this juggling the tariff soon was yielding $200,000 a month, a sum sufficient to maintain the Government and to pay interest on the debt.

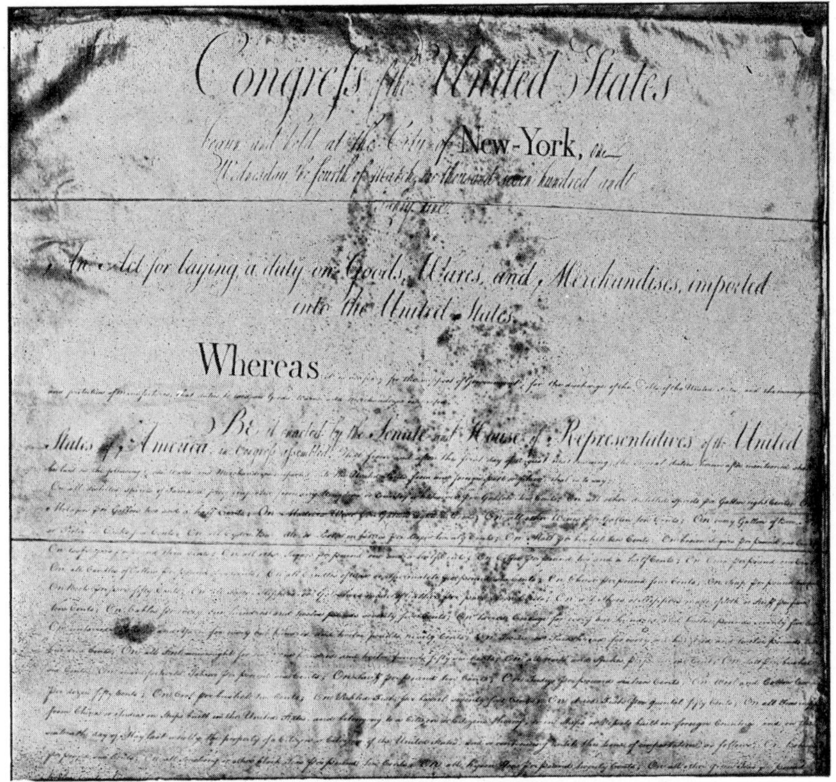

Congress of the United States

New-York,

An Act for laying a duty on Goods, Wares, and Merchandises, imported into the United States.

Whereas

Be it enacted by the Senate and House of Representatives of the United States of America

399 First sheet of the Tariff Act of 1789, from the original inscribed on vellum in the State Department, Washington

400 Thomas Jefferson, 1743–1826, from the pastel portrait, about 1798, by James Sharples (1751–1811) in Independence Hall, Philadelphia

401 Alexander Hamilton, 1757–1804, from the portrait, about 1792, by John Trumbull in the Metropolitan Museum of Art, New York

402 Edmund Randolph, 1753–1813, from a copy of an original now lost, in the Virginia State Library, Richmond

403 Major-General Henry Knox, 1750–1806, from the portrait by Gilbert Stuart in the Museum of Fine Arts, Boston

404 Samuel Osgood, 1748–1813, from the portrait by John Trumbull, courtesy of William B. Osgood Field, New York

THE ORGANIZATION OF ADMINISTRATIVE DEPARTMENTS

With the tariff out of the way, Congress turned its attention to the organization of the administration. In May it was decided to continue, under new titles, the three old departments of the former Government. Acts of July 27, August 7, and September 2 created State, and War and Navy departments. Later, provision was made for an Attorney-General and a Postmaster-General. Jefferson, trained in diplomatic intercourse, was selected as Secretary of State. For the head of the Treasury, Washington called upon the energetic and able Hamilton. General Knox was continued at the war office. Edmund Randolph of Virginia became Attorney-General, and Samuel Osgood of New York Postmaster-General.

THE JURISDICTION OF COURTS IS SETTLED

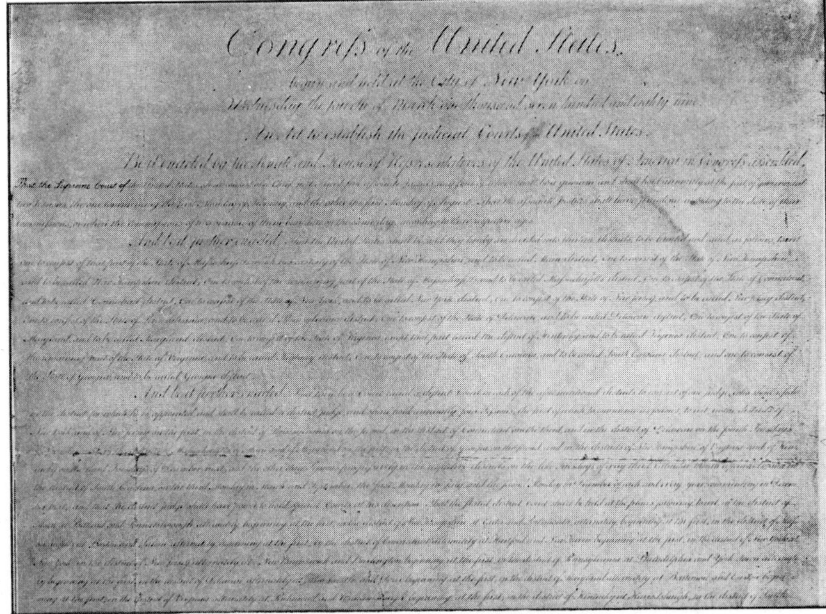

Congress of the United States,
begun and held at the City of New York on
Wednesday the fourth of March one thousand seven hundred and eighty nine.
An Act to establish the judicial Courts of the United States.
Be it enacted by the Senate and House of Representatives of the United States of America in Congress assembled,

405 Title and first page of the Judiciary Act of 1789 from the original in the Department of State, Washington

NEXT came up for consideration the court system. The Constitution provided simply that there should be a Supreme Court and such other courts as the Congress might establish. There was little difficulty about the former; but a difference of opinion arose concerning the inferior courts. Many wished the state courts to be given jurisdiction over federal cases, with appeal to the Supreme Court. This did not meet with the approval of the Federalists, who wanted a strong national government independent of the states in the discharge of its functions. The result was the act of September 24, largely the work of Oliver Ellsworth, a stanch Federalist. Senator Maclay of Pennsylvania, a leader of the opposition, wrote, "It certainly is a vile law system, calculated for expense and with a design to draw by degrees all law business into the Federal Courts. The Constitution is meant to swallow the State Constitutions by degrees, and thus to swallow by degrees all the State Judiciaries." The separate court system so created has never been abandoned; and the Judiciary Act of 1789, with few important changes, has remained law to the present time.

406 Chief Justice John Jay, 1745–1829, from the portrait by Gilbert Stuart in the Metropolitan Museum of Art, courtesy of Peter Augustus Jay

EMINENT LAWYERS ARE PUT ON THE BENCH

To fill these positions was now the President's task. Their importance he fully recognized. In a letter of September 27 he wrote: "Impressed with a conviction that the true administration of justice is the firmest pillar of good government, I have considered the first arrangement of the judicial department as essential to the happiness of our country and the stability of its political system. Hence the selection of the fittest characters to expound the laws and dispense justice has been an invariable subject of my anxious concern." There were several possibilities for the Chief Justiceship — among them James Wilson, John Rutledge, John Jay and Robert R. Livingston. Jay was finally chosen. As his associates, Washington selected John Blair of Virginia, William Cushing of Massachusetts, James Wilson of Pennsylvania, John Rutledge of South Carolina, and Robert H. Harrison of Maryland. The last refused, and the vacancy was filled by James Iredell of North Carolina. All were eminent lawyers; most of them had had judicial experience. Jay, in particular, had over a long period of years and in many offices given proof of courage and statesmanship. All, moreover, had taken a hand in bringing the new government into being.

Congress of the United States,
begun and held at the City of New-York, on Wednesday the fourth of March one thousand seven hundred and eighty nine.

Article the First.
Article the Second.
Article the Third.
Article the Fourth.
Article the Fifth.
Article the Sixth.
Article the Seventh.
Article the Eighth.
Article the Ninth.
Article the Tenth.
Article the Eleventh.
Article the Twelfth.

Attest,
John Beckley, Clerk of the House of Representatives.
Sam. A. Otis Secretary of the Senate.
Frederick Augustus Muhlenberg Speaker of the House of Representatives.
John Adams, Vice-President of the United States, and President of the Senate.

407 First Twelve Proposed Amendments, facsimile of the original engrossed draft, in the Emmet Collection, New York Public Library

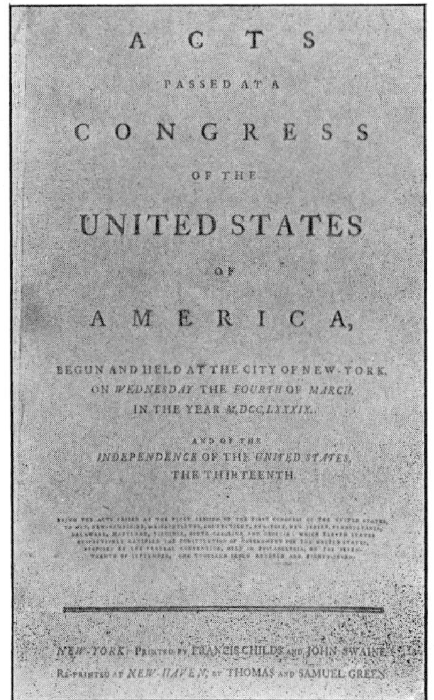

ACTS
PASSED AT A
CONGRESS
OF THE
UNITED STATES
OF
AMERICA,
BEGUN AND HELD AT THE CITY OF NEW-YORK,
ON *WEDNESDAY* THE *FOURTH* OF *MARCH*,
IN THE YEAR M,DCC,LXXXIX.
AND OF THE
INDEPENDENCE OF THE *UNITED STATES*,
THE THIRTEENTH.

NEW-YORK: PRINTED BY FRANCIS CHILDS AND JOHN SWAINE.
RE-PRINTED AT *NEW-HAVEN*; BY THOMAS AND SAMUEL GREEN.

408 From the copy published at New York, 1789, in the New York Public Library

AMENDMENTS FORM A BILL OF RIGHTS

FIVE of the states had ratified the Constitution on the express condition that certain amendments should be made at the earliest possible moment. This was a moral obligation upon the first Congress which, for a time, it seemed to ignore. Complaints finally forced its hand. The suggested amendments were referred to a committee. Weeding out from them all that affected the structure or powers of the Government, Congress sent to the states a dozen propositions, ten of which were adopted and to this day form the Bill of Rights of the Constitution. The Constitution, in addition to creating the outlines of a government, stressed property rights; the first ten amendments stressed those human rights, the demand for which had appeared again and again both before and during the Revolution.

THE GOVERNMENT STARTS WITHOUT PARTY LINES

ON September 29, 1789, the Congress, adjourned. It had successfully started the new Government. A judicial system had been created, administrative departments established, appropriations for ordinary expenses voted, salaries fixed, a tariff laid, an Indian policy formulated. These measures were recognized by all as necessary; divisions of opinion had not noticeably crept into Congressional debate. But with the second session, opening January 4, 1790, came matters of policy upon which party lines formed. This situation developed out of the financial condition of the country, and with it is inextricably woven the names of Thomas Jefferson and Alexander Hamilton.

HAMILTON FILLS IMPORTANT PUBLIC POSTS

After Yorktown, where he took an active part, Hamilton studied law at Albany under his father-in-law. In 1782 he was admitted to practice, only to be sent by the New York Assembly to the Continental Congress. In 1786 he attended the Annapolis Convention and with Madison secured the call for the Philadelphia Convention, of which he became a member. His effective aid in securing the ratification of the Constitution has already been described (p. 158). His appointment to the post of Secretary of the Treasury was generally acclaimed as fitting. In that office he served till January, 1795, when he withdrew to resume private practice. His interest and activity in public and political affairs did not cease and his articles signed "Camillus," were a welcome aid to Washington in the contest over the Jay Treaty. When the war scare of 1798 came, he was made Major-General in charge of military preparations. The following years saw his struggle with Burr in New York and national politics, ending so disastrously in July of 1804. Slight in stature, Hamilton was of erect and courtly bearing and conduct. Inclined to stand aloof from the "great beast" that was the people, he had many enemies in the growing democracy. But enemies as well as friends bore testimony to his preëminent ability as statesman and financier. With Jefferson, his great rival, he shaped the national democracy that is America.

409 Alexander Hamilton, from the portrait by John Trumbull in the New York City Hall

HAMILTON ORGANIZES NATIONAL FINANCES

Underlying all of Hamilton's actions while in Washington's cabinet was one central effort — to attach to the Federal Government the vital interests of the influential groups of the country. He realized that the Government would be no stronger than the allegiance of its citizens. With him that allegiance was to be won through the purse. When, therefore, the Congress called upon him to prepare a report on the state of the finances, he eagerly evolved a plan that would simultaneously reëstablish the national credit, gain the support of the moneyed classes, and draw the nation together into a unity resting upon a strong national government. This plan was presented to Congress in a series of masterly reports. The first, dated January 14, 1790, dealt with the public credit. Hamilton pointed out that the national debt exceeded $54,000,000, the market price for which was as low as 25% of par. This debt he proposed to refund at par. Objection at once arose. For speculators, getting wind of the movement to refund, had bought up much of the domestic debt. Was the Government now going to enable them to profiteer? From the rural constituencies came vehement protest. Madison, pushed by Henry and the debtor farmers of Virginia, offered a compromise, the impracticability of which finally led to the adoption of Hamilton's scheme, substantially unchanged.

410 Alexander Hamilton, from the engraving by J. Rogers after the "Talleyrand Miniature"

Congress of the United States:
At the Second Session, begun and held at the city of New York, on Monday the fourth of January one thousand seven hundred and ninety.
An Act making provision for the debt of the United States.

411 Title and first page of the Assumption Act, 1790, from the engrossed copy in the Department of State, Washington

HAMILTON PROPOSES ASSUMPTION OF STATE DEBTS

HIS second proposition startled the country. The national government, he urged, should assume such parts of the debt of the several states as had been incurred in support of the common revolution against England. Such a step, he considered, was both sound finance and sound politics; for it would attach to the national government the money interests without whose support it could not stand. The states that had paid little of their debt — Massachusetts, Connecticut, South Carolina — favored assumption. Not so with the others that had little or no debt. These states, notably Virginia, were not eager to help their sisters carry their burdens. Madison now definitely broke with Hamilton. After weeks of discussion the bill was, on May 25, rejected by the House.

POLITICAL COMPROMISE PLACES THE CAPITOL AT WASHINGTON

BUT Hamilton did not despair. Since 1788 there had been much talk about the location of the permanent capital of the new nation. Debate had reduced the sites to two, one somewhere in Pennsylvania, and the other on the Potomac near Georgetown. Southerners favored the latter, but could not master sufficient votes to carry the plan. Hamilton, caring little about the issue, seized upon it as a lever to secure the passage of the Assumption Bill. Jefferson invited Hamilton and Madison to dinner and the bargain was struck. To appease the Pennsylvanians the Government was to be located for ten years at Philadelphia, while the new city, planned by the President, Andrew Ellicott, and Major L'Enfant, with Versailles as a model, was in course of construction. On July 26, 1790, the Assumption was voted, thirty-two to twenty-nine, in the House of Representatives.

412 The White House, from an engraving by N. King, published in 1805, in the Library of Congress, Washington

CONGRESS PROVIDES FOR A NATIONAL BANK

To the third session of the First Congress Hamilton presented the next plank in his platform, for the creation of a national bank. This, as has been noted, had long been a favorite notion. There were in 1790 but three banks in the country, at Philadelphia, New York and Boston. A national bank would be of inestimable service to expanding business interests, encouraging the development of land and manufactures. At the same time it would serve as fiscal agent for the Government. Against these arguments the opposition brought all their force without avail; in 1791 the bill was sent to Washington for his approval. The President, following his custom of relying upon his department heads for advice, asked for written opinions concerning its constitutionality, a point that had been raised in Congress. Jefferson and Randolph advised a veto. Hamilton, who had seen Jefferson's elaborate opinion against the constitutionality of the measure, on February 23 wrote his own, in which for the first time was laid down the doctrine of broad construction, to be followed closely in 1819 by Chief Justice Marshall. Two days later the bill became law.

period as his other duties would permit, to the subject of Manufactures; and particularly to the means of promoting such as will tend to render the United States independent on foreign Nations, for military and other essential supplies. And he thereupon respectfully submits the following Report. —

The expediency of encouraging manufactures in the United States, which was not long since deemed very questionable, appears at this time to be pretty generally admitted. The embarrassments, which have obstructed the progress of our external trade, have led to serious reflections on the necessity of enlarging the sphere of our domestic commerce: the restrictive regulations, which in foreign markets abridge the vent of the increasing surplus of our Agricultural produce, serve to beget an earnest desire, that a more extensive demand for that surplus may be created at home: And the complete success, which has rewarded manufacturing enterprise, in some valuable branches, conspiring with the promising symptoms, which attend some less mature essays, in others, justify a hope, that the obstacles to the growth of this species of industry are

414 Extract from Hamilton's Report on Manufactures, Dec. 5, 1791, from the engrossed copy in the Library of Congress, Washington

Treasury Department, December 13th 1790.

In obedience to the order of the House of Representatives of the ninth day of August last requiring the Secretary of the Treasury to prepare and report on this day such further provision as may in his opinion, be necessary for establishing the public Credit; The said Secretary further respectfully reports

That from a conviction (as suggested in his report No. 1 herewith presented) That a National Bank is an Institution of primary importance to the prosperous administration of the Finances, and would be of the greatest utility in the operations connected with the support of the Public Credit — his attention has been drawn to devising the plan of such an institution, upon a scale, which will intitle it to the confidence, and be likely to render it equal to the exigencies of the Public.

Previously to entering upon the detail of this plan, he entreats the indulgence of the House, towards some preliminary reflections naturally arising out of the subject, which he hopes will be

413 First page of Hamilton's Report on a National Bank, Dec. 13, 1790, from the engrossed copy in the Library of Congress, Washington

INDUSTRIAL DEVELOPMENT IS URGED

To round out his policy of utilizing the national Government to promote the interests of the nation, Hamilton submitted to the Second Congress his famous Report on Manufactures. "To form a more perfect union" it was necessary to cultivate a manufacturing industry that could balance the existent agricultural and commercial activities. "Not only the wealth, but the independence and security of a country, appear to be materially connected with the prosperity of manufactures. Every nation, with a view of these great objects, ought to endeavor to possess within itself all the essentials of national supply. These comprise the means of subsistence, habitation, clothing and defence. The possession of these is necessary to the perfection of the body politic; to the safety as well as to the welfare of the society. The want of either is the want of an important organ of political life and motion." Although it discussed with profound ability the problems of political economy, this Report was received at the time with small enthusiasm.

415 Alexander Hamilton in the uniform of a Major-General, from the portrait, 1791, by C. W. Peale in the New York Historical Society

AN EXCISE TAX LEADS TO THE "WHISKY REBELLION"

HAMILTON, indeed, had overreached himself. As, one by one, his policies were presented to Congress, antagonism grew. They were regarded as attempts to form a perpetual alliance between the national Government and the wealthy classes; they were excoriated as evidences of a desire to annihilate the states, the temples of self-government, by consolidating all powers at the center. The spirit of discontent first manifested itself in the Whisky Insurrection. As part of his financial program, Hamilton had in March, 1791, secured an Act to impose an excise tax on the manufacture of spirituous liquors. His aim had been at once to increase the revenues and to bring home to the individual citizen the fact of the national Government's existence and power. This truth proved unpalatable along the frontier. Crude means of transportation to the seaboard compelled the hardy settlers of western Pennsylvania to condense their corn and grain into whisky, which became their currency and their major source of income. The tax thus bore with special and, as it seemed to them, unfair severity upon the mountaineers. In 1794 murmurings broke into open revolt. A mass meeting near Pittsburgh decided to resist the law by force of arms. The Governor of Pennsylvania awaited action by the national government. It was a situation exactly to the taste of Hamilton. On the seventh of August the President issued a proclamation against the rebels and called for fifteen thousand militia from the states of Pennsylvania, Maryland, Virginia and New Jersey.

THE INSURGENTS YIELD TO NATIONAL POWER

IN the mind of Washington was the query, will these citizen troops march against their fellows of a neighboring state to enforce a national law? March they did, with Hamilton in the forefront. Such an overwhelming show of national power was more than enough. By the time the army reached Pittsburgh the insurgents had melted away. Hamilton was for driving home the lesson, but milder counsels prevailed. The tax, however, was retained. The Government had proved its power.

416 The End of the Whisky Rebellion, scene from The Chronicles of America motion picture *Alexander Hamilton*

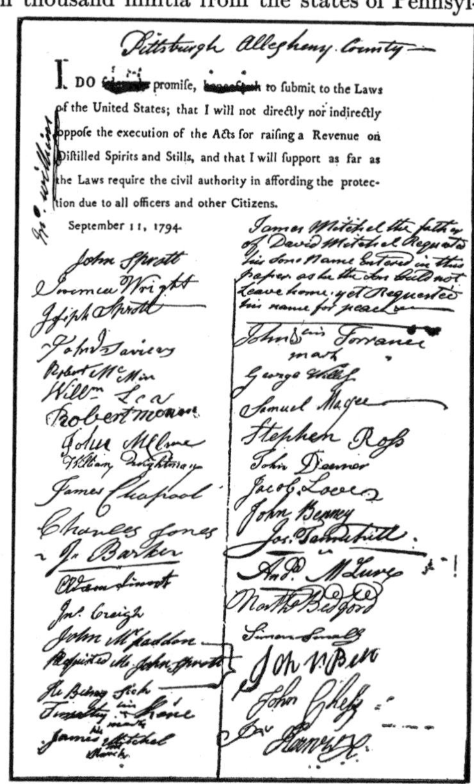

Pittsburgh Allegheny County

I DO [illegible] promise, [illegible] to submit to the Laws of the United States; that I will not directly nor indirectly oppose the execution of the Acts for raising a Revenue on Distilled Spirits and Stills, and that I will support as far as the Laws require the civil authority in affording the protection due to all officers and other Citizens.

September 11, 1794.

417 Oath of Submission by Pennsylvanians, from the original in the Library of Congress, Washington

Fellow Citizens,

YOU have this moment been witnesses to one of the noblest spectacles that the eyes of freemen ever beheld. You have seen the first patriot of his country, raised by the unanimous voice of his fellow-citizens to the highest station in it, standing in the august presence of the people, and binding himself by a solemn oath to support the constitution established by their deliberate and voluntary consent. How must the heart of every good citizen exult upon this happy occasion, an occasion which is the triumph of freedom, the triumph of Americans—the triumph of humanity!

But it is not enough, fellow-citizens, to rejoice on this occasion. It is your duty to act, you are bound by all the ties of interest and consistency to ask ourselves what further remains to be done, and immediately to set about it. You owe it to yourselves and the rest of the United States to remove, as far as depends on you, every source of embarrassment which may threaten the successful administration of the government which you have concurred in establishing.

To those, who will not suffer themselves to be seduced by the busy agents of anti-federalism, no policy can be more plain than that of removing from the highest office of our state government the man, who is looked up to by the adversaries of the national constitution, not only in this state but throughout the Union, as the great bulwark of their cause. Federalists who do not pursue this policy manifest by their conduct, that however they may be friends to the constitution, they are greater friends to its greatest enemy.

Let me therefore conjure such of you, as may not already have given your votes, to hasten, with hearts glowing with federalism, to the polls of the several wards in which you reside, and there by your suffrages, in favor of Judge Yates, to maintain the character of your city and prove to the rest of the United States that New-York is unvariably true to the cause she has espoused.

FEDERALIST

April 30, 1789

418 Handbill on New York Politics, 1789, from the copy in the New York Historical Society

FELLOW CITIZENS,

THE man who, on this day of general joy and satisfaction, will attempt to improve the solemn spectacle to which you have been witnesses, to the purposes of fomenting party spirit, and keeping up distinctions which ought to be forgotten, must be influenced by diabolical motives.

Every honest heart glows at the reflection, that WASHINGTON is at the head of our government—And shall the feelings of any one be wounded by conjuring up the name of anti-federal, to answer the purpose of a party?—It has been done; fellow citizens, by a writer who signs himself " A FEDERALIST."—He is no federalist; he is some spirit, swoln with ambition, and impelled by malice, and revenge, black as the infernal regions.

Be not deceived, my country-men; ask yourselves, has not JUDGE YATES been as much opposed to the new government as GOVERNOR CLINTON? The latter you have tried, he is a good man, and a good magistrate. He has possessed, and still holds, the confidence of the GREAT WASHINGTON, whom may heaven long preserve.

As honest and independent men, therefore, come forward and disappoint PARTY RAGE, and UNREASONABLE ENVY, by giving CLINTON your votes.

A FRIEND TO UNION, AND THE NEW CONSTITUTION.

APRIL 30, 1789.

419 Handbill on New York Politics, 1789, from the copy in the New York Historical Society

PARTY LINES APPEAR

HAMILTON's measures served to sharpen and bring into the national arena the conflict between two schools of thought that had their origin as far back as the Revolution. The differences between the debtor-farmers and the conservative classes in the days before the Constitution were emphasized with the result that two political parties appeared, each ignoring state lines in its membership. On one side, under the Secretary of the Treasury, were ranged the large merchants, the manufacturers, the bondholders, the lawyers and the clergy — those who above all desired stability and prosperity. Against this compact minority was arrayed the mass of the people, the impoverished farmers, the self-reliant pioneers, the apprentices — those who saw no need for a strong government, much less for a strong central government. Of this party Thomas Jefferson became the recognized leader.

Gazette of the United States.

National Gazette.

420 From copies of both newspapers in the New York Public Library

THE PRESS PLAYS A LARGE PART IN POLITICS

To both sides the issue seemed clear-cut and fundamental. The followers of Jefferson charged that the administration leaders were under British influence, and that they were utilizing their power to favor a special and sectional class. We were "galloping into monarchy." The Hamiltonians, in turn, regarded their opponents as wild anarchists whose talk of liberty and democracy could mean nothing else than a desire to bring in the rule of the mob. The press took up the battle. Indeed, John Fenno, editor of the *Gazette of the United States*, founded in New York, 1787, had early found in Hamilton a patron. Philip Freneau, the poet, in 1791 was persuaded to edit the *National Gazette*, founded in that year to support Jefferson. By Fenno and Freneau bitterest invective and personal spite were unleashed in the party struggle.

421 The "Republican Court," from the engraving by A. H. Ritchie (1822–95) after the painting *Lady Washington's Reception* by Daniel Huntington (1816–1906), original in the Brooklyn Museum

THE "REPUBLICAN COURT"

THE pomp and ceremony thrown about Washington and his administration came in for especial derision and satire. Hamilton's suggestion that coins be struck with the image of the President of the day, the Senate's weighty deliberations on the matter of the presidential title — should it be "His Highness the President of the United States of America and Protector of their Liberties," or simply "His Patriotic Majesty" — Washington's cream-colored carriage bedecked with medallions, all these Freneau held up to fierce ridicule. He took particular delight in ridiculing Mrs. Washington's receptions, the "Republican Court" of the Monocrats. Their frigid formality furnished an occasion rarely lost, despite the obvious distress of the President.

422 The Storming of the Bastille, from the *Collection Complete des Tableaux Historiques de la Revolution Française*, Paris, 1798, in the New York Public Library

THE INFLUENCE OF THE FRENCH REVOLUTION

MEANWHILE in France a series of events were taking place which were to influence the internal politics of the United States for a score of years. The opening acts of the French Revolution, and particularly such dramatic events as the storming of the Bastille, aroused great enthusiasm throughout the United States. It seemed as though France were about to follow the footsteps of the American colonies by casting off tyranny and establishing a constitutional government.

423 The Execution of Louis XVI, from the *Collection Complete des Tableaux Historiques de la Revolution Française*, Paris, 1798

REACTION AGAINST FRENCH VIOLENCE

But as the Revolution in France progressed and assumed a violent character, a distinct reaction took place among certain classes of the American people. The execution of Louis XVI was the turning point. This act, together with stories of the flouting of the Christian religion, turned conservative Americans against the Revolution. Democratic Americans, however, became even more enthusiastic as a result of the execution of the King and the proclamation of a Republic. This division of sentiment was carried over to the internal political struggles of the country and added to the growing hostility between the Federalists and the Republicans.

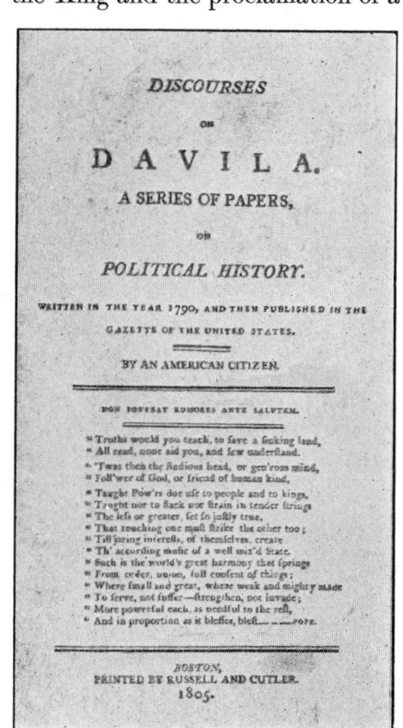

DISCOURSES

ON

DAVILA.

A SERIES OF PAPERS,

ON

POLITICAL HISTORY.

WRITTEN IN THE YEAR 1790, AND THEN PUBLISHED IN THE GAZETTE OF THE UNITED STATES.

BY AN AMERICAN CITIZEN.

NON PONEBAT RUMORES ANTE SALUTEM.

"Truths would you teach, to save a sinking land,
"All read, none aid you, and few understand.
"'Twas then the studious head, or gen'rous mind,
"Foll'wer of God, or friend of human kind,
"Taught Pow'rs due use to people and to kings,
"Taught nor to slack nor strain its tender strings
"The less or greater, set so justly true,
"That touching one must strike the other too;
"Till jaring interests, of themselves, create
"Th' according music of a well mix'd State.
"Such is the world's great harmony that springs
"From order, union, full consent of things;
"Where small and great, where weak and mighty made
"To serve, not suffer—strengthen, not invade;
"More powerful each, as needful to the rest,
"And in proportion as it blesses, blest.—— ——POPE.

BOSTON,
PRINTED BY RUSSELL AND CUTLER.
1805.

424 Title-page of John Adams' essays, first published in 1790, in the New York Public Library

ARGUMENTS ON THE FRENCH REVOLUTION

Prominent Americans took sides in the clash between the exponents of the principles of the French Revolution and the conservatives. In 1790, John Adams published a weighty argument on the principles of government to show that public affairs should be trusted to "the rich, the well-born and the able." Then in 1791 appeared Thomas Paine's *Rights of Man*, written in reply to Burke's *Reflections on the Revolution in France*, 1790, and welcomed by Jeffersonians as political gospel. Its circulation was a million and a half copies.

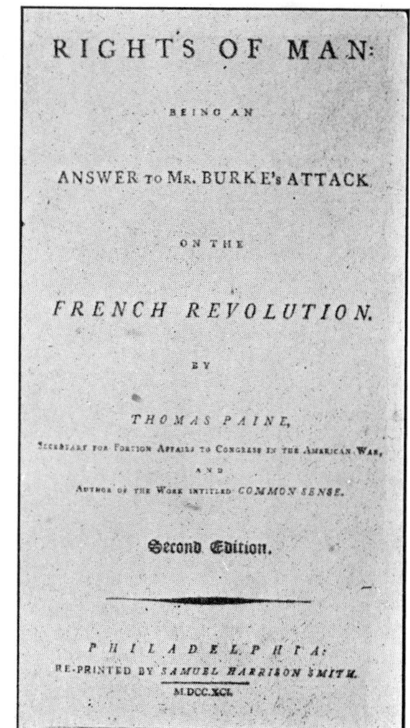

RIGHTS OF MAN:

BEING AN

ANSWER TO MR. BURKE's ATTACK

ON THE

FRENCH REVOLUTION.

BY

THOMAS PAINE,

SECRETARY FOR FOREIGN AFFAIRS TO CONGRESS IN THE AMERICAN WAR,

AND

AUTHOR OF THE WORK INTITLED *COMMON SENSE.*

Second Edition.

PHILADELPHIA:
RE-PRINTED BY *SAMUEL HARRISON SMITH.*
M.DCC.XCI.

425 Title-page of Thomas Paine's reply to Burke, in the New York Public Library

(17.)

George Pfeffer
James Boylan
Stewart Cummin
William Milnor
Nathan Boys

Each of the above members paid to Edward Fox. Treasurer pro tem: the Sum of Half a Dollar; making together, six Dollars.

The Society then adjourned to the 3d day of July next.

July 3rd 1793

The Society met pursuant to their adjournment of the 20th June last

Citizen William Coates, Vice President, in the Chair —

Citizens David Jackson, Alexander James Dallas, Jonathan D. Sergeant, Elisha Gordon Joseph D. Hamelin and John Wigton.

Signed the Constitution and paid each half a Dollar to the Treasurer

The Minutes of the proceeding Meeting were read.

Mr Dallas from the Committee of Correspondence

426 Extracts from the minutes of the first meeting, 1793, of the Democratic-Republican Society of Philadelphia, from the original in the Historical Society of Pennsylvania

AMERICAN RADICALS IMITATE THE FRENCH

Enthusiasm for the French Revolution among the followers of Jefferson expressed itself in the erection of Liberty poles. The term "Republican" now became the favored title of the party. Some of Jefferson's followers went to the extent of direct imitation of the French Revolutionists. "Democratic clubs" were formed in various cities, based on the model of the Jacobin Club in Paris. These clubs held secret meetings and their members addressed each other as "citizen," in the manner of the French.

SATIRES ON THE JEFFERSONIANS

Political lampoons were used by both parties. *The Jacobiniad* was a satire upon the followers of Jefferson, who are pictured as ignorant and illiterate boors aping the radicalism of the Jacobin clubs of France.

THE JACOBINIAD. 21

No. VII.

OUR readers are, doubtleſs, all impatience to hear the great Vinal, whom we left on the point of ſpeaking. But we muſt entreat them to poſtpone their curioſity, for a few moments, until we have introduced the following literary curioſity, which we have juſt received from a correſpondent, who pledges himſelf for its authenticity.

COPY of a COMPACT,

to be ſigned by every candidate, previous to his admiſſion into the conſtitutional ſociety (alias jacobin club) at Boſton: the *compoſition*, by brother Tommy: the *ſpelling*, by the secretary, verbatim et literatim.

"*WHEREASS it apeers to uſs, that the*
"*libertys off our cuntry are much endanger*
"*from ariſtokratical prinſipuls beeing ſpred a-*
"*mung uſs, and that the prezidant is miſsled*
"*by bad advizers, wee, the ſubſhribears, have*
"*inturred into an aſſoſiaſhun to inflerce elex-*
"*ſhuns, and as fur as in us lys, pull down*
"*the federal goverment: and as grate ſek-*
"*recy, is much wanted in this biſneſs, wee*
"*bindc ourſelfes, not to lett any thing, ſed or*
"*dun in our ſocity, git abraud, leſt wee over-*
"*ſett,*

427 From J. S. J. Gardiner, *Remarks on the Jacobiniad*, Boston, 1795

THE FRENCH ENVOY ARRIVES

TRICOLOR cockades and Democratic societies sprang up everywhere. In the midst of this agitation the French envoy, Genêt, arrived at Charleston. After ten days of hilarious welcome, he began a triumphal progress to Philadelphia, traveling through a region disgruntled with the administration — an administration which naturally eyed this exuberance with suspicion.

428 Edmond Charles Genêt, 1765–1834, from the portrait by Ezra Ames in the Albany (N. Y.) Institute and Historical and Art Society

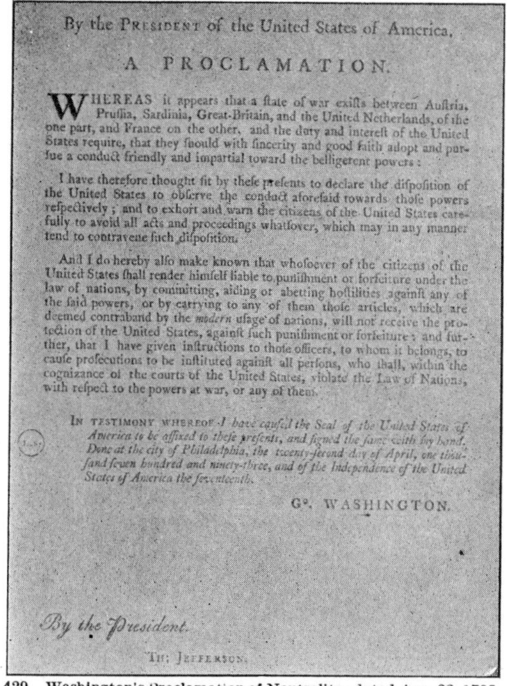

By the PRESIDENT of the United States of America,

A PROCLAMATION.

WHEREAS it appears that a ſtate of war exiſts between Auſtria, Pruſſia, Sardinia, Great-Britain, and the United Netherlands, of the one part, and France on the other, and the duty and intereſt of the United States require, that they ſhould with ſincerity and good faith adopt and purſue a conduct friendly and impartial toward the belligerent powers:

I have therefore thought fit by theſe preſents to declare the diſpoſition of the United States to obſerve the conduct aforeſaid towards thoſe powers reſpectively; and to exhort and warn the citizens of the United States carefully to avoid all acts and proceedings whatſoever, which may in any manner tend to contravene ſuch diſpoſition.

And I do hereby alſo make known that whoſoever of the citizens of the United States ſhall render himſelf liable to puniſhment or forfeiture under the law of nations, by committing, aiding or abetting hoſtilities againſt any of the ſaid powers, or by carrying to any of them thoſe articles, which are deemed contraband by the *modern* uſage of nations, will not receive the protection of the United States, againſt ſuch puniſhment or forfeiture; and further, that I have given inſtructions to thoſe officers, to whom it belongs, to cauſe proſecutions to be inſtituted againſt all perſons, who ſhall, within the cognizance of the courts of the United States, violate the Law of Nations, with reſpect to the powers at war, or any of them.

IN TESTIMONY WHEREOF *I have cauſed the Seal of the United States of America to be affixed to theſe preſents, and ſigned the ſame with my hand. Done at the city of Philadelphia, the twenty-ſecond day of April, one thouſand ſeven hundred and ninety-three, and of the Independence of the United States of America the ſeventeenth.*

G°. WASHINGTON.

By the President.

TH: JEFFERSON.

429 Washington's Proclamation of Neutrality, dated Apr. 22, 1793, from a printed copy in the New York Public Library

AMERICA IS NEUTRAL IN THE FRANCO-BRITISH WAR

WHILE Genêt was being fêted in Charleston, news of war between France and Great Britain caused the cabinet grave concern. America was tied by bonds of gratitude and treaty to France. That country, indeed, had been promised, in case of attack, special privileges in American ports. Should, then, Genêt be received as the representative of the favored nation? What would this mean to American commerce, most of which was with England? Hamilton favored cancellation of the French treaties as no longer effective; Jefferson would countenance anything short of war with Britain. The upshot was an agreement to receive Genêt, but to interpret the treaty privileges of France with strictness; and, lastly, to issue a Presidential proclamation warning all citizens to refrain from acts hostile to any of the belligerents. Jefferson, as Secretary of State, played an important part in the development of the American system of neutrality.

FOR THE GAZETTE.

MR. FENNO,

AS attempts are making very dangerous to the peace, and it is to be feared not very friendly to the conſtitution of the United States—it becomes the duty of thoſe who wiſh well to both to endeavor to prevent their ſucceſs.

The objections, which have been raiſed againſt the proclamation of neutrality lately iſſued by the Preſident, have been urged in a ſpirit of acrimony and invective, which demonſtrates that more was in view than merely a free diſcuſſion of an important public meaſure; that the diſcuſſion covers a deſign of weakening the confidence of the people in the author of the meaſure, in order to remove or leſſen a powerful obſtacle to the ſucceſs of an oppoſition to the government, which however it may change its form, according to circumſtances, ſeems ſtill to be adhered to and purſued with perſevering induſtry.

This reflection adds to the motives connected with the meaſure itſelf to recommend endeavors, by proper explanations, to place it in a juſt light. Such explanations at leaſt cannot but be ſatisfactory to thoſe who may not have leiſure or opportunity for purſuing themſelves an inveſtigation of the ſubject and who may wiſh to perceive, that the policy of the government is not inconſiſtent with its obligations or its honor.

The objections in queſtion fall under four

430 Extract from the first of Hamilton's letters signed "Pacificus" in support of neutrality, from the *Gazette of the United States*, June 29, 1793, in the New York Public Library

HAMILTON DEFENDS NEUTRALITY

THE proclamation angered the opponents of the administration. Their newspapers lauded Genêt and virulently attacked the administration and the President. The French agent wrote to his superiors at Paris: "You could appreciate the value of the declarations of neutrality which have been made if you knew the enthusiasm and the entire devotion of our friends in the United States." He even asserted that the President had exceeded his powers in issuing such a declaration. This was seized upon by Jefferson and the Republicans as an ingenious weapon with which to strike the administration. Hamilton's pen came to the rescue. In the *Gazette of the United States* appeared seven letters from "Pacificus," ably defending the action of April 22.

Gazette of the United States.

A NATIONAL PAPER, PUBLISHED WEDNESDAYS AND SATURDAYS BY JOHN FENNO, No. 34, NORTH FIFTH-STREET, PHILADELPHIA.

[No. 129 of Vol. IV.] SATURDAY, AUGUST 24, 1793. [Whole No. 451.]

FOR THE GAZETTE.

MR. FENNO,

Pleaſe to give a place in your Gazette to the following obſervations. The Printers who may have republiſhed the pieces, ſigned PACIFICUS, *are alſo requeſted to republiſh theſe, and will no doubt be candid enough to do ſo.*

NUMBER I.

SEVERAL pieces with the ſignature of PACIFICUS were lately publiſhed, which have been read with ſingular pleaſure and applauſe, by the foreigners and degenerate citizens among us, who hate our republican government, and the French revolution; whilſt the publication ſeems to have been too little regarded, or too much deſpiſed by the ſteady friends to both.

Had the doctrines inculcated by the writer, with the natural conſequences from them, been nakedly preſented to the public, this treatment might have been proper. Their true character would then have ſtruck every eye, and been rejected by the feelings of every heart. But they offer themſelves to the reader in the dreſs of an elaborate diſſertation; they are mingled with a few truths that may ſerve them as a paſſport to credulity; and they are introduced with profeſſions of anxiety for the preſervation of peace, for the welfare of the government, and for the reſpect due to the preſent head of the executive, that may prove a ſnare to patriotiſm.

In theſe diſguiſes they have appeared to claim the attention I propoſe to beſtow on them; with a view to ſhew, *from the publication itſelf*, that under colour of vindicating an important public act, of a chief magiſtrate, who enjoys the confidence and love of his country, principles are advanced which ſtrike at the vitals of its conſtitution, as well as at its honor and true intereſt.

As it is not improbable that attempts may be made to apply inſinuations which are ſeldom ſpared when particular purpoſes are to be anſwered, to the author of the enſuing obſervations, it may not be improper to premiſe, that he is a friend to the conſtitution, that he wiſhes for the preſervation of peace, and that the preſent chief magiſtrate has not a fellow-citizen, who is penetrated with deeper reſpect for his merits, or feels a purer ſolicitude for his glory.

This declaration is made with no view of courting a more favorable ear to what may be ſaid than it deſerves. The ſole purpoſe of it is, to obviate imputations which might weaken the impreſſions of truth; and which are the more likely to be reſorted to, in proportion as ſolid and fair arguments may be wanting.

The ſubſtance of the firſt piece, ſifted from its inconſiſtencies and its vague expreſſions, may be thrown into the following propoſitions:

That the powers of declaring war and making treaties are, in their nature, executive powers:

That being particularly veſted by the conſtitution in other departments, they are to be conſidered as exceptions out of the general grant to the executive department:

That being, as exceptions, to be conſtrued ſtrictly, the powers not ſtrictly within them, remain with the executive:

That the executive conſequently, as the organ of intercourſe with foreign nations, and the interpreter and executor of treaties, and the law of nations, is authoriſed, to expound all articles of treaties, thoſe involving queſtions of war and peace, as well as others;—to judge of the obligations of the United States to make war or not, under any caſus federis or eventual operation of the contract, relating to war;—and, to pronounce the ſtate of things reſulting from the obligations of the United States, as underſtood by the executive:

That in particular the executive had authority to judge whether in the caſe of the mutual guaranty between the United States and France, the former were bound by it to engage in the war:

That the executive has, in purſuance of that authority, decided that the United States are not bound:—And,

That its proclamation of the 22d of April laſt, is to be taken as the effect and expreſſion of that deciſion.

The baſis of the reaſoning is, we perceive, the extraordinary doctrine, that the powers of making war and treaties, are in their nature executive; and therefore comprehended in the general grant of executive power, where not ſpecially and ſtrictly excepted out of the grant.

Let us examine this doctrine; and that we may avoid the poſſibility of miſtating the writer, it ſhall be laid down in his own words: a precaution the more neceſſary, as ſcarce any thing elſe could outweigh the improbability, that ſo extravagant a tenet ſhould be hazarded, at ſo early a day, in the face of the public.

His words are—"Two of theſe [exceptions and qualifications to the executive powers] have been already noticed—the participation of the Senate in the *appointment of officers*, and the *making of treaties*. A *third* remains to be mentioned—the right of the legiſlature to *declare war, and grant letters of marque and repriſal*."

Again—"It deſerves to be remarked, that as the participation of the Senate in the *making treaties*, and the power of the legiſlature to *declare war*, are *exceptions* out of the general *executive power*, veſted in the Preſident, they are to be conſtrued *ſtrictly*, and ought to be extended no farther than is *eſſential* to their execution."

431 Extract from the first letter of "Helvidius," from the *Gazette of the United States*, Aug. 24, 1793, in the New York Public Library

MADISON REPLIES TO HAMILTON

THESE letters were too much for Jefferson. He appealed to Madison for aid. "For God's sake, my dear sir, take up your pen . . . and cut him to pieces in the face of the public." Madison responded under the name of "Helvidius." It was a battle between two of the best minds of the day and its results, so far as influencing public opinion, were inconclusive.

THE FRENCH ENVOY

MEANWHILE the conduct of Genêt had been alienating his friends. With cool disregard of international etiquette, he began his business without first presenting his credentials to the Government. He commissioned privateers, appointed consuls and prepared measures of offense against the Spanish settlements in Louisiana. Received with hauteur by Washington on May 18, he used the press to denounce the cowardice of France's turncoat ally and to appeal over the heads of the Government to the people. To Jefferson Washington then wrote: "Is the minister of the French Republic to set the acts of this Government at defiance with impunity?" His cabinet answered, "No!" The most exacting country could no longer counsel forbearance, and Jefferson agreed that the French Government should be asked to recall their tactless and insolent envoy. Jefferson's work as Secretary of State during the formative first years under the Constitution were as important in shaping American foreign relations as were Hamilton's in determining the nation's financial policy. Jefferson took the lead in establishing the principle (in the case of France after the execution of Louis XVI) of recognizing *de facto* governments which has become a regular practice in international law. He also made a distinction between political and ordinary crimes, and refused extradition of political exiles. His achievements gave him high rank among the men who have helped to shape American foreign policy.

432 From the painting *Washington's First Meeting with Citizen Genêt* by Howard Pyle for Woodrow Wilson, *A History of the American People*. © Harper & Bros.

DIPLOMATIC COMPLICATIONS ARISE

JEFFERSON'S action had its political aspect. On August 3 he wrote to Madison concerning Genêt: "He will sink the Republican interest if they do not abandon him. Hamilton presses eagerly an appeal — *e.g.*, to the people. Its consequences you may readily seize, but I hope we shall prevent it." Though the Republican cause thus suffered, feeling for France remained friendly, as is shown by the activities of the numerous "Democratic Societies" (No. 426). To this, grievances against England largely contributed. She had not yet executed several of the provisions of the treaty of 1783; the United States was still refused privileges of trade with British colonies; with the outbreak of war between France and England new sources of irritation appeared. France threw open to American vessels her West Indian ports, while our trade with European ports expanded. England hastened to claim the right to seize, as contraband of war, provisions bound for France and vessels attempting to run her blockade of French ports. In execution of these regulations she proceeded to search American vessels on the high seas and to impress any sailors found to be of English birth. Early in 1794 war with England seemed inevitable. This situation the Republicans tried to exploit to their own advantage. In January, Madison presented to the House seven resolutions urging economic retaliation for Britain's harsh measures. Bills to fortify harbors, to build frigates, to strengthen the army, were rushed through the Congress. In March a temporary embargo was laid on British commerce.

433 John Jay, from the miniature in oil, 1793, by John Trumbull in the School of the Fine Arts, Yale University

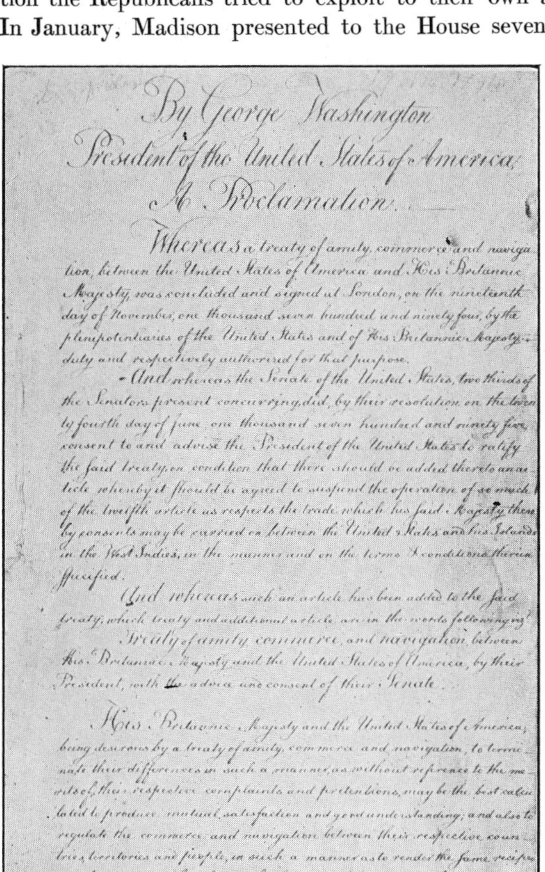

By George Washington
President of the United States of America,
A Proclamation.

Whereas a treaty of amity, commerce and navigation, between the United States of America and His Britannic Majesty, was concluded and signed at London, on the nineteenth day of November, one thousand seven hundred and ninety four, by the plenipotentiaries of the United States and of His Britannic Majesty, duly and respectively authorised for that purpose.

And whereas the Senate of the United States, two thirds of the Senators present concurring, did, by their resolution on the twenty fourth day of June one thousand seven hundred and ninety five, consent to and advise the President of the United States to ratify the said treaty, on condition that there should be added thereto an article whereby it should be agreed to suspend the operation of so much of the twelfth article as respects the trade which his said Majesty thereby consents may be carried on between the United States and his Islands in the West Indies, in the manner and on the terms & conditions therein specified.

And whereas such an article has been added to the said treaty, which treaty and additional article are in the words following viz!

Treaty of amity commerce, and navigation between His Britannic Majesty and the United States of America, by their President, with the advice and consent of their Senate.

His Britannic Majesty and the United States of America, being desirous by a treaty of amity, commerce and navigation, to terminate their differences in such a manner, as without reference to the merits of their respective complaints and pretensions, may be the best calculated to produce mutual satisfaction and good understanding; and also to regulate the commerce and navigation between their respective countries, territories and people, in such a manner as to render the same reciprocally beneficial and satisfactory, they have, respectively named their plenipoten-

434 Title and first page of Washington's Proclamation on the Jay Treaty, 1794, from the engrossed copy in the Department of State, Washington

THE JAY TREATY

IN April, 1794, Washington dispatched Chief Justice John Jay to England as a special envoy. The British had not surrendered the frontier forts in accordance with the terms of the treaty of 1783; old American debts to British merchants remained unpaid, with the merchants prevented from taking legal action. It was Jay's task to prevent the two nations from drifting into war. The treaty which bears his name pleased no one, but it represented the best the young United States, with practically no international prestige, could obtain from the mother country. England agreed to surrender the forts; the debts were to be referred to a claims commission; the British grievance that the Loyalists had not been indemnified for their losses was balanced against the American grievance that the British army during the war had carried off many valuable slaves. The East Indian trade was opened to American vessels but the much desired trade with the West Indies was restricted to vessels of seventy tons or less, with other provisions to prevent the carrying of sugar and other subtropical products from America to Europe. The Senate after a bitter debate ratified the treaty but eliminated the clause relating to the West Indies.

435 Jay Burned in Effigy, from B. J. Lossing, *Our Country*, New York, 1905, after a drawing by F. O. C. Darley

POPULAR PROTEST GREETS THE TREATY

WHEN, in the summer of 1795, the treaty came to public knowledge, protest was vehement. Jay became the most unpopular man in America. In Boston and Charleston he was burned in effigy. Hamilton was stoned in New York when he endeavored to speak for Jay. The treaty was labeled pro-British and anti-French. State legislatures declared it unconstitutional. It became the football of furious party politics.

FISHER AMES' SPEECH

ONLY after a hard struggle, marked by the brilliant and persuasive oratory of Fisher Ames of Massachusetts, did the House, in the ensuing winter, vote the appropriations necessary to effectuate it. The vote was close, the resolution being carried by fifty-one to forty-eight. New England cast only four votes against it and from the South there were but four votes in its favor. The prospect of the nullification of the treaty had alarmed the merchants; and their petitions addressed to the Congress played no small part in the final result.

436 Fisher Ames, 1758–1808, from the portrait by Gilbert Stuart in Memorial Hall, Harvard University

437 Christopher Gore, 1758–1827, from the portrait by John Trumbull in Memorial Hall, Harvard University

THE JAY TREATY BRINGS SOME ADVANTAGES

As a means of avoiding war, the Jay Treaty was an act of wisdom. And in its less contentious clauses America profited by it. Under its provisions commissions were established to settle a variety of claims of the two parties and their nationals. Christopher Gore, later Senator from Massachusetts, was one of the commissioners to England; William Pinkney of Maryland, later Attorney-General under Madison and Minister to England and to Russia, was another. The damages awarded to the citizens of the United States proved greater than those received by British subjects, and in yet another way the treaty served well.

438 William Pinkney, 1764–1822, from the portrait by Rembrandt Peale (1778–1860) in possession of Mrs. Isabelle McCoy Jones, Washington, D. C., courtesy of the Frick Art Reference Library, New York

RIGHTS ON THE MISSISSIPPI

For years Spain had insisted upon the exclusive right of navigation on the Mississippi. Her efforts to enforce this claim aroused the ire of the people of Kentucky and Tennessee to such a point that they threatened to take the matter into their own hands. At this juncture the President sent Thomas Pinckney, Minister at London, to Madrid to negotiate a treaty. He arrived at a favorable moment.

By George Washington,

President of the United States of America.

A Proclamation.

Whereas a Treaty of Friendship, Limits and Navigation, between the United States of America and His Catholic Majesty, was concluded and signed at St. Lorenzo el Real on the twenty seventh day of October, one thousand seven hundred and ninety five, by the Plenipotentiaries of the United States and of his Catholic Majesty duly and respectively authorized for that purpose; which treaty, is in the words following viz.t

His

439 From the engrossed copy of Washington's Proclamation of the Treaty of San Lorenzo, 1795, in the Department of State, Washington

And Whereas the said Treaty has by me, by and with the advice and consent of the Senate of the United States, on the one part, and by his Catholic Majesty on the other, been duly approved and ratified; and the ratifications were duly exchanged at Aranjuez on the twenty fifth day of April, one thousand seven hundred and ninety six: Now therefore, to the end that the said Treaty may be executed and observed with punctuality and the most sincere regard to good faith, on the part of the United States, I hereby make known the premises; and enjoin and require all persons bearing Office civil or military, within the United States, and all others, citizens or inhabitants thereof, or being within the same, to execute and observe the said Treaty accordingly.

In Testimony whereof, I have caused the seal of the United States of America to be affixed to these presents, and signed the same with my Hand.

Done at the City of Philadelphia the second day of August, in the year of our Lord one thousand seven hundred and ninety six, and of the Independence of the United States of America, the twenty first.

G. Washington

By the President

Timothy Pickering,

Secretary of State

440 From the engrossed copy of Washington's Proclamation of the Treaty of San Lorenzo, 1795, in the Department of State, Washington

Art. XXIII.

The present Treaty shall not be in force untill ratified by the Contracting Parties, and the ratifications shall be exchanged in six months from this time, or sooner if possible.

In Witness whereof We the underwritten Plenipotentiaries of His Catholic Majesty and of the United States of America have signed this present Treaty of Friendship, Limits and Navigation and have thereunto affixed our Seals respectively.

Done at San Lorenzo el Real this seven and twenty day of October one thousand seven hundred and ninety five.

Art. XXIII.

El presente Tratado no tendra efecto
Partes Contratantes le hayan ratif
tificaciones se cambiaran en el te
meses, ó antes si fuere posible contan
En fe de lo qual Nosotros los
Plenipotenciarios de S. M. Catolic
dos Unidos de America hemos f
tud de nuestros plenos poderes este
Amistad, Limites, y Navegacion, y
puesto nuestros sellos respectivos
Hecho en San Lorenzo el Rea
siete de Octubre de mil setecient
y cinco.

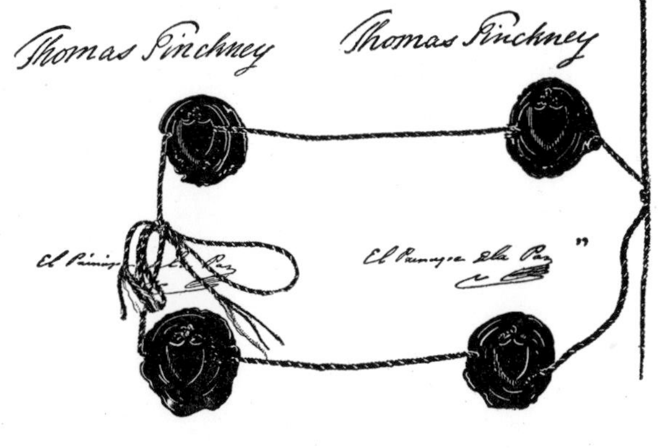

441 Last page of the Treaty of San Lorenzo, in the Department of State, Washington

THE TREATY OF SAN LORENZO

Godoy, the Spanish Premier, was a Liberal. In 1794 news reached Madrid of the Jay Treaty (No. 434). Pinckney, wearied by fruitless negotiations, asked for his passports, announcing that he was going to London. Godoy, fearing an alliance between the United States and England, therefore agreed to the Treaty of San Lorenzo. The boundary between the United States and Florida was fixed, and the Mississippi was thrown open to American navigation, with the privilege of using New Orleans as a port. The West had gained a route to the outer world.

442 Thomas Pinckney, 1750–1828, from a miniature in oil, 1791, by John Trumbull, in the School of the Fine Arts, Yale University

JOHN ADAMS ELECTED PRESIDENT

THE uproar over the Jay Treaty had not subsided before the election of 1796 began to stimulate party passions, already fierce. Washington let it be known that he wished to retire; thus for the first time the Presidency was thrown open to contest. Congressional caucuses were held to select candidates. Hamilton, Federalist leader, had little popular following; Jay was disqualified by the treaty; John Adams was therefore chosen. He was an aristocrat in thought and speech, but his many years in public life had made his name a household word.

JEFFERSON CHOSEN VICE-PRESIDENT

ADAMS was heartily disliked by his party leader. Honest, intelligent, partiotic, he did not possess the art of winning and working with his fellows. Stubborn and proud, he refused to subordinate himself to Hamilton, who during Washington's administration had been the leader of the Federalist party. The latter therefore resorted to a questionable political trick whereby Adams' companion on the Federalist ticket, Thomas Pinckney, popular because of the Spanish treaty, would be returned as President. But the scheme became known, the Adams electors refused to vote for Pinckney, and Jefferson, head of the Republican ticket, was elected vice-president.

443 John Adams in court dress, from the portrait painted in England in 1783 by J. S. Copley, in Memorial Hall, Harvard University

444 John Adams, from the pastel portrait by Sharples in Independence Hall, Philadelphia

ADAMS IS HANDICAPPED BY FACTIONS

THE new President, therefore, entered office after an election that showed real strength in the opposing party and factions within his own. Under such conditions, his effort to carry on the non-partisan policies of Washington proved unfortunate. His proposals to appoint Jefferson or Madison as Minister to France alienated the Hamiltonians; while his retention of the Washington cabinet, most of the members of which looked to Hamilton for leadership, served to weaken his administration and to strengthen the Republicans. John Adams may have been a profound student of government, but he was very slow in learning the lessons of practical politics.

445 Pierre Auguste Adet, 1763–1832, from the pastel portrait by Sharples in Independence Hall, Philadelphia

MONROE PROVES AN INDISCREET MINISTER

ALMOST at the outset Adams was faced with a serious foreign problem. In 1794, to supplant the Federalist Gouverneur Morris, Washington had sent, as Minister to France, James Monroe, disciple of Jefferson. Monroe found France perturbed by the pending Jay Treaty. In his efforts to appease the Directory he overstepped the bounds of diplomatic discretion, and was recalled in the autumn of 1796. Before departing he intimated that should Jefferson be elected in the campaign of 1796, compensation would be forthcoming for the offensive treaty. Acting upon the hint, the French Minister in the United States, Adet, worked more or less openly for the success of the Republicans. Such tactics still further increased Federalist dislike of France.

446 James Monroe, 1758–1831, from the pastel portrait by Sharples, about 1798, in Independence Hall, Philadelphia

447 Charles Maurice Talleyrand-Perigord, 1754–1838, from an engraving for the *European Magazine*, 1814, after a portrait by François P. Gérard (1770–1837)

448 Charles Cotesworth Pinckney, 1746–1825, from the portrait by Gilbert Stuart, owned by Julian Mitchell, Charleston, S. C.

AMERICA RESENTS INDIGNITY BY FRANCE

CHARLES COTESWORTH PINCKNEY, Federalist successor to Monroe, was humiliatingly refused the "card of domicile" which would permit him to remain in France. When news of this rebuff reached America, public indignation was intense. Adams called Congress in special session in May, 1797, and, telling the members forcefully that the Directory had "treated us neither as allies nor as friends nor as a sovereign state," recommended the taking of measures of defense, to show the world that "we are not a degraded people humiliated under a colonial spirit of fear."

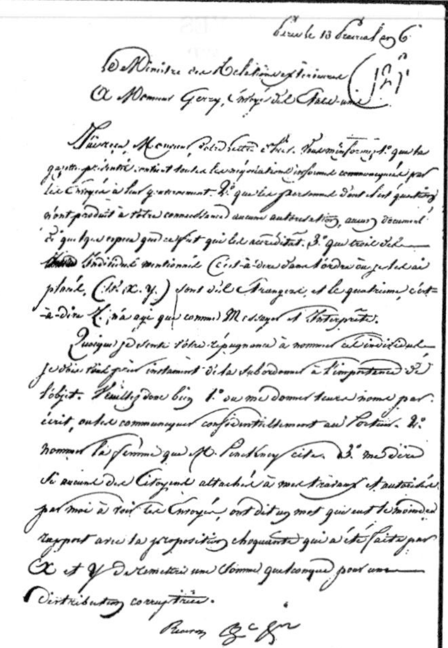

Paris le 13 Prairial an 6.

Le Ministre des Relations extérieures

A Monsieur Gerry, Envoyé des Etats-unis.

J'ai reçu, Monsieur, votre lettre d'hier. Vous m'informez 1° que la gazette présentée contient toutes les négociations informes communiquées par les Envoyés à leur gouvernement. 2° que les personnes dont il est question n'ont produit à votre connaissance aucune autorisation, aucun document de quelque espèce que ce fût qui les accréditât. 3° que trois des individus mentionnés (c'est-à-dire dans l'ordre où je les ai placés, (W. X. Y.) sont des Etrangers, et le quatrième, c'est-à-dire Z, n'a agi que comme Messager et Interprète.

Quoique je sente votre répugnance à nommer ces individus, je dois [illegible] prier instamment de la subordonner à l'importance de l'objet. Veuillez donc bien 1° ou me donner leurs noms par écrit, ou les communiquer confidentiellement au Porteur. 2° nommer la femme que M. Pinckney cite. 3° me dire si aucun des Citoyens attachés à mes travaux et autorisés par moi à voir les Envoyés, ont dit un mot qui eut le moindre rapport avec la proposition choquante qui a été faite par X et Y de remettre une somme quelconque pour une distribution corruptrice.

Recevez &c &c

449 Talleyrand's Letter to Gerry, 1798, from the original in the Ministère des Affaires Etrangères, Paris

TALLEYRAND SLIGHTS THE ENVOYS

ADAMS, however, thought peaceful relations might still be preserved. He therefore appointed, with the confirmation of the Senate, John Marshall and Elbridge Gerry to join Pinckney in Paris. Gerry was a Massachusetts Republican and so not altogether objectionable to the Federalists, while his presence might mollify the testy French Directory. In October all three were informally received by Talleyrand as Foreign Minister. A few days later they were approached by three persons, later distinguished as X, Y and Z, as agents of the Minister. They suggested that a gift of 1,200,000 francs might prove an aid to negotiations. "No, no, no, not a penny," responded Pinckney. Then, after months of futile exchanges between the two parties, the commissioners gave up in disgust. Talleyrand prevailed upon Gerry to remain, which encouraged the Directory to hope for a change of front by the United States, and intensified the foreign issue in American politics.

(Translation)

Paris, 13 Prairial, 6.

The Minister of Foreign Affairs [Talleyrand]
to Mr. Gerry, Envoy of the United States.

I have received, Sir, your letter of yesterday. You inform me, 1st, that the journal presented contains all the informal negotiations communicated by the envoys to their government; 2nd, that the persons in question have not produced to your knowledge any authorization or document of any kind that would accredit them; 3rd, that three of the individuals mentioned (designating them in the order in which I have placed them as W, X, Y) are foreigners, and that the fourth, or Z, has acted only as messenger and interpreter.

Although I understand your reluctance to name these individuals, I must beg you at once to subordinate this to the importance of the matter. Will you please, therefore, 1st, either give me their names in writing, or tell them confidentially to the bearer; 2nd, name the woman referred to by Mr. Pinckney; 3rd, tell me whether any of the citizens attached to my staff and authorized by me to see the envoys have said one word which has the least relation to the shocking proposal that has been made by X and Y to remit any sum whatever for corrupt distribution.

450 From a contemporary cartoon *The Times; A Political Portrait*, in the New York Historical Society

WAR WITH FRANCE IS THREATENED

WHILE Adams awaited news from Paris, the war party was with difficulty restrained. But when, on April 3, 1798, the President sent to Congress the dispatches from the commissioners describing their treatment, the resentment was unbounded. As the correspondence was published, Republicans joined with Federalists in calling for war. "Millions for defense, but not one cent for tribute" became the universal rallying cry. Commerce with France and her possessions was ordered stopped, the French treaties were abrogated, a direct tax was voted, and a large volunteer army, with Washington at its head, organized. All this pleased the Federalists, and especially Hamilton, who became the second in command of the new army.

A NAVY DEPARTMENT IS ESTABLISHED

AMONG the various measures for waging the undeclared war was an act establishing a navy department, at the head of which Adams placed Benjamin Stoddert of Maryland, Revolutionary soldier and Georgetown merchant. Equipment for the new frigates, the *Constitution*, *Constellation*, and *United States* was voted; the merchant marine was permitted to arm for defense and offense; and in July, 1798, three squadrons sailed against the French in the West Indies.

451 Benjamin Stoddert, 1751–1813, from the portrait by E. F. Andrews in the office of the Secretary of the Navy, Washington

CONGRESS RESTRICTS INTERNATIONAL COMMUNICATION

THE war spirit ran high. France had injured America more than once. The impudence of Genêt and Adet (Nos. 428, 445) was not forgotten. Scores of American merchantmen had been captured by French privateers. Then came George Logan's trip to Paris for the purpose of averting war. Talleyrand received him with marked courtesy. For in truth France wanted no war with the United States. Talleyrand's conduct had been bluster to win America at least to benevolent neutrality. But Logan was a Republican and his action was an unwarranted and partisan interference in diplomacy. So the Logan Act was passed, forbidding an individual citizen to take part in a controversy with a foreign power.

FIFTH *CONGRESS* OF THE UNITED STATES:
At the Third Session,
Begun and held at the city of *Philadelphia*, in the ftate of PENNSYLVANIA, on *Monday*, the third of *December*, one thoufand feven hundred and ninety-eight.

An ACT *for the punishment of certain crimes therein specified.*

Be it enacted by the SENATE and HOUSE of REPRESENTATIVES of the United States of AMERICA, in Congress assembled, [illegible]

Jonathan Dayton Speaker of the House of Representatives
Th: Jefferson Vice. President of the United States, and President of the Senate

I certify that this Act did originate in the House of Representatives
[illegible] Clerk.

January 30 1799 Approved
John Adams
President of the United States

452 The Logan Act, 1799, from the original in the Department of State, Washington

453 William Vans Murray, 1762–1803, from the miniature in the possession of V. Murray Sulivane, Cumberland, Md.

A CONVENTION IS SIGNED WITH FRANCE, 1800

But Adams received Logan and welcomed the suggestion that Talleyrand was anxious for peace, and would give a proper reception to any Minister sent. The President wanted war as little as the French. He saw an opportunity to end it. Never lacking in courage, he now took the initiative. Without consulting a hostile cabinet, he sent to the Senate, in February, 1799, the nomination of William Vans Murray, then Minister to Holland, as Minister to France. To the Republicans the action of Adams was endorsement from an unexpected quarter of their own contention, that it was foolish to talk of war with a country that was only too willing to be friendly if she in turn were not discriminated against. To the Federalists his action brought consternation. In the heat of his first reaction, a Federalist leader wrote to Hamilton, "Had the foulest heart and the ablest head in the world been permitted to select the most embarrassing and ruinous measure, perhaps it would have been precisely the one which has been adopted." Taking the initiative for his party, Hamilton insisted that the negotiations be placed in the hands of a commission, to include the new Minister, rather than of an individual. Adams finally agreed, nominating Oliver Ellsworth and Patrick Henry. When Henry declined the nomination, William R. Davie of North Carolina was substituted. After many months of discussion, a convention was signed at Paris in September, 1800, which gave mutual satisfaction. Napoleon, now in power, did not insist on a renewal of the treaties of 1778; while America did not press certain damage claims. Thus formally came to an end the only treaty of alliance between the United States and a European power.

FOREIGNERS IN AMERICA MEET RESTRAINTS

The ultra-Federalists were at the height of their power in the spring of 1798 when the XYZ affair had aroused a spirit of militant patriotism. The opportunity was not lost on those who felt that a check should be placed on democracy. The Whisky Rebellion, the Democratic societies so warmly espousing the doctrines of the French revolutionists, the scurrilous press which stopped at nothing to denounce public officials — these were signs of a decay of the constitutional theory that government was to protect property and to be administered by the able. Many Republican leaders, notably Albert Gallatin — who had sympathized with the Whisky uprising — were of foreign birth, and so also were several of the more intemperate publicists. Hence the repressive measures of 1798. The term of residence for naturalization was raised from five to fourteen years; the President was given discretionary power to deport any obnoxious alien, and to arrest, imprison, and deport dangerous enemy aliens. Jury trial was not required.

FIFTH *CONGRESS* OF THE UNITED STATES:

At the Second Session,

Begun and held at the city of *Philadelphia*, in the state of Pennsylvania, on *Monday*, the thirteenth of *November*, one thousand seven hundred and ninety-seven.

An ACT *respecting alien enemies.*

Be it enacted by the Senate and House of Representatives of the United States of America, in Congress assembled, *That whenever there shall be a declared war between the United States and any foreign nation or government, or any invasion or predatory incursion shall be perpetrated, attempted, or threatened against the territory of the United States, by any foreign nation or government ...*

454 Title and first page of the Alien Enemies Act, 1798, from the original in the Department of State, Washington

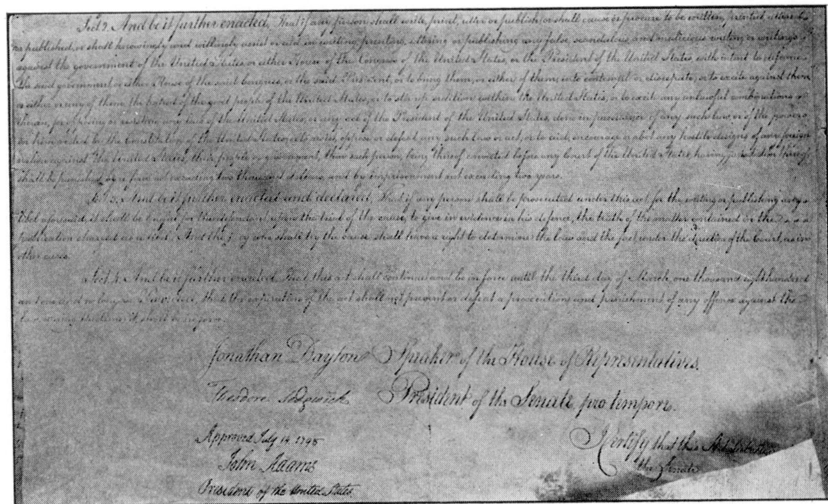

Sect. 2. And be it further enacted, That if any person shall write, print, utter or publish, or shall cause or procure to be written, printed, uttered or published, ...

Sect. 3. And be it further enacted and declared, That if any person shall be prosecuted under this act for the writing or publishing any libel aforesaid, ...

Sect. 4. And be it further enacted, That this act shall continue and be in force until the third day of March, one thousand eight hundred and one, ...

Jonathan Dayton Speaker of the House of Representatives.

Theodore Sedgwick President of the Senate pro tempore.

Approved July 14, 1798
John Adams
President of the United States

I certify that this Act [illegible]
the Senate [illegible]

455 Section 2, 3, and 4 of the Sedition Act, 1798, from the original in the Department of State, Washington

CONGRESS PROVIDES AGAINST SEDITION

These drastic measures were designed to counteract the exertions of French and Irish radicals within the country. Some thought Gallatin, Republican leader, was a special objective of the acts. But the effects of the statutes were far-reaching. Hamilton predicted that "If we push things to an extreme, we shall then give to faction body and solidity." So it happened. The Republican press at once made an outcry. To muzzle it came the Sedition Act, later to serve as a model for the espionage acts in the war of 1917–18. This made it a crime to publish any false or malicious writings against the Government, Congress, or the President, with intent to excite popular hatred of or resistance to them, or to bring them into contempt. It was aimed at a few Republican editors, perhaps unduly ardent in their political activity. But the law did not single out the Republicans; nor were they alone in the use of unrestrained language. "Fire-eating salamanders" and "poison-sucking toads" were some of the epithets of Fisher Ames, arch-Federalist, when he tried to describe his political opponents.

CONGRESS AT ODDS OVER THE SEDITION ACT

Adams made no effort to enforce the alien acts, for the more obnoxious French agitators left the country of their own accord; while the President, to the disgust of the extreme Federalists, derided the prospect of a foreign invasion. Yet, like the rest of his party, he wished that respect should be shown to public officials; and prosecutions under the Sedition Act received his approval. The first to suffer was Matthew Lyon, member of Congress from Vermont. A fiery Irishman, Lyon had worked up from poverty to the proprietorship of a newspaper which he called *The Scourge of Aristocracy and Repository of Important Political Truth.* As a rabid Republican, he was thoroughly hated by the Federalists and became the butt of their gibes. In January, 1798, irritated by Griswold, Federalist from Connecticut, Lyon in a passion spat in the face of his tormentor. The House took up the case, but the Federalists could not muster the two-thirds necessary for expulsion of a member. Griswold took matters into his own hands and on the fifteenth of February suddenly attacked Lyon with a heavy bludgeon. The latter retaliated as best he could. The following day a resolution to expel both members was brought in, but nothing came of it. Scarcely had the Sedition Act passed when Lyon was arrested for publishing a letter accusing Adams of "unbounded thirst for ridiculous pomp, foolish adulation, and selfish avarice." He was fined one thousand dollars and given four months in jail, during which time he was triumphantly reëlected to Congress. Many years later the fine was refunded, with interest. On his release from jail, his fine was paid through the aid of Jefferson, Madison, Gallatin, and other Republicans of prominence.

456 From a cartoon *Congressional Pugilists*, in *The Echo*, Hartford, 1807, published by Noah Bailey

JEFFERSON OPPOSES RESTRICTIONS ON POPULAR LIBERTY

Prosecutions for a time continued, but their political effect soon caused the Government to abandon the laws. The measures had been aimed at radical aliens and their Jacobin sympathizers, the Republicans. The latter were loud in condemnation of them. Jefferson in October wrote to a friend: "The X,Y,Z fever has considerably abated through the country, and the alien and sedition laws are working hard. I fancy that some of the State Legislatures will take strong ground on this occasion. For my own part, I consider those laws as merely an experiment on the American mind, to see how far it will bear an avowed violation of the Constitution. If this goes down, we shall immediately see attempted another act of Congress, declaring that the President shall continue in office during life, reserving to another occasion the transfer of the succession to his heirs, and the establishment of the Senate for life." In short, Jefferson saw in the rising tide of objection to the administration and its acts fine campaign material. To ensure that "strong ground of the State legislatures," he drafted a set of resolutions which he placed in the hands of John Breckinridge of the Kentucky legislature, where, with minor changes, they were enthusiastically adopted. But Jefferson saw more than campaign material in the sedition law. The enactment impaired the right of free speech and free press without which the governmental experiment in the United States must fail. The common people rallied to his support as he led the attack upon the Federalist aristocracy.

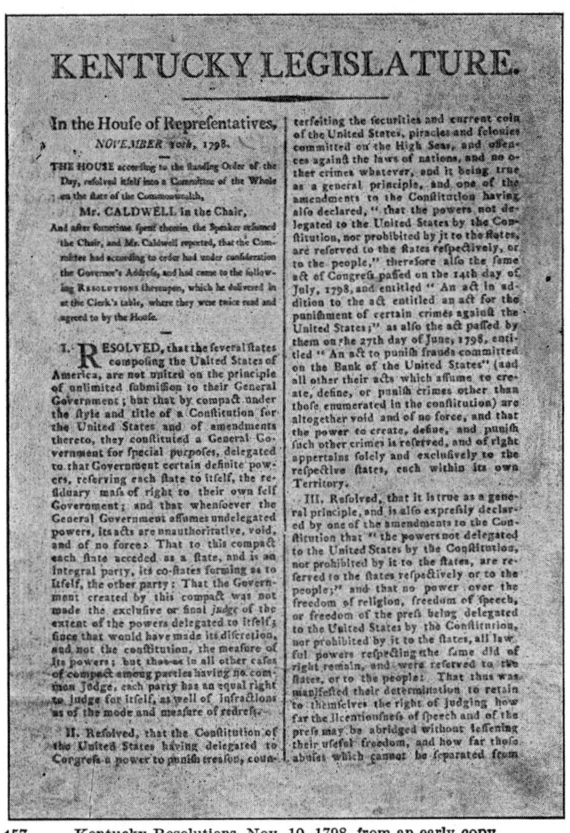

KENTUCKY LEGISLATURE.

In the Houfe of Reprefentatives,
NOVEMBER 10th, 1798.

THE HOUSE according to the ftanding Order of the Day, refolved itfelf into a Committee of the Whole on the ftate of the Commonwealth,

Mr. CALDWELL in the Chair,

And after fometime fpent therein the Speaker refumed the Chair, and Mr. Caldwell reported, that the Committee had according to order had under confideration the Governor's Addrefs, and had come to the following Resolutions thereupon, which he delivered in at the Clerk's table, where they were twice read and agreed to by the Houfe.

I. RESOLVED, that the feveral ftates compofing the United States of America, are not united on the principle of unlimited fubmiffion to their General Government; but that by compact under the ftyle and title of a Conftitution for the United States and of amendments thereto, they conftituted a General Government for fpecial purpofes, delegated to that Government certain definite powers, referving each ftate to itfelf, the refiduary mafs of right to their own felf Government; and that whenfoever the General Government affumes undelegated powers, its acts are unauthoritative, void, and of no force: That to this compact each ftate acceded as a ftate, and is an integral party, its co-ftates forming as to itfelf, the other party: That the Government created by this compact was not made the exclufive or final *judge* of the extent of the powers delegated to itfelf; fince that would have made its difcretion, and not the conftitution, the meafure of its powers; but that as in all other cafes of compact among parties having no common Judge, each party has an equal right to judge for itfelf, as well of infractions as of the mode and meafure of redrefs.

II. Refolved, that the Conftitution of the United States having delegated to Congrefs a power to punifh treafon, counterfeiting the fecurities and current coin of the United States, piracies and felonies committed on the High Seas, and offences againft the laws of nations, and no other crimes whatever, and it being true as a general principle, and one of the amendments to the Conftitution having alfo declared, "that the powers not delegated to the United States by the Conftitution, nor prohibited by it to the ftates, are referved to the ftates refpectively, or to the people," therefore alfo the fame act of Congrefs paffed on the 14th day of July, 1798, and entitled "An act in addition to the act entitled an act for the punifhment of certain crimes againft the United States;" as alfo the act paffed by them on the 27th day of June, 1798, entitled "An act to punifh frauds committed on the Bank of the United States" (and all other their acts which affume to create, define, or punifh crimes other than thofe enumerated in the conftitution) are altogether void and of no force, and that the power to create, define, and punifh fuch other crimes is referved, and of right appertains folely and exclufively to the refpective ftates, each within its own Territory.

III. Refolved, that it is true as a general principle, and is alfo exprefsly declared by one of the amendments to the Conftitution that "the powers not delegated to the United States by the Conftitution, nor prohibited by it to the ftates, are referved to the ftates refpectively or to the people;" and that no power over the freedom of religion, freedom of fpeech, or freedom of the prefs being delegated to the United States by the Conftitution, nor prohibited by it to the ftates, all lawful powers refpecting the fame did of right remain, and were referved to the ftates, or to the people: That thus was manifefted their determination to retain to themfelves the right of judging how far the licentioufnefs of fpeech and of the prefs may be abridged without leffening their ufeful freedom, and how far thofe abufes which cannot be feparated from

457 Kentucky Resolutions, Nov. 10, 1798, from an early copy in the Massachusetts Archives

STATE RIGHTS RESOLUTIONS PASS IN VIRGINIA

Jefferson persuaded Madison to draft for the Virginia legislature resolutions similar to those of Kentucky. This was done. These two documents, destined later to encourage doctrines of nullification and of secession, though condemned by other states, made a profound sensation. Many years later Madison wrote of them: "The Resolutions were for political effect, intended as a party platform to arouse the Republican sentiment throughout the country and secure a general condemnation of the Federalist centralization." If this was the purpose, they were highly successful.

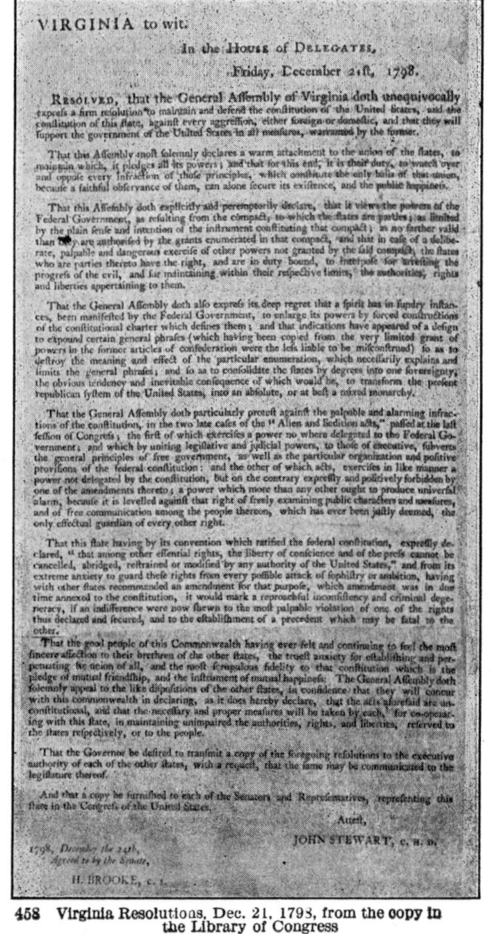

VIRGINIA to wit.

In the House of Delegates,

Friday, December 21ft, 1798.

Resolved, that the General Affembly of Virginia doth unequivocally exprefs a firm refolution to maintain and defend the conftitution of the United ftates, and the conftitution of this ftate, againft every aggreffion, either foreign or domeftic, and that they will fupport the government of the United States in all meafures, warranted by the former.

That this Affembly moft folemnly declares a warm attachment to the union of the ftates, to maintain which, it pledges all its powers; and that for this end, it is their duty, to watch over and oppofe every infraction of thofe principles, which conftitute the only bafis of that union, becaufe a faithful obfervance of them, can alone fecure its exiftence, and the public happinefs.

That this Affembly doth explicitly and peremptorily declare, that it views the powers of the Federal Government, as refulting from the compact, to which the ftates are parties; as limited by the plain fenfe and intention of the inftrument conftituting that compact; as no farther valid than they are authorifed by the grants enumerated in that compact, and that in cafe of a deliberate, palpable and dangerous exercife of other powers not granted by the faid compact, the ftates who are parties thereto have the right, and are in duty bound, to interpofe for arrefting the progrefs of the evil, and for maintaining within their refpective limits, the authorities, rights and liberties appertaining to them.

That the General Affembly doth alfo exprefs its deep regret that a fpirit has in fundry inftances, been manifefted by the Federal Government, to enlarge its powers by forced conftructions of the conftitutional charter which defines them; and that indications have appeared of a defign to expound certain general phrafes (which having been copied from the very limited grant of powers in the former articles of confederation were the lefs liable to be mifconftrued) fo as to deftroy the meaning and effect of the particular enumeration, which neceffarily explains and limits the general phrafes; and fo as to confolidate the ftates by degrees into one fovereignty, the obvious tendency and inevitable confequence of which would be, to transform the prefent republican fyftem of the United States, into an abfolute, or at beft a mixed monarchy.

That the General Affembly doth particularly proteft againft the palpable and alarming infractions of the conftitution, in the two late cafes of the "Alien and Sedition acts," paffed at the laft feffion of Congrefs; the firft of which exercifes a power no where delegated to the Federal Government; and which by uniting legiflative and judicial powers, to thofe of executive, fubverts the general principles of free government, as well as the particular organization and pofitive provifions of the federal conftitution: and the other of which acts, exercifes in like manner a power not delegated by the conftitution, but on the contrary exprefly and pofitively forbidden by one of the amendments thereto; a power which more than any other ought to produce univerfal alarm, becaufe it is levelled againft that right of freely examining public characters and meafures, and of free communication among the people thereon, which has ever been juftly deemed, the only effectual guardian of every other right.

That this ftate having by its convention which ratified the federal conftitution, exprefly declared, "that among other effential rights, the liberty of confcience and of the prefs cannot be cancelled, abridged, reftrained or modified by any authority of the United States," and from its extreme anxiety to guard thefe rights from every poffible attack of fophiftry or ambition, having with other ftates recommended an amendment for that purpofe, which amendment was in due time annexed to the conftitution, it would mark a reproachful inconfiftency and criminal degeneracy, if an indifference were now fhewn to the moft palpable violation of one of the rights thus declared and fecured, and to the eftablifhment of a precedent which may be fatal to the other.

That the good people of this Commonwealth having ever felt and continuing to feel the moft fincere affection to their brethren of the other ftates, the trueft anxiety for eftablifhing and perpetuating the union of all, and the moft fcrupulous fidelity to that conftitution which is the pledge of mutual friendfhip, and the inftrument of mutual happinefs: The General Affembly doth folemnly appeal to the like difpofitions of the other ftates, in confidence that they will concur with this commonwealth in declaring, as it does hereby declare, that the acts aforefaid are unconftitutional, and that the neceffary and proper meafures will be taken by each, for co-operating with this ftate, in maintaining unimpaired the authorities, rights, and liberties, referved to the ftates refpectively, or to the people.

That the Governor be defired to tranfmit a copy of the foregoing refolutions to the executive authority of each of the other ftates, with a requeft, that the fame may be communicated to the legiflature thereof.

And that a copy be furnifhed to each of the Senators and Reprefentatives, reprefenting this ftate in the Congrefs of the United States.

Atteft,

JOHN STEWART, C. H. D.

1798, December the 24th,
Agreed to by the Senate,

H. BROOKE, C. S.

458 Virginia Resolutions, Dec. 21, 1798, from the copy in the Library of Congress

Monumental Inſcription.

"That life is long which anſwers Life's great end"

YESTERDAY EXPIRED,
Deeply regretted by MILLIONS of grateful Americans,
And by *all* GOOD MEN.
The FEDERAL ADMINISTRATION
Of the
GOVERNMENT of the *United States*:
Animated by
A WASHINGTON, an ADAMS ;—a
HAMILTON, KNOX, PICKERING, WOLCOTT, M'HENRY, MARSHALL,
STODDERT and DEXTER.
Æt. 12 years.

Its death was occaſioned by the
Secret Arts, and Open Violence;
Of Foreign and Domeſtic Demagogues:
Notwithſtanding its whole Life
Was devoted to the Performance of every Duty
to promote
The UNION, CREDIT, PEACE, PROSPERITY, HONOR, and
FELICITY OF ITS COUNTRY.

At its birth it found
The Union of the States diſſolving like a Rope of ſnow;
It hath left it
Stronger than the Threefold cord.

It found the United States
Bankrupts in Eſtate and Reputation;
It hath left them
Unbounded in Credit; and reſpected throughout
the World.
It found the *Treaſuries* of the United States and
Individual States *empty*.
It hath left them *full and overflowing*.
It found
All the Evidences of Public Debts worthleſs as rags;
It hath left them
More valuable than Gold and Silver.

It found
The United States *at war* with the
Indian Nations;—
It hath concluded *Peace* with them all.
It found
The Aboriginels of the ſoil *inveterate
enemies of the whites*;
It hath exerciſed towards them *juſtice* and *generoſity*,
And *hath left them faſt friends*.

It found
Great-Britain in poſſeſſion of all
the *Frontier Poſts*;
It hath demanded their ſurrender, and
it leaves them in the poſſeſſion
of the United States.
It found
The American ſea-coaſt utterly *defenceleſs*;
It hath left it *fortified*.
It found our *Arſenals* empty; and *Magazines*
decaying;
It hath left them full of *ammunition*
and *warlike Implements*.
It found our country dependent on Foreign Nations
for *engines of defenſe*;
It hath left
Manufactories of *Cannon* and *Muſquets*
in full work.
It found
The American Nation at *War* with
Algiers, *Tunis*, and *Tripoli*;
It hath
Made *Peace* with them all.
It found
American Freemen in Turkiſh ſlavery, where
they had languiſhed in chains for years;
It hath
Ranſomed them, and ſet them free.

It found the war-worn, invalid *Soldier*
ſtarving from want;
Or, like BELISARIUS, *begging his refuſe
meat from door to door*;
It hath left
Ample proviſion for the regular
payment of his *penſion*.

It found
The *Commerce* of our country confined
almoſt to *Coaſting Craft*;
It hath left it
Whitening every ſea with its canvaſs, and
cheering every clime with its *ſtars*.

It found our
Mechanics and *Manufacturers* idle in
the ſtreets for want of employ;
It hath left them
Full of buſineſs, proſperous, contented
and happy.
It found
The Yeomanry of the country oppreſſed with
unequal taxes;—their farms, houſes and barns
decaying; their cattle ſelling at the
ſign poſts; and they driven to
deſperation and *Rebellion*;
It hath left
Their coffers in caſh; their houſes in repair;
their barns full; their farms overſtocked; and
their produce commanding ready money,
and a high price.
In ſhort—
It found them *poor, indigent Malcontents*;
It hath left them
Wealthy Friends to Order and good Government.

It found
The United States *deeply in debt to
France* and *Holland*;
It hath *paid* ALL *the demands* of the former, and
the principal part of the latter.
It found the Country in a ruinous
Alliance with *France*;
It hath honorably diſſolved the connexion,
and ſet us free.

It found
The United States without a ſwivel
on float *for their defenſe*;
It hath left
A NAVY—compoſed of Thirty-four ſhips of
war; mounting 918 guns; and manned
by 7350 gallant tars.

It found
The EXPORTS of our country, a mere ſong, in
value;
It hath left them worth
Above SEVENTY MILLIONS of Dollars per annum.
In one word,
It found AMERICA *diſunited, poor, inſolvent,
weak, diſcontented, and wretched*;
It hath left HER
*United, wealthy, reſpectable, ſtrong,
happy* and *proſperous*.
Let the faithful Hiſtorian, in after times,
ſay theſe things of its Succeſſor, if it can.
And yet—notwithſtanding all theſe ſervices and
bleſſings there are found
Many, very many, weak, degenerate Sons,
who, loſt to virtue, to gratitude,
and patriotiſm,
Openly exult, that this Adminiſtration
is no more.
And that
The "Sun of Federaliſm is ſet for ever."
"Oh ſhame where is thy bluſh?"

As one Tribute of Gratitude in theſe Times,
This MONUMENT
Of the Talents and Services of the deceaſed;
is raiſed by
The Centinel.

March 4th, 1801.

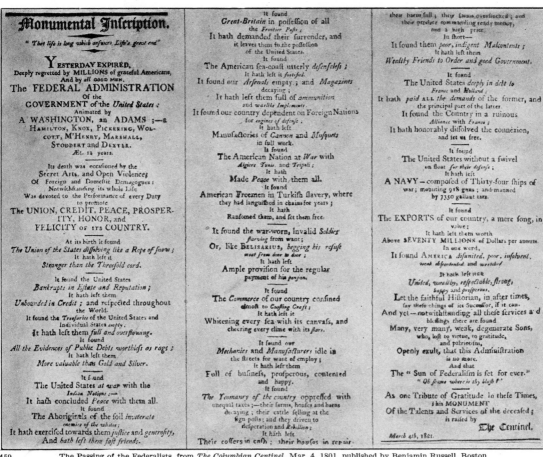

459 The Passing of the Federalists, from *The Columbian Centinel*, Mar. 4, 1801, published by Benjamin Russell, Boston

CENTRALIZED POWER RECEIVES A SETBACK

No more bitter election campaign has ever been fought than that of 1800. The Federalists, intrenched in public office, arraigned their opponents as Jacobins and raised the bugaboo of a French plot to sever Kentucky from the Union. But the people did not listen. In despair the Federalists appealed to the "friends of society, religion, and good order" to support an administration whose record of service was so full. Upon that record the Republicans, deftly led by Jefferson and Burr, concentrated their attack. Centralization of power, suppression of constitutional liberties, increased and direct taxation, swollen civil service, all came in for reproof. Disaffection in Federalist ranks added to their troubles. As state after state swung to Jefferson the Federalists became frantic. When, despite Hamilton, Burr carried New York for the Republicans, the result was practically certain. The Federalists had fallen. Never again did the party elect a President of the United States.

460 Senate Chamber of the First Congress, Sixth and Chestnut Streets, Philadelphia, from a photograph

CHAPTER VIII

THE VIRGINIA DYNASTY

THE party that came into power on the wave of the Revolution of 1800 was preeminently the party of Jefferson. As a party leader, Jefferson is without a peer. "In his understanding of mass psychology, he had no equal. When a measure was passed or a policy adopted in Philadelphia, he knew the reactions in the woods of Georgia without waiting for letters and papers. This rare insight into the mass mind made him a brilliant propagandist. . . . In his leadership we find more of leading than of driving. He had a genius for gently and imperceptibly insinuating his own views into the minds of others and leaving them with the impression that they had conceived the ideas and convinced Jefferson. . . . Jefferson was the original 'Easy Boss.' . . . Jefferson was the most resourceful politician of his time. For every problem he had a solution. He teemed with ideas. These were his shock troops. If he seemed motionless, it was because by a nod or look he had put his forces on the march. Like the wiser of the modern bosses, he knew the virtue of silence. When in doubt, he said nothing. When certain of his course, he said nothing — to his foes. It was impossible to smoke him out when he preferred to stay in. In the midst of abuse he was serene. And he was a stickler for party regularity. He appreciated the possibilities of organization and discipline. When money was needed for party purposes, his friends would receive a note: 'I have put you down for so much.' . . . He was never too big for the small essential things, and he was a master of detail. . . . His energy was dynamic and he was tireless. He never rested on his arms or went into winter quarters. His fight was endless." — CLAUDE G. BOWERS, *Jefferson and Hamilton*, 1925, pp. 107–111. Such was the man who came to the Presidency in 1801.

The degree of success attained by Jefferson and the causes of his failures as well as of his achievements may be found embodied in the remarkable words of Josiah Quincy, polished orator and arch-Federalist. In the course of the debate in the House of Representatives on the suspension of the Embargo (1808), Quincy said: "We are but a young nation. The United States are scarcely yet hardened into the bone of manhood. The whole period of our national existence has been nothing else than a continued series of prosperity. The miseries of the Revolutionary war were but as the pangs of parturition. The experience of that period was of a nature not to be very useful after our nation had acquired an individual form and a manly constitutional character. It is to be feared we have grown giddy with good fortune, attributing the greatness of our prosperity to our own wisdom, rather than to a course of events, and a guidance, over which we had no influence. It is to be feared that we are now entering that school of adversity, the first blessing of which is to chastise an overweening conceit of ourselves." Quincy, in short, believed that the progress of the country was due, not to the somewhat undiscerning though eager experimentation of the Republicans, but to factors imbedded in nonpolitical institutions. These institutions, chiefly economic, Jefferson had found none too pliant. Less doctrinaire devices than his were needed to promote the general welfare. The times of adversity prophesied by Quincy came in 1812. Yet from the clouds of the War of 1812 the country emerged with a new, unchastened spirit of optimism. The "Era of Good Feeling" was a time of rejoicing, when men felt that their country had been tested and found good. The nation was vigorous, self-reliant, hopeful.

THOMAS JEFFERSON BECOMES PRESIDENT, 1801

THE success of Jefferson was honestly dreaded by numerous intelligent folk. The Reverend Timothy Dwight, President of Yale, prophesied that "the Bible would be cast into a bonfire, our holy worship changed into a dance of Jacobin phrensy, our wives and daughters dishonored, and our sons converted into the disciples of Voltaire and the dragoons of Marat." Little wonder that, when it was learned that the electoral vote had been a tie between Jefferson and Burr, the Federalist caucus chose to support the latter as the lesser of two evils. Only the pressure of Hamilton secured, on the thirty-sixth ballot, the selection of Jefferson, who he thought would "pursue a temporizing rather than a violent system."

461 Thomas Jefferson, 1743–1826, from the portrait painted in 1805 by Rembrandt Peale, in the New York Historical Society

JEFFERSON'S MYSTIFYING PERSONALITY

THE man so distrusted was indeed a perplexing individual. Born, in 1743, of good Virginia aristocracy, he was a lifelong believer in the people and in their desire and capacity to govern themselves. Studious and retiring, he nevertheless for a generation led a political party with deftness and aplomb. A cultivated gentleman who with reluctance left the brilliant life of Paris to join Washington's cabinet, he in a few short years was condoning the Terror as a mere incident in a beneficent development. His partisanship dates from this period, and as time passed his mystifying personality unfolded still further. In May, 1787, he was described as "an American who is at once a musician, skilled in drawing, a geometrician, an astronomer, a natural philosopher, legislator and statesman. It seemed as if from his youth he had placed his mind, as he had done his house (Monticello), upon an elevated situation, from which he might contemplate the universe." Thomas Jefferson and Benjamin Franklin were two of the most versatile men that America has produced. Both were deists and were influential in the development of deistic thought in their day. Both were men of science. Though the terms were not then in vogue, Franklin tended more to pure and Jefferson to applied science. If Franklin was the greater diplomat, Jefferson was the greater political leader. Jefferson knew well both how to compromise, when the occasion seemed to demand it, and how to fight. He made bitter enemies and constant friends. Although at the end of his administration he suffered the humiliation of seeing his policy of "peaceable coercion" abandoned, his prestige was not impaired. For more than a decade after his retirement he remained the "Sage of Monticello" to whose drawing room journeyed men of all sorts seeking counsel and guidance. Though Jefferson has been dead for more than a century, his thought and his ideals still influence the development of the American people.

462 From the portrait of Jefferson by Mather Brown (1761–1831), painted in London about 1785, courtesy of Charles Francis Adams, Boston

463 Jefferson in 1799, from the portrait by Gilbert Stuart in the Bowdoin Museum of Fine Arts, Bowdoin College, Brunswick, Maine

MACLAY'S PEN PORTRAIT OF JEFFERSON

In 1790, Senator Maclay thus described the Democratic leader: "Jefferson is a slender man, has rather the air of stiffness in his manner. His clothes seem too small for him. He sits in a lounging manner, on one hip commonly, and with one of his shoulders elevated above the other. His face has a sunny aspect. His whole figure has a loose shackling air. He has a rambling vacant look, and nothing of that firm, collected deportment which I expected would dignify the presence of a secretary or minister. I looked for gravity, but a laxity of manner seemed shed about him. He spoke almost without ceasing, but even his discourse partook of his personal demeanor. It was loose and rambling; and yet he scattered information wherever he went, and some even brilliant sentiments sparkled from him." There is a striking contrast between the portrayal of the third President by the politician Maclay, and the artist, Stuart.

JEFFERSON WANTS A "WISE AND FRUGAL GOVERNMENT"

Jefferson's creed was simple, and understood by his followers. Nowhere is it better stated than in the inaugural address, delivered by him in the new capitol. "Let us, with courage and confidence, pursue our own Federal and Republican principles; our attachment to union and representative government. Kindly separated by nature and a wide ocean from the exterminating havoc of one-quarter of the globe; too high-minded to endure the degradations of the others; possessing a chosen country, with room enough for our descendants to the thousandth and thousandth generation; entertaining a due sense of our equal right to the use of our own faculties, to the acquisition of our own industry, to honor and confidence from our fellow-citizens, resulting not from birth, but from our actions and from our sense of them; enlightened by a benign religion, professed indeed and practised in various forms, yet all of them inculcating honesty, truth, temperance, gratitude, and the love of man; acknowledging and adoring an overruling Providence, which, by all its dispensations, proves that it delights in the happiness of man here, and his greater happiness hereafter; with all these blessings, what more is necessary to make us a happy and prosperous nation? Still one thing more, fellow-citizens, a wise and frugal government which shall restrain men from injuring one another, shall leave them free to regulate their own pursuit of industry and improvement, and shall not take from the mouth the bread it has earned. This is the sum of good government and this is necessary to close the circle of our felicities."

464 From the portrait of Jefferson, 1821, by Thomas Sully (1783–1872) in the Library of the United States Military Academy, West Point, N. Y.

JEFFERSON'S CHIEF ADVISERS

Jefferson's cabinet selections still further illuminate the man. Three, Henry Dearborn and Levi Lincoln of Massachusetts and Gideon Granger of Connecticut, came from the stronghold of Federalism, which had given Jefferson but one vote in the electoral college. Robert Smith of Maryland became head of the Navy Department. These men were either of mediocre ability or in charge of military administration, a matter in which the President took little interest. His real advisers were two, Madison as Secretary of State and Gallatin at the Treasury. Albert Gallatin was the ablest financier among the Republicans. A graduate of the University of Geneva, he had come to America in 1780. Since his election to the House of Representatives in 1795 he had made public finance his special study. In that body he had become the recognized Republican leader. Gallatin's thirteen years as Secretary of the Treasury developed a policy pleasing to his leaders and their supporters. His major care at this time was to reduce the public debt. His economy was on a fair way to achievement when foreign disturbances came to disrupt his thrifty plans.

465 Albert Gallatin, 1761–1849, from the portrait by Gilbert Stuart in the Metropolitan Museum of Art, New York

CONGRESS IS GUIDED BY RANDOLPH

With a working majority in both Houses, the administrative program fared well. Persons still confined under the Sedition Act were pardoned; the Hamiltonian whisky tax was repealed, the residence requirement for naturalization reëstablished at five years, and the army, navy and diplomatic corps reduced. The President's spokesman was John Randolph of Roanoke, who had entered the House on the wave of opposition to the Alien and Sedition Acts and was to prove a consistent strict constructionist. This led him later to break with Jefferson. But now he was administration leader and his keen wit and sarcasm were employed against the Federalist enemies. The first clash with the Federalists came early. On February 13, 1801, the hang-over Congress had passed a Judiciary Act (No. 404) which set up a machinery of courts which the Republicans considered needlessly expensive. Worse than this, Adams had in the last hours of his administration filled the sixteen new judgeships with stanch Federalists, among them defeated Congressmen. The incoming Republicans regarded the measure, and with some cause, as a partisan device designed to perpetuate Federalist power. Repeal was accomplished on March 31, 1802. "Judges created for political purposes, and for the worst of purposes under a republican government, for the purpose of opposing the National will, from this day cease to exist," rejoiced the *National Intelligencer.*

466 John Randolph of Roanoke, 1773–1833, from the portrait by Chester Harding (1792–1866) in the Corcoran Gallery of Art, Washington, D. C.

467 John Marshall, 1755–1835, from the portrait by John Wesley Jarvis (1780–1840) in the possession of R. S. Marshall, Portsmouth, Va., courtesy of the Frick Art Reference Library, New York

JEFFERSON AND MARSHALL HAVE OPPOSING VIEWS

In June, two of the new judges sitting in the Supreme Court had instructed the District Attorney to prosecute the editor of the *National Intelligencer* for libel against the Judiciary. Though the matter was dropped, it had spurred Jefferson's zeal to get rid of such partisans. Another event soon after strengthened this desire. On January 20, John Adams had nominated John Marshall of Virginia, acting Secretary of State, to be Chief Justice. Marshall had long been the subject of Jefferson's dislike, while Marshall thought no better of the new President. The opinions of the Chief Justice in the famous case of *Marbury* vs. *Madison*, 1803, were regarded by Jefferson with high indignation as an unwarranted and partisan "attempt in subversion of the individuals of the Executive Cabinet within their peculiar departments." Indeed, the contemporary criticism of Marshall's opinion was chiefly of this character; almost no attention was paid to the enunciation of that principle of judicial review that has since made *Marbury* vs. *Madison* a "leading case."

THE REPUBLICANS ATTACK THE JUDICIARY

Bit by bit, the Republicans became convinced that they could not hope to govern the country with the judiciary in the hands of hostile partisans. Hence began a general attack on the judges. They first dealt with John Pickering of the Federal District court in New Hampshire. As he was a drunkard and mentally incapacitated, it was easy to secure his impeachment by the House and removal by the Senate. Then charges were brought against Samuel Chase of the Supreme Court. Chase had been a Revolutionary hero, but since 1796 his conduct on the bench had been notoriously partisan. His handling of cases under the Alien and Sedition Acts was remembered by Republicans with hatred. He had actively campaigned for Adams in 1800. This was no unusual action for the judges of the day; but when, in May, 1803, in the course of charging a grand jury, Chase attacked the President and his principles, Jefferson gave the word to prosecute. But the House, and its manager, John Randolph, overdid it. The Senate refused to find Chase guilty. The attack on the judiciary had failed. Not until 1811 did a majority of the Supreme Court owe their selection to the Republicans; even then Marshall's personality and views continued to dominate.

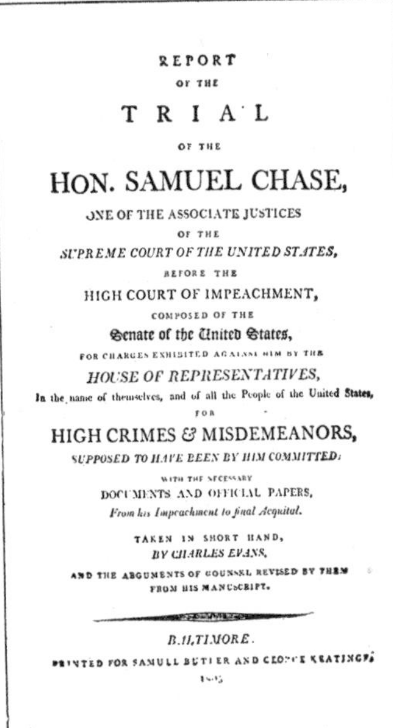

REPORT
OF THE
TRIAL
OF THE
HON. SAMUEL CHASE,
ONE OF THE ASSOCIATE JUSTICES
OF THE
SUPREME COURT OF THE UNITED STATES,
BEFORE THE
HIGH COURT OF IMPEACHMENT,
COMPOSED OF THE
Senate of the United States,
FOR CHARGES EXHIBITED AGAINST HIM BY THE
HOUSE OF REPRESENTATIVES,
In the name of themselves, and of all the People of the United States,
FOR
HIGH CRIMES & MISDEMEANORS,
SUPPOSED TO HAVE BEEN BY HIM COMMITTED:
WITH THE NECESSARY
DOCUMENTS AND OFFICIAL PAPERS,
From his Impeachment to final Acquital.
TAKEN IN SHORT HAND,
BY CHARLES EVANS,
AND THE ARGUMENTS OF COUNSEL REVISED BY THEM
FROM HIS MANUSCRIPT.

BALTIMORE.
PRINTED FOR SAMUEL BUTLER AND GEORGE KEATINGE,
[illegible]

468 Title-page of the pamphlet in the New York Public Library

469 Samuel Chase, 1741–1811, from the portrait by C. W. Peale in Independence Hall, Philadelphia

THE LOUISIANA COLONY BECOMES A CHILD OF FRANCE

MEANWHILE, the shifting currents of European politics were creating a new issue. Napoleon was master of France and eager to extend his power. War with England was closing; Talleyrand pointed to America as a fruitful scene for new glory. So on Oct. 1, 1800, by the secret treaty of San Ildefonso, Spain was persuaded to cede Louisiana to France. In March, 1802, the Peace of Amiens threw open to France the high seas. These developments perturbed the United States. No man in the country was more interested in the welfare of the West than the President. Now, when the settlement of 1763 with Spain seemed about to be reopened to the disadvantage of America he wrote Robert R. Livingston, Minister at Paris: "There is on the globe one single spot, the possessor of which is our natural and habitual enemy. It is New Orleans. . . ." So long as that outlet for the Mississippi country was in the lax and indolent hands of Spain trouble could be avoided, but once let the strongest of European countries, controlled by the indomitable ambition of Napoleon, enter the country, and American interests were at hazard.

PROCLAMATION.

AU NOM DE LA REPUBLIQUE FRANCAISE.

VERTU, PATRIE.

Le Général de Division VICTOR, Capitaine Général de la LOUISIANE.

AUX LOUISIANAIS.

CHERS LOUISIANAIS!

PAR un Traité fait entre le GOUVERNEMENT FRANCAIS ET SA MAJESTÉ LE ROI D'ESPAGNE, LA LOUISIANE est redevenue une Propriété de la République Française. Je viens au nom de son Premier Magistrat, l'immortel BONAPARTE, prendre possession de votre intéressante Colonie, & associer son sort aux brillantes destinées du Peuple Français.

Jusqu'à présent, chers Louisianais; malgré votre sage conduite, & tous vos efforts pour l'agrandissement de votre Colonie, vous n'avez pû qu'y imprimer le mouvement de votre activité, que vous conserver dans le cercle étroit de vos anciennes possessions; vous n'avez pu profiter de toutes les ressources que vous offroit pour l'agriculture, un territoire vaste & fécond; vous n'avez pu faire tourner au profit d'un commerce plus agrandi, toutes les richesses de votre heureux sol.

Je viens au nom de notre Gouvernement, vous offrir les moyens qui doivent multiplier vos jouissances; je vous apporte des loix qui ont fait la gloire de la Nation Française, comme elles assurent sa tranquilité & son bonheur. Entouré de Magistrats probes & éclairés, nous rivaliserons avec les vôtres pour établir au milieu de vous une justice incorruptible. Une administration Sage & prévoyante donnera le mouvement & la vie à l'agriculture & à toutes les branches de l'industrie & du commerce. Je vous amene enfin de nouveaux frères qui comme moi vous connoissoient assez avant de se réunir à vous, pour vous estimer & vous chérir. Désormais tous délicieusement confondus, nous n'allons plus former qu'une seule famille dont tous les membres travailleront au bonheur de chacun & à la prospérité générale. Devenu votre père, j'en aurai toute la tendresse; sans cesse j'éveillerai la sollicitude de la mere-patrie pour ajouter à ce qui pourroit manquer à la Colonie.

Chers Louisianais! ne craignez rien de cette masse imposante de Guerriers qui m'environne. La gloire qu'ils ont acquise dans les combats leur a déja mérité votre estime, les vertus qui les distinguent vous porteront à les aimer. Ils respecteront & feront respecter vos droits & vos propriétés, dans le cas où on voudroit y porter atteinte, & vous n'aurez je vous l'atteste, qu'à vous louer de leur conduite.

Quant à moi, Chers Louisianais, j'aurai assez fait pour mon bonheur si je puis assurer le vôtre par mes veilles & par mes soins.

VICTOR.

470 The French Proclamation to the people of Louisiana, 1802, from the copy in the New York Historical Society

(Translation)

In the name of the French Republic, Victor, General of Division, Captain General of Louisiana, to the Louisianians.

Dear Louisianians:

By a treaty made between the French Government and His Majesty the King of Spain, Louisiana has become a property of the French Republic. I come in the name of its First Consul, the immortal Napoleon, to take possession of your interesting Colony, and to join your fortunes to the brilliant destinies of the French People.

Up to the present time, dear Lousianians, in spite of your wise conduct, and all your efforts for the aggrandizement of your Colony, you have been able to stamp the result of your activities only within the narrow circle of your old possessions; you have not been able to take advantage of all the resources offered for agriculture in this vast and fecund territory; you have not been able to turn to the profit of a larger commerce all the rich fruits of your happy soil.

I come in the name of our Government to offer you means to multiply your pleasures; I bring you the laws that have made the glory of the French Nation, for they assure its tranquillity and its happiness. Surrounded by just and enlightened magistrates, we shall vie with you in establishing incorruptible justice in your midst. A wise and far-sighted administration will give movement and life to agriculture and to all branches of industry and of commerce. I bring you brothers like myself who even though we have not previously met you, know you well enough to esteem and cherish you. Henceforth all delightfully mingling together, we shall form a family, each one of whose members shall work for the happiness and prosperity of all. I shall feel for you the tenderness of the father that I have become; I shall show unceasingly the solicitude of the mother-country to provide the Colony with anything that it may need.

Dear Lousianians, do not fear the imposing group of warriors who surround me. The glory that they have acquired in battle merits your esteem; the virtues that distinguish them will permit you to love them. They shall respect your rights and your properties, and I assure you that you can only praise their conduct. As for myself, dear Louisianians, my happiness will be assured if I can assure your own by my watchfulness and my care.

VICTOR

471 Robert R. Livingston, 1746–1813, from the portrait about 1796 by St. Memin, in the New York Public Library

JEFFERSON USES DIPLOMACY TO AVOID WAR

RUMOR of the treaty of cession came to Washington. Before it was a certainty, the Spanish Government in New Orleans closed the port on the technical ground that the United States had failed to apply for the extension of the privilege as provided for in the Pinckney treaty of 1795. The West was aroused; but Jefferson, abhorring war, thought diplomacy might succeed. Livingston was instructed to impress France with our determination to keep the Mississippi open, and with that end in view to sound Napoleon on the purchase of West Florida and New Orleans. Monroe, Jefferson's favorite diplomat, was dispatched to aid Livingston.

472 From a sculptured group *Signing the Louisiana Treaty* by Karl Bitter (1867-1915) on the Louisiana Monument, Louisiana Purchase Exposition, St. Louis

NAPOLEON SELLS LOUISIANA TO THE UNITED STATES

THE ultimate success of the American policy was aided by several events. Napoleon's colonizing scheme rested upon the rich island of Santo Domingo, Hayti. But a successful slave uprising and the appearance of yellow fever persuaded Napoleon to abandon the island. Louisiana was now useless to him; moreover, another war with England was brewing for which he needed money. So in April, 1803, Barbé-Marbois made an offer to Livingston to sell, not simply Orleans and West Florida, but all Louisiana. After some haggling, the bargain was struck for $15,000,000. Livingston, Monroe, and Marbois signed the treaty, which added to American sovereignty more land than was contained in all the original thirteen states.

Treaty

Between the United States of America and the French Republic

The President of the United States of America and the First Consul of the French Republic in the name of the French People desiring to remove all Source of misunderstanding relative to objects of discussion mentioned in the Second and fifth articles of the Convention of the {8th Vendémiaire an 9 / 30 September 1800} relative to the rights claimed by the United States in virtue of the Treaty concluded at Madrid the 27 of October 1795, between His Catholic Majesty, & the Said United States, & willing to Strengthen the union and friendship which at the time of the Said Convention was happily reestablished between the two nations have respectively named their Plenipotentiaries to wit: The President of the United States, by and with the advice and consent of the Senate of the Said States; Robert R. Livingston Minister Plenipotentiary of the United States and James Monroe Minister Plenipotentiary and Envoy extraordinary of the Said States near the Government of the French Republic; And the First Consul in the name of the French people, Citizen Francis Barbé Marbois Minister of the public treasury who after having respectively exchanged their full powers have agreed to the following

POSSESSION OF LOUISIANA DISARMS CRITICISM

JEFFERSON was pleased and yet perturbed. The trans-Appalachian people were now assured of a trade route; but acquisition of the new territory conflicted with the doctrine of the strict construction of the Constitution he had so often announced. He even prepared an amendment to cover the matter, but fear lest Napoleon might change his mind, and also pressure from the frontier, caused it to be given up. The President summoned Congress into special session, the treaty was ratified on October 26, 1803, and the delicate point of constitutional law was overborne by the fact of actual possession.

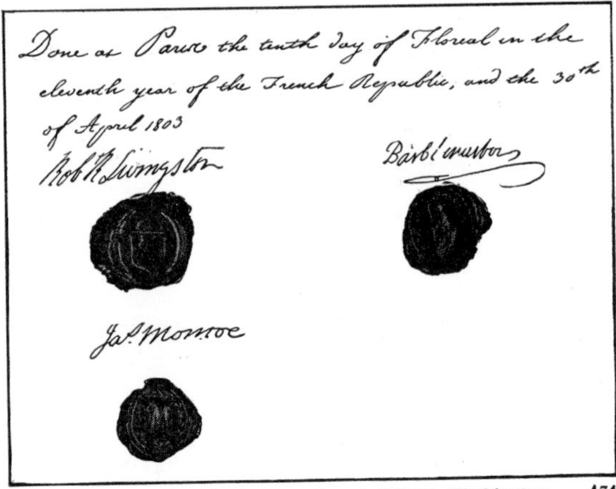
Done at Paris the tenth day of Floreal in the eleventh year of the French Republic, and the 30th of April 1803

Robt R Livingston

Barbé Marbois

Jas. Monroe

473 First and last pages of the English version of the Louisiana Treaty, April 30, 1803, original in the Department of State, Washington 474

IRRECONCILABLES SUGGEST A MOVE TOWARD DISUNION

THE Federalists could not oppose the Louisiana Purchase on grounds of strict construction, but their dislike for the "lordlings of the South" found a pretext for opposition. The treaty provided for the ultimate admission of the ceded territory into the Union as a state or states, and this meant a lessening of New England's importance in the National Government. So they advanced the doctrine that although under the Constitution territory could be annexed as a colony, admission of such territory as a state would require at least a constitutional amendment, involving the consent of three-fourths of the states. When this proposition failed of acceptance, a few irreconcilables, led by Timothy Pickering and Roger Griswold of Massachusetts, broached the advisability of secession; and, although discouraged in their designs by such Federalists as Fisher Ames and George Cabot, they considered that if they could enlist New York's support the scheme would succeed. But New York was Democratic-Republican. How could it be won? The Federalists placed their hopes on Aaron Burr.

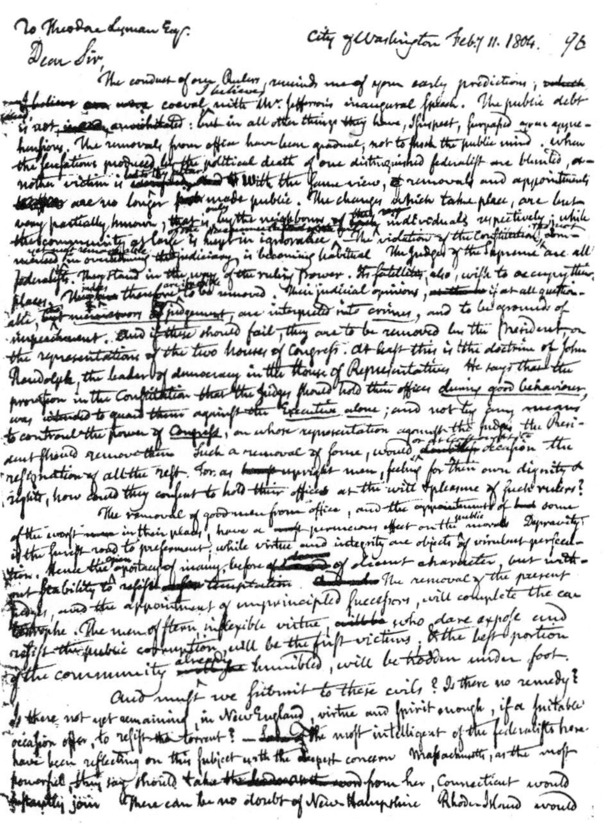

To Theodore Lyman Esq. City of Washington Feby 11. 1804. 96

Dear Sir,

The conduct of our Rulers, reminds me of your early predictions, I believe coeval with Mr. Jefferson's inaugural speech. The public debt is not annihilated: but in all other things have, I suspect, surpassed your apprehensions. The removals from office have been gradual, not to shock the public mind. When the sensations produced by the political death of one distinguished federalist are blunted, another victim is led to the altar. With the same view, removals and appointments are no longer made public. The changes which take place, are but very partially known, only by the neighbours of the individuals respectively; while the community at large is kept in ignorance. The violation of the Constitution, [illegible] in overturning the judiciary, is becoming habitual. The Judges of the Supreme are all federalists. They stand in the way of the ruling power. Its satellites, also, wish to occupy their places. The judges therefore are to be removed. Their judicial opinions, if at all questionable, the mere errors of judgment, are interpreted into crimes, and to be grounds of impeachment. And if these should fail, they are to be removed by the President, on the representation of the two houses of Congress. At least this is the doctrine of John Randolph, the leader of democracy in the House of Representatives. He says that the provision in the Constitution that the Judges should hold their offices during good behaviour, was intended to guard them against the Executive alone; and not by any means to controul the power of Congress, on whose representation against the Judges the President should remove them. Such a removal of some, would, or at least ought to occasion the resignation of all the rest. For as upright men, feeling for their own dignity & rights, how could they consent to hold offices at the will & pleasure of such rulers?

The removal of good men from office, and the appointment of some of the worst in their places, have a pernicious effect on the public morals. Depravity is the surest road to preferment; while virtue and integrity are objects of virulent persecution. Hence the open apostacy of many, before deemed of decent character, but without stability to resist temptation. The removal of the present Judges, and the appointment of unprincipled successors, will complete the catastrophe. The men of stern inflexible virtue, who dare expose and resist corruption, will be first victims; & the best portion of the community already humbled, will be trodden under foot.

And must we submit to these evils? Is there no remedy? Is there not yet remaining, in New England, virtue and spirit enough, if a suitable occasion offer, to resist the torrent? — The most intelligent of the federalists here have been reflecting on this subject with the deepest concern. Massachusetts, as the most powerful, they say should take [illegible] from her, Connecticut would instantly join. There can be no doubt of New Hampshire. Rhode Island would

475 First page of the letter from Timothy Pickering to Theodore Lyman, Feb. 11, 1804, referring to possible dissolution of the Union, original in the Massachusetts Historical Society

476 Aaron Burr, 1756–1836, from the portrait by John Vanderlyn in the New York Historical Society

FEDERALIST RELIANCE ON AARON BURR

No American career has been more checkered than Burr's. Son of Princeton's first President and grandson of Jonathan Edwards, he began life auspiciously. After serving with distinction during the war, he began in 1783 the practice of law in New York City. Owing partly to the restrictions then imposed upon Loyalist lawyers, his practice soon became highly lucrative. He also began a public career that showed him a master politician. From state offices he went in 1791 to the United States Senate. His services in the 1800 campaign were indispensable to the Republican cause; but his complicity in the Federalist jobbery resulting from that election lost him any remaining shreds of regard by the leaders of the party. Henry Adams thus characterizes the Burr of the early nineteenth century: "An aristocrat imbued with the morality of Lord Chesterfield and Napoleon Bonaparte, Colonel Burr was chosen the head of the Northern democracy. He was the idol of the wards of New York City, and aspirant to the highest offices he could reach by means legal or beyond the law; or, as he pleased himself with saying, after the manner of the First Consul of the French Republic, 'Great souls care little for small morals.'"

NEW-YORK EVENING POST.

WEDNESDAY, JULY 19.

The statement containing the facts that led to the interview between General Hamilton and Col. Burr, published in the Evening Post on Monday last, studiously avoided mentioning any particulars of what past at the place of meeting. This was dictated by suitable considerations at the time, and with the intention, that whatever it might be deemed proper to lay before the public, should be made the subject of a future communication. The following is therefore now submitted.

In the interviews that have since taken place between the gentlemen that were present, they have not been able to agree in two important facts that passed there—for which reason nothing was said on those subjects in the paper lately published as to other particulars in which they were agreed.

Mr. P. expressed a confident opinion that General Hamilton did not fire first—and that he did not fire at all *at Col. Burr.* Mr. V. N. seemed equally confident in opinion that General H. did fire first—and of course that it must have been *at* his antagonist.

General Hamilton's friend thinks it to be a sacred duty he owes to the memory of that exalted man, to his country, and his friends, to publish to the world such facts and circumstances as have produced a decisive conviction in his own mind, that he can not have been mistaken in the belief he has formed on those points—

1st. Besides the testimonies of Bishop Moore, and the paper containing an express declaration, under General Hamilton's own hand, inclosed to his friend in a packet, not to be delivered but in the event of his death, and which have already been published, General Hamilton informed Mr. P. at least ten days previous to the affair, that he had doubts whether he would not receive and not return Mr. Burr's first fire. Mr. P. remonstrated against this determination, and urged many considerations against it, as dangerous to himself and not necessary in the particular case, when every ground of accommodation, not humiliating, had been proposed and rejected. He said he would not decide lightly, but take time to deliberate fully. It was incidentally mentioned again at their occasional subsequent conversations, and on the evening preceding the time of the appointed interview, he informed Mr. P. he had made up his mind *not to fire at Col Burr the first time, but to receive his fire, and fire in the air.* Mr. P. again urged him upon this subject, and repeated his former arguments. His final answer was in terms that made an impression on Mr P.'s mind which can never be effaced. "My friend, it is the effect of A RELIGIOUS SCRUPLE, and does not admit of reasoning; it is useless to say more on the subject, as my purpose is definitively fixed."

2d His last words before he was wounded afford a proof that this purpose had not changed. When he received his pistol, after having taken his position, he was asked if he would have the hair spring set?—His answer was, "*Not this time.*"

3d. After he was wounded, and laid in the boat, the first words he uttered after recovering the power of speech, were, (addressing himself to a gentleman present, who perfectly well remembers it) "*Pendleton knows I did not mean to fire at Col. Burr the first time.*"

4th. This determination had been communicated by Mr. P. to that gentleman that morning, before they left the city.

5th. The pistol that had been used by General Hamilton, laying loose over the other apparatus in the case which was open; after having been some time in the boat, one of the boatmen took hold of it to put it into the case. General Hamilton observing this, said "*Take care of that pistol—it is cocked.—It may go off and do mischief.*" This is also remembered by the Gentleman alluded to.

This shews that he was not sensible of having fired at all. If he had fired *previous* to receiving the wound, he would have remembered it, and therefore have known that the pistol could not go off; but if *afterwards* it must have been the effect of an involuntary exertion of the muscles produced by a mortal wound, in which case, he could not have been conscious of having fired.

6. Mr. P. having so strong a conviction that if General Hamilton had fired first, it could not have escaped his attention, (all his anxiety being alive for the effect of the first fire, and having no reason to believe the friend of Col. Burr was not sincere in the contrary opinion,) he determined to go to the spot where the affair took place, to see if he could not discover some traces of the course of the ball from General Hamilton's pistol. He took a friend with him the day after General Hamilton died, and after some examination they fortunately found what they were in search of. They ascertained that the ball passed through the limb of a ceder tree, at an elevation of about twelve feet and an half, perpendicularly from the ground, between thirteen and fourteen feet from the mark on which General Hamilton stood, and about four feet wide of the direct line between him and Colonel Burr, on the right side; he having fallen on the left. The part of the limb through which the ball passed was cut off and brought to this city, and is now in Mr. Church's possession.

No inferences are pointed out as resulting from these facts, nor will any comments be made. They are left to the candid judgment and feelings of the public.

477 Contemporary comment on the Burr-Hamilton episode, from the *New York Evening Post*, July 19, 1804

THE BURR–HAMILTON DUEL

THE Federalist conspirators found Burr in complaint mood. He was in the midst of a bitter struggle for supremacy in New York politics. The antagonism of Jefferson had thrown all patronage to Burr's rivals, the Clintons and the Livingstons. He was thus in the market for support, and accepted Federalist backing in the gubernatorial race of 1804. This alliance met with the stubborn opposition of Hamilton, friend of union and foe of Burr. Burr, defeated, laid the cause at the door of Hamilton, as he had done in 1800. Angry to the core, he called upon Hamilton to make good the charges the latter had sponsored in the campaign. The duel that followed in 1804 was a momentous event. The Federalists lost a great leader, the "Northern Confederacy" foundered, and Burr was compelled to flee as a murderer.

478 Blennerhassett's Island, from an engraving by F. E. Jones after a sketch by Lizzie Forbes for *The Ladies Repository*, Feb. 1859

BURR GOES WEST

BROKEN in the East, Burr's audacious ambition led him to the West. Crossing the Alleghanies, he drifted to Blennerhassett's Island in the Ohio, near Marietta. It was the show place of the West, thanks to the mansion and estates of Harman Blennerhassett, a wealthy Irishman of good blood, born in England, who had settled here in 1798. He had surrounded himself with all the culture possible and whiled away his time with philosophy, music, and the arts.

BURR ENLISTS SUPPORT FOR A VAGUE SCHEME

With Blennerhasset was his talented wife, afterward to attain some fame as a poet. To them Burr broached a scheme which has never been fully understood. They fell in with his design and contributed money, energy, and supplies. The island became a hive of military activity. Further to insure success, Burr won the support of General Wilkinson, then in command of the army and Governor of the Louisiana Territory, and as two-faced a villain as ever served the United States Government. Other leaders of the turbulent West Burr won through magnificent fabrications of his fertile mind, the mind of a romantic politician in a romantic age.

480 General James Wilkinson, 1757–1825, from the portrait, 1808, by St. Memin in the Corcoran Gallery of Art, Washington

479 Harman Blennerhassett, 1765–1831, from William H. Safford, *The Blennerhassett Papers*, Cincinnati, 1864, after the engraving by A. H. Ritchie (1822–95)

BURR CAPTURED AND TRIED FOR TREASON

Through 1805 and 1806 Burr carried on his involved negotiations. Rumor was rife throughout the West, but the Federal authorities were slow to act. At last Jefferson became convinced of the seriousness of the movement. A presidential proclamation of November 27, 1806, called for the arrest of all involved. Wilkinson and others deserted and Burr found himself a miserable fugitive. Finally caught in Alabama, he was brought to Virginia for trial on the charge of treason.

The case was an event of unparalleled social and political interest. It was tried in the United States Circuit Court sitting at Richmond. Burr's charming daughter Theodosia won him the sympathy of many, and the court room was packed to hear and see the eminent participants. Chief Justice Marshall presided. Luther Martin and Edmund Randolph were counsel for the accused, and William Wirt for the Government. John Randolph was foreman of the grand jury. The trial was widely regarded as a test of strength between the Chief Justice and the President. Certainly Burr's acquittal on technical grounds did not lessen Jefferson's animosity toward the leader of the Federalist bench. Burr was again tried on a charge of misdemeanor and was again acquitted.

481 From the painting *The Trial of Aaron Burr* by C. W. Jefferys (1869–) in the possession of the publishers

482 The British Attack by the *Leander*, from a contemporary print published by J. J. Barralet in the collection of N. S. Bartow, courtesy of the American Art Association, New York

AMERICA SUFFERS FROM THE BRITISH–FRENCH QUARREL

MEANWHILE, despite factional quarrels arising from the centralizing tendencies of the administration, Jefferson had been triumphantly reëlected in 1804. His troubles seemed to have vanished. In December he wrote: "Peace is smoothing our path at home and abroad." In this he was unfortunately mistaken. The Peace of Amiens had been broken in the final struggle between Napoleon and England. Each employed all efforts to cripple the other, let neutrals suffer as they might. The chief neutral was the United States. After Trafalgar in 1805 England felt free to tighten her control of the seas. The competition of the American mercantile marine was proving damaging to the British merchant. The rule of 1756, forbidding neutral trade to ports closed to them in time of peace, was revived, and strengthened by an admiralty case in 1805. If France would not permit Americans to share in the trade of the French West Indies in time of peace, she should not be permitted to throw open these West Indian ports after war had been declared and after the British navy had driven the French merchant fleet from the Atlantic. In May, 1805, Fox's blockade closed French ports from Ostend to Brest to American vessels. Finding it more convenient to blockade the American coast than the European, British vessels were stationed off New York. Their policing proved highly obnoxious and occasionally warlike. The killing of John Pierce by a shot from the *Leander*, a British warship off Sandy Hook, April 28, 1806, was an unwarranted act of barbarity that aroused American resentment.

THE BLOCKADE IS TIGHTENED

NAPOLEON countered with the Berlin Decree of November, 1806, declaring a blockade of the British Isles, and confiscation of all vessels coming from England to a French port. The English ministry replied with two Orders-in-Council, of January and November, 1807, which extended Great Britain's blockade to every European port from Copenhagen to Trieste. There followed Napoleon's Milan Decree of December. By the end of 1807 any ship bound for Europe, except for Russia, Sweden, or Turkey, was liable to capture by one or the other of the warring parties.

Numb. 15990. [33]

The London Gazette.

Published by Authority.

From Tuesday January 6, to Saturday January 10, 1807.

AT the Court at the *Queen's Palace*, the 7th of *January* 1807,

PRESENT,

The KING's Most Excellent Majesty in Council.

WHEREAS the French Government has issued certain Orders, which, in Violation of the Usages of War, purport to prohibit the Commerce of all Neutral Nations with His Majesty's Dominions; and also to prevent such Nations from trading with any other Country in any Articles the Growth, Produce, or Manufacture of His Majesty's Dominions; and whereas the said Government has also taken upon itself to declare all His Majesty's Dominions to be in a State of Blockade, at a Time when the Fleets of France and her Allies are themselves confined within their own Ports by the superior Valour and Discipline of the British Navy; and whereas such Attempts on the Part of the Enemy would give to His Majesty an unquestionable Right of Retaliation, and would warrant His Majesty in enforcing the same Prohibition of all Commerce with France, which that Power vainly hopes to effect against the Commerce of His Majesty's Subjects, a Prohibition which the Superiority of His Majesty's Naval Forces might enable him to support, by actually investing the Ports and Coasts of the Enemy with numerous Squadrons and Cruizers, so as to make the Entrance or Approach thereto manifestly dangerous; and whereas His Majesty, though unwilling to follow the Example of His Enemies, by proceeding to an Extremity so distressing to all Nations not engaged in the War, and carrying on their accustomed Trade, yet feels Himself bound by a due Regard to the just Defence of the Rights and Interests of His People, not to suffer such Measures to be taken by the Enemy, without taking some Steps on His Part to restrain this Violence, and to retort upon them the Evils of their own Injustice; His Majesty is thereupon pleased, by and with the Advice of His Privy Council, to order, and it is hereby ordered, that no Vessel shall be permitted to trade from one Port to another, both which Ports shall belong to or be in the Possession of France or her Allies, or shall be so far under their Controul as that British Vessels may not freely trade thereat; and the Commanders of His Majesty's Ships of War and Privateers shall be, and are hereby instructed, to warn every Neutral Vessel coming from any such Port, and destined to another such Port, to discontinue her Voyage, and not to proceed to any such Port; and any Vessel after being so warned, or any Vessel coming from any such Port, after a reasonable Time shall have been afforded for receiving Information of this His Majesty's Order, which shall be found proceeding to another such Port, shall be captured and brought in, and, together with her Cargo, shall be condemned as lawful Prize. And His Majesty's Principal Secretaries of State, the Lords Commissioners of the Admiralty, and the Judges of the High Court of Admiralty and Courts of Vice-Admiralty, are to take the necessary Measures herein as to them shall respectively appertain.

W. Fawkener.

Die Mercurij, 31° Decembris 1806.

ORDERED, by the Lords Spiritual and Temporal, in Parliament assembled, That this House will not receive any Petition for a private Bill after Friday the 27th of February next.

Ordered, That this House will not receive any Report from the Judges upon Petitions presented to this House for private Bills, after the first Day of Meeting after the Recess at Easter.

483 British Order-in-Council, dated Jan. 1807, from the *London Gazette*, 1807

THE EUROPEAN WAR IS CARRIED INTO AMERICA

In theory, there was little to choose between the two belligerent nations. At first Americans sided with one or the other as party tradition dictated. The Federalists fancied war with France, the Republicans war with England. At any rate, a foreign issue was once again intruded into American politics and Jefferson's hopes for peace were rudely shattered. Jefferson desired peace and endeavored to maintain an honorable neutrality. But Britain's command of the sea rendered her conduct more odious in effect than the equally dictatorial policy of Napoleon. So it was against England that Jefferson directed his neutralization scheme. For long he had believed that America could maintain peace under such trying conditions by the use of a policy of commercial discrimination. He had witnessed the success of the non-importation agreements of colonial days; he revived the method now. In March, 1806, a Non-Importation Act was passed excluding such British goods as were not essential to America. Before this mild measure became operative he sent William Pinkney to London to negotiate a treaty which should restore mutual confidence. But the treaty proved so advantageous to Great Britain that Jefferson rejected it without submitting it to the Senate.

The finiſhing

STROKE.

Every Shot's a Vote,

And every Vote

KILLS A TORY!

DO YOUR DUTY, REPUBLICANS

Let your exertions this day

Put down the Kings

AND TYRANTS OF BRITAIN.

LAST DAY.

April, 1807.

484 Republican broadside, 1807, directed against "British" Federalists, from the copy in the New York Historical Society

Wednesday, July 8, 1807.

BY THOMAS JEFFERSON,

PRESIDENT OF THE U. STATES OF AMERICA,

A Proclamation.

During the wars which, for some time, have unhappily prevailed among the powers of Europe, the United States of America, firm in their principles of peace, have endeavored by justice, by a regular discharge of all their national and social duties, and by every friendly office their situation has admitted, to maintain, with all the belligerents, their accustomed relations of friendship, hospitality, and commercial intercourse.—Taking no part in the questions which animate these powers against each other, nor permitting themselves to entertain a wish but for the restoration of general peace, they have observed with good faith the neutrality they assumed, and they believe that no instance of a departure from its duties can be justly imputed to them by any nation. A free use of their harbors and waters, the means of refitting and of refreshment, of succour to their sick and suffering, have, at all times, and on equal principles, been extended to all, and this too amidst a constant recurrence of acts of insubordination to the laws, of violence to the persons, and of trespasses on the property of our citizens, committed by officers of one of the belligerent parties received among us. In truth these abuses of the laws of hospitality have, with few exceptions, become habitual to the commanders of the British armed vessels hovering on our coasts, and frequenting our harbors. They have been the subject of repeated representations to their government. Assurances have been given that proper orders should restrain them within the limit of the rights and of the respect due to a friendly nation: but those orders and assurances have been without effect; no instance of punishment for past wrongs has taken place.

At length, a deed, transcending all we have hitherto seen or suffered, brings the public sensibility to a serious crisis, and our forbearance to a necessary pause. A frigate of the U. States trusting to a state of peace, and leaving her harbor on a distant service, has been surprised and attacked by a British vessel of superior force, one of a squadron then lying in our waters and covering the transaction, and has been disabled from service, with the loss of a number of men killed and wounded. This enormity was not only without provocation or justifiable cause, but was committed with the avowed purpose of taking by force, from a ship of war of the United States, a part of her crew; and that no circumstance might be wanting to mark its character, it had been previously ascertained that the seamen demanded were native citizens of the United States. Having effected his purpose, he returned to anchor with his squadron within our jurisdiction. Hospitality under such circumstances ceases to be a duty: and a continuance of it, with such uncontrolled abuses, would tend only by multiplying injuries and irritations, to bring on a rupture between the two nations. This extreme resort is equally opposed to the interest of both, as it is to assurances of the most friendly dispositions on the part of the British government, in the midst of which this outrage has been committed. In this light the subject cannot but present itself to that government and strengthen the motives to an honorable reparation of the wrong which has been done, and to that effectual control of its naval commanders, which alone can justify the government of the United States in the exercise of those hospitalities it is now constrained to discontinue.

In consideration of these circumstances and the right of every nation to regulate its own police, to provide for its peace and for the safety of its citizens, and consequently to refuse the admission of armed vessels into its harbors or waters, either in such numbers or of such descriptions, as are inconsistent with these, or with the maintenance of the authority of the laws, I have thought proper in pursuance of the authorities specially given by law to issue this my Proclamation, hereby requiring all armed vessels bearing commissions under the government of Great Britain, now within the harbors or waters of the United States, immediately and without any delay to depart from the same, and interdicting the entrance of all the said harbors and waters to the said armed vessels, and to all others bearing commissions under the authority of the British government.

And if the said vessels, or any of them, shall fail to depart as aforesaid, or if they or any others so interdicted, shall hereafter enter the harbors or waters aforesaid, I do in that case forbid all intercourse with them or any of them, their officers or crews, and do prohibit all supplies and aid from being furnished to them or any of them

And I do declare and make known, that if any person from, or within the jurisdictional limits of the U. States, shall afford any aid to any such vessel, contrary to the prohibition contained in this proclamation, either in repairing any such vessel, or in furnishing her, her officers or crew, with supplies of any kind, or in any manner whatsoever, or if any pilot shall assist in navigating any of the said armed vessels, unless it be for the purpose of carrying them in the first instance beyond the limits and jurisdiction of the U. S. or unless it be in the case of a vessel forced by distress, or charged with public dispatches, as hereinafter provided for, such person or persons shall, on conviction, suffer all the pains and penalties by the laws provided for such offences.

And I do hereby enjoin and require all persons bearing offices civil or military within or under the authority of the U. States, and all others, citizens or inhabitants thereof, or being within the same, with vigilance and promptitude to exert their respective authorities, and to be aiding and assisting to the carrying this proclamation and every part thereof into full effect.

Provided nevertheless, That if any such vessels shall be forced into the harbors or waters of the United States, by distress, by the dangers of the sea, or by the pursuit of an enemy, or shall enter them charged with the dispatches or business from their government, or shall be a public packet for the conveyance of letters and dispatches, the commanding officer immediately reporting his vessel to the collector of the district, stating the object or causes of entering the said harbors or waters, and conforming himself to the regulations in that case prescribed under the authority of the laws, shall be allowed the benefit of such regulations respecting repairs, supplies, stay, intercourse and departure as shall be permitted under the same authority.

In testimony whereof, I have caused the seal of the United States to be affixed to these presents and signed the same.

Given at the city of Washington the second day of July, in the year of our Lord one thousand eight hundred and seven, and of the sovereignty and independence of the United States the thirty-first.

TH: JEFFERSON.

BY THE PRESIDENT.

JAMES MADISON,

Secretary of State

485 Proclamation of July 2, 1807, barring British warships from American harbors, from the copy in the New York Historical Society

JEFFERSON RESISTS BRITISH IMPOSITIONS

Shortly thereafter a further strain was placed upon Jefferson's conciliatory temper. Great Britain had never ceased to insist upon the inalienability of British allegiance, as applied to sailors in foreign service. Now, with American commerce flourishing, high wages brought many desertions from the English merchant marine and navy. So the policy of impressment was resumed. This came to a head in June, 1807, when the *Leopard* fired upon, stopped, and took several men from the United States frigate *Chesapeake.*

TENTH CONGRESS OF THE UNITED STATES;

At the First Session,

Begun and held at the city of Washington, in the territory of Columbia, on Monday the twenty-sixth of October, one thousand eight hundred and seven.

AN ACT laying an embargo on all ships and vessels in the ports and harbors of the United States.

Be it enacted by the Senate and House of Representatives of the United States of America, in Congress assembled, That [illegible]

486 The Embargo Act, 1807, from the original in the Department of State, Washington

FOREIGN COMMERCE IS FORBIDDEN

Such incidents convinced the President that stiffer measures must be taken. He, therefore, pushed the Non-Importation Act further in the Embargo Act of December, 1807. All foreign commerce was, for an indefinite future, prohibited.

SMUGGLING THRIVES UNDER EMBARGO

Enforcement of such a drastic policy proved harder than enactment. Shipowners and merchants were loath to surrender a highly profitable, if dangerous, trade. As prices fell, even the farmers began to resent the policy of passive coercion. Smuggling throve, despite rigorous enforcement measures, passed in 1808; even rowboats were subject to surveillance.

THE EMBARGO,

A SONG COMPOSED AND SUNG AT DOVER. *JULY* 4th, 1808.

[*TUNE—Come let us prepare—*]

DEAR Sirs, it is wrong
To demand a *New Song*;
I have let all the breath I can ſpare, go;
With the Muſe I've confer'd,
And ſhe won't ſay a word,
But keeps laughing about the EMBARGO.

I wiſh that I could
Sing in *Alegro* mood,
But the times are as ſtupid as *Largo*;
Could I have my choice,
I would ſtrain up my voice,
'Till it *ſnapt* all the *ſtrings* of EMBARGO.

Our great politicians,
Thoſe dealers in viſions,
On *paper* to all lengths will dare go;
But when call'd to decide,
Like a *turtle* they hide,
In their own pretty *ſhell* the EMBARGO.

In the time that we try,
To put out Britains *eye*,
I fear we ſhall let our own *pair* go;
But yet we're ſo wiſe,
We can ſee with French eyes,
And then we ſhall like the EMBARGO.

A French privateer
Can have nothing to fear; [go;
She may load, and may hear or may there
Their friendſhip is ſuch
And we love them ſo much,
We let them ſlip thro' the EMBARGO.

Our ſhips all in motion
Once whiten'd the ocean;
They ſail'd and return'd with a Cargo
Now doom'd to decay,
They are fallen a prey,
To Jefferſon, worms, and EMBARGO.

Leſt Britain ſhould take
A few men by miſtake,
Who under falſe colors may dare go;
We're manning their fleet
With our Tars, that retreat
From poverty, ſloth, and EMBARGO.

What a *fuſs* we have made,
About rights and *free trade*,
And ſwore we'd not let our own ſhare go;
Now we can't for our ſouls
Bring a Hake from the *ſhoals*,
'Tis a breach of the *twentieth* EMBARGO.

Our Farmers ſo gay,
How they gallop'd away,
'Twas money that made the old mare go;
But now ſhe wont ſtir,
For the whip or the ſpur,
'Till they take off her *clog*, the EMBARGO.

If you aſk for a debt,
The man turns in a *pet*,
"I pay ſir? I'll not let a hair go;
"If your officer comes,
"I ſhall put up my thumbs,
"And clap on his breath an EMBARGO."

Thus Thommy deſtroys,
A great part of our joys;
Yet we'll not let the beautiful fair, go;
They all will contrive
To keep commerce alive,
There's nothing they hate like EMBARGO.

Since rulers deſign,
To deprive us of wine,
'Tis beſt that we now have a *rare go*;
Then each to his poſt,
And ſee who will do moſt,
To knock out the blocks of EMBARGO.

PRINTED and for ſale by J. K. REMICH, at his Printing Office on Dover Landing.

487 A British political song on the Embargo, from the copy in the New York Historical Society

REAL FRENCH PIRACY.

AMERICANS!
See the EXECUTION of BONAPARTE's Orders to Burn, Sink, and Destroy your Ships!

Look on this Picture! Read the transactions on which it is founded; and then Vote for *Sullivan*, or any other Partizan of France if you can!!

BOSTON, March 30.

American Commerce in Flames;
OR REAL FRENCH
PIRACY AND BARBARI[TY]

☞ AMERICANS! Ye who y
of French Benevolence! Who yet
French Alliance! And who yet f
the Friends of *French Measures!*
REFLECT! And then before you
listen to the warnings of your Consci

FACTS ON OATH.

On Monday last, arrived here, the ship
hontas commanded by Capt. HARRIS of
ton, in 32 days from Liverpool; and ha
protest before a Notary Public, of the fa
the following statement:—

That on March 1, 1808, in lat. 4
10 W. she was brought to, and b
from the French Frigate La Hermion
Hortense, of 40 guns each: which h
been to the West Indies with troops,
on the return, and were then cruizi
the mouth of the Channel. Immed
on the French officers' boarding,
Harris was ordered on board the F
Commodore; and directions were
that the stores should be removed
the Pocahontas, and the ship BUR
These orders were afterwards co
manded; the stores returned, and
Harris was compelled to take on
Forty-Seven Persons, belonging to t
lowing American SHIPS, which ha
TAKEN and BURNT by the Fren
tional frigates, viz.

William, Rockwell, from Liverpool f
vannah—

Brutus of Duxbury, Smith, from
pool.

Eliza, Dunbar, from Liverpool, for
York.

The Pocahontas thus escaped conflag
from the necessity the French were u
getting rid of the American prisoners, b
want of provisions; but before they l
they flung into the sea all the crates o
they could come at; seized the letters,
&c. and wantonly destroyed them; an
Harris was then compelled to steer to th
ward. On the passage, Capt. H. fell
the ship Baltic, Capt. Delano, who h
goodness to take twenty of the Americ
cluding Capts. Rockwell and Dunbar,
—the others including Capt. Smith,
here in the Pocahontas, and are living w
of this wickedness and wantonness of
outrages.

FURTHER FACTS.

The William and Brutus, before men
sailed in company from Liverpool with t
cahontas; they all had salt and crates on
Several other American vessels sailed in c
ny, some of whom were supposed to be
eastward of the frigates: That the Fren
wished to fall in with some vessel wi
goods, and intended to look out for th
Capt. Lewis, of this port, who was to s
after, the Ceres, Capt. Webber, and other
the American vessels belonging to this po

REFLECTIONS.

If we complain of the decisions of the British Admiralty Courts, when without any treaty to guide them,—if we condemn the conduct of

488 Federalist broadside on French piracy, published at Boston, 1808, from the copy in the American Antiquarian Society, Worcester, Mass.

THE EMBARGO IS THE CAMPAIGN ISSUE

UNDER such circumstances occurred the election of 1808. Madison was the administration candidate; C. C. Pinckney of South Carolina stood again for the Federalists. John Randolph attempted to win support for Monroe in opposition to the Government. Throughout the states the election turned upon the issue of the embargo. Federalists denounced the Government for ruining trade and accused it of blindness to French maltreatment. The Republicans replied in kind, in manifestoes exploiting British truculence toward America. Once again, a foreign issue threw a shadow over domestic policy, and caused threats of secession to be made. New England after eight years of Republican rule and with four more in prospect was growing restive.

British Barbarity and Piracy!!

The Federalists say that Mr. Christopher Gore ought to be supported as Governor—for *his attachment to Britain.*—If British influence is to effect the suffrages of a free people, let them read the following melancholy and outrageous conduct of British Piracy, and judge for themselves.

The "LEOPARD OUTSPOTTED" or Chesapeak Outrage outdone.

The account of the *outrageous* proceeding of the British on American vessels and property at Canton must have been known here by the arrival of the brig Caravan, Capt. Gilchrist but the owners are the relations of TIMOTHY PICKERING whose attachment to Britain prevented his attacking British troops after they had killed his countrymen.

The Caravan Capt. Gilchrist, arrived last monday at noon, and belongs to Timothy Williams and Mr. Pratt of Boston—and all information relative to the following infamous transaction has been suppressed here.

From the New York Gazette and General Advertiser of monday March 21st. The following narrative of the transaction at China in 1807, appeared in the evening paper of Saturday—We understand that the documents in support of the statement have been forwarded on to the secretary of state at Washington.

FACTS

Respecting the treatment of Americans by the commanders of British vessels of war, within the neutral waters of the empire of China, in 1807.

The brig Caravan, captain Gilchrist, arrived at Macao, and was boarded by an officer from his majesty's brig Diana Lieutenant Kempthorne commander. The officers had orders to take out a Frenchman, who had been impressed by the captain of a British vessel in the Straits of Malacca, but returned by order of the commander in chief on that station. Captain Gilchrist refused to deliver him, alleging his engagements to perform the voyage, and reminding the officer of his former impressments. The next morning the Caravan was again boarded, and the demand for the Frenchman renewed, when the officer was informed that he had left the brig, and was allowed to search. As his search was unsuccessful, he took a Dutchman, who was shortly after returned, and informed captain Gilchrist he had orders to take his carpenter, provided the Frenchman could not be found. He was told in reply, that the Frenchman was not on board, and that he should not have the carpenter. At this time, the Caravan having her pilot on board, had got underway to run up the river, and the Diana was under way to the windward of her. As soon as the officer reached the Diana she bore away, just stern on the Caravan, when lieutenant Kempthorne, and thirty or forty men armed with cutlasses and pistols, boarded and demanded the Frenchman or the carpenter.

Captain Gilchrist replied, that no man should be taken but himself, and ordered his carpenter below. Kempthorne ordered his seamen to seize some of the crew, which capt. Gilchrist opposing, Kempthorne directed them to seize him. This they attempted to do; as he was rescuing one of his seaman, cut him across the hand, disarmed and threw him upon deck, where they tied him and his first officer. They next tied a rope round his second officer, threw him overboard, and dragged him on board the Diana!

This outrageous exercise of power, ended by the release of captain Gilchrist and the return of his officer, and permission to proceed to Whampoa. A few days after arrived the schooner Topaze, captain Nichols, owned by Messrs. Smith† and Buchanan of Baltimore, and was examined by an officer from the Diana. The next day, the 8th of August, three English and one American seamen, belonging to the schooner, sent a letter to lieutenant Kempthorne, expressing a wish to leave the schooner and enter his Majesty's service, and requesting a boat might be sent for them which was done, and a demand made by Kempthorne for their wages, which being refused, he found some money of the schooner's, by directions of one of the runaway seamen, paid them himself, and returned on board his vessel. He was there informed by these sailors, that the schooner had been committing piratical depredations on the South west coast of America, firing at and plundering under English colours, three Spanish brigs. Without questioning their veracity, he immediately armed his boats, and proceeded for the schooner. She was under way running in for the Portuguese harbor, called the Type, by permission of the governor of Macao. As the boat approached, captain Nichols desired them to keep off; determined as is supposed, not to suffer the same insults that had been offered to capt. Gilchrist; and as the boats still approached, he presented a blunderbuss at the nearest; the men from which boarded almost immediately. Lieutenant Kempthorne was slightly wounded on the temple, and knocked overboard. The boat then dropped astern to pick him up, which having done, they boarded on each quarter, wounded two men and a boy, and forced their whole crew to retreat forward, where capt. Nichols was *shot through the body* by the sailing master of the brig, and expired immediately. The remainder of the crew fled to the forecastle, and the schooner remained entirely in the possession of the British, who mov'd her alongside the Diana, and shifted her * cargo into the latter without further ceremony.

Shortly after arrived the Phaeton, Capt. Pellew, who approved of Lieut. Kempthorne's conduct, took the deposition of the seamen belonging to the schooner, and although not a circumstance transpired to induce the public to place any belief in the assertions of the disaffected seamen, ordered her for Bombay for trial on suspicion of piracy. A request was made a few hours afterwards to Lieut. Kempthorne, by an American gentleman at Macao, for the body of Capt. Nichols, who informed him that it was *already buried*.‡ The Americans soon learnt with mingled emotions of *regret and indignation, that it had been committed to the waves without form or ceremony.* They were however to be further insulted by Capt. Pellew. He had impressed from the Belisarius‡ several American seamen, and although proofs were forwarded, taken by the American Consul, Mr. Carrington, of their citizenship, not only refused to give them up, but returned an insolent reply to the letter which accompanied them. He had on board his ship a British seaman, impressed from the ship Fair American, Capt. Conckling, two years preceding, and who had received from Capt. Concklin, duplicate drafts for his wages, upon a House in London. As the sailor had kept one of the drafts, an application was made to Capt. Concklin on his arrival at Macoa, in the Gen. Clarkson, for the payment of it. This was refused, unless the other could be produced, or a protest to shew it had not been paid by his agents in London. The Gen. Clarkson proceeded for Whampoa, though Capt. Pellew threatened if the draft was not paid to fire into her while getting under way. The draft was shortly forwarded to Mr. Carrington, with a demand for payment, and for the payment of the wages due the men impressed from the Belisarius; and a threat, that in case of refusal, he would send his boats and take out six men from the Clarkson, in addition to the two he had before taken. Ere any reply had been returned to this letter, another was received by Mr. Carrington, importing, that Capt. Pellew had heard of a combination among the American captains, to defend their vessels from being boarded at Whampoa, and to render each other assistance in case the Phaeton's boats should attempt it; and that he was determined, in case the bill was not immediately paid, together with the wages, before demanded, to send 200 men on board the Company's ship Retreat, lying at Whampoa, haul her along side the Clarkson, and enforce his demands. This letter was by Mr. Carrington communicated to the American captains at Canton, who immediately made such arrangements as were thought necessary to repel an attack. Fortunately the Hang Merchants became alarmed, and by a speedy interference obliged Capt. Pellew to relinquish his intentions.

The British ships anchor at the mouth of the river Tigris, and bring too and examine all vessels. As they have the power, they contend for the right of exercising jurisdiction within the neutral waters of China, and as the Chinese honor is not sensible to insult of this nature, it is propable they will continue the exercise of their assumed rights, till the American government shall interfere for its prevention.

† *Samuel Smith of Baltimore, one of the owners, is a senator from Maryland.*

* *One hundred and sixty thousand dollars in specie.*

† *Thrown overboard.*

‡ *Belisarius, Brown, of Boston.*

BOSTON, March 25, 1808.

489 A Republican broadside, Boston, March 25, 1808, from the copy in the New York Historical Society

490 James Madison, 1751–1836, from the portrait by Asher B. Durand (1796–1886) in the New York Historical Society

MADISON BECOMES PRESIDENT

All the New England states, except Vermont, cast their votes for Pinckney, alleging that Jefferson's tactics were aimed at ruining their section of the country. Madison, however, won a majority of the electoral college and entered the presidency. He had behind him a long and distinguished career in the public service, but he had worked largely in the capacity of lieutenant to some more vigorous captain. An excellent staff officer, Madison proved a weak leader. He is described as "possessing a calm expression and a penetrating blue eye; he looked like a thinking man." Small and plump, he was slow of speech and action. Though Jefferson retained an active interest in affairs, his master-hand was absent. Congressional factions assumed the power which Madison knew not how to use.

NEW ENGLAND AGITATES FOR EMBARGO REPEAL

Even before the close of Jefferson's administration the embargo had fallen. As its burden grew steadily greater, agitation in New England called for its repeal. Town meetings hotly debated the issue and sent petitions to Congress.

Town Meeting.

To the Inhabitants of the Town of Salem.

Fellow Citizens,

You well know that your Selectmen have been decidedly of opinion that it was altogether *unnecessary*, *inexpedient*, and *improper* for the Town of Salem to interfere with the General Government upon the question of removing the Embargo:—but as a legal number of the inhabitants of this town have requested them to call a meeting for the purpose of petitioning Congress on the subject, they have deemed it their duty pursuant to the request of Benjamin Pickman, jun. Esq. and others, to issue and publish the following warrant, &c.

Per Order.

JOHN PUNCHARD, *Town Clerk.*

To ——— ——— *one of the Constables of the Town of Salem.*

You are hereby required forthwith to notify and warn the Freeholders and other Inhabitants of the Town of Salem, qualified to vote in Town affairs in Ward No. —, to assemble at the Meeting house called the Tabernacle in said Salem on Wednesday, the 26th inst. at 9 o'clock, A.M. to know if the Town will adopt the following Petition, to be presented to Congress as soon as may be after their next meeting.

[*Signed by the Selectmen.*]

PROPOSED PETITION.

"*To the Honorable the Senate, and the Honorable the House of Representatives of the United States, in Congress assembled.*

The Inhabitants of Salem in the State of Massachusetts, convened in legal Town Meeting, respectfully represent,

That in consequence of their local situation they are almost wholly dependant upon foreign commerce for their subsistence. They have therefore seen with the deepest concern the continuance of the late laws which have interdicted all such commerce, and subjected the coasting trade to unusual and severe restrictions. By the operation of these laws, the people, particularly the poorer and middling classes, have already suffered great distress, and the season is rapidly approaching when they are to feel with still greater severity the want of those necessaries of life which they have heretofore been able to obtain by their habitual employment.

It now appears that these restrictive measures which have been defended on the expectation that they would induce the belligerents to rescind their unjust decrees and orders, have wholly failed of producing that effect. But amidst the distress which exists, it gives your Petitioners singular satisfaction that a prospect is offered of opening a beneficial trade with the kingdoms of Spain and Portugal, and their colonies, by the patriotic exertions of those nations who are struggling for a government of their own choice, and for their national Independence. And if it is a duty, it must be a gratification to the feelings of the people of the United States to aid by a mutually advantageous commerce, the generous efforts of that nation which was the first to recognize the independence of our own Country.

Your Petitioners further represent, that they consider Commerce as essential to the strength and prosperity of the United States, and to the support and encouragement of Agriculture and the Fisheries, and they cannot for a moment admit an idea that it is to be forever abandoned for the establishment of Manufactures. Under these convictions, and from an apprehension that Commerce if long diverted from, may never return into its accustomed channels, as well as from a regard to their own rights, and those of their posterity,—they pray that the several laws laying these interdictions may be repealed.

The foregoing is a copy of the substance of the warrant, and a true copy of the proposed Petition.

Attest, JOHN PUNCHARD, *Town Clerk.*

To all real Americans and Friends of the Country.

You are called upon solemnly, to attend the Town-Meeting, as warned above, to act on the foregoing petition. The government of your country have been endeavoring to maintain your rights and liberties as an independent nation against G. Britain and France; to protect our Seamen from impressment, and our trade from destruction; to resist taxation by the British Government upon our fair and honorable commerce; and to save our property from the avarice and injustice of privateers and ships of war. The embargo has been laid for these purposes, and the foregoing petition calls upon you to desert the government and give yourselves up to the mercy and injustice of the belligerent powers. Have you no confidence in the government of your own choice? Are you willing continually to encourage foreign nations to infringe your rights by publicly avowing your determination not to bear any inconvenience to which a vindication of them will subject you? —If, like the Patriots of 1775, you are willing to bear all things rather than submit to be taxed by Great Britain, come forth and declare it, AND VOTE AGAINST THIS PETITION.

A CAUCUS will be held by the *True Americans*, this Evening at 6 o'clock, at

WASHINGTON HALL.

Attend, and shew your enemies the strength of the good old cause of Independence.

Salem, Oct. 25, 1808.

491 Town Meeting broadside, Salem, Mass., Oct. 25, 1808, from the copy in the American Antiquarian Society, Worcester, Mass.

At a General Assembly of the State of Connecticut holden at New Haven on the Second Thursday of October A.D. 1808. ——

The interests of all classes of our citizens, being deeply and extensively affected, by acts interdicting our commerce, and it being, by this assembly, considered expedient, in such a crises, to express the sentiments of this state:

Res. I. Resolved; that altho' the share, which, the People have, in the government, of the United States, is, on ordinary occasions, the best security, of the public welfare; and altho' the good people of this state rely with unabated confidence, on the wisdom and integrity, of the Senators, and Representatives, from this state, in the congress of the United States; yet, in this unprecedented crisis, silence on the part of this legislature, might be construed, to imply the want of a disposition to protect, or an intention to betray, the dearest rights of our constituents. —

Resolved; that deeply impressed with these truths we have deliberately examined into the tendency and operation of the acts, interdicting foreign commercial enterprizes; and while we yield to none, in an affectionate attachment to the constitution of the United States; and claim no right of immediate interference, in the foreign relations of our country; we maintain; that the right freely, to navigate the ocean, was like our soil, transmitted to us, as an inheritance from our forefathers; and that, the enjoyment of this right, is secured to us, as a free and sovereign state, by the plighted faith, of the United States. —

Resolved; that while we admit the power, vested in congress, to regulate commerce, to restrain or suspend it, for short and definitive periods, as a measure of precaution or internal police, preliminary to efficient measures of ulterior defences, we cannot refrain from expressing an opinion, that to interdict it indefinitely, is a measure, partial in its operation not only imposing unequal and intolerable burden on the carrying and commercial states, but abandoning invaluable rights reserved and guaranteed by solemn compact. —

Resolved; that on this fair exposition of the great charter of our rights, we consider the acts, interdicting foreign commerce, incompatible with justice and good faith, in regard to the carrying and commercial states, and deplore the existence of a system of statutes and

492 Connecticut Resolutions on the Embargo, Oct. 1808, from the original in the Connecticut State Archives, Hartford

regulations so novel in principle and not enforced through the mild medium of courts of justice, but by executive edicts, and military and maritime force; That we view with regret, this extension of the executive power and the continuance of a policy ruinous to ourselves and inefficient in preventing the aggressions of foreign nations. —

Resolved; that while we deprecate wars, waged from motives of ambition, partiality or prejudice or for national aggrandizement, or in the uncertain expectation of results which if realized, have no practical value and bring with them no compensation for the calamities, through which they are gained: yet steady and persevering in the usages, habits, and principles of our forefathers; and, like them, born free, we retain the strongest love of liberty; and will never surrender it to the artifice or arms, of any foreign power; that for the security of a blessing so inestimable it becomes a great and magnanimous nation to cherish and employ efficient means of defence. —

Resolved; that the good people of this state are enduring restrictions upon their commerce, which on cool and impartial consideration appear to this assembly to be unnecessary and grievous; that we rely nevertheless in their further patient and faithfull regard to public order in the hope that the congress of the United States will at their approaching session, on a knowledge of their distresses speedily decide that a removal of them is compatible with the peace, honor, and happiness of the United States. — — —

General Assembly Octr. session 1808. } John Cotton Smith Speaker of the House of Representatives —

Jona Trumbull Govr

Attest Samuel Wyllys Secretary

493 Connecticut Resolutions on the Embargo, Oct. 1808, from the original in the Connecticut State Archives, Hartford

NORTHERN STATES RESENT THE POWER OF THE CENTRAL GOVERNMENT

THE doctrine of state rights was for the moment borrowed from the Republicans and applied to the measures of Jefferson. Partisan legislatures in Massachusetts, Connecticut, Rhode Island and Delaware passed resolutions denouncing the tyranny of the central government. The Connecticut Resolutions on the Embargo concluded, on behalf of the aggrieved people, with the "hope that the Congress of the United States will, at their approaching session, on a knowledge of their distresses, speedily decide that a removal of them is compatible with the peace, honor and happiness of the United States."

This Assembly have attended with anxious concern to the several acts of Congress interdicting foreign commerce and more especially to an act approved on the 9th day of January last by the President of the United States under the title of "An Act to enforce and make more effectual an act laying an Embargo on all ships and vessels in the ports and harbours of the United States"

After solemn deliberation and advisement thereon the General Assembly are decided in opinion and do Resolve that the acts aforesaid are a permanent system of measures abandoning unalienable rights, introducing the exercise of unconstitutional privileges, and unprecedented on the annals of nations, and do contain provisions for exercising arbitrary powers grievous to the good people of this State dangerous to their common liberties, incompatible with the Constitution of the United States and encroaching upon the immunities of this State.

Resolved That to preserve the Union and support the Constitution of the United States, it becomes the duty of the Legislatures of the States in such a crisis of affairs vigilantly to watch over and vigorously to maintain the powers not delegated to the United States but reserved to the States respectively or to the people. And that a due regard to this duty will not permit this Assembly to assist or concur in giving effect to the aforesaid unconstitutional acts.

Resolved That this Assembly highly approve of the conduct of his Excellency the Governor in declining to designate persons to carry into effect by the aid of military power the Act of the United States enforcing the Embargo; And that his letter addressed to the Secretary for the department of War, containing his refusal to make such designation be recorded in the public records of this State as an example to persons who may hold places of distinguished trust in this free and independent republic.

Resolved That the persons holding executive offices under this State are restrained by the duties which they owe this State from affording any official aid or cooperation in the execution of the Acts aforesaid and that his Excellency the Governor be requested as Commander in Chief of the military force of this State to cause these resolutions to be published in General Orders: And that the Secretary of this State be and he is hereby directed to transmit copies of the same to the several Sheriffs and Town Clerks.

Resolved That his Excellency the Governor be requested to communicate the foregoing resolutions to the President of the United States with an assurance that this Assembly regret that they are thus obliged under a sense of paramount public duty to assert the unquestionable rights of this State, to abstain from any agency in the execution of measures which are unconstitutional and despotic.

Resolved That this Assembly accord in sentiment with the Senate and House of Representatives of the Commonwealth of Massachusetts that it is expedient to effect certain alterations in the Constitution of the United States; and will zealously cooperate with the Commonwealth and any other of the States, in all legal and constitutional measures for procuring such amendments to the Constitution of the United States as shall be judged necessary to obtain more effectually protection and defence for Commerce; and to give to the commercial States their fair and just consideration in the Union and for affording permanent security, as well as present relief from the oppressive measures under which they now suffer.

7. Resolved that his Excellency the Governor be requested to transmit copies of the foregoing resolutions to the President of the Senate, and Speaker of the house of Representatives in the Commonwealth of Massachusetts and to the Legislatures of such of our Sister States as manifest a disposition to concur, in restoring to commerce the former activity and preventing the repetition of measures which have a tendency not only to destroy it but to dissolve the Union, which ought to be inviolate.

Extra Session
February 1809.

Passed in the House of Representatives with the following amendments, to wit by striking out the last word in the second resolution and inserting these words "act professing to enforce the embargo" - also by striking out the word acts in the fourth line of the fourth resolution and insert in lieu thereof the word "act"

Concurred in the Upper House
Test Saml Wyllys Secretary — Saml Rowland Clerk

494 Connecticut Resolutions on the Embargo, Feb. 1809 (Extra Session), from the original in the Connecticut State Archives, Hartford

CONNECTICUT DEFIES THE SECRETARY OF WAR

In Connecticut, where were large commercial interests — Federalist in politics — opposition went to the extreme of nullification. On receipt of a letter from the Secretary of War, asking the Governor to assign militia officers "of known respect for the laws" to aid in enforcement of the embargo, Governor Trumbull sent a declination, and called the legislature into special session. To that body he presented his justification. "Whenever our national legislature is led to overleap the prescribed bounds of their constitutional powers, on the state legislatures, in great emergencies, devolves the arduous task — it is their right — it becomes their duty, to interpose their protecting shield between the right and liberty of the people, and the assumed power of the general government." This stand the legislature approved, and in a series of resolutions restated the condemnation of the "Enforcement Act." It issued an "Address to the People," and angled for support from the other New England states. One spirited response to the measure was *The Embargo*, by William Cullen Bryant at the time a boy of fourteen (see Vol. XI, p. 128).

495 From a cartoon on the Non-Intercourse Act by "Peter Pencill," 1809, reproduced in the Bancker Collection catalogue, 1898, courtesy of S. V. Henkels

A NON-INTERCOURSE ACT SUPPLANTS THE EMBARGO

SUCH defiance forced the hand of the reluctant Jefferson. The Federalists in Congress, led by Josiah Quincy of Massachusetts, were joined by disgruntled Republicans such as John Randolph and Joseph Story. On March 1, 1809, the embargo was supplanted by a Non-Intercourse Act which allowed trade with all the world except Great Britain and France. The President was empowered to suspend the prohibition against the latter whenever either of them rescinded her restrictions upon neutral commerce. The cartoon thrusts by the Federalist opposition are at Jefferson and the failure of his embargo policy. "Intercourse" and "Non-intercourse" are sarcastically contrasted. Under the former, American trade suffers from foreign competition; under the latter, the American consumer feels the lack of commodities which had customarily come from abroad.

496 From a cartoon by "Peter Pencill," 1809, reproduced in the Bancker Collection catalogue, in 1898, courtesy of S. V. Henkels

By the Virtue, Firmness and Patriotism of

JEFFERSON & MADISON,

Our Difficulties with England are settled—our Ships have been preserved, and our Seamen will, hereafter, be respected while sailing under our National Flag.

NEW-YORK, SATURDAY MORNING, APRIL 22, 1809.

IMPORTANT.

By the President of the United States.—A Proclamation.

WHEREAS it is provided by the 11th ſection of the act of Congreſs, entitled "An "act to interdict the commercial intercourſe between the United States and Great Bri- "tain and France, and their dependencies; and for other purpoſes,"—and that "in "caſe either France or Great Britain ſhall ſo revoke or modify her edicts as that they "ſhall ceaſe to violate the neutral commerce of the United States," the Preſident is authoriſed to declare the ſame by proclamation, after which the trade ſuſpended by the ſaid act and by an act laying an Embargo, on all ſhips and veſſels in the ports and harbours of the United States and the ſeveral acts ſupplementary thereto may be renewed with the nation ſo doing. And whereas the Honourable David Montague Erſkine, his Britannic Majeſty's Envoy Extraordinary and Miniſter Plenipotentiary, has by the order and in the name of his ſovereign declared to this Government, that the Britiſh Orders in Council of January and November, 1807, will have been withdrawn, as reſpects the United States on the 10th day of June next. Now therefore I James Madiſon, Preſident of the United States, do hereby proclaim that the orders in council aforeſaid will have been withdrawn on the tenth day of June next; after which day the trade of the United States with Great Britain, as ſuſpended by the act of Congreſs above mentioned, and an act laying an embargo on all ſhips and veſſels in the ports and harbors of the United States, and the ſeveral acts ſupplementary thereto, may be renewed.

Given under my hand and the seal of the United States, at Washington, the nineteenth day of April, in the year of our Lord, one (L. S) thousand eight hundred and nine, and of the Independence of the United States, the thirty-third.

JAMES MADISON.

By the President,
RT. SMITH, *Secretary of State.*

497 A Republican broadside, Apr. 22, 1809, from the copy in the New York Historical Society

A FLUCTUATING POLICY AFFECTS INTERCOURSE

THIS relaxation of Jeffersonian policy brought a momentary gleam of hope at the opening of Madison's administration. Canning, British Minister of Foreign Affairs, instructed David Erskine, Minister at Washington, to offer the withdrawal of the Orders-in-Council on certain conditions. Erskine, exceeding his authority, represented the case to Madison in an unduly favorable light. The latter eagerly accepted the Minister's advances at face value, and on April 19 proclaimed a suspension of non-intercourse with Great Britain, to be effective June 10. In commercial circles Madison was hailed as a wizard-statesman; without delay a thousand ships were outfitted and dispatched to British ports to reopen the old profitable trade. But when Canning learned of Erskine's action, the arrangement was disavowed and the Minister recalled. In deep chagrin, Madison had no recourse but to revive the Non-Intercourse Act against Great Britain. The policy of the Administration became increasingly unpopular. At length, in the spring of 1810, a further step toward its abandonment was taken. Macon's Bill No. 2 removed all restrictions on commerce, but authorized the President to reëstablish them against one nation should it not within three months follow the action of the other in repealing its offensive regulations.

MADISON IS DECEIVED BY NAPOLEON'S SUBTLE POLICY

NAPOLEON had meanwhile been playing a crafty game. His actions had been as inconsiderate of the rights of neutrals as those of Great Britain, but because of his naval weakness not so oppressive to the United States. He feared, moreover, an alliance between America and Great Britain. When, however, the fiasco of the Erskine negotiations stimulated American dislike of his enemy, Napoleon issued the Rambouillet Decree of March, 1810, confiscating all American vessels in ports under his control. This conduct, he hoped, would lead to the reëstablishment of the embargo, less injurious to him than to Great Britain. All this was changed by the Macon Act, which opened to his enemy a fruitful market. He therefore told Madison that on November 1, 1810, the Berlin and Milan Decrees would cease to operate, "it being well understood that in consequence the English are to revoke their Orders-in-Council and renounce the blockade." Madison fell into the trap. The President gave notice on November 2 that the French restrictions were removed, and asked Great Britain to revoke her orders. The latter refused. Madison thereupon issued a proclamation, under the authority of the Macon Act, restoring non-intercourse with Great Britain as of February 2, 1811. As news continued to come that Napoleon was still seizing all vessels breaking the decrees, the whole country, and particularly commercial New England, became intensely aroused. Then, at the critical moment, Napoleon released the vessels, and the war fever in America swung against Great Britain.

Late and Highly Important Intelligence from *FRANCE!!!*

☞ The French Decrees NOT repealed, on the 13th of March!!

☞ American Vessels AGAIN Sequestered!!

☞ No American Ship can leave France without FIRST obtaining a Special LICENCE!!

☞ Most all the American Masters will ABANDON their property, and return home in a CARTEL to New-York!!

☞ It is now ascertained: that the few American Vessels released from France, cost their owners, the *full amount of them!!*

From the Freeman's Journal.

PHILADELPHIA, April 17.

Capt. Cullen, [illegible] arrived yesterday, in 30 days from Bayonne, which place [illegible] March. The verbal and written news by this vessel are of such [illegible] extinguish hope. *Not only was the American property (which was faithfully promised to be restored on the 2d February,) not given up on the 13th March, but all American vessels arriving in France were refused an entry,* were put under sequestration and their papers sent to Paris. On the 8th of March the Director General of the customs announced to the merchants of Bordeaux, that the emperor had adjourned the expression of his opinion respecting the admitting [A]merican vessels to entry.—Another letter states that the Director General of the customs had declared that no more applications for admitting American vessels to an entry, would be received. Of course they will remain under sequestration. *The vessels which sailed from America under Napoleon's special licences were equally sequestered with those which had none—no distinction being made!!*

No American vessel is permitted to leave France, except under a special licence, which it is very difficult to procure, and costs a large sum.

"What the event will be (says a letter which we have seen) no one can tell—but beware, and advise your friends also to beware, of shipping any more property to this country."

From all we have been able to gather by this arrival, there appears not the least probability of Napoleon restoring American property, or rescinding his Berlin and Milan decrees, which are still in most rigorous operation.

From the Philadelphia Daily Advertiser.

By the Eagle and Fox, arrived here last evening from Bayonne, it appears that the Emperor had postponed the final decision of the question "Shall the American vessels that have arrived in the ports of France since the repeal of the non-intercourse," be admitted to an entry? and desired that no farther application should be made;—*thus are these vessels provisionally sequestered,* until his imperial majesty, (who loves the Americans,) shall have made up his royal mind!!!

In this situation of affairs, it was expected that many of the *masters and crews, would abandon the property and return home* in the brig Rose in Bloom, a cartel, preparing to leave Bayonne for N. York.

The Eagle has despatches for Government, and a file of French papers for Gen. Armstrong.

From the Philadelphia True American.

Yesterday arrived, brig Fox, Cullen, from Bayonne, in France. This is one of the vessels sequestered by Bonaparte, at St. Sebastians, in 1809, and was together with the Eagle, Hawk, and a number other American vessels carried to Bayonne, and as the captain informs all, together with their cargoes, sold by order of the plunderer of the world.

After having purchased his vessel at the sale, he got a freight of brandy, wine and dry goods, when he got permission and left that port March 15, in co. with the Eagle, Alfton, with passengers for this port.

At the time of sailing, the 15th March, Capt. Cullen, says, nothing that he heard, had been done in the repeal of the French decrees, or liberation of the American trade, as the schr. Spencer, Moffat; schr. Purse, and brig Ann, all of whom had arrived at Bayonne from New York, were laying with their cargoes on board waiting the *ipse dixit* of Bonaparte from Paris.—The brig Meteor Hauiy, is said to be arrived at Bordeaux from this port and said to be in the same condition.

In the Fox came passenger, capt. Chevers of Salem and 4 sailors who had been prisoners among the French for some time.

Extract of a letter from a gentleman who came passenger in the Fox, arrived in Philadelphia from France, to his friends in that city.

"The political disposition of the French government as respects this country, was, at the time of my departure, as unpropitious as it has ever been, and there were no hopes entertained that there would be any relaxation of the system of spoliation that she has so long maintained.——If I except the actual and immediate confiscation, I may safely say that the same vexation to which our commerce was exposed prior to the 2d of November last exists at present. For those vessels which have arrived subsequent to that period, and upon the [illegible] faith of the repeal of Milan, Berlin and other decrees, are still kept in a state of sequestration; or what is tantamount, no decision can be obtained as to what will be their fate. Such as arrived, were obliged to transmit their papers to Paris, to be submitted to the examination of the emperor, and I know of no instance wherein any notice has been taken of them, but in such as were provided with licences.——So far from there being any amelioration of our prospects the reverse was the fact, as I saw letters of good authority from Paris dated the 7th March, wherein it was said, that the emperor had issued orders to all the custom houses, not to permit the admission of any American vessel and property, to seize such as should arrive, and not to report on the case of any whatsoever that had arrived."

498 From a Federalist handbill of 1811 in the American Antiquarian Society, Worcester, Mass.

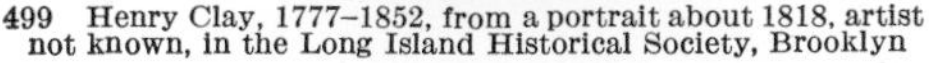

499 Henry Clay, 1777–1852, from a portrait about 1818, artist not known, in the Long Island Historical Society, Brooklyn

500 John C. Calhoun, 1782–1850, from the portrait, 1826, by Charles Bird King in the Corcoran Gallery of Art, Washington

NEW BLOOD ENLIVENS THE TWELFTH CONGRESS

Popular resentment against Europe and the Administration was reflected in the election of 1810. Seventy new men appeared in the Twelfth Congress. Up to this time the political leaders were men of Revolutionary days, trained to temporizing caution. The new men were young, filled with an unreasoned patriotism and buoyancy. These "War Hawks" were more numerous in the House. Henry Clay of Kentucky, John C. Calhoun, Langdon Cheves and William Lowndes of South Carolina, and Felix Grundy of Tennessee were among the new spokesmen of the western spirit and western interests.

501 Felix Grundy, 1777–1840, from the portrait in the Tennessee Historical Society, Nashville

502 Langdon Cheves, 1776–1857, from a miniature, 1819, by Charles Fraser, owned by Mrs. Louisa R. McCord Smythe, Charleston, S. C.

VILE AND DETESTABLE DEMOCRATICK TRICK EXPOSED!!

THE last effort which has been made, to deceive the People of this County, as to the measures of the Federal Party, and the characters of the men they are pledged to support, is perhaps the most flagrantly wicked of any which has yet been adopted.—On Thursday last an inflammatory Handbill issued from the Ægis Office in Worcester, headed "CRUSH TREASON! DEFEAT INTRIGUE! SAVE THE UNION!"—MR. STRONG, the "*Patriotick Proceedings*"—and JOHN HENRY!" This Handbill has been most industriously circulated, throughout the County.—It purports to be made up of extracts from Federal Newspapers, published in 1809, & is intended to produce an impression, that the Federal Party, with GOVERNOR STRONG at their head, were then conspiring with a British Spy, to bring about, a separation between the Eastern and Southern States.—On comparing the extracts contained in the handbill with the passages, in the papers, from which the extracts are said to be made, it has been discovered, that these passages have been garbled and mutilated in the most infamous manner, and so as to change entirely the sense intended to be expressed.

It is not practicable at this late hour, to expose *all* the deformity of this vile and abominable "Plot."—A few short extracts from the handbill, compared with the original publications, will serve to convince the Publick, that there is no stratagem too base to be adopted, by the Democratick Party, in this time of trial and tribulation, which may have a tendency to accomplish their nefarious schemes.

FROM THE HANDBILL.

Extract from the doings of the Federalists in the town of Northampton, where Mr. Strong resides.—[TAKEN FROM THE CENTINEL OF JAN. 18, 1809.]

"AT a numerous meeting from different towns in the County of Hampshire, convened at *North-Hampton*, on the 12th Jan. 1809, *to take into consideration the present alarming condition of the U. States, and of this Commonwealth*, the following Resolutions, &c. were passed:

"Considering the awful and eventful struggle now making in Europe, on the one hand, to *subjugate* and *enslave* AN INNOCENT and UNOFFENDING nation, [*England*] and on the other, to resist the efforts of a cruel and relentless tyranny—That our common country has been, and still is suffering unusual and extraordinary burthens *from the measures adopted by the National Government*—That causes are continually occurring which tend to produce a DISSOLUTION OF THE UNION—Therefore,

"*Resolved*, That we highly approve of the conduct of the Legislature of this Commonwealth, and of their doings and proceedings at their last session, *respecting our differences with Great Britain, and of the laws laying an Embargo*—That we have the fullest confidence in *their* wisdom and firmness, *in taking all such measures in future*, as are in their power, to relieve from the evils generally felt—*That we look to them* to see that ample provision be made to secure and protect the inhabitants of this Commonwealth, *from general and unreasonable search, &c.*"

FROM THE CENTINEL OF JANUARY 18, 1809.

"Considering the awful and eventful struggle now making in Europe, on the one hand to subjugate and enslave an innocent and unoffending nation, [*Spain*] and on the other to resist the efforts of a cruel and relentless tyranny—a struggle which the history of a few years past demonstrates, may be deeply interesting to the people of the United States—that our common country has been and still is suffering unusual and extraordinary burthens from the measures recently adopted and pursued by the national government—That within our own commonwealth its treasures have been squandered and applied to private use, principles & practices deliberately and officially avowed and advocated, totally inconsistent with the preservation of our republican form of government—That causes are continually occuring which tend to produce A MOST CALAMITOUS EVENT—a *Dissolution of the Union*—and finally, that it is the right and duty of those who love their country, and desire to perpetuate its liberty and independence, in times of publick danger, boldly to call upon and urge their fellow citizens of all parties to exert themselves to promote the general welfare.—Therefore,

Resolved, That we highly approve of the conduct of the Legislature of this Commonwealth in the choice of Electors of President and Vice-President, and of their doings and proceedings at their last session respecting our differences with Great Britain, and of the laws laying an Embargo—That we have the fullest confidence in their wisdom and firmness, in taking all such measures in future, as are in their power, to relieve from the evils generally felt by the citizens, and more severely by our brethren in the eastern part of the Commonwealth, and to avert the fatal effects of those with which we are threatened—That we look to them to see that ample provision be made to secure and protect the inhabitants of the Commonwealth in the enjoyment of those invaluable privileges secured by the bill of rights, and guaranteed by the federal constitution, among which, we hold as most important, the subordination of military powers to the civil—the right of exemption from general and unreasonable search, and the right of seeking and finding sure and speedy redress for injuries sustained."

In the above passages, it is sufficient to point out two of the most gross and palpable perversions of the meaning of the Federalists assembled at Northampton. The "INNOCENT and UNOFFENDING NATION" referred to in the resolutions, is "*Spain*," which every body knows was then gloriously struggling against the "*cruel and relentless tyranny*" of BONAPARTE. The handbill charges the supporters of these resolutions, of whom Governour Strong is said to be one, with eulogizing "England" *as an innocent and unoffending nation.*"—This is not all.—The resolutions speak of the dissolution of the Union as "A MOST CALAMITOUS EVENT."—The hand-bill by basely omitting this expression, intended to produce a belief that this "dissolution" was the object which the Federalists were endeavouring to accomplish. Let the two extracts be carefully compared, and no one can fail to percieve that the whole passage has been most infamously mutilated with a view to mislead the Publick Sentiment, as to the views of the Federal Party,

In the other passage selected, the same attempt has been made to produce a false impression as to the language of the Legislature.

FROM THE HANDBILL.

"In the Legislative Electioneering Address to the People, which was got up on the 2d of March, 1809, just before the Spring election, and which helped MR. GORE into office, is the following:—

"When they [this Legislature] perceive that you [the People] are prepared to *break the chains* imposed by a *fatal* and *mistaken policy*, [Embargo] and that ALL THE CONSTITUTED AUTHORITIES OF NEW ENGLAND are united in SENTIMENT and PURPOSE;—when they are sensible that you are ABLE *to resist*, and that *self preservation* will make RESISTANCE a DUTY, they will reflect upon your *claims* AND YIELD TO THE JUSTICE OF YOUR PRETENSIONS! And they will feel, that the CONFEDERATION is intended for the *general welfare!*"

FROM THE LEGISLATIVE ADDRESS PUBLISHED IN THE CENTINEL OF MARCH 11, 1809.

It would indeed be a grateful occupation to the Legislature to apply an immediate remedy to the evils of which the Petitioners complain and which we fear will be aggravated by a continuance of the existing commercial restrictions, or substitutes not less oppressive and fatal, though veiled under new titles. But they are compelled to avow that it is with the people themselves that every efficient plan of redress must originate.—While the advocates for British war and the contemners of commerce can calculate upon your divisions, they will advance in their mad and presumptuous course, and rely upon your Governors and your Representatives to neutralize your opposition to their measures. But when they [*the National Government*] perceive that you are prepared to break the chains imposed by a fatal and mistaken policy, and that all the constituted authorities of New England are united in sentiment and purpose; when they are sensible that you are able to resist, and that self-preservation will make resistance a duty, they will reflect upon your claims, and yield to the justice of your pretensions. They will feel that the confederation is intended for the general welfare, and that it is only by paying some regard to this object, we can maintain that union which common interest should make perpetual."

The object of the handbill is to prove that the Legislature of Massachusetts were inviting the People of New-England to revolt from the Union and establish a government of their own. The genuine extract from their address, proves most unequivocally that their object was to induce them to adopt such measures as "WOULD MAINTAIN THAT UNION WHICH COMMON INTEREST REQUIRED SHOULD BE PERPETUAL!"

Instead of inviting the People to "break the chains of the Union,"—they exhort them only to adopt such firm and energetic measures as will convince the National Government, of their hostility to the EMBARGO, and the anticommercial system they were then pursuing.—These measures *were* adopted.—The NATIONAL GOVERNMENT RECEDED FROM the GROUND they HAD taken.—AND THE UNION WAS PRESERVED!!!

Such is this outrageous attempt to lead the People to believe that Governor STRONG was conspiring with JOHN HENRY to dissolve the Union!—The "*Plot*" is detected; and another hideous trait in the character of Democracy is exhibited to the calm and dispassionate view of the People!

SPY OFFICE, *Worcester, April* 4, 1812.

N. B. News has this moment arrived by express, that, on Tuesday last, the Committee of Foreign Relations had decided upon the measure of an *immediate* EMBARGO, AS PREPARATORY TO WAR!!!

503 Facsimile of part of a handbill issued from *The Spy* office, Worcester, Mass., Apr. 4, 1812, original in the American Antiquarian Society, Worcester, Mass.

"VILE AND DETESTABLE DEMOCRATICK TRICK EXPOSED!!"

WHEN the War Hawks came to Washington, in November, 1811, they were eager to avenge the insults of the past twenty years of neutrality. They elected Henry Clay Speaker of the House, in those days the more important of the two legislative bodies. They then proceeded to secure, through the aid of the Speaker, control of the more important committees. Many of them believed that England was aiding the Indians of the Ohio valley to make war upon the frontier. With most of the War Hawks an inbred antipathy demanded war against England, though some, like Calhoun, more logically wanted to war on both England and France. So enthusiastic and dexterous were they that Madison's timidity was overcome. In the spring of 1812 he made public some letters purchased from one John Henry, a British subject (referred to in No. 503). Henry had sounded New England Federalists regarding separation, and his letters were sent by the Governor-General of Canada to Lord Castlereagh, the British foreign minister, a price of $125,000 being put on them which Castlereagh refused to pay. Madison then bought them for the United States for $50,000. While there was little in them not already known, their publication at this time further excited the militant passions and the sectional bitterness of New England.

MADISON IS SPURRED TO WAR PREPARATIONS

THE Twelfth Congress, convened ahead of time by presidential proclamation, devoted its attention to the country's foreign relations. Especially in the House, where Clay had been chosen Speaker, was the war spirit noticeable. Early in the session a House committee reported that Great Britain, "instead of retracting that unjustifiable attack on neutral rights, in which she professed to be only the reluctant follower of France, had advanced with bolder and continually advancing strides, demanding as a condition of her revoking her orders, that France and her allies should admit into their territories the products and manufactures of Great Britain." The committee therefore recommended increasing the military force, refitting the navy, and authorizing merchant vessels to arm in self-defense. After heated debate, these motions were adopted.

On April 1, 1812, Madison, now fully under the dominance of the War party — which threatened to refuse him renomination for the presidency unless he sided with them — and of James Monroe, freshly returned from his European humiliation, recommended a sixty-day embargo, preparatory to open war.

EMBARGO BY EXPRESS.

BOSTON, FRIDAY EVENING, APRIL 3, 1812—*6 o'clock.*

The following letter is this moment handed me by express.

HARRISON G. OTIS.

"Mr. CALHOUN, of South Carolina, a Member of the Committee of Foreign Relations, has this moment informed Mr. QUINCY, that the Committee of Foreign Relations, have decided to lay a Proposition for an EMBARGO on the table of the House of Representatives to-morrow.—This information may be depended on from the respectability of the source from whence it is derived; and the measure to be recommended, it is understood, meets the approbation of the Executive.

JAMES LLOYD,
JOSIAH QUINCY,
JAMES EMOTT.

"*Washington, Tuesday, March* 31, 1812, 2 *o'clk, P. M.*

The Honorable H. G. Otis, Boston.

SPRINGFIELD, APRIL 4th, 1812.

In confirmation of the above, letters have been this day received in town from WM. ELY, Esq. at Washington, stating that an Embargo was to be immediately laid on, preparatory to a declaration of War.

Information is this moment received from Mr. BYERS of this town, now on his way to Philadelphia, that an Embargo is actually laid.

It is said that drafts are to be made from the militia within twenty days.

504 From a handbill, April 4, 1812, announcing an embargo preparatory to war, in the American Antiquarian Society, Worcester, Mass.

505 Josiah Quincy, 1772–1864, from the portrait by Gilbert Stuart in the Museum of Fine Arts, Boston

CONGRESS DECLARES WAR AGAINST ENGLAND

THESE measures were not adopted without a struggle. In Josiah Quincy of Boston the Federalists found a leader, stanch in support of the commercial interests of his people. He had opposed the annexation of Louisiana, even to the point of suggesting secession; he had played a part in the protest against the Enforcement Acts. Now, joined by John Randolph and a few Republicans, he managed in some degree to check the giddy flight of the War Hawks. Additions to the navy were voted down. So were taxes, forcing the government to float a loan upon a market which refused to absorb it. But, nothing daunted, the younger men pushed aside all opposition. On June 1, 1812, Madison presented to Congress the most forceful of his state papers, asking for an immediate declaration of war against England. On the 18th, Congress assented. Two days later, the House committee on foreign relations, through Calhoun, made a report summarizing the acts of aggression of Great Britain, beginning in 1806, and endorsing the President's recommendation. Behind closed doors the matter was considered, until, on the eighteenth, the Congress was announced as having concurred in the opinion of Madison.

506 From a contemporary cartoon by William Charles (– 1820); courtesy of Stan V. Henkels

THE WAR IS UNPOPULAR IN NEW ENGLAND

THE United States had entered a war that was needless, rash, impolitic, and illogical. It was illogical because Napoleon had ignored American rights equally with Great Britain, and because the alleged causes for now declaring war had existed, and in more acute form, for years past. It was rash because the country was sadly unprepared. The navy, of excellent quality, counted seven good frigates and nine smaller vessels. The regular army in June, 1812, contained fewer than seven thousand troops, poorly equipped, inefficiently officered, and dispersed along the extensive frontier. The first Bank of the United States had been refused a new charter in 1811, and Gallatin, Secretary of the Treasury, struggled against tremendous odds to finance, even inadequately, an unexpected war. It was impolitic because the country was as a whole apathetic, and in spots bitterly opposed. The declaration had been carried by votes of seventy-nine to forty-nine in the House, and nineteen to thirteen in the Senate; and thereafter thirty-four congressmen signed and circulated a vigorous protest. To the Federalists the war seemed due to a "Virginia Cabal" in alliance with "madmen of Kentucky and Tennessee" and with Napoleon. New England church bells were tolled when news of the declaration came, and flags were at half-mast.

507 DeWitt Clinton, 1769–1828, from the portrait, 1807, by John Trumbull in the New York Chamber of Commerce

MADISON IS RE-ELECTED BY A NARROW MARGIN

THE early test of strength came in the elections of 1812. The war party renominated Madison, with Elbridge Gerry of Massachusetts as a running-mate, to win votes in the Federalist stronghold. Federalists and anti-war Republicans united behind DeWitt Clinton, vigorous and talented nephew of George Clinton, for so long leader of the New York Republicans. After a campaign in which the issue was war or no war, Madison was reëlected, but by a narrow and significant vote. The thirteen original states, split at the Potomac, gave Clinton eighty-nine votes and Madison ninety; the issue was determined by the West, whose votes went solidly for Madison and war.

508 From the contemporary cartoon by William Charles in the Historical Society of Pennsylvania

THE AMERICAN NAVY

THE war was unnecessary because at the time of its declaration Great Britain was on the point of conceding the American demands. Impoverished merchants and laborers pressed for a repeal of the obnoxious Orders-in-Council; and on June 16, two days before the American declaration, their withdrawal was promised. But injured feelings remained; so the War Hawks carried on. The Administration planned to rely chiefly on a land campaign that would win Canada and enable the United States to dictate terms from Halifax. Ignominious defeats along the border effectually frustrated this scheme; while the navy, of whose success no one dreamed in 1812, was winning spectacular victories on the lakes and the ocean. The news of Perry's victory on Lake Erie astounded the British public, and confessions of weakness began to appear in the English newspapers. One of the cartoons refers to the naval duel between the *Hornet* and the *Peacock* in which the latter suffered defeat, the other to Perry's victory. (For the War of 1812 see Vol. VI.)

509 From the contemporary cartoon by William Charles in the Historical Society of Pennsylvania

DEATH OF THE EMBARGO, WITH ALL ITS "RESTRICTIVE ENERGIES."

A wit first celebrated this great event in the FEDERAL REPUBLICAN, in the manner to be seen below; but he has had the politeness to revise and correct the article for the Evening Post, with additions: in this improved state it is now presented to our readers, aided by an appropriate engraving devised by the author and admirably executed by one of our fellow-citizens. Here it comes—

"TO THE GRAVE GO SHAM PROTECTORS OF "FREE TRADE AND SAILORS' RIGHTS"—AND ALL THE PEOPLE SAY AMEN!"

TERRAPIN'S ADDRESS.

Reflect, my friend, as you pass by;
As *you* are, *now*, so, once, was *I*;
As *I* am *now*, so *you* may be:—
Laid on your back to die like me!
I was, indeed, true Sailor born;
To quit my friend, in death, I scorn.
Once Jemmy *seem'd* to be my friend,
But, basely, brought me to my end!
Of head bereft, and light, and breath,
I hold *Fidelity*, in death:—
For "*Sailor's Rights*" I still will tug:
And, Madison to death I'll hug,
For his perfidious zeal disploy'd,
For "*Sailor's Rights and for Free Trade.*"
This small atonement I will have—
I'll tug down Jemmy to the grave.
Then Trade and Commerce shall be free
And Sailors have their liberty—
Of head bereft, and light, and breath,
The *Terrapin*, still true in death,
Will punish Jemmy's perfidy:
Leave Trade, and *brother Sailors Free!*

PASSENGERS REPLY.

Yes Terrapin, bereft of breath,
We see thee faithful still, in death:
Stick to't—"*Free Trade and Sailor's Right*:
Hug Jemmy—press him—hold him—bite—
Ne'er mind thy head—thou'lt live without it,
Spunk will preserve thy life—don't doubt it—
Down to the grave t'atone for sin,
Jemmy must go, with Terrapin.
Bear *him* but off, and we shall see
Commerce restor'd and *Sailors Free!*
Hug, Terrapin, with all thy might,
Now for "*Free Trade* and *Sailor's Right*:"
Stick to him, Terrapin, to thee the nation
Now eager looks:—then die for her salvation.

FLOREAT RESPUBLICA.

Banks of Goose Creek,
City of Washington,
15th April 1814.

510 From the *New York Evening Post*, April 25, 1814, engraving on the repeal of the embargo by Alexander Anderson (1775–1870) after a drawing by John Wesley Jarvis

ECONOMIC PRESSURE LIFTS THE EMBARGO

SUCH victories, hailed with delight, were illusory. It was simply a question of time before Britain could concentrate her vast fleet upon American waters and blockade her ports. In the spring of 1814, Napoleon's abdication enabled England to bend all her energies upon the American war. Internal disaffection in America, moreover, rose rather than declined. The governors of Massachusetts, Rhode Island, and Connecticut ignored Madison's call for militia; the New England bankers boycotted the national treasury; the farmers and merchants went still further. In August, 1814, the British authorities wrote to London that "two-thirds of the army in Canada are at this moment eating beef provided by the American contractors, drawn principally from Vermont and New York." To meet this illicit barter Madison pushed through, in December, 1813, a drastic embargo. There followed widespread unemployment and open defiance by New England. In April the law was repealed, an event celebrated with speeches and bonfires along the coast.

NEW ENGLAND CALLS A CONVENTION OF PROTEST AT HARTFORD

IN the spring of 1813, the Federalists regained control of the Massachusetts government. Josiah Quincy, who declined reëlection to Congress, became the leader in the state in opposition to the war policy. In June a Remonstrance against War was adopted; in February, 1814, there followed one against the Embargo. Taking a leaf from Madison's Virginia Resolutions of 1798, the General Court asserted that, "Whenever the national compact is violated, and the citizens of this state are oppressed by cruel and unauthorized laws, their legislature is bound to interpose its power, and wrest from the oppressor his victim." Then in October it issued a call for a convention of the New England States, to meet at Hartford in December. Here the delegates, among whom were leading Federalists such as George Cabot, Theodore Dwight and Harrison Gray Otis, in secret session formulated their demands on the national government. Senator Pickering, hoping for radical action, awaited its work with eagerness. The hostile cartoonist represents New England about to leap into the lap of England.

511 From the contemporary cartoon by William Charles in possession of the publishers

PEACE COMES BEFORE THE HARTFORD PROJECTS ARE PRESENTED

But more cautious counsel prevailed. After adjournment in January there was published an address which contained little more than a restatement of the Kentucky and Virginia Resolutions. Seven amendments to the national constitution were proposed, and the participating states were called upon to present the demands to Congress. If the national government took no action within six months, another convention was to be held. Massachusetts and Connecticut thereupon sent commissioners to lay the projects before the Government. Before they could do this news came of Jackson's victory at New Orleans and of the peace treaty signed at Ghent the preceding December. In a trice the movement collapsed, leaving nothing behind but odium for the participants.

THE

PROCEEDINGS

OF A

Convention of Delegates,

FROM THE STATES OF

MASSACHUSETTS, CONNECTICUT, AND RHODE-ISLAND;

THE

COUNTIES OF CHESHIRE AND GRAFTON,

In the State of New-Hampshire;

AND THE

COUNTY OF WINDHAM,

In the State of Vermont:

CONVENED AT

HARTFORD, IN THE STATE OF CONNECTICUT,

December 15th, 1814.

HARTFORD:—Printed.

RE-PRINTED AT NEW-HAVEN, BY OLIVER STEELE.

Jan. 1815

512 Title-page of the pamphlet in the New York Public Library

THE RUSSIAN BEAR OFFERS TO MEDIATE

Negotiations for peace had begun shortly after the outbreak of hostilities. Russia, to protect her new and thriving commerce with America, had embarked upon a war with France. But now America, instead of siding with Russia in the effort to subdue France, was fighting France's enemy. This was little to the liking of Russia; for during the war French interests would be favored by America at the expense of Russia; and at its conclusion either France or Great Britain, but not Russia, would reap the benefits of American trade. To enable Great Britain to concentrate her strength against France, Russia's enemy, and to resuscitate her commercial dealings with America, Russia offered to mediate between the English-speaking countries.

513 From the contemporary cartoon by William Charles in the New York Historical Society

514 From an engraving after a painting *Peace of Ghent, 1814, and Triumph of America*, by Mme. Plantou, "Citizen of the United States," published by P. Price, Jr., Philadelphia

PEACE IS MADE ON CHRISTMAS EVE, 1814

THIS offer Madison accepted in the spring of 1813. He appointed James Bayard, Federalist senator from Delaware, and Albert Gallatin to join John Quincy Adams, Minister at St. Petersburg, as peace commissioners. England, however, rejected Russia's mediation, preferring direct negotiations. These were opened at Ghent in August, 1814. Jonathan Russell, formerly Chargé d'Affaires in London, and Henry Clay had been added to America's delegation. The British representatives were men of little importance. They were instructed to make no concessions to the main demands of the United States — impressments, the blockade, and indemnity for maritime losses. Indeed, they were to push for several concessions from America. For a time the conference was deadlocked. Then came news from America of the British defeat at Plattsburg (Vol. VI). In addition to this, a shift in the European diplomatic situation proving unfavorable, England receded from her intransigent attitude. On Christmas Eve, 1814, an agreement was reached.

THE PEACE TREATY FAILS TO SETTLE DISPUTED ISSUES

THE treaty simply provided for cessation of hostilities and a return to the pre-war situation. Impressment of seamen — the issue which Madison had most stressed — went unmentioned. The long-standing disputes about boundaries, the Newfoundland fisheries, and navigation of the Mississippi were postponed for future discussion, so that the treaty of peace was inconclusive.

Treaty of
Peace and Amity
between
His Britannic Majesty
and
The United States of America

His Britannic Majesty and the United States of America desirous of terminating the War which has unhappily subsisted between the two Countries and of restoring upon principles of perfect reciprocity, Peace, Friendship, and good Understanding between them, have for that purpose appointed their respective Plenipotentiaries, that is to say, His Britannic Majesty on his part has appointed the Right Honourable James Lord Gambier, late Admiral of the White, now Admiral of the Red Squadron of

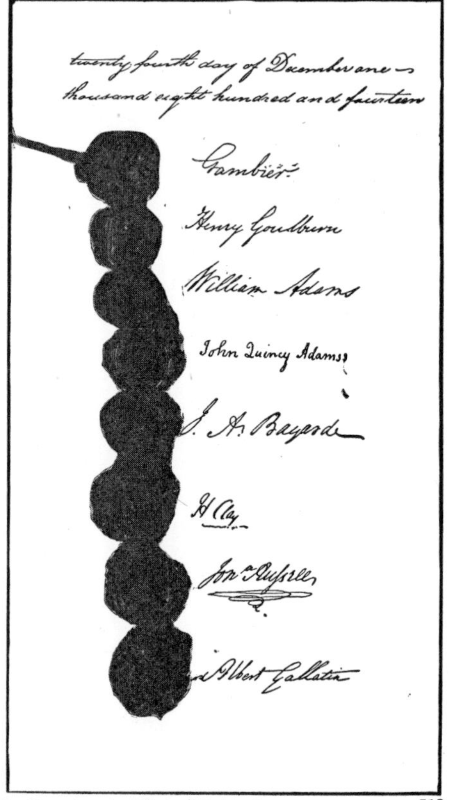

twenty fourth day of December one thousand eight hundred and fourteen

Gambier
Henry Goulburn
William Adams
John Quincy Adams
J. A. Bayard
H Clay
Jon. Russell
Albert Gallatin

515 First and last pages of the original in the Department of State, Washington 516

PEACE ELIMINATES FOREIGN DISTRACTIONS

Yet, thanks to peace in Europe, violation of our rights was no longer of value to Great Britain. In America, at any rate, peace was hailed with delight, for every one was tired of war. The struggle, moreover, had shown the folly of permitting French and English issues to dominate domestic politics and to engender disaffection. It stimulated a national patriotism and commercial independence of Europe. After 1815, chief attention was devoted for the first time since 1776 to American problems.

517 From the painting *Signing the Treaty of Ghent*, by A. Forestier (1790–1872) in the State Department, Washington

of the United States, all and every person and persons, by and with whose order, agreement, consent, approbation, and connivance such unlawful advance or loan, shall have been
made, upon conviction thereof, shall forfeit and pay for every such offence, treble the value or amount of the sum or sums, which have been so unlawfully advanced or lent
one fifth thereof to the use of the informer, and the residue thereof to the use of the United States. Sec: 14. And be it further enacted, That the bills or notes of
the said corporation originally made payable, or which shall have become payable on demand, shall be receivable in all payments to the United States, unless otherwise
directed by act of Congress. Sec: 15. And be it further enacted, That during the continuance of this act, and whenever required by the Secretary of the Treasury, the
said corporation shall give the necessary facilities for transferring the public funds from place to place, within the United States, or the territories thereof, and for distributing
the same in payment of the public creditors without charging commissions or claiming allowance on account of difference of exchange, and shall also do and perform
the several and respective duties of the Commissioners of Loans for the several states, or of any one or more of them whenever required by law. Sec: 16 And be it further
enacted, That the deposits of the money of the United States, in places in which the said Bank and branches thereof may be established, shall be made in said Bank
or Branches thereof, unless the Secretary of the Treasury shall at any time otherwise order and direct; in which case the Secretary of the Treasury shall immediately lay before Congress

518 From the original Act for a National Bank, 1816, in the Department of State, Washington

if in session, and if not, immediately after the commencement of the next session, the reasons of such order or direction. Sec: 17. And be it further enacted, That the said corporation
shall not at any time suspend or refuse payment, in gold and silver, of any of its notes, bills, or obligations; nor of any monies received upon deposite in said Bank, or in any of its
offices of discount and deposite, and if the said corporation shall at any time refuse or neglect to pay on demand, any bill, note or obligation, issued by the corporation, according to
the contract, promise or undertaking therein expressed; or shall neglect or refuse to pay on demand any monies received in said Bank, or in any of its offices aforesaid, on deposite to
the person or persons entitled to receive the same, then and in every such case, the holder of any such note, bill, or obligation, or the person or persons entitled to demand and receive
such monies as aforesaid shall respectively be entitled to receive and recover interest on the said bills, notes, obligations, or monies, until the same shall be fully paid and satisfied
at the rate of twelve per centum per annum, from the time of such demand as aforesaid, Provided, That Congress may at any time hereafter enact laws enforcing and regulating
the recovery of the amount of the notes, bills, obligations, or other debts of which payment shall have been refused as aforesaid with the rate of interest above mentioned, vesting
jurisdiction for that purpose in any courts, either of law or equity, of the Courts of the United States or Territories thereof, or of the several states, as they may deem expedient.
Sec: 18. And be it further enacted, That if any person shall falsely make, forge, or counterfeit, or cause or procure, to be falsely made, forged or counterfeited, or willingly aid
or assist, in falsely making, forging or counterfeiting any bill or note in imitation of, or purporting to be a bill or note issued by order of the president, [illegible] and Company of

519 From the original Act for a National Bank, 1816, in the Department of State, Washington

THE FEDERAL POWER IS STRENGTHENED

The difficulties of reconstruction were blithely faced by the youthful leaders of the new-model Republican party. Under stress of circumstances, their strict constructionist doctrine had in practice been dropped bit by bit. To the 14th Congress, meeting in December, 1815, Madison sent a memorable message, calling for an adequate army and navy, a protective tariff, national aids for roads and canals, the reëstablishment of a national bank. The response was generous; as Josiah Quincy said, the Republicans "out-Federalized Federalism."

520 James Monroe, 1758–1831, from the portrait by Gilbert Stuart in the Pennsylvania Academy of the Fine Arts, Philadelphia

MONROE IS THE LAST OF THE VIRGINIA DYNASTY

THAT the Republicans were acting in accord with general opinion was shown in the election of 1816. With little opposition from the dying Federalist party, the last of the Virginia dynasty became President. Monroe had early attached his fortunes to those of Jefferson. Without the brilliance of his leader, he possessed a stolid ability to manage routine that served him well in a period of mounting prosperity, when new problems had not yet become ominous. He had, moreover, sufficient discernment to surround himself with able advisers. J. Q. Adams, William H. Crawford, William Wirt and J. C. Calhoun were in his cabinet. A tour of the country at the outset of his administration further strengthened his position. Monroe looked forward to a happy administration. In his inaugural address he said, "Equally gratifying is it to witness the increased harmony of opinion which pervades the union. Discord does not belong to our system. Union is recommended, as well by the free and benign principles of our Government, extending its blessings to every individual, as by the other eminent advantages attending it."

521 James Monroe, from the portrait, 1822, by John Vanderlyn in the New York City Hall, courtesy of the Municipal Art Commission

522 From a sketch for the painting *Election Day at the State House*, about 1818, by John Lewis Krimmel (1787–1821) in the Historical Society of Pennsylvania

FEBRUARY, 1810. 87

FLETCHER *v.* PECK.

FLETCHER v. PECK.

ERROR to the circuit court for the district of Massachusetts, in an action of covenant brought by Flecher against Peck.

The *first* count of the declaration states that Peck, by his deed of bargain and sale dated the 14th of May, 1803, in consideration of 3,000 dollars, sold and conveyed to Fletcher, 15,000 acres of land lying in common and undivided in a tract described as follows: beginning on the river Mississippi, where the latitude 32 deg. 40 min. north of the equator intersects the same, running thence along the same parallel of latitude a due east course to the Tombigby river, thence up the said Tombigby river to where the latitude of 32 deg. 43 min. 52 sec. intersects the same, thence along the same parallel of latitude a due west course to the Mississippi; thence down the said river, to the place of beginning; the said described tract containing 500,000 acres, and is the same which was conveyed by Nathaniel Prime to Oliver Phelps, by deed dated the 27th of February, 1796, and of which the said Phelps conveyed four fifths to Benjamin Hichborn, and the said Peck by deed dated the 8th of December, 1800; the said tract of 500,000 acres, being part of a tract which James Greenleaf conveyed to the said N. Prime, by deed dated the 23d of September, 1795, and is parcel of that tract which James Gunn, Mathew M'Allister, George Walker, Zachariah Cox, Jacob Walburger, William Longstreet and Wade Hampton, by deed dated 22d of August, 1795, conveyed to the said James Greenleaf; the same being part of that tract which was granted by letters patent under the great seal of the state of Georgia, and the signature of George Matthews, Esq. governor of that state, dated the 13th of January, 1795, to the said James Gunn and others, under the name of James Gunn, Mathew M'Allister, and George

If the breach of covenant assigned be, that the *state* had no authority to sell and dispose of the land, it is not a good plea in bar to say that the *governor* was legally empowered to sell and convey the premises, although the facts stated in the plea as inducement, are sufficient to justify a direct negative of the breach assigned.

It is not necessary that a breach of covenant be assigned in the very words of the covenant. It is sufficient if it show a substantial breach.

The court will not declare a law to be unconstitutional, unless the opposition between the constitution and the law be clear and plain.

The legislature of Georgia, in 1795, had the power of disposing of the unappropriated lands within its own limits

523 From *Report of Cases Argued and Adjudged in the Supreme Court, 1810,* by William Cranch, New York, 1812

316 CASES IN THE SUPREME COURT

1819.
M'Culloch v. State of Maryland.

(CONSTITUTIONAL LAW)

M'CULLOCH v. The STATE OF MARYLAND *et al.*

Congress has power to incorporate a Bank.

The government of the Union is a government of the People; it emanates from them; its powers are granted by them; and are to be exercised directly on them, and for their benefit.

The government of the Union, though limited in its powers, is supreme within its sphere of action; and its laws, when made in pursuance of the constitution, form the supreme law of the land.

There is nothing in the Constitution of the United States, similar to the articles of Confederation, which exclude incidental or implied powers.

If the *end* be legitimate, and within the scope of the constitution, all the *means* which are appropriate, which are plainly adapted to that end, and which are not prohibited, may constitutionally be employed to carry it into effect.

The power of establishing a corporation is not a distinct sovereign power or end of government, but only the means of carrying into effect other powers which are sovereign. Whenever it becomes an appropriate means of exercising any of the powers given by the constitution to the government of the Union, it may be exercised by that government.

If a certain means to carry into effect any of the powers, expressly given by the constitution to the government of the Union, be an appropiate measure, not prohibited by the constitution, the degree of its necessity is a question of legislative discretion, not of judicial cognizance

The act of the 10th April, 1816, c. 44., to "incorporate the subscribers to the Bank of the United States," is a law made in pursuance of the constitution.

The Bank of the United States has, constitutionally, a right to establish its branches or offices of discount and deposit within any State.

The State, within which such branch may be established, cannot, without violating the constitution, tax that branch.

The State governments have no right to tax any of the constitutional means employed by the goverment of the Union to execute its constitutional powers.

524 From *Report of Cases Argued and Adjudged in the Supreme Court, 1819,* by Henry Wheaton, New York, 1819

MARSHALL BROADENS THE POWER OF THE SUPREME COURT

NATIONALISM was further strengthened by a number of important decisions handed down by the Supreme Court, still dominated by Marshall. In 1810 it was determined that a state might not break a contract made with a private person (*Fletcher* vs. *Peck*); nine years later this protection was broadened in the famous Dartmouth College case. *United States* vs. *Peters* (1819), *Martin* vs. *Hunter's Lessee* (1816), and *Cohens* vs. *Virginia* (1821), immensely extended the jurisdiction of the national judiciary over state cases. In *McCulloch* vs. *Maryland* (1819), Hamilton's doctrine of implied powers and policy of liberal construction of the Constitution received judicial sanction; in *Gibbons* vs. *Ogden* (1824), the court hinted at the vast field of power resident in the interstate commerce clause of the Federal Constitution. Private and public protest at these "encroachments upon the rights of the States" were unheeded.

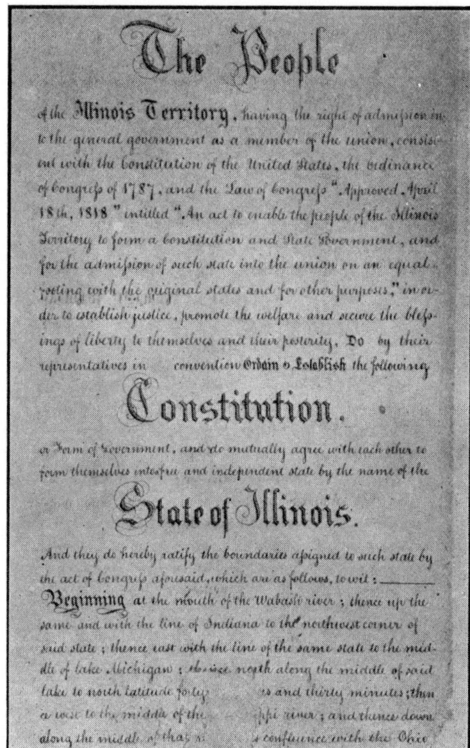

The People of the Illinois Territory, having the right of admission into the general government as a member of the union, consistent with the Constitution of the United States, the ordinance of Congress of 1787, and the Law of Congress "Approved April 18th, 1818" entitled "An act to enable the people of the Illinois Territory to form a Constitution and State Government, and for the admission of such state into the union on an equal footing with the original states and for other purposes," in order to establish justice, promote the welfare and secure the blessings of liberty to themselves and their posterity, Do by their representatives in convention Ordain & Establish the following

Constitution.

a Form of Government, and do mutually agree with each other to form themselves into a free and independent state by the name of the

State of Illinois.

And they do hereby ratify the boundaries assigned to such state by the act of Congress aforesaid, which are as follows, to wit: ——

Beginning at the mouth of the Wabash river; thence up the same and with the line of Indiana to the northwest corner of said state; thence east with the line of the same state to the middle of Lake Michigan; thence north along the middle of said lake to north latitude forty [illegible] and thirty minutes; then [illegible] to the middle of the [illegible] river; and thence down along the middle of that [illegible] confluence with the Ohio

525 Facsimile of the first page of the Illinois Constitution, in the Department of State, Springfield, Ill.

SLAVE STATES ARE PAIRED WITH FREE

THE great slavery struggle broke in upon the peace of Monroe's administration. The question had smoldered since Congress in 1807 closed the foreign slave trade. Interest in emancipation had persisted, while an economic motive appeared for the institution's defense. The South discovered that her predominance in national affairs, so far as it was based on population, was waning. To preserve the balance between North and South in the Senate, the scheme was hit upon of admitting new states in pairs, one slave, one free, thus: Indiana (1816) and Mississippi (1817); Illinois (1818) and Alabama (1819).

526 Jesse Burgess Thomas, 1777–1853, from the portrait in the Illinois State Historical Society, Springfield

THE MISSOURI COMPROMISE CLOSES HOT DEBATE

The issue was joined in February, 1819, when James Tallmadge, Jr., of New York, during consideration of a bill enabling Missouri to form a state constitution, moved an amendment which prohibited the further extension of slavery and provided for gradual abolition within Missouri. Once started, the debate raged throughout the country. Jefferson wrote, "A geographical line, coinciding with a marked principle, moral and political, once conceived and held up to the angry passions of men, will never be obliterated; and every new irritation will mark it deeper and deeper." The Missouri question led to violent discussion, the North condemning any attempt to increase the number of slave states, the South contending for slave owners' rights under the Constitution. For a time, however, a way out was found in the Compromise of 1820, which, offered by Senator Jesse B. Thomas of Illinois, by amendment admitted Missouri without restriction, but prohibited slavery north of 36° 30′ north latitude (this being Missouri's southern boundary) in the remainder of the Louisiana Purchase. Maine was admitted as a free state to balance the admission of Missouri. Excitement subsided, for it was thought that the issue was settled, that the Union was saved.

SPEECH

OF

THE HONORABLE

JAMES TALLMADGE, Jr.

OF

Duchess County, New-York,

IN THE

House of Representatives of the United States,

ON

SLAVERY.

TO WHICH IS ADDED, THE PROCEEDINGS OF THE

MANUMISSION SOCIETY

OF THE CITY OF NEW-YORK,

AND THE

CORRESPONDENCE OF THEIR COMMITTEE

WITH

Messrs. Tallmadge and Taylor.

NEW-YORK:

PRINTED BY E. CONRAD,

Frankfort-street.

1819.

526 Title-page of the copy in the New York Public Library

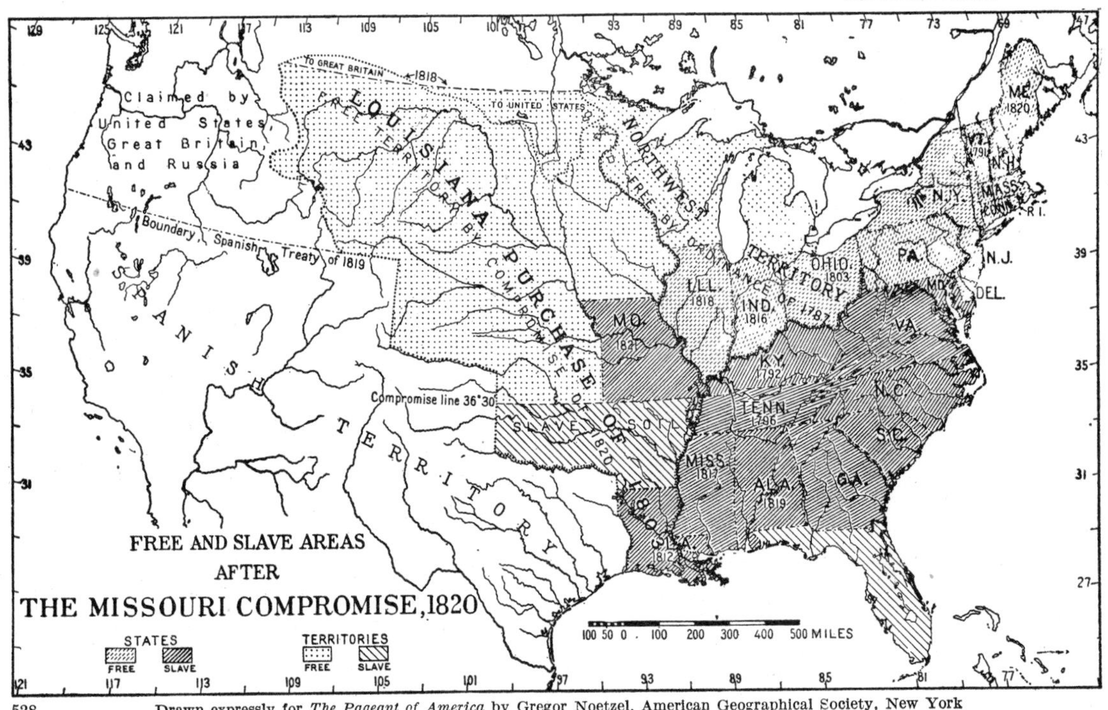

528 Drawn expressly for *The Pageant of America* by Gregor Noetzel, American Geographical Society, New York

SPAIN CEDES FLORIDA

MEANWHILE external affairs reëngaged the attention of the Administration. It began with the question of the Florida purchase. Negotiations to this end had been opened by Jefferson; often interrupted, often renewed, they now came to a head. The Napoleonic wars had weakened Spain's control of her American colonies. South America was winning independence. In Florida little effort was made by the Spanish authorities to preserve order; Jackson's invasion in 1818 brought home their impotence. (See Vol. II.) So, thanks to the able diplomacy of John Quincy Adams, Spain ceded what she could not hold; the treaty also placed the disputed western boundary of Louisiana at the Sabine River.

GREAT BRITAIN SUGGESTS ALLIANCE WITH AMERICA

NEW troubles soon harassed the Spanish Government in the form of a republican revolution. The King then called for help from the other European powers joined with him in the Holy Alliance. France, as their agent, went to Spain's aid. It was widely believed that the next venture would be to subdue Spain's colonies and the struggling young republics in South America. This displeased Great Britain. She had looked with some favor, not lessened by a growing trade, upon the liberal revolts in the southern continent. Canning, Foreign Minister, therefore suggested in August, 1823, that the United States unite with England in protesting against the impending invasion.

529 Article 3 of the Treaty with Spain, 1819, fixing the western boundary of Louisiana, original in the Department of State, Washington

530 Page of James Monroe's letter to Jefferson, Oct. 17, 1823, referring to Canning's proposal of "a co-operation between Great Britain and the United States against the Holy Alliance," original in the Library of Congress

531 Page of Jefferson's letter to Monroe, Oct. 20, 1823, referring to Great Britain as "the nation which can do us the most harm of any one, or all, on earth; and with her on our side we need not fear the whole world," original in the Library of Congress

most enlightened citizens, and under which we
have enjoyed unexampled felicity, this whole
nation is devoted. We owe it therefore to candor,
and to the amicable relations existing between
the United States and those powers, to declare that
we should consider any attempt on their part to
extend their system to any portion of this Hemis-
-phere, as dangerous to our peace and safety.
With the existing Colonies or dependencies of any
European power we have not interfered, and shall
not interfere. But with the Governments who have
declared their Independence, and maintained
it, and whose Independence we have, on great
consideration, and on just principles, acknowledged,
we could not view any interposition for the purpose
of oppressing them, or controlling in any other
manner, their destiny, by any European power,
in any other light, than as the manifestation of
an unfriendly disposition towards the United
States. In the war between those new Governments
and Spain, we declared our neutrality at the
time of their recognition, and to this we have

532 The Monroe Doctrine in Monroe's handwriting, from the message to Congress, Dec. 2, 1823, original in the Library of Congress

ADAMS PERSUADES MONROE TO ADOPT THE FAMOUS "DOCTRINE"

Adams, however, did not desire that the United States should "come in as a cock-boat in the wake of the British man-of-war." He believed that England would act whether we coöperated or not; and that the United States was the leading power in America and should declare an independent policy. In this position he was strengthened by the knowledge that Great Britain would not be loath to acquire new territory in the western hemisphere. The arguments of the able Secretary of State convinced Monroe, whose public was made ready by popular sympathy with the South American republics. The annual message to Congress was selected as the vehicle, and on December 2, 1823, "the Monroe Doctrine" took its place in the list of American political "stereotypes."

CHAPTER IX

JACKSONIAN DEMOCRACY

BORN of the sturdy nationalism springing up after the War of 1812, came Jacksonian Democracy. Out of the West, to perturb the sanguine and contented East, rose a new hurly-burly spirit. To the frontiersman and the worker in the city there seemed something awry with the system which gave to men prosperous freedom, but denied them the power to direct the flow of that prosperity more fully and more equitably. The self-confidence that had been bred by the social and economic conditions of the American frontier now asserted that the Virginia Dynasty, and King Caucus, must give place to a scheme of things more consonant with the times, more democratic.

Thus, on an irresistible wave of protest there came into power that strange thing called Jacksonian Democracy. Stubborn, honest, outspoken, eager, it tried with fumbling hands to redirect the course of events. Government henceforth was to be administered, not simply in the interest of the people, but also by the people. This ambition to rule was furthermore stimulated by a widespread suspicion that government in the past had not in all cases been carried on for the welfare of the common people, that government had been controlled by the few for the benefit of the few. Hence the common man must assume control; the man of little learning but of immense good will was representative of the mass, and to him must power be given; upon his counsel the public servants were to rely. Power to rule was to be justified, not by the accident of office, but by the character of the man. Thus were the people to come into their own.

Of all the men of the day, Andrew Jackson seemed most fully to embody the popular aspirations. To him, therefore, were gladly given the reins of power. One of themselves, he could be trusted. That such a delegation of power to the President might still further weaken the hold of the people upon their government was not foreseen, except by those who liked neither Jackson nor his ideas. They watched him accumulate power into his own hands, and predicted disaster. They dubbed him King Andrew, and asserted that the new situation was worse than anything that had been charged against the Virginia Dynasty. Jackson soon gave them plenty of cause for worry, for expostulation, for denunciation. It appeared that he had no respect for tradition, for the accepted decencies of political conduct. It became a matter of course that men of the older school should oppose the Democrats on every issue, large or small.

Thus, under Jackson, the character of the national government underwent transformation. The Presidency was exalted as never before; the cabinet became openly and completely subject to the will of the chief; the Congress lost all claim to direct the actions of the administration, and became a critic of, rather than a guide for, the President. Even the independence of the courts was threatened. No wonder the conservatives within the country were aghast; no wonder that, once they had recovered their powers of speech and action, they should begin a bitter battle against King Mob.

In the midst of this titanic struggle there appeared an issue that was to prove so momentous as to transcend all others. Unforeseen by most, unwelcome to all, a question began to distort the answers attempted for all others: What was the nature of these United States? Was it a loose, convenient league of sovereignties? Or a permanent consolidated union?

STATE OF TENNESSEE,

IN GENERAL ASSEMBLY,

OCTOBER 17th, 1813.

***RESOLVED** by the General Assembly of the State of Tennessee,* That our Senators in Congress be instructed, and our Representatives requested, to use their best endeavours to prevail upon Congress, to propose to the several States for their adoption, an amendment to the Constitution of the United States, so as to reduce the term of service of Senators in Congress, from six to that of four years, from the time they enter upon the duties of their appointments.

Resolved, That the Executive of this state be requested to transmit a copy of the foregoing resolution to each of our Senators and Representatives in Congress, and to each of the Executives of the several states, with a request that they submit it to the consideration of their respective Legislatures.

Th: Claiborne

Speaker of the House of Representatives,

Robt C. Foster,

Speaker of the Senate.

ATTEST,

W Alexander *Clk. H. Rep.*

James Rogers *Clk. Senate.*

533 Tennessee Proposal to Amend the Constitution, Oct. 17, 1813, from the copy of the resolution in the New York Historical Society

THE WEST CALLS THE EAST UNDEMOCRATIC

EVEN before Monroe's election, the West was beginning to make itself felt and heard. The hardy frontiersman cherished notions of democracy that met with obstacles in many of the political institutions established on the seaboard. Property qualifications for the suffrage and for office, long tenure of office, the indirect election of Senators and President — these were devices to maintain the aristocrat in power. They met with little favor in the West. There were murmurings against the congressional caucus as an unconstitutional and undemocratic device. This caucus was a meeting of the members of the same political party who sat in the Senate and the House for the purpose of nominating the party candidate for the Presidency. The United States was too large and transportation facilities were too poorly developed to make a national nominating convention possible. This ground swell of opposition reached the national political shore in the election of 1824. The Federalist party had disappeared, leaving no opponent for the Republicans. Monroe was not the man to maintain party discipline; nor was there any outstanding candidate for the succession. Hence the election became a personal rather than a partisan struggle under which lay an unavowed sectionalism.

NEW BLOOD FROM THE WEST SHOWS POLITICAL STRENGTH

THE caucus candidate was William H. Crawford, Secretary of the Treasury, whose greatest strength lay in Virginia, mother of Presidents. Crawford had been born in Amherst County, Virginia, although he was at this time a resident of Georgia. But the West was tiring of the Virginia Dynasty. Already the legislatures of Kentucky and Tennessee had put forward Henry Clay and Andrew Jackson as their favorites. Early in 1823 Massachusetts placed John Quincy Adams in the running. All were in name Republicans, all tried to appeal for support to every part of the country. But Crawford was handicapped by illness, and by the widespread belief that he was little more than an intriguing politician, a suspicion perhaps justified by his Tenure of Office Act of 1820. Nomination by the Caucus, moreover, had by now become a liability rather than an asset. This was the more true in that Crawford's nomination had been made at a meeting attended only by that minority of Republicans favoring his candidacy.

534 William H. Crawford, 1772–1834, from the portrait by Charles Bird King in the Redwood Library, Newport, R. I.

535 From a campaign cartoon, 1824, by Crackfardi, in the New York Historical Society

JACKSON'S CANDIDACY MAKES A POPULAR APPEAL

Adams was strong, but almost solely in the North. Clay in the West represented similar interests. Jackson proved the only candidate with a national appeal. His strength was based partly upon his military record, partly upon his simple manners, partly upon the fact that he was untainted by long political service. He stood for a change. As the campaign progressed his strength grew; Clay finished the contest in fourth place.

CLAY GIVES THE PRESIDENCY TO JOHN QUINCY ADAMS

Jackson received the largest number of votes in the electoral college but not a majority. Under the provisions laid down by the Constitution the election went to the House of Representatives. Clay, the genial speaker of the House, held the balance of power. Though personally unfriendly toward Adams, and differing from him immensely in character, Clay found the New England man the candidate to support. While the views of Adams were much like his own, the former's unpopularity hindered a second term; this would enable Clay in 1828 to join northwest and northeast in a successful campaign against his bitter enemy, Jackson. So, on the first ballot, Adams received the vote of thirteen states, Jackson of seven, and Crawford of four. On being informed of the result of the election, the President-elect addressed a letter of acceptance to the House. He reminded them of the novel conditions under which he had been chosen, conditions unprecedented in the short history of the Republic, and called for their aid in making his administration successful.

536 From the painting *The Old House of Representatives*, by S. F. B. Morse (1791–1872) in the Corcoran Gallery of Art, Washington

537 John Quincy Adams, 1767–1848, from the portrait, about 1840, by Chester Harding in the Redwood Library, Newport, R. I.

ADAMS IS HANDICAPPED

Adams brought to the Presidency integrity of character, a wide experience in foreign affairs and a deep knowledge of the needs of the country. He was a thorough-going nationalist and his administration was characterized by increased federal expenditures for public improvements. In temperament he was less suited to the office. Ungracious and unbending, he rarely made warm friends and always made warm enemies. The political situation aggravated these characteristics. The administration was a time of party realignment, with continuous jockeying for position in Congress and before the people. Jackson denounced the appointment of Clay to the chief cabinet post as the reward for a corrupt bargain; the election of Adams was, moreover, a defeat of the popular will, which had favored Jackson above all others. Around "Old Hickory" gathered all the many elements antagonized by the implacable Puritan. Electioneering for the next campaign began in 1824. The opposition of the militant Jackson made it impossible for President Adams to proceed far with his statesman-like plans for the nation.

JACKSON'S FOLLOWERS ATTACK ADAMS

Even more than the campaign of 1824, that of 1828 was a battle of personalities. The intervening years had embittered former political friends. The downfall of "King Caucus" called into being new and more elaborate party machinery, controlled by such masters as Clay, and Martin Van Buren of New York. Campaigning was nationalized. National party committees took charge, preparing literature, devising appeals, directing tactics. The campaign of 1828 began almost with the inauguration of President Adams. A persistent effort was made by Jackson's followers to discredit the administration with the corrupt bargain charge. The illustration, "Adams and Liberty," is typical of the campaign material which was distributed as Adams neared the end of his term. It depicts the use of electioneering methods that were somewhat novel at the time, but which within the next few years came to be accepted as a matter of course.

Centreville, July 19th, 1828.

Dear Sirs,—You were appointed at a county meeting of the friends of the Administration, held in this place, in May, 1827, a committee of vigilance for your district, and being uncertain whether you have been informed of that appointment, we beg leave now to notify you of it, and at the same time to solicit your co-operation and unremitting exertions to the duties which will be required of you. It is probably not unknown to you, that our opponents are daily making privately, as well as publicly, the most strenuous efforts, and unless we meet them in a correspondent manner, *showing an imposing front*, and a *bold, determined courage*, we may be defeated, although we believe that

when there KEPT IN VIEW by the persons who convey them, UNTIL THEY HAVE VOTED; each committee man to be as active and industrious as possible on the day of election, *a part of whom, the MOST POWERFUL, both in PERSONAL STRENGTH and COURAGE*, not less than six, must be appointed to stand constantly at the polls for the purpose as well of defending the rights of our friends, as to object to illegal voters, many of whom, particularly young men, nearly of age, will no doubt be pushed forward. The chairman and secretary ought immediately to add to your number of committee men, at least twenty, or more if necessary—*taking them out of every neighborhood* in the district, and also *taking care to*

538 From a campaign circular of 1828 in possession of the publishers

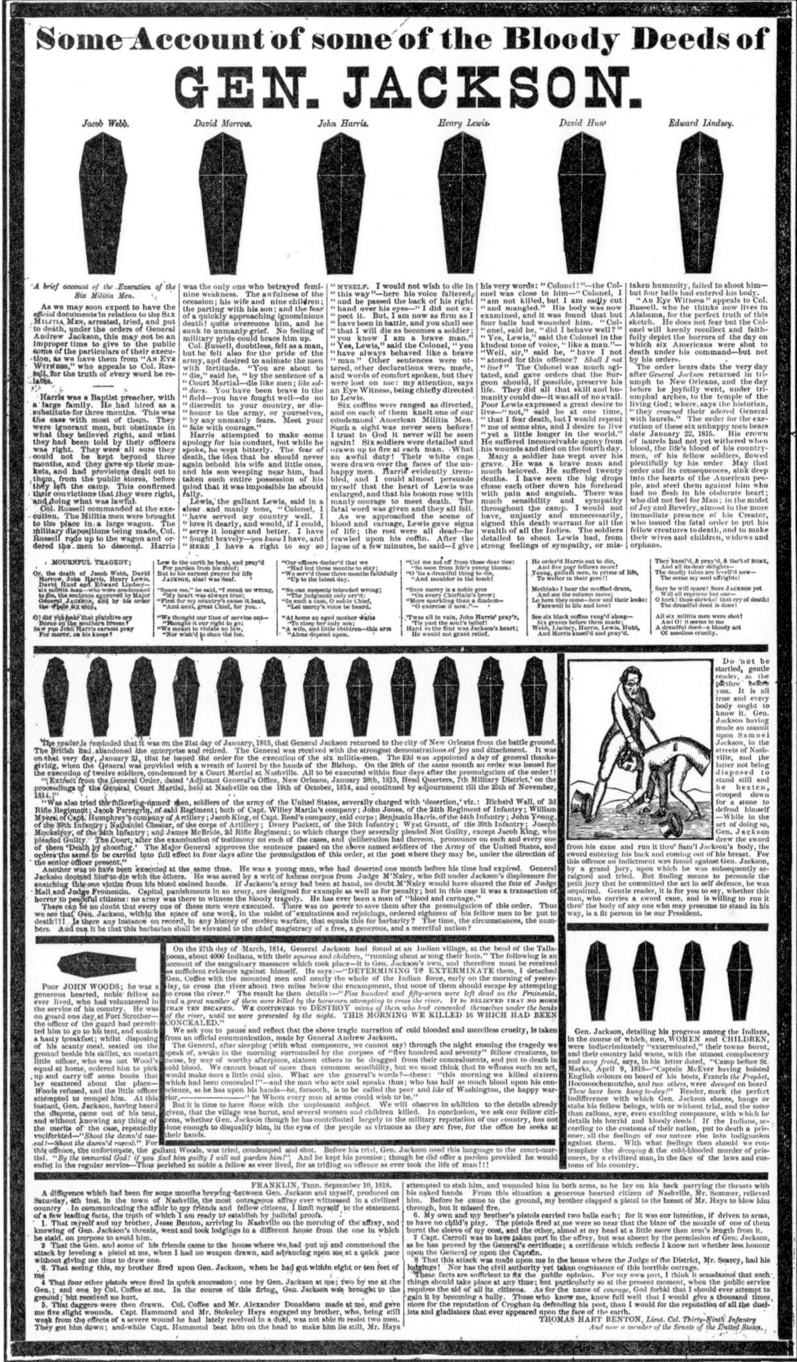

Some Account of some of the Bloody Deeds of GEN. JACKSON.

Jacob Webb. David Morrow. John Harris. Henry Lewis. David Hunt. Edward Lindsey.

A brief account of the Execution of the Six Militia Men.

As we may soon expect to have the *official* documents in relation to the SIX MILITIA MEN, arrested, tried, and put to death, under the orders of General Andrew Jackson, this may not be an improper time to give to the public some of the particulars of their execution, as we have them from "AN EYE WITNESS," who appeals to Col. Russell, for the truth of every word he relates.

Harris was a Baptist preacher, with a large family. He had hired as a substitute for three months. This was the case with most of them. They were ignorant men, but obstinate in what they believed right, and what they had been told by their officers was right. They were all sure they could not be kept beyond three months, and they gave up their muskets, and had provisions dealt out to them, from the public stores, before they left the camp. This confirmed their convictions that they were right, and doing what was lawful.

Col. Russell commanded at the execution. The Militia men were brought to the place in a large wagon. The military dispositions being made, Col. Russell rode up to the wagon and ordered the men to descend. Harris was the only one who betrayed feminine weakness. The awfulness of the occasion; his wife and nine children; the parting with his son; and the fear of a quickly approaching ignominious death! quite overcome him, and he sunk in unmanly grief. No feeling of military pride could brace him up.

Col. Russell, doubtless, felt as a man, but he felt also for the pride of the army, and desired to animate the men with fortitude. "You are about to "die," said he, "by the sentence of a "Court Martial—die like men; *like sol-"diers.* You have been brave in the "field—you have fought well—do no "discredit to your country, or dis-"honor to the army, or yourselves, "by any unmanly fears. Meet your "fate with courage."

Harris attempted to make some apology for his conduct, but while he spoke, he wept bitterly. The fear of death, the idea that he should never again behold his wife and little ones, and his son weeping near him, had taken such entire possession of his mind that it was impossible he should rally.

Lewis, the gallant Lewis, said in a clear and manly tone, "Colonel, I "have served my country well. I "love it dearly, and would, if I could, "serve it longer and better. I have "fought bravely—*you know* I have, and "HERE I have a right to say so "MYSELF. I would not wish to die in "this way"—here his voice faltered, "and he passed the back of his right "hand over his eyes—"I did not ex-"pect it. But, I am now as firm as I "have been in battle, and you shall see "that I will die as becomes a soldier; "you know I am a brave man." "Yes, Lewis," said the Colonel, "you "have always behaved like a brave "man." Other sentences were uttered, other declarations were made, and words of comfort spoken, but they were lost on me: my attention, says an Eye Witness, being chiefly directed to Lewis.

Six coffins were ranged as directed, and on each of them knelt one of our condemned American Militia Men. Such a sight was never seen before! I trust to God it never will be seen again! Six soldiers were detailed and drawn up to fire at each man. What an awful duty! Their white caps were drawn over the faces of the unhappy men. Harris evidently trembled, and I could almost persuade myself that the heart of Lewis was enlarged, and that his bosom rose with manly courage to meet death. The fatal word was given and they all fell.

As we approached the scene of blood and carnage, Lewis gave signs of life; the rest were all dead—he crawled upon his coffin. After the lapse of a few minutes, he said—I give his very words: "Colonel!"—the Colonel was close to him—"Colonel, I "am not killed, but I am sadly cut "and mangled." His body was now examined, and it was found that but four balls had wounded him. "Col-"onel, said he, "did I behave well?" "Yes, Lewis," said the Colonel in the kindest tone of voice, "like a man."—"Well, sir," said he, "have I not "atoned for this offence? *Shall I not "live?*" The Colonel was much agitated, and gave orders that the Surgeon should, if possible, preserve his life. They did all that skill and humanity could do—it was all of no avail. Poor Lewis expressed a great desire to live—"not," said he at one time, "that I fear death, but I would repent "me of some sins, and I desire to live "yet a little longer in the world." He suffered inconceivable agony from his wounds and died on the fourth day.

Many a soldier has wept over his grave. He was a brave man and much beloved. He suffered twenty deaths. I have seen the big drops chase each other down his forehead with pain and anguish. There was much sensibility and sympathy throughout the camp. I would not have, unjustly and unnecessarily, signed this death warrant for all the wealth of all the Indies. The soldiers detailed to shoot Lewis had, from strong feelings of sympathy, or mistaken humanity, failed to shoot him—but four balls had entered his body.

"An Eye Witness" appeals to Col. Russell, who he thinks now lives in Alabama, for the perfect truth of this sketch. He does not fear but the Colonel will keenly recollect and faithfully depict the horrors of the day on which six Americans were shot to death under his command—but not by his orders.

The order bears date the very day after *General Jackson* returned in triumph to New Orleans, and the day before he joyfully went, under triumphal arches, to the temple of the living God; where, says the historian, "they *crowned* their adored General with laurels." The order for the execution of these six unhappy men bears date January 22, 1815. His crown of laurels had not yet withered when blood, the life's blood of his countrymen, of his fellow soldiers, flowed plentifully by his order. May that order and its consequences, sink deep into the hearts of the American people, and steel them against him who had no flesh in his obdurate heart; who did not feel for Man; in the midst of Joy and Revelry, almost in the more immediate presence of his Creator, who issued the fatal order to put his fellow creatures to death, and to make their wives and children, widows and orphans.

MOURNFUL TRAGEDY;

Or, the death of Jacob Webb, David Morrow, John Harris, Henry Lewis, David Hunt and Edward Lindsey—six militia men—who were condemned to die, the sentence approved by Major General JACKSON, and by his order the whole six shot.

O! did you hear that plaintive cry
Borne on the southern breeze?
Saw you John Harris earnest pray
For mercy, on his knees?

Low to the earth he bent, and pray'd
For pardon from his chief;
But to his earnest prayer for life
JACKSON, alas! was deaf.

"Spare me," he said, "I mean no wrong,
"My heart was always true;
"First for my country's cause it beat,
"And next, great Chief, for you.

"We thought our time of service out—
"Thought it our right to go;
"We meant to violate no law,
"Nor wish'd to shun the foe.

"Our officers declar'd that we
"Had but three months to stay;
"We serv'd those three months faithfully
"Up to the latest day.

"No one suspects intended wrong;
"The judgment only err'd:
"In such a case, O noble Chief,
"Let mercy's voice be heard.

"At home an aged mother waits
"To clasp her only son;
"A wife, and little children—this arm
"Alone depend upon.

"Cut me not off from those dear ties:
"So soon from life's young bloom:
"O 'tis a dreadful thing to die,
"And moulder in the tomb!

"Sure mercy is a noble gem
"On every Chieftain's brow;
"More sparkling than a diadem—
"O exercise it now."—

'Twas all in vain, John Harris' pray'r,
'Tis past the soul's belief!
Hard as the flint was Jackson's heart;
He would not grant relief.

He order'd Harris out to die,
And five poor fellows more!
Young, gallant men, in prime of life,
To welter in their gore!!

Methinks I hear the muffled drum,
And see the column move;
Lo here they come—how sad their looks:
Farewell to life and love!

See six black coffins rang'd along—
Six graves before them made;
Webb, Lindsey, Harris, Lewis, Hunt,
And Morris kneel'd and pray'd.

They kneel'd, & pray'd, & tho't of HOME,
And all its dear delights—
The deadly tubes are levell'd now—
The scene my soul affrights!

Sure he will spare! Sure JACKSON yet
Will all reprieve but one—
O hark! those shrieks! that cry of death!
The dreadful deed is done!

All six militia men were shot!
And O! it seems to me
A dreadful deed—a bloody act
Of needless cruelty.

The reader is reminded that it was on the 21st day of January, 1815, that General Jackson returned to the city of New Orleans from the battle ground. The British had abandoned the enterprise and retired. The General was received with the strongest demonstrations of joy and attachment. It was on that very day, January 21, that he issued the order for the execution of the six militia-men. The 23d was appointed a day of general thanksgiving, when the General was provided with a wreath of laurel by the hands of the Bishop. On the 28th of the same month an order was issued for the execution of twelve soldiers, condemned by a Court Martial at Nashville. All to be executed within four days after the promulgation of the order!!

"[Extract from the General Order, dated 'Adjutant General's Office, New Orleans, January 28th, 1815, Head Quarters, 7th Military District,' on the proceedings of the General Court Martial, held at Nashville on the 19th of October, 1814, and continued by adjournment till the 25th of November, 1814.]"

"Was also tried the following-named men, soldiers of the army of the United States, severally charged with 'desertion,' viz.: Richard Wall, of 3d Rifle Regiment; Jacob Perregrin, of said Regiment; both of Capt. Willey Martin's company; John Jones, of the 24th Regiment of Infantry; William Myers, of Capt. Humphrey's company of Artillery; Jacob King, of Capt. Reed's company, said corps; Benjamin Harris, of the 44th Infantry; John Young, of the 39th Infantry; Nathaniel Chester, of the corps of Artillery; Drury Puckett, of the 24th Infantry; Wyat Grantt, of the 39th Infantry; Joseph Muckelroy, of the 24th Infantry; and James McBride, 2d Rifle Regiment; to which charge they severally pleaded Not Guilty, except Jacob King, who pleaded Guilty. The Court, after the examination of testimony on each of the cases, and deliberation had thereon, pronounce on each and every one of them 'Death by shooting.' The Major General approves the sentence passed on the above named soldiers of the Army of the United States, and orders the same to be carried into full effect in four days after the promulgation of this order, at the post where they may be, under the direction of the senior officer present."

Another was to have been executed at the same time. He was a young man, who had deserted one month before his time had expired. General Jackson doomed him to die with the others. He was saved by a writ of habeas corpus from Judge M'Nairy, who fell under Jackson's displeasure for snatching this one victim from his blood stained hands. If Jackson's army had been at hand, no doubt M'Nairy would have shared the fate of Judge Hall and Judge Fromentin. Capital punishments in an army, are designed for example as well as for penalty; but in this case it was a transaction of horror to peaceful citizens: no army was there to witness the bloody tragedy. He has ever been a man of "blood and carnage."

There can be no doubt that every one of these men were executed. There was no power to save them after the promulgation of this order. Thus we see that Gen. Jackson, within the space of one week, in the midst of exultations and rejoicings, ordered eighteen of his fellow men to be put to death!!! Is there any instance on record, in any history of modern warfare, that equals this for barbarity? The time, the circumstances, the numbers. And can it be that this barbarian shall be elevated to the chief magistracy of a free, a generous, and a merciful nation?

Do not be startled, gentle reader, at the picture before you. It is all true and every body ought to know it. Gen. Jackson having made an assault upon Samuel Jackson, in the streets of Nashville, and the latter not being disposed to stand still and be beaten, stooped down for a stone to defend himself—While in the act of doing so, Gen. Jackson drew the sword from his cane and run it thro' Sam'l Jackson's body, the sword entering his back and coming out of his breast. For this offence an indictment was found against Gen. Jackson, by a grand jury, upon which he was subsequently arraigned and tried. But finding means to persuade the petit jury that he committed the act in self defence, he was acquitted. Gentle reader, it is for you to say, whether this man, who carries a sword cane, and is willing to run it thro' the body of any one who may presume to stand in his way, is a fit person to be our President.

Poor JOHN WOODS; he was a generous hearted, noble fellow as ever lived, who had volunteered in the service of his country. He was on guard one day, at Fort Strother—the officer of the guard had permitted him to go to his tent, and snatch a hasty breakfast; whilst disposing of his scanty meal, seated on the ground beside his skillet, an upstart little officer, who was not Wood's equal at home, ordered him to pick up and carry off some bones that lay scattered about the place—Woods refused, and the little officer attempted to compel him. At this instant, Gen. Jackson, having heard the dispute, came out of his tent, and without knowing any thing of the merits of the case, repeatedly vociferated—"*Shoot the damn'd rascal!—Shoot the damn'd rascal.*" For this offence, the unfortunate, the gallant Woods, was tried, condemned and shot. Before his trial, Gen. Jackson used this language to the court-martial. "*By the immortal God! if you find him guilty I will not pardon him!*" And he kept his promise; though he did offer a pardon provided he would enlist in the regular service—Thus perished as noble a fellow as ever lived, for as trifling an offence as ever took the life of man!!!

On the 27th day of March, 1814, General Jackson had found at an Indian village, at the bend of the Tallapoosa, about 4000 Indians, with their *squaws* and *children*, "running about among their huts." The following is an account of the sanguinary massacre which took place—it is Gen. Jackson's own, and therefore must be received as sufficient evidence against himself. He says:—"DETERMINING TO EXTERMINATE them, I detached Gen. Coffee with the mounted men and nearly the whole of the Indian force, early on the morning of yesterday, to cross the river about two miles below the encampment, that none of them should escape by attempting to cross the river." The result he then details:—"*Five hundred and fifty-seven were left dead on the Peninsula, and a great number of them were killed by the horsemen attempting to cross the river.* IT IS BELIEVED THAT NO MORE THAN TEN ESCAPED. WE CONTINUED TO DESTROY *many of them who had concealed themselves under the banks of the river, until we were prevented by the night.* THIS MORNING WE KILLED 16 WHICH HAD BEEN CONCEALED."

We ask you to pause and reflect that the above tragic narration of cold blooded and merciless cruelty, is taken from an official communication, made by General Andrew Jackson.

The General, after sleeping (with what composure, we cannot say) through the night ensuing the tragedy we speak of, awoke in the morning surrounded by the corpses of "five hundred and seventy" fellow creatures, to cause, by way of worthy afterpiece, sixteen others to be dragged from their concealments, and put to death in cold blood. We cannot boast of more than common sensibility, but we must think that to witness such an act, would make ours a little cold also. What are the general's words?—these: "this morning we killed sixteen which had been concealed!"—and the man who acts and speaks thus; who has half as much blood upon his conscience, as he has upon his hands—he, forsooth, is to be called the peer and *like* of Washington, the happy warrior,—————"he Whom every man at arms could wish to be."

But it is time to have done with the unpleasant subject. We will observe in addition to the details already given, that the village was burnt, and several women and children killed. In conclusion, we ask our fellow citizens, whether Gen. Jackson though he has contributed largely to the military reputation of our country, has not done enough to disqualify him, in the eyes of the people as virtuous as they are free, for the office he seeks at their hands.

Gen. Jackson, detailing his progress among the Indians, in the course of which, men, WOMEN and CHILDREN, were indiscriminately "exterminated," their towns burnt, and their country laid waste, with the utmost complacency and *sang froid*, says, in his letter dated, "Camp before St. Marks, April 9, 1818—"Captain McEver having hoisted English colours on board of his boats, Francis *the Prophet*, Hocomochemutcho, and *two others*, were *decoyed* on board *These have been hung to-day!*" Reader, mark the perfect indifference with which Gen. Jackson shoots, hangs or stabs his fellow beings, with or without trial, and the more than callous, aye, even exulting composure, with which he details his horrid and bloody deeds! If the Indians, according to the customs of their nation, put to death a prisoner, all the feelings of our nature rise into indignation against them. With what feelings then should we contemplate the *decoying* & the cold-blooded murder of prisoners, by a civilized man, in the face of the laws and customs of his country.

FRANKLIN, Tenn. September 10, 1818.

A difference which had been for some months brewing between Gen. Jackson and myself, produced on Saturday, 4th inst. in the town of Nashville, the most outrageous affray ever witnessed in a civilized country. In communicating the affair to my friends and fellow citizens, I limit myself to the statement of a few leading facts, the truth of which I am ready to establish by judicial proofs.

1. That myself and my brother, Jesse Benton, arriving in Nashville on the morning of the affray, and knowing of Gen. Jackson's threats, went and took lodgings in a different house from the one in which he staid, on purpose to avoid him.

2 That the Gen. and some of his friends came to the house where we had put up and commenced the attack by leveling a pistol at me, when I had no weapon drawn, and advancing upon me at a quick pace without giving me time to draw one.

3. That seeing this, my brother fired upon Gen. Jackson, when he had got within eight or ten feet of me

4 That four other pistols were fired in quick succession; one by Gen. Jackson at me; two by me at the Gen.; and one by Col. Coffee at me. In the course of this firing, Gen. Jackson was brought to the ground; but received no hurt.

5. That daggers were then drawn. Col. Coffee and Mr. Alexander Donaldson made at me, and gave me five slight wounds. Capt. Hammond and Mr. Stokeley Hays engaged my brother, who, being still weak from the effects of a severe wound he had lately received in a duel, was not able to resist two men. They got him down; and while Capt. Hammond beat him on the head to make him lie still, Mr. Hays attempted to stab him, and wounded him in both arms, as he lay on his back parrying the thrusts with his naked hands. From this situation a generous hearted citizen of Nashville, Mr. Summer, relieved him. Before he came to the ground, my brother clapped a pistol to the breast of Mr. Hays to blow him through, but it missed fire.

6. My own and my brother's pistols carried two balls each; for it was our intention, if driven to arms, to have no child's play. The pistols fired at me were so near that the blaze of the muzzle of one of them burnt the sleeve of my coat, and the other, aimed at my head at a little more than arm's length from it.

7 Capt. Carroll was to have taken part in the affray, but was absent by the permission of Gen. Jackson, as he has proved by the General's certificate; a certificate which reflects I know not whether less honour upon the General or upon the Captain.

8 That this attack was made upon me in the house where the Judge of the District, Mr. Searcy, had his lodgings! Nor has the civil authority yet taken cognisance of this horrible outrage.

These facts are sufficient to fix the public opinion. For my own part, I think it scandalous that such things should take place at any time; but particularly so at the present moment, when the public service requires the aid of all its citizens. As for the name of *courage*, God forbid that I should ever attempt to gain it by becoming a bully. Those who know me, know full well that I would give a thousand times more for the reputation of Croghan in defending his post, than I would for the reputation of all the duelists and gladiators that ever appeared upon the face of the earth.

THOMAS HART BENTON, *Lieut. Col. Thirty-Ninth Infantry*
And now a member of the Senate of the United States.

539 From a copy of a campaign poster known as the "Coffin Hand Bill," referring to the war record of Jackson, in possession of the publishers

PERSONAL ABUSE MARKS THE CAMPAIGN OF 1828

THE main objective of the Democrats in the election of 1828 was to oust the "Ins"; that of the National Republicans, to prevent the victory of the mob, led by the "arch-demagogue" Jackson. Decorous manners were forgotten. Campaign papers were devoted to scurrilous abuse of the opposing leaders. Jackson was characterized as a duellist, a gambler, a cockfighter, a drunkard, a murderer. Adams had bought the Presidency; he was a Freemason, a Unitarian, stingy, extravagant. Worst of all, he had purchased, with public money, a billiard table for the White House!

540 General Andrew Jackson, 1767–1845, from the portrait by Rembrandt Peale, courtesy of John Frederick Lewis, Philadelphia

JACKSON'S ELECTION ROUTS TRADITIONS

JACKSON, with Calhoun as Vice-president, was swept into power with the electoral votes of all the transmontane states. They had, in addition, carried two strategic eastern commonwealths. "Old Hickory's" popularity won Pennsylvania; Van Buren's management won New York. The old official class with its training and its traditions had been ingloriously routed. "King Mob," wrote Justice Story, "seemed triumphant." In Jackson they had found a perfect symbol and leader. He is thus sketched by Burgess (*The Middle Period*, p. 135): "Ignorant and irascible indeed, but virtuous, brave and patriotic beyond any cavil or question; faithful and devoted in his domestic life, absolutely unapproachable by pecuniary inducements; the best of friends and the most implacable of enemies; quick, hasty in forming his judgments and tenacious beyond expression in holding to them; prone to elevate every whim and impulse to a behest of conscience; earnest, terrible in the inflexibility of his purposes; . . . here were certainly qualities calculated to rouse the enthusiasm of the masses, if not of the classes."

AMBITION MAKES JACKSON A GENTLEMAN FARMER

JACKSON was the first President whose humble origin was exploited for political purposes. Though Washington had been a surveyor's assistant, and John Adams was dubbed a "cobbler's son," both had been aristocrats and regarded as such. Now had come a change: the mass had one of their own kind in the chief office in the land. Curiously enough, however, Jackson in one important respect carried on the best Virginia tradition. Like the Virginia presidents, his heart's desire was to be a gentleman farmer. To the Hermitage plantation, purchased in 1804, he gave as much care and thought as to the problems of state.

541 The Hermitage, home of Andrew Jackson, near Nashville, Tenn., from a drawing after a photograph

542 Andrew Jackson as a Planter, from the portrait, 1835, by R. E. W. Earl at the Hermitage

VAN BUREN BECOMES SECRETARY OF STATE

Jackson had come into power on a protest vote. During the campaign and in the building up of his cabinet, he gave little indication of the policies he would favor. Cabinet offices were, indeed, bestowed not because of administrative ability or political attitude, but as party rewards. The first office went to Van Buren, the clever little politician of Kinderhook on the Hudson, who had risen to political importance as the head of a political organization in New York State known as the "Albany Regency," and had been recently chosen Governor of the Empire State. Unknown to Jackson, Van Buren, like Vice-president Calhoun, cherished an ambition to become President. This fact soon played its part in the drama. In Ingham of Pennsylvania, Berrien of Georgia, and Branch of North Carolina, Calhoun secured three supporters in the cabinet. The others were Jackson's personal friends. None had previous experience in national administration; of them all, Van Buren alone proved a power in the new Government. These appointments to the cabinet, awaited with much interest by the triumphant populace, offered the first official inkling of the new character that the national government was assuming.

543 Martin Van Buren, 1782–1862, from the portrait, 1828, by Henry Inman (1801–46) in the City Hall, New York, courtesy of the Municipal Art Commission

544 Amos Kendall, 1789–1869, from an engraving, about 1840, by the Bureau of Engraving & Printing, Washington

SHREWD POLITICIANS FORM A KITCHEN CABINET

It soon became clear that the status of the cabinet had changed. Jackson regarded himself as the people's representative and relied for advice quite as much on outsiders as upon the heads of the departments. Gradually he gathered about him a group of country editors and personal friends whose counsel was so often sought — often in places less pretentious than the council room — that they were nicknamed the "Kitchen Cabinet." Chief among them were Amos Kendall of Kentucky, Isaac Hill of New Hampshire, Major William B. Lewis of Tennessee, Jackson's first campaign manager, and Francis P. Blair, editor of the *Washington Globe*. Nowhere could be found a shrewder group of politicians, nor one more ingenious in controlling the hurly-burly of the party press. The place given them in the process of government was a second indication of the democratization of the system set up forty years before, and a recognition of the part to be played in politics by the newspaper press.

545 John C. Calhoun, 1782–1850, from a miniature, 1827, by John Trumbull in the School of the Fine Arts, Yale University

THE VICE-PRESIDENT WANTS TO BE PRESIDENT

The power of the Kitchen Cabinet was in part due to the growing hostility between the President and Calhoun. In many ways the two men were alike. Both were Carolinians, both were born masters of men, of great courage and honesty. For many years they had been friends. But the resemblance was one of externals. Jackson was the uncultured man of impulse whose prejudices sometimes led to rashness; Calhoun the educated philosopher, who believed in action controlled by reason.

Entering Congress as a War Hawk in 1811, Calhoun had at once become a resourceful leader in debate, a national figure in politics. In 1824 he had yielded the presidential race to Jackson. In 1828 he joined him as Vice-president. For 1832 he was the expected candidate. To this end he bent his great energy. At his behest Duff Green had made the *National Telegraph* a powerful party paper. All who might be influential in politics were assiduously cultivated.

SOUTH CAROLINA CONDEMNS THE HIGH TARIFF

Calhoun found the issue upon which to wage his fight in the discontent of his fellow cotton planters of the South. In the expiring days of the Adams administration, party maneuvers had resulted in the enactment of the "Tariff of Abominations." John Randolph said it was intended "to rob and plunder one half of the Union for the benefit of the residue." In South Carolina long-pent-up feelings of hostility to the tariff exploded. In December, 1828, the legislature adopted an "Exposition" of their views that a protective tariff was unconstitutional and subject to avoidance by state action. Calhoun sympathized with their grievance. His casting vote had defeated the Tariff of 1827; he was the real author of the *Exposition*. From this situation he now hoped to frame an issue which would at once win him the Presidency, revive the prosperity of his state, and stave off the danger of secession.

EXPOSITION

AND PROTEST,

REPORTED

BY THE SPECIAL COMMITTEE

OF THE

HOUSE OF REPRESENTATIVES,

ON

THE TARIFF;

READ AND ORDERED TO BE PRINTED,

Dec. 19*th*, 1828.

COLUMBIA, S. C.

D. W. SIMS, STATE PRINTER.

1829.

546 Title-page of the copy in the New York Public Library

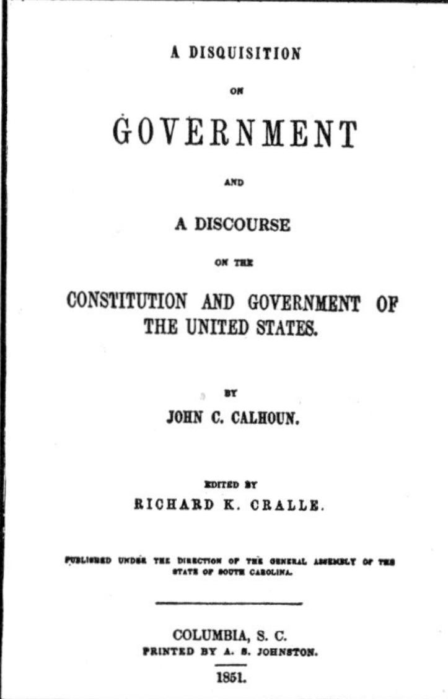

A DISQUISITION

ON

GOVERNMENT

AND

A DISCOURSE

ON THE

CONSTITUTION AND GOVERNMENT OF THE UNITED STATES.

BY

JOHN C. CALHOUN.

EDITED BY

RICHARD K. CRALLE.

PUBLISHED UNDER THE DIRECTION OF THE GENERAL ASSEMBLY OF THE STATE OF SOUTH CAROLINA.

COLUMBIA, S. C.

PRINTED BY A. S. JOHNSTON.

1851.

547 Title-page of the copy in the New York Public Library

CALHOUN MAKES A CONTRIBUTION TO POLITICAL THOUGHT

Metaphysically inclined, Calhoun developed to cover the situation a philosophy of government that still stands as the most original and incisive contribution to American political thought since *The Federalist*. He regarded government as a natural institution which, if left in the hands of the popular majority, would always be utilized by them to tyrannize over minorities. Some device was therefore needed to protect the latter. This he found, in the United States, to rest in the doctrine of "concurrent majorities," whereby no action of importance to any group or section should be taken without their consent. This theory he developed with great acuteness of reasoning in his *Disquisition on Government*, written a short time before his death.

548 Robert Y. Hayne, 1791–1839, from the portrait, about 1823, by S. F. B. Morse in possession of Mrs. William A. Hayne, San Francisco

SOUTHERNERS CLASH WITH NEW ENGLAND INTERESTS

THE first test of Calhoun's strength came early in 1830. In January, Senator Foote of Connecticut introduced a resolution for inquiring into the expediency of limiting land sales in the West. The Southerners seized the occasion to win the dominant West, as represented by Jackson and the Democrats, to their side in the impending struggle with the manufacturing Northeast. Their spokesman was Senator Robert Y. Hayne of South Carolina, a charming gentleman and an able lawyer who had already won laurels as an orator. His vigorous denunciation of the Federalists of New England won wide applause. The Democrats were jubilant; even Jackson wrote him a congratulatory letter. When Hayne approached the subject of nullification, Calhoun, from the chair, openly dispatched by messengers suggestions for the speaker's guidance. The whole speech was generally regarded as a telling shot in the party warfare.

HAYNE DIRECTS HIS ATTACK AT WEBSTER

HAYNE'S attack had been directed at the most conspicuous Federalist in the Senate. Webster's reputation as an orator was already world-wide. But his political career made him easy prey for the Democrats. Early in the war of 1812 he had become leader of the New Hampshire opposition; and it was for this reason that he had been returned to Congress in 1813. Throughout the war he opposed the administration with intemperate fervor that at times approached sedition. When, therefore, on a bitter winter's day he arose to reply to Hayne, the fashionable gallery expected fireworks. His effort was not disappointing. Defense of the war policy of the Federalists was difficult and none too convincing, but his exposition of the Constitution as supreme and binding, and of the Union as indissoluble was masterly.

549 From the painting *Webster's Reply To Hayne*, by G. P. A. Healy (1813–94) in Faneuil Hall, Boston

550 From the painting *Our Federal Union — It Must be Preserved*, by C. W. Jefferys, in possession of the publishers

JACKSON IS ROUSED TO SPEAK FOR THE UNION

To Jackson the encounter at first appeared purely a partisan affair in which his sympathies lay with Hayne. In all probability the danger of disunion had been unnoticed by him, as by most of the leaders, until the Great Debate. Then his eyes were fully opened to the threat. In the spring of 1830, the nullifiers planned a banquet, ostensibly to celebrate Jefferson's birthday, really to associate their doctrine with that of the father of Democracy, and to sound out the President. Jackson and Van Buren divined the motive and together prepared the President's toast for the occasion. "Thus armed," later wrote Van Buren, the "Red Fox," "we repaired to the dinner with feelings on the part of the Chief akin to those which would have animated his breast if the scene of this preliminary skirmish in defense of the Union had been the field of battle instead of the festive board." When, after Jackson's words had electrified the gathering, Calhoun, ever loyal to his convictions, responded with "The Union: next to our liberty, the most dear; May we all remember that it can only be preserved by respecting the rights of the States and by distributing equally the benefits and burdens of the Union," the issue was drawn.

551 From a cartoon by Edward W. Clay (1792–1837), dated Washington, 1831, original in the Historical Society of Pennsylvania, Philadelphia

JACKSON BREAKS WITH CALHOUN AND MAKES CABINET CHANGES

THE final break between Jackson and Calhoun came a month later, when the President for the first time heard that the latter had, in 1818, advised Monroe that General Jackson deserved censure for his conduct in Florida. Jackson, most loyal of friends, could not understand how a professed friend could so act. In May, 1831, he severed all relations with the Vice-president. This was followed by a shake-up in the cabinet. Van Buren, in "King Andrew's" favor, withdrew to give his Chief a free hand. Calhoun's supporters were forced out. These shifts the opposition tried to turn into political capital. In truth, they simply indicated that Jackson would in future have a harmonious and anti-Calhoun cabinet. This consolidation of the ranks of the Jacksonians against the leader of the South was at the time hidden. The press imputed the cabinet dismissals and resignations to the notorious affair of Mrs. Eaton, and quite overlooked their political implications.

ABLER MEN BECOME JACKSON'S ADVISERS

THE new cabinet was composed of abler men. Edward Livingston was Secretary of State. Of the famous New York family, he had moved to Louisiana immediately after the Purchase; there he had long been a prominent Democrat, an ardent nationalist, and Jackson's friend. He was internationally famous for his Code on Reform and Prison Discipline. Roger B. Taney became Attorney-General. He was at this time leader of the Maryland bar and a brilliant pleader before the United States Supreme Court over which he was soon to preside as Chief Justice.

552 Edward Livingston, 1764–1836, from the portrait painted by John Trumbull in 1805 for the City of New York, courtesy of the Municipal Art Commission

SOUTH CAROLINA DEFIES THE NATIONAL GOVERNMENT

THE nullification movement did not halt with speeches and toasts. South Carolina, finding the tariff of 1832 unsatisfactory, met in convention at Columbia. With the Governor as chairman, the assemblage declared the Acts of 1828 and 1832 null and void in South Carolina, as of February, 1833; authorized the calling out of the militia, and asserted that should the National Government try to use force the state would set up its own Government. This defiance aroused the testy Jackson. In December he issued a proclamation, drafted by Livingston, in which South Carolina was warned of what might follow from her conduct. The language was not less nationalistic than that of Webster.

of the People of the United States, whose delegates framed, and whose conventions approved it. The most important among these objects, that which is placed first in rank, on which all the others rest, is "to form a more perfect union." Now, is it possible that even if there were no express provision giving supremacy to the Constitution and laws of the United States over those of the States—can it be conceived that an instrument made for the purpose of "forming a more perfect union" than that of the confederation, could be so constructed by the assembled wisdom of our country as to substitute for that confederation a form of government dependent for its existence on the local interest, the party spirit of a State, or of a prevailing faction in a State? Every man of plain unsophisticated understanding, who hears the question will give such an answer as will preserve the Union.—Metaphysical subtlety, in pursuit of an impracticable theory, could alone have devised one that is calculated to destroy it.

I consider then the power to annul a law of the United States, assumed by one State, incompatible with the existence of the Union, contradicted expressly by the letter of the Constitution, unauthorized by its spirit, inconsistent with every principle on which it was founded, and destructive of the great object for which it was formed.

After this general view of the leading principle, we must examine the particular application of it which is made in the ordinance.

The preamble rests its justification on these grounds:—It assumes as a fact, that the obnoxious laws,—

at the City of Washington, this tenth day of December, in the year of our Lord one thousand eight hundred and thirty-two, and of the Independence of the United States the fifty-seventh

By the President Andrew Jackson

Edw Livingston Secretary of State.

553 From the original "nullification" proclamation of Jackson, Dec. 10, 1832, in the Department of State, Washington

Section 5. And be it further enacted, That whenever the President of the United States shall be officially informed, by the authorities of any State, or by a judge of any Circuit or District Court of the United States, in the State, that, within the limits of such State, any law or laws of the United States, or the execution thereof, or of any process from the Courts of the United States is obstructed by the employment of military force, or by any other unlawful means, too great to be overcome by the ordinary course of judicial proceeding, or by the powers vested in the marshal by existing laws, it shall be lawful for him, the President of the United States, forthwith to issue his proclamation, declaring such fact or information, and requiring all such military and other force forthwith to disperse; and if at any time after issuing such proclamation, any such opposition or obstruction shall be made, in the manner or by the means aforesaid, the President shall be, and hereby is, authorized, promptly to employ such means to suppress the same, and to cause the said laws or process to be duly executed, as are authorized and provided in the cases therein mentioned by the act of the twenty-eighth of February,

554 Section 5 of the Act for Enforcing the Tariff, Mar. 2, 1833, from the original in the Department of State, Washington

THE TARIFF IS LOWERED AND SOUTH CAROLINA YIELDS

South Carolina remained obdurate. Calhoun resigned the vice-presidency to be free to fight the President from the floor of the Senate. The President then showed statesmanship. He advised downward modification of the tariff. South Carolina suspended nullification to await action by Congress. That body, after much debate, adopted a compromise bill framed by Clay in conference with Calhoun. This provided for a gradual reduction of the higher tariff rates, until in 1842 there would be a flat rate of twenty per centum. With this peace offering went the Force Act, giving the President adequate power to handle any like situation in the future. The Carolina Convention reassembled, expressed itself as satisfied, withdrew its nullification resolution of the tariff acts and made the gesture of nullifying the Force Act. The incident was closed. Conflict had been avoided, the Union preserved, and South Carolina had secured a lowering of the tariff.

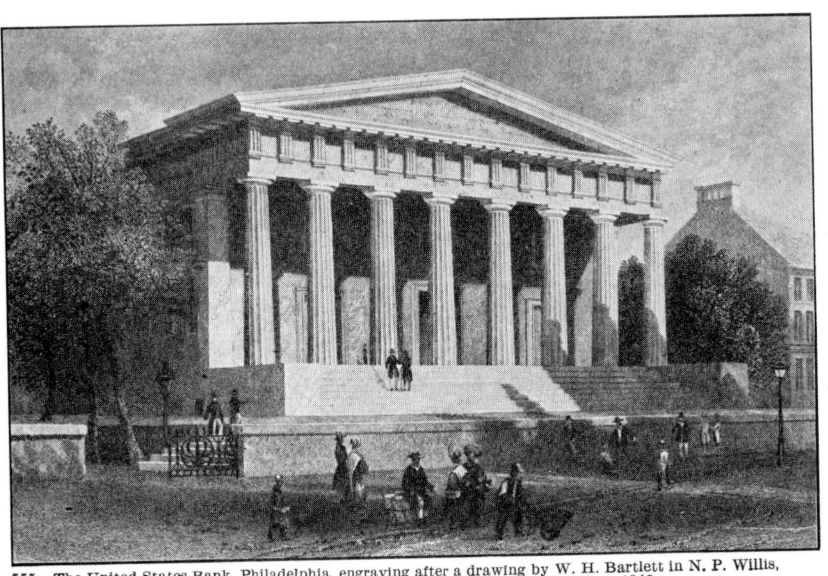

555 The United States Bank, Philadelphia, engraving after a drawing by W. H. Bartlett in N. P. Willis, *American Scenery Illustrated in a Series of Views*, London, 1840

THE NATIONAL BANK EXCITES THE WEST

Meanwhile another issue had come to the foreground. Jackson's political strength lay on the frontier, where easy money was in demand. Credit for expansion was sought from the banks. But state banks were hampered by the competition of the National Bank, with headquarters at Philadelphia. It was, to the West, monopolizing the money market and standing for the money power of the East.

JACKSON VETOES THE NATIONAL BANK'S CHARTER

THE Bank's charter expired in 1836. Nicholas Biddle, the president, was anxious to discover Jackson's attitude. Throughout the summer of 1829, the President put him off with evasion or silence. Then, in his first annual message, he opened the attack. He urged Congress that it was not too soon to consider the question of a new charter. "Both the constitutionality and the expediency of the law creating this bank are well questioned by a large portion of our fellow-citizens; and it must be admitted by all that it has failed in the great end of establishing a uniform and sound currency." This was far from pleasing to the aggressive Biddle. He was, however, in a quandary. Should he continue to endeavor to win Jackson's favor, or should he join the party opposition with the Bank as the campaign issue? Clay, leader of the opposition, and searching for an issue, pressed Biddle to the latter course. The apparent hesitancy of Jackson to push the matter encouraged Clay to believe that on such a plank he could win the election of 1832. "My own belief," he wrote Biddle, "is that, if now called upon, he would not negative the bill [for recharter], but that if he should be re-elected the event might and probably would be different." Biddle was won over; on the 9th of January, 1832, he applied for a new charter. The Democrats, led in the Senate by Benton of Missouri, and in the House by Polk of Tennessee, proceeded to the fight, with Clay and McDuffie opposing. Biddle himself came to the capital to superintend. In July the Whigs carried the day. Jackson, however, was adamant. With most of the cabinet against him, he sent to the Senate his veto message, phrased as a campaign document. The Democrats had stolen a march on the Whigs. The latter had forced the Bank as the issue for 1832; the former outdid them in making political capital out of it.

556 Nicholas Biddle, 1786–1844, from the portrait, 1826, by Thomas Sully in possession of Charles Biddle, Andalusia, Pa.

ILLUSTRATIONS
OF
MASONRY,
BY
ONE OF THE FRATERNITY.
WHO HAS DEVOTED THIRTY YEARS TO THE SUBJECT.

"And God said, Let there be light,
And there was light."

ROCHESTER.
PRINTED FOR THE AUTHOR.
1827.

557 Title-page of the copy in the New York Public Library

THE RISE OF ANTI-MASONRY

THE campaign which followed was in many ways significant of the growing political life. The first nomination had been made by a new and remarkable party. One William Morgan of Batavia, New York, had published a book purporting to reveal the secrets of Freemasonry. His subsequent disappearance led many to believe that he had been abducted and murdered by Masons. Through New York, New England, and Pennsylvania spread the suspicion that the Masonic order, with members mainly from the wealthier classes, was a secret political society whose influence swayed legislatures and juries.

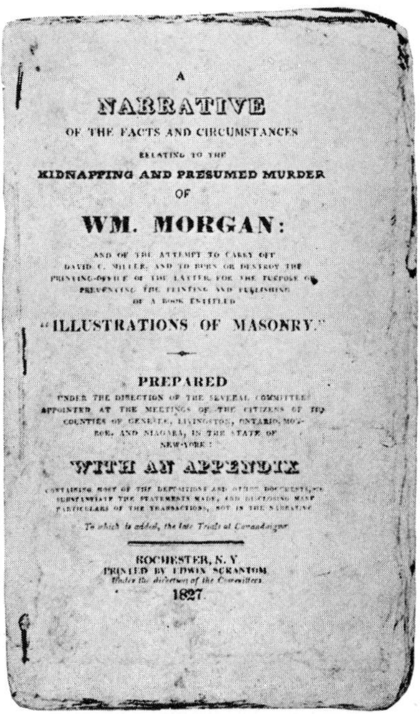

A
NARRATIVE
OF THE FACTS AND CIRCUMSTANCES
RELATING TO THE
KIDNAPPING AND PRESUMED MURDER
OF
WM. MORGAN:
AND OF THE ATTEMPT TO CARRY OFF
DAVID C. MILLER, AND TO BURN OR DESTROY THE
PRINTING-OFFICE OF THE LATTER, FOR THE PURPOSE OF
PREVENTING THE PRINTING AND PUBLISHING
OF A BOOK ENTITLED
"ILLUSTRATIONS OF MASONRY."

PREPARED
UNDER THE DIRECTION OF THE SEVERAL COMMITTEES
APPOINTED AT THE MEETINGS OF THE CITIZENS OF THE
COUNTIES OF GENESEE, LIVINGSTON, ONTARIO, MONROE, AND NIAGARA, IN THE STATE OF
NEW-YORK:
WITH AN APPENDIX
CONTAINING MOST OF THE DEPOSITIONS AND OTHER DOCUMENTS, TO
SUBSTANTIATE THE STATEMENTS MADE, AND DISCLOSING MANY
PARTICULARS OF THE TRANSACTIONS, NOT IN THE NARRATIVE.
To which is added, the late Trials at Canandaigua.

ROCHESTER, N. Y.
PRINTED BY EDWIN SCRANTOM.
Under the direction of the Committees.
1827.

558 Title-page of the copy in the New York Public Library

559 "William Morgan writing his *Illustrations of Masonry*," from *The Anti-Masonic Almanac*, Rochester, N. Y., 1829

POLITICIANS MAKE CAPITAL OF THE NEW MOVEMENT

SEVERAL demagogic young politicians, such as Thurlow Weed and William H. Seward in New York, and Thaddeus Stevens in Pennsylvania, seized upon the movement to promote their own ambitions. The party carried on campaigns in several other states in this election, and met with some success. To magnify the issue and to strengthen their position in national politics, they held, in September, 1830, a national convention at Philadelphia where it was determined to organize a national party. This was America's first national party convention, and the precedent established by the Anti-Masons was soon followed by the older parties. A year later, meeting in Baltimore, the Anti-Masons nominated William Wirt of Maryland as their presidential candidate. He was a well known man of letters, author of didactic essays in the manner of *The Spectator*, on oratory, the fine arts, education, etc.

561 William Wirt, 1772–1834, from the portrait by Henry Inman in the Boston Athenæum

560 "William Morgan taken from Batavia by a mob of Masons and confined in Canandaigua jail under false pretences," from *The Anti-Masonic Almanac*, Rochester, N. Y., 1829

ANTI-MASONS WANT THE WHIGS TO ACCEPT WIRT

WIRT was a brilliant lawyer who had been Attorney-General under Monroe. He was, moreover, an intimate friend of Clay and held similar views of politics. It was the hope of the Anti-Masons that Wirt would prove an acceptable candidate to the Whigs, thus consolidating opposition to Jackson.

CLAY IS NOMINATED BY THE YOUNG REPUBLICANS

562 From a contemporary cartoon by Edward W. Clay in the New York Historical Society

Clay, however, would not surrender his ambition. The National Republicans, aping the Anti-Masons, held in December a convention at which he was unanimously nominated. In the following May, Clay's "Infant School" of young Republicans met at Washington and issued a platform endorsing internal improvements and protection. Clay at first wished Wirt to withdraw in his favor. This Wirt desired to do; but the politicians discovered that with him nominally in the race there was a greater chance of winning New York and Pennsylvania from Jackson. Thus an unannounced coalition was formed. Clay was also angling for the support of Calhoun and the Nullifiers. The cartoon illustrates the game as viewed by the Whigs. Clay, confident of victory on the issues fixed and with Wirt as secret ally, is about to take the stakes — the votes of New York and Pennsylvania — from under the eyes of the harassed and astounded Jackson. Calhoun discreetly withholds his cards from play.

THE NATIONAL BANK DEPOSITS ARE REMOVED TO STATE BANKS

The result was a thorough drubbing for the coalition. Their intrigue had overlooked a fact never forgotten by the clever politicians of the Kitchen Cabinet — namely, that the election was to be decided by the masses, not by the business man, the banker and the manufacturer. Jackson interpreted the election as a complete endorsement of his views, and proceeded to execute them. "Emperor Nicholas" (Biddle), who had thrown himself and the Bank actively into the campaign, did not despair. He saw that sudden closure of the Bank in 1836 would bring on a crisis to avoid which Jackson might be forced to recharter the institution. To forestall the reëntry of the Bank into politics, detrimental to his interests, Jackson, under pressure from Amos Kendall and Frank Blair, ordered the removal of the deposits to state banks. Loyal "Downing" Democrats rejoiced at the energetic decision of their leader. His strokes had brought down the temple of financial corruption on to the heads of its defenders. The grafting hangers-on; the National Republicans, Clay and Webster; Silas Wright, leader of the New York opposition; the bribed editors of the *National Gazette* and of minor organs of the Bank, were overthrown.

563 From a contemporary cartoon in possession of the publishers

564 From a contemporary cartoon in the New York Historical Society

JACKSON'S ORDER IS CENSURED IN THE SENATE

On the publication (September 25) of Jackson's famous "Paper to the Cabinet," the Bank took counsel. At Webster's suggestion, a memorial to Congress was prepared the arrogant tone of which indicated the confidence with which the financiers approached the struggle with the President. There were, indeed, grounds for confidence. Van Buren and conservative Democrats believed that scarcity of money and widespread distress would follow the placement of public funds in small and irresponsible local banks. Biddle took care to drive home the lesson by progressive curtailments of the Bank's credit. In January, 1834, he wrote to a friend: "Our only safety is in pursuing a steady course of firm restriction — and I have no doubt that such a course will ultimately lead to restoration of the currency and the recharter of the Bank." It was in truth a struggle between two giants. In it Biddle ruthlessly employed the financial power that was his, until the oppressed began to suspect that their distress was due fully as much to the Bank as to Jackson. Bit by bit, the business interests of the country then began to desert Biddle. But the politicians, less quick in judgment, continued the fight on the floor of Congress, long after the country had lost interest. The House sustained the removal by a vote of 118 to 103. In the Senate the opposition was in control, and, led by Clay, there followed "the longest period which had been occupied in a single debate, in either House of Congress, since the organization of the Government," ending on March 27, 1834, in a vote of twenty-six to twenty censuring the action of the President. A voluminous literature deals with this "bank war," a notable feature of which is the series of letters in which Biddle vindicates his own course of action.

JACKSON AND THE SENATE'S CENSURE

THE censure stung Jackson to fight back. Three weeks later he presented to the Senate his Protest, in which he vigorously denounced the resolutions and berated the Senate for "proceedings . . . subversive of that distribution of powers of government which the Constitution has ordained and established, . . . and calculated . . . to concentrate in the hands of a body, not directly amenable to the people, a degree of influence and power dangerous to their liberties and fatal to the Constitution of their choice." This demurrer was greeted with delight by the people: the Senate refused to place it upon their minutes. Then followed Benton's dramatic and persistent effort to have stricken from the records the censure of his chief. Austere, conceited, a prolix and diffuse speaker, he was, nevertheless, a commanding figure in American politics and long a leader of Democracy. His fight to pass an expunging resolution, successful in 1837, kept the Bank issue in politics during the election of 1836.

565 Thomas H. Benton Addressing the Senate on the Resolution of Censure, from a sketch in the *United States Magazine and Democratic Review*, Oct. 1837

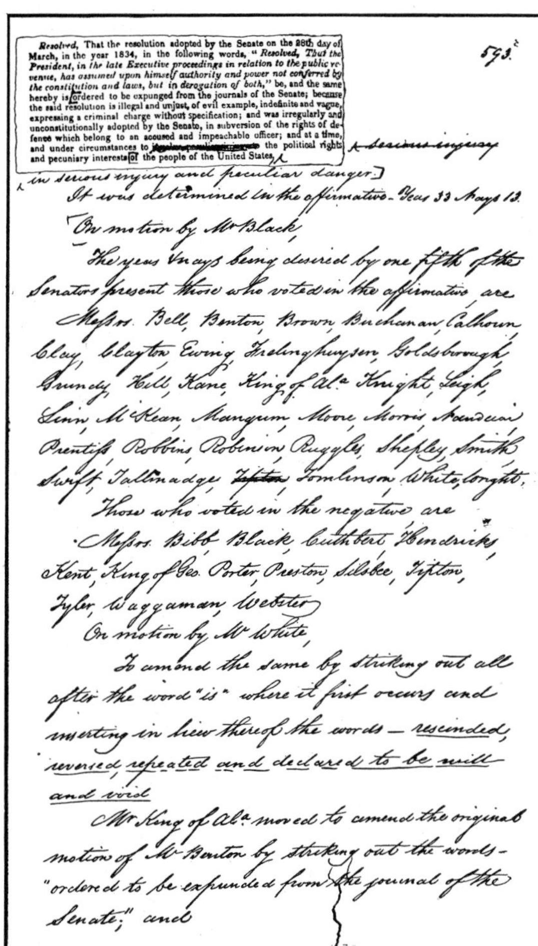

593.

Resolved, That the resolution adopted by the Senate on the 28th day of March, in the year 1834, in the following words, "*Resolved, That the President, in the late Executive proceedings in relation to the public revenue, has assumed upon himself authority and power not conferred by the constitution and laws, but in derogation of both,*" be, and the same hereby is ordered to be expunged from the journals of the Senate; because the said resolution is illegal and unjust, of evil example, indefinite and vague, expressing a criminal charge without specification; and was irregularly and unconstitutionally adopted by the Senate, in subversion of the rights of defence which belong to an accused and impeachable officer; and at a time, and under circumstances to ~~[illegible]~~ the political rights and pecuniary interests of the people of the United States, ~~a serious injury~~ in serious injury and peculiar danger.]

It was determined in the affirmative - Yeas 33 Nays 13.

On motion by Mr Black,

The yeas & nays being desired by one fifth of the Senators present those who voted in the affirmative are

Messrs. Bell, Benton, Brown, Buchanan, Calhoun, Clay, Clayton, Ewing, Frelinghuysen, Goldsborough, Grundy, Hill, Kane, King of Ala, Knight, Leigh, Linn, McKean, Mangum, Moore, Morris, Naudain, Prentiss, Robbins, Robinson, Ruggles, Shepley, Smith, Swift, Tallmadge, ~~Tipton~~, Tomlinson, White, Wright,

Those who voted in the negative are

Messrs. Bibb, Black, Cuthbert, Hendricks, Kent, King of Geo. Porter, Preston, Silsbee, Tipton, Tyler, Waggaman, Webster

On motion by Mr White,

To amend the same by striking out all after the word "is" where it first occurs and inserting in lieu thereof the words — rescinded, reversed, repealed and declared to be null and void

Mr King of Ala. moved to amend the original motion of Mr Benton by striking out the words - "ordered to be expunded from the journal of the Senate," and

566 From the Journal of the Senate of the Twenty-third Congress, debate on the Jackson resolution to expunge; with a printed copy of the resolution of censure pasted in the journal

EFFECT OF THE CENSURE FIGHT

FROM one angle the censure fight may be regarded as an incident in a significant constitutional development. More than once, on the floor of Congress, it was urged that the President's actions in his executive capacity were subject to legislative control. The victory of Jackson may be regarded as a victory for presidential over parliamentary government. So at least certain leading politicians read the event. This is shown in the change of party name, in the spring of 1834. Niles' *Register* for April 12 reported: "In New York and Connecticut the name 'Whig' is now used by the opponents of the Administration when speaking of themselves, and they call the Jackson men by the offensive name of 'Tories.'" It was a conscious effort to stigmatize Jacksonism as executive usurpation, to identify the National Republicans with the historic struggle against royal prerogative. The same feeling appeared in Calhoun's elaborate report on "the extent of federal patronage and the expediency of reducing the same," in which the Whigs combined party politics with constitutional principle. They proposed (1) an annual distribution of the surplus revenue; (2) a law to regulate executive selection of public depositories; and (3) a repeal of the law limiting the tenure of customs officers. Thus it was hoped executive tyranny and the Democratic machine could be curbed.

567 Hugh Lawson White, 1773–1840, from a portrait in the State Library, Nashville, Tenn., courtesy of the Tennessee Historical Society

THE DEMOCRATS ARE DIVIDED OVER CANDIDATES

EVEN among the Democrats a division had appeared. Van Buren had long been regarded as the Crown Prince, picked to ascend the throne in 1836. His candidacy was, however, unacceptable to many of Jackson's supporters. Jackson, with all his faults, was recognized as honest; "Mattie," the "Red Fox," was looked upon as an intriguer. He was, moreover, a northerner. To the southern gentleman of breeding and wealth these were not appealing characteristics. Jackson had lost strength in the South. Advocates of state rights were distressed by his treatment of South Carolina; the wealthier planters were horror-struck at his attack on the Bank, the strict constructionist at his many vigorous actions. Above all, they shuddered at the intimacy between Jackson and the spoils politician symbolized by the Tammany Society. This disaffection found a candidate in Judge Hugh L. White of Tennessee, an old friend of Jackson, who, as early as 1834, had left the fold. Ponderous, dignified, White was a Senator of the old school. The Whigs were appealed to by his grudge against the President; and for a time considered the possibility of making him their own candidate. His taciturnity, however, militated against his availability for the spirited campaign in sight. He was left to draw southern votes away from Van Buren.

VAN BUREN IS ELECTED AS JACKSON'S FAVORITE

JACKSON, therefore, had little trouble in nominating his favorite, although Virginia rebelled at the selection of Richard M. Johnson of Kentucky for Van Buren's running-mate, an action which later threw the election of the Vice-president into the Senate. The Whigs finally fixed upon William Henry Harrison, the popular victor of Tippecanoe, as a candidate who would appeal to the frontier democracy and the olden virtues. Massachusetts remained loyal to Webster; while Calhoun's supporters continued their separatist tactics by backing Senator W. P. Mangum of North Carolina. The dying Anti-Masonic party found a candidate to their liking in Judge John McLean of Ohio. With so many candidates in the field, appealing to such a wide variety of political tastes, the opposition hoped to draw from Van Buren sufficient strength to throw the election into the House. Van Buren, though never popular and somewhat timid, was nevertheless elected as Jackson's man, pledged to "follow in the footsteps of his illustrious predecessor."

568 From a contemporary cartoon in the New York Historical Society

ILLUSORY PROSPERITY PRECEDES THE PANIC OF 1837

569 From a contemporary cartoon *The Modern Balaam and His Ass*, in the New York Historical Society

The walking was rough. In his farewell address, issued on the day on which he retired from the Presidency, Jackson had much to say about the prosperous condition in which he left the country. But such prosperity as existed was largely illusory. The destruction of the United States Bank and the distribution of the Treasury surplus had opened the way for a flood of "wild-cat" currency; "wild-cat" banking had led to feverish speculation; speculation in public lands had prompted the issue of the Specie Circular which required all payments to the government to be made in recognized national currency instead of local bank notes; and soon after Van Buren was installed, the Specie Circular proved the forerunner of a severe financial panic. Credit staggered and fell; trade was prostrated; prices shot upward; bread riots broke out; business houses by the score were driven to the wall.

570 From a contemporary cartoon by E. W. Clay in the New York Public Library

THE PANIC HAS DISCONCERTING POLITICAL EFFECTS

Here we have an anti-Jackson cartoonist's idea of disconcerting developments at a Democratic feast. The cotton planters and the Tammany man are making merry. But Van Buren, who as President is reaping the whirlwind sowed by others, has eyes only for the specter that has slipped into his chair at the head of the table; while Jackson, in the role of *Lady Macbeth*, explains away his successor's perturbation as best he can.

571 From a "Shinplaster" cartoon, published in 1837 by H. R. Robinson, New York, in the American Antiquarian Society, Worcester, Mass.

VAN BUREN CALLS CONGRESS TO PLAN RELIEF

Petitions poured in, asking for relief. Van Buren yielded to the pressure, and, withdrawing somewhat from the bullionist element of his party, led by the dauntless Jackson and the dogged Benton, called Congress into special session, in the autumn of 1837, to consider remedies.

THE SUB-TREASURY BILL PASSES CONGRESS

In this move he was influenced largely by a partisan revolt in his home state. Here a group of laborers, filled with doctrinaire notions of the desirability of returning to the "first principles" expounded by Jackson, had rebelled from Tammany rule and the Albany Regency. They denounced all banks and special privileges and believed that hard money was a panacea. As a result of their defection, the Whigs carried the city of New York in the autumn of 1837. This disturbed the "Little Magician." He therefore suggested to Congress an extension of the principle of the Specie Circular; in addition, he urged the establishment of an Independent Treasury whereby the government would care for its own money in sub-treasuries in each of the larger cities. This did not please the old Bank men, who labeled his bill the Divorce Bill because it divorced public and private business. Jackson, however, wrote an open letter from the Hermitage approving the plan, and Calhoun, seeing its real merit, swung to its support. It was finally carried in June, 1840.

572 From a contemporary cartoon in the New York Historical Society

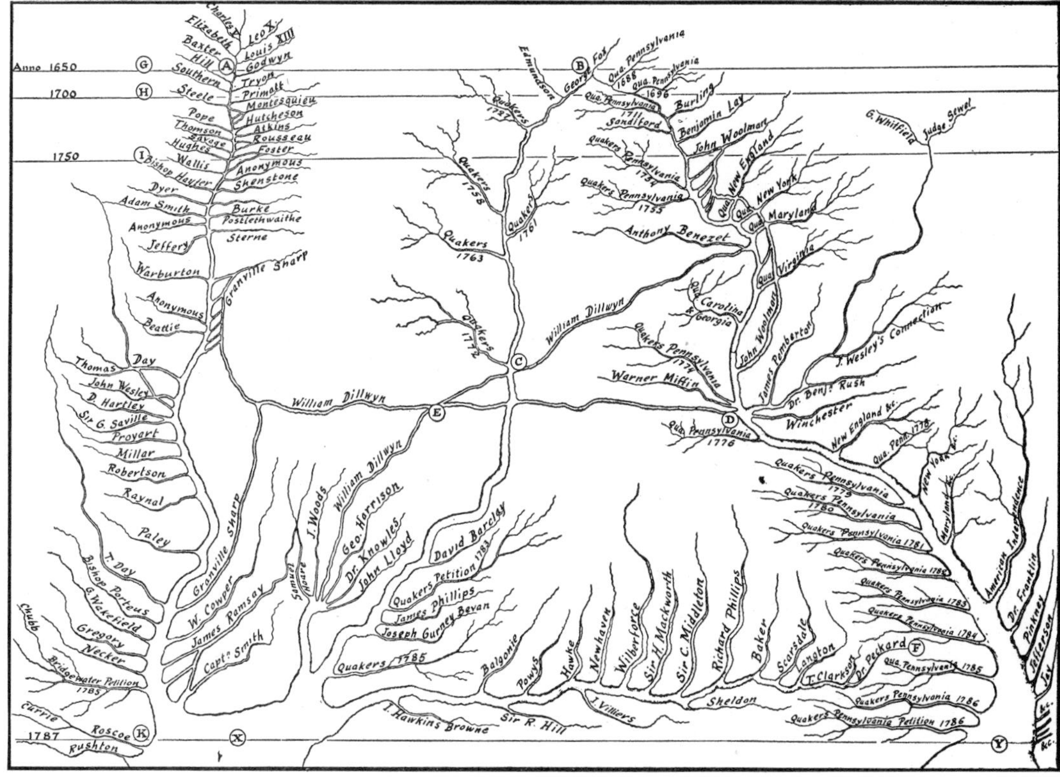

573 Map of the "Stream of Abolition," from M. A. Clarkson, *The History of the Rise, Progress and Accomplishment of the Abolition of the African Slave Trade by the British Parliament*, London, 1808

THE SLAVERY ISSUE ASSERTS ITSELF AFRESH

THROUGHOUT Van Buren's term the panic and its aftermath held public attention, while another issue returned to disturb the country. Since the Missouri Compromise, the slavery question had never entirely dropped from view. Indeed the problem was older than the United States. In the eighteenth century many of the colonial leaders, notably Franklin, Jefferson and Jay, had spoken and worked for abolition. Slavery, however, was subjected to less criticism as time passed. Only its more cruel features, such as the foreign slave trade, received general disapproval. And this had been abolished by the Act of 1807.

A QUAKER WORKS FOR EMANCIPATION

WHILE the new nation was finding its feet, the slavery issue rested, only to emerge suddenly in the Missouri question. At that time, and for a decade after, anti-slavery advocates were pursuing a conciliatory policy. The leading spirit was Benjamin Lundy, New Jersey Quaker of fine mind and ideals. He founded and published *The Genius of Universal Emancipation*, which persistently but tactfully urged gradual emancipation. Traveling extensively through the South, Lundy won moral and financial support from many slaveholders. In 1816 was founded the American Colonization Society which, under such men as Bushrod Washington, Clay, and Madison, sent some thousand negroes to Liberia on the west coast of Africa.

574 Benjamin Lundy, 1789–1839, after a water-color portrait in the possession of the family, reproduced in the *Journal of the Illinois State Historical Society*, July 1913

575 William Lloyd Garrison, 1804–79, from a photograph, about 1860, in possession of the Garrison family

A NEW FIGURE APPEARS AGAINST SLAVERY

Now appeared a new and forceful figure in the person of William Lloyd Garrison of Massachusetts. In 1829 he had associated himself with Lundy as joint editor in Baltimore. Here he denounced slavery in such flaming terms that he was imprisoned for libel. This experience convinced him that Lundy's methods were futile: immediate emancipation became his objective, to be attained by an unrelenting attack from the North upon the South.

GARRISON IS INEXORABLE FOR ABOLITION

Obtaining the necessary funds by antislavery lectures, Garrison issued in Boston the first number of *The Liberator*, on the first of January, 1831. He deeply felt the moral wrong of slavery, and passionately demanded its abolition. His first words were characteristic: "I *will be* as harsh as truth, and as uncompromising as justice. On this subject, I do not wish to think, or speak, or write, with toleration. . . . I will not equivocate — I will not excuse — I will not retreat a single inch — *and I will be heard.*"

576 From a copy of *The Liberator* in its first year, 1831, in the New York Public Library

THE LIBERATOR LIVES TILL ITS OBJECT IS ATTAINED

Garrison kept his word, and for thirty-five years he waged war against an institution he regarded as sinful. He was the avowed leader of the abolitionist radicals. Until his life-work was ended he never relented.

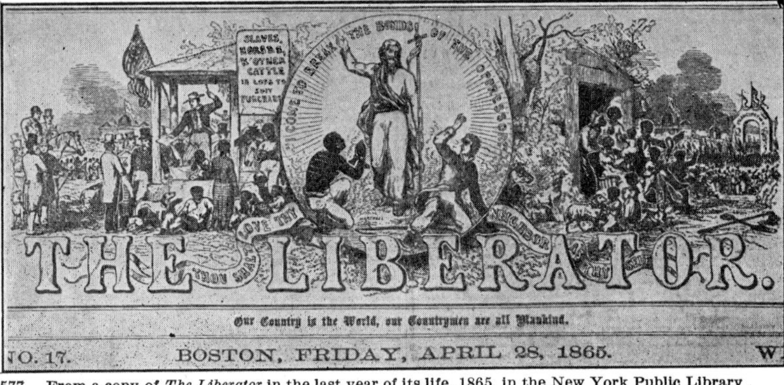

577 From a copy of *The Liberator* in the last year of its life, 1865, in the New York Public Library

A QUAKER SCHOOLMISTRESS PERSECUTED FOR TEACHING COLORED GIRLS

SUCH tactics were bound to arouse resentment. The immediate effect in the North was to alienate law-abiding people, who saw in Garrison an enemy of society. The radical social doctrines and intemperate language of the abolitionists stirred the latent intolerance of vested interests. One of the unpopular tenets of the group was equal freedom of activity for women and men. At Canterbury, Connecticut, Prudence Crandall, a Friend, conducted a school for girls to which she admitted persons of color. The townsfolk and the officials protested and forbade enrollment of negroes from without the state, except by special permit. The principal was persecuted by her neighbors and imprisoned, and her schoolhouse was destroyed by a mob.

578 Prudence Crandall, 1803–90, from the portrait by Francis Alexander (1800–81), painted in 1838 for the Anti-Slavery Society, in the Library of Cornell University, Ithaca, N. Y.

GARRISON IS MOBBED IN BOSTON

IN Boston, upon the occasion of a lecture, October 21, 1835, Garrison was mobbed and dragged through the streets with a rope around his neck. He was finally rescued by the mayor, who placed him in the city jail for safety. At the time, one of his co-workers, George Thompson, recently arrived from Scotland, escaped only by donning woman's garb. Thompson's visit had aroused so much indignation that President Jackson publicly denounced him. He eventually fled in a rowboat to a British vessel bound for St. John, New Brunswick.

579 From a contemporary cartoon in the New York Historical Society

AMERICA HAS A "MARTYR AGE"

THIS violent spirit spread over the North. In 1837 the Reverend Elijah P. Lovejoy, editor of an antislavery paper, whose press had been destroyed three times by mobs, was murdered in Alton, Illinois. With his friends he defended the office-building, but on opening the door was instantly struck by five bullets. The trustees of Bowdoin College attempted to remove a professor suspected of abolitionism.

580 Elijah Parish Lovejoy, 1802–37, from a silhouette portrait in Randall Parish, *Historic Illinois*, Chicago, 1905, courtesy of A. C. McClurg & Co.

THE FOES OF ABOLITION RIOT IN PHILADELPHIA

IN Philadelphia the abolitionists erected a hall at a cost of $40,000, only to have it set on fire the day after the first meetings were held therein. For three nights the city was the scene of riots in which many houses occupied by negroes were attacked.

581 Burning of Pennsylvania Hall, Philadelphia, May 17, 1838, from a sketch drawn on the spot and engraved by John Sartain, reproduced from *The Story of Pennsylvania Hall*

582 From a contemporary cartoon by E. W. Clay in the New York Historical Society

FREE NEGROES SUFFER FROM THE ANTI-ABOLITIONISTS

SOUTHERN feeling against the abolitionists was intense. Conduct which in the North offended moral standards received in the South additional opprobrium as exciting violence among the negroes and as destructive of law and order. Uprisings such as Nat Turner's insurrection of slaves in Virginia, in 1831, were laid at the door of the northern fanatic. Turner, a negro who believed he was chosen by the Lord to lead his people to freedom, had set out with a band of disciples to destroy the entire white race. An early response to such outrages was a tightening of the Black Codes which governed the activities of the negroes. In many cities freedmen were numerous; their presence was now regarded as dangerous to public peace. The southern point of view was expressed in 1837 by one of their most cultivated writers, W. G. Simms: "By emancipation and the pettings of philanthropy the coarse and uneducated negro became lifted into a condition to which his intellect did not entitle him, and to which his manners were unequal: — he became presumptuous, accordingly, and consequently offensive." In the North a similar opinion was adopted, and the free negro, in many places denied citizenship, became the victim of legal and social humiliations and economic discriminations.

THE INCONSISTENCY OF THE SOUTH IS SATIRIZED

THOSE who dared to express sympathy with the abolitionist too often received summary treatment at the hands of their neighbors. The picture is an abolitionist rejoinder, and a burlesque on the incompatibility of slavery with American liberty. The same theme was often used in English caricatures of America.

583 From a contemporary cartoon issued by the American Anti-Slavery Society, in the American Antiquarian Society, Worcester, Mass.

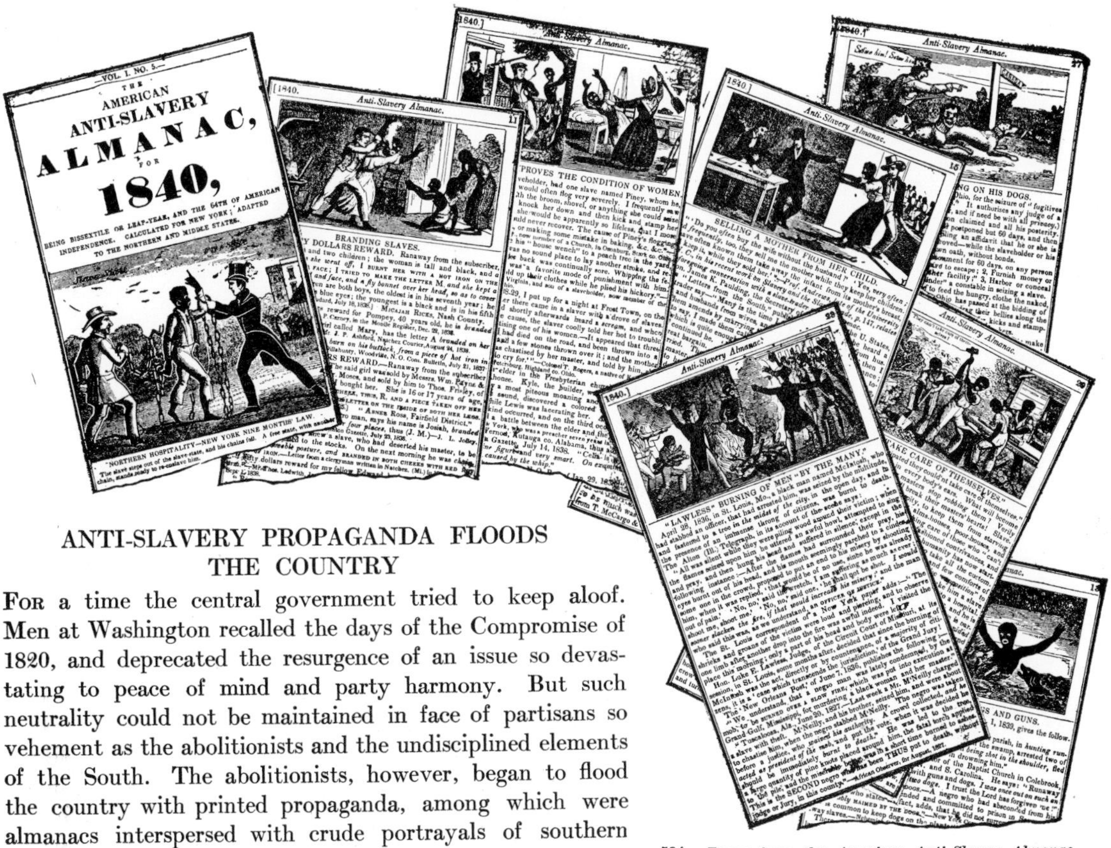

584 Pages from the *American Anti-Slavery Almanac for 1840*, Boston, in possession of the publishers

ANTI-SLAVERY PROPAGANDA FLOODS THE COUNTRY

FOR a time the central government tried to keep aloof. Men at Washington recalled the days of the Compromise of 1820, and deprecated the resurgence of an issue so devastating to peace of mind and party harmony. But such neutrality could not be maintained in face of partisans so vehement as the abolitionists and the undisciplined elements of the South. The abolitionists, however, began to flood the country with printed propaganda, among which were almanacs interspersed with crude portrayals of southern cruelty and northern indifference to the slave.

585 From an antislavery broadside, *Southern Ideas of Liberty*, representing an attack on the Post Office at Charleston, S. C., in the American Antiquarian Society, Worcester, Mass.

A PRO-SLAVERY MOB BREAKS POSTAL LAWS

THE

WAR IN TEXAS;

A

REVIEW OF FACTS AND CIRCUMSTANCES,

SHOWING THAT

THIS CONTEST IS THE RESULT

OF A LONG PREMEDITATED

CRUSADE AGAINST THE GOVERNMENT,

SET ON FOOT BY

Slaveholders, Land Speculators, &c.

WITH THE VIEW OF

RE-ESTABLISHING, EXTENDING, AND PERPETUATING

THE SYSTEM OF

SLAVERY AND THE SLAVE TRADE

IN THE

REPUBLIC OF MEXICO.

BY A CITIZEN OF THE UNITED STATES.

PHILADELPHIA:
PRINTED FOR THE AUTHOR,
BY MERRIHEW AND GUNN,
No. 7, Carters' Alley.
1836.

586 Title-page of Benjamin Lundy, *The War in Texas*, Philadelphia, 1836, in the New York Public Library

MUCH of the antislavery propaganda was deliberately sent into the South. Inflammatory pamphlets and papers were sent broadcast into the South, arousing strong resentment. Attacking the post office, a mob in Charleston seized and burned a mail sack full of such literature. The postmaster of New York thereupon refused to forward such mail destined for southern points, and in this summary procedure he was upheld by Amos Kendall, the Postmaster-General. This ruling aroused heated debate in Congress, where Calhoun endeavored to secure a statute prohibiting the use of the mails for abolition literature addressed to points where its circulation would be illegal. His plan was, however, defeated. To give to postal officials the right to discriminate among the pieces of mail presented to them was to establish a dangerous practice and one likely to produce greater evils than the sending of abolitionist propaganda into the South.

JACKSON RECOGNIZES TEXAN INDEPENDENCE

INTO still another political field the slavery issue was injected. Since the early 'twenties, Americans had been settling in the Mexican provinces north of the Rio Grande. Several times Adams and Jackson had suggested the purchase of Texas, only to be rebuffed by Mexico. At last came the Texan Revolution, resulting in a declaration of independence — signed chiefly by Americans — and in 1836 a request for annexation to the United States. Abolitionists in the North shouted wolf; this was simply a southern plot to increase slave territory. John Quincy Adams declared against annexation, Webster counseled delay, and Congress merely authorized the President to recognize Texan independence (March 3, 1837).

THE "GAG RULES" KILL PETITIONS AGAINST SLAVERY

JAIL IN WASHINGTON,—SALE OF A FREE CITIZEN TO PAY HIS JAIL FEES!

587 From the broadside *Slave Market of America*, published at New York, 1836, by the American Anti-Slavery Society, original in the New York Historical Society

FURTHER excitement was aroused by the attitude taken by the House of Representatives toward antislavery petitions. A group of abolitionists had determined to secure congressional action for their goal, so far as the National Government had power over the matter. Beginning in the session of 1833–34, petitions poured in calling for acts abolishing slavery in Florida and the District of Columbia, and for control of the interstate slave traffic. Bit by bit, southern ire rose, until in the winter of 1835–36 the House spent bitter days fighting over the constitutional right of petition and over slavery in the District. In May, 1836, it determined that all such petitions should "without being printed and referred, be laid upon the table." This was a red flag to the abolitionists; the volume of petitions grew, until in 1840 the House provided that no such memorials "be received . . . or entertained in any way whatever." This simply inflamed abolitionist ardor, and kept the cause in the political arena. Not until 1844, after the mischief had been done, were these gag rules abandoned. The unwavering and courageous leader of the fight against the gag rules, John Quincy Adams, now a member of the House of Representatives, rose again to greatness.

THE BIBLE AND SLAVERY

THE attack upon slavery roused the gentlemen planters of the South to thought regarding their peculiar institution. A profound religious awakening had stirred southern communities in the first third of the century. Many southerners turned to the Bible as the literally inspired Word of God. On its pages, both in the Old and the New Testaments, they found references to slavery, even rules governing the relation of master and slave. They came to the sincere conclusion that slavery was a divine institution, and that negro slavery was God's way of bringing civilization to the savage African. Slavery, therefore, was a positive good to both black and white. Its evils could be mitigated by the spreading of the gospel. The Southerner pointed to patriarchal slavery in the South where the master and mistress looked after feeding, clothing and doctoring their people. He called attention to the loyalty of thousands of slaves to their owners and to the close bond of affection which often developed. Then, by way of contrast, he pointed to the horrible conditions in the industrial cities of England where free labor was ruthlessly exploited in the midst of wretchedness and need. The argument was a telling one.

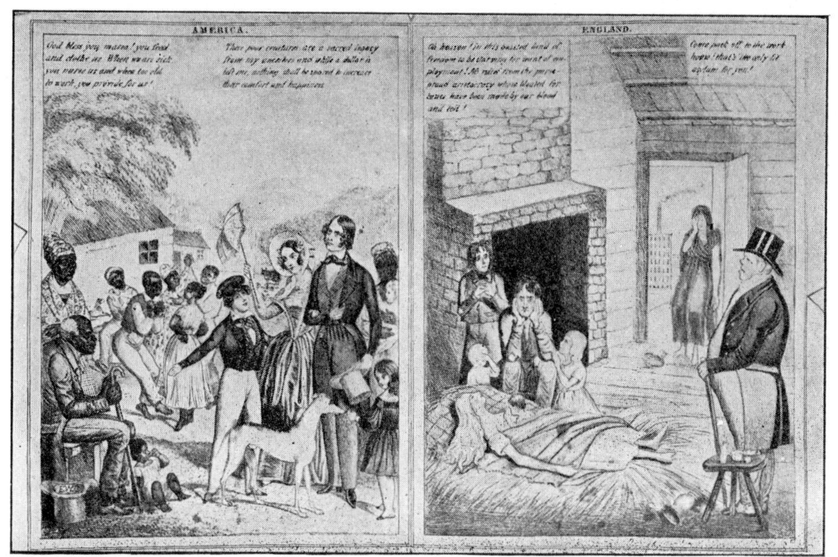

588 From a caricature *Black and White Slaves*, by E. W. Clay, in the New York Historical Society

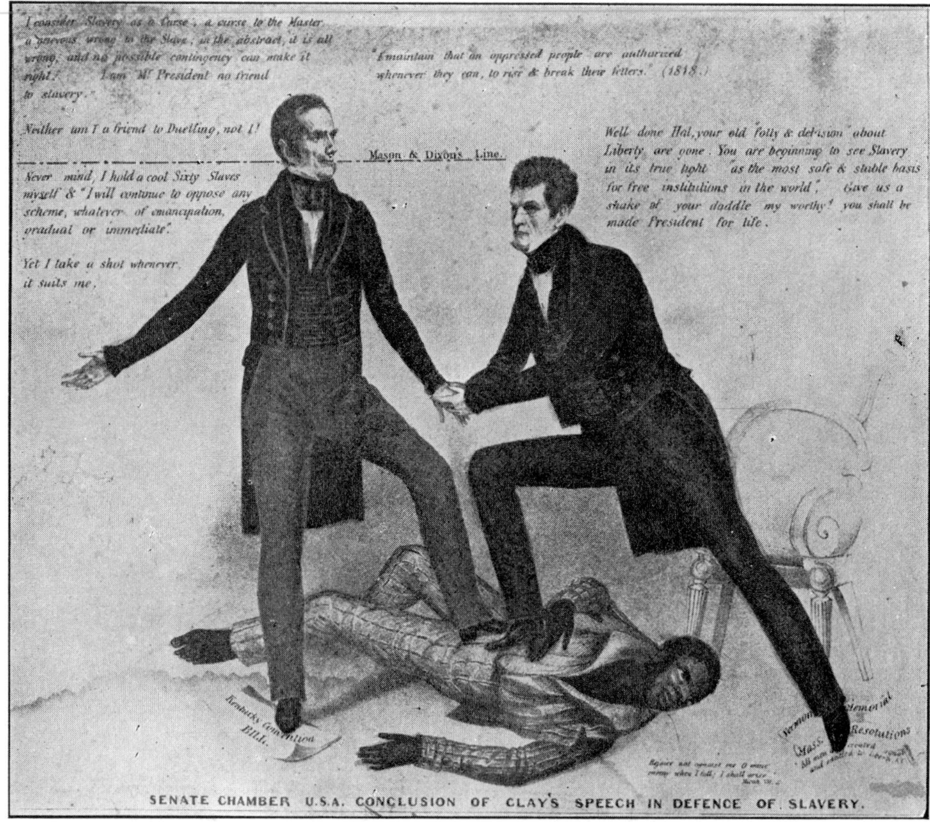

589 From a contemporary cartoon in the Historical Society of Pennsylvania

HENRY CLAY

Clay in his defense of slavery followed a more devious course. He talked much of the difference between equality in the abstract and in human society, of the state of nature as against long-established social institutions, of ethics as against law, of the dangers to life and property which would follow upon emancipation. While Calhoun, the philosopher of state rights, in the face of this new issue, trampled upon the antislavery petition of the sovereign state of Vermont, Clay was seeking a *via media* that would satisfy all factions of a political party whose sole bond of union was desire to preserve property interests from Jacksonism. His efforts to conciliate the South won him the hatred of abolitionists. In a famous speech of February 7, 1839, he announced that he had opposed the calling of a constitutional convention in Kentucky in 1838, for fear that the abolitionists would dominate its deliberations. He continued: "If I were now a citizen of any of the planting states — the Southern and Southwestern states — I would continue to oppose any scheme whatever of emancipation, gradual or immediate, because of the danger of an ultimate ascendancy of the black race, or of a civil contest which might terminate in the extinction of one race or another." Seizing upon this reasonable proposition, the abolitionists interpreted it as sounding an alliance between the Great Pacificator and the champion of slavery.

590 Hard Times Token (obverse and reverse) issued in the Jackson period, courtesy of the American Numismatic Society, New York

CHAPTER X

THE ROARING 'FORTIES

THE eager Jacksonian Democrats had concerned themselves chiefly with domestic problems. These had been approached with the zeal of the reformer, and manhandled to solution. But these rough and ready methods brought in their train other problems, which could not so easily be settled by the decree of *vox populi*. The Democrats, however, did not at first realize that there were limitations upon the effectiveness of their tactics. This is well illustrated in the history of America's foreign relations during the period. For in the years following Jackson's administration the same bumptious patriotism that had brought him to the Presidency found expression in a militant nationalism that for a time threatened to overwhelm the better sense of the people. The cry of "Fifty-four Forty or Fight" embodied the popular solution of the Oregon question. The apparent success of such diplomatic procedure led to the extension of that rallying-cry into "Manifest Destiny." It was foreordained that the United States should absorb Canada, Cuba, Mexico, the whole of the Americas. But thanks to President Polk, Calhoun and Webster, the methods of the boisterous Democrats received the restraint they needed. In the field of domestic issues, a similar shift in tactics was to prove necessary. The attitude of the Jacksonian Democrat toward such issues is vividly portrayed in a passage in Van Buren's Autobiography written in the 'fifties: "Never," ... was this Country so thoroughly convulsed, never before was the vital principle — that of the sovereignty of the popular will — ... so seriously menaced, never before were our material interests so severely and wantonly injured as they were by the successive struggles of the second Bank of the United States to obtain a renewal of its charter. Those who lived at that day and were conversant with public affairs know that all the branches of the Federal Government, ... as well as those of the State Governments, were profoundly agitated by those struggles. They obtruded themselves into all the ramifications of society, shed their baleful influence upon all its interests and for a season suspended, if they did not permanently weaken, the recognition of some of its most vital obligations." — J. C. Fitzpatrick (editor), *The Autobiography of Martin Van Buren*, 1918.

That menace was met in typical Jacksonian fashion, for, as has been well said, "Jacksonian Democracy did not fear central government as such; it only feared central government directed by its political enemies." — F. L. Paxson, *History of the American Frontier*, 1924, p. 319. Such methods were bound to arouse opposition. The character of that opposition was affected by the concurrent external policies of the Government; and it found a philosophy of conduct in the principles enunciated by Calhoun. The annexation of extensive lands, and proposals to annex others, raised serious problems — above all, that of the status of slavery in the territories. The problem, which had slumbered since the Missouri Compromise, now started a series of events leading to a final solution of the slavery question. In the 'forties the question was more acute than before, thanks to the issues raised by South Carolina in 1832. The tactics of Jacksonism made "states rights" a doctrine under which centralization could be opposed and slavery protected. Clearly, the slavery issue was joined to the knotty problem of the relation between the National Government and the states. The time was approaching when the continuance of the former issue was to endanger the Union.

591 From a contemporary cartoon in the New York Historical Society

THE MEETING AT SARATOGA

Clay, in his famous speech on February 7, 1839, had taken great pains to push his claims for the Presidency; and after its delivery he returned to Kentucky, confident of success at the party convention in December. With the exception of Webster, no other Whig was so prominent, and none was his peer in party and public service. Webster, however, did not possess the attributes that make a popular presidential candidate. During the summer, rumors reached Clay that all was not well in New York State, where Thurlow Weed, the astute political manager, had been friendly. Hence he set out, ostensibly upon a journey for his health, to discover what was happening. Early in August, he came to Saratoga, where, as elsewhere, he was received with apparent enthusiasm. To the welcoming assemblies attended by the élite came Clay supporters in fantastic hirsute adornment — for they had sworn not to shave until Clay was President. Here the aspiring Kentuckian met Van Buren, whose opponent Clay soon hoped to be. Here also Clay conferred with Weed, who told him that he could not be elected. In point of fact, Weed was at the moment taking steps to pledge the New York delegation to General Scott, in order to keep it from voting for Clay.

POLITICIANS SEEK A NEW CANDIDATE

Weed's real candidate was Harrison, native of Virginia but now resident of Ohio. For Weed, above all a politician, was concerned with the prospect of victory in 1840. He saw the many weaknesses of the Whigs. Their two great leaders, Clay and Webster, were jealous of one another and unwilling to yield precedence. The party had no common convictions and no common program, except that of ousting the Democrats. Under such conditions, principle, thought Weed, must be subordinated to expediency. A candidate must be chosen who would poll votes. This meant that Clay could not be selected. He had been too long in the arena, and his position was too well known to permit straddling. He had recently offended the abolitionists. He was a Mason whom the strong Anti-Masonic group within the party would not favor. He had, also, twice been defeated for the Presidency. In short, he was distinctly not the best candidate. General Harrison, on the other hand, possessed those attributes which Clay lacked, and at the same time did not arouse the manifold prejudices directed against the Kentuckian.

592 William Henry Harrison, 1773–1841, from the portrait by George Catlin (1796–1872), courtesy of the Ehrich Galleries, New York

593 From a broadside published in New York, 1840, at the office of the *Harrison Almanac*, original in the New York Historical Society

CLAY LOSES THE NOMINATION TO HARRISON

Harrison had a military record that would appeal. During the War of 1812 he had served with distinction in the Northwest. He was the hero of Tippecanoe. Except for his strong candidacy in 1836, he had not recently been active in politics. He was, moreover, the son of a "signer." His views upon current issues were scarcely known. In fine, he would be a great vote-getter. So the wire-pulling of Weed and Greeley resulted in the defeat of Clay's ambitions and the nomination of Harrison. To allay the bitterness aroused by this decision, the convention managers selected as the General's running-mate a man known to be Clay's friend. This was John Tyler of Virginia. The campaign of 1840 began as soon as the Whig convention adjourned in December, 1839. There was no need to await the action of the Democratic convention to be held in Baltimore in the following May; for Van Buren's renomination was a certainty. The Whigs, wisely avoiding the internal dissension that would arise from the attempt, adopted no platform. To hide their lack of principle and of unity, they embarked upon a campaign in which emotion was to swamp reason.

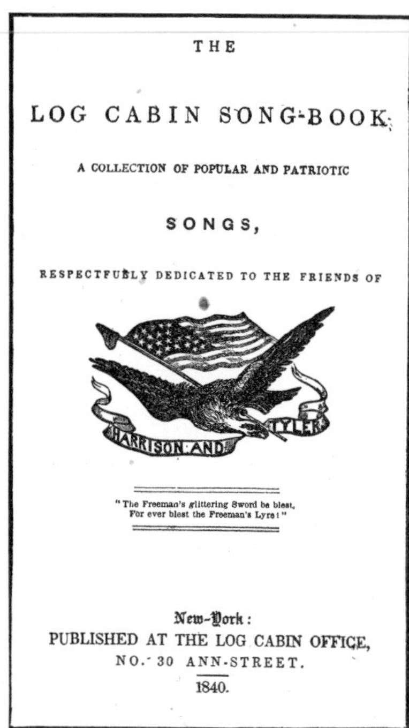

THE

LOG CABIN SONG-BOOK:

A COLLECTION OF POPULAR AND PATRIOTIC

SONGS,

RESPECTFULLY DEDICATED TO THE FRIENDS OF

"The Freeman's glittering Sword be blest,
For ever blest the Freeman's Lyre!"

New-York:
PUBLISHED AT THE LOG CABIN OFFICE,
NO. 30 ANN-STREET.
1840.

594 Title-page of the original issue, New York, 1840, from a copy in the New York Public Library

595 From *General Harrison's Log Cabin March & Quickstep*, published in 1840 at Baltimore by Samuel Carusi

CAMPAIGN SONGS

THE Democrats affected to treat the Whigs and their tactics with contempt. At the time of the Harrisburg convention, the *Hartford Times* had suggested that the Whig nominee, when chosen, should be called "the federal-whig-abolition-amalgamation-conservative-anti-masonic-striped-pig-foreign-missionary candidate." After the nomination another prominent eastern paper wrote derisively of Harrison as a man better fitted, if provided with a pension, to remain in his log cabin with a barrel of hard cider than to enter the White House. The remark was unfortunate. The people of Ohio had just passed through the log-cabin era; with the log cabin they associated the hardships and privations which "Mattie's" panic of 1837 had renewed. Resenting the imputation in the article, these people seized upon the log cabin as a symbol of liberty and democracy. At the Whig state convention at Columbus in February, 1840, was introduced the "log-cabin song," written to the swinging tune of *Highland Laddie*. Other songs quickly followed and were sung up and down the country. Horace Greeley, a young New York journalist, saw his opportunity, and established a campaign paper, *The Log Cabin*, which soon had a circulation of eighty thousand copies.

THE HARD CIDER CAMPAIGN

EVERYWHERE log cabins were erected as headquarters for the Whig politicians. Here were held mass meetings to which from many miles around came farmers with their families to spend days and nights in singing songs and shouting "Tippecanoe and Tyler too." It became impossible to count them, and surveyors were employed to measure the throngs by the acre. At every gathering appeared the jug of cider and the coonskin, tokens of Harrison's love of the people. A campaign biographer of the candidate said that "his table, instead of being covered with exciting wines, is well supplied with the best cider." (See Nos. 568, 600.) In contrast with the "Honest Farmer of North Bend," possessed of all the homely virtues of the true American, Van Buren became the aristocrat who lived in a palace and dressed himself before elaborate French mirrors, callous to the sufferings brought upon the people by his policies and the corruption of his administration.

596 From a lithograph by J. T. Bowen after an aquatint *Log Cabin Politicians*, by William Hall, courtesy of J. F. Sabin, New York

AN APPEAL TO THE PEOPLE

THE politicians who had engineered Harrison's nomination overlooked no method of appeal for votes. The masses were carried along upon a swelling wave of enthusiasm. It was like a religious revival. Never before in America's political history has there been seen such immense conventions, such crowds, such stupendous processions, whole towns and counties turned their population into a line of march often five miles long and sometimes stretching from one state into another. Clay and Webster soon threw themselves fervidly into the campaign. Clay declared: "The battle is now between the log cabins and the palaces, between hard cider and champagne." Webster publicly apologized for not having been born in a log cabin, and pointed with pride to the fact that his elder brothers and sisters had that honor. "If ever I am ashamed of it," he added, "may my name and the name of my posterity be blotted forever from the memory of mankind."

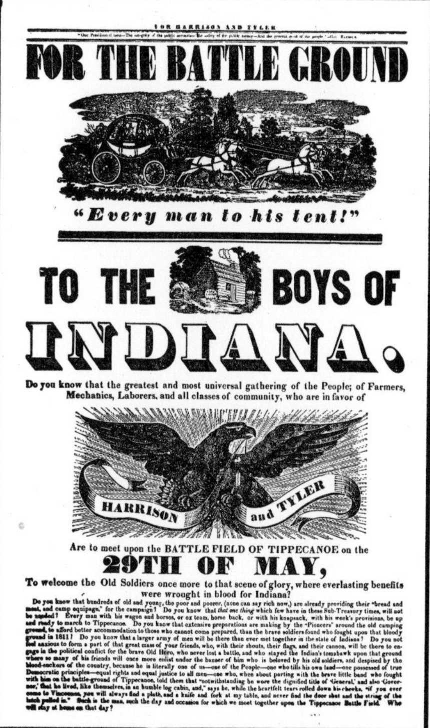

FOR THE BATTLE GROUND

"Every man to his tent!"

TO THE BOYS OF INDIANA.

Do you know that the greatest and most universal gathering of the People, of Farmers, Mechanics, Laborers, and all classes of community, who are in favor of

HARRISON and TYLER

Are to meet upon the BATTLE FIELD OF TIPPECANOE on the

29TH OF MAY,

To welcome the Old Soldiers once more to that scene of glory, where everlasting benefits were wrought in blood for Indiana?

Do you know that hundreds of old and young, the poor and poorer, (none can say rich now,) are already providing their "bread and meat, and camp equipage," for the campaign? Do you know that *that one thing* which few have in these Sub-Treasury times, will not be needed? Every man with his wagon and horses, or ox team, horse back, or with his knapsack, with his week's provisions, be up and ready to march to Tippecanoe. Do you know that extensive preparations are making by the "Pioneers" around the old camping ground, to afford better accommodation to those who cannot come prepared, than the brave soldiers found who fought upon that bloody ground in 1811? Do you know that a larger army of men will be there than ever met together in the state of Indiana? Do you not feel anxious to form a part of that great mass of your friends, who, with their shouts, their flags, and their cannon, will be there to engage in the political conflict for the brave Old Hero, who never lost a battle, and who stayed the Indian's tomahawk upon that ground where so many of his friends will once more enlist under the banner of him who is beloved by his old soldiers, and despised by the blood-suckers of the country, because he is literally one of us—one of the People—one who tills his own land—one possessed of true Democratic principles—equal rights and equal justice to all men—one who, when about parting with the brave little band who fought with him on the battle-ground of Tippecanoe, told them that "notwithstanding he wore the dignified title of 'General,' and also 'Governor,' that he lived, like themselves, in an humble log cabin, and," says he, while the heartfelt tears rolled down his cheeks, "if you ever come to Vincennes, you will always find a plate, and a knife and fork at my table, and never find the door shut and the string of the latch pulled in." Such is the man, such the day and occasion for which we meet together upon the Tippecanoe Battle Field. Who will stay at home on that day?

597 From *The Spirit of '76*, issue of May 9, 1840, in the Indiana State Library, Indianapolis

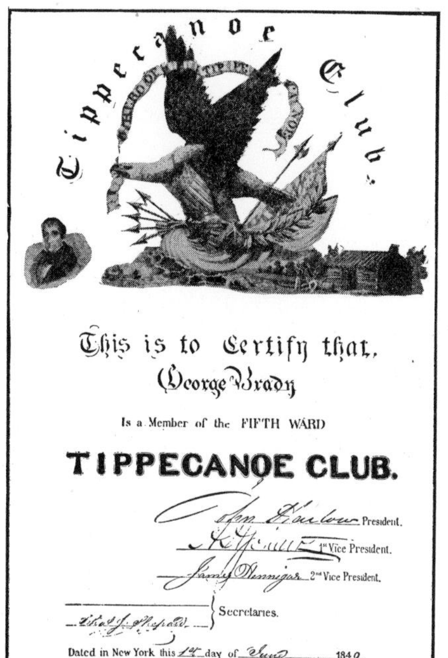

Tippecanoe Club.

This is to Certify that, George Brady

Is a Member of the FIFTH WARD

TIPPECANOE CLUB.

President.

1st Vice President.

2nd Vice President.

Secretaries.

Dated in New York this 1st day of June 1840

598 Certificate of membership in the Tippecanoe Club, New York, dated June 1, 1840, from the original in the New York Historical Society

599 From a lithograph after a drawing by A. C. Smith, published at Baltimore, 1840, in the City Library, Baltimore

NATIONAL CONVENTION OF WHIG YOUNG MEN

To an immense gathering at Baltimore in May, there was rolled, from Kentucky, a large ball, whence originated the phrase, "Keep the ball a-rolling." Before this throng, Clay exclaimed: "This is no time to argue; the time for argument has passed; the nation has already pronounced its sentence."

600 From a contemporary cartoon published by H. R. Robinson, New York, in the New York Historical Society

HARRISON EVADES EXPRESSION OF POLITICAL OPINIONS

THE Democrats could not withstand such campaigning. The Baltimore convention had issued a platform declaring against the protective tariff, national aid to internal improvements, and a United States Bank, as involving the exercise of "doubtful constitutional powers." But these issues could make no headway against the cries of the Whigs. Banners with the legend "Matty's policy, fifty cents a day and French soup; our policy, two dollars a day and roast beef," carried more weight than did arguments of a more reasoned character. When Van Buren called upon Harrison for an expression of views, hoping that political capital might be made for the Democrats, the hard-cider men turned aside the effort to introduce real issues by contrasting the habits of life of the two candidates.

HARRISON ELECTED PRESIDENT

LONG before election day it was evident that Van Buren would be defeated. Nothing that he and his supporters could do was sufficient to prevent his downfall. He lost his own state — indeed, Illinois was the only northern state which went Democratic — and received only sixty votes out of the two hundred and ninety-four in the electoral college. The defeated candidate accepted the verdict with his usual composure, hoping that in 1844 he would be more fortunate.

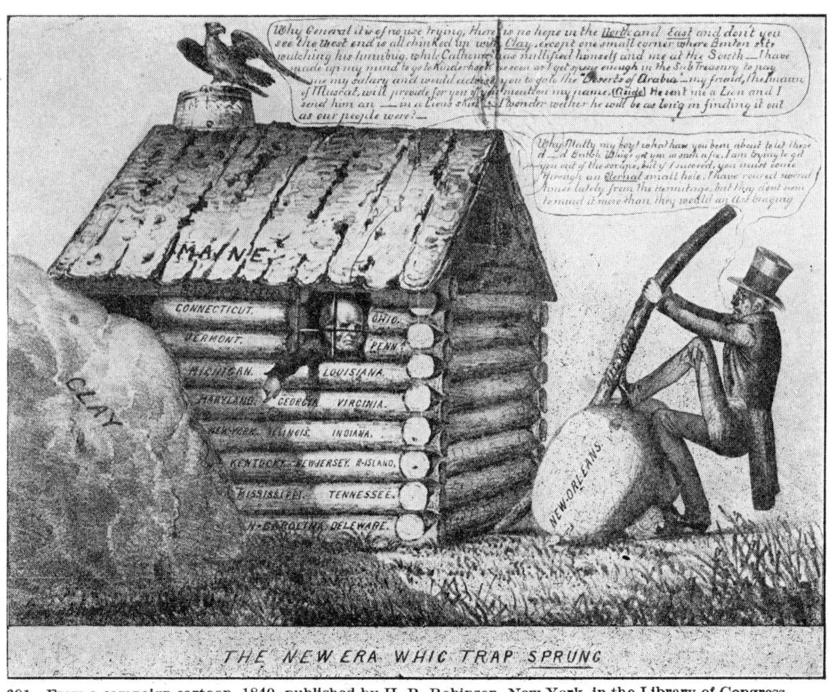

601 From a campaign cartoon, 1840, published by H. R. Robinson, New York, in the Library of Congress

TYLER SUCCEEDS TO THE PRESIDENCY

The Whig rejoicings were short-lived. Although they had carried most of the states of the Union, Harrison's popular vote was only about six per cent larger than Van Buren's. The Whigs, moreover, had come into power with divided counsels. Harrison's policies were still largely a matter of guesswork, although Clay seemed to have secured the post of unofficial adviser. On one point only were the Whigs certain. They wanted office. So persistent were their demands for spoils that Harrison's strength was overtaxed; and on April 4, 1841, just a month after the inauguration, the President died. For the first time there succeeded to the chief magistracy a man who had been elected Vice-president. John Tyler had been nominated by the Whigs, not because he was thought to be of presidential caliber, or because he was sympathetic with the views of the dominant faction within the party, but as a means of conciliating a minority faction. For thirty years he had adhered with pride to a fixed political principle, that of strict construction. When the party of his choice seemed to him to stray from that principle, he had not hesitated to change party. That this had brought him political success did not weaken his convictions. The nationalistic Whigs foresaw trouble.

602 John Tyler, 1790–1862, from the portrait by G. P. A. Healy in the United States National Museum, Washington

TYLER AND THE WHIGS

Under pressure from Clay, Harrison had summoned Congress to meet in special session on May 31, 1841. Tyler fell in with his plan; he also kept in office Harrison's cabinet, packed with Clay's friends. Clay now determined to assert his leadership openly. On June 7 he introduced into the Senate six resolutions which were to be the Whig platform, to be enacted under the guidance of the Kentuckian. The program had three chief planks: first, abolition of the independent treasury and reëstablishment of a national bank; second, upward revision of the tariff; and third, distribution among the states of the proceeds of sales of public lands. At first all went well. The repeal of the Independent Treasury Act was speedily accomplished, with Tyler's approval. Then came the hitch. Tyler's strict constructionist views were well known; yet Clay and his supporters were confident. Tyler's remarks on the matter in his message of June 1, 1841, had seemed conciliatory. So Clay continued with his program, only to have it blocked by two successive vetoes. This made the breach between the President and the Whigs complete. Clay's partisans in the cabinet resigned, followed by others until Webster alone remained. In Congress and out, Tyler's followers were so few as to be nicknamed "The Corporal's Guard." The party was broken; the elections of 1842 gave the Democrats control of the House; and the prospects for 1844 were gloomy.

603 From a contemporary cartoon published by H. R. Robinson, New York, in the New York Historical Society

604 Lord Ashburton, 1774–1848, from the portrait by G. P. A. Healy in the Department of State, Washington

605 Daniel Webster, 1782–1852, from the portrait by G. P. A. Healy in the Department of State, Washington

THE WEBSTER-ASHBURTON TREATY

Article XII.

The present Treaty shall be duly ratified, and the mutual exchange of ratifications shall take place in London, within six months from the date hereof, or earlier if possible.

In faith whereof, we, the respective Plenipotentiaries, have signed this Treaty, and have hereunto affixed our seals.

Done, in duplicate, at Washington, the ninth day of August, Anno Domini one thousand eight hundred and forty two.

Danl Webster Ashburton

606 Last page of Ashburton Treaty, Aug. 9, 1842, from the original in the Department of State, Washington

WEBSTER had remained in the cabinet as Secretary of State in order to conclude certain matters of moment then pending with Great Britain. In an effort to settle all outstanding difficulties between the two countries, Lord Ashburton, who knew and liked America, was in 1841 sent as special Minister to the United States. Webster, backed by the President's constant support, negotiated with him. In the summer of 1842, an agreement was reached upon a number of important matters. Some years earlier, Great Britain had forbidden English vessels to engage in the slave trade. Afterward she had made arrangements with many other nations authorizing her navy to enforce their laws prohibiting the trade. The United States had not entered into such an arrangement, with the result that many slavers hid under the American flag. Great Britain therefore asserted a right to search vessels to determine whether they were properly carrying the American flag. To this the United States, remembering what had happened before the War of 1812, refused assent. The Webster-Ashburton Treaty now settled this dispute. Both nations were to maintain patrolling squadrons off the African slave coast. Thus Great Britain gained suppression of the trade, while the United States did not accede to any right of search. The treaty also settled the Maine-New Brunswick boundary, long a troublesome point in the relations between the two countries.

"ALL OF TEXAS, ALL OF OREGON"

As the election of 1844 approached, Clay and Van Buren appeared as the most likely candidates of their respective parties. The Whigs, who had turned against Clay four years before, had been chastened by the events of Tyler's administration. Van Buren, in spite of his defeat of 1840, had not lost his hold on the organization of the Democratic party. In the spring of 1844, returning from a visit to Andrew Jackson at the Hermitage, he called upon Henry Clay. Both prospective candidates agreed in fearing the disruptive possibilities of the issue of the annexation of Texas. They seem to have agreed that the Texas question should be eliminated from the party platforms. On April 20, when Clay was in Raleigh, North Carolina, and Van Buren was at his home in New York State, the country was surprised to read letters given out by both Clay and Van Buren decrying a discussion of Texas annexation. There was a sharp popular reaction against this concerted attempt to sidetrack an issue in which everyone was interested. With the Democratic convention scarcely a month away, Senator Robert J. Walker of Mississippi undertook the task of defeating the "Little Magician." Walker already had boldly demanded the "re-annexation of Texas and the re-occupation of Oregon" — all Oregon. This had laid the foundation for a union between the South and the West. When Clay and Van Buren published their "self-denying ordinances," Walker assumed the management of the Democratic party. With the opening of the Democratic convention at Baltimore he renewed and vitalized the two-thirds rule. "He procured the passage of this resolution by a mere majority vote, and thus Van Buren, who had a majority of the delegates instructed to vote for him, was deprived of the leadership of the party. The Walker slogan, 'All of Texas, all of Oregon,' was adopted by the convention, and James K. Polk, formerly Speaker of the House of Representatives, was nominated for the Presidency." — W. E. Dodd, *Expansion and Conflict*, pp. 129–30.

607 Robert J. Walker, 1801–69, from a photograph in the Department of Archives and History, Jackson, Miss.

608 James K. Polk, 1795–1849, from a daguerreotype in the collection of L. C. Handy. Washington

POLK SUITS THE SOUTHERNERS

"He was the least conspicuous man who had ever been nominated for President." — Fish, *Development of American Nationality*, p. 305. As a friend of Jackson, a native of North Carolina, and a resident of Tennessee, Polk suited the southern branch of the Democratic party better than Van Buren. The platform, moreover, declared strongly for the annexation of Texas. Thus the campaign of 1844 drew sharply a definite and important issue, that of expansion.

609 From a cartoon by E. W. Clay, published by H. R. Robinson, New York, in the New York Historical Society

THE CAMPAIGN OF 1844

President Tyler, disliked by both the Whigs and the Democrats, attempted to build up a party of his own, but withdrew from the race before the campaign was over. Calhoun supported Polk, and hoped that the coalition of South and West which had put the Tennessean forward would advance his own candidacy in 1848. Webster, Clay's great rival for the leadership of the Whigs, said little during the campaign. The contest centered about territorial expansion and slavery. Polk, whose platform supported both propositions, found himself in a highly favorable strategic position. Clay, whose prestige and personal popularity were vastly greater than that of his opponent, was put on the defensive at the very outset of the campaign.

POLK AS A PROTECTIONIST

The candidate and the main plank of the Democrats were pleasing to the South. To avoid the cry of sectionalism, and to win the Northwest, they added a demand for the "re-occupation" of Oregon. To assure victory, it remained to satisfy the Northern Democrats. These, in general, were offended at the rejection of Van Buren, while many feared lest the domination of the southern Democrats would endanger the protective tariff under which the northern elements prospered. Clay, moreover, was vigorously exploiting the virtues of the American system, and, in particular, those of the Tariff of 1842. To counter the Whig campaign and to mollify the doubting Democrats of the North, Polk wrote a letter which was given wide publicity, and which, at the hands of his partisans, was dexterously interpreted to favor the principle of protection.

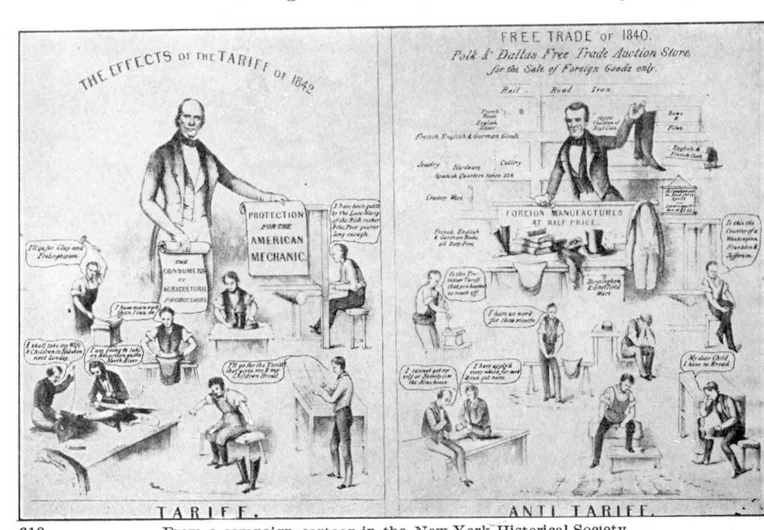

610 From a campaign cartoon in the New York Historical Society

611 Great Whig Procession in New York, from *The Illustrated London News*, Nov. 24, 1844

WHIG ENTHUSIASM

As the campaign developed, it seemed that the attitude of the people of New York State would decide the election. Here, where the antislavery Whigs were strong, Clay was at first the leading candidate. But as he began to hedge upon the issue of the annexation of Texas, his supporters became lukewarm. In the end, enough voted for Birney, candidate of the Liberty party, openly opposed to annexation, to swing the state into the Democratic column.

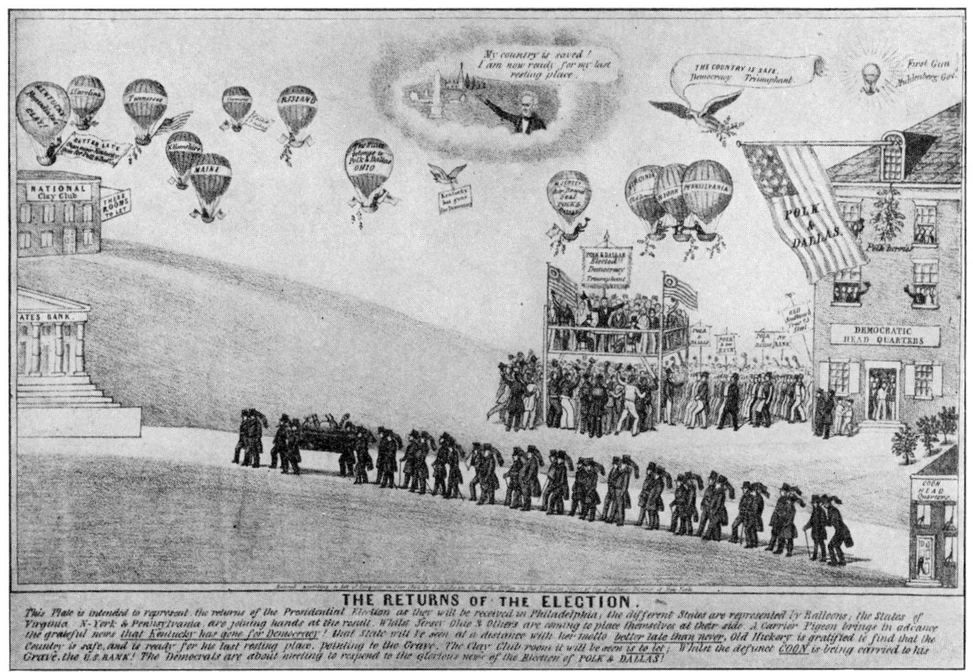

612 From a cartoon published, 1844, by J. Childs, New York

POLK IS ELECTED

As the returns were received, Polk's victory became clear. He carried the Gulf states and the Northwest; Clay won in New England, while the middle and upper Southern States were divided. Though the electoral vote was one hundred and seventy to one hundred and five, Polk's popular plurality was only forty thousand.

613 James Gillespie Birney, 1792–1857, from a portrait from life, artist not known, courtesy of William J. Farrington, Saratoga, Cal.

THE CANDIDATE OF THE LIBERTY PARTY

THE campaign of 1844 saw the reappearance of the Liberty party with James Gillespie Birney as its candidate. A figure in sharp contrast to that of William Lloyd Garrison, Birney was a Kentucky planter. With his father's slaves he had inherited his father's desire to do away with the institution of slavery. Before the publication of the first issue of *The Liberator* in 1831, Birney for some years had been a regular contributor to the American Colonization Society. In 1832–33 he traveled among his fellow planters in the Southwest in the interest of the Colonization Society. In 1834 he freed his own negroes. In 1830 Birney, who had been a recognized leader of Clay's party in the South, broke with the great Kentuckian because he would not lead a crusade to abolish slavery in Kentucky. Driven out of the South by the persecution of the slaveholding opponents, Birney established himself in Cincinnati, where he launched an antislavery paper of moderate tone. Yet Birney spoke with force and candor through the columns of his paper. "There will be no cessation of conflict until slavery shall be exterminated or liberty destroyed. Liberty and slavery cannot live in juxtaposition." He became the leader of the less radical abolitionists. He did not follow Garrison in his attack upon the Constitution or in his policy of no political action. Birney believed that only through politics could civil war be averted. His followers, unsuccessful in securing recognition for their views by either political party, organized the Liberty party in 1840 and nominated Birney for the Presidency. He polled seven thousand votes. In 1844 he was again put forward. This time his vote was sixty thousand. He is credited with drawing enough support from Clay in the critical state of New York to throw the electoral vote of that state, and with it the election, to Polk. The year after the election Birney was disabled by paralysis, caused by a fall from his horse, and from this time withdrew from active participation in public life. But he continued to contribute to the press, and the principle he stood for did not die.

THE LIBERATOR.

BOSTON:

FRIDAY MORNING, NOV. 6, 1840.

Third Political Party.

We have yet to see one good argument advanced in favor of the third party movement. There is no reason whatever why we should oppose it, if we could perceive any thing good in it, near or remote. Standing aloof as we do from any direct participation in the politics of the country, we are quite sure that we occupy as disinterested and impartial a position, in respect to the political bearings of the anti-slavery cause, as do those who are striving to obtain, or who have no objections to receive, the loaves and fishes of office.' We have been careful to peruse the political lucubrations of the Emancipator, the Friend of Man, the Abolitionist, and some other papers friendly to the third party; but their logic and their declamation have alike failed to make any impression upon us. While we see nothing to alter our opinion, that it originated in selfishness and ambition, and is prosecuted in the spirit of desperation against the most fearful odds, we have no doubt that there are some who support it from an honest belief that it will subserve the interests of the anti-slavery cause.

It is worthy of remark that some of the most prominent supporters of the movement have already been put in nomination for office—Gerrit Smith, James G. Birney, Thomas Earle, Henry B. Stanton, John G. Whittier, &c. &c: It is hardly probable that they will be elected, seeing they are opposed by a large majority of the abolitionists in the United States, as well as the two great existing parties!

It is also worthy of remark, that almost all who go for a third party are either openly or secretly in favor of new organization—and new organization is not trustworthy, either morally or politically. It is an evil spirit, full of self-seeking, and swayed by ambitious and sectarian motives. In New-England, it has made the new political movement a *dernier resort* to save it from an immediate overthrow. To illustrate this point, we quote the following passage from 'the detected letter' of Elizur Wright, Jr. to Henry B. Stanton, written one year ago:

'One thing *I know*. Unless you do take such a step, [get up a third party,] our new organization here is *a gone case* It has been, *inter nos*, shockingly mismanaged. Every thing has been made to turn upon the *woman question*. The political has been left to fall out of sight. It won't do for *us* to start the national politics. But if the parent society does so, and not by *our* move, then we can take hold with all our might—the non-resistants will have to be out upon us under true flag (!)—the *confounded* woman question will be forgotten—and we shall take a *living* position. You certainly *see* this. Take my solemn assurance that *it is life and death with us*. Make the move, and we will follow and *live*.'

New organization will find, in the sequel, that

614 Garrison's editorial opposing the Liberty party, from *The Liberator*, Nov. 6, 1840

THE OREGON QUESTION

POLK had been elected on an expansionist platform, and throughout his administration foreign policy was predominant. Tyler, anxious to carry through his program of annexation before leaving office, had persuaded the short session of Congress, meeting in December, 1844, to offer Texas acceptable terms of admission to the Union. Thus upon his inauguration Polk found one of his main planks already adopted. He turned to the Oregon question. The whole of this great country was claimed by both the United States and Great Britain. Polk's first move was to offer a compromise that had been proposed earlier, namely, that of dividing the territory by the forty-ninth parallel, the present international boundary. When England summarily rejected this, popular feeling in America became intense.

615 From a cartoon in *Punch*, 1845, probably by John Leech

THE ACQUISITION OF OREGON

THE expansionists within the country cried for war, unless England would cede American claims as far north as 54°40′. Polk was firm. The moderate element hoped that England's repeal of the corn laws, which threw open her ports to American grain, would pacify the West. But the President was eager to settle the issue, and to settle it in America's favor. He reiterated his belief that the United States had valid claims to lands north of 49°, and suggested to Congress that it should take measures to effectuate them. England had watched these developments closely, and finally agreed to reconsider her earlier rejection of the compromise offer. In the summer of 1846 a treaty was signed which made the forty-ninth parallel the basis of division. The United States now, for the first time, held undisputed foothold upon the Pacific coast.

616 From a cartoon, 1846, by E. W. Clay, in the Library of Congress

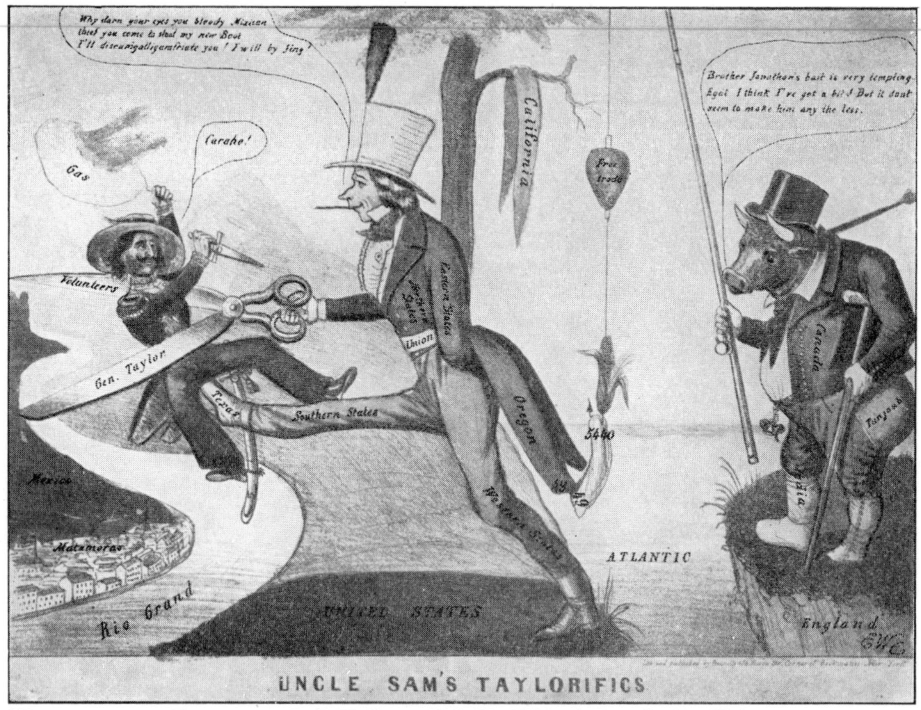

617 From a cartoon by E. W. Clay, published in 1846 by A. Donnelly, New York

CONGRESS DECLARES WAR ON MEXICO

Polk was the more ready to accept the settlement of the Oregon line as trouble was brewing upon the southern border. Mexico had refused to recognize the independence of Texas and had protested against its annexation to the United States. The southern boundary of Texas, moreover, was in dispute. These matters might have been arranged amicably had Polk and the expansionists not entertained ambitious dreams of a greater United States. Polk wished to secure California, an immense Mexican possession to the West. This Mexico refused to sell. Feeling along the border became strained. Near Matamoras, on the Rio Grande, the troops of the two countries came into conflict; and on May 11, 1846, the President recommended to Congress the adoption of a declaration of war, on the ground that "War exists, and notwithstanding all our efforts to avoid it."

Texas
California
THE GREEDY BOY.
VICTORIA.—YOU GREEDY YOUNG YANKEE! YOU WON'T LEAVE A CRUMB FOR LITTLE FREDERICK ALBERT.
LOUIS PHILIPPE.—SOYEZ TRANQUILLE MA CHERE; YOU ARE VARY FOND OF INDIAN BONBONS, AND I LOAF VARY MOSH ZE TABAC D'ALGIERS MYSELF WE SHALL MOSH BETTER BOTH BE QUIET.

618 From a cartoon in *Yankee Doodle*, New York, 1846–47

THE TREATY OF PEACE

After spirited resistance by the aroused Mexicans, the American troops under Taylor and Scott (see Vol. VI) made such inroads into the country that peace became inevitable. By this time the expansionists in the United States were calling for the annexation of the whole of Mexico. But Polk was content with the cession, in March, 1848, for fifteen million dollars, of more than five hundred thousand square miles of territory in California and the Southwest.

PARTY UNITY IS STRAINED

THESE accessions of territory quickly caused trouble. Immediately after the acquisition, if not, indeed, before it, arose the question that was to work such havoc. Should the new territories be slave or free? Here was an issue manifestly calling for announcement of principle. For the time, however, the politicians did their best to avoid giving an answer. While the country was debating Calhoun's doctrine of "Non-interference," the Western idea of "squatter sovereignty" and the Wilmot Proviso, which sought to exclude slavery from the territory acquired from Mexico, the election of 1848 approached. "The preservation of party unity became a problem of the greatest difficulty, taking the utmost skill of the politicians." — FISH, *Development of American Nationality*, p. 317. The Democrats, dodging the slavery issue, nominated Lewis Cass, a northerner who was popular in the South. Cass had been associated with General Harrison in a commission to treat with the Indians who had been hostile to the United States in the War of 1812. He had subsequently been superintendent of Indian Affairs and Secretary of War in Jackson's cabinet.

619 Lewis Cass, 1782–1866, from the portrait by G. P. A. Healy, in the possession of Mrs. M. C. Ledyard

620 David Wilmot, 1814–68, from a photograph taken while in Congress, courtesy of Mrs. L. M. Dusinberre, Wellsboro, Pa.

A CARTOON OF THE DAY

THIS was a transitional period in which the American people, not less than the politicians, were unsettled in their minds regarding many questions that affected the nation as a whole. The cartoonist has attempted to illustrate the discordant elements out of which in the process of time was to rise the one great issue destined to divide the country. Garrison, Calhoun, Wilmot and Greeley were actors in a drama whose climax, while it had to be deferred, was none the less inevitable. "Bubble, bubble, toil and trouble! Boil, Free Soil, the Union spoil; Come grief and moan, Peace be none, Till we divided be!"

THE HURLY-BURLY POT.

621 From a cartoon published in 1850 by James Bailey, New York, in the Library of Congress

622 Thurlow Weed, 1797–1882, from a photograph by Brady

THE WHIG NOMINATION OF 1848

The Whigs also tried the policy of evading the slavery issue. As their nominee they selected, under the guidance of Thurlow Weed, General Taylor, the hero of the war, whom the Democratic administration had seemed to slight. As he was a southerner and a slaveholder, his popularity in the South seemed certain; while his military record was to carry him through the North. The scheme of the party managers was discerned by Lowell in *The Biglow Papers:*

> Another pint thet influences the minds of sober jedges
> Is thet the Gin'ral hez n't gut tied hand an' foot with pledges,
> He hez n't told ye wut he is, an' so there ain't no knowin'
> But wut he may turn out to be the best there is agoin'.

AN AVAILABLE CANDIDATE.
THE ONE QUALIFICATION FOR A WHIG PRESIDENT.

623 From a contemporary cartoon in the New York Historical Society

CLAY ON SLAVERY

Clay had desired the Whig nomination; but again he had injured his chances by an unfortunate statement. In 1847, when the Mexican army was completely defeated, he had made a speech, declaring that there should be a generous peace, and insisting that the party should renounce any "wish or desire on our part to acquire any foreign territory whatever, for the purpose of propagating slavery, or of introducing slaves from the United States." Such frankness was objectionable to the party leaders, and Clay was set aside for a man whose views were not so well known.

624 From a Democratic cartoon, published in 1848 by H. R. Robinson, New York, in the New York Historical Society

THE FREE SOIL PARTY

SUCH evasion of the slavery issue by the major parties was displeasing to many in the North. Since 1844 a faction of the Democrats in New York, known as the Barn-burners, and followers of Van Buren, had been openly on the antislavery side. In the Democratic convention this faction had been slighted by the administration forces, in favor of the rival New York faction, the Hunkers. Now, under the influence of ardent antislavery men, such as Benjamin Butler the elder, former law partner of Van Buren, a coalition was formed between the Barn-burners and the Liberty party. Van Buren was nominated for the Presidency, with Charles Francis Adams of Massachusetts as running-mate. As the Free Soil party, the group entered the campaign "upon the national platform of freedom."

625 From a cartoon published at New York in 1848, in the New York Historical Society

THE VICTORY OF THE WHIGS

DESPITE the efforts of both Whigs and Democrats, the slavery question was intruded into the campaign. The Democrats suffered as a result of the unpopularity of the Mexican war in certain sections of the North. The Whigs were aided by the prestige of the victor of Buena Vista (Vol. VI).

The split in the ranks of the New York Democrats proved fatal. In the election Taylor received a plurality of the popular votes, and one hundred and sixty-three of the two hundred and ninety electoral votes. By their opponents the election was hailed as a death-blow for the Democrats. More to the point, however, was the strength shown by the Free Soil party. Van Buren received nearly 300,000 votes — all from the free states of the North and Northwest. In New Hampshire and Ohio the Free Soilers elected Senators. In eleven states they held the balance between the old parties. Such results should have demonstrated to men of all political faiths that the vital issue of the day could not be much longer ignored with impunity. The politicians, however, preferred to give a less disconcerting interpretation to the election returns. To them it meant the downfall of the Democrats and the long-sought victory of the Whigs. This was a simple explanation, but satisfying to no one who examined the problems that faced the new administration.

626 From a cartoon published by Abel & Durang, Philadelphia, in the Historical Society of Pennsylvania

CHAPTER XI

A HOUSE DIVIDED AGAINST ITSELF

TO further the alliance between the doctrine of state rights and the cause of slavery, Calhoun bent every effort. In every question that came before the government he saw something of concern to the slave-holding South. Almost every action and suggested action of the national government seemed to him to presage an irresistible conflict in which the supporters of slavery must choose between submission and secession. In this view he was not alone. Many in the North and the West saw what was impending and did their utmost to prevent its occurrence.

In the Compromise of 1850 they thought that the outbreak had been forestalled. The passage of the measures constituting that compromise was met with a sigh of relief from those who realized the danger that had been escaped. Having, however, avoided, as they thought, that danger, they proceeded to consider slavery as a settled issue.

Had the slavery question not been so closely tied up with other pressing problems, the decision of 1850 might have endured. It was, however, not an isolated matter that could be dismissed so easily; rather, it permeated everything that required political consideration. Acquisition of new territory, establishment of territorial governments, admission to the Union of territories, treatment of the Indians, construction of transcontinental railroads — in each of these there lurked the political bogey so much feared by the politician of the day. The juncture between these problems and the slave question becomes obvious upon the slightest perusal of the numerous resolutions passed by state legislatures and mass meetings held in the 'fifties. This interweaving of numerous issues is well illustrated, for example, in a Resolve of the Connecticut Legislature, adopted in the spring of 1850:

> "Resolved, That the integrity and permanence of American power on the Pacific Ocean, the increase of our commerce and wealth, the extension of our institutions, and the cause of human freedom on this continent, require the immediate admission of California into this Union, with her present Constitution, and the boundaries therein defined, without any reference to any other question or measure whatever."

Since the slavery issue was so involved with others, it not unnaturally cropped up anew in 1854. This time there were not at hand the men who had, by experience, become adept at "compromising." Webster, Clay and Calhoun were dead; their places were taken by men less skillful, more intransigent. The result was that the Kansas-Nebraska decisions in no way laid the ghost of the slavery issue.

On the contrary, the issue became increasingly complicated not only by its economic, political, and sectional associations; but by the fact that it was, as analyzed by Jefferson and Lincoln, a race problem. The majority of the people in the Northwest were opposed to the entry into that section of the negro, either slave or free. In Illinois, for example, a series of anti-negro laws was passed, followed in 1853 by an act of the General Assembly of that State, the object of which was "to prevent the immigration of free negroes into the State." The law made it a misdemeanor for a negro or a mulatto, bond or free, to enter Illinois with the intention of taking up permanent residence.

TAYLOR OPPOSES THE EXTENSION OF SLAVERY

President Taylor was the successful candidate of a party that in the campaign of 1848 had endeavored to evade the slavery issue. He was honest, independent, but without experience in statecraft or politics. He had been nominated as a man whose southern connections and military record would win the favor of all sections of the Whig party. The South hoped that he would lean toward her interests; but early in his administration he came to rely upon William H. Seward, antislavery Whig senator from New York. This bent became more pronounced with the exigency arising from the discovery of gold in California, which made it imperative to establish orderly government at once in the new Southwestern territories. Without waiting for Congressional action, Taylor advised California and New Mexico to form constitutions and to apply for admission to the Union. He hoped thus to dispose, at least in part, of the problem of slavery in the territories. In August, 1849, he announced that "The people of the North need have no apprehension of the further extension of slavery."

627 Zachary Taylor, 1784–1850, from the portrait by G. P. A. Healy, after Jaques Amans (1801–88), in the Corcoran Gallery of Art, Washington

THE GROWTH OF ABOLITION

1840.] *Anti-Slavery Almanac.* 17

Oh my child my child

WOMEN AT WORK IN THE FIELD.

Mr. Lemuel Sapington, a native of Maryland, formerly a slave-trader, now a respectable citizen of Lancaster, Pa., in a letter dated January 21, 1839, speaking of slaves in the southern part of Virginia, says:—

"Among the gangs, are often young women, who bring their children to the fields, and lay them in a fence corner, while they are at work. When a child is three weeks old, a woman is considered in working order. I have seen a woman, with her child strapped to her back, laboring the whole day, beside a man, perhaps the father of the child, and he not being permitted to give her any assistance, himself being under the whip."

Rev. Francis Hawley, pastor of the Baptist church, Colebrook, Ct., who lived seventeen years in North and South Carolina, says:—

"Those who are with child are driven to their task till within a few days of the time of their delivery; and when the child is a few weeks old, the mother must again go to the field. If it is far from her hut, she must take her babe with her. If the child cries, she cannot go to its relief; the eye of the overseer is upon her: and if, when she goes to nurse it, she stays a little longer than the overseer thinks necessary, he commands her back to her task. Brother, you cannot begin to know what the poor slave mothers suffer on thousands of plantations at the south."

Rev. Horace Moulton, of the Methodist Episcopal church, says:—

"Women are seen bringing their infants into the field to their work, and leading others, who are not old enough to stay in the cabins with safety. When they get there, they must set them down in the dirt and go to work. Some, who have *very young* ones, fix a little sack, and place the infants on their back and work. One reason is, the child will not cry so much when it can hear a mother's voice. Another is, the mothers fear the *poisonous snakes*. I never knew any place where the land is so infested with venomous snakes, as in the low lands round about Savannah. To secure their infants from poisonous snakes, females *often* work with their infants on their backs."

"The South-west, by a Yankee," was published by the Harpers, N. Y., 1835. The writer takes great pains to impress his readers with the beauties of slavery. Yet he says, (vol. ii. p. 125,) "On most plantations females are allowed a month's cessation from ☞FIELD labor before and after confinement. But it cannot be denied that on some plantations, nothing but *actual confinement* releases them from the field, to which the mother soon after returns, leaving an infant *a few days old* (! ! !) at the "quarters."

628 From the *Anti-Slavery Almanac*, 1840, in possession of the publishers

Settlement was not to be such a simple affair. Sectional feeling had become more intense than in the early days of the abolition societies. The antislavery movement had increased vastly in importance and in its strength throughout the North and West. The days when abolitionists in this region were the subject of riotous assaults had passed as dislike for slavery spread. In this widespread hostility to the peculiar institution of the South lay a threat to the integrity of the nation. In this development such publications as the *Anti-Slavery Almanac*, among others, had a positive influence.

A

SCRIPTURAL, ECCLESIASTICAL, AND HISTORICAL

VIEW OF SLAVERY,

FROM THE

DAYS OF THE PATRIARCH ABRAHAM, TO THE NINETEENTH CENTURY.

ADDRESSED TO THE

RIGHT REV. ALONZO POTTER, D.D.,

BISHOP OF THE PROT. EPISCOPAL CHURCH, IN THE DIOCESE OF PENNSYLVANIA.

BY

JOHN HENRY HOPKINS, D.D., LL.D.,

BISHOP OF THE DIOCESE OF VERMONT.

[Fourth Thousand.]

New-York:

W. I. POOLEY & CO., HARPER'S BUILDING, FRANKLIN SQUARE.

629 From the original in the possession of Matthew Page Andrews, Baltimore

630 Wendell Phillips, William Lloyd Garrison, and George Thompson, an English antislavery advocate, from a daguerreotype taken about 1851, owned by the Garrison family

ABOLITIONIST LEADERS

GARRISON remained, as the antislavery movement grew in strength, its most radical leader. His *Liberator* continued its untiring attack upon the men of the South who owned and trafficked in human chattels. In the 'thirties George Thompson, a Scotsman (picture adjoining), who had been prominent in the British abolition movement, collaborated with Garrison. In 1835 Thompson was quoted as saying in a public address that "Southern slaves ought, or at least had a right, to cut the throats of their masters." Wendell Phillips was scarcely second to Garrison in the vehemence of his attack upon slavery. In 1861, he placed on an honor-roll which included Cromwell and Washington the name of Toussaint L'Ouverture, who had led the great slave insurrection in Haiti at the opening of the nineteenth century which drove the French from that rich colony. With such men preaching the cause of human freedom in the North, the politicians faced almost insuperable obstacles in determining the national policy with regard to slavery. (For slavery as a domestic institution see Volume III.)

THE SLAVE TRADE

THE domestic slave trade was a feature of the peculiar institution of the South that roused the fiercest opposition in the North. Such an invoice as that of John W. Pittman made abolitionists by the score. Few northern women could read without being deeply stirred such sentiments as these which are expressed in the last paragraph of the invoice: "I did intend to leave Nancy child but she made such a damned fuss I had to let her take it I could of got fifty Dollars for so you must add forty Dollars to the above." To southern women this aspect of slavery was a sad but necessary accompaniment of an inevitable institution. They strove to reduce it to the smallest possible proportions. But amelioration was not abolition; and more than once the fanatics in the North capitalized such conduct as benevolent despotism endeavoring to disguise the inherent evil of human slavery.

An invoice of ten negroes sent this day to John B Williamson by Geo Kremer named & cost as follows

To wit		
	Betsey Kackley	$410.00
	Nancy Aulick	515.00
	Harry & Helen Miller . .	1200.00
	Mary Kootz	600.00
	Betsey Ott	560.00
	Isaac & Fanny Brent .	992.00
	Lucinda Luckett	467.50
	George Smith	510.00
Amount of my traveling expences & boarding		5254.50
of lot No 9 not included in the other bills		39.50
Kremers expences Transporting lot No 9 to Richd		51.00
Carryall hire . .		6.00
		$5351.00

I have this day delivered the above named negroes costing including my expences and other expences five thousand three hundred & fifty dollars this May 26th 1835

John W. Pittman

I did intend to leave Nancy child but she made such a damned fuss I had to let her take it I could of got fifty Dollars for so you must add forty Dollars to the above

631 Invoice of a Sale of Negroes, 1835, from the original in the Library of Congress

BEECHER'S PARODY OF A SLAVE AUCTION

632 From *The Ladies Home Journal*, Nov. 1896, drawing by T. de Thulstrup. © Curtis Publishing Company, reproduced by permission

Henry Ward Beecher, perhaps the greatest preacher of his day, identified himself actively with the cause of anti-slavery. On June 1, 1856, he won a triumph. Before an audience that filled every inch of space in Plymouth Church he staged a demonstration of a slave auction. "The solemn, impressive silence of that vast Plymouth assemblage was absolutely painful as a young woman slowly ascended the stairs leading to the pulpit and sank into a chair by Mr. Beecher's side. Instantly assuming the look and manner of a slave auctioneer he called for bids. 'Look,' he exclaimed, 'at this marketable commodity — human flesh and blood, like yourselves. You see the white blood of her father in her regular features and high, thoughtful brow. Who bids? You will have to pay extra for that white blood because it is supposed to give intelligence. Stand up, Sarah! Now look at her trim figure and her wavy hair! . . . She is a Christian woman — I mean, a praying nigger — and that makes her more valuable, because it insures her docility and obedience to your wishes. Servants, obey your masters! you know. She believes in that doctrine. How much for her? Will you allow this praying woman to be sent back to Richmond to meet the fate for which her father sold her?'" — Mrs. Henry Ward Beecher, in the *Ladies Home Journal*, Nov., 1896.

LIBERTY LINE.

NEW ARRANGEMENT--NIGHT AND DAY.

The improved and splendid Locomotives, Clarkson and Lundy, with their trains fitted up in the best style of accommodation for passengers, will run their regular trips during the present season, between the borders of the Patriarchal Dominion and Libertyville, Upper Canada. Gentlemen and Ladies, who may wish to improve their health or circumstances, by a northern tour, are respectfully invited to give us their patronage.

SEATS FREE, *irrespective of color.*

Necessary Clothing furnished gratuitously to such as have *"fallen among thieves."*

"Hide the outcasts—let the oppressed go free."—*Bible.*

☞For seats apply at any of the trap doors, or to the conductor of the train.

J. CROSS, *Proprietor.*

N. B. For the special benefit of Pro-Slavery Police Officers, an extra heavy wagon for Texas, will be furnished, whenever it may be necessary, in which they will be forwarded as dead freight, to the "Valley of Rascals," always at the risk of the owners.

☞Extra Overcoats provided for such of them as are afflicted with protracted *chilly-phobia.*

633 Facsimile of advertisement of the Underground Railroad, from *The Western Citizen*, July 13, 1844

THE UNDERGROUND RAILROAD

The South had awakened to the threatened danger and jealously guarded her rights. In the North the Underground Railroad, with efficiency and expedition, aided fugitive slaves to escape to Canada. There were "stations" at regular intervals in the northern towns, especially in New York and the New England states, and many prominent men acted as "conductors." The southern people, in turn, held mass meetings at which such auctions were denounced. The cry of disunion was raised. From Mississippi a call was issued for a southern convention, to meet at Nashville in June, 1850, to deliberate upon measures to be taken in the crisis.

634 Levi Coffin, 1798–1877, reputed President of the Underground Railroad, from an engraving by R. O'Brien, in the Friends Historical Society, Philadelphia

"LIBERTY, EQUALITY, FRATERNITY.

DEDICATED TO THE SMARTEST NATION IN ALL CREATION.

635 From a cartoon by John Leech in *Punch*, 1848, by permission of the proprietors

AN ENGLISH THRUST AT SLAVERY

Across the Atlantic, English artists satirized the "land of the free" in biting cartoons. In such a drawing as "Liberty, Equality, Fraternity, dedicated to the smartest nation in all creation," is plainly expressed the attitude toward Americans of a considerable body of the English people.

NORTHERN RIDICULE OF ABOLITIONISTS

The Abolitionists, as reformers are prone to do, went to extremes. Garrison advocated the abandonment of the Union if the slaves were not freed. Though more and more Northern people became hostile to slavery, the opposition to and ridicule of the radical Abolitionists continued.

636 From a caricature *Ye Abolitionists in Council*, in *Harper's Weekly*, May 28, 1859

CLAY RETURNS TO THE SENATE

The nation was confronted with a crisis in 1850 when California applied for admission to the Union as a free state. "The task of working out a compromise which should reconcile the various conflicting interests, and of securing its acceptance, fell to Henry Clay. It was the most difficult political task since the adoption of the Constitution. Just that line of agreement had to be drawn which would satisfy one section without causing repugnance in the other, for it was not enough to secure the passage of an act of Congress, but it was necessary to win for it the approval of a majority in both sections. . . . Clay's seventy-four years had been crowded with political experience, and he knew every pathway through the maze of national affairs. . . . The fact that he had at last given up his presidential ambition, and that after eight years' absence he had returned to the Senate for the express purpose of bringing peace to his distracted country, gave him prestige with all his colleagues, while his feeble health added a rather pathetic interest to his efforts." — Fish, *Development of American Nationality*, pp. 322–23.

637 Henry Clay at seventy-one, from a daguerreotype, taken 1848, in Philadelphia, by Marcus A. Root, in the Historical Society of Pennsylvania

638 From an engraving by R. Whitechurch after the painting *Clay Addressing the Senate on the Compromise of 1850*, by Peter F. Rothermel (1817–95)

CLAY PLEADS FOR HIS COMPROMISE PLAN

On January 29, 1850, Clay presented his plan to the Senate. In the form of a series of resolutions, it purported to settle all of the controverted issues. California was to be admitted with her free-soil constitution; the other territories were to be organized without congressional dictation as to slavery therein; Congress was to enact a fugitive slave law that would adequately protect slave-owners; and the slave-trade within the District of Columbia was to be prohibited. A week later, the author of the measures, in a memorable speech, pleaded for them as a compromise honorable to both sections.

CALHOUN'S LAST SPEECH

On the fourth of March, Calhoun replied. He was so ill that his speech had to be read for him. But in his advocacy of the cause of the South he did not falter. He denounced the compromise as a betrayal of his section, as another indication of the dominance of the North in the nation's councils. He felt that one by one the cords of union were snapping. The nation could be saved only by constitutional readjustments which would restore the balance between the sections. "If you who represent the stronger portions," he urged upon the Northern senators, "cannot agree to settle them (*i.e.*, the questions at issue between the two sections) on the broad principles of justice and duty, say so, and let the states we represent agree to separate and part in peace. If you are unwilling we should part in peace, tell us so, and we shall know what to do, when you reduce the question to submission or resistance. If you remain silent you then compel us to infer what you intend." This was Calhoun's last great act. Soon afterward, the leading statesman of the South was dead.

639 From a cartoon signed W. T. C., published in 1848 by H. R. Robinson, New York, in the New York Historical Society

640 Daniel Webster, 1782–1852, from a daguerreotype taken in 1851, in the Massachusetts Historical Society

VOTERS, Read This!

EXTRACT FROM A

SPEECH

DELIVERED BY THE

Hon. Daniel Webster,

IN THE SENATE OF THE UNITED STATES, ON THE 7th OF MARCH, 1850.

"If the infernal Fanatics and Abolitionists ever get the power in their hands, they will override the Constitution, set the Supreme Court at defiance, change and make Laws to suit themselves. They will lay violent hands on those who differ with them politically in opinion, or dare question their infallibility; bankrupt the country and finally deluge it with blood."

641 From a handbill giving an extract from Webster's Seventh of March Speech, 1850, in the New York Historical Society

WEBSTER'S SEVENTH OF MARCH SPEECH

A FEW days later, the third great figure in the Senate rose to speak. Throughout the North, Webster was looked upon as the pilot under whom the storm of slavery could be weathered. The antislavery element now hoped that he would turn all his powers against the extension of slavery. But Webster valued the Union above all else; when it was in danger, all lesser matters must give way. So he declared for the compromise. His chief task was to conciliate the South. He admitted that the North had defaulted in its duty of returning fugitive slaves; he charged the abolitionists with conduct that was certain to arouse southern resentment; and, fearing secession, he asked the North to be fair, to accept the compromise. "To break up this great government! To dismember this great country! . . . No, sir! No, sir! There will be no secession. Gentlemen are not serious when they talk of secession." This "Seventh-of-March Speech" was approved by the more moderate people of the North. The radicals, however, were enraged. Webster was compared with Benedict Arnold, accused of bidding for southern support for the Presidency, and denounced in many public meetings.

THE COMPROMISE IS ENACTED, SEPT., 1850

WEBSTER'S support did not ensure the passage of Clay's measures. Debate became general, both in and out of Congress, and continued for months. Jefferson Davis succeeded Calhoun as the leader of the South; Chase of Ohio and Seward of New York were the spokesmen for the extremists in the North. The deadlock seemed interminable. But events proved favorable to Clay's scheme. The Southern Convention, meeting in June, was controlled by moderates, who contented themselves with temperate demands. The death, on July 9, of General Taylor brought Millard Fillmore, whose political career began and ended with the birth and extinction of the Whig party, into the Presidency; and he evidenced his support of the compromise by appointing Webster Secretary of State. Furthermore, it was found that, by voting on each item of the compromise separately, majorities for all could be obtained. In the first weeks of September, they received the President's signature.

Fugitive Slave Bill.

As passed by the Senate and House of Representatives, Sept. 12, 1850, and approved September 18, 1850, by President FILLMORE.

AN ACT to amend, and supplementary to the act entitled, "An act respecting fugitives from justice, and persons escaping from the service of their masters," approved, Feb. 12, 1793.

SECTION 1. That persons who have been or may hereafter be, appointed Commissioners in virtue of any act of Congress, by the Circuit Courts of the United States, and who in consequence of such appointments, are authorised to exercise the powers that a *justice of the peace or other magistrate* of any of the United States may exercise in respect to offenders for any crime or offence against the United States, by arresting, imprisoning, or bailing the same under and by virtue of the thirty-third section of the act of the 24th of September, 1789, entitled "An act to establish Judicial Courts of the United States," shall be and are hereby *authorized and required to exercise and discharge all the powers and duties conferred by this act.*

SEC 2. And be it further enacted, That the Superior Court of *each organized territory* of the United States, shall have the same power to appoint commissioners to take acknowledgements of bail and affidavits, and to take depositions of witnesses in civil causes which is now possessed by the Circuit Courts of the United States; all commissioners who shall be appointed for such purposes by the Superior Court of *any organized territory* of the United States, shall possess all the powers and exercise all the duties conferred by law upon the commissioners appointed by the Circuit Court of the United States for similar purposes, and shall moreover exercise and discharge all the powers and duties conferred by this act.

SEC. 3. And be it further enacted, That the circuit courts of the United States and the superior courts of each organized territory of the United States, shall, from time to time, *enlarge the number of commissioners, with a view to afford reasonable facilities to reclaim fugitives from labor*, and to the discharge of the duties imposed by this act.

SEC. 4. And be it further enacted, That the commissioners above named shall have concurrent jurisdiction with the Judges of the Circuit and District Courts of the United States, in their respective circuits and districts within the several States, and the judges of the superior courts of the territories, severally and collectively, in term time and vacation; and shall grant certificates to such claimants, upon *satisfactory proof* being made with *authority to take and remove such fugitives from service or labor*, under the restrictions herein contained, to the State or territory from which such persons may have escaped or fled.

SEC. 5. And be it further enacted, That it shall be the duty of all marshals and deputy marshals to obey and execute all warrants and precepts issued under the provisions of this act, when to them directed; and should any marshal or deputy marshal *refuse* to receive such warrant or other process, when tendered, or use all proper means diligently to execute the same, he shall on conviction thereof, be *fined in the sum of ONE THOUSAND DOLLARS to the use of such claimant* on motion of such claimant, by the circuit or district court of the district of such marshal; and after arrest of such fugitive by such marshal or his deputy, or whilst at any time in his custody under the provisions of this act, should such fugitive escape, *whether* WITH OR WITHOUT THE ASSENT OF SUCH MARSHAL OR HIS DEPUTY, such marshal shall be liable on his official bond to be prosecuted for the benefit of such claimant, for the *full value* of the service or labor of said fugitive in the State, territory or district whence he escaped; and the better to enable the said commissioners when thus appointed, to execute their duties faithfully and efficiently; in conformity with the requirements of the Constitution of the United States and of this act, they are hereby authorized and empowered, *within their counties* respectively to appoint in writing under hands *any one or more suitable persons* from time to time, to execute all such warrants and other process as may be issued by them in the lawful performance of their respective duties, with authority to such commissioners or the person to be appointed by them to execute process as aforesaid, to summon and CALL TO THEIR AID THE BYSTANDERS, or *posse comitatus* of the proper county, when necessary to insure a faithful observance of the clause of the constitution referred to, in conformity with the provisions of this act—AND ALL GOOD CITIZENS ARE HEREBY COMMANDED TO AID AND ASSIST IN THE PROMPT AND EFFICIENT EXECUTION OF THIS WHENEVER THEIR SERVICES MAY BE REQUIRED as aforesaid for that purpose; and said warrants shall run and be executed by said officers anywhere in the State, within which they are executed.

SEC. 6. And be it further enacted, That when a person held to service or labor in any State or territory of the United States, *has heretofore or shall hereafter* escape into another State or territory of the United States, the person or persons to whom such services or labor may be due, or his, her or their agent or attorney, duly authorized, by power of attorney, in writing acknowledged and certified under the seal of some legal officer of court of the State or territory in which the same may be executed, may pursue and reclaim such fugitive person, either by procuring a warrant from some of the courts, judges or commissioners aforesaid, of the proper circuit, district or county for the apprehension of such fugitive from service or labor, or by seizing and arresting such fugitive, where the same can be done *without process*, and by taking or causing such person to be taken, forthwith before such court, judge or commissioner, whose duty it shall be to hear and determine the case of such claimant *in a* SUMMARY MANNER; and upon *satisfactory proof* being made, by *deposition or affidavit*, in writing, to be taken and certified by such court, judge or commissioner, or by *other satisfactory testimony*, duly taken and certified by some court, magistrate, justice of the peace, or other legal officer authorized to administer an oath and take depositions under the laws of the State or territory from which such person owing service or labor may have escaped, with a certificate of such magistracy or other authority, as aforesaid, with the seal of the proper court or officer thereto attached, which seal shall be sufficient to establish the competency of the proof, and with proof also by affidavit, of the *identity* of the person whose service or labor is said to be due as aforesaid, that the person so arrested does in fact owe service or labor to the person or persons claiming him or her, in the State or territory from which such fugitive may have escaped, as aforesaid, and that said person escaped, to make out and deliver to such claimant, his or her agent or attorney, a *certificate* setting forth the substantial facts as to the service or labor due from such fugitive to the claimant, and of his or her escape from the State or territory in which such service or labor was due, to the State or territory in which he or she was arrested, *with authority to such claimant or his or her agent or attorney, to use such reasonable force and restraint as may be necessary*, under the circumstances of the case, to take and remove such fugitive person back to the State or territory from whence he or she may have escaped as aforesaid. IN NO TRIAL OR HEARING UNDER THIS ACT SHALL TESTIMONY OF SUCH ALLEGED FUGITIVE BE ADMITTED IN EVIDENCE; and *the certificates in this and the first section mentioned* SHALL BE CONCLUSIVE OF THE RIGHT OF THE PERSON OR PERSONS IN WHOSE FAVOR GRANTED, *to remove such fugitive to the State or territory from which he escaped, and shall prevent all molestation of said person or persons by any process issued by any court, judge, magistrate or other person whomsoever.*

SEC. 7. And be it further enacted, That any person who shall knowingly or willingly obstruct, hinder or prevent such claimant, his agent or attorney, or *any person or persons*, lawfully assisting him, her or them, from arresting such fugitive from service or labor EITHER WITH *or* WITHOUT PROCESS as aforesaid; or shall rescue, or attempt to rescue such fugitive from service or labor, from the custody of such claimant, his or her agent or attorney, or other person or persons lawfully assisting as aforesaid when so arrested, pursuant to the authority herein given and declared; OR SHALL AID, ABET, OR ASSIST SUCH A PERSON SO OWING SERVICE OR LABOR AS AFORESAID, DIRECTLY OR INDIRECTLY TO ESCAPE from such claimant, his agent or attorney, or other person or persons legally authorized as aforesaid, or SHALL HARBOR or CONCEAL such fugitive, so as to prevent the discovery and arrest of such person, after notice or knowledge of the fact that such person was a fugitive from service or labor as aforesaid, shall, for either of said offences be subject to *a fine not exceeding* ONE THOUSAND DOLLARS *and* IMPRISONMENT NOT EXCEEDING SIX MONTHS, by indictment and conviction before the district court of the United States for the district in which such offence may have been committed, or before the proper court of criminal jurisdiction if committed within any one of the *organized territories* of the United States; *and shall, moreover, forfeit and pay by way of civil damages to the party injured by such illegal conduct, the sum of* ONE THOUSAND DOLLARS FOR EACH FUGITIVE SO LOST, as aforesaid, to be recovered by action for debt, in any of the district or territorial courts aforesaid, within whose jurisdiction the said offence may have been committed.

SEC. 8. And be it further enacted, That the marshals, their deputies, and the clerks of the said district and territorial courts, shall be paid for their services the like fees as may be allowed to them for similar services in other cases; and where such services are rendered exclusively in the arrest, custody and delivery of the fugitive to the claimant, his or her agent or attorney, or where such supposed fugitive may be discharged out of custody for want of sufficient proof as aforesaid, then such fees are to be paid in the whole by such claimant, his agent or attorney; and in all cases where the proceedings are before a commissioner, he shall be entitled to a fee of TEN DOLLARS in full for his services in each case, *upon the delivery of the said certificate to the claimant*, his or her agent or attorney; or a fee of FIVE DOLLARS *in cases where the proof shall not in the opinion of such commissioner, warrant such certificate and delivery*, inclusive of all services incident to such arrest and examination, to be paid, in either case, by the claimant, his or her agent or attorney. The person or persons authorized to execute the process to be issued by such commissioners for the arrest and detention of fugitives from service or labor, as aforesaid, shall also be entitled to a fee of *five dollars each* for said person he or they may arrest and take before any such commissioner as aforesaid, at the instance and request of such claimant, with such other fees as may be deemed reasonable by such commissioner for such additional services as may be necessarily performed by him or them; such as attending at the examination, keeping the fugitive in custody, and providing him with food and lodging during his detention, and until the final determination of such commissioner; and in general for performing such other duties as may be required by such claimant, his or her attorney or agent, or commissioner in the premises, such fees to be made up in conformity with the fees usually charged by the officers of the courts of justice within the proper district or county, as near as may be practicable, and paid by such claimants, their agents or attorneys, whether such supposed fugitives from service or labor, be ordered to be delivered to such claimants by the final determination of such commissioner or not.

SEC. 9. And be it further enacted, That upon affidavit made by the claimant of such fugitive, his agent or attorney, after such certificate has been issued, that he has reason to apprehend that *such fugitive will be rescued by force* from his or their possessions before he can be taken beyond the limits of the State in which the arrest is made, it shall be the duty of the officer making the arrest to *retain the fugitive in his custody, and to remove him to the State whence he fled*, and there to deliver him to said claimant, his agent or attorney. And to this end, the officer aforesaid is hereby AUTHORIZED AND REQUIRED TO EMPLOY SO MANY PERSONS AS HE MAY DEEM NECESSARY to overcome such force, and to retain them in his service so long as circumstances require. The said officer and his assistants, while so employed to receive the same compensation, and to be allowed the same expenses as are now allowed by law for transportation of criminals, to be certified by the judge of the district within which the arrest is made, and PAID OUT OF THE TREASURY OF THE UNITED STATES.

SEC. 10. And be it further enacted, That when any person held to service or labor in any State or Territory, or in the District of Columbia, shall escape therefrom, the party to whom such service or labor shall be due, his, her or their agent or attorney may apply to any court of record therein, or judge thereof in vacation, and make satisfactory proof to such court or judge in vacation, of the escape aforesaid, and that the person escaping owed service or labor to such party. Whereupon the court shall cause a record to be made of the matter as proved, and also a general description of the persons escaping with such convenient certainty as may be, and a transcript of such record authenticated by the attestation of clerk and seal of the said court being produced in any other State, Territory or District in which the person so escaping may be found, and being exhibited to any judge, commissioner or other officer authorized by the law of the United States to cause persons escaping from service or labor to be delivered up, *shall be held and taken to be full and conclusive evidence of escape, and that the service or labor of the person escaping is due to the party in such record mentioned.* And upon the production by the said party of other and further evidence, *if necessary either oral or by affidavit*, in addition to what is contained in the said record of the identity of the person escaping, *he or she shall be up to the claimant.*—And the said court, commissioner, judge or other person authorized by this act to grant certificates to claimants of fugitives, shall upon the production of the record and other evidences aforesaid, grant to such claimant a certificate of his right to take any such person identified and proved to be owing service or labor as aforesaid, which certificate shall authorize such claimaint to seize or arrest and transport such person to the State or Territory from which he escaped. Provided,

That nothing herein contained shall be construed as requiring the production of a transcript of such record as evidence as aforesaid. But in its absence the claim shall be heard and determined upon other satisfactory proofs competent in law.

Approved, September 18, 1850.

MILLARD FILLMORE.

THE BLACK LIST.

Total vote from free States in favor of the Fugitive Slave bill

DEMOCRATS—*Maine*—Messrs. Fuller, Gerry, Littlefield—3.

New Hampshire.—Messrs. HIBBARD and PEASLEE—2.

New York—Mr Walden—1.

New Jersey—Mr Wildrick—1.

Pennsylvania—Messrs Dimmick, Job Mann, McLanahan, Robbins, Ross and James Thompson—6.

Ohio—Messrs. Hayland and Miller—2.

Indiana—Messrs. Alberston, William J. Brown, Dunham, Gorman, McDonald—5.

Illinois—Messrs. Bissel, T. L. Harris, McClernand, Richardson, Young—5.

Michigan—Mr A. W. Buel—1.

Iowa—Mr Leffler—1.

California—Mr Gilbert—1. Total 27.

WHIGS.—Messrs. Elliot, of *Mass.*; McGaughey of *Ind.*; John L. Taylor, of *Ohio*—Total, 3

Total Ayes from free states, 30.

642 From a broadside, 1850, in the New York Historical Society

PREAMBLE AND RESOLUTIONS

OF

THE SOUTHERN CONVENTION.

SOUTHERN CONVENTION,
November ~~OCTOBER~~ 18th, 1850.

The following Preamble and Resolutions were reported by the Committee on Resolutions, and adopted by the Convention:

We, the delegates assembled from a portion of the States of this Confederacy, make this exposition of the causes which have brought us together, and of the rights which the States we represent are entitled to under the compact of union.

We have amongst us two races, marked by such distinctions of color, and physical and moral qualities, as forever forbid their living together on terms of social and political equality.

The black race have been slaves from the earliest settlement of our country, and our relations of master and slave have grown up from that time. A change in those relations must end in convulsion, and the entire ruin of one or both races.

When the constitution was adopted, this relation of master and slave, as it exists, was expressly recognized and guarded in that instrument. It was a great and vital interest, involving our very existence as a separate people, then as well as now.

The States of this Confederacy acceded to that compact each one for itself, and ratified it as States.

If the non-slaveholding States, who are parties to that compact, disregard its provisions, and endanger our peace and existence by united and deliberate action, we have a right, as States, there being no common arbiter, to secede.

The object of those who are urging on the Federal Government in its aggressive policy upon our domestic institutions, is, beyond all doubt, finally to overthrow them, and abolish the existing relation between master and slave. We feel authorized to assert this from their own declarations, and from the history of events in this country for the last few years.

To abolish slavery or the slave trade in the District of Columbia—to regulate the sale and transfer of slaves between the States—to exclude slaveholders with their property from the territories—to admit California under the circumstances of the case, we hold to be all parts of the same system of measures, and subordinate to the same end they have in view, which is openly avowed to be, the total overthrow of the institution.

We make no aggressive move. We stand upon the defensive. We invoke the spirit of the Constitution, and claim its guaranties.—Our rights—our independence—the peace and existence of our families—depend upon the issue.

The Federal Government has within a few years acquired, by treaty and by triumphant war, vast territories. This has been done by the councils and the arms of all, and the benefits and rights belong alike and equally to all the States. The Federal Government is but the common agent of the States united, and represents their conjoined sovereignty over subject matter granted and defined in the compact.

The authority it exercises over all acquired territory, must, in good faith, be exercised for the equal benefit of all the parties. To prohibit our citizens from settling there with the most valuable part of our property, is not only degrading to us as equals, but violates our highest constitutional rights.

Restrictions and prohibitions against the slaveholding States it would appear, are to be the fixed and settled policy of the Government—and those States that are hereafter to be admitted into the Federal Union from their extensive territories will but confirm and increase the power of the majority; and he knows little of history who cannot read our destiny in the future if we fail to do our duty now, as free people.

We have been harrassed and insulted by those who ought to have been our brethren in their constant agitation of a subject vital to us and the peace of our families. We have been outraged by their gross misrepresentations of our moral and social habits, and by the manner in which they have denounced us before the world. We have had our property enticed off and the means of recovery denied us by our co-States. We have been denied our rights in the Territories of the Union, which we were entitled to as political equals under the constitution. Our peace has been endangered by incendiary appeals. The Union instead of being considered a fraternal bond, has been used as the means of striking at our vital interests.

The admission of California, under the circumstances of the case confirms an unauthorized and revolutionary seizure of public domain, and the exclusion of near half the States of the Confederacy from equal rights therein—destroys the line of 36°30' which was originally acquiesced in as a matter of compromise and peace, and appropriates to the Northern States 120,000 square miles below that line, and is so gross and palpable a violation of the principles of justice and equality as to shake our confidence in any security to be given by that majority who are now clothed with power to govern the future destiny of this confederacy.

The recent purchase of territory by Congress from Texas, as low down as 32 degrees on the Rio Grande, also indicates that the boundaries of the slaveholding States are fixed, and our doom prescribed, so far as it depends upon the will of a dominant majority, and nothing now can save us from a degraded destiny but the spirit of freemen who know their rights and are resolved to maintain them, be the consequences what they may.

We have no powers that are binding upon the States we represent. But in order to produce system and concerted action, we recommend the following resolutions, viz:

Resolved, That we have ever cherished, and do now cherish a cordial attachment to the constitutional Union of the States and that to preserve and perpetuate that Union unimpaired, this Convention originated and has now re-assembled.

Resolved, That the Union of the States is a Union of equal and independent sovereignties, and that the powers delegated to the Federal Government, can be resumed by the several States, whenever it may seem to them proper and necessary.

Resolved, That all the evils anticipated by the South, and which occasioned this Convention to assemble have been realized, by the failure to extend the Missouri line of Compromise to the Pacific Ocean; By the admission of California as a State; By the organization of Territorial Governments for Utah and New Mexico, without giving adequate protection to the property of the South; By the dismemberment of Texas; By the abolition of the slave trade and the emancipation of slaves carried into the District of Columbia for sale.

Resolved, That we earnestly recommend to all parties in the slaveholding States, to refuse to go into, or countenance any National Convention, whose object may be to nominate candidates for the Presidency and Vice Presidency of the United States, under any party denomination whatever, until our constitutional rights are secured.

Resolved, That in view of these aggressions, and of those threatened and impending, we earnestly recommend to the slaveholding States, to meet in a Congress or Convention, to be held at such time and place as the States desiring to be represented, may designate, to be composed of double the number of their Senators and Representatives in the Congress of the United States, entrusted with full power and authority to deliberate and act with the view and intention of arresting farther aggression, and if possible, of restoring the Constitutional rights of the South, and if not to provide for their future safety and independence.

Resolved, That the President of this Convention be requested to forward copies of the foregoing preamble and resolutions to the Governors of each of the slaveholding States of the Union, to be laid before their respective Legislatures at their earliest assembling.

CHAS. J. McDONALD, President.
REUBEN CHAPMAN, Vice President.

E. G. EASTMAN, Secretary.

643 Printed copy of the Preamble and Resolutions of the Southern Convention, held at Nashville, 1850, in the Library of Congress

THREATS OF SECESSION

WHILE the debates over the compromise had gone on in Congress there had been ominous developments in the South. Threats of secession were heard in many places. The southern people were resolved that their rights should be recognized. A convention of delegates from the slave states assembled at Nashville in 1850 ostensibly to discuss commercial matters but actually to take preliminary steps to unite the section if developments should go against the South in Washington. The convention caused copies of its resolutions to be forwarded "to the Governors of each of the slave-holding states of the Union, to be laid before their respective Legislatures at their earliest assembling." It soon appeared that Unionists were in control, and in June the convention was adjourned to reassemble, in spite of the fact that Judge Sharkey, the Unionist president, refused to issue the call. But the membership was so reduced that the convention did not dare do more than denounce the Compromise of 1850, reassert the right of secession, and recommend political noncoöperation by the South in the national parties "until our constitutional rights are secured."

JEFFERSON DAVIS ASPIRES TO SOUTHERN LEADERSHIP

THE passing of Calhoun left the South without a national leader. Many southerners of a younger generation aspired to the position of the great South Carolinian. Among them was a Mississippi planter, Jefferson Davis. In 1845, when thirty-seven years of age, he married as his second wife Miss Varina Howell, a granddaughter of a former Governor of New Jersey. He had entered politics two years before. The year after his marriage he left his bride to take command of the Mississippi Rifles, the first regiment raised in his state for service in the Mexican War. He was a member of the United States Senate during the eventful session in which the Compromise of 1850 was passed. He was a zealous advocate of state rights. He disapproved of the Compromise, resigned his seat and sought the office of Governor of his native state. He was unsuccessful in this candidacy, although by his personal popularity he reduced the Union majority from 7500 to 999. His defeat at the hands of Foote, who favored the measures, was evidence that a majority of his neighbors were determined to abide by the settlement which Congress had worked out.

644 Jefferson Davis, 1808-89, at the age of thirty-seven, with his bride, Varina Howell, from a daguerreotype in the possession of their granddaughter, Mrs. George B. Webb, Colorado Springs, Colorado

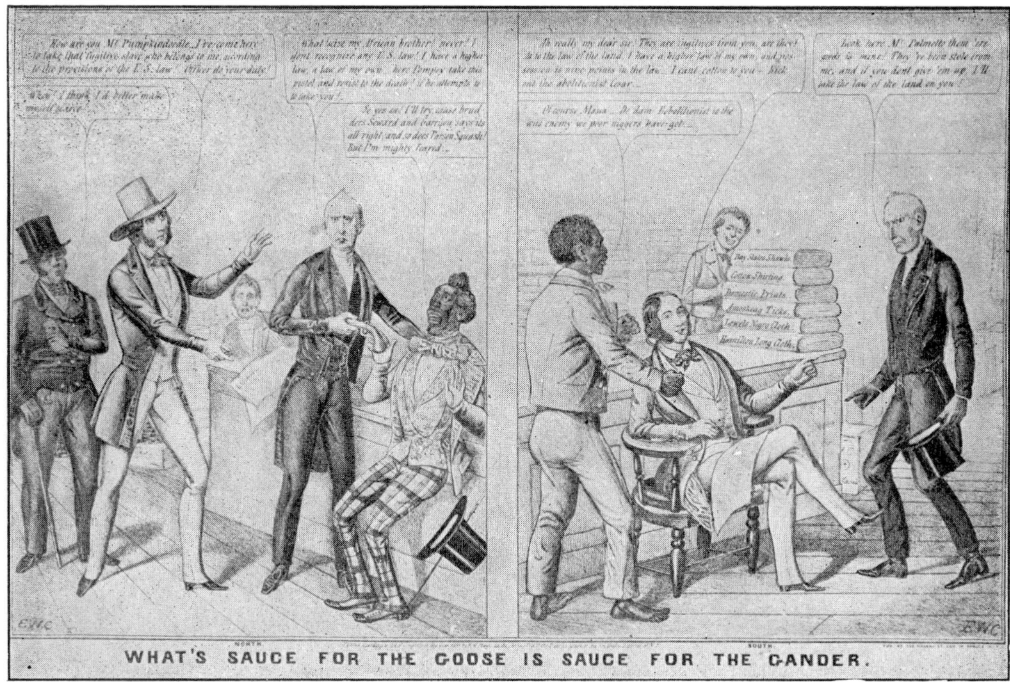

WHAT'S SAUCE FOR THE GOOSE IS SAUCE FOR THE GANDER.

645 From a cartoon, 1851, by E. W. Clay in the New York Historical Society

NORTH AND SOUTH GRADUALLY ACCEPT THE COMPROMISE

Though the compromise was now upon the statute books, it was still to be accepted by the people North and South. In Georgia, Mississippi and South Carolina, the irreconcilables were strong. Special state conventions were called to consider secession. Bit by bit, however, cooler counsels prevailed. In Georgia, leaders of both parties united behind the Compromise. In Mississippi, Jefferson Davis was defeated in his race for Governor by Foote, who favored the settlement.

RESISTANCE TO THE FUGITIVE SLAVE LAW

In short, the South determined to refrain from overt action, provided the North lived up to the letter of the Compromise — particularly in respect to the fugitive slaves. In its determination to accept the Compromise, the South had the powerful support of Webster, upon whom was vented all the fury of the abolitionists. As cases of the rendition of escaped slaves began to occur, these people made it clear that they were prepared to forcibly resist the execution of the law — a palpable menace to the Union.

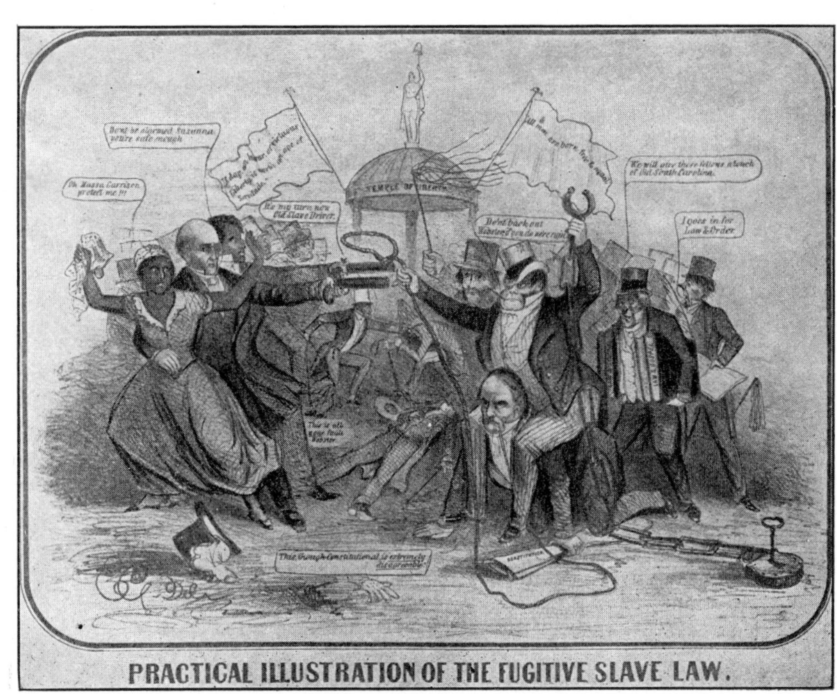

646 From a contemporary cartoon by E. W. Clay, in the New York Historical Society

647 From *Gleason's Pictorial*, Boston, May 3, 1851

NORTHERN ELOQUENCE IS POURED OUT AGAINST SLAVERY

FROM the pulpit the measure was denounced by Henry Ward Beecher as a violation of the law of God. Indeed, many eloquent men seized upon Seward's sensational assertion that there was "a higher law than the Constitution" to rouse the people to protect the fugitives from the South. The speaker in the illustration was Wendell Phillips.

THE FUGITIVE SLAVE LAW GENERALLY ACCEPTED

SEWARD, on the floor of Congress, as the mouthpiece of the radicals of the North, had announced: "We deem the principle of the law for the recapture of fugitives, as thus expounded, unjust, unconstitutional and immoral; and thus, while patriotism withholds its approbation, the consciences of our people condemn it." The response from the North seems to accept his statement as a correct interpretation of its stand. Against this clamor more temperate men for a time raised their voices in vain. Webster spent his vast energies in a speaking tour in which he tried to appease the radicals and to point out the necessity for compliance with the compromise. Clay, Douglas, Rufus Choate, Buchanan and other political leaders assured the country that the Fugitive Slave Law was constitutional and that it was the duty of the North to observe it to the letter. In his message to Congress in December, 1850, President Fillmore gave the law unequivocal support. Sentiment began to change; open opposition to decline. This was due in part to the persuasion of the leaders; in part to the Underground Railway, which furnished an effective means of evading the law.

648 From the painting *Fugitive Slaves Arriving at the Home of Levi Coffin* by C. W. Jefferys (1869–), in the possession of the publishers

649 From *Punch*, 1847, cartoon by Richard Doyle (1824–83), by permission of the proprietors

NATIONAL PRIDE AND BRITISH RIDICULE

WEBSTER also utilized his office of Secretary of State to divert popular attention from domestic matters to foreign affairs. To a friend he wrote, in explanation of a somewhat aggressive note he had sent to Hülsemann, the Austrian representative, who had protested against the sending of an American agent to Hungary, then revolting from Austria, that he wished to "touch the national pride and make a man feel sheepish and look silly who should speak of disunion." This was relatively easy to do, for the jingoistic spirit of the 'forties was still prevalent. Yet many of the gibes directed at America dealt with the slavery question (see No. 635), so that the issue was kept before the public.

THE GADSDEN PURCHASE

One of the major problems of the time was that of effectively linking up the states east of the Mississippi and the new territory on the Pacific coast. The dry western plains and the Rocky Mountains rendered this difficult. Engineers decided that the best routes for a transcontinental railroad lay to the South. To use them, however, would make it necessary to cross territory belonging to Mexico; and the turbulent state of affairs in that country gave little assurance of adequate protection. This difficulty was finally removed by the Gadsden Purchase of 1853, whereby the United States acquired the needed territory from northern Mexico. Thus, by peaceful methods, the United States gained a large territory for which the patrioteers supporting the doctrine of Manifest Destiny might have been persuaded to fight.

three leagues from land, opposite the mouth of the Rio Grande as provided in the fifth article of the treaty of Guadalupe Hidalgo, thence as defined in the said article, up the middle of that river to the point where the parallel of 31° 47' north latitude crosses the same, thence due west one hundred miles, thence south to the parallel of 31° 20' north latitude, thence along the said parallel of 31° 20' to the 111 th meridian of longitude west of Greenwich, thence in a straight line to a point on the Colorado river twenty english miles below the junction of the Gila and Colorado rivers, thence up the middle of the said river Colorado until it intersects the present line between the United States and Mexico.

650 Article 1 of the Gadsden Treaty with Mexico, Dec. 30, 1853, from the engrossed copy in the Department of State, Washington

651 James Gadsden, 1788–1858, from the portrait by George Flagg (1816–97), courtesy of Mrs. George S. Holmes, Charleston, S. C.

652 Tigre Island, off Honduras, a subject of dispute between England and the United States, after a sketch in the *Illustrated London News*, Aug. 17, 1850

653 John M. Clayton, 1796–1856, from the portrait by H. C. Pratt in the State House, Dover, Del.

THE CLAYTON–BULWER TREATY

Until the time when a transcontinental railroad should be something more than a dream, a more practicable plan was that of building a canal across the isthmus of Central America. At the time, most American commerce and travel from coast to coast passed over this area, and some steps had already been taken to protect American interests there. With the discovery of gold in California the situation took on even greater importance. It was now found that Great Britain was a rival. She had settlements of long standing, and special interests locally recognized, in Central America. Secretary Clayton, therefore, began negotiations with the British Minister resident at Washington; and in April, 1850, the two agreed to a treaty which provided that any canal which might be built should be neutralized and that neither party should "assume or exercise dominion over" any part of Central America.

654 General Narciso Lopez, 1799–1851, from an engraving in *Gleason's Pictorial*, Sept. 27, 1851

FILIBUSTERING IN CUBA

OF more widespread interest was the effort to annex Cuba. The expansionists had long looked covetously upon this island, which, indeed, was by many deemed essential to the protection of American navigation of the Mississippi. With the resurgence of the slavery question, the southerners became particularly interested in the island. They especially disliked that part of the Compromise of 1850 which admitted California as a free state; and many regarded the acquisition of Cuba as a reasonable compensation for this loss. Since 1848, the press had been filled with stories about Cuba; so that popular interest in the island was intense. In the succeeding years, three methods of acquisition were tried: purchase from Spain, conquest, and annexation after a Cuban revolution which was to be made successful by American aid. This last plan was, indeed, tried first. Various filibustering expeditions, under the Cuban leader, General Narciso Lopez, were organized in the United States and dispatched to Cuba, only to meet with disaster.

THE AMERICAN ROVER-GENERAL WOT TRIED TO STEAL A CUBA.

655 From a cartoon in *Punch*, 1850, by permission of the proprietors

ENGLAND AND THE CUBAN EPISODE

GREAT BRITAIN was at first amused by these American adventures. But as it appeared that the American Government was privy to them, she became disturbed, and in 1851 she ordered her navy to prevent unauthorized landings in Cuba. In April of the following year, at the suggestion of the Spanish Government, England proposed a tripartite agreement, of which Great Britain, France and the United States should mutually renounce any purpose of annexing Cuba. Edward Everett, Webster's successor at the State Department, refused to enter into any such arrangement and issued a vigorous dispatch which roused American nationalism and momentarily diverted popular interest from the slavery issue.

MASTER JONATHAN TRIES TO SMOKE A CUBA, BUT IT DOESN'T AGREE WITH HIM!!

656 From a cartoon in *Punch*, 1850, by permission of the proprietors

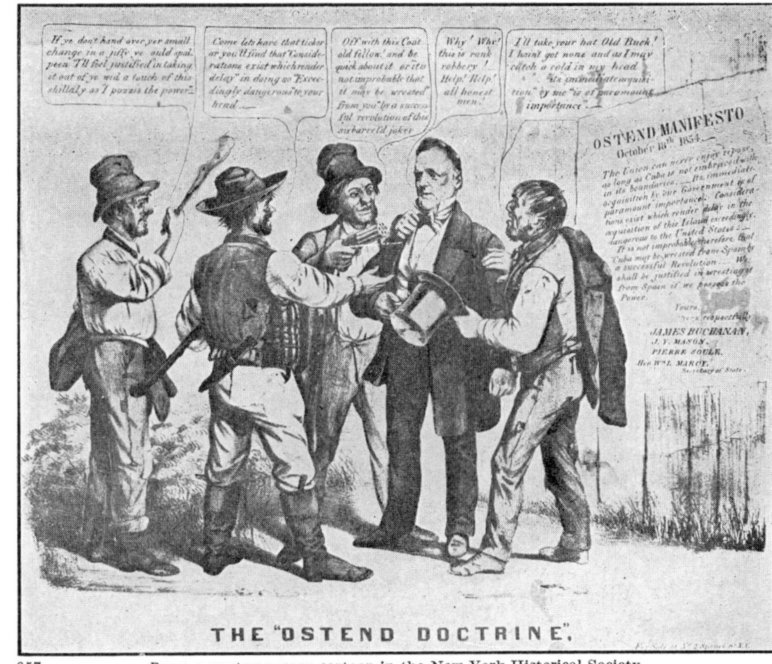

657 From a contemporary cartoon in the New York Historical Society

THE POLICY OF IMPERIALISM

So successful was this move that for a time Democratic leaders considered making "Cuba and Canada" the slogan for the campaign of 1852. The plan was abandoned because the acquisition of Canada was chimerical, while to advocate that of Cuba alone might antagonize the antislavery North. But after the election of 1852, the Pierce administration continued to agitate expansion. In his inaugural address the President announced his policy: "It is not to be disguised that our attitude as a nation and our position on the globe render the acquisition of certain possessions not within our jurisdiction eminently important for our protection." The whole affair reached its culmination in 1854. Under instructions from Washington, the American Ministers to England, France and Spain met at Ostend and there formulated a Cuban policy. The Ostend Manifesto declared that Cuba's position made its acquisition by the United States imperative. Should Spain refuse to sell, "then, by every law, human and divine, we shall be justified in wresting it from Spain if we possess the power; and upon the very same principle that would justify an individual in tearing down the burning house of his neighbor if there were no other means of preventing the flames from destroying his own home." Such imperialism proved a boomerang; Marcy, Secretary of State, refused to act upon the policy so enunciated; domestic questions reabsorbed public attention.

A HUNGARIAN PATRIOT VISITS AMERICA

In addition to these and other diplomatic incidents, foreign affairs in one other way noticeably affected domestic politics. The unsettled state of Europe, signalized by the revolutionary outbreaks of 1830 and of 1848, led many people to emigrate to America. "From 1850 to 1860 the foreign-born population of the United States increased eighty-four per cent, and most of these newcomers settled in the states and territories of the North. There they naturally gravitated to the party that opposed slavery and stood for an indivisible Union; for they were unaccustomed to slavery in Europe, and many of them were veterans of wars for national unification. Moreover, they brought with them the traditions of a defiant and bitter republicanism." — A. M. Schlesinger, *Political and Social History of the United States*, p. 134. Louis Kossuth, exiled from Hungary for leading an insurrection, came to the United States in 1852 to procure aid for the establishment of Hungarian independence. He spoke English fluently and aroused great enthusiasm but the policy of non-interference in European politics prevailed and Kossuth returned home disappointed.

658 The Arrival of Kossuth in New York, from *Gleason's Pictorial*, Dec. 27, 1851

659 From a cartoon of the campaign of 1852, published by N. Currier, New York, in the New York Historical Society

THE CAMPAIGN OF 1852

THE efforts of the political leaders to calm the country had met with a certain degree of success. People were prosperous and wished to avoid unsettling influences. As the election of 1852 approached, northern opposition to the Fugitive Slave Law subsided, and it was clear that both parties would accept the compromise acts as final. The Democrats, meeting at Baltimore on the first of June, and finding the ambitions of their leaders — such as Douglas, Cass and Buchanan — dangerous to party harmony, united upon a dark horse in the person of Franklin Pierce of New Hampshire. He was a man with a good military record, some eloquence, and no troublesome political record. The Whigs also found difficulty in selecting a candidate. Webster and Fillmore led the field; but both were unsatisfactory to the northern wing of the party which, under the leadership of Seward, was strenuously opposed to the Fugitive Slave Law. The southerners succeeded in getting a platform favoring the Compromise, and were then persuaded to accept as candidate General Winfield Scott, the military hero of the day. Thus, in a campaign in which the chief issue was that of holding to the Compromise of 1850, the Whigs attempted to please one section with their platform and the other section with their candidate.

660 Franklin Pierce, 1804–69, from a photograph of a daguerreotype. © L. C. Handy

THE ELECTION OF PIERCE

SUCH tactics met with a serious rebuff. Pierce, who was nearly everywhere considered a sincere supporter of the Compromise, was elected with two hundred and fifty-four electoral votes to forty-two for General Winfield Scott, the Whig candidate. In their attempt to please North and South, the Whigs pleased no one, "so that the settlement of the territorial question had been at the expense of one of the great national parties, which had constituted an important bond of union." — C. R. FISH, *Development of American Nationality*, p. 329. This, however, was not at the time discerned, for at the end of Fillmore's term "the quiet of the country in regard to the slavery question was more complete than it had been since 1830." — J. W. BURGESS, *The Middle Period*, pp. 380–81, and the new administration at once began its aggressive foreign policy with a view to guiding public attention into less divisive channels. "I fervently hope," said Pierce in his inaugural address, "that the question is at rest, and that no sectional or ambitious or fanatical excitement may again threaten the durability of our institutions or obscure the light of our prosperity."

661 The Funeral Procession of Henry Clay in New York, from *Gleason's Pictorial*, July, 1852

AMERICA MOURNS THE DEATH OF CLAY AND WEBSTER

In the heat of the presidential campaign of 1852 the two greatest of the Whig leaders passed away. Clay died in Washington on the twenty-ninth of June. He pronounced upon himself a just judgment: "If anyone desires to know the leading and paramount object of my public life, the preservation of this Union will furnish him the key." In the following October, Webster died at his home in Marshfield, Massachusetts. The whole nation mourned the passing of these giants of the middle of the nineteenth century. For the Whig party in which for so many years they had been rival leaders their loss was irreparable. The presidential election of 1852 was the last in which the Whigs played any important part for the party was unable to agree upon a national policy toward slavery.

662 Henry Clay, from a bust by Joel T. Hart (1810–77), in the Kentucky State Historical Society

663 The Funeral Procession of Daniel Webster at Marshfield, Mass., from *Gleason's Pictorial*, Nov. 1852

664 From a contemporary Whig cartoon in the New York Historical Society

THE GROWTH OF SECTIONALISM

Sectional feeling increased in the times of Pierce. It seemed to cling to every public question. and to grow ever more menacing. The cartoon here shown well illustrates this tendency as it appeared in these unsettled days. The President, assuming a post of determined independence, is shown borne aloft by Linn Boyd of Kentucky, Speaker of the House. Thus is indicated the delicate union within the party of North and South; while Boyd's evident satisfaction pictures the pleasure of the South when it found Pierce favoring it in his cabinet appointments. Marcy, one of the cabinet men, stands on Boyd's left, lamenting the difficulties into which the administration's jingoistic foreign policy had brought them. Most portentous of trouble, however, is the appearance on the other hand of Stephen A. Douglas, with his Nebraska issue and his advocacy of squatter sovereignty in the territories. That was a program the adoption of which was to evoke bitterness throughout the country and split wide open the ranks of the national political parties.

665 Robert Toombs, 1810–85, from a photograph. © H. P. Cook, Richmond, Va.

TWO SOUTHERNERS DESERT THE WHIGS

In the election of 1852 an important shift had occurred in the politics of the South. Robert Toombs of Georgia and Alexander H. Stephens of Georgia deserted the Whig party to join forces with the Democrats. This strengthened the political organization of the planters which was seeking to control the policies of the Democratic party, particularly on all questions involving southern interests. This group had selected Pierce for nomination and was to have easy access to the White House during his administration.

666 Alexander H. Stephens, 1812–83, from a photograph by Brady

JEFFERSON DAVIS, SECRETARY OF WAR

President Pierce selected Jefferson Davis as his Secretary of War, an office which Davis discharged with great distinction and with real benefit to the nation. He organized engineer companies and sent them into the Rocky Mountains to explore several proposed routes for a transcontinental railroad. He enlarged the army and modernized its equipment. He revised the system of tactics, perfected the signal corps service and increased coast and frontier defenses. He appointed subordinates on merit and in defiance of party considerations. His record in the Mexican struggle and in the War Department gives point to the often expressed opinion that the great tragedy in his life was that he was elected president of the Southern Confederacy instead of being allowed, as he ardently desired, to assume a high command in the Confederate army. While active in the work of his department he was one of a group composed, besides himself, of John Slidell of Louisiana and Jesse D. Bright of Indiana, which was the real power behind the Pierce administration.

667 Jefferson Davis as Secretary of War, from a miniature made by an English artist, in the possession of his granddaughter, Mrs. Gerald B. Webb, Colorado Springs, Col.

668 Jesse D. Bright, 1812–75, from an engraving in *Gleason's Pictorial*, Mar. 5, 1853

DOUGLAS ADVOCATES POPULAR SOVEREIGNTY

Douglas, Senator from Illinois, was the "Little Giant" of the Democrats of the Northwest. He ardently believed in the Northwest and its future. With many others, he had refused to accept the dictum of the engineers that the most feasible route for a transcontinental railroad was in the South. A northern route, however, was hampered by the absence of territorial government west of Missouri and Iowa; and organization there was opposed by the South, since under the terms of the Missouri Compromise the territories and states so established would be free soil. Douglas, as chairman of the Senate committee on territories, in the winter of 1853 hit upon a plan which he thought would do all that he desired for the West and would also promote his cherished ambition to be President. As a self-made man of the raw West, Douglas believed in the potency of local self-government to handle political questions. Upon this panacea he now staked his fortune and in January, 1854, he reported to the Senate his Nebraska Bill for the organization of the territory. The question of slavery was to be determined upon the principle of "squatter sovereignty," which he renamed popular sovereignty. The people of the territories should decide for themselves whether or not they would have slavery. This, he thought, would remove the vexed issue from national politics, would win southern support — for under this scheme the South could still hope for territorial extension of slavery — and would throw open the new lands for westward expansion

669 John Slidell, 1793–1871, from an engraving after a photograph by Brady, in *Harper's Weekly*, Mar. 27, 1858

670 Stephen A. Douglas, 1813–61, from a carte de visite by Fredricks, New York

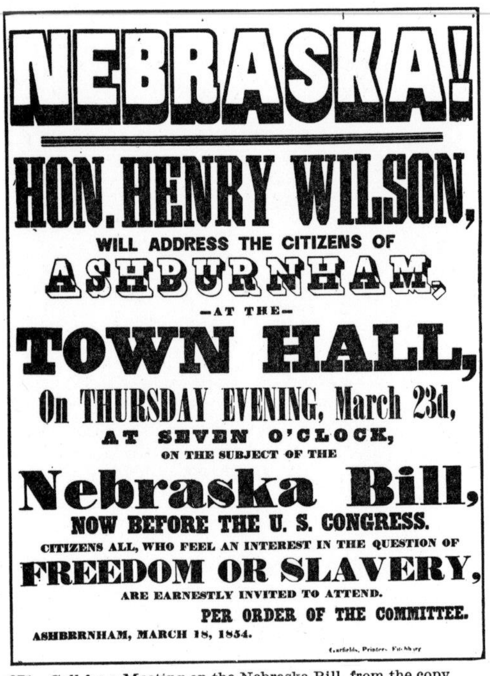

NEBRASKA!
HON. HENRY WILSON,
WILL ADDRESS THE CITIZENS OF
ASHBURNHAM,
—AT THE—
TOWN HALL,
On THURSDAY EVENING, March 23d,
AT SEVEN O'CLOCK,
ON THE SUBJECT OF THE
Nebraska Bill,
NOW BEFORE THE U. S. CONGRESS.
CITIZENS ALL, WHO FEEL AN INTEREST IN THE QUESTION OF
FREEDOM OR SLAVERY,
ARE EARNESTLY INVITED TO ATTEND.
PER ORDER OF THE COMMITTEE.
ASHBURNHAM, MARCH 18, 1854.

671 Call for a Meeting on the Nebraska Bill, from the copy in the American Antiquarian Society, Worcester, Mass.

POPULAR REACTION TO THE NEBRASKA BILL

THUS suddenly was reopened the question which all had hoped would prove to have been settled by the Compromise of 1850. The debate in the Senate was bitter. Throughout the North, Douglas was the object of attack and execration.

Sec. 14. And be it further enacted, That a delegate to the House of Representatives of the United States, to serve for the term of two years, who shall be a citizen of the United States, may be elected by the voters qualified to elect members of the legislative assembly, who shall be entitled to the same rights and privileges as are exercised and enjoyed by the delegates from the several other Territories of the United States to the said House of Representatives, but the delegate first elected shall hold his seat only during the term of the Congress to which he shall be elected. The first election shall be held at such time and places, and be conducted in such manner, as the governor shall appoint and direct; and at all subsequent elections the times, places, and manner of holding the elections, shall be prescribed by law. The person having the greatest number of votes shall be declared by the governor to be duly elected; and a certificate thereof shall be given accordingly. That the constitution, and all laws of the United States which are not locally inapplicable, shall have the same force and effect within the said Territory of Nebraska as elsewhere within the United States, except the eighth section of the act preparatory to the admission of Missouri into the Union, approved March sixth, eighteen hundred and twenty, which, being inconsistent with the principle of non-intervention by Congress with slavery in the States and Territories, as recognized by the legislation of eighteen hundred and fifty, commonly called the compromise measures, is hereby declared inoperative and void; it being the true intent and meaning of this act not to legislate slavery into any Territory or State, nor to exclude it therefrom, but to leave the people thereof perfectly free to form and regulate their domestic institutions in their own way, subject only to the constitution of the United States: Provided, That nothing herein contained shall be construed to revive or put in force any law or regulation which may have existed prior to the act of sixth March, eighteen hundred and twenty, either protecting, establishing, prohibiting, or abolishing slavery.

672 Section 14 of the Kansas-Nebraska Act of May 30, 1854, repealing the Missouri Compromise of 1820, from the engrossed copy in the State Department, Washington

DOUGLAS ERECTS TWO NEW TERRITORIES

DOUGLAS soon found that his measure was not altogether pleasing to the South. He therefore amended it to provide for the erection of two territories, Kansas and Nebraska, with the fortieth parallel as the dividing line. His southern supporters hoped to be able to win Kansas for slavery. In this form the bill passed, by the vote of the southern members and of about one half of the northern Democrats.

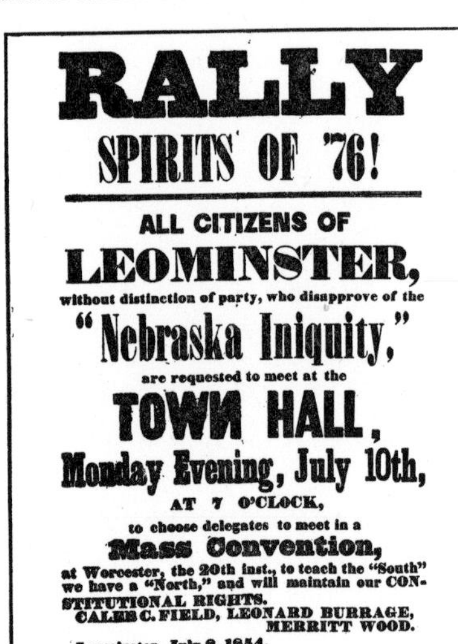

RALLY
SPIRITS OF '76!
ALL CITIZENS OF
LEOMINSTER,
without distinction of party, who disapprove of the
"Nebraska Iniquity,"
are requested to meet at the
TOWN HALL,
Monday Evening, July 10th,
AT 7 O'CLOCK,
to choose delegates to meet in a
Mass Convention,
at Worcester, the 20th inst., to teach the "South" we have a "North," and will maintain our CONSTITUTIONAL RIGHTS.
CALEB C. FIELD, LEONARD BURRAGE,
MERRITT WOOD.
Leominster, July 8, 1854.

673 Call for a Meeting on the "Nebraska Iniquity," from the copy in the American Antiquarian Society, Worcester, Mass.

THE BIRTH OF THE REPUBLICAN PARTY

THE Nebraska Bill completely disrupted party lines, in Congress and out. Even before its passage, the congressional campaign of 1854 had begun. The Whig party dropped from view; the Democrats in the North found little in common with those in the South; while new parties, notably the Republican, emerged. The result of the elections showed sectionalism more prevalent than before. In many parts of the North the candidates who favored "popular sovereignty" went down to defeat before men opposed to the extension of slavery; in the South those who espoused Calhoun's doctrine that the Constitution kept all territories open to slavery were favored. The Congress which assembled in December, 1855, was deadlocked for two months over the selection of a speaker, until by compromise the Republican candidate, Nathaniel P. Banks, was named. The political leaders who regretted that Douglas had reopened the provocative issue found themselves forced to take sides or to endanger their political future.

EMIGRATION TO KANSAS

674 Eli Thayer, 1819–99, from the portrait by E. R. Waite in the City Hall, Worcester, Mass.

MEANWHILE the country was weighing the merits of Douglas' scheme of local option. On all sides it was soon recognized that there would be no slavery in Nebraska. But Kansas lay just west of Missouri, and its climate seemed favorable to slave culture. That region, therefore, became the scene of bitter sectional rivalry. Emigrants from the South and from the North were aided by local partisans in their journey to the West. The South was first in the field, for many Missourians moved across the line into Kansas early in the summer of 1854. But the North possessed larger resources, human and material, and great organizing ability. At Worcester, Massachusetts, there was formed, under Eli Thayer and others, the New England Emigrant Aid Society. Thousands of free-state settlers went out under the guidance of such agencies. This subsidized emigration from the North caused deep resentment in the South. The planters, coupling this with northern refusal to accept the Fugitive Slave Law, came to feel that the North was unwilling to abide by decisions of the National Congress. The northerners responded with equally vigorous assertions that slavery was to be kept out of the new territory, at all costs and in preservation of the fundamental principles of American liberty.

"BORDER RUFFIANS"

Two groups in Kansas soon came into conflict. The slavery advocates in Missouri took precautions to ensure their victory. March 30, 1855, was fixed as the day for the election of the first territorial legislature. On that morning there appeared at the polls in eastern Kansas "an unkempt, sun-dried, blatant, picturesque mob of five thousand men with guns upon their shoulders, revolvers stuffing their belts, bowie-knives protruding from their boot-tops, and generous rations of whiskey in their wagons." — S. T. L. ROBINSON, *Kansas*, p. 27. These were "border ruffians" from western Missouri, and with the aid of their votes the legislature which met in July at Pawnee was strongly pro-slavery in sentiment. It adopted for Kansas the Missouri code of laws and drafted a state constitution. Meanwhile armed immigrants from the North were pouring into Kansas to win the territory for freedom.

675 From an engraving by John Rogers after a drawing *Missourians Going to Kansas to Vote*, by F. O. C. Darley

FREE STATE CONVENTION!

All persons who are favorable to a union of effort, and a permanent organization of all the Free State elements of Kansas Territory, and who wish to secure upon the broadest platform the co-operation of all who agree upon this point, are requested to meet at their several places of holding elections, in their respective districts on the 25th of August, instant, at one o'clock, P M., and appoint five delegates to each representative to which they were entitled in the Legislative Assembly who shall meet in general Convention at

Big Springs, Wednesday, Sept. 5th '55,

at 10 o'clock A M., for the purpose of adopting a Platform upon which all may act harmoniously who prefer Freedom to Slavery.

The nomination of a Delegate to Congress, will also come up before the General Convention.

Let no sectional or party issues distract or prevent the perfect co-operation of Free State men. Union and harmony are absolutely necessary to success. The pro-slavery party are fully and effectually organized. No jars nor minor issues divide them. And to contend against them successfully, we also must be united.—Without prudence and harmony of action we are certain to fail. Let every man then do his duty and we are certain of victory.

All Free State men, without distinction, are earnestly requested to take immediate and effective steps to insure a full and correct representation for every District in the Territory. "United we stand; divided we fall."

By order of the Executive Committee of the Free State Party of the Territory of Kansas, as per resolution of the Mass Convention in session at Lawrence, [illegible] and 16th, 1855.

J K GOODIN, Sec'y **C. ROBINSON, Chairman.**

Herald of Freedom, Print.

676 Call for a Free State Convention in Kansas, August 1855, from the copy in the Kansas State Historical Society, Topeka

FREE STATE CONVENTION

The national administration seemed inclined to recognize this packed legislature as the legitimate Government of the territory. But the free-soil settlers at once set on foot an undertaking designed to overcome the advantage held by the pro-slavery party. Under the guidance of Dr. Charles Robinson of Fitchburg, Massachusetts — a prominent Forty-niner and a leader in the New England Emigrant Aid Society — they adopted the tactics that California had earlier employed. Their plan was to hold a territorial convention for the purpose of framing a free-state constitution with which they would go directly to Congress asking admission to the Union. Thus, while ignoring the pro-slave legislature, the free-soil men could justify themselves under the doctrine of popular sovereignty.

THE KANSAS DEADLOCK

The plan of the free-state men was executed in the autumn of 1855, resulting in a convention at Topeka in October. This convention drew up a free-state constitution, which was submitted for popular ratification, preparatory to submission to Congress, in December. The pro-slavery men abstained from voting, with the result that the charter was overwhelmingly approved. In January, 1856, elections under this constitution were held, and Dr. Robinson was chosen Governor. By this time, however, armed conflict between the two factions had broken out, and the deadlocked Congress, far from being rid of the slavery question, was presented with the issue in an especially acute form.

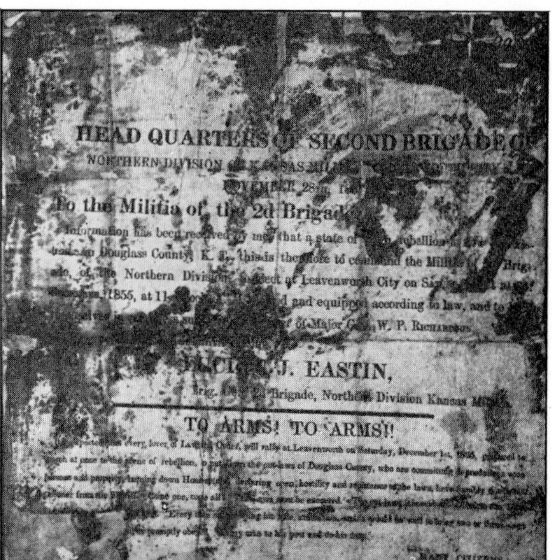

677 Kansas Militia broadside, Nov.-Dec. 1855, calling on men to put down rebellion, from the copy in the Kansas State Historical Society, Topeka

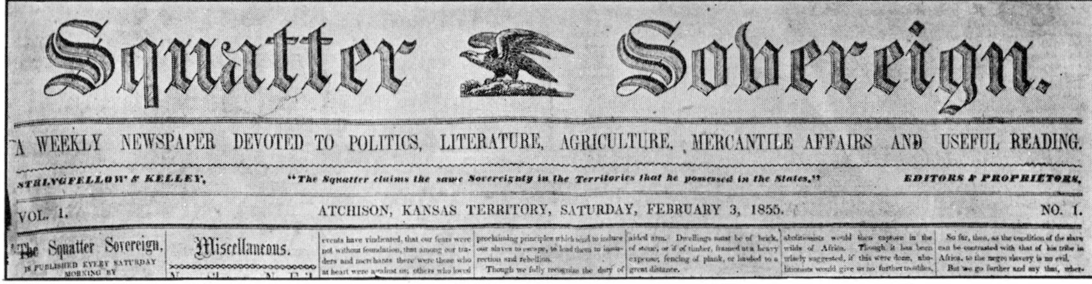

Squatter Sovereign.

A WEEKLY NEWSPAPER DEVOTED TO POLITICS, LITERATURE, AGRICULTURE, MERCANTILE AFFAIRS AND USEFUL READING.

STRINGFELLOW & KELLEY, "The Squatter claims the same Sovereignty in the Territories that he possessed in the States." EDITORS & PROPRIETORS.

VOL. 1. ATCHISON, KANSAS TERRITORY, SATURDAY, FEBRUARY 3, 1855. NO. 1.

The Squatter Sovereign, IS PUBLISHED EVERY SATURDAY MORNING BY

Miscellaneous.

678 Title of Stringfellow's newspaper published in advocacy of Douglas' plan of "squatter sovereignty"

THE KNOW-NOTHING PARTY

WITH such uncertainty and confusion in Congress, the people turned to the election of 1856. The Compromise of 1850, and its abrogation in 1854, had wrought havoc with established party organization and policy. This worked to the advantage of the newly formed American party, built up around a secret society whose members were called Know-Nothings because when questioned concerning the mysteries of the order they denied all knowledge of them. The party was, in fact, primarily anti-alien and anti-Catholic; the members took oath to support for public office only American-born Protestants. This prejudice against the foreigner, stimulated by the growing immigration of the 'forties and 'fifties, had been sporadically expressed for some years. In the elections of 1854–55 the Know-Nothings carried Massachusetts, Connecticut, Rhode Island, New Hampshire, Kentucky and California; and accordingly they looked to the election of 1856 with high hopes.

679 Torchlight Meeting of Know-Nothings at New York, from the *Illustrated London News*, Nov. 24, 1855

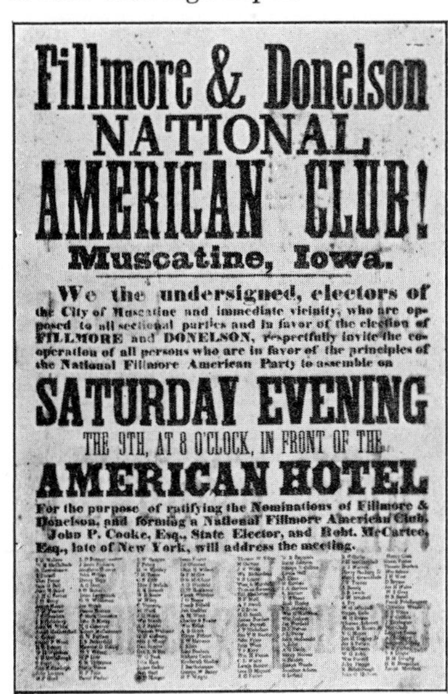

Fillmore & Donelson
NATIONAL
AMERICAN CLUB!
Muscatine, Iowa.

We the undersigned, electors of the City of Muscatine and immediate vicinity, who are opposed to all sectional parties and in favor of the election of FILLMORE and DONELSON, respectfully invite the co-operation of all persons who are in favor of the principles of the National Fillmore American Party to assemble on

SATURDAY EVENING
THE 9TH, AT 8 O'CLOCK, IN FRONT OF THE
AMERICAN HOTEL

For the purpose of ratifying the Nominations of Fillmore & Donelson, and forming a National Fillmore American Club. John P. Cooke, Esq., State Elector, and Robt. McCartee, Esq., late of New York, will address the meeting.

680 From a campaign poster of the "American" or "Know-Nothing" party, in the American Antiquarian Society, Worcester, Mass.

THE KNOW-NOTHING CANDIDATES

MEETING in convention at Philadelphia in February, 1856, the Know-Nothings, or the American party, found sectionalism intruding even into their organization. Indeed, after angry debate, most of the antislavery delegates withdrew, leaving the southern wing in control. With a platform that attempted to divert attention from the slavery question by crying up the foreign peril, the party went into the campaign with Fillmore and Donelson as its candidates.

681 From a contemporary cartoon published by Currier & Ives, New York, in the New York Historical Society

BUCHANAN NOMINATED BY THE DEMOCRATS

THE Democrats tried hard to present an appearance of harmony. Since the Douglas principle of popular sovereignty was to be their major plank, it was expected that either the Little Giant or Pierce would be the nominee. But the North so opposed the proceedings in Kansas that the leaders were passed over for a man less closely connected with recent domestic events. As Minister to England, James Buchanan had been abroad during the more trying times. His availability was enhanced because his name was linked with that aggressive foreign policy which had been employed to distract the country from internal troubles. (See No. 657.) Acceptable to the South, he could be supported also by the conservative elements of the North.

682 From a contemporary Democratic cartoon published by Currier & Ives, original in the Library of Congress

THE PARTY OF THE REFORMERS

THE Whig party, practically defunct, contented itself with endorsing the candidates of the American party. There was thus need for a party which would stand foursquare against the Democrats and the extension of slavery. This need was filled by the Republican party, which had grown with surprising rapidity since 1854. To it had thronged a miscellany of malcontents, a fact of which its rivals made the most. "It got its programme from the Free-Soilers, whom it bodily absorbed; its radical and aggressive spirit from the abolitionists, whom it received without liking; its liberal views upon constitutional questions from the Whigs, who constituted both in numbers and in influence its commanding element; and its popular impulse from the Democrats, who did not leave behind them, when they joined it, their faith in their old party ideals." — WOODROW WILSON, *Division and Reunion*, p. 188. In spite of such heterogeneity, the party showed remarkable solidarity. Assembling in Philadelphia on the anniversary of Bunker Hill, the delegates, passing over the more prominent leaders — such as Chase of Ohio and Seward of New York — selected John C. Fremont of California, a young man little known in politics, but with a well-advertised record as an explorer of the Far West. The platform vigorously denounced the pro-slavery and jingoistic activity of recent years. The cartoon below pictures the early hopes of the new Republican party that its middle-of-the-road platform would draw to its support all who dreaded the extremes implicit in the policies advocated by its rivals.

GREAT EXCITEMENT!!

Arrival in this City of

THE NONDESCRIPT!

OR

WOOLLY HORSE

And will be exhibited

ONCE IN A WHILE,

At the Hut, corner of Asylum and High Streets, until Nov. 4th, previous to taking its departure for Salt River.

Nature seems to have exhausted all her ingenuity in the production of this

WONDERFUL AND ASTONISING ANIMAL,

He is a complex, made up of the Elephant, Deer, Horse, Jackass, Buffalo, Camel, Calf, and Negro!

Is the full size of the Horse. Has a negro head, abolition body, tail of the snake, and feet like an elephant. A fine black curled WOOL covers his head and EYES, and he easily bounds to the highest kind of political majorities at a single jump. Naturalists and Political Antiquarians say that his antecedents are but LITTLE KNOWN in Natural History. Philosophers Free Love Greely, Bennett, and others have labored hard to give some scientific diagnosis of this truly

WONDERFUL ANIMAL,

But no two of them agree as to his origin, religion, character and habits. He is indisputably, and undoubtedly,

Nature's First and Last of his Species.

He will be exhibited only in the evening, as that is the only time when he exhibits his wonderful strength of lungs and limbs. He assumes during the day a comatose and sleepy state, apparently recruiting his energies for his *extraordinary exertions* during the night.

A full and accurate description of his habits, religion, &c will be elaborately given by Rev. H. WARD BEECHER, commander of the "Holy Rifles," who was instrumental in his capture, and is now traveling throughout the New England States, exhibiting this NONDESCRIPT animal in all his curious feats of

GROUND AND LOFTY TUMBLING.

He will exhibit several "Patent Shricks for Kansas." In order to make the Exhibition more interesting, several Shackles, &c. which were worn in Kansas by Free State Men, have been added. Negotiations are on foot for the capture of Stringfellow and Jim Lane. A perfect size of life Plaster Figure of Bleeding Kansas, from the original at Meriden, is present.

CAUTION.

The managers of this extraordinary Nondescript, have heard that a similar animal—the very duplicate of theirs—has been found in Maryland; but it proves to be false. No such animal is in existence. The one professed to have been discovered by Free Love Greeley differs in every particular, and there is not the

SLIGHTEST RESEMBLANCE BETWEEN THE TWO!

The owners and managers of this Hermaphrodite Beast, are happy to be able to refer to any number of "Political Parsons" throughout the Northern States, who have lent their sacred influence and position to the advancement of our private interest.

The audience will be entertained by music from the

"SILK STOCKING GLEE CLUB,"

To the tune of "Hard Times," "De Dah Dah!" "Pennsylvania is a hard road to travel," &c. &c.

Niggers and females will occupy the gallery, as the animal has a strong and peculiar affinity for that class of nature's productions.

☞Tickets can be procured at the Note Shaving Banking House, and at the door of the Fourth Church during Prayer Meetings.

☞P. S. For sale 1,000,000,000 shares of Mariposa Stock. Subscriptions taken up for Bleeding Kansas and political purposes

683 Poster on the new Republican Party, printed at Hartford, Conn., in the New York Historical Society

684 From a contemporary cartoon in the New York Historical Society

685 From a contemporary Democratic cartoon published by Currier & Ives, New York, in the New York Historical Society

686 Horace Greeley, 1811–72, from a photograph by Brady

A JIBE AT THE REPUBLICANS

THE Republicans launched a campaign that in vigor and spectacle resembled that of 1840. With "Bleeding Kansas" as their cry, they appealed, through the agency of newspaper editors such as Horace Greeley of the *New York Tribune*, James Gordon Bennett of the *New York Herald*, Henry J. Raymond of the *New York Times*, and General J. Watson Webb of the *Courier and Enquirer*, New York, to the northerners' dread lest the "Buchaneers" expand their domain of slavery. In the cartoon Greeley, with his brother editors, Bennett and Raymond, is seen astride the "woolly horse" of the new Union party. (See No. 683.) Fremont is caricatured as an incompetent who was being misled by his over-enthusiastic guides.

687 James Gordon Bennett, 1795–1872, from a contemporary caricature in the American Antiquarian Society, Worcester, Mass.

688 From a contemporary cartoon published by Currier & Ives, New York, in possession of the publishers

REFORMERS HANDICAP REPUBLICAN POPULARITY

In particular, the opposition played upon the widespread dislike for the abolitionists as a means of discrediting the Republicans. The eccentric personalities of the reformers, their extravagant acts and still more extravagant words were a heavy burden for the new party to carry.

SECTIONALISM OF THE REPUBLICAN PARTY

As the campaign developed, it appeared that the Republicans were too sectional in their appeal and not sufficiently organized to carry the country. Buchanan gained many adherents who had become alarmed by the apparent radicalism of the Fremont followers. Fillmore took occasion to announce that Fremont's election would endanger the Union. In the South, it need hardly be said, "black republicanism" was identified by many with all the "isms" in the dictionary.

689 From a contemporary cartoon published by Currier & Ives, New York, in the Historical Society of Pennsylvania, Philadelphia

RIDICULE OF RADICALS MARKS THE CAMPAIGN

The poster "For Salt River" admirably shows the spirit of the opposition to the new Republican party and the attacks which were made upon it. Henry Ward Beecher gained his sobriquet from an episode early in the migration to Kansas. At a meeting for the encouragement of emigration he subscribed for a rifle to be presented to a prospective settler. Thereafter equipping emigrants with "Beecher's Bibles" was common. Fred Douglass, one of the "stokers" of the Fremont ship, was perhaps the most remarkable negro of his time. For two decades before the Civil War he was an effective advocate of abolition. Banks, referred to as a "steward," was to become Governor of Massachusetts and one of the prominent "political generals" who fought on the Federal side in the sectional struggle. "Foxy" Raymond and "Sauney" Bennett were editors.

690 Frederick Douglass, 1817–95, from a photograph by Warren, Boston

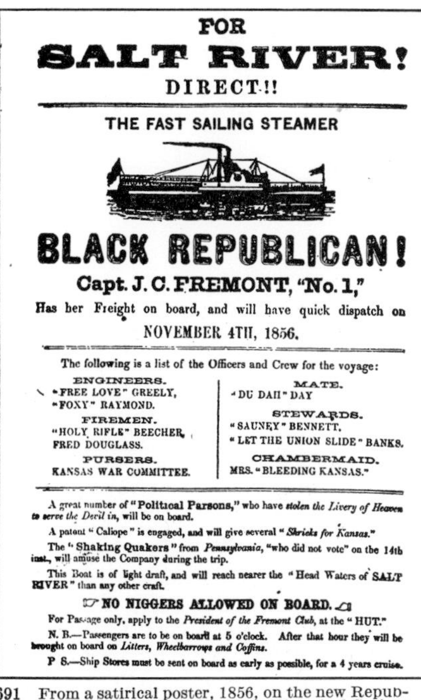

FOR

SALT RIVER!

DIRECT!!

THE FAST SAILING STEAMER

BLACK REPUBLICAN!

Capt. J. C. FREMONT, "No. 1,"

Has her Freight on board, and will have quick dispatch on

NOVEMBER 4TH, 1856.

The following is a list of the Officers and Crew for the voyage:

ENGINEERS.
"FREE LOVE" GREELY,
"FOXY" RAYMOND.

FIREMEN.
"HOLY RIFLE" BEECHER,
FRED DOUGLASS.

PURSERS.
KANSAS WAR COMMITTEE.

MATE.
"DU DAH" DAY

STEWARDS.
"SAUNEY" BENNETT.
"LET THE UNION SLIDE" BANKS.

CHAMBERMAID.
MRS. "BLEEDING KANSAS."

A great number of "**Political Parsons,**" who have *stolen the Livery of Heaven to serve the Devil in*, will be on board.

A patent "Caliope" is engaged, and will give several "*Shrieks for Kansas.*"

The "**Shaking Quakers**" from *Pennsylvania*, "who did not vote" on the 14th inst., will amuse the Company during the trip.

This Boat is of light draft, and will reach nearer the "Head Waters of SALT RIVER" than any other craft.

NO NIGGERS ALLOWED ON BOARD.

For Passage only, apply to the *President of the Fremont Club*, at the "HUT."

N. B.—Passengers are to be on board at 5 o'clock. After that hour they will be brought on board on *Litters, Wheelbarrows and Coffins.*

P S.—Ship Stores must be sent on board as early as possible, for a 4 years cruise.

691 From a satirical poster, 1856, on the new Republican party, in the New York Historical Society

THE ELECTION GOES TO THE DEMOCRATS

The contest was rather close. Buchanan received one hundred and seventy-four electoral votes to one hundred and fourteen for Fremont, while Fillmore received eight from Maryland. The Democrats had had a close call; and the size of the Republican vote gave the old-line leaders cause to worry for the future.

692 From a contemporary cartoon published by Currier & Ives, New York, in the New York Historical Society

BUCHANAN AND HIS CABINET

Buchanan had been selected as the candidate of the party because he was "regular" and because he was in favor with the South. When in office he surrounded himself with men of like views. The cabinet, which was confirmed by the Senate on March 6, included Howell Cobb at the Treasury, Floyd as Secretary of War, Thompson at the Interior Department, Isaac Toucey as Secretary of the Navy, and Brown at the head of the Post Office, most of them from slave states. At the head of the group he placed Lewis Cass of Michigan, with whose aid he hoped to continue emphasis upon diplomatic successes in order to quiet the country.

693 James Buchanan, 1791–1868, from a photograph

694 President Buchanan and his Cabinet, from *Harper's Weekly*, Mar. 13, 1858

A SOUTHERNER HEADS THE TREASURY

Howell Cobb, who held such an important position in President Buchanan's political family, had long been a striking figure in southern politics. He was a Georgian. He had entered Congress as a Democrat in 1843 and served by successive reëlections till 1851, distinguishing himself as a debater. He had sided with President Jackson in his stand on the question of nullification in South Carolina. Believing ardently in the extension of slavery, he had efficiently supported Polk's administration. When the Compromise of 1850 had been agreed upon, he became one of its stanch supporters as a Union Democrat. On the issue of the Compromise he was elected Governor of Georgia by a large majority. In 1860, when the struggle between the sections came to a head, he abandoned the cause of the Union to become a leader of the secession movement. He was president of the convention of the seceded states which framed the constitution of the Confederacy. During Buchanan's administration he was an efficient secretary and one of the most important of the President's political advisers.

695 Howell Cobb, 1815–68, from a wood engraving after a photograph

CHARLES SUMNER ATTACKED IN THE SENATE

On May 22, 1856, Charles Sumner, Senator from Massachusetts, made a bitter and vituperative speech on the question of Kansas. In the course of the address he attacked Senator Butler of South Carolina. "The Senator from South Carolina has read many books of chivalry, and believes himself a chivalrous knight, with sentiments of honor and courage. Of course he has chosen a mistress to whom he has made his vows, and who, though ugly to others, is always lovely to him; though polluted in the sight of the world, is chaste in his sight. I mean the harlot Slavery. Let her be impeached in character, or any proposition be made to shut her out from the extension of her wantonness, and no extravagance of manner or hardihood of assertion is then too great for the Senator." "When Sumner concluded, the gathering storm broke forth. Cass of Michigan, after saying that he had listened to the address with equal surprise and regret, characterized it as 'the most un-American and unpatriotic that ever grated on the ears of the members of that high body.' . . . Two days later Sumner was sitting alone at his desk in the Senate chamber after adjournment when Preston Brooks, a nephew of Senator Butler and a member of the lower House, entered and accosted him with the statement that he had read Sumner's speech twice and that it was a libel on South Carolina and a kinsman of his. Thereupon Brooks followed his words by striking Sumner on the head with a cane. Though the Senator was dazed and blinded by the unexpected attack, his assailant rained blow after blow until he had broken the cane and Sumner lay prostrate and bleeding at his feet. Everywhere throughout the South, in the public press, in legislative halls, in public meetings, Brooks was hailed as a hero." — Jesse Macy, *The Anti-Slavery Crusade*, pp. 175–76. Brooks, before the attack, had pressed Sumner to apologize. Though Sumner's physician soon after the affray reported him capable of performing his duties, he undertook a journey around the world as an invalid while still retaining his office.

696 Charles Sumner, 1811–74, from a photograph taken when he was forty-five, in the Harvard College Library

FRIDAY, MAY 23, 1856.

THE LATEST NEWS.

BY MAGNETIC AND PRINTING TELEGRAPHS.

Assault on Senator Sumner in the Senate Chamber.

Washington, May 22, 1856.

About half past one, after the Senate adjourned, Col. Preston S. Brooks, M. C., of South Carolina, approached Senator Sumner, who was sitting in his seat, and said to him—

Mr. Sumner, I have read your speach against South Carolina, and have read it carefully, deliberately and dispassionately, in which you have libelled my State and slandered my white haired old relative, Senator Butler, who is absent, and I have come to punish you for it.

Col. Brooks then struck Senator Sumner with his cane some dozen blows over the head. Mr. Sumner at first showed fight, but was overpowered. Senator Crittenden and others interfered and separated them.

Mr. Keith, of South Carolina, did not interfere, only to keep persons off.

Senator Toombs declared that it was the proper place to have chastised Mr. Sumner.

The affair is regretted by all.

The stick used was gutta percha, about an inch in diameter, and hollow, which was broken up like a pipestem.

About a dozen Senators and many strangers happened to be in the chamber at the moment of the fight. Sumner, I learn, is badly whipped. The city is considerably excited, and crowds everywhere are discussing the last item. Sumner cried—"I'm most dead! oh! I'm most dead!" After Sumner fell between two desks, his own having been overturned, he lay bleeding, and cried out—"I am almost dead—almost dead!"

697 From the New York *Herald*, May 23, 1856

THE DRED SCOTT DECISION

Any hopes Buchanan may have entertained that the slavery issue could be evaded were dashed by a decision of the Supreme Court handed down two days after his inauguration. Dred Scott was a slave who had been carried by his master into the free state of Illinois and the territory of Minnesota, free soil under the Missouri Compromise. Subsequently he had voluntarily returned to Missouri. A test case then had been started to determine whether Scott's residence in free areas had made him permanently a freedman. In his decision Chief Justice Taney determined that negroes could not be citizens of the United States, and hence could not, under the conditions of the present case, sue in the federal courts.

698 Dred Scott, from a portrait from life by Louis Schultze in the Missouri Historical Society

699 Chief Justice Roger B. Taney, 1777–1864, from the portrait by G. P. A. Healy in the United States Supreme Court, Washington

TANEY ACCUSED OF FAVORING THE SOUTH

NOT content with thus disposing of the matter, Taney went on to declare that even though Scott could properly bring suit in the courts, he had not gained freedom by residence in free territory because the Compromise of 1820 was unconstitutional. This was true, it was held, because the Constitution recognized slaves as property, of which Congress could with due process of law deprive no one. No decision of the Supreme Court has caused more public discussion. The South applauded it as opening all national territory to slavery, and thus nullifying the legal arguments of the northerners. The latter were bitter in their criticism of the court, and pointed out that Justices Curtis and McLean had dissented from its judgment, and that Taney had gone out of his way to give aid and comfort to the slave section. The passage in Taney's decision that aroused most unfavorable comment was that in which he said that the negroes "had for more than a century before been regarded as beings of an inferior order . . . so far inferior, that they had no rights which the white man was bound to respect."

REPUBLICANS GROW BITTER OVER "BLEEDING KANSAS"

THE cartoon, "Liberty the Fair Maid of Kansas in the Hands of the Border Ruffians," shows the bitterness of the Republicans, who charged the Democratic administration with inflicting unspeakable suffering and barbaric cruelties upon the people of Kansas.

700 From a contemporary Republican cartoon in the New York Historical Society

THE DIS-UNITED STATES—A BLACK BUSINESS.

701 From a cartoon in *Punch*, Nov. 8, 1856, by permission of the proprietors

THE AMERICAN TWINS, OR NORTH AND SOUTH.

702 From a cartoon in *Punch*, Sept. 27, 1856, by permission of the proprietors

ENGLAND SYMPATHIZES WITH THE SOUTH

English observers watched the developments of events in the United States with growing concern. They saw two hostile civilizations emerging in the republic across the Atlantic. British sentiment began to clarify. *Punch's* cartoon, "The Dis-United States" should be compared with that of "Liberty, Fraternity, Equality," published eight years previous. (See No. 635.) In the earlier drawing the jibe is at America, in the latter the negro appears in the rôle of ignorant destroyer. Not without significance is the contrast in figures representing the North and South. The uncouth northern farmer is the Yankee democrat who had been so often ridiculed in England. The southerner is a gentleman. The contrast is an early expression of the sympathy of the British upper classes with the South in spite of the fact that the southern aristocracy was based on slavery.

CIVIL WAR IN KANSAS

The Dred Scott decision was a challenge to the Republican party. If the Missouri Compromise was unconstitutional and if the slave owner could take his property anywhere in the national domain, the platform of the Republican party, demanding no further extension of slavery in the territories, was unconstitutional. The decision only served to strengthen the determination of the antislavery forces of the North. Some months before the decision was handed down, civil war had broken out in Kansas. In May, 1856, Lawrence, the center of the Free Soil party, had been attacked by a pro-slavery force from the eastern end of the territory and sacked. In reprisal for some lives lost by the antislavery people, John Brown led a band of men in a series of cold-blooded murders of slavery sympathizers at Dutch Henry's Crossing on the Pottawattomie. This affair marked the appearance upon the national stage of the fanatic who was destined to aid materially in bringing the North and South to war. Yet such was the temper of the times that men of honor and standing in the North applauded Brown for his massacres, gave him money and held meetings in his honor. His is one of the many puzzling personalities in the drama of slavery and abolitionism.

703 John Brown, 1800–59, from a photograph taken in 1855, in the Kansas State Historical Society, Topeka

704 John Brown, from a photograph taken in 1859

705 The Hall of Representatives, with the members in session, from *Harper's Weekly*, Feb. 6, 1858

THE REVOLT OF DOUGLAS

In December, 1857, Buchanan's first Congress assembled. There was excitement from the opening of the session because the Kansas question had reached a crisis. Buchanan had sent the unwilling Robert J. Walker to Kansas as Governor. He had called an election for a constitutional convention. Again the Missourians had come over the border and had filled the ballot boxes with pro-slavery votes. The Lecompton constitution, guaranteeing the slave owners in Kansas possession of their property, was the result. The Free State men, who greatly outnumbered their opponents, had demanded that the constitution be submitted to a fair vote of the people, as provided for in Douglas' Kansas-Nebraska Act. The convention had refused. Walker had appealed to the President to compel submission. Buchanan had declined and Walker had resigned. When Congress assembled in December, one of the most dramatic battles in our legislative history was pending. Buchanan recommended admission under the pro-slavery constitution and intimated that Democrats who refused to follow him would receive no mercy from the administration. All eyes were upon the Senator from Illinois. In the most effective speech of his life Douglas denounced the President and led a secession of the northwestern Democrats from the dominant party of the South. After a prolonged and acrimonious debate a compromise was reached. Kansas was to be admitted when the Lecompton constitution was approved by a popular vote. If the vote were favorable, Kansas was to receive large grants of public lands within her borders; if unfavorable, admission to the Union was to await a substantial increase in population. Despite this weighting of the scales, the Kansans rejected the constitution by a vote of eleven thousand to eighteen hundred.

LINCOLN RIDING THE CIRCUIT

Shortly after the "revolt of Douglas," an inconspicuous Illinois lawyer suddenly became a national figure. In 1858 Douglas sought reëlection to his seat in the Senate. The Republicans of Illinois pitted against him a man known and respected throughout the state for his character and his political ability. Douglas looked upon Lincoln as an antagonist who would force him to his best efforts. The ensuing campaign was destined to become the most famous fight for a Senatorial seat in American history.

706 From *Collier's Weekly*, Feb. 13, 1909, after a drawing by Rollin Kirby (1874–), courtesy of P. F. Collier & Son Company

ABRAHAM LINCOLN, 1809–65

Lincoln opened the campaign with a carefully prepared speech, at the Republican State Convention, meeting in Springfield, Illinois, June 16, 1858. He began by saying that the country was in the fifth year since the adoption of Douglas' policy of "popular sovereignty" which was to put an end to the slavery agitation. Far from being ended, agitation had steadily increased. "In my opinion," said Lincoln, "it will not cease until a crisis has been reached and passed. A house divided against itself cannot stand. I believe this government cannot endure permanently half slave, half free. I do not expect the Union to be dissolved. I do not expect the house to fall; but I do expect it will cease to be divided. It will become all one thing or all the other. Either the opponents of slavery will arrest the further spread of it, and place it where the public mind shall rest in the belief that it is the course of ultimate extinction, or its advocates will push it forward till it shall become alike lawful in all the states, old as well as new, North as well as South." This bold pronouncement excited the fears of Lincoln's timid friends and laid him open to the conventional attacks of the supporters of slavery. Lincoln, however, never lowered his lofty tone of opposition to slavery.

707 Lincoln at forty-nine, from an ambrotype taken the day after the debate with Douglas at Galesburg, Ill., Oct. 7, 1858, courtesy of F. R. Jelliffe, Galesburg

THE LINCOLN–DOUGLAS DEBATES

A series of debates between the two candidates was arranged. In the course of this famous interchange, Lincoln showed, first, that Douglas would not serve the Republicans, since his principle of squatter sovereignty was an insecure basis for the establishment of free-soil states; second, that Douglas was no longer a fit candidate for the southern Democrats, for he forced Douglas, in the debate at Freeport, to quibble on the effect of the Dred Scott case until the South labelled him "heretic." Douglas won the seat in the Senate, but at the expense of his chances for the Presidency in 1860.

708 Lincoln's Debate with Douglas at Charleston, Ill., from J. F. Newton, *Lincoln and Herndon*, courtesy of The Torch Press, Cedar Rapids, Iowa

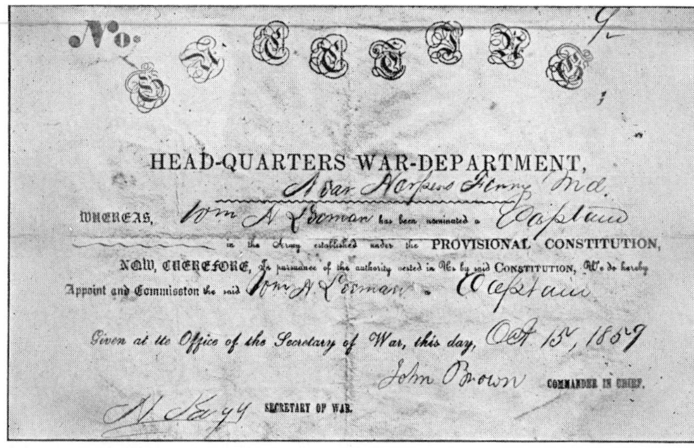

No. 9

HEAD-QUARTERS WAR-DEPARTMENT,
Near Harpers Ferry Md.

Whereas, Wm H Leeman has been nominated a Captain in the Army established under the PROVISIONAL CONSTITUTION,

Now, Therefore, In pursuance of the authority vested in Us by said Constitution, We do hereby Appoint and Commission the said Wm H Leeman a Captain

Given at the Office of the Secretary of War, this day, Oct 15, 1859

John Brown COMMANDER IN CHIEF.

H Kagy SECRETARY OF WAR.

709 Commission issued by John Brown and his Secretary of War Kagy, reproduced by courtesy of Mrs. Augustine J. Todd

JOHN BROWN'S RAID

In October, 1859, the country was startled by news of a night attack on the Government arsenal at Harper's Ferry, Virginia. John Brown believed that the time had come to rouse the slaves to rebel and throw off their shackles. His plan was that of a madman. With a handful of followers he surprised and captured the arsenal which was to provide the arms for the slave insurrection. He then called upon the slaves to rise against their masters. Before midnight the village was patroled by his armed men, six of whom had been ordered to bring in a number of neighboring planters with their slaves. He had seized several leading citizens as hostages, but had allowed a railway train to pass through the town northward, and this of course carried the news. Governor Wise of Virginia promptly sent the state militia to the scene. Colonel Robert E. Lee led a small force of United States troops against the disturbers of the peace. The slaves did not rise. Brown and his band were surrounded in a little building called the engine house, and were shot down one by one. Brown refused to surrender and when some of his men aimed at passers-by he said: "Don't shoot! That man is unarmed." Then Brown was captured, though not until he had been badly wounded. A thrill of horror ran through the slave states as the people of the South pictured to themselves what the result would have been had Brown succeeded in starting an insurrection of the negroes. In the North, Brown was widely acclaimed a hero. When such a deed could arouse such different emotions, there could be no doubting that the Union was in danger.

710 John Brown's Fort at Harper's Ferry, as it appeared some years after the raid. © Rau Studios, Inc.

THE TRIAL OF JOHN BROWN

Brown's trial aroused great excitement in both North and South. It followed speedily upon his capture. Able counsel was furnished him and his case received fair handling. But the result was never in doubt. On the last day of October, 1859, he was convicted of treason, of advising slaves and others to rebel, and of murder in the first degree. He was sentenced to be hanged on Friday, the second of December. Strong pressure was brought to bear on Governor Wise of Virginia to commute the sentence. Even his life was threatened. To the threats and appeals Wise replied: "I am warned that hanging will make him a martyr. Ah! Will it? Why? The obvious answer to that question shows me above everything else the necessity for hanging him."

711 John Brown arraigned before the court at Charlestown, Va., from a sketch made at the time by James E. Taylor

THE AFTERMATH OF THE RAID

THE southern people demanded the execution of Brown as a just punishment of a heinous crime. Emerson called him "that new saint, than whom none purer or more brave was ever led by love of men into conflict and death." Men in both sections, however, tried to minimize the significance of Harper's Ferry. Thus, a southern correspondent for *Harper's Weekly* wrote of the trial: "Here, in all probability, is an end of old John Brown — saint or sinner, martyr or murderer, famous or infamous, as the case may be. We may yet all have to acknowledge that we owe him for one good turn: with desperate hand he has blown up the whole magazine of abolition pyrotechnics — pray God there may not be a cracker or a squib remain unburned! Brethren of the North, when hereafter any man shall attempt to profane your rostrums or your pulpits with incendiary abuse and revilings against any section of our common country, I charge you smite him on the mouth — with the word Harper's Ferry."

A PREMATURE MOVEMENT.
JOHN BROWN. "Here! Take this, and follow me. My name's Brown."
CUFFEE. "Please God! Mr. Brown, dat is onpossible. We ain't done seedin' yit at our house."

712 From a cartoon in *Harper's Weekly*, Nov. 26, 1859

713 A Union Meeting outside the New York Academy of Music, Dec. 19, 1859, from *Harper's Weekly*, Jan. 7, 1860

UNION MEETINGS IN THE NORTH

IN the North huge meetings were held to laud the Union and urge its preservation. The very enthusiasm shown at these meetings, like the hidden warning in the writings of the southerner, indicate the tenseness of public feeling. The Congress which assembled shortly after John Brown's execution spent its time in tossing defiance from one side to the other and back again. Senator Grimes of Iowa wrote his wife: "The members on both sides are mostly armed with deadly weapons, and it is said that the friends of each are armed in the galleries." Throughout the country militia companies were forming and military exhibitions came to be of common occurrence. Such demonstrations and conduct of this kind were at bottom very different from the rough and ready methods customary in American politics. There was now a tenseness of feeling that expressed dread of an impending crisis.

714 The Democratic Convention at Charleston, S. C., from *Harper's Weekly*, April 28, 1860

THE SPLIT IN THE DEMOCRATIC CONVENTION

SUCH was the spirit in which the parties approached the election of 1860. The Democratic convention met at Charleston, South Carolina, in April. Douglas was the recognized leader of the northern branch of the party; but in February, the southerners had, in the form of resolutions presented in Congress by Jefferson Davis, tested his sympathy for the extreme pro-slavery view and found him wanting. When, therefore, a majority at Charleston voted to stand by the Douglas doctrine enunciated at Freeport, the delegates from seven slave states withdrew.

715 William L. Yancey, 1814–63, from an engraving after a daguerrotype

716 Meeting of the Southern Seceders at St. Andrew's Hall, Charleston, April 30, 1860, from *Harper's Weekly*, May 12, 1860

SECEDERS CHEER FOR A SOUTHERN REPUBLIC

THE break-up of the Charleston convention was a dramatic event. William L. Yancey, who as radical advocate of secession had been the counterpart in the South of William Lloyd Garrison in the North, led the Alabama delegation from the hall. One after another, other delegates followed after speeches of explanation. That night the seceders and their friends held a jubilee and marched about the streets with a band. Yancey addressed crowds wild with excitement, cheering for a southern republic. The rupture of the Democratic party meant that an important bond holding the North and South together had snapped.

TWO DEMOCRATS ARE NOMINATED FOR PRESIDENT

Each wing of the Democratic party put a candidate into the field. The southerners advanced John C. Breckinridge of Kentucky as their standard-bearer. To Breckinridge went the support of the Buchanan administration. Breckinridge stood on a platform which declared: "That the government of a territory . . . is provisional and temporary; and during its existence, all citizens of the United States have an equal right to settle with their property in the territory, without their rights, either of person or of property, being destroyed or impaired by congressional legislation" and "that it is the duty of the Federal government, in all its departments, to protect, when necessary, the rights of persons and property in the territories, and wherever else its constitutional authority extends." Meanwhile, the northern rump at the Charleston convention of the party became deadlocked. Douglas, standing firmly by his well-known doctrine of popular sovereignty, was the leading candidate for the presidential nomination; but he could not muster supporters in number equal to two thirds of the original full membership of the convention. So the body adjourned to Baltimore, where, through a change in the rules for nominating candidates, Douglas was chosen over the opposition of the Buchanan administration.

717 John C. Breckinridge, 1821–75, from a photograph by Brady

718 From a cartoon published in 1860 by Currier & Ives, New York, in the Historical Society of Pennsylvania

719 Candidates for the Republican Nomination in 1860, from photographs by Brady in *Harper's Weekly*, May 12, 1860

ABRAHAM LINCOLN NOMINATED FOR PRESIDENT

THE Republicans met at Chicago in May, in the new "wigwam" built by local political clubs for the purpose. The party leaders realized that a man of moderate, but decisive, views was desirable, one, moreover, who would undermine Douglas' strength in the Northwest. Seward of New York was the most prominent candidate. In 1850 he had spoken of a "higher law" than the Constitution; in 1858 he had told the North that it was engaged in an "irrepressible conflict" that must make the nation all slave or all free.

"The Republicans had no division among themselves upon doctrine. Such division as existed was due to the ordinary rivalry of political leaders. In the opinion of all his enemies and of most Americans, Seward was the Republican man of the hour. During much of 1859 he had discreetly withdrawn from the country and had left to his partisans the conduct of his campaign, which seems to have been going well when he returned in the midst of the turmoil following the death of John Brown. Nevertheless, he was disturbed over his prospects, for he found that in many minds both North and South he was looked upon as the ultimate cause of all the turmoil. His famous speech on the 'irrepressible conflict' was everywhere quoted as an exultant prophecy of these terrible latter days. It was long the custom to deny Seward any good motive in a speech which he now delivered, just as it was to deny Webster any good motive for his famous 7th of March speech. . . . Both men were seeking the Presidency; both, we may fairly believe, were shocked by the turmoil of political currents; each tried oiling the waters, and in the attempt each ruined his candidacy. Seward's speech in condemnation of John Brown in February, 1860, was an appeal to the conservative North against the radical North and to many of his followers it seemed a change of front. It certainly gained him no new friends and it lost him some old ones so that his star as presidential candidate began its decline. The first ballot in the Republican convention surprised the country. Of the votes, two hundred and thirty-three were necessary for a choice. Seward had only one hundred and seventy-three and one half. Next to him, with one hundred and two votes, stood none of the leading candidates, but the comparatively obscure Lincoln. A gap of more than fifty votes separated Lincoln from Cameron, Chase and Bates. On the second ballot, Seward gained eleven votes while Lincoln gained seventy-nine. The enemies of Seward, finding it impossible to combine on any of the conspicuous candidates, were moving toward Lincoln, the man with the fewest enemies. The third ballot gave Lincoln the nomination." — NATHANIEL W. STEPHENSON, *Abraham Lincoln and the Union*, The Chronicles of America Series, Vol. 29, pp. 75–6, New Haven, 1920.

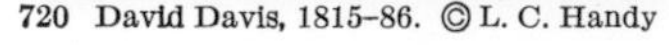

720 David Davis, 1815–86. © L. C. Handy

721 The Republican Nominating Convention, 1860, from *Harper's Weekly*, May 19, 1860

WHAT CAUSED LINCOLN'S NOMINATION

SEWARD's February speech had, in short, led too many northerners to see in him a compromising character unfitted for the strenuous days ahead. The choice, therefore, fell upon Lincoln. This result was brought about in part by the able management of David Davis, Lincoln's aide at Chicago, and in part because the little that was known in the East about Lincoln gave him the reputation of being a determined opponent of slavery. A fourth convention was held early in May, at Baltimore, composed of men who hoped to be able to cling to the historic order of things. As the Constitutional Union party, they adopted a platform declaring for "no political principle other than the Constitution of the country, the union of the States, and the enforcement of the laws." The candidates were John Bell of Tennessee and Edward Everett of Massachusetts. The convention was composed, for the most part, of highly respectable, middle-aged and elderly men who, alarmed at the bitterness of the sectional controversy, had met with the idea of saving the imperiled Union.

722 John Bell, 1797–1869, from the portrait in the Tennessee State Library, courtesy of the Tennessee Historical Society

723 Edward Everett, 1794–1865, from an engraving in the collection of the Bostonian Society, Boston

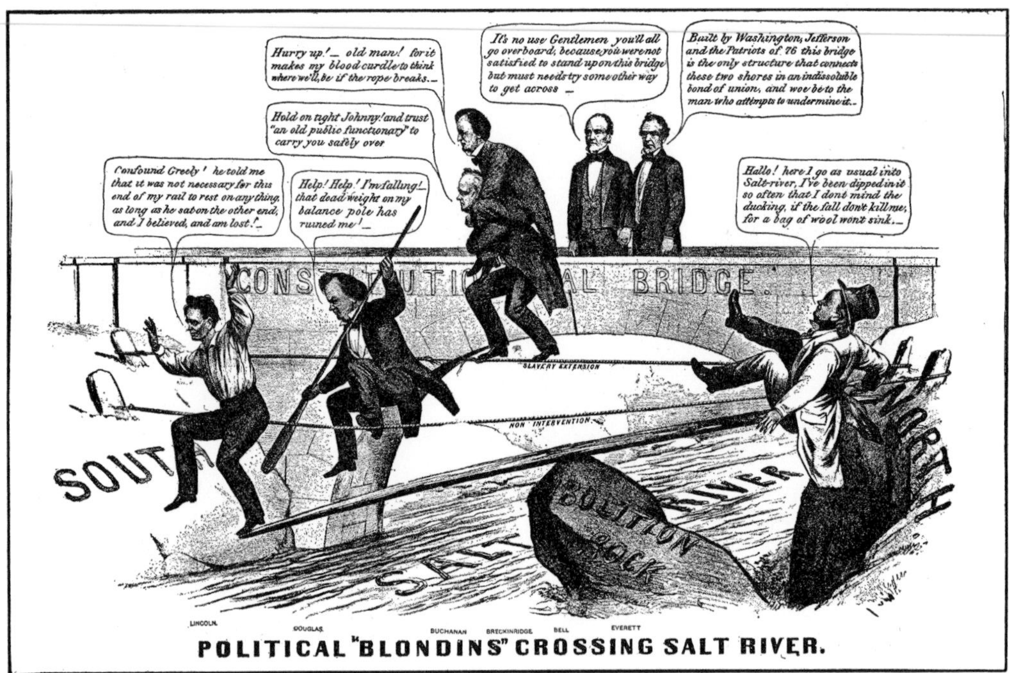

724 From a contemporary campaign cartoon published by Currier & Ives, New York, in possession of the publishers

A CRITICAL CAMPAIGN

THE ensuing campaign was exciting. Many felt that momentous changes were impending. The timid, shrinking from the extremes of the Republican and Democratic platforms, found apparent security in the program of the Bell-Everetts, as representing a moderate course to which all could safely subscribe.

725 From a contemporary campaign cartoon published by Currier & Ives, in possession of the publishers

RIDICULE OF THE REPUBLICANS

AGAINST the Republican party and its candidates were revived the accusations that had been made in 1856. Its rivals held it up to the people as composed of a variegated and ill-assorted group of freethinkers, held together by the liberal but vague promises of Greeley in his *Tribune*, and by glittering generalities from the candidate. The cartoon represents the Republican procession on its way to the lunatic asylum.

726 From a contemporary campaign cartoon published by Currier & Ives, in possession of the publishers

THE REPUBLICANS ARE ACCUSED OF STRADDLING

In the North the Republicans were fighting the field; in the South they made little headway. In Pennsylvania they stressed the desirability of a protective tariff; in urban communities they advocated "Free Homes for the Homeless"; while they eagerly sought the foreign vote. So varied were the types of appeal that their opponents contended that the party was quibbling and straddling issues.

727 From a contemporary campaign cartoon published by Currier & Ives, in possession of the publishers

LINCOLN POPULAR WITH THE YOUNG VOTER AND THE LABORING CLASS

Lincoln, however, proved a popular candidate with the young men and with the laboring class. The latter was easily aroused to favor a man of the people whose election would mean a house-cleaning at the capitol.

728 From a contemporary campaign cartoon published by Currier & Ives, in possession of the publishers

A REPUBLICAN VIEW OF THE CONTEST

AND as the campaign developed in the North, it began to be perceived that Lincoln's personality and his principles were greater assets than the schemes of his rivals. The superficial traits of the former backwoodsman were gradually forgotten, as the courage, integrity and broad humanity of the candidate became more and more evident to all. The Democrats, moreover, found their leaders pulling in opposite directions, to the destruction of all hopes for victory.

729 From a contemporary campaign cartoon published by Currier & Ives, in possession of the publishers

REPUBLICAN TACTICS

From the outset of the campaign the split in the Democratic party was looked upon by political wiseacres as the decisive factor in the contest. Douglas made a brilliant fight. He took the stump and campaigned throughout the North. His motive seems to have been not so much hope of election in 1860 as a desire to maintain the enthusiasm and discipline of his party against the next presidential campaign when he hoped that the northern and southern factions could be brought together. The Republicans, taking every advantage of their tactical opportunity, organized their followers into "Wide Awake Clubs." The "Wide Awakes" enlivened many a night in the autumn of 1860 with their torch-light processions. They marched, not only in great cities like New York but in small country towns, creating enthusiasm for Lincoln and conviction of Republican victory.

730 Procession of "Wide Awakes" at New York, Oct. 3, 1860, from *Harper's Weekly*, Oct. 13, 1860

DOUGLAS PLEADS FOR THE UNION

Toward the end of the struggle, Douglas, frightened by secession talk in the South, abandoned his campaign in the North and made a tour in the slave states in a last-minute endeavor to swing that section from Breckinridge to Bell, who was pledged to maintain the Union. This meant the surrender of his own region to the Republicans, and an abandonment of his own hopes of election. He pleaded with the South not to secede in the event of Lincoln's election.

731 From a contemporary campaign cartoon published by Currier & Ives, in the American Antiquarian Society

732 From photographs of Lincoln taken by Hesler in June 1860, at Springfield, Ill. 733

ABRAHAM LINCOLN ELECTED

THE election showed clearly the political separation between North and South. Lincoln carried the North solidly, except for New Jersey; Breckinridge the South. In the border states, where sentiment was divided, the vote was split between the conservative candidates, Bell and Douglas. "Northern radicalism won the North, Southern radicalism won the South, and the middle region was for inaction with regard to slavery." — C. R. FISH, *Development of American Nationality*, p. 358. The extreme partisans of slavery did not even wait for the election of Lincoln before they began to make active preparations for insurrection.

734 From a contemporary campaign cartoon published by Currier & Ives, in possession of the publishers

SOUTH CAROLINA SECEDES

AIDED by a divided opposition, the Republicans had won the Presidency. But they failed to secure a majority in either House of Congress. The more temperate men, therefore, hoped that the final break between the sections could be averted. "But the psychology of the situation played inevitably into the hands of the extremists. Twenty-five years of increasing sectional bitterness had caused the two branches of the American people to lose faith in each other." — A. M. SCHLESINGER, *Political and Social History of the United States*, p. 170. In South Carolina, where the radicals were stronger than elsewhere in the South, the Governor had told the legislature, on November 5, that if Lincoln were elected, a state convention would be summoned, similar to that of 1788, to consider the advisability of secession. On December 17, therefore, the convention met at Charleston; and three days later it unanimously repealed the act of 1788 ratifying the Constitution and dissolved the "union now subsisting between South Carolina and other States, under the name of the United States of America." Commissioners were dispatched to Washington to settle questions concerning the division of national property in the state and of the national debt, and to other slave states to win their coöperation.

735 Secession Meeting in front of the Mills House, Charleston, S. C., from *Frank Leslie's Illustrated Newspaper*, Dec. 1, 1860

737 Facsimile of the South Carolina Ordinance of Secession, in the American Antiquarian Society, Worcester, Mass.

736 Robert Barnwell Rhett, 1800–76, framer of the Ordinance of Secession, courtesy of A. Burnet Rhett, Charleston

738 A Street View in Charleston, S. C., from *Frank Leslie's Illustrated Newspaper*, Dec. 1860

THE ORGANIZATION OF THE CONFEDERACY

In these states there was division of opinion, not as to the constitutionality of secession, but as to its present expediency. In Georgia, in particular, the struggle was close. Alexander Stephens counseled delay, declaring that Lincoln could do nothing "unless backed by power in Congress," and in Congress he would not have a majority. Opposed to Stephens was Robert Toombs, a leading "fire-eater" of the South. In the end Toombs was victorious, and on January 19 Georgia seceded. Before the first of February, seven other Gulf states followed. On the fourth, delegates met at Montgomery to form a southern confederation; and on the eighth they adopted a provisional constitution, expressly sanctioning slavery, and elected Jefferson Davis and Alexander Stephens provisional president and vice-president.

739 From a contemporary cartoon published by J. L. Magee, Philadelphia, in the New York Historical Society

BUCHANAN UNWILLING TO COERCE SECEDING STATES

Responsibility for meeting these developments fell upon Buchanan and the Congress which assembled in December, 1860. Buchanan, by nature timid, feared that forceful measures would throw fuel upon flames which, if left alone, might expire for lack of encouragement. In his message, therefore, while declaring secession unconstitutional, he stated that he believed the National Government had no right to coerce a state. Congress was left to deal with the crisis without executive guidance. Once more it attempted compromise. Under the lead of Senator Crittenden of Kentucky, various plans to placate the slave states were debated, without avail.

740 John J. Crittenden, 1787–1863, from a photograph by L. C. Handy

FORT SUMTER LEADS TO A STATE OF WAR

Meanwhile, South Carolina had bestirred herself to actions that threatened to force the Government's hand. In Charleston harbor lay Fort Sumter, occupied by Federal troops under Major Anderson. After much urging, the President dispatched the *Star of the West* with military supplies and provisions to the aid of the fort. Upon her arrival in the harbor, on January 9, Confederate batteries opened fire. Ignorant of the plans of his superiors, Major Anderson was not prepared to aid the vessel, which returned to New York. Though confronted with a *casus belli*, Buchanan failed to act. Effective management of the situation remained a problem to be faced by the new President, who took office on March 4, 1861.

741 From a contemporary cartoon published by Currier & Ives, in the New York Historical Society

NOTES ON THE PICTURES

1. Another portrait, after an original by Van Dyck, is in Vol. I, p. 211.
2. The Cotton portrait by Smibert is in Vol. I, p. 213.
3. This rare volume came from the press of Hezekiah Usher.
5. According to the record, there were four commissioners to negotiate with Berkeley. The picture shows but three.
11. Lely, born in Westphalia, studied in Holland, then painted in England under the patronage of Charles I. He became eminent as the portraitist in England of celebrities of his time.
12. A portrait of Clarendon after Gerard Soest is in Vol. I, p. 264.
13. There has been controversy as to whether the Connecticut charter in the State Library is the original or whether the original is the one in the Connecticut Historical Society at Hartford. The charter was executed in duplicate May 10, 1662, the one that was first sealed being the original. The claim is made for the Historical Society's possession that it bears internal evidence of being the original in that it has the words "per fine five pounds" written on it, which do not appear on the State Library's historical duplicate.
15. Picture an imaginary conception of a custom of which few details have been handed down.
16. By a Virginia-born artist and illustrator of ability who was known for conscientious work; architectural details open to criticism.
18. Pyle's fanciful picture is valuable as expressing the spirit of an occasion of which few details are known. Artist known for his close study of American history and of period costume. For other examples of his work see Vol. I.
22. The order-in-council and the proclamation were printed together as a four-page leaflet.
28. Original in the Old South Church, Boston.
29. See 18.
31. The Charter Oak was destroyed in a hurricane in August, 1856. Charles De Wolf Brownell was known as one of the Connecticut valley painters. His painting, formerly owned by ex-Governor Jewell, is framed in wood sawed from the tree. Poems have been written about this tree, among them the lines of Mrs. L. H. Sigourney:

> Out laughed that hoary Oak, and op'd
> Its bosom's secret cell,
> And brought the entrusted treasure forth
> Which it had guarded well.

35. Drawn probably by W. L. Shepperd. See 16.
37. Statue erected in memory of Leisler, who as Governor of New York in 1689 bought land now the site of New Rochelle as a place of refuge for persecuted Huguenots.
39. An earlier portrait is in Vol. XII, section on Graphic Arts, p. 225.
40. A discussion on this broadside, by some regarded also as a newspaper, appears in *Publications of the Colonial Society of Massachusetts*, Vol. 9, p. 421.
44. The Board of Trade met first at the Palace of Whitehall after its appointment in 1696, occupying at first temporary and then permanent quarters probably located in the neighborhood of the other offices east or south of the banqueting hall. After the fire of 1698 which destroyed part of the central portion of the palace, the board moved to the reconstructed Cock-pit. The new office was the home of the board for seventeen years, and was situated just inside of the Holbein gateway to the right and consequently a little south of where the portico of Dover House is to-day. The Secretaries of State had their offices prior to 1761 in Whitehall, at first before the fire in the old palace and afterwards in the Cock-pit on the ground floor facing the street.
50. Charles Bridges, an English artist, was in Virginia from 1730 to 1750. Many portraits formerly attributed to Sir Godfrey Kneller were painted by Bridges. He made portraits of the family of William Byrd, who recommended him to Gov. Spotswood as "worthy to be the 'sergeant painter' of Virginia."
55. In this picture the workman, Dennis Lawrence, who built the State House, is talking with Andrew Hamilton, deputy-Governor, and the figure in the background is Dr. John Kearsley, member of the committee.
64. William Cogswell, 1819–1903, a portrait painter chiefly self-taught.
72. The dismembered snake device is believed to have been designed and cut by Benjamin Franklin, having appeared first in his paper, *The Pennsylvania Gazette*, on May 9, 1754, following an account of the capture of Captain Trent's men, wherein Franklin refers to the "disunited state of the colonies." This was just before Franklin left for Albany to present his plan for a union to the Congress of the Colonies. The snake device was reproduced the following week (May 13, 1754) in the *New York Gazette*

as shown, and continued in use for twenty years thereafter among the colonies.

75, 76, 77. Only known original of a Writ of Assistance.

78. Another portrait of Otis by Blackburn is in Vol. XI, p. 51.

80. Portrait painted in England after Bernard's return from America.

96. For an exhaustive account of the Patrick Henry miniature and other Henry portraits see C. H. Hart, *Proceedings of the Numismatic and Antiquarian Society of Philadelphia*, Vol. 26, 1913.

99. The Virginia Resolutions, as here printed, differ in phraseology, but not materially in substance, from Henry's original draft. One of the resolutions as adopted does not appear in the published version.

108. British political caricatures of the eighteenth century were done by free-lance draftsmen and sold to London publishers who issued them on separate sheets. They were purchased not only by individuals, but by publishers of books and magazines to illustrate the text on Colonial affairs. T. Bowles was one of the principal publishers of such "penny" caricatures which were referred to as "humorous prints." Few were signed. They were sometimes accompanied by doggerel verse, and in general were anti-ministerial in tone and essentially coarse in conception. See 113, 170, 176, 205.

113. A contemporary version of this rare caricature has the following explanation: "The Hero of this Print is the gentle Mr. *Stamper*, who is carrying to the Family Vault his favourite Child, in a Coffin, Miss AME-STAMP, about 12 Months old. *Anti-Sejanus*, who reads the Burial Service, is the first in the Procession. — After him follow Two Pillars of the Law, supporting Two Black Flags: on which are the usual Stamps, consisting of the *White Rose* united with the *Thistle*, supposed to have been originally contrived on the *Tenth of June*. The expressive Motto of *Semper eadem* is preserved: but the Price of the Stamp is changed to *Three Farthings*, which the *Budget* explains: and the *small Numbers*, which are pointed at, are too contemptible to deserve Notice *by the Majority*. The Chief Mourner, *Sejanus*, follows Mr. *Stamper*. Then Two remarkable Personages, the celebrated *Weaver* and Lord *Gawkee:* after them *Jemmy Twitcher*, with his Friend and *Partner*, Lord *H——*. Two B——s conclude the Procession. Upon the Fore Ground are two large Bales of Black Cloth and Stamps returned from *America*."

121. For other Copley portraits, see 148, 157, 207, 247, 254, 443, also Vol. XII.

122. Fictitious portrait typical of several other portraits of Revolutionary leaders that appeared in England to satisfy public curiosity regarding men and affairs in the colonies. See paper by C. H. Hart, *Frauds in Historical Portraiture*, Annual Report of the American Historical Association, 1915, pp. 87–99.

128. Augustus Charles Pugin, famous as an authority on English architecture of the time, supplied the architectural details and Rowlandson, the English caricaturist, the figures.

130. Original of the illustration was by Hubert François Gravelot, a noted French illustrator of late eighteenth-century books.

134. Paul Revere (1735–1818) worked as a copperplate engraver, die-sinker, silversmith, and founder of church bells. He is reputed to have been a rapid engraver. *The Boston Massacre* (No. 148) is his most noted work in this line. See also Vol. XII, No. 372.

141. This caricature, according to James Parton, *Caricature and other Comic Art*, New York, 1877, has been attributed to Benjamin Franklin, who was living in London at the time and writing anonymous articles in favor of the American cause. In this issue of *The Political Register* is an unsigned article criticizing Britain's treatment of the Colonies, followed by the King's speech referring to the Crown's possible loss of the American Colonies through their "disobedience."

145. Imaginary reconstruction, correct in spirit, by a painter of "patriotic" subjects for popular consumption.

147. By a painter of American history known for careful study of period costume and historical detail. For other examples of his work see Vols. I and VI.

148. See 134. The original of the "Massacre" is now believed to have been drawn by Henry Pelham, J. S. Copley's half-brother.

149. For other Copley portraits, see 121, 157, 443, also Vol. XII.

152. See 31.

164. By a leading American mural painter. For other examples of his work see Vols. I and XII.

167. François Godefroy and Nicolas Ponce were French artists who in 1783–84 issued a collection of sixteen engravings of which this was one. The series was called the *First French Book on the United States of America*.

168, 169. These caricatures are two of a series executed in mezzotint and issued in 1774–75 by the London publishers Sayre & Bennett referring to the Boston Port Bill. They are attributed by R. T. H. Halsey to Phillip Dawe, an English artist who studied with Hogarth and had much of his clever humor. Dawe is credited also with the caricatures 179, 199, 200, 211. They show remarkable knowledge of colonial politics of the day and are pro-American in tone. Their effect and probably their purpose was to satirize the policies of the British government. For further discussion of them see R. T. H. Halsey, *Boston Port Bill*, published in 1904 by the Grolier Club, New York.

170. See 108.

176. See 108.

177. This caricature was undoubtedly copied by Paul Revere from an original under the same title which appeared in *The London Magazine*, April 1774, two months before it appeared in the *Royal American Magazine*.

178. The first American edition of this pamphlet was printed in 1774 at Williamsburg, Va. Jefferson's own copy is in the Library of Congress.

179. See 168.

185. See 18.

188. Matteson, a prolific painter of pictures on American history whose "popular" appeal has done much to perpetuate false or exaggerated notions of events. See Vol. XI, p. 37.

190. Deland, a Philadelphia painter of the modern historical school, whose work is characterized by conscientious endeavor to reconstruct history from close study of essential facts.

199, 200. See 168.

205, 208. See 108.

211. See 168.

218. See 18.

219. This engraving is after an allegorical picture by West, which represents Britannia receiving under her mantle, supported by Justice and Religion, a group of American loyalists, among them Sir William Pepperell, Benjamin Franklin's son and Governor William Franklin of New Jersey.

229. Ferris, a pupil under French masters, has painted fifty or more canvases, now in Independence Hall, on American history. They are marked by rich color effects and deep sentimental feeling, and reveal close study of colonial and revolutionary costume.

230. Pine's picture is useful for the authenticity of his portraits. He came from England in 1784 to Philadelphia, where he met some of the signers. In 1785 he spent three weeks at Mt. Vernon, painting a portrait of Washington.

231. This is Jefferson's original rough draft of the Declaration and is so marked by him in the margin of the fourth sheet. The draft contains on sheet one, two verbal changes, one each by Franklin and John Adams; on sheet two, one by Adams and one by Franklin; on sheet three, two by Franklin, and on sheet four, one by Franklin. J. C. Fitzpatrick, in *The Spirit of the Revolution*, 1924, says Franklin should have been credited with eleven changes. The interlineations, excisions and substitutions seen in the original draft, notably in the third and fourth sheets, indicate the vigorous editing the document received at the hands of Congress. The last sheet was considerably altered, liberal deletions and revisions being made in the text as written by Jefferson. This is indicated by the note in the margin, end of the third line of the draft, "a different phraseology inserted." Jefferson in his *Notes*, in speaking of these changes, says: "The idea that we had friends in England worth keeping terms with still haunted the minds of many. For this reason those passages which conveyed censures on the people of England were struck out, lest they should give them offense. The clause too, reprobating the enslaving the inhabitants of Africa was struck out — in compliance to South Carolina and Georgia, who had never attempted to restrain the importation of slaves, and who on the contrary still wished to continue it. Our northern brethren also I believe felt a little tender under those censures; for tho' their people have very few slaves themselves yet they had been pretty considerable carriers of them to others."

235. Trumbull wrote to Jefferson that this picture contained forty-seven portraits, thirty-six of which Trumbull had painted from life, including all the signers who were living in 1791. He began to paint the picture in 1787 while in Europe. Two of the portraits he had painted from memory and nine he had copied from portraits done by others. Jefferson is shown in the group that drew up the Declaration. Trumbull's painting has no historical value as a true representation of the event. His effort was rather toward giving to posterity a picture containing actual portraits of the men whose names were attached to the immortal document. (In two cases, John Dickinson and Thomas Willing of Pennsylvania, the portraits are not of signers.) Trumbull spent much time in preparation. The stiffness and formal appearance of the signers betray the handicap the artist gave himself when he essayed this noble but inartistic conception. The picture had to run the gauntlet of mild criticism not long after its completion in 1824. Edmund Randolph referred sarcastically to the display of Congressional "legs," and Greenough, the sculptor, replied pointing out that this applied only to the legs of ten members. The architectural details of the chamber in which the Declaration was signed are different in Pine's and Trumbull's pictures; Pine's version (No. 230) is the more correct.

238. Portrait painted while Paine was in England, location not known.

240. The statue was pulled down on July 9, 1776, just after the Declaration of Independence had been first read in New York. The head

of the statue was preserved by Loyalists, while the lead body was taken to Litchfield, Conn., and there molded by patriotic ladies into bullets to be used against the King's troops. The artist Johannes A. Oertel, 1823–1909, painted the picture in 1852, and it was published as a steel engraving. Oertel produced many religious pictures, including the *Rock of Ages* which became a popular "chromo."

247. See 108.

254. See 108.

262. This and similar pictures helped, perhaps designedly, to influence French public opinion to support the American alliance and in this sense were propaganda.

267, 268. These obviously French cartoons were dated Boston, 1778, probably in derision of the British.

271. The cartoon gives possibly the earliest representation of Brother Jonathan.

272, 273. See 108.

275, 276. See 108.

279, 280, 282. See 108.

283. West gave as a reason for not finishing this picture that he had no portrait of the British Commissioner, who died without leaving a likeness.

291. The artist made pencil studies at the scenes of Franklin's life in America before painting a series of murals for the Franklin Union, shown in this chapter.

300. The original portrait of Franklin by Chamberlin was formerly in the possession of Joshua Bates, 1788–1864, an American financier of the firm of Barring Brothers & Co., London. It passed to his grandson, Victor Vander Weyer, of London. A copy by C. D. Leslie is in the Harvard University collection.

301. Benjamin Wilson succeeded Hogarth in 1761 as "Sergeant Painter" of England. He painted George III and the Queen in 1776.

305. Schuessele, born in Alsace, studied in Paris under Delaroche and painted this picture in Philadelphia in 1856; later other pictures on American history which were engraved as large prints by John Sartain.

306. This Franklin letter to Strahan was not sent.

310. This portrait was made by Charles Nicolas Cochin the younger, who belonged to a famous French family of artists.

314. Baron André Edouard Jolly, born at Brussels in 1799, was a Belgian officer, who painted historical and genre pictures about 1835–40. Mirzbach cites him as an art patron and amateur painter.

315. In the cartoon the group of figures representing the four quarters of the Earth — Europe impersonated by D'Alembert, Asia by Catherine II of Russia, Africa by Prince Orinoco, America by Benjamin Franklin — are being warned to desist from paying homage to Voltaire by the winged and blindfolded figure of Prejudice and Ignorance. On Voltaire's tomb an inscription reads:

> In this sad and fatal tomb rests the shadow of Voltaire, Weep, ye Beaux Arts, you no longer have a Father — and the Universe has lost its Torch.

Voltaire and Franklin had met amid great enthusiasm in Paris in 1778, just after the conclusion of the treaty between France and America. Voltaire died a few months later.

317. Andreas Stöttrup, 1754–1812, a German portrait painter and engraver.

327. Another portrait of Morris by Gilbert Stuart will be found in Vol. VI.

348. Pinckney had this portrait painted by Stuart when he was on a visit to England. The original remained in the Pinckney family for a long time. In recent years it was obtained by Charles Henry Hart for Alexander S. Cochran, who deposited it in Philipse Manor Hall.

350. The background of the picture is inaccurate; the portraits on the wall are a nineteenth century addition. "The scene is Philadelphia; Washington is in the chair behind a table on a low dais. To the right foreground are Madison, with cloak on arm, and Alexander Hamilton, standing. Farther back near Washington stands Jefferson talking to another delegate whose back is turned. In the group of four men standing to the left in the foreground, the characteristic face of Benjamin Franklin gives a familiar look. His unpowdered hair hangs loose about his neck." — Brochure issued by the State of Wisconsin.

357. Charles B. J. Fevret de St. Memin, artist of the French nobility, came to America in 1793 to escape persecution. He engraved seven hundred portraits of prominent Americans from 1796 to 1810, working south from New York through Washington to South Carolina.

365. For Gilbert Stuart as a portrait painter, see Vol. XII.

366. See 230.

371. Regarding this portrait, Washington wrote to Joseph Reed: "Mr. Campbell *whom I never saw* to my knowledge, has made a very formidable figure of the commander-in-chief, giving him sufficient portion of terror in his countenance." According to C. H. Hart, *Frauds in Historical Portraiture*, Annual Report of the American Historical Association, 1915, pp. 87–99, as many as 147 fictitious portraits of Washington are known.

372. Artist's paintings on American history show careful and conscientious renderings of events marked by intelligence and insight.

373. The artist was elected an N.A. in 1848. He studied at Paris, Rome and Düsseldorf, and

executed several historical canvases of note. According to Washington Irving, the members of Congress "were seated and covered as representatives of the sovereignty of the Union." Trumbull's painting of the same event is in the Yale School of the Fine Arts. (See Vol. I, No. 400.)

378. See 372.

380. Original painted for reproduction as a steel plate to satisfy the demand for popular prints on American history.

381. See 147.

382. See 188.

383. Washington lived in this house on Franklin Square only until March, 1790, when he moved into the Macomb mansion, on the site of the present No. 39 Broadway.

384. Of this portrait Trumbull in his *Reminiscences* says: "I represented him in full uniform, standing by a white horse, leaning his arm upon the saddle; in the background, a view of Broadway in ruins, as it then was, the old fort at the termination; British ships and boats leaving the shore, with the last of the officers and troops of the evacuating army, and Staten Island in the distance. Every part of the detail of the dress, horse, furniture, etc., as well as the scenery was accurately copied from the real objects."

387. See 229.

391. See 357.

396. Peter Lacour, a French artist (1745–1814). For other engravings by Doolittle see Vols. VI and XII.

400. Sharples, an English painter in pastel, made many crayon portraits in America between 1796 and 1811. See Notes on the Pictures, Vol. I, p. 310.

409. Portrait was painted a few months after Hamilton's death. Trumbull's memorandum of Dec. 22, 1804, says: "Did a whole-length portrait of General Hamilton for the City, from Cerracchi's bust." The bust by Joseph Cerracchi was modeled in 1794, when Hamilton was thirty-seven years old.

410. The famous "Talleyrand miniature" was made in France after Hamilton's death, from an original crayon drawing done by James Sharples, when Hamilton was about forty years of age. Talleyrand had admired the Sharples portrait and he took it from the wall of the Hamilton home when he made his adieux on sailing for France. After Hamilton's untimely death Mrs. Hamilton wrote to Talleyrand, asking for the portrait. Before he returned it, Talleyrand had the French artist Chartres make two miniature copies, one of which he sent to the Hamilton family with the original drawing.

421. Daniel Huntington, painter of portraits and historical pictures, was twice president of the National Academy. For estimate of his work see Vol. XII. "On Friday evening, May 29th, (1780) Mrs. Washington held her first 'levee' which was attended by the fashionable society of New York. She afterwards held a reception every Friday evening from eight until ten o'clock. These 'levees' were arranged on the plan of the English and French drawing rooms, visitors entitled to the privilege by reason of official or social position, came without special invitation. Full dress was required of all. President Washington usually attended." — Irving, *Life of Washington.*

427. The cartoon represents the secretary of the Boston Constitutional party reading the compact, with its wretched spelling, to the members.

433. Trumbull's miniatures of celebrities of the day, to the number of 56, are in the Yale School of the Fine Arts.

444. See 400.

451. Eliphalet F. Andrews, an Ohio artist born in 1835, studied in Europe and later painted portraits in Washington.

456. This crude caricature is one of the earliest attempts to visualize Brother Jonathan.

458. This portrait is said to have been painted by Stuart in 1824 when Webster was forty-two years old.

471. See 357.

480. See 357.

500. Charles Bird King, 1785–1862, studied in London, painted in Philadelphia and Washington. Many of his pictures are in the Redwood Library, Newport, R. I., and several at Harvard University.

506. Charles, born in Scotland, came to America and designed, engraved and published caricatures in the English manner. This is one of two in which Washington appears.

508. See 506.

509. Brother Jonathan and Master Jonathan were appellations given by English cartoonists successively to the young republic of the United States. "Brother Jonathan" is said to have referred originally to Jonathan Trumbull, Governor of Connecticut during the Revolution. Washington used to say, "We must consult Brother Jonathan," and it became a cognomen for the people. John Doyle used "Brother Jonathan" in *Punch* in 1847, "Master Jonathan" appeared in *Punch* in 1850 (see No. 656). *The Lantern*, New York, in 1852 had several cartoons drawn by Frank Bellew of the figure of Jonathan in high hat and striped trousers. Thomas Nast in *Harper's Weekly* took over Bellew's conception, added whiskers and put stars on the vest of Jonathan, making the famous Uncle Sam that has been the model of most cartoonists since Nast's day. (For Uncle Sam, see also Vol. IX.)

511, 512. See 506.

514. Madame Plantou painted historical pictures and miniatures in Washington and Philadelphia about 1820 to 1825.

521. Vanderlyn (see his *Columbus*, Vol. I, No. 203) after his return from abroad painted portraits with considerable success.

522. Krimmel (see also Vol. XII) was German-born and painted in Philadelphia. The picture contains portraits of local politicians of the day. Dunlap speaks of its composition as "masterly," and the figures as "beautifully drawn."

535. A good example of the rude beginnings of American caricature in which less emphasis is laid upon the draftsmanship than upon the coarse jests and witless text inscribed in the "balloons."

536. Samuel Finley Breese Morse was an inventor (see Vol. V) as well as an artist. While first President of the National Academy of Design, he invented the electric telegraph, which Congress utilized in a line between Baltimore and Washington in 1844. (See also Vol. XII.)

542. Ralph E. W. Earl, 1786–1837, married a niece of Andrew Jackson and while living at the Hermitage, made several portraits of the General.

545. See 433.

548. See 536.

549. The painting is said to contain one hundred and thirty portraits.

550. Jeffreys a successful illustrator and close student of American history. See also Vol. III.

551. Edward W. Clay, engraver and lithographer, gained fame as a prolific caricaturist of the period 1820 to 1845, first through his conception of *Rats Leaving a Falling House.* Clay had served as a midshipman in the navy and later studied art in Europe. His work is not always initialed, and many cartoons of the Jackson period and later are undoubtedly by his hand. See also 562, 570, 582, 609, 616, 617.

562. See 551.

584. The cuts, sometimes cleverly drawn, in the *Anti-Slavery Almanac* undoubtedly had an influence in shaping public opinion against the South, especially in farming communities of the North and Middle West.

588. See 551.

592. Catlin painted portraits before he devoted himself to depicting the American Indian. (See Vol. I.)

609. See 551.

616. See 551.

627. Amans, portrait painter of New Orleans, has left no record of his life except some creditable portraits.

628. Rothermel, a Philadelphia painter who did several other pictures of the "patriotic" school — Patrick Henry, Gettysburg, etc. This picture was extensively distributed as a large framing print. Portraits may be identified of Calhoun, Webster, Douglas, Benton and other national figures of the day.

645, 646. See 551.

648. See 550.

656. See 509.

659. From 1832 to 1857 Nathaniel Currier of New York issued "colored engravings" or "chromos" illustrating current history, rural and sporting scenes and personalities. In 1857 he took as partner James Merritt Ives, and under the firm name of Currier & Ives, copyrighted prints, many in color, appeared from May 6, 1857. These are now acknowledged to be an important record of American history during these years, especially for the Civil War period. Some of the productions of Currier & Ives are fine examples of this form of art. Among the artists who made the designs were George Inness, the painter; J. H. Bufford, lithographer; Louis Maurer, cartoonist; J. M. Ives; Mrs. F. F. Palmer, who specialized in rural scenes; Charles Parsons, painter and illustrator for Harper's; A. F. Tait, J. Cameron, and G. H. Durrie. The prints were issued as separate sheets, and buyers used them for publication or for posting in shops and homes. Of some of the more successful issues of the Civil War period as many as 50,000 prints were sold. (See also Vol. XII, p. 310.)

681, 685, 688, 689. See 659.

724, 725, 729, 731, 734. See 659.

INDEX

Titles of books under author are in italics; titles of illustrations under producer are in quotation marks.